Lecture Notes in Computer Scienc

Commenced Publication in 1973
Founding and Former Series Editors:
Gerhard Goos, Juris Hartmanis, and Jan van Leeuwen

T0237889

Maria A. Wimmer   Hans J. Scholl
Marijn Janssen   Roland Traunmüller (Eds.)

Electronic Government

8th International Conference, EGOV 2009
Linz, Austria, August 31 - September 3, 2009
Proceedings

 Springer

Volume Editors

Maria A. Wimmer
University of Koblenz-Landau, Institute for IS Research
Universitätsstraße 1, 56070 Koblenz, Germany
E-mail: wimmer@uni-koblenz.de

Hans J. Scholl
University of Washington, The Information School
Seattle, WA 98195-2840,USA
E-mail: jscholl@u.washington.edu

Marijn Janssen
Delft University of Technology
Faculty of Technology, Policy, and Management
Jaffalaan 5, 2628 BX Delft, The Netherlands
E-mail: M.F.W.H.A.Janssen@tudelft.nl

Roland Traunmüller
University of Linz
Institute of Informatics in Business and Government
Altenbergerstraße 69, 4040 Linz, Austria,
E-mail: traunm@iwv.jku.at

Library of Congress Control Number: 2009932688

CR Subject Classification (1998): K.4, K.5, K.6.5, C.2, H.5, H.4

LNCS Sublibrary: SL 3 – Information Systems and Application, incl. Internet/Web and HCI

ISSN   0302-9743
ISBN-10   3-642-03515-9 Springer Berlin Heidelberg New York
ISBN-13   978-3-642-03515-9 Springer Berlin Heidelberg New York

springer.com

© Springer-Verlag Berlin Heidelberg 2009
Printed in Germany

Typesetting: Camera-ready by author, data conversion by Scientific Publishing Services, Chennai, India
Printed on acid-free paper   SPIN: 12733354   06/3180   5 4 3 2 1 0

Preface

Years of worldwide economic depression do not only shatter private-sector firms and strain public-sector budgets, they also test the viability of academic conferences and other scholarly events. Given this context it is remarkable how well the eighth EGOV conference maintained its standing as an annual international conference with a global reach. Submissions from Europe increased over those from other parts of the globe. However, the conference upheld its attractiveness to scholars from around the world as a venue of high reputation. The 2009 EGOV conference brought together scholars and practitioners from five continents and 32 countries.

Previous EGOV conferences were dedicated to three main areas, which overlap in part: eGovernment, eGovernance, and eParticipation. While the overlap still exists, a vibrant and sizable community has formed around topics of participation, inclusion, and democracy in the digital age. For the first time, with ePart this topical strand organized its own conference with separate proceedings. ePart aims to review research advances in both social and technological scientific domains, seeking to demonstrate new concepts, methods and styles of eParticipation. The Chairs of both conferences consider it important to maintain close links and are committed to co-locating the two events in the years to come.

Similar to the year before, the 2009 EGOV "Call for Papers" attracted 119 paper submissions and 5 workshop and panel proposals. Among those submissions, which included full research papers, work-in progress papers on ongoing research as well as project and case descriptions, 34 full research papers (empirical and conceptual) were accepted for Springer's LNCS proceedings. These papers have been clustered under the following headings:

- Reflecting eGovernment research
- Administrative reform and public sector modernization
- Performance management and evaluation
- Aspects in government-to-citizen interactions
- Building blocks in eGovernment advancements

Accepted papers on ongoing research and general development issues, on case and project descriptions, as well as workshop abstracts are published by Trauner Druck in a complementary proceedings volume.

As in the past couple of years and per the recommendation of the Paper Awards Committee, the EGOV Organizing Committee granted *outstanding paper* awards in three distinct categories:

- The most interdisciplinary and innovative research contribution
- The most compelling critical research reflection
- The most promising practical concept

Due to the early editorial deadline for these proceedings, the winners in each category cannot be presented here. However, the award ceremony has become a well-attended highlight at the end of each EGOV conference, where the winners are presented.

In February, the eGovernment community received the sad news of Valerie Gregg's passing. Val had served as a co-program manager for the Digital Government Program at the US National Science Foundation for many years. She took up and successfully advanced many projects, one of which was to bring the European and the US eGovernment communities more closely together. She also served as co-director and co-founding faculty of the iGov Research Institute, which gives doctoral students the opportunity to meet and study together under the guidance of senior scholars in this domain of study. Valerie Gregg died from cancer at the age of only 55. We will always remember her and already gravely miss her deep passion, energizing spirit, creative vision, and her joyful smile, with which she inspired everyone who had the privilege of working with her.

Many people make large events like this conference happen. We thank the 55 members of the EGOV 2009 Program Committee and 52 additional reviewers for their great efforts in reviewing the submitted papers. Gabriela Wagner of the DEXA organization as well as the DEXA staff deserve special thanks for taking care of the organizational issues of EGOV. Lisa Sturm of the University of Koblenz-Landau (Germany) supported us in the administrative management of the review process and in compiling the proceedings of EGOV 2009.

Austria's high-regarded Johannes Kepler University (JKU) hosted the 2009 edition of the DEXA cluster of conferences including the EGOV conference. JKU and the city of Linz in Austria were chosen not by coincidence to host the event. Linz is the hometown of the DEXA organization, which this year celebrated its 20th anniversary. In 2009, Linz was also the European Capital of Culture. The city's cultural life is rich and in 2009 even richer through numerous additional programs and cultural events throughout the year. We thank our hosts at JKU and quite a number of local institutions for the support provided in the organization of the event. It was a pleasure to visit the wonderful city of Linz during this special year in its history.

August/September 2009

Maria A. Wimmer
Hans J. (Jochen) Scholl
Marijn Janssen
Roland Traunmüller

Organization

Executive Committee

Maria A. Wimmer	University of Koblenz-Landau, Germany
Jochen Scholl	University of Washington, USA
Marijn Janssen	Delft University of Technology, The Netherlands
Roland Traunmüller	University of Linz, Austria

Program Committee

Ashraf Hassan Abdelwahab	Deputy to the Minister of State for Administrative Development, Egypt
Shadi Al-Khamayseh	University of Technology (UTS), Australia
Vincenzo Ambriola	University of Pisa, Italy
Yigal Arens	Digital Government Research Center, USC/ISI, USA
Karin Axelsson	Linköping University and Örebro University, Sweden
Molnar Balint	Corvinus University, Hungary
Frank Bannister	Trinity College Dublin, Ireland
Victor Bekkers	Erasmus University Rotterdam, The Netherlands
Lasse Berntzen	Vestfold University College, Norway
John Bertot	Florida State University, USA
Yannis Charalabidis	National Technical University of Athens, Greece
Wichian Chutimaskul	King Mongkut's University of Technology Thonburi, Thailand
Ahmed M. Darwish	Minister of State for Administrative Development, Egypt
Jim Davis	Oxford University, UK
Sharon Dawes	CTG, University at Albany, USA
Rahul De'	Indian Institute of Management Bangalore, India
Iván Futó	Corvinus University of Budapest, Advisor for E-Government, Hungary
Rimantas Gatautis	Kaunas University of Technology, Lithuania
Olivier Glassey	IDHEAP, Switzerland
Dimitris Gouscos	University of Athens, Greece
Luis Guijarro-Coloma	University of Valencia, Spain

Helle Zinner Henriksen	Copenhagen Business School, Denmark
Tomasz Janowski	United Nations University - IIST, Macau, China
Marijn Janssen	Delft University of Technology, The Netherlands
Luiz Antonio Joia	Brazilian School of Public and Business Administration, Getulio Vargas Foundation, Brazil
Ralf Klischewski	German University in Cairo, Egypt
Trond Knudsen	Research Council, Norway
Christine Leitner	Danube University Krems, Austria
Katarina Lindblad-Gidlund	Mid Sweden University, Sweden
Miriam Lips	Victoria University of Wellington, New Zealand
Alexander Makarenko	Institute for Applied System Analysis at National Technical University of Ukraine (KPI), Ukraine
Josef Makolm	Federal Ministry of Finance, Austria
Gregoris Mentzas	National Technical University of Athens, Greece
Carl Erik Moe	University of Agder, Norway
Bjoern Niehaves	European Research Center for Information Systems, Germany
Theresa Pardo	CTG, University at Albany, USA
Vassilios Peristeras	DERI, Ireland
Rimantas Petrauskas	Mykolas Romeris University, Lithuania
Reinhard Posch	Technical University of Graz, CIO of the Federal Government, Austria
Andreja Pucihar	University of Maribor, Slovenia
Peter Reichstädter	Federal Chancellery of Austria
Nicolau Reinhard	University of São Paulo, Brazil
Reinhard Riedl	Bern University of Applied Sciences, Switzerland
Hans Jochen Scholl	University of Washington, USA
Maddalena Sorrentino	University of Milan, Italy
Witold Staniszkis	Rodan Systems S.A., Poland
Efthimios Tambouris	CERTH/ITI and University of Macedonia, Greece
Yao-Hua Tan	Vrije Universiteit Amsterdam, The Netherlands
Roland Traunmüller	University of Linz, Austria
Tom M. van Engers	University of Amsterdam, The Netherlands
Mirko Vintar	University of Ljubljana, Slovenia
Maria A. Wimmer	University of Koblenz-Landau, Germany

Additional Reviewers

Jörg Becker, Germany
Melanie Bicking, Germany
Bojan Cestnik, Slovenia
Giovanni A. Cignoni, Italy
Laurens Cloete, South Africa
Enrico Ferro, Italy
Leif S. Flak, Norway
Enrico Francesconi, Italy
Andreás Gábor, Hungary
Fernando Galindo, Spain
Francisco Javier García Marco, Spain
Göran Goldkuhl, Sweden
Catherine Hardy, Australia
Steve Harris, UK
Timo Herborn, Germany
Marcel Hoogwout, The Netherlands
Ed Hovy, USA
Jiri Hrebicek, Czech Republic
Jan Huntgeburt, Austria
Arild Jansen, Norway
Bernhard Karning, Austria
Bram Klievink, The Netherlands
Yoon Ko, Korea
Irene Krebs, Germany
Herbert Kubicek, Germany
Pilar Lasala, Spain
Mario Jorge Leitao, Portugal
Euripides Loukis, Greece

Marian Mach, Slovakia
Ann Macintosh, UK
Scott Moss, UK
Robert Müller-Török, Austria
Thomas Mundt, Germany
Jacob Nørbjerg, Denmark
Eleni Panopoulou, Greece
Gnther Pernul, Germany
Willem Pieterson, The Netherlands
Wolfgang Polasek, Austria
Alexander Prosser, Austria
Gerald Quirchmayr, Austria
Tomas Sabol, Slovakia
Andreas Schaad, Germany
Sabrina Scherer, Germany
Daniel M. Schmidt, Germany
Christian Schneider, Germany
John Shaddock, UK
Jamal Shahin, The Netherlands
Mauricio Solar, Chile
Ignace Snellen, The Netherlands
Costas Vassilakis, Greece
Reka Vas, Hungary
Melanie Volkamer, Germany
Silke Weiss, Austria
Petra Wolf, Germany

Table of Contents

Performance Management and Evaluation

Aspects in Government-To-Citizen Interactions

Building Blocks in E-Government Advancements

Profiling the EG Research Community and Its Core

Hans J. (Jochen) Scholl

University of Washington, Box 352840, Seattle, WA 98195-2840, USA
jscholl@u.washington.edu

Abstract. Electronic Government Research (EGR) has progressed beyond its stages of infancy and has unfolded into a respected domain of multi- and cross-disciplinary study. A sizable and dedicated community of researchers has formed. So far, however, few, if any, accounts exist which sufficiently analyze the profile of the electronic government research community. The contribution of this paper is to describe this profile and give a detailed account of the core researcher community, name the most prolific researchers, determine their disciplinary backgrounds, and identify their preferred standards of inquiry. The study also identifies and quantifies the preferred publishing outlets in EGR, distinguishing between core journals and core conferences, on the one hand, and non-core sites, on the other hand. This study advances the understanding of the emerging structure and profile of the academic domain of EGR and helps researchers identify adequate publishing outlets for their domain-related research.

Keywords: Electronic Government Research, EGR, core EGR community, core EGR journals, core EGR conferences, prolific EGR scholars, disciplinary breakdown, multi-disciplinary EGR, EGOV EndNote Reference Library, EGRL.

1 Introduction and Research Questions

Previous Analyses of the Electronic Government (EG) Study Domain: EG owes the first sign of self-recognition as a separate domain of research to Grönlund who in 2003 attempted to formulate a foundational EG theory [5]. In several follow-up studies the author suggested that the study of EG and EG Information Systems (EGIS) should encompass the political, the administrative, and the societal spheres of government [6]. EG, he asserted, was an immature field lacking academic rigor in many, if not most, contributions [6-9].

Two reviews of the early EG literature [1, 10] produced contrasting and contradicting results, one supporting Grönlund's claims, the other dismissing them. While these authors mainly viewed EG from their own mono-disciplinary perspectives, other EG scholars pointed at the transdisciplinary nature of the phenomena under study in EG, which precluded any single discipline to declare sole ownership of the domain and of the phenomena of study [4, 11, 12]. While these analyses and discussions revolved around the foundations and the acceptable standards of inquiry in EG research (EGR), the forming of the EGR community itself and the roles and orientations of their leading members had not been included in those studies. Up to this time it has not even been known how many researchers the EG community formed and what their backgrounds were.

M.A. Wimmer et al. (Eds.): EGOV 2009, LNCS 5693, pp. 1–12, 2009.

The Body of Knowledge in Electronic Government: Elsewhere [13], it has been argued that EG as a domain of study has progressed beyond its stage of infancy and that EGR has produced a steady stream of no less than three hundred, English-language, peer-reviewed articles per annum ever since 2004. For a young domain of study, this is a remarkably high output volume. It was further found that roughly half of the annual research volume is published in so-called EG core journals (ibid).

An additional third of this annual output is published in the proceedings of one of three annual EG core conferences, that is, the Electronic Government Track at the Hawaii International Conference on System Sciences (HICSS), the dg.o conference organized by the Digital Government Society of North America (DGSNA), and the Europe-based DEXA/EGOV conference, each of which has been conducted for about a decade and has produced a sizable contribution to the academic knowledge in EGR (ibid). Over five sixths of EGR, hence, is published in EGR core journals or proceedings of EGR core conferences.

After the record year of 2005 with almost 500 peer-reviewed publications, EGR went through a short phase of declining publication numbers, until 2008, when an increase of some 17 percent to 368 EG publications was recorded. The topical breakdown showed that half of EG publications were dedicated to (1) *organization, management, and transformation*. With around ten percent each, four topics followed: (2) *digital democracy*, (3) *e-services*, (4) *design studies and tools*, and (5) *policy, governance, and law*. The topic of (6) *infrastructure, integration, and interoperability* ranks in sixth place with a little under seven percent followed by the two small topical areas of (7) *information security* and (8) *foundations and standard of inquiry* (ibid).

The analysis also uncovered that 85 percent of all EG publications were non-technical in nature. Most publications were empirically based. Over 3,500 authors were recorded; however, more than three quarters of those authors had published only a single article or paper. In other words, around 800 individuals had published more than one article or paper on EG, suggesting that the core community of EG researchers, that is, individuals with at least one EG-related publication per annum over the past four years, would be even smaller.

Contribution and Research Questions: It is the aim and contribution of this paper to produce insights in and advance the understanding of the composition of the EGR community. In particular, the following research questions will be addressed:

(R1) Which individuals form the inner core of this community of EG researchers, and how many are there?
(R2) Which disciplines do the core EG researchers represent/were they trained in?
(R3) Which general methods (quantitative/qualitative) do they prefer in their research?
(R4) Which outlets for publications do the core EG researchers prefer?

The results of these analyses point to where the EG study domain might be headed, and what the prospects for interdisciplinary projects in EG might be.

Paper Organization: This paper is organized as follows: First, the data source and method are presented; then, the results are presented; third, the findings are discussed; and finally, conclusions are drawn and future research is outlined.

2 Data and Method

2.1 Data

The data source for this analysis is the publicly available EG reference library (EGRL) 2008 version 4.4. (EGRL08), which contained a total of 2,632 reference entries. These entries had to meet the following criteria for inclusion:

At a minimum a paper or an article had to

a) Have passed an academic peer review process,
b) Be published in the proceedings of an academic conference or in an academic journal,
c) Be published in English (or, if published in another language, an English-language translation had to be publicly available),
d) Be of at least seven pages (or equivalently, 3,700 words) in length (including references) for a non-technical article, or
e) Be of at least four pages (2,250 words) in length (including references) for a technical article.

While these criteria allow for inclusion in the reference library of research notes and research-in-progress papers as well as full-length technical papers, in computer science, for example, they explicitly exclude non-academic accounts, posters, birds-of-a-feather reports, workshop summaries, symposium summaries, conference and event introductions, extended abstracts, commentaries, editorial notes, book reviews, and other rudimentary or light pieces of work.

As an exception, some twenty non-peer-reviewed papers with a high citation count in the academic literature, such as Balutis' introduction to EG in Public Manager [2, 3] were purposefully included to maintain the reference library's comprehensiveness and ease of use.

The EGRL08 was populated with reference records found through keyword and full-text searches, both by hand and electronically, in journals and academic conference proceedings, when they met the above-specified criteria. The core journal outlets in EGR, pubic administration research (PAR), political science research (PSR), information systems research (ISR), and other domains and disciplines were included in the searches as well as the proceedings of HICSS, DEXA/EGOV, and dg.o. Also included in the searches were the proceedings of the ICIS and AMCIS conferences as well as some regional or special-topic conferences in EG. Since EG has attracted the attention of numerous disciplines and their publishing outlets, iterative keyword searches have been conducted across the archives of JSTOR, Project MUSE, Science Direct, EBSCO, the ACM Digital Library, IEEE Xplore, and Springerlink among quite a few others.

Keywords used in the searches included "e-Government," "digital government," "e-Governance," "PMIS" (that is, Public Management Information Systems), "IT" or "ICT (that is, information technology or information and communication technology) in Public Administration or public sector," "e-democracy," "digital democracy," "e-participation," "e-inclusion," "digital divide," "e-Services in government," "e-voting," "e-campaigning," "e-rulemaking," and the acronyms "G2G, G2B, G2E, G2C, IEE" (which stand for government-to-government, government-to-business, government-to-employee, government-to-citizen, and internal effectiveness and efficiency) and also spelling and acronym variations of those.

From its first release in 2006, the number of entries in the EGRL had grown from some 1,500 to a total of 2,632 by fall of 2008 (version 4.4). This latter version served as the basis for the analysis presented below. Please note that EGRL08 does not contain references published after September of 2008 but a well-informed estimate of the number of publications for the final quarter of that calendar year was made [13].

2.2 Method

The following scheme was used for coding the 2,632 entries in EGRL08:
- (a) Type of publication outlet (core EG journal; core EG conference; other (non-core EG) journal; other (non-core EG) conference, book section, edited book, monograph, and other publication).
- (b) Topical orientation of article (foundations and standards of inquiry; organization, management, and transformation; infrastructure, integration, and interoperability; services; participation, inclusion, voting, and e-democracy; policy, governance, law, and trust; design studies, information systems development (ISD), algorithms, and tools; security; and other topical orientations).
- (c) Type of article (technical publication, non-technical publication, hybrid, and other type).
- (d) Basis of article (empirical, conceptual, review, hybrid, and other basis).

Core Journals: The following criteria were used to determine which journals would be considered core outlets for EG publications:

(1) A clearly stated and enacted focus on EG in the editorial objectives and scope, (2) editorial board comprised of leading EG scholars, (3) strictly upheld high review and acceptance standards to ensure that published articles are of higher-quality, (4) consistently large output volume of EG research articles, (5) leading EG scholars frequently and repeatedly publish their work in the outlet; (6) a global geographical reach as indicated by institutional origin of submitting authors, (7) publisher's sustained commitment to EG, (8) publisher's academic reputation, and (9) journal's academic reputation. Journals with a wider scope definition than EG, which had a particularly strong publication record regarding EG (criterion #4) and a good reputation as an academic journal (criterion #9) were also considered for inclusion.

Using these criteria, the initial list of core journals encompassed

(1) Inderscience's *Electronic Government, An International Journal* (EGaIJ),
(2) ACI's *Electronic Journal of E-Government* (EJEG),
(3) Elsevier's Government Information Quarterly (GIQ),
(4) IOS Press' *Information Polity* (IP),
(5) IGI's *International Journal of Electronic Government Research* (IJEGR),
(6) Taylor & Francis' *Journal of Information Technology and Politics* (formerly Journal of E-Government/ (JITP/JEG), and
(7) Emerald's *Transforming Government: Process, People, and Policy* (TGPPP).

The short academic track records of the majority of these journals prevented them from scoring high in terms of academic reputation (criterion #9); so, no ranking of these journals has been attempted.

Core Conferences: For identifying core conferences in EG, similar criteria as for core journals were used:

(1) A clearly stated and enacted focus on EG in the call for papers, (2) a relatively long track record of regular annual recurrences of the conference, (3) a consistently large output volume of completed EG research papers, (4) strong gravitational power; that is, a global geographical reach as indicated by institutional origin of submitting authors and participants, (5) strictly upheld high review and acceptance standards, leading to high-quality papers, (6) proceedings available from a publisher of high reputation, and (7) a major and recurring EG community event attached to the conference such as an annual meeting of a professional EG association, an EG symposium, a doctoral consortium on EG, an EG workshop series, or an EG job placement center.

Three aforementioned conferences met the specified criteria:

(1) The EG track at HICSS,
(2) DEXA EGOV, and
(3) DGSNA's dg.o conference.

As also mentioned above, for almost a decade, these three conferences have consistently attracted a large number of high-quality submissions from a wide subsection of active EG scholars. Review and acceptance standards for submissions to these three conferences have been aligned to maintain high-quality papers, and the proceedings of these three conferences (published by IEEE, ACM, and Springer respectively) are restricted to include only completed research papers.

Core EG Researchers: In the period from its early beginnings in the late 1990s until this research was conducted in 2008, the study domain's academic output had peaked in 2005 [13]. However, most publications were recorded in the second half of that decade. Therefore, it was reasoned that researchers with less than four publications in EG within five years had to be considered non-core, while authors with four to seven publications within half a decade would count as extended EGR community. Researchers with eight or more publications or one or more publication per year, hence, would reasonably qualify as members of the core EGR community.

For every author found in the EGRL08 the number of publications was counted, and the results were sorted from highest to lowest. For the members of the above-defined core EGR community with eight publications or more, a web-based research was conducted to identify these researchers' disciplinary backgrounds and academic trainings. For the core EGR group the topical orientation was analyzed based on publications as well as regarding the general methods (quantitative/qualitative) that the researchers of the core group had employed in their research. Further, publication outlets were analyzed which the core EG researchers had preferred.

3 Findings

3.1 Research Question (R1): Which Individuals Form the Inner Core of This Community of EG Researchers, and How Many Are There?

When addressing the research question it is helpful to understand the overall composition of the EG research community: How many individuals actually form the core community and the extended core community, and how many individuals are occasional contributors to the body of knowledge in EG? The analysis of the EGRL08 provided a clear answer to this question: The core community (including the extended core community) comprises 225 scholars from around the world.

The vast majority of contributors (93.6 percent) must be categorized as non-core, when the criteria for peer-reviewed publications are applied (more than three publications in five years). Even if the standards were lowered to only more than two publications in five years for making it to the core, the effect would be minimal (241 as opposed to 225 core members) and still 93.1 percent of authors would qualify only as occasional or non-core contributors. In other words, the extended worldwide EG core community is rather small. Figure 1 shows a breakdown of the EG community in terms of numbers of publications and core-to-non-core ratios.

PUBLICATIONS PER AUTHOR	#	CUMULATIVE COUNT	PERCENTAGE	TYPE OF ENGAGEMENT
8 or more	55	55	1.6%	Core Community
6 to 7	47	102	1.3%	Extended community
4 to 5	123	225	3.5%	Extended community
2 to 3	588	813	16.8%	Non-core
1	2693	3,506	76.8%	Non-core
	3,506		100.0%	

Fig. 1. EG Community As Defined By Number of Publications (2008)

As shown in Figure 2, fifty-five scholars were identified who had published eight or more peer-reviewed articles on EG. Together these scholars published a total of 749 articles. Since this sum contains double counts due to co-authorships, the total volume of publications recorded in EGRL08 which core EG researchers had authored represents less than 28.5 percent of the whole body of academic knowledge in EG.

3.2 Research Question (R2): Which Disciplines Do the Core EG Researchers Represent / Which Disciplines Were They Trained in?

Twelve core EG researchers (or 21 percent) had an academic training background in three or more disciplines, while 23 (or 41 percent of the) researchers had a pure mono-disciplinary training and research background. Another 21 (or 37 percent of) EG scholars were trained in at least two separate disciplines. Scholars with pure mono-disciplinary backgrounds mainly came from two disciplines: Computer Science with nine (or 16 percent) of all core EG scholars, and Public Administration with seven (or 12.5 percent) of all core EG scholars. In Figure 3 the various disciplines participating in EGR are enumerated.

Core EG Researcher Community

Rank	# Pubs	Researcher	Region *)	Rank	# Pubs	Researcher	Region *)	Rank	# Pubs	Researcher	Region *)
1	44	Gil-Garcia, J. R.	NoAm		12	Weerakkody, V.	Europe		9	Georgiadis, P.	Europe
2	38	Pardo, T. A.	NoAm	22	11	Bekkers, V.	Europe		9	Horan, T. A.	NoAm
3	35	Scholl, H. J.	NoAm		11	Ferro, E.	Europe		9	Joia, L. A.	LaAm
4	27	Janssen, M.	Europe		11	Fletcher, P. D.	NoAm		9	Nichaves, B.	Europe
5	26	Dawes, S. S.	NoAm		11	Garson, G. D.	NoAm		9	Pan, S. L.	NoAm
6	23	Macintosh, A.	Europe		11	Henriksen, H. Z.	Europe	46	8	Ambite, J. L.	NoAm
7	22	Cresswell, A. M.	NoAm		11	Hovy, E.	NoAm		8	Ebbers, W.	Europe
	22	Grönlund, A.	Europe		11	Irani, Z.	Europe		8	Flak, L. S.	Europe
	22	Wimmer, M. A.	Europe		11	Jaeger, P. T.	NoAm		8	Gouscos, D.	Europe
10	19	Wagenaar, R. W.	Europe		11	Klischewski, R.	Africa		8	Helbig, N. C.	NoAm
11	18	Andersen, K. V.	Europe		11	Tarabanis, K.	Europe		8	Krimmer, R.	Europe
12	14	Norris, D. F.	NoAm	32	10	Carter, L. D.	NoAm		8	Mentzas, G.	Europe
	14	Welch, E. W.	NoAm		10	Choudrie, J.	Europe		8	Moon, M. J.	NoAm
14	13	Becker, J.	Europe		10	Kim, S. T.	NoAm		8	Samet, H.	NoAm
	13	Chen, H.	NoAm		10	Lenk, K.	Europe		8	West, D. M.	NoAm
	13	Reddick, C. G.	NoAm		10	Roy, J. P.	NoAm	56	7	*intentionally left blank*	
	13	Shulman, S. W.	NoAm		10	Tambouris, E.	Europe			*intentionally left blank*	
	13	Traunmüller, R.	Europe		10	Vintar, M.	Europe			*intentionally left blank*	
19	12	Dwivedi, Y. K.	Europe		10	Xenakis, A.	Europe			*intentionally left blank*	
	12	Luna-Reyes, L. F.	NoAm	40	9	Fountain, J. E.	NoAm			*intentionally left blank*	

*) NoAM = North America (w/ Mexico) / LaAm = Latin America (w/o Mexico)

Fig. 2. The 55 Most Prolific EG Researchers by # of Publications (2008)

RANK	DISCIPLINE / FIELD	FREQUENCY	%	RANK	DISCIPLINE / FIELD	FREQUENCY	%
1	Public Administration	17	34%	13	Accounting	1	2%
2	Political Sciences	14	28%		American Studies	1	2%
3	Management of Information Systems	13	26%		Biology	1	2%
4	Business Administration	12	24%		Chemistry	1	2%
	Computer Science	12	24%		Economics	1	2%
6	Information Science	5	10%		Library and Information Sciences	1	2%
7	Educational Administration	4	8%		Operations Research	1	2%
	Mechanical Engineering	4	8%		Organizational Behavior	1	2%
9	Law	3	6%		Organizational Psychology	1	2%
10	Civil Engineering	2	4%		Psychology	1	2%
	Industrial Engineering	2	4%		Social Sciences	1	2%
	Physics	2	4%		Technical Science	1	2%

Fig. 3. Disciplines of the 55 Most Prolific EG Researchers (2008)

In summary, the five most frequent disciplinary backgrounds in EGR are Public Administration, Political Science, Management of Information Systems, Business Administration, and Computer Science.

3.3   Research Question (R3): Which General Methods (Quantitative/Qualitative) Do Core EG Researchers Prefer in Their Research?

When analyzing this aspect of EGR, it became clear that EG scholars draw from a wide range of methods with Action Research and grounded-theory based qualitative studies at one end of the continuum and purely quantitative methods including algorithmic studies and simulations at the other end of the continuum. This study merely distinguished between "qualitative" and "quantitative" studies in order to gain an overall perspective.

Methods Used	Number of Authors	Percentage
Both / Mixed	25	45.45%
Purely Quantitative	25	45.45%
Purely Qualitative	5	9.1%
Total	55	100.0%

Fig. 4. Methods Used by Most Prolific EG Researchers

Both qualitative as well as quantitative methods include a whole range of methodological approaches supporting fairly diverse epistemological stances and ontological claims, whose stated purpose of study was not within the scope of this research (see Figure 4). Interestingly, seven of the top-ten most prolific EG scholars used both quantitative and qualitative methods in their research, while two used mainly qualitative, and one used predominantly quantitative methods in their studies. EGR provides a home to multiple methodological approaches, which exceed the methodological range of a number of disciplines engaged in EGR. Hence, when EGR-related research is submitted to more narrowly structured mono-disciplinary outlets, including some non-core EGR outlets, difficulties in the paper acceptance process might occur.

3.4   Research Question (R4): Which Outlets for Publications Do the Core EG Researchers Prefer?

Unsurprisingly, EG-oriented conferences appeared earlier (1999/2000) than journals dedicated to the domain of study (2003-2007). As discussed before, some journals (GIQ, IP) and conferences (HICSS, AMCIS) extended their scope, while other journals and conferences remained mildly interested.

Rank	Core Journal	# of Pubs
1	GIQ	41
2	EGAIJ	29
3	IJEGR	23
4	IP	17
5	EJEG	12
6	TGPPP	10
	JITP	10

Rank	Core Journal	# of Authors
1	GIQ	22
2	IJEGR	14
3	EGAIJ	13
4	EJEG	9
5	IP	7
	TGPPP	7
7	JITP	6

Fig. 5. Number of Publications from Core EG Researchers per Core Journal (left); Number of Core EG Researchers Publishing in Core Journals (right)

The core journals attracted numerous publications from the most prolific EG researchers, with GIQ and EGAIJ combining the lion's share of publications (see Figure 5, left table). Among the core EG research community, GIQ and IJEGR had the best reach into the core community (see Figure 5 – right table). For example, 22 (or 40 percent) of the 55 most prolific EG researchers had published in GIQ at least once.

Of course, the core group also published elsewhere. The following outlets were most frequently used: *Communications of the ACM* (CACM); Computer; *Decision Support Systems* (DSS); *Information Systems Journal* (ISJ); *Information Technology & Management* (IT&M); *International Journal of Electronic Governance* (IJEG); *International Journal of Public Admin*istration (IJPA); *Journal of the American Society of Information Science & Technology* (JASIST); *Journal of Enterprise Information Management* (JEIM); *Journal of Government Information* (JGI); *Journal of Public Administration Research and Theory* (JPART); *Public Administration Review* (PAR); *Public Performance & Management Review* (PPMR); *Social Science Computer Review* (SSCR) among other journals.

In terms of number of publications from the core group, SSCR and CACM lead the field (see Figure 6 – left table); with regard to number of authors preferring non-core outlets, again, CACM and SSCR lead the field (see Figure 6 – right table). About 46 percent (25 of 55) of the EG core group also used other publishing outlets for a total of 38 articles (see Figure 6).

With regard to conferences, the core group favored the three core conferences (DEXA/EGOV, dg.o, and HICSS) clearly over other conferences for presenting their research. As shown in Figure 7 (upper left table), the EG core community had most articles published at DEXA/EGOV and HICSS. These two conferences also had the farthest reach into the core community with 67 percent (HICSS) and 60 percent (DEXA/EGOV) (see Figure 7, upper right table). While non-core conferences attracted up to 20 members from the core group, no single non-core conference was able to even remotely match the core conferences in number of publications (see Figure 7, lower left table). Interestingly, Americas Conference on Information Systems (AMCIS) had a reach almost as far as the dg.o conference and attracted 27 percent of core EG researchers (dg.o: 31 percent).

Rank	Non-Core Journal	# of Pubs
1	SSCR	9
2	CACM	8
3	JEIM	7
4	ISJ	6
5	IJPA	6
6	PAR	6
7	IJEG	5
8	JASIST	5
9	Computer	4
10	PPMR	4
11	DSS	3
12	IT&M	3
13	JGI	3
14	JPART	2
	Other Journals	38

Rank	Non-Core Journal	# of Authors
1	CACM	8
2	SSCR	8
3	JEIM	7
4	ISJ	6
5	IJEG	5
6	IJPA	5
7	JASIST	4
8	PPMR	4
9	Computer	3
10	IT&M	3
11	JGI	3
12	PAR	3
13	DSS	2
14	JPART	1
	Other Journals	25

Fig. 6. Number of Publications from Core EG Researchers per Non-core Journal (left); Number of Core EG Researchers Publishing in Non-core Journals (right)

Rank	Core Conferences	# of Pubs
1	DEXA/ EGOV	141
2	HICSS	105
3	dgo	56

Rank	Core Conferences	# of Authors
1	HICSS	37
2	DEXA/ EGOV	33
3	dgo	17

Rank	Non-core Conferences	# of Pubs
1	AMCIS	26
2	ASPA	6
3	ICEGOV	5
4	Other Conf	45

Rank	Non-core Conferences	# of Authors
1	AMCIS	15
2	ICEGOV	4
3	ASPA	2
4	Other Conf	20

Fig. 7. Number of Publications from Core EG Researchers per Core Conference (upper left); Number of Core EG Researchers Publishing in Core Conferences (upper right); Number of Publications from Core EG Researchers per Non-core Conference (lower left); Number of Core EG Researchers Publishing in Non-core Conferences (lower right)

4 Discussion and Conclusion

At first glance, it might be disillusioning to find that the core EG community is relatively small (55 individuals), and even the extended core community comprises only a total of 225 scholars, while the vast majority of contributors (that is, 3,281 scholars) engages only occasionally in EGR. However, as the rapidly expanding body of academic knowledge in EG demonstrates, this community has been highly productive. More research would be necessary to better understand the level of productivity and the relative size of this community when compared with other disciplinary and multi-disciplinary domains.

Most researchers listed in the core group (Figure 2) have their primary institutional affiliations either in Europe (27 EG researchers) or in North America (26 EG researchers). Only one scholar of the core group is based in Africa and another one in Latin America (excluding Mexico). No core EG researcher was found in Asia or in Oceania. This seems to indicate that EGR is predominantly conducted at institutions in Europe and North America.

What had already been suggested on the basis of casual observations has been confirmed by this research: Almost 60 percent of EG researchers have obtained multiple disciplinary trainings in their academic careers. Those trained in just one discipline have frequently engaged in collaboration with researchers from different training backgrounds. This suggests that, in principle, openness exists with regard to methods and standards of inquiry, which helps enable cross-disciplinary collaboration. While six disciplines (Public Administration, Political Science, MIS, Business Administration, Computer Science, and Information Science) were most frequent among core EG scholars, it is noteworthy that another seventeen disciplines are represented in that core group of EG scholars.

The wealth of diverse academic backgrounds also translates into a diversity and richness of methodological instruments and tools of inquiry among EG scholars. Almost every other researcher in the core group routinely uses mixed (that is, both quantitative and qualitative) methods, while 45 percent of the core scholars rely solely on quantitative methods. These results suggest that research conducted by the core group has more quantitative than qualitative orientations; yet, the qualitative elements in EG are strong, since more than 50 percent of core EG researchers regularly employ qualitative methods in their studies.

Whether or not the EG community will be able to support seven core journals over the long haul remains to be seen. However, in the core researcher group, GIQ, EGAIJ, and IFEGR have the strongest standing in terms of both number of articles and number of authors. In terms of non-core journals, SSCR, CACM, JEIM, ISJ, and IJPA are most prominent among core EG scholars. It is remarkable that the flagship journals in US Public Administration (PAR, *Administration & Society*, *American Review of Public Administration*, JPART) or Public Policy (*Journal of Policy Analysis and Management* and *Policy Science*) do not play any significant role in EGR.

The three EG core conferences attract the overwhelming number of papers and authors. So far, AMCIS is the only non-core conference with noticeable attractiveness to core scholars. It remains to be seen how other conferences such as ICEGOV or ECIS/PACIS can gain ground among the core scholars. Traditional public administration conferences such as APPAM or ASPA do not play any recognizable role in EGR.

Summary. The contribution of this study has been to shed light on the composition of the core EGR community and to provide a sharp profile of its core researcher group detailing disciplinary backgrounds and publishing preferences. As a result, major disciplinary backgrounds have been determined, preferred methods could be quantified, and preferred publishing outlets and conferences could be identified.

So far, only the number of publications per author has been counted without any attempt to rank order or weigh the publications or the authors' contributions. While the sheer publication count can serve as a good initial indicator of authors' interest in and commitment to EGR, it certainly does not sufficiently describe any particular author's relative standing and influence in the EGR community. For such a purpose, a dedicated citation analysis needs to be undertaken, which will be one of the logical follow-on studies to this research.

Future research also needs to explore in more detail the topical orientations of the extended EGR community. It will also be worthwhile to observe whether or not the EG researcher community will expand or contract over the next decade depending on the research project funding situation in the various regions.

Acknowledgement. I am indebted to my graduate assistants Jean Lee and Christine Lee who worked with me at the Information School of the University of Washington, and who have tirelessly helped me prepare and maintain the EGRL.

References

[1] Andersen, K.V., Henriksen, H.Z.: The First Leg of E-Government Research: Domains and Application Areas 1998-2003. International Journal of Electronic Government Research 1, 26–44 (2005)

[2] Balutis, A.P.: E-government 2001, Part I: Understanding the Challenge and Evolving Strategies. The Public Manager 30, 33–37 (Spring 2001)

[3] Balutis, A.P.: E-government 2001, Part II: Evolving strategies for action. The Public Manager 30, 41 (2001)

[4] Delcambre, L., Giuliano, G.: Digital government research in academia. Computer 38, 33–39 (2005)

[5] Grönlund, Å.: Framing e-gov: e=mc3. In: Traunmüller, R. (ed.) EGOV 2003. LNCS, vol. 2739, pp. 191–198. Springer, Heidelberg (2003)

[6] Grönlund, Å.: State of the Art in e-Gov Research – A Survey. In: Traunmüller, R. (ed.) EGOV 2004. LNCS, vol. 3183, pp. 178–185. Springer, Heidelberg (2004)

[7] Grönlund, Å.: State of the Art in E-Gov Research: Surveying Conference Publications. International Journal of Electronic Government Research 1, 1–25 (2005)

[8] Grönlund, Å.: What's in a Field–Exploring the eGovernment Domain. In: Proceedings of the 38th Annual Hawaii International Conference on System Sciences (HICSS 2005) - Track 5 Island of Hawaii (Big Island), p. 125a. Computer Societry Press (2005)

[9] Grönlund, A., Andersson, A.: e-gov research quality improvements since 2003: More rigor, but research (Perhaps) redefined. In: Wimmer, M.A., Scholl, H.J., Grönlund, Å., Andersen, K.V. (eds.) EGOV 2006. LNCS, vol. 4084, pp. 1–12. Springer, Heidelberg (2006)

[10] Norris, D.F., Lloyd, B.A.: The Scholarly Literature on E-Government: Characterizing a Nascent Field. International Journal of Electronic Government Research 2, 40–56 (2006)

[11] Scholl, H.J.: Central research questions in e-government, or which trajectory should the study domain take? Transforming Government: People, Process and Policy 1, 67–88 (2007)

[12] Scholl, H.J.: Discipline or interdisciplinary study domain? Challenges and Promises in Electronic Government Research. In: Chen, H. (ed.) Digital Government, pp. 19–40. Springer, New York (2007)

[13] Scholl, H.J.: Electronic Government: A Study Domain Past its Infancy. In: Scholl, H.J. (ed.) Electronic Government: Information, Technology, and Transformation. M.E. Sharpe, Armonk (in press, 2009)

Mapping the E-Government Research
with Social Network Analysis

Nuša Erman and Ljupčo Todorovski

Univeristy of Ljubljana, Faculty of Administration
Gosarjeva 5, SI-1000 Ljubljana, Slovenia
{nusa.erman,ljupco.todorovski}@fu.uni-lj.si

Abstract. About fifteen years of e-government research (EGR) lead to a research field that is looking forward to define an identity as a proper and autonomous scientific discipline. This paper proposes the use of social network analysis as a methodology for building a map of EGR and consequently contributing to the process of establishing EGR identity. The paper analyzes the network of citation between authors induced by papers published in the four proceedings of this conference (International Conference on e-Government) in the period from 2005 to 2008. The analysis helps us identify the authors that had most influence on the EGR field development and relate them to the thematic topics that prevailed the conference papers in the last four years.

Keywords: e-government research analysis, social networks, citation analysis.

1 Introduction

e-Government research (EGR) focuses on studying the use of information and communication technology in public administration and government activities. For about fifteen years of its existence the interest for EGR has dramatically grown: from the sporadic appearances of the e-government term in various research papers and government documents to an established research field with a number of specialized academic programs, annual conferences, and conference journals. Despite (or due to) the evident and intensive short-term growth, many authors still consider the EGR to be a rather young research field that still seeks its identity and looks forward to establish itself as a proper scientific discipline [14].

As a consequence, a number of authors studied and analyzed the development process and current development stage of the e-government research field. Studies vary both in terms of the central focus of the EGR analysis as well as analytical methodology used. Grönlund focuses on development of model for measuring EGR maturity. The results of two consecutive studies performed in 2003 [5] and 2005 [6] show, on one hand, increased research collaboration between various institutions as well as increase in the publication standards in terms of number of referenced papers and research rigor. On the other hand, studies show only slight progress in terms of theory forming and testing. Heeks and Bailur [7] analyze EGR along several dimensions, such as impact perspectives, theoretical basis, and methodological approaches. The

M.A. Wimmer et al. (Eds.): EGOV 2009, LNCS 5693, pp. 13–25, 2009.

results of the analysis confirm the findings of previous studies related to lack of clarity, rigor, and generalization that would lead to a common e-government theoretical framework. The establishment of such a ground theory is closely related to the process of forming EGR identity.

Note however, that the above exemplary studies of the EGR field also show diversity of methodological approaches taken and a lack of common analysis framework. This paper, tries to overcome this lack. It introduces methodologies for social network and citation analysis as a common analytical framework and uses them to build an initial map of the EGR field and its development. In particular, we first build a data set of references in the papers published in the proceedings of the International Conference on e-Government (EGOV conference) in the period of four years from 2005 to 2008. Second, we transform the data set into a network of citations between authors. Finally, we perform social network analysis [11] on the obtained network, to obtain the list of most influential authors and relate them to most influential topics that prevailed the EGOV conference papers.

The rest of this paper is organized as follows. Section 2 introduces the data used in this study, the process used to obtain them, and the resulting network of citations between authors induced by the EGOV conference papers. In Section 3, we present the results of the network analysis. Section 4 discusses and analyses the results, putting them in the context of related work. Finally, Section 5 concludes the paper and lays out the directions for further research.

2   Establishing the Citation Network

The data we used in this study include all the papers published in seven proceeding of the annual International Conference on e-Government (EGOV conference) held in the period between 2002 and 2008. We used electronic versions of the papers, available through SpringerLink service, as a source for building the data set and citation network. In the rest of this section, we describe the process of gathering data, present a brief summary of the collected data, and their transformation to citation networks.

2.1   References Data

All the papers published in the proceedings of the EGOV conference follow the same formatting template, which made the data extraction from papers fairly simple. We developed a simple parser that collected two clusters of data for each paper:

- *paper-specific data*: list of authors, list of countries of authors' affiliations, paper title, and year of publication;
- *references data*; for each reference cited in a paper, we collected: list of authors, title, type of publication, publication venue (conference proceedings or journal, where applicable), and year of publication.

The parser was able to collect data from the first cluster accurately enough so only few manual corrections were necessary. However, the huge differences in references formats used by different authors, posed non-negligible challenges to the parser, requiring a lot of manual data cleansing in the second data cluster.

The results of the semi-automatic procedure is a data set, where the complete clean data from the first cluster is gathered for all the papers published in 2002-2008 period, that is 399 papers. These papers include about 5000 references. However, due to the amount of manual labor required to clean the data, the data set currently includes references data only for the papers published in the four proceedings published in the period of last four years, from 2005 to 2008. The data and supplementary materials related to the presented analysis are available at http://daisy.fu.uni-lj.si/egran-wiki/.

Figure 1 shows the number of published papers in the seven proceedings. The number steadily increased in the first three years, and significantly dropped from 100 to 30 in 2005. The decrease is due to improved review process [6] and increased acceptance criteria. Papers that are not accepted for publication in the main conference proceedings are considered for publication in the second-tier (communication) proceedings (these papers are not included in our study).

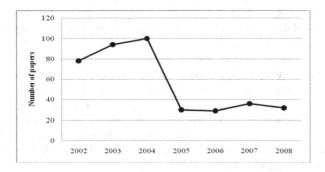

Fig. 1. Number of papers published in the proceedings of the EGOV conference in the period between 2002 and 2008

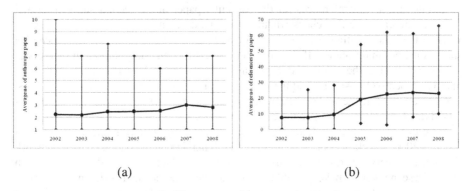

(a)   (b)

Fig. 2. Average number of authors per paper (a, left-hand side) and average number of references per paper (b, right-hand side) for all the papers published in the proceedings of the EGOV conference. The vertical line that accompanies each data point represents the range (minimal and maximal value) of the corresponding numbers.

Figure 2 shows the average number of authors (left-hand side) and average number of references per paper (right-hand side) in each year proceedings. According toFigure 2a, presenting the average number of authors per paper, we can ascertain minor increase in average number of authors per paper. Maximal number of authors changes more significantly, from 10 in 2002 to steady 6-7 in the last four years.Figure 2b shows rapid growth of the number of references per paper from 2004 to 2006, reaching a steady plateau of about 25 references per paper in the last three years. Minimum and maximum number of references per paper change more dynamically: while it was quite usual to find a paper without references in the first three proceedings, currently the minimal number of references reached 10. Similarly, maximal number of references increased from the initial 30 to a steady 60-70.

2.2 Network of Citations between Authors

From this point on, we focus our attention to the papers published in the proceedings of the last four years, from 2005 to 2008, where fully specified and cleaned data on references is available. From the collected data, we are going to prepare networks to be used for social network analysis.

Otte and Rousseau [12] distinguish between two main approaches to social network analysis: the ego network analysis and the global network analysis. While the ego network analysis focuses on the network of one person, the global network analysis deals with all the relations between the network participants. In our study, we perform global network analysis, where network participants are authors, and relations between them are citations. The outcome of the analysis will help us identify the most cited (and therefore most influential) authors, which, in turn, we map to the most influential topics that prevail in the papers presented at the EGOV conference.

The data set, presented in the previous section, can be easily transformed to a network of citations between authors, following a simple procedure. For each paper in the proceedings, we collect the list of paper authors (A_P) from the first data cluster. Then we go through the list of references for the particular paper in the second data cluster and for each reference, we first check whether it is an auto-citation or not. To do so, we test whether the lists of authors of the paper (A_P) and the list of authors of the reference (A_R) share some common names. If they do, the reference is an auto-citation and we disregard it. Otherwise, the citation is proper, and for each pair of authors (a_P, a_R) from A_P and A_R, respectively, we first add the nodes a_P and a_R corresponding to the two authors, if necessary (i.e., if the nodes are not already in the network), and second, add the directed link (arc) from a_P to a_R to the citation network.

Note that the data set includes data about papers from four consecutive years from 2005 to 2008, which allows us to observe the dynamic change of the citation network through the years. To do so, we first construct four different networks; one for each year. These networks make possible to outline the structure and differences between networks in the four observed years. Table 1 summarizes the characteristics of these single-year networks. The dynamic change of these properties follow the patterns of change observed in the previous section, we observe a steady increase in number of authors and citations from 2005 to 2007 with a plateau of about 1000 authors and 3000 citations reached in the last two years. Percentage of citations made to EGOV conference papers more than doubled in the period from 2005 to 2006 and reached over 10%, and from 2006 to 2008 it slightly decreased and reached a steady state of about 8%.Density of the network [9] indicates a number of arcs in a network as a proportion to the maximum number of possible arcs (corresponding to a network, where every pair of vertices is connected with an arc). Since the network density is inverse proportional to the network size, density decreases in the observed period. For all four networks, we can ascertain low values of density (networks are sparse), since the networks contain only a good 0.3% of all possible arcs.

Table 1. General properties (number of vertices, number of arcs, and density) of the networks of citations built on data from a single year proceedings

	2005	2006	2007	2008
#vertices (authors)	597	846	996	985
#arcs (citations)	1385	2208	3284	3240
%EGOV citations	4.19	10.91	8.71	8.40
network density	0.0039	0.0031	0.0033	0.0033

In continuation of our study, we also construct four "cumulative" citation networks. In each of this data from 2005 to the current year are included. These networks are truly information rich and they enable to expose the dynamics of the structure characteristics through the four years of the conference. Table 2 summarizes the characteristics of the cumulative networks. As one would expect, the size of cumulative networks steadily increase (both in terms of the number of vertices and arcs), where the size increase being followed by density decrease. In a whole 2005-2008 network there is present only a good 0.1% of all possible arcs.

Note also, that authors rarely cite papers from the EGOV conference. In 2005, only 4% of the pure citations were to papers published at the EGOV conference. The percentage increased since, to reach a plateau of about 8.5% in the last two years, leaving much space for increase in the coming years.

Table 2. General properties of the "cumulative" citation networks built on data from 2005 to the current year

	2005	2005-2006	2005-2007	2005-2008
#vertices (authors)	597	1345	2131	2870
#arcs (citations)	1385	3594	6879	10120
%EGOV citations	4.19	8.32	8.50	8.47
network density	0.0039	0.0020	0.0015	0.0012

Having built the citation networks, we are prepared to perform exploratory social network analysis. As the citation analysis is related to social network analysis [12], we will apply the notions of the latter one to the former. If social network analysis offers the techniques and concepts to analyze social relations, citation analysis enables the use of these techniques and concepts in analyzing relations, based on citations or references of the papers, or in our case, authors of the papers.

3 Analyzing the Citation Network

Before proceeding with the analysis, let us introduce the term citation analysis. Citation analysis can be defined as a method for research of the frequency, patterns, and graphs of citations or references in journal articles, books and conference proceedings [11]. As a very useful method of bibliometric research [2], it is often applied in scientometrics, a scientific discipline that deals with measuring and analyzing science. In this respect, the main purpose of citation analysis is to establish relationships among authors or their work according to the citations in scholarly works. On this foundation, various links can be observed, e.g. links between authors, scholarly works, journals, conferences, or between different scientific fields. In the present paper we concentrate on the citations links between authors.

3.1 Structural Prestige of the Nodes

Among most interesting aspects of the citation network analysis, where authors represent units and the focus is on links between them, is the search for the most prominent authors. These correspond to the network nodes with the highest number of citations, i.e., incoming network links. By exploring this aspect of the EGR citation network we are able discover the authors and, in turn, the thematic topics that stand out, has major influence, or characterize the study within the EGR field.

The best way to proceed with this aspect of the citation analysis is to study the input relations between the network nodes (authors), which indicate positive choices among them. According to Nooy [11], the network nodes with many positive choices are referred to be more prestigious. In this sense, we identify the most prestigious authors in our networks according to three different measures of input degree, size of the input domain, and proximity prestige.

The simplest measure of structural prestige is the input degree of a node. A higher input degree indicates the higher structural prestige. Due to the fact that this measure is an absolute measure, which means that the comparison between two different networks is not possible, we have to use the normalized values of input degree to compare networks. The main deficiency of the input degree as a measure of structural prestige is that it concentrates exceptionally on direct choices, so it does not matter whether the choices are made from prestigious or un-prestigious authors. To extend prestige to indirect choices we extend our attention to the whole input domain of a node. The size of the input domain presents the portion of all other vertices from which, considering the directions of connections, we can reach the selected author. This measure is quite the opposite from the input degree, as it flattens out the differences between direct and indirect choices, though the first ones are usually more important than the latter ones.

In this respect, "proximity prestige" measure trades off between the two extremes. Proximity prestige is calculated on the basis of the input domain, where influence of the input choice is divided by the mean distance from all vertices in the input domain of the observed node. Thus, proximity prestige attaches more importance to a choice by a close neighbor. According to this, a great input domain and short distances lead to high values of proximity prestige.

Figure 3 shows the maximum proximity prestige values of the "single year" and "cumulative" citation networks. Figure 3a shows that the maximal proportion of positive choices increase through the years, with an exceptional and rather large decrease from 2006 to 2007. Note that the maximal value of 0.0296 is reached in 2008. The observed value corresponds to the fact that one of the authors in 2008 network receives almost 3% of all positive choices, regarding the authors in his input domain and the average distance of these authors.

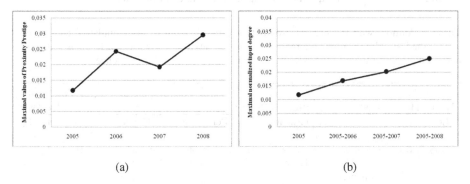

(a)   (b)

Fig. 3. Maximal proximity prestige of the nodes in the single year citation networks (a, left-hand side) and cumulative citation networks (b, right-hand side)

This increase might be interpreted as a sign of field maturation, where citations are being concentrated among several authors. This observation is confirmed also in Figure 3b, since the maximal proximity prestige steadily increases, with the largest change (increase) being observed in 2006. As the citation network grows, the maximal proximity prestige slowly and steadily increases, which means that the choices are getting more and more specific and clustered around narrowing group of authors. These authors are the ones that have major contribution to the identity of the developing e-government research field.

3.2 Most Influential Authors and Topics

Table 3 presents the dynamic change of the list of the most influential authors through the last four years. In each "cumulative" citation network, we identified the ten authors with highest proximity prestige. We adjusted the selection threshold, where necessary, to include all the authors with the same proximity prestige. Thus, the length of the lists varies from nine in 2005 network to eleven in the other ones. The constant changes in the list are related to the rapid growth of the e-government research field. The EGR field has not reached a maturity lever, where there is a stable elite of frequently cited authors that has a major influence in the field. And again, the list shows convergence, since there is a considerable overlap in the last tow lists for the 2005-2007 and 2005-2008 networks.

Despite the dynamic change of the list, there is a core group of nine authors that reappear (at least twice) as the most prestigious ones in more than one citation network: Grönlund, Hood (each of them has three appearances in the lists), Heeks, Wimmer,

Lee J.W., van Dijk, Layne, Hargittai, and Orlikowski. Note that only four (less than half) of them have contributed papers to the EGOV conference, others are cited through books, articles and papers published elsewhere. Note also that majority of the authors from Table 3 are not only outside the community of authors of papers published at the EGOV conference, they can be hardly considered members of the EGR community. This finding leads us to the first conclusion that the most influential authors in EGOV community come from other (neighboring) scientific fields, which might be considered to be another indicator of the field immaturity.

Table 3. Authors with the highest proximity prestige in each of the cumulative citation networks; the last column shows the range of the proximity prestige measure. Emphasized author name indicates that the author has contributed papers to the EGOV conference.

Network	List of most cited authors	Proximity Prestige
2005	Ahn, Katsikas, Gritzalis, Lopez, Pernul, Sandhu, Coyne, Feinstein, Youman	0.012
2005-2006	**Grönlund**, **Traunmüller**, Hood, Hirschheim, van de Ven, Margetts, Horrocks, Andersen, Watson, Bannister, Remenyi	0.011-0.017
2005-2007	Heeks, **Grönlund**, Hood, **Wimmer**, Hargittai, Layne, Lee J.W., **Scholl**, Orlikowski, **van Dijk**, Nielsen	0.016-0.020
2005-2008	**Grönlund**, Heeks, Hood, **Wimmer**, Lee J.W., Webster, **van Dijk**, Layne, Margetts, Hargittai, Orlikowski	0.019-0.025

In the final stage of our analysis, after identifying the most frequently cited authors, we extracted the lists of references citing their articles and papers and examined the latter. We looked into the thematic topics covered in these papers and articles, since they reflect the prevailing topics of the EGOV conference papers in the last four years. In the continuation of the section, we present these topics.

Most of the references to the two most cited authors, Grönlund and Heeks, are to their papers that provide analysis or state-of-the-art overview of the e-government research. Each of them also edited a volume dedicated to the providing a broad overview of the research within the field; we also clustered references to these edited volumes under the thematic topic of state-of-the-art e-government research. This topic is definitely, and this comes by no surprise, the most frequently cited one.

The second most influential thematic topic, identified mostly through the papers authored by Wimmer and her colleagues, is the topic of integrating e-services in public administration. The topic is relevant by itself, its popularity being probably reinforced by numerous research and development projects related to it, funded by European Commission within its 5th and 6th Framework Program. Papers in this thematic cluster introduce and analyze different frameworks for and approaches to seamless user-centric integration and interoperability of e-government services.

While first two thematic topics are induced from the papers published within the EGOV conference community, the rest of the thematic topics are external to EGR. Orlikowski, through her cited articles and papers, brings in another frequently cited topic of organization transformation under the influence of information and communication technology. This comes by no surprise, since e-government studies often try to evaluate the influence of technology on the public administration domain, especially the way government provide services to citizens and businesses. Another influential topic, brought in by papers authored by Hargittai is the topic of digital divide. Here the focus is mainly concentrated on the study beyond the digital divide, for which the authors use the term "digital inequality". The issue is relevant for e-government, since it identifies groups of Web users with significantly different/diverse Web usage skills. The e-government research often refers to the inequalities between these groups and tries to integrate them in the empirical studies and models of e-government acceptance, take-up, and usability.

A single paper, authored by Layne and Lee J.W., introduces an issue of establishing a unifying e-government model as the fifth most frequently cited thematic topic. With maturation of the EGR field, one would expect the topic of establishing a unifying e-government theories and models to become one of the most important and influential issues. This however, does not currently hold true for the papers published in the EGOV conference proceedings.

Finally, through the most cited authors, we also identified four almost equally frequent topics, which are less frequent then the top five, discussed above: the paradigm of new public management (Hood), factors of success or failure of e-government projects (Heeks), user profiling and services personalization in public administration (van Dijk), and roadmaps for future e-government research (Wimmer).

Regarding proximity prestige measure presented in Table 3, Grönlund is the most cited author in three of four "cumulative" networks and the preference of this author is obvious from 2006 onwards. Figure 4 presents the authors, which are according to input relations adjacent to Grönlund, i.e., the network of authors that cite his works.

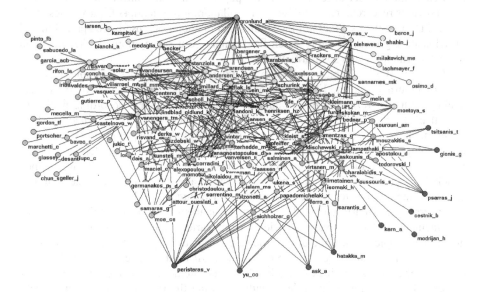

Fig. 4. The subnetwork of the 2005-2008 citation networks containing authors that cite papers authored by Grönlund

Figure 4 presents the 3 levels of neighborhood of the node corresponding to Grönlund and consists of 129 authors, which are directly (make direct citations to his work) or indirectly connected to him. Thirty-eight authors make direct citations to Grönlund's papers (in Figure 4 the corresponding nodes are colored yellow) and 90 authors (green and red nodes) are indirectly connected to him. The latter ones are connected to the most prestigious author over one (green vertices) or two (red vertices) intermediary authors. Note that Grönlund's neighborhood does not contain other authors from the list of most cited ones, presented in Table 3. This might be considered as a first sign of maturation of the EGR field, in terms of formation of sub-communities of authors in the field; each community developing an independent line of research. This hypothesis is yet to be confirmed with further network analysis.

4 Discussion

As we emphasized in the introduction, the rapid development of the e-government research field (EGR), motivated many authors to analyze the current state and the dynamics of EGR. There are three studies by Grönlund [5,6], Heeks and Bailur [7], and Andersen and Henriksen [1] that our paper strongly relates to. Grönlund proposes a model for measuring the maturity of the field focusing on the phases through which the research fields pass in the process of becoming mature. He uses two different datasets in the study: in the first one papers published in the proceedings of the EGOV conference (as well as papers from two other major e-government conferences) in 2003 and in the second one the papers from EGOV conference in 2005. He observes an increase in the authors' efforts to comply with the research publication standards, increase in the number of references in the papers, which indicates better involvement with previous research, and increase in the collaboration of authors from various institutions. Despite the exactness of the studies and methodology used, the applied model of delineating growth of the research field cannot be used anymore, as the change in founding principles was so enormous [6].

Heeks and Bailur [7] base their study on a data set that includes a sample of papers from two journals and the EGOV conference. They concentrated solely on the papers dealing with e-government *per se* and they characterize papers according methodological issues related to: statements authors make about impacts associated with e-government, statements about underlying research philosophy, evidence of research methodology and methods used, and use of particular theories or models (and/or the impact of absence thereof in the EGR field). On the basis of further analysis, they concluded that the change over time seems limited and they proposed some solutions and recommendations for further research in e-government field.

Andersen and Henriksen [1] also perform an analysis of EGR research on a data set that includes 110 peer-reviewed articles from various journals that address the e-government topic. Again, the aim of the research is to identify the type of methodological approaches and research populating the EGR field. The results show that most of EGR focus on capabilities of applications and interactions with citizens and businesses, while only few studies deals with exploring the role of government in technology diffusion and citizen participation in political and democratic discourse.

There are several important differences between approaches taken in the presented studies of EGR field development and the one presented here. First, the data set used in our study is a *systematic one* that includes *all the papers* published in the proceedings of the EGOV conference in the last four years and not on a sample of papers. We are aware that focusing on a single publication venue can be considered as a limitation of our study, which we further address in the final section. Second, as opposed to the focus on methodological approaches in the other studies, we identify here the thematic topics that take most of the attention of the authors contributing to the EGOV conference. Third, our study relies on standard scientometric method widely used to analyze other research fields.

The principal idea of inclusion of social network and citation analysis into EGR field is similar to the use of these methods for analysis of other scientific fields. The citation analysis has been proposed and used for exploration of structural characteristics in case of several journals, conferences, and research disciplines. Various approaches to citation analysis were taken, such as word co-occurrence analysis, bibliographic coupling, co-citation analysis, intercitation analysis, and co-authorship analysis. All these approaches were used to explore and describe the state of development of the particular discipline [8], the impact of conferences on other scientific areas [3], the history and sociology of particular scientific area [12], or to analyze an actual social network based on bibliography database [13].

Note finally that the utility of social network analysis in e-government studies has been already demonstrated. The studies concentrate primarily on connections between principal actors working together to implement e-government project [4] or on partnership networking for implementing local e-government policies [9]. In this kind of studies, we are usually confronted with mixed methods studies, since, beside the social network analysis, as an exploratory method, these studies include other qualitative and quantitative methods, such as interviews and surveys.

5   Conclusions and Further Work

Scientific research is a collaborative activity, where researchers establish collaboration through coauthoring papers or through building upon research results accomplished by others and citing their work. The collaborative aspect of scientific research can be nicely captured using social network analysis, as illustrated in this paper. Following standard citation analysis methods, we identify most cited authors in the EGR field and through analysis of the references to their papers, we identify the most prominent research topics that occupy the interests of researches in the field. We consider that result to be an important cornerstone in the process of establishing a map of the EGR field map. Another important contribution of our study is the establishment of a first systematic bibliographic data set of e-government research.

However, the data set is far from being exhaustive. The first obvious limitation is its focus on a single publication venue that is the proceedings of the EGOV conference. Although it represents a nice start, the immediate task for further work in extension of the data set with data on papers from other e-government conferences (such as the annual conference the Digital Government Society of North America) and journals (e.g., *Government Information Quality* and *Information Polity*).

In the present paper we focused on the citation networks, where nodes correspond to authors and links correspond to citations. Our data set allows for establishment and analysis of other types of networks as well, on which we will focus in our future work. One possibility is to analyze the network of co-authors, where each link corresponds to the fact that the two connected authors has co-authored a paper [10]. Another possibility is the analysis of the citation networks in terms of publication venues where the referenced papers come from. The result of such analysis would reveal what are the most influential "neighboring" scientific fields and publication venues that strongly influence the development and shape of the EGR field. Furthermore, all the networks included in our study has nodes that correspond to authors, while, in general, nodes in citation networks can correspond to publication units (papers, articles, and books). Note however, that it will be quite a challenge to uniquely identify publication units in the rather "noisy" data set of references.

Acknowledgments. This material is based in part upon work supported by the Slovenian Research Agency through the funds for training and financing young researchers. We would also like to thank the three anonymous reviewers for their comments that helped us improve the presentation of the analysis results.

References

1. Andersen, K.V., Henriksen, H.Z.: The first leg of e-government research: domains and application areas 1998-2003. International Journal of Electronic Government Research 1(4), 26–44 (2005)
2. Bibliometrics,
   http://www.ischool.utexas.edu/~palmquis/courses/biblio.html
3. Clausen, H., Wormell, I.: A bibliometric analysis of IOLIM conferences 1977-1999. Journal of Information Science 27(3), 157–169 (2001)
4. Cotterill, S., King, S.: Public Sector Partnerships to Deliver Local E-Government: A Social Network Study. In: Wimmer, M.A., Scholl, J., Grönlund, Å. (eds.) EGOV 2007. LNCS, vol. 4656, pp. 240–251. Springer, Heidelberg (2007)
5. Grönlund, A.: State of the Art in e-Gov Research – A Survey. In: Traunmüller, R. (ed.) EGOV 2004. LNCS, vol. 3183, pp. 178–185. Springer, Heidelberg (2004)
6. Grönlund, A., Andersson, A.: e-Gov Research Quality Improvements Since 2003: More Rigor, but Research (Perhaps) Redefined. In: Wimmer, M.A., Scholl, H.J., Grönlund, Å., Andersen, K.V. (eds.) EGOV 2006. LNCS, vol. 4084, pp. 1–12. Springer, Heidelberg (2006)
7. Heeks, R., Bailur, S.: Analyzing e-government research: Perspectives, philosophies, theories, methods, and practice. Government Information Quarterly 24, 243–265 (2007)
8. Liu, Z., Wang, C.: Mapping interdisciplinarity in demography: a journal network analysis. Journal of Information Science 31(4), 308–316 (2005)
9. Medaglia, R.: Local networking for e-services: A UK case study. In: Wimmer, M.A., Scholl, H.J., Grönlund, Å., Andersen, K.V. (eds.) EGOV 2006. LNCS, vol. 4084, pp. 256–268. Springer, Heidelberg (2006)
10. Newman, M.E.J.: Scientific collaboration networks. I. Network construction and fundamental results. Phisycal review E 64 (2001)

11. de Nooy, W., Mrvar, A., Batagelj, V.: Exploratory social network analysis with Pajek. Cambridge University Press, New York (2005)
12. Otte, E., Rousseau, R.: Social network analysis: a powerful strategy, also for the information sciences. Journal of Information Science 28(6), 441–453 (2002)
13. Sabo, S., Grčar, M., Fabjan, D.A., Ljubič, P., Lavrač, N.: Exploratory analysis of the ILPnet2 social network (2007),
    http://kt.ijs.si/Dunja/SiKDD2007/Papers/Sabo_PajekILPNet.pdf
14. Scholl, H.J.: Is E-Government Research a Flash in the Pan or Here for the Long Shot? In: Wimmer, M.A., Scholl, H.J., Grönlund, Å., Andersen, K.V. (eds.) EGOV 2006. LNCS, vol. 4084, pp. 13–24. Springer, Heidelberg (2006)

Qualitative Data Analysis of Issue Interrelations and Interdependencies for E-Government Research Planning

Maria A. Wimmer and Melanie Bicking

University of Koblenz-Landau, Institute for Information Systems,
Universitätsstr. 1, 56070 Koblenz, Germany
{wimmer,bicking}@uni-koblenz.de

Abstract. Science and technology roadmapping is currently a popular method to develop long-term strategies for e-government. In the scope of the EC-co-funded research project eGovRTD2020, an innovative methodology has been developed, which combines scenarios and roadmapping to support long-term strategic policy-making for e-government research. This approach bases on systematically analyzing qualitative data throughout the whole roadmapping process based on individual issues and their interrelations. The paper explores the complex analysis of the network of relations and interdependencies between these issues. We introduce a concept for the systematic analysis of interlinks between single issues, which helps improving the quality of analysis and advances the consolidation of results to form well grounded strategic policy-making. A case example extracted from the project serves as proof of concept.

Keywords: Qualitative data analysis, roadmapping, strategic policy planning, e-government.

1 Introduction

The concept of good governance "describes the principles, approaches and guidelines for good governance and public administration to promote interaction and formation of political will with regard to societal and technological changes" [17]. Already in 2001, the European Commission (EC) has formulated five principles for good governance: openness, participation, accountability, effectiveness and coherence [3]. For a number of years, governance and strategic policy-making were addressed separately, and were not researched with the focus of using ICT. Yet in the course of good governance, strategic planning of research and technology development (RTD) has become a crucial success factor in global competition, both in the private and the public sector. Technology support thereby becomes more and more important. Consequently in November 2008, the EC has published a research call in Framework Program 7 with the objective 7.3 dedicated to "ICT for governance and policy modeling"[1]. This call specifically focuses the involvement of the general public in policy-making and in strategic decision-making thereby exploiting advanced ICT.

---

[1] http://cordis.europa.eu/fp7/ict/ (accessed 4th June 2009)

M.A. Wimmer et al. (Eds.): EGOV 2009, LNCS 5693, pp. 26–39, 2009.
© Springer-Verlag Berlin Heidelberg 2009

In preparation to this call, within the EC's 6th Framework Program of Information Society Technologies (IST), the eGovRTD2020[2] project was carried out to sketch e-government in 2020 roadmap and, thereby, identifying future strategic research fields for the development of e-government and the public sector as such [3]. The project methodology linked scenario building and technology roadmapping for long-term strategic policy-making and e-government research. With the identification and recommendation of thirteen key research areas in the next future, the methodology provided guidelines for e-government research programs and national long-term e-government policies [3].

In this context, the project consortium developed a qualitative data analysis approach based on the definition of four explicit process steps (cf. [3] pp. 13-36):

- Investigating the *State-of-Play* of e-government research: Strategic documents were studied to identify current e-government research and implementation foci in existing European and national strategies and policies of governments [1].
- Building *Scenarios* to envision potential long-term futures of e-government and respective settings: The scenarios depicted potential future settings of governments, society and economics, as well as modern ICT used in performing government activities and in interacting with their constituencies [7].
- Conducting a *Gap Analysis* to compare the research foci of both state-of-play and scenarios and to identify research gaps: The gaps were assessed according to their relevance and their impact to the overall governance model (i.e. policy formulation, policy execution and policy enforcement (cf. [7] and [3] p. 31f). For gaps identified with high relevance and impact, gap storylines were developed. Hence, the needs of future research emerging from the scenarios, as well as risks and weaknesses in current research were argued and fed naturally into the next step of roadmapping [12].
- *Roadmapping* e-government research by formulating, prioritizing and phasing e-government research themes and actions (based on gaps identified): The final results were a set of thirteen research roadmaps for contributing to strategic policy-making of public sector innovation through government modernization supported by ICT use. Each roadmap proposed a research theme and measurable actions which were prioritized and set into a timeframe to be implemented (cf. [3] pp. 121--161).

Each of these steps of the eGovRTD2020 strategic planning methodology collected, structured and analyzed qualitative data and, thereby, produced new outcome, as well as input for the next step.

The targeted addressees of the eGovRTD2020 results were organizations managing research funds and therewith being responsible for the proper use of these funds. Such organizations and the respective decision-makers must rely on qualitative information and arguments well grounded and well reasoned in order for them to make the best possible choices for future investments towards economic growth and prosperous developments. Hence, traceability - i.e. tracing the line of argumentation from the final result (roadmap) back to its roots (original text passage of strategic documents) – was crucial to verify the argumentation of the interpretation.

---

[2] http://www.egovrtd2020.org/

To provide well grounded and well reasoned arguments for future developments, and with the request for a holistic approach for e-government 2020 (cf. [3], pp. 13-17, [16]), the eGovRTD2020 approach had to be based on a rigorous research method. Applying a holistic approach results, however, in a complex endeavor and requires effective tool support. Above all, it requires consideration of interrelations and inter-dependencies between individual dimensions as set out in the holistic framework for e-government (cf. [3], pp. 13-17, [16]). Managing and computing the interrelations and interdependencies of a variety of dimensions and issues calls for proper ICT tool support in qualitative data analysis.

The paper is organized as follows: next section reviews approaches to qualitative data analysis. Section 3 introduces the qualitative data analysis method used in eGovRTD2020 and respective requirements resulting from the demands of improving the performance and management of traceability and replicability in qualitative data interpretations. Section 4 presents a concept to make qualitative data analysis more visible and clear. An exemplary case from eGovRTD2020 serves as proof of concept (section 5). We conclude with a reflection of work and an outlook for further work.

2   Approaches to Qualitative Data Analysis

Working along the eGovRTD2020 project evidenced that interdependencies among issues may strongly bias the resulting recommendations to give. Analyzing and tracing such interdependencies was perceived crucial in ensuring high quality of analysis and well grounded results, in particular since the interpretation of the qualitative data should be replicable and easily comprehensible.

Qualitative methods are now widely used and increasingly accepted in a variety of fields and domains (e.g. [2], [5]). However, critics often blame qualitative research of not ensuring quality criteria and standards of empirical research such as objectivity, reliability and validity due to subjectivity and arbitrariness in the interpretation of the collected data (no unified and standardized data collection schema). Over the last years, researchers (see e.g. [2], [7], [10]) have worked on improving the quality of qualitative research. Qualitative data analysis (QDA) methods such as Grounded Theory [15], Objective Hermeneutic [13], Qualitative Content Analysis [10], Documental Method [2] etc. have emerged as a response to afore mentioned criticism. These QDA approaches provide documented and inter-subjective arguable methods.

As a matter of fact these well grounded QDA methods are specifically tailored to the application in social sciences. Consequently, they are not completely applicable to the e-government domain. Yet as stated in ([6] pp. 12-17 and 25f), the investigation of social science concepts and solutions is a chance to learn from excellence, as well as from examples and extract what practitioners need. If the problems are the same, but the context is different, the lessons learned might be still valuable, although adaptations need to be made.

Current discussions about quality criteria and standards in the field of qualitative data analysis also evidence the importance of inter-subjective traceability and replicability in QDA domains [14]. eGovRTD2020's underlying qualitative data analysis concept sought a methodically controlled and holistic concept to be kept visible. In consequence, interrelations and interdependencies for coping with the holistic approach had to be addressed, made visible and traced properly.

3 Qualitative Data Analysis in eGovRTD2020

Preparation of the raw qualitative data material started with a synthesis based on the reduction of the data complexity. This took place by means of qualitative data analysis thereby standardizing the level of generality and increasing it stepwise. With a growing level of abstraction the extent of data material decreased, since single issues (i.e. units of meanings) were integrated and clustered. Then the aspired level of abstraction was defined[3]. The steps followed to generalize issues towards a high level of abstraction were [10]:

- Reduction through *selection*, i.e. removing issues with exact the same meaning(s)
- Reduction through *clusters*, i.e. constructing and integrating issues at the same level of abstraction, as well as compiling a catalogue of new statements as a system of categories thereby reviewing and - if necessary - revising the synthesized system of categories on the basis of the original material (i.e. inductive development of categories).

In this respect qualitative data analysis took place through synthesizing (complexity reduction through abstraction but keeping the key contents) and structuring (structure material using predefined classification criteria) regarding a multi-disciplinary approach [3].

The data analysis of both stat-of-play and scenarios were processed alike. Figure 1 depicts the approach (figure adopted from [3] p. 27f, and [12]). Thereby, state-of-play documents and scenario documents were analyzed to identify relevant issues, which were categorized into topics of interest or dimensions, and further on grouped and categorized into dimensions.

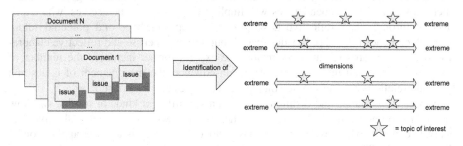

Fig. 1. eGovRTD2020 methodology for qualitative data analysis of text-based documents

For common understanding, we herewith recall the definitions of the terms used for clustering and generalizing (cf. [3], p. 6):

---

[3] Examples of qualitative data collected are available from the respective deliverables: state-of-play, scenario building, gap analysis and roadmapping under http://www.egovrtd2020.org/ and in [3].

- *Issues* are aspects/elements in a text. A text combines various aspects/elements of e-government and its settings. An issue can be either a dimension or topic of interest.
- *Topics of Interest* are single points along a dimension and are a particular type of issue. One topic of interest may belong to more than one dimension, e.g. the trust dimension can contain certification authorities as a topic of interest. Certification authority can also belong to the security dimension.
- A *dimension* is a variable depicting two opposing extremes on the future of e-government and is a particular type of issue. For example, in the dimension "trust in government", one extreme is distrust in government and the other extreme is a high trust in government. A dimension has at least two opposing topics, (i.e. denoting the extremes) and can contain further topics along the scale.
- A *category* refers to a cluster or group of similar dimensions leading to a more holistic understanding of e-government. As such, categories denote a domain or interactions between domains of the holistic framework of e-government (see also [3] p. 15f).

Underlying data of the first two methodological steps (state-of-play and scenario analysis materials) resulted in two lists of categories (one per methodological step). Each category represented a cluster of similar relevant issues identified and extracted from text. For traceability and replicability purposes, the text passages were coded and assigned to predefined categories thereby counting the number of occurrences of issues in order to identify relevant foci and emphases. In a second step, the list of issues was divided into two lists per category, a list of topics of interest and a list of dimensions described through extremes.

Up to this step, the qualitative data analysis and the results extracted were easily traceable und replicable. Further elaboration resulted in steady decrease of traceability and replicability, because the subsequent interpretation of data based mainly on the knowledge of the experts who were structuring, synthesizing and interpreting the material, i.e. only the experts knew about the original interrelations and interdependencies between the single topics of interests and the dimensions. The knowledge about these interrelations and interdependencies was implicit to the experts themselves, who explicated it through their reflective descriptions by gap storylines and potential future research demands (cf. [11]). Besides that, through their expertise and reflective elaboration of gaps towards research roadmaps, the experts further increased the number of topics of interest and interrelations. As a consequence, the management of issues and their interrelations becomes more complex and requires proper tool support.

In order to visualize and distinguish between the different kinds of results, and how they relate to one another or imply each other, we herewith introduce a qualitative data analysis concept, which bases on text-based document analysis and the application of the eGovRTD2020 policy planning methodology thereby relying on visualization of dependencies.

4   Visual Concept to Analyze Interrelations and Interdependencies

Before presenting the concept, we introduce the notions of reliability, validity and transparency of results, as these features are the drivers for the concept. In the eGovRTD2020 methodology's qualitative data analysis, reliability is achieved if the results are consistent and if the results of the study are replicable under a similar methodology [7]. Therefore the line of argumentation and the interrelations as well as interdependencies between issues need to be traced and well-presented. By contrast validity refers to quality and trustworthiness thereby establishing confidence in the findings [9]. Confidence is a powerful determinant of achieving validity; therefore concepts need to build and ensure trust in the results gained. The concept of transparency "denotes the property of transmitting light so as to make what lies beyond completely visible" [4]. Adopting the definition for the scope of this paper, transparency aims at generating approval for long-term strategic decisions. This can be achieved through a concept which allows tracing issues as well as interrelations and interdependencies among issues from the final result back to its origins and thereby making the complex structure of qualitative data analysis visible to outsiders.

Figure 2 illustrates a generic visualization of issues identified in the state-of-play analysis, and the corresponding interdependencies among the issues. Likewise, Figure 3 visualizes the exemplary issues and their interrelations identified in scenarios.

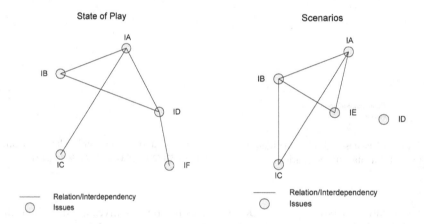

Fig. 2. A generic graphical sketch of issues identified, and their interdependencies identified in the State-of-play

Fig. 3. A generic graphical sketch of issues identified, and their interdependencies identified in Scenarios

A synthesis of the issues in the state-of-play vs. scenarios results in the following constellations of issues and relations:

- Issues included in both, state-of-play and scenarios: IA, IB, IC, ID
- Issues and their corresponding relations which are included in both state-of-play and scenarios: IA--IB, IA--IC
- Issues only mentioned in the state-of-play: IF
- Issues only emerged in scenarios: IE
- Issues and their corresponding relations which are only included in the state-of-play: IA--ID, ID--IF

– Issues and their corresponding relations which are only included in the scenarios: IB--IC, IB--IE, IA--IE.

In a first step, the graphical sketch of issues and their interrelations facilitates thorough analysis of both, state-of-play and scenarios separately. In a second step, it also supports in the gap analysis through the visualization of issues and their interrelations. Therewith, the concept supports the juxtaposition of state-of-play and scenario results, as depicted in Figure 4, Figure 5 and Figure 6. Based on these interrelations, qualitative data analysis can be made visible and therewith traceable. This supports further on in the gap analysis, and in the subsequent roadmapping activity, where further issues and interrelations may be identified and brought into play.

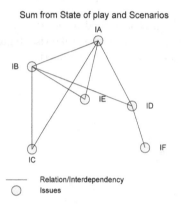

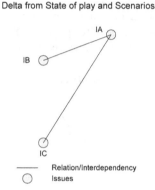

Fig. 4. Sum of issues and relations identified in both, State-of-play and Scenarios

Fig. 5. Delta of issues and relations from both, the state-of-play and the scenarios

The visualization of issues and interdependencies in Figure 4 gives an idea about the scope of the whole domain of study with its elements and their relations. A comparative analysis of Figure 2, Figure 3 and Figure 4 provides first insights into the gaps between as-is-situation (described through the state-of-play) and the potential to-be-situation (outlined through the scenarios), both in terms of issues and their interrelations. Consequently, the following alternative conclusions may be drawn from the synthesis, which support the subsequent gap analysis in eGovRTD2020:

– An issue and/or a relation only exist in the state-of-play. As the issue or relation does not exist in the future, no gap or need for action in strategic planning exists.
– An issue and/or a relation only exist in scenarios. Here, a gap and need for action is identified, which calls for proper strategic planning.
– An issue and/or a relation exist in both, the state-of-play and the scenarios. In this case, a more thorough synthesis is required. Thereby, all issues and relations, which are included either only in the state-of-play or only in the scenarios, are eliminated from the summary graph, hence creating the delta graph as depicted in

Figure 5. In further qualitative analysis of the issues and relations, two alternative results are possible:

- No gap exists. Future needs are completely tackled by current strategic and research activities. Analysis of the issue and/or relation terminates at this point.
- A potential gap exists. As current research only reflects parts of the identified future demands, the issue or relation needs to be further investigated.

By creating a database with the individual issues grouped into dimensions and further on into categories, and their interrelations, a first step of qualitative data analysis is supported. Through the visualization, the qualitative - and even a quantitative - synthesis are supported. The synthesis can further be supported with annotating the quality of relations in the juxtaposition of state-of-play and scenario results as depicted in Figure 6. In this case, the summary graph of Figure 4 is taken as the basis, and the results of synthesis described above are added to the relations (cf. legend of figure on right hand side for coding of quality). Apart from that, further expert-based relations which are identified through the synthesis are added (broken line relation).

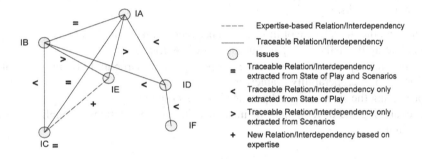

Fig. 6. Expanding the visual model of issues and relations with the assessment of relations and additional expert-based identification of relations

Through the expansion of the visual model of a domain, its issues and relations by adding qualitative assessments in the database and the visualization (see Figure 6), it is now possible to juxtaposition phases of analysis, synthesis and development of a roadmap and therewith support full traceability and replication of a strategic plan from the state-of-play via the scenarios and gaps identified to roadmap themes or activities in a strategic plan. With this concept, we demonstrated how to counteract the criticism of subjectivity in qualitative data analysis ("interpretation of data only taking place in the mindsets of experts who process the analysis") by introducing traceability of analysis and synthesis steps through the visualization, qualitative annotation and argumentation in the juxtaposition of evolving results (state-of-play vs. scenarios; state-of-play vs. roadmap, scenarios vs. roadmap).

Through a respective tool support (application integrating text-based qualitative data analysis and database with annotation and visualization facilities), a traceable and replicable line of argumentation can be navigated back and forth from state-of-play to final roadmaps and/or strategy plans. An important advantage of such a tool support is further on, that the results can be reused and lay the ground for further iterations of roadmap developments and strategy planning.

For strategy developers and those experts, who conduct qualitative data analysis, the concept serves as means to evidence the quality of their results and to make their analytical work much easier since the concept allows them at any point in the process to go back to the original material and therewith trace and replicate their own works.

An important requirement for the tool implementation is to support alternative result paths through versioning and, therewith, to allow strategic decision-makers to reason about costs, public value and impact of different alternatives.

5 Applying the Concept to an Example from eGovRTD2020

The example chosen for the proof of concept is "interoperability". For demonstration purposes, the state-of-play example is limited to issues extracted from the IDABC program[4]. IDABC aims to improve the effectiveness of European public administrations and cooperation between them thereby supporting and promoting the development of pan-European e-government services and the underlying interoperable telematic networks. Focus is put on:

- enabling the interchange of information between public administrations
- facilitating the delivery of pan-European user-centric services
- getting interoperability across different policy areas, particularly on the basis of a European Interoperability Framework (EIF)
- promoting the spread of good practice in e-government
- encouraging the development of innovative telematic solutions in public administrations.

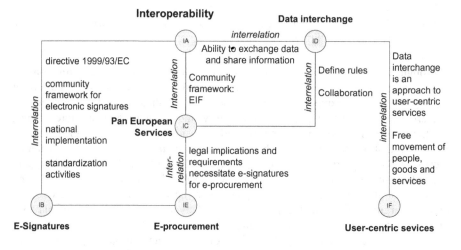

Fig. 7. Interoperability issues and relations extracted from the state-of-play

[4] IDABC: Interoperable Delivery of Pan-European e-government Services to Public Administrations, Business and Citizens, cf. http://europa.eu/scadplus/leg/en/lvb/l24147b.htm

A particular focus within IDABC is Public procurement by electronic means (e-procurement) in order to improve and simplify the way government procurement operates. E-procurement is tackled to help enterprises identifying contract opportunities and supplying their goods and services across Europe's Internal Market thereby contributing to Europe's competitiveness and economic growth. E-signatures are thereby still a barrier to be overcome in conducting business across Europe. Besides, implementation activities focus on facilitating electronic public procurement by providing functional requirements, common tools or generic services for the contracting authorities.

Figure 7 shows five issues related to interoperability (which is an issue, too). The interrelations between the single issues are detailed to show interlinks in interoperability research and implementation.

Next, an example extracted from the scenario entitled "Mature (e)-government in the united federal states of Europe"[5] is given, which embodied interoperability as an important dimension with a number of topics. Central idea of the scenario was that "Europe's member states closely work together and national thinking shifts to European thinking in 2020. Technology is used everywhere and is part of daily life therefore interoperability is of utmost importance and is fully deployed".[5] The issues extracted from the scenario are shown in Table 1.

Table 1. Issues extracted from scenario "Mature (e)-government in the united federal states of Europe"[5]

Europeanization	Ageing society	Transparency
Multi-channel access	E-inclusion	Reforms in administration
Mobility	E-voting	Eliminate relics
One-stop Government	User-friendly services	Simplify processes
Services for the elderly	Cheaper services	Automating of the back-office
Networked systems	Data protection	Monitoring and control
Identification and authentication	Regulatory framework	Standardization Interoperability
Translation technologies	Central databases	User-friendly technology
E-payment	E-procurement	Integration

Issues in grey cells present those, which are directly or indirectly related to interoperability according to the scenario example. Only these issues are considered for simplification for the case analysis. Their interrelations are shown in Figure 8.

Since the state-of-play and the scenario analysis take place one after the other, complexity of interrelations and interdependencies is manageable. In gap analysis, both results are brought together. Hence, complexity rises extremely and therefore the interrelations can only be managed with proper tool support. We therefore can only present a limited extraction of the example.

Gaps are not simply and strictly referred to as the differences between the 'as is' and the 'to be' situation, since they may cover different issues emerging from a wide-ranging comparison of the state-of-play with the alternative possible futures depicted

---

[5] See Deliverable 2.1 (p. 49) available online at http://www.egovrtd2020.org/

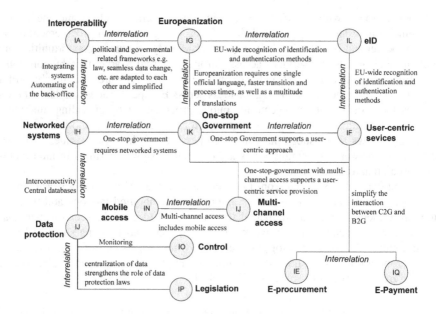

Fig. 8. Interoperability issues and relations extracted from scenario description

in the scenarios. In order to express a well grounded line of argumentation of gaps, the differences need to be extracted carefully and transformed into visible assessments of interrelations, as proposed in the concept presented in section 3. Figure 9 presents the application of the concept to the respective gap assessment of the case example.

As shown in Figure 9, three common issues exist in both, state-of-play and scenarios (dark grey nodes IA, IE, IF): interoperability, e-procurement and user-centric services. Interrelations among issues, which were in the state-of-play, have been coded with "<". Interrelations identified only in the scenario have been coded with "<". In this example, there are no direct relations existing in both, state-of-play and scenarios (hence no "="). However, from the graph one can identify second order interrelations via intermediate issue, e.g. interoperability and user-centric services are connected via data interchange in the state-of-play, and via Europeanization and eID in the scenarios. Europeanization and pan-European services play an important role in both. In terms of interoperability in the scenario, networked systems are key. Hence, a number of expert-based relations have been added, as these issues strongly interrelate with interoperability in the context of the future scenario.

The visualization of the different kinds of relations either existing in current research and/or policy documents or in future scenarios lays the foundation for the subsequent step in the eGovRTD2020 roadmapping methodology. First of all, the assessment of gaps by experts is facilitated a lot with a tool support that visualizes issues of a domain in its current state as well as in potential future images. Further on, the tool support enables annotation of issues and relations with gaps and gap assessments in terms of very high, high, middle, low, no relevance to e-government ([12], [11]). Being supported with extraction of only the gaps which are assessed as

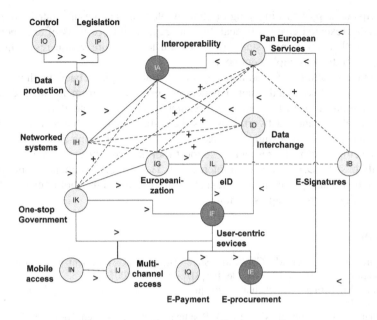

Fig. 9. Assessment of research and implementation gaps in the interoperability case example

very high or highly relevant, next steps are facilitated as well. Only those gaps which are assessed as very high and high relevant are considered for developing gap story-lines (cf. [3] p. 6), which lay the ground for the roadmap themes. The gap storylines aim at giving a deeper understanding of needs emerging in future scenarios, as well as the risks and weaknesses in current research. Adding these lines of argumentation to the assessment completes the grounds for traceable and replicable development of roadmaps and strategic plans.

The whole eGovRTD2020 approach demands a great deal of qualitative data analysis support through a proper ICT tool. A central part of the concept for a col-laboration and communication tool is the visualization needed to support the compari-son of the state-of-play and the scenario issues and relations. Thereby it must support the inclusion of scientific expertise of the analysts and enable networked knowledge for collective analysis.

6 Conclusions and Outlook

The eGovRTD2020 science and technology roadmapping methodology [3] presents a comprehensive and thorough approach to assess and understand e-government as a complex and dynamic socio-technical domain. The methodology includes both, broad vision and detailed analysis for roadmapping and strategic planning, based on a holistic concept. Through a proper QDA tool, the analysis of the major discontinuities, un-knowns, and contrasts between the state-of-play and the possible future scenarios can effectively be supported. Likewise, through the annotation of gaps identified, and their assessment of importance and relevance in respect to the domain under consideration, the subsequent step of roadmapping or strategy planning can be facilitated. Above all, the concept presented enables traceability and replicability of lines of argumentation back and forth from current status of a domain to its future vision resulting in the roadmap or strategy to implement next.

Through traceability of roadmap results or strategic plans back to their starting points, decision-makers and other outsiders are given an instrument to better understand the evolution of results and to argue them. Such an extended visual QDA tool supports reliability and trustworthiness, as the results are traceable and replicable by anybody that wants to investigate the results of a strategy planning activity.

The development of the respective support tool is currently under way. First steps of visually based QDA have been implemented. The tool development has progressed until simple gap analysis mapping. Next steps are to expand the tool to enable the last step of tracking the roadmap evolution.

References

1. Bicking, M., Bowern, M., Cook, M.: State-of-play in eGovernment research and implementation in Europe and worldwide. In: [3], pp. 37–56 (2007)
2. Blaxter, M.: Criteria for evaluation of qualitative research. Medical Sociology News 22, 68–71 (1996)
3. Codagnone, C., Wimmer, M.A. (eds.): Roadmapping eGovernment Research: Visions and Measures towards Innovative Governments in 2020. MY Print snc di Guerinoni Marco & C, Clusone (2007)
4. De Klerk, P.: Transparency, Confidence-Building and Verification and the Peaceful Use of Nuclear Energy. In: International Topical Workshop on Proliferation-Resistance in Innovative Reactors and Fuel Cycles, International Atomic Energy Agency (IAEA) & LNCV, Como, July 2-6 (2001)
5. Firth, L., Mellor, D., Pang, J.: Qualitative research across cultures: data quality issues. In: Qualitative market research: approaches and applications, pp. 127–140. Icfai University Press, Hyderabad (2007)
6. Huntingford, J., Frosini, P.: Knowledge and Innovation for Regional Growth. Recommendations based on European good Practices. ERIK (European Regions Knowledge based Innovation) Network 4 (2007)
7. Janssen, M., Wimmer, M.A., Bicking, M., Wagenaar, R.W.: Scenarios of governments in 2020. In: [3], pp. 55–84 (2007)
8. Lenk, K., Traunmüller, R.: Öffentliche Verwaltung und Informationstechnik - Perspektiven einer radikalen Neugestaltung der öffentlichen Verwaltung mit Informationstechnik. R.v.Decker's Verlag, Heidelberg (1999)
9. Lincoln, Y.S., Guba, E.G.: Naturalistic inquiry. Sage, Beverly Hills (1985)
10. Mayring, P.: Qualitative Content Analysis. Forum: Qualitative Social Research [On-line Journal], vol. 2 (June 2000),
    http://qualitative-research.net/fqs/fqs-e/2-00inhalt-e.htm
    (Date of access: May 9, 2008)
11. Pucihar, A., Bogataj, K., Wimmer, M.A.: Gap analysis methodology for identifying future ICT related eGovernment research topics - case of ontology and semantic web in the context of eGovernment. In: Markus, M.L., Hampe, J.F., Gricar, J., Pucihar, A., Lenart, G. (eds.) Proceedings of 20th Bled eConference eMergence: Merging and Emerging Technologies, Processes, and Institutions, Digital Proceedings,
    http://domino.fov.uni-mb.si/proceedings.nsf/2007/
    (accessed: 5th June 2009)

12. Pucihar, A., Bogataj, K., Wimmer, M.A., Janssen, M., Malinauskiene, E., Bicking, M., Petrauskas, R., Klein, M., Ma, X., Amadori, G., Traunmüller, R.: Gap analysis: the process and gap storylines. In: [3], pp. 85–120 (2007)
13. Reichertz, J.: Objective Hermeneutics and Hermeneutic Sociology of Knowledge. In: Flick, U., et al. (eds.) Companion to Qualitative Research. Sage, London (2004)
14. Steinke, I.: Kriterien qualitativer Forschung. Ansätze zur Bewertung qualitativ-empirischer Sozialforschung. Juventa, Weinheim (1999)
15. Strauss, A.L., Corbin, J.: Grounded Theory Research: Procedures, Canons and Evaluative Criteria. Zeitschrift für Soziologie 19, 418 et. seq. (1990)
16. Wimmer, M.A.: The Role of Research in Successful E-Government Implementation. In: Zechner, A. (ed.) E-Government Guide Germany. Strategies, Solutions and Efficiency, pp. 79–87. Fraunhofer IRB Verlag, Stuttgart (2007)
17. Wimmer, M.A., Stadach, M., Morland, P.: Glossary. In: Zechner, A. (ed.) E-Government Guide Germany. Strategies, Solutions and Efficiency, pp. 431–456. Fraunhofer IRB Verlag, Stuttgart (2007)

Caste Structures and E-Governance in a Developing Country

Rahul De'

Indian Institute of Management Bangalore, Bannerghatta Road,
Bangalore 560076, India
`rahul@iimb.ernet.in`

Abstract. Castes, or endogamous kinship relationships, are prevalent in communities across the world and particularly in developing countries. Caste plays a strong role in determining community structures and political power. However, the role of caste as a factor in shaping e-governance design and outcomes is absent in the literature. This paper addresses this particular gap by examining some cases from India.

The paper specifically considers whether the priorities of dominant caste groups determine e-governance design and implementations, to the exclusion of marginal and non-dominant castes. Further, it examines if e-governance introductions change or affect the relations of caste groups. The research relies on Structuration theory to provide a framework through which to study these issues. Data from three case studies from India are used to conduct the analysis, and these include the Bhoomi project from Karnataka, the Gyandoot project from Madhya Pradesh, and the VKC project from Puducherry. All three are information kiosk-based projects for providing e-governance services for citizens living in villages and rural areas.

Keywords: e-governance, development, caste, Structuration, technology, India.

1 Introduction

Many e-governance programmes in developing countries reach into the furthest regions of the rural countryside. These programmes intend to bring governance services, via digital means, to citizens who have little access to modern governance mechanisms. This technology 'contact' brings with it new assumptions and new relations of governance; it emerges in a field that is already dense with social relations that are both historically defined and are changing and re-forming in response to the onslaught of modernity.

Prior research has examined the impact of e-governance in rural areas, the manner in which the systems are designed to best serve governance needs, and the manner in which participation of rural citizens can be improved, amongst other issues. This research has examined the artifact of e-government systems in the given situation, though not much effort has gone into considering the

M.A. Wimmer et al. (Eds.): EGOV 2009, LNCS 5693, pp. 40–53, 2009.

manner in which the artifact affects social structures and networks of relations. In particular, in the case of India, research ignores the manner in which e-governance affects and is affected by the structures of caste in India. This paper attempts to address this gap in the literature.

Caste relations in India are a complex subject to study and understand. There is a notional understanding of caste, and an in-practice understanding based on *jati* and brotherhoods, which are visible through social practices such as rites, ceremonies, marriage relations, and through political formations. Castes and caste groups are changing and dynamic in nature, as they respond to the priorities and challenges of the social-political environment.

The paper begins with a basic framework of caste and caste dynamics in India. This framework is used as a backdrop to understand the design, implementation and impact of a few e-governance programmes that have been implemented in rural regions. To conduct this analysis the paper relies on Structuration theory, a theory that provides a substantial analytical framework to understand the minute details of everyday practices and relations within society. The structure of the paper is as follows: a review of the literature on caste in India; a review of e-governance research in developing countries, mainly India; an outline of Structuration theory; a brief outline of three e-governance projects; analysis of the influence of caste in the projects; and conclusions.

2   Background Theory and Research Questions

2.1   Caste in India

Caste in India is best captured by the phrase "idioms of association far more powerful than any other single category of community" ([1]; page 7). Caste is a term applied by the British colonial rulers to understand the myriad complexities of the systems of kinship, endogamy, Vedic *varna* categories and profession-based communities that existed across India. The most widely held view of caste is that it consists of four broad varna categories arranged in a rough hierarchy - the brahmins, the kshatriyas, the vaishyas, the shudras - that drew their provenance from ancient scriptures. However, the current composition of castes is very complex - for example, the most populous castes, currently referred to as Other Backward Classes (OBCs), constitute a wide range of castes corresponding to the middle castes in the varna order. In addition, there are the Scheduled Castes (SCs), also called *Dalits*, corresponding to traditional manual professions, and Scheduled Tribes (STs), originally from forested tracts, who are outside the varna order.

Caste plays an important and significant role in the everyday lives of individuals. In village India, the result of being in a caste implies that beginning from childhood individuals are taught rituals, responsibilities, family and community status and differences, as understood from within their caste position. Differences are sharpened and clarified, and also notions of purity for some castes are established. Everyday practices, calendrical and life cycle rituals are determined by the caste credo. Caste also shapes the political and social contours of village life, [2] determining fault lines of contest and emerging affiliations.

Central to understanding caste in villages in India is the notion of the dominant caste [3]. The dominant caste is identified as one having either numerical strength or a dominant status (despite not having numerical strength), which is obtained through various means, such as land ownership, Sanskritisation (adopting Vedic daily rituals) or Westernisation. The dominance provided by these two modes of living also present opportunities for caste mobility, or the ability to move away from the inherited caste to one that is perceived to be higher in the social order.

Forms of modernity introduced first in the colonial period, and later, have provided means for certain caste groups to mobilise. School education introduced by the British, and the railways, provided newer forms of access and physical mobility that also enabled caste mobility.

In most of colonial India, the British introduced a system of administration of villages and districts that deliberately ignored the caste dynamics on the ground. Administrators from different regions, and mostly of the Brahmin caste, were brought in to have a 'neutral' administration. This practice became widespread and was adopted by feudal rulers of princely estates who served the British. Post India's Independence, this practice continued and led to a widening gap between the local elite, who held sway over village politics, and the national elite who were responsible for implementing national policies in these same villages. This tension led to the slow movement of local dominant caste groups to demand and obtain state power through electoral politics as well as through penetration in the administrative class. National politics in India is now dominated by caste groups and caste affiliation dynamics[4]. This, also, results in a politics of 'appeasement' where certain caste groups are given privileges through policy measures, in preference to others.

In the popular discourse, caste biases have a negative connotation, as something abhorrent, an evil too. They are oppressive and demeaning, as, for example, those who were called 'untouchables' (some Dalit castes). This aspect of caste is reinforced in the media, popular literature, films, novels, and other works of art. Caste biases are viewed as racist in origin and devoid of either an objectivist or a humanist sensibility that argues for eschewing caste considerations in social interactions.

2.2   Review of e-Governance in Developing Countries

There are two broad streams of literature on e-governance in developing countries. One stream identifies, describes and then evaluates projects as to their effectiveness in delivering some governance service[5,6,7]. This research makes an implicit assumption that e-governance is needed in developing countries, is almost necessary, and the objective of the research is to uncover why it has succeeded (or not) and then to learn from and replicate those results. This research often assumes that technology introductions are deterministic in nature and, further, the impact of such introductions can be measured through simple and visible parameters.

A second stream of research explicitly acknowledges the complexities involved in technology introductions and takes a less definite and more reflexive approach towards examining e-governance in developing countries. In this research, technology is not assumed to be a fixed and over-determined entity but a plastic catalyst that introduces change, and is also shaped by it [8]. When information technology is introduced to assist in the process of governance it comes into a confrontation with existing modes of working and culture [9,10]; it modifies existing practices and processes and is actively resisted [11,12]; it impinges upon developmental issues of access, power, the role of the market and individual liberties and freedoms [13,14,15].

Though research in this stream has considered the contextual particularities [9,16] of the local situation, the literature is largely lacking in an explicit analysis of caste groups and how they impact or are impacted by information technology introductions. This is a serious gap in the literature, given that caste politics and relations form some of the most important and fundamental social structures in developing countries, and particularly so in India. Any developmental or social innovation in India is introduced into a field that has a pre-existing and evolving social dynamic that will engage with the innovation. This engagement has to be understood theoretically and also in its practical instantiation.

2.3   Review of Structuration Theory

Structuration is a theory of sociology that explains, or draws cause-and-effect relations for, human actions and events in society. This theory builds on the idea of 'structures' that are abstract rules or ways of doing, or the meanings associated with seeing and doing, and operate through implicit and explicit codes. Structures have three dimensions, those of signification, domination and legitimation. Structures of signification provide meaning and associations for everyday objects and acts. These structures reside in objects and artifacts of daily use that justify the structures themselves and reinforce their signification as humans continue to use them. Structures of domination are relations of power evident in conversations, writing and other forms of discourse and in human action. These structures are reinforced by humans acknowledging and acquiescing to power relations, such as to those in authority. Structures of legitimation are those rules of conduct and action that are considered appropriate and are sanctioned. These structures determine what is acceptable and habitual in the everyday practices of humans.

Structures are not fixed or unchangeable [17]. They are created through practice, by humans, and thus reside in the everyday and ordinary activities of communities of people. The theory of structuration deliberately avoids prior theories that relied on fixed structures in society, thus making human action passive, and also theories that relied inherently on human action, while ignoring the issues of power, social relations and constraints [18]. Structuration argues that structures existing in society and human action are mutually constitutive and form a duality. So observed social phenomena are not a product of one or the other but of both.

Structuration theory enables a richer understanding of the issues that pertain to the use and management of information technology in organisations. For instance, important interactional influences of IT within organisations [19] are: shaping of IT by humans, facilitation of human action by IT, embedded norms in technology, and the shaping of structures with IT.

These interactions arise in an ever-changing and evolving context of the organisation. Structuration theory enables *interpretive flexibility* [19], which assumes that technology is never objectively fixed and its nature is changing based on its use. Further, structuration achieved with the introduction of technology is emergent and recursive by nature. More specifically, the "...structures of technology use are constituted recursively as humans regularly interact with certain properties of a technology and thus shape the set of rules and resources that serve to shape their interaction" [20].

2.4   Research Questions

Caste practices are a form of structuration on their own. Caste affiliations and *jati* practices create structures of signification, domination and legitimation in village life: use of caste symbols (by choice of clothes, as marks on the forehead) on an everyday basis signal caste position and power, as also reinforce the position; access to village resources and affiliation with those in power mark caste domination through everyday living; and living in caste-segregated villages provides legitimation of caste-based practices.

Introduction of e-governance in villages in India creates a set of interactions between technology and human relations. It is hypothesised that relations between those in different caste groups are affected by the technology, may be mediated by it, and caste groups and affiliations impact the manner in which the technology is designed, implemented and used. In this context the two important research questions that arise are:

1. Do the design and implementation of e-government systems reflect existing caste priorities and practices? Are the systems designed, implicitly or explicitly, to address the priorities of the dominant caste?
2. Do e-government systems change or affect in any way the existing caste order and practices? Do they impact the existing relations between different caste groups?

2.5   Methodology

The research questions are addressed by considering three e-governance projects from India. The three projects are the Bhoomi project from Karnataka, the Gyandoot project from Madhya Pradesh, and the Village Knowledge Centres (VKC) project from Puducherry. These projects were chosen as they are all mature projects, they have sustained for more than five years, are widely used, and all have a focus on rural populations.

Data for two projects, Bhoomi and VKC, were obtained from primary sources - multiple site visits, several hundred field interviews, and structured surveys - as also from published secondary sources. (Details of the extensive primary data collection are omitted for reasons of space.) Data for the Gyandoot project was obtained only from secondary sources. All secondary sources are cited.

3   Data and Analysis

3.1   The Bhoomi Project

The Bhoomi (meaning 'land') project of Karnataka was launched in 2001 in a state-wide effort to computerise land records. Bhoomi kiosks enable two services, of providing copies of land records to farmers and of providing a queue system for logging land mutation (sale or transfer) requests. The kiosks are located in all 177 sub-districts of the state and cover the entire revenue land (agricultural land). Farmers go to the kiosks to obtain land records, which are essentially records of their land holdings (listing the pattern of farming, a record of loans taken, etc) that they can obtain for a nominal fee and also quite quickly. Bhoomi kiosks are widely used, particularly for obtaining land records that are later used to obtain loans from banks.

The kiosks were designed with the specific intent of giving easy access to land records for farmers. Traditionally, the records were maintained and issued by village accountants (VAs), officials of the revenue department located in villages, and they were known to take a long time to process the records and also demanded bribes [21]. Now, the records are maintained at a kiosk located at a sub-district office, and are updated three times a year by the village accountants with data on crops grown by the farmers. The kiosks are managed by fresh, young hires who were specifically trained for the job.

3.2   Caste Interaction with Bhoomi

In Karnataka [22,23] the dominant caste groups are divided principally into *Lingayats* and *Vokkaligas*. Lingayats are a coalition of castes that formed from a particular religious movement, whereas Vokkaligas are landed peasants who also belong to different endogamous castes. These two groups have dominated village-level politics in Karnataka, and in the post-Independence era also at the state level. An important aspect of this dominance is that almost all chief ministers, who have come from these caste groups, have always played to the interests of these communities, with few exceptions. Government policies, handouts, jobs, schemes, scholarships etc were all targeted at these two communities with the neglect of others, particularly the lower caste groups. As these caste groups began to gain political power, they started replacing Brahmins and non-Hindus in the bureaucracy. This further strengthened their political power in the state.

At the village level the bureaucratic functions of revenue collection and land settlement was also dominated by the two caste groups, led by the village headman, and their allies. This combined with the fact that most farmers in Karnataka were owner-cultivators presented a strong class interest of farmers that was dominated by the caste-group interests.

Bhoomi's introduction in Karnataka followed the priorities of the dominant landed castes. It was designed to provide easy access to land records and to make efficient the land sale or transfer process. These benefited the land-owning castes the most, as they were in the best position to use the easy availability of land records to obtain loans and also participate in land transactions. Dalit and lower castes work mainly as landless labour and as tenant farmers in the state and they had marginal use of the Bhoomi system. In a study [24] of two different land-tenure regions, one in which the majority of farmers were owner-cultivators (the district of Mandya in Karnataka) and one in which the majority were tenant farmers (the district of Koppal), it was found that Bhoomi clearly benefited larger farmers over small farmers, and also land-owning farmers over tenant or landless farmers.

In Koppal, elimination of VAs from the land records issue process helped the land-owning and absentee land-owners to ensure that their titles did not get diluted (Koppal is dominated by landlords who allow tenants to farm on their lands; if this fact is recorded on the land record by the VA, it could mean loss of rights for the owner). Any entry in the record now requires approval at the sub-district offices, which the land-owning castes have better access to and they can control adverse recordings (eg. name of the legitimate tenant cultivator). The fact that since the time of the introduction of Bhoomi no fresh tenancy applications have been filed in the office of the Koppal district administrator (as also the use of Bhoomi data for disposing off any pending tenancy applications) points to the insignificance of Bhoomi for the non-dominant tenant castes of Koppal.

A strong motive for Bhoomi's design and implementation was to reduce/curtail the powers of the village accountant [25]. The VAs invariably belonged to the dominant castes and traditionally served the dominant groups well, however, they were also the most helpful officials for Dalit and lower castes in all matters related to access to government services - such as scholarships, subsidies, certificates, loans, etc. With a reduction of the powers of the VA, the non-dominant populations are affected as their everyday access to governance and services is also reduced.

In the everyday practices of Dalit and landless farmers, Bhoomi has not acquired significance. It remains remote and alien, also physically removed from the site of living and work. Bhoomi remains disconnected from and irrelevant for acquiring seeds, negotiating with moneylenders, sowing, etc. It is not a carrier of information about prices, weather, subsidies, government schemes, etc. In its distance from the village, it privileges those who can travel to the sub-district headquarters, can afford to lose a day's wages, can apply for and get bank loans, and have property to transact.

3.3   The Gyandoot Project

The Gyandoot Telecentres were launched in the Dhar district of the state of Madhya Pradesh, in the year 2000. The telecentres or kiosks were small rooms consisting of a computer connected to a network via modem, a printer, an uninterruptible power supply (UPS) box, some furniture, and some additional peripheral equipment (like scanners). 34 kiosks were set up initially, in various towns and villages in the district, with one kiosk in each town, and each was connected to the rest via a local area network and to the district headquarters, in Dhar town. The kiosks were initiated and funded on a public-private partnership basis, with local youth being selected as the kiosk operators or *soochaks*. The project champion was the District Collector (the senior-most official in the district and also a member of the elite Indian Administrative Service (IAS)).

Gyandoot kiosks were designed to provide e-governance services such as complaint registration, access to government forms, purchase of land records, applications for government schemes, along with a host of commercial services such as commodity price reporting, sale of goods, and information exchange.

Gyandoot was launched under a formal committee called the Gyandoot Samiti that selected the soochaks and the location for the kiosks. The objective of the Samiti was to have local control, through *panchayats* (village councils) over the kiosks. The soochaks had to pay an annual fee of Rs 5000 to the Samiti to retain their access to the networks. They earned revenues by levying nominal charges for all services rendered through the kiosks.

Gyandoot did not have the impact that was initially promised. The project was awarded the Stockholm Challenge Award in 2000, soon after its initiation, based more on the concept and its bold objectives. Gyandoot had been located in the Dhar district particularly because this was a 'backward' district, with about 60% of the population below the poverty line. After the initial phase, and particularly after the champion was transferred out of the district (which is routine for IAS officers), the governance services declined dramatically as the departments responsible for addressing the needs arising from the kiosks lost interest in servicing them. Studies show [26,27] that there was not much impact on uplifting the poor residents of the district; and the few interesting cases of redress of complaints, better price availability for sale of products, faster response for crop diseases, remained isolated cases with no substantial impact. The kiosks also suffered from problems of connectivity and a steady supply of electricity.

Gyandoot kiosks do survive and are in use. Recent studies show that they are thriving on providing a host of services in addition to those they were designed for; the most sought after services continue to be for accessing land records [28], followed by information on market and prices, and the access to exam results from school boards.

3.4   Caste Interaction with Gyandoot

The state of Madhya Pradesh is located in the what is known as the 'Hindi belt' that is characterised by a majority of the population speaking the Hindi language. It is also a state that has historically been dominated by the upper castes, as it was amalgamated from princely estates after India's Independence. Political power was consolidated within the three varna castes, also based on their access to control over most agricultural land in the state. Post Independence, the Congress party dominated politics and held power continuously, with all the chief ministers drawn from the dominant castes. The Congress party retained a long history of factionalism within the state and no individual chief minister could sustain complete control for too long. However, the later leaders made sure that their base was consolidated by incorporating some of the backward castes, SCs, OBCs, and STs, which constitute a fifth of the population in the state.

The Gyandoot project was initiated with the explicit developmental intention of addressing the needs of the poorest people in Dhar, those below the poverty line, and this meant largely the SCs, the STs and a fraction of the OBCs. Gyandoot's three-part objectives of information and service enhancement, entitlement enablement, and capability enhancement [28], were implemented in a manner that enabled the landed middle-class and literate population to have a far better use for its services than the marginal populations [29,28]. STs are typically marginal/subsistence farmers who do not produce surplus that they have to market, typically do not have title access to land and so have no need for land records (one of the most popular applications of Gyandoot), and do not have the literacy or wherewithal to use the facilities for training in computing technology.

Gyandoot kiosks were of two kinds, those controlled by the village councils, and funded by them, and those controlled privately. The soochaks were appointed by open advertisement and competitive selection by the village councils; they were trained to use the equipment and were provided assistance with setting up the kiosks. There is evidence that the private kiosks were assigned more on the basis of connections and caste affiliation - a particular case in point [30] is in Badnaver town, where an upper caste soochak was able to set up a kiosk despite there being one in existence already, on the grounds that he was able to entertain the district officials at his home.

Surveys of users and non-users [29,28] show two prominent tendencies: when a kiosk is located within the village or town, the community is more likely to use its facilities; and there is high awareness about its facilities amongst most non-users. The first point is apparently 'obvious,' that proximity enables use, but it also underscores the fact that for an alien technology to be integrated into the daily practices of a community, it is legitimated by proximity and a familiarity with the kiosk operators. The second finding shows that awareness does not translate into use; e-governance is brought to the local community by a central power, its mandate is more to centralise services rather than to decentralise [25], and as such it represents a prohibitive symbol of state power that is captured and manipulated by the local elite [30]. Since the awareness of and knowledge about the kiosks carries mainly through word-of-mouth [29], it substantiates the power relations already existing within the caste structures of the communities.

3.5   The Village Knowledge Centres Project

The Village Knowledge Centres (VKCs) project of the M.S. Swaminathan Research Foundation (MSSRF), an NGO based in Chennai, is a developmental initiative targeted at using information and communication technologies for development. These knowledge centres follow a kiosk model of providing computing technology to rural communities, a part of which includes providing governance information and services. (As opposed to Gyandoot, the VKCs were not designed for providing mainly governance services.)

Currently located in the Union Territory of Puducherry, itself a small land mass surrounded on the east by the Bay of Bengal and on the other sides by the state of Tamil Nadu (two districts of Puducherry are not in this land mass), the VKCs provide kiosks that connect the village community through a local network to MSSRF's resource centres from which information is transferred and exchanged. 15 VKC centres are located in Puducherry, around the central facility at Puliyarkuppam. The centres provide information on market activities, data on government schemes, computing facilities for local industry (such as milk and dairy production), training for computing skills, and Internet surfing (this last is charged). The centres are financially supported by MSSRF through international funding.

MSSRF is a prominent non-governmental organisation (NGO) in India that was set up in the late 80s. When MSSRF conceived of the VKCs in the late 90s, they actively engaged the local communities in villages to determine what services to offer, where to locate the kiosks, whom to employ for manning the kiosks, and how to manage them. There was an explicit emphasis on inclusion of women and Dalits in running and usage of the kiosks.

The VKCs currently run quite successfully in that they are actively used in most of the villages they are available in. Their financial viability was never an issue as they are funded by MSSRF. Most of the usage is for training in computer skills, which is sought by young persons seeking employment in nearby towns and cities, for information on market prices and for maintaining accounts for local milk producers. Many of the kiosk operators are women and there is a large participation of women in the kiosk usage, though less than that of men.

3.6   Caste Interaction and VKCs

The region of the Kaveri river delta, where the VKCs are located, is a site of intense caste-based politics. Many villages in that region are strongly divided, physically, along caste lines. For example, in a village of Sripuram, in the district of Tanjore in Tamil Nadu, Beteille (1996) noted the existence of three distinct neighbourhoods, those for the Brahmins, called the *agraharam*, those for the Non-Brahmins (a collection of many middle-castes, including OBCs), and those for the Dalits (or lower-castes), called *cheri* [31]. It was common practice for members of either community not to visit the neighbourhoods of the others, and if by chance they had to, they performed rituals to 'cleanse' themselves. All living practices and rituals were conducted in the region bound by caste lines, and within these bounds too there existed divisions along sub-castes. In the hierarchical order of belief, the Brahmins considered themselves to be the highest and the Dalits to be the lowest. Part of this dominant order also arose from land rights, where Brahmins historically had access to land whereas the Dalits worked as landless labour. The middle-caste Non-Brahmins were land owners but did not have the political power of the Brahmins.

A political movement of the Dalits, referred to as the Dravida movement, began in the 1920s, which brought a sense of assertiveness and political organisation to the Dalit groups [32]. After independence the Congress party dominated politics in the state of Tamil Nadu, but by the 1970s the Dravida movement asserted itself, based on a call for Tamil assertion and also a rejection of North Indian language imposition. State politics was taken over by the Dravida party, which in the course of time developed its own internecine differences and split. By the late 90s and early 2000s, the Dravida parties had fractured into many, with two dominating the political process, however several parties relying on the middle-castes (Non-Brahmin castes) had also gained political power through sheer numbers. Over the years, affirmative action policies by successive state governments had replaced the mostly Brahmin bureaucracy by persons from the Dalit and middle castes. These actions have also led to claims for and contest for power, leading to violence amongst caste groups [33].

When the VKCs were introduced in the late 90s, the promoters explicitly engaged in a dialogue with people in the villages to understand the manner in which caste would interact with the usage of the kiosks. One of the issues that had to be resolved was the location of the kiosks. They had to be in a place considered to be neutral for access. Certain temples and panchayat offices were considered to be suitable for the kiosk offices as they were accessible by many different castes [31]. After the kiosks were set up, some were actively resisted by certain caste groups as it was not in their part of the village and they used political pressure to have them relocated [34].

The VKC kiosks remain largely unused by Dalits [34,35]. The services and facilities provided are of no use for them. The kiosks have no meaning for their everyday practices as landless farmers. The kiosks are modern inventions that are used by the upper and dominant castes, for accessing various government services and for learning new skills. Even in a village where the kiosk is located in the Dalit areas, the usage is low as the main residents do not have much use for the kiosk's services, and also because upper caste residents will not venture into the facility, it being outside their caste boundary.

4   Conclusions

We revisit the research questions and examine answers to them in the light of the three case studies presented above.

The first question was whether the design and implementation of e-government systems reflected the priorities of the dominant castes. For the Bhoomi and Gyandoot cases there is clear evidence to conclude that the services of the systems meet the needs of primarily the dominant castes. Inscribed into the implementations of the kiosks was a rationality that clearly favoured the practices and priorities of the dominant castes in Karnataka and Madhya Pradesh. For the case of the VKCs, there was a deliberate attempt to include the needs of non-dominant and marginal castes, however, through use and emergent configurations, the priorities of the dominant castes prevailed.

Caste, an "idiom of association," manifested itself in everyday practices of access to, mobility around, sharing of knowledge about, and use of the kiosks. Caste affiliation and privilege played directly into the equation for extracting the new resources made available by a powerful technology. Everyday practices of the dominant castes facilitated, and were facilitated by, the easy appropriation of the technology.

The second question was whether the technology introduction changed or affected the existing caste order. The evidence from all three cases is conclusive: although the non-dominant castes may not be worse off from the presence of the e-government systems, the dominant castes are certainly better off. With easy and better access to markets, information and governance services, the dominant castes have improved their own relative economic advantage. There is strong evidence for this in the Bhoomi and Gyandoot cases.

Historically, caste mobility was possible by effective appropriation of new technologies by caste groups, and this appears to be the case with e-governance also. With some caste groups being able to leverage the new technologies better, they are in a position to mobilise their *jati* with respect to others. In the fiercely competitive space of political and economic dominance, e-governance plays its, possibly, intended role.

Caste and kinship groups exist in all communities of the world, and, in particular, in the developing world. So far, research in e-governance has ignored the interactions that such technological innovations have with caste groups (and this paper makes a first attempt to fill this gap in the literature). The findings of this paper underscore the fact that caste concerns not only impact the design and implementation of e-government systems, but also are themselves impacted by the technology.

Structuration theory provided the lens by which to examine the everyday practices of individuals in communities as also to examine and interpret the recursive influences of technology and social structures. It helped constitute an *a priori* theoretical framework with which to read the particular context of e-governance introductions in a rural community. Another strong contribution of this paper is in demonstrating that Structuration theory is valuable in understanding the sociology of caste and e-governance.

References

1. Dirks, N.: Castes of Mind. Princeton University Press, Princeton (2001)
2. Nicholas, R.W.: Structures of politics in the villages of Southern Asia. In: Singer, M., Cohn, B.S. (eds.) Structure and Change in Indian Society, pp. 243–284. Aldine Transaction (1968)
3. Srinivas, M.: Mobility in the caste system. In: Singer, M., Cohn, B.S. (eds.) Structure and Change in Indian Society, pp. 189–200. Aldine Transaction (1968)
4. Harriss, J.: Comparing political regimes across Indian states: A preliminary essay. Economic and Political Weekly (1999)
5. Bhatnagar, S.: Development and telecommunications access: Cases from South Asia. In: Avgerou, C., Rovere, R.L.L. (eds.) Information Systems and the Economics of Innovation, pp. 33–52. Edward Elgar, Cheltenham (2003)

6. Bhatnagar, S.: E-Government: From Vision to Implementation. Sage Publications, New Delhi (2004)
7. Rao, T., Rao, V., Bhatnagar, S., Satyanarayana, J.: E-governance assessment frameworks. Technical report, National Institute for Smart Government, Hyderabad (2004)
8. Williams, R., Edge, D.: The social shaping of technology. Research Policy 25, 856–899 (1996)
9. Walsham, G., Sahay, S.: GIS for district-level administration in India: Problems and opportunities. MIS Quarterly 23(1), 39–66 (1999)
10. Madon, S.: Computer-based information systems for decentralized rural development administration: A case study in India. Journal of Information Technology 7, 20–29 (1992)
11. De', R.: E-Government systems in developing countries: Stakeholders and conflict. In: Wimmer, M.A., Traunmüller, R., Grönlund, Å., Andersen, K.V. (eds.) EGOV 2005, vol. 3591, pp. 26–37. Springer, Heidelberg (2005)
12. Silva, L., Hirschheim, R.: Fighting against windmills: Strategic information systems and organizational deep structures. MIS Quarterly 31(2), 327–354 (2007)
13. Avgerou, C., McGrath, K.: Power, rationality, and the art of living through sociotechnical change. MIS Quarterly 31(2), 295–315 (2007)
14. Madon, S.: Evaluating the developmental impact of e-governance initiatives: An exploratory framework. The Electronic Journal of Information Systems in Developing Countries 20(5), 1–13 (2004)
15. Prakash, A., De', R.: Importance of developement context in ICT4D projects: A study of computerization of land records in India. Information Technology & People 20(3), 262–281 (2007)
16. Puri, S.K.: Integrating scientific with indigenous knowledge: Constructing knowledge alliances for land management in India. MIS Quarterly 31(2), 355–379 (2007)
17. Giddens, A.: The Constitution of Society. Polity Press, Cambridge (1984)
18. Jones, M.R., Karsten, H.: Gidden's structuration theory and information systems research. MIS Quarterly 32(1), 127–157 (2008)
19. Orlikowski, W.J., Robey, D.: Information technology and the structuring of organizations. Information Systems Research 2(2), 143–169 (1991)
20. Orlikowski, W.J.: Using technology and constituting structures: A practice lens for studying technology in organizations. Organization Science 11(4), 404–428 (2000)
21. Chawla, R., Bhatnagar, S.: Bhoomi: Online delivery of land titles in Karnataka, India. Web Document (December 2001) (accessed in April 2005)
22. Manor, J.: Karnataka: Caste, class, dominance and politics in a cohesive society. In: Frankel, F., Rao, M. (eds.) Dominance and State Power in Modern India, vol. 1, pp. 322–361. Oxford University Press, Oxford (1990)
23. Manor, J.: Structural changes in Karnataka politics. Economic and Political Weekly (1977)
24. Prakash, A.: Development Paradigms, Social Contexts and Patterns of Technology Use: Study of Land Record Computerization in India. PhD thesis, Indian Institute of Management Bangalore (2008)
25. De', R.: Control, de-politicization and the eState. In: Wimmer, M.A., Scholl, H.J., Ferro, E. (eds.) EGOV 2008. LNCS, vol. 5184, pp. 61–72. Springer, Heidelberg (2008)
26. Kothari, B.: Comment (Gyandoot: When you look closer, the moon has craters). Regional Development Dialogue 23(2), 60–64 (2002)

27. Cecchini, S., Raina, M.: Electronic government and the rural poor: The case of Gyandoot. Information Technologies and International Development 2(2), 65–75 (2004)
28. Tiwari, M., Sharmistha, U.: ICTs in rural India: User perspective study of two different models in Madhya Pradesh and Bihar. Science, Technology & Society 13(2), 233–258 (2008)
29. Jafri, A., Dongre, A., Tripathi, V., Aggrawal, A., Shrivastava, S.: Information communication technologies and governance: The Gyandoot experiment in Dhar district of Madhya Pradesh, India. Working Paper 160, Overseas Development Institute (2002)
30. Sreekumar, T.: Decrypting e-governance: Narratives, power play and participation in the Gyandoot intranet. The Electronic Journal on Information Systems in Developing Countries 32(4), 1–24 (2007)
31. Beteille, A.: Caste, Class and Power: Changing Patterns of Stratification in a Tanjore Village. Oxford University Press, Oxford (1996)
32. Gorringe, H.: Taming the Dalit Panthers: Dalit politics in Tamil Nadu. Journal of South Asian Development 2(1), 51–73 (2007)
33. Vincentnathan, S.G.: Caste politics, violence, and the panchayat in a South Indian community. Comparative Studies in Society and History 38(3), 484–509 (1996)
34. Parthasarathy, B.: Information and communication technologies for developement: A comparative analysis of impacts and costs from India. Technical report, International Institute of Information Technology Bangalore (2004)
35. Kenny, C.: Behind the digital divide. The Economist 374(8417), 22–25 (2005)

Towards Coordination Preparedness of Soft-Target Organisation

Mohammed Shahadat Uddin and Liaquat Hossain

Project Management Graduate Programme, University of Sydney, Australia

Abstract. In this paper, we introduce a network enabled coordination model to examine the coordination preparedness of soft-target organisations such as common public access areas including transit hubs, schools, parks, and sports areas. It is apparent that little attention is given in recent research focusing on the use of network analysis as a way to explore coordination preparedness for this type of organisation. In this study, we emphasise this type of soft-target organisation and propose a model to examine the coordination preparedness to any disasters by testing hypothesis related to network relationship and coordination preparedness. We analyse the dataset entitled *Preparedness of Large Retail Malls to Prevent and Respond to Terrorist Attack, 2004*, which contains a total of 120 completed surveys of security directors of retail malls. The following questions form the basis of this study: What do soft-target organisations need to be better prepared to respond to disaster? How does network relationship between soft-target organisation and emergency agencies affect the coordination preparedness of soft-target organisation for disaster recovery? Which degree of centrality measure needs to be followed to measure network variables in order to analyse the coordination preparedness? Result shows that soft-target organisation with high level of network relationship with other emergency agencies are better prepared to disaster response. Using this result, the preparedness of a soft-target organisation might be judged for successfully participation in an actual emergency.

Keywords: Soft-Target Organisation, coordination preparedness, network relation.

1 Introduction

We define *soft-target organisation (STO)* as an organisation where a large number of people gather regularly, which has multiple entrances and exits making them vulnerable to terrorist attack, and where there is more possibility of higher number of casualties in case of any terrorist attack. This type of organisation does not participate in any emergency response; instead they have to prepare themselves to respond and recover from any kind of disaster. Therefore, there is a need to maintain strong relationship with public emergency agencies, which puts them in a star or wheel (Figure 1) network communication structure with emergency agencies where they are in the center of the network. To measure the network position of this type of actor, degree centrality is found useful, which can be defined as the number of ties incident upon a node [7].

M.A. Wimmer et al. (Eds.): EGOV 2009, LNCS 5693, pp. 54–64, 2009.

Coordination is evident in a network when multiple actors pursue goals together. Coordination can be defined as the additional information processing performed when two or more connected actors pursue goals that a single actor pursuing the same goals would not perform [14]. More precisely, coordination can be referred to as managing dependencies between activities [15]. The following components of coordination form basis for our proposed model: (a) set of actors, public emergency agencies with which *STO* is connected and *STO* itself; (b) who perform tasks, all involved security staff in the network from emergency agencies and *STO*; and, (c) to achieve goals, better coordination preparedness [1] [13].

Studies on disaster coordination suggest that lack of coordination preparedness causes more loss in respect of casualties and finance in extreme events regardless of whether it is naturally occurring such as *The New Orleans hurricane* or man-made like the *World Trade Centre (WTC) bombing* [10]. Coordination preparedness encompassing an emergency plan, which describes required services by allowing all actors to provide support and coordination among actors, and instructional guidelines to follow in case of emergency, is considered to be the necessary precondition for handling an emergency effectively. In this paper, we analyse and hypothesise an actor's network relationship and its perceived coordination preparedness. To do so, we use variables to represent both network relationship and coordination preparedness for an actor, and use dataset to test our proposed hypothesis. We argue that an actor who maintains a strong network relationship is able to show better coordination preparedness in a disaster response.

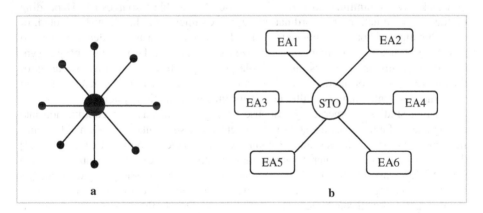

Fig. 1. (a) a star (b) Similar network structure of STO with emergency agencies (EA)

The rest of the paper is organized as follows: a background description of coordination is described in section 2. Then in section 3 proposed coordination preparedness model for *STO* is presented. We also develop a set of hypotheses for the study in this section. An overview of data collection as well as the methods used for data preparation and data analysis is described in section 4. This is followed by a discussion of the findings and conclusions.

2   Coordination

Coordination facilitates social interactions where multiple actors work towards a common goal. Coordination is something that occurs within an organisation or discipline and therefore, it is internal to the organisation. Inter-organisational coordination, on the other hand, is defined as managing capability of inter-organisational collaborations and relationships, which can be in many forms including inter-organisational teams, partnerships, alliances, and networks [8]. It is very difficult to measure coordination due to difficulties to detect the type and nature of group interactions, which define its dependent variables. For example, in an emergency response network, coordination can be measured from how often all organisations in the network share information, and rehearse its emergency protocols. Therefore, we first need to find out key coordination processes, and then measure effectiveness of those processes in order to quantify coordination. In extreme events such as disaster, organisations frequently develop formal and informal network relationships in order to save lives and return a society to a state of "business as usual" [4], and hence, a proper coordination among those organisations make it easy to achieve these goals.

Approaches to coordination can be diverse, which mainly depends on the nature of network under consideration. Traditionally, coordination has been justified as hierarchical control mechanism based on top-to-bottom approach. The idea is to maintain coordination by control from the top authority, a 'coordination by command' approach [6]. Selecting a suitable governing body make this traditional approach to coordination a contentious issue for a long time. Organisation approaches to coordination seek how to minimize cost by efficient use of available resources [9]. Depending on the way of functioning, coordination might be either centralized, or distributed, or a combination of both at organisational level. A central coordinator decomposes and distributes tasks among others in centralized coordination. To maintain proper synchronization among sub-tasks and a single point of failure are the disadvantages of this approach of coordination [2]. Tasks are often distributed among actors who can work independently and in parallel in a distributed coordination system.

Existing studies of emergency response have given emphasis on coordination and management of emergency agencies in the events of crisis. Kruke and Olsen [11] identified coordination challenges during complex emergencies. Comfort and Kapucu [4] developed a guideline for inter-organisational coordination in extreme situations. Also, a study by Riley and Hoffman [18] implies the key properties of emergency coordination in terms of having an awareness of others within the network, defining the accessibility of information flow through the network, and the quality of information that a particular organisation is able to obtain. However, research on measuring coordination preparedness from the perspective of network structure of *STO* is lacking to date. Though these types of organisations do not participate in case of crisis of others, they need to maintain strong coordination preparedness as they are possible target for terrorist attack [5].

3   Coordination Preparedness through Social Network (SN)

SN theory plays an important role in identifying and quantifying informal network, which functions at level beyond the formal and traditional organisational structure of relationships. Prior research suggest that investigations of informal networks are very useful in identifying network properties such as which actor is the most influential, what kind of relationship exist among the actors [16]. Network centrality such as degree centrality of SN theory is very efficient in assessing network behavior, which can unfold existing informal network patterns that are not invented before [3]. The selected approach to studying a social network may be determined by the type of network under investigation and its associate level of data collection.

Social network analysis (SNA) is the mapping and measuring of relationships between actors. It has been successfully applied to understand networks and their participants by evaluating locations of actors in the network. Measuring a network location of an actor is finding the centrality of that actor. There are three primary measures of network centrality: (a) degree centrality, (b) closeness, and (c) between-ness. The number of direct links connecting a node determines degree centrality of that node. It highlights the node with the most ties to other actors in the network; indicating having more direct contrast and adjacency than all other actors in the network [19]. Degree measurements mainly relevant in the studies of popularity and activity of actors as it primarily concerns with local point centrality. In the study of coordination, degree centrality is useful depending on the nature of network for measuring local authority, and might be used to compare network conditions and the state of coordination. As STO have a star type of network, degree centrality might be useful in making such a comparison.

3.1 Our Proposed Model

The framework of our proposed model, as illustrated in the Figure 2, is intended for the assessment of coordination preparedness during a non-crisis period in order to optimize network performance. The model is constructed with a view to assess the current state of coordination preparedness as a product of attributes of network rela-tion. There is a single moderating variable defined as *training score,* which is used to cluster our dataset, and also for completing a micro-level analysis.

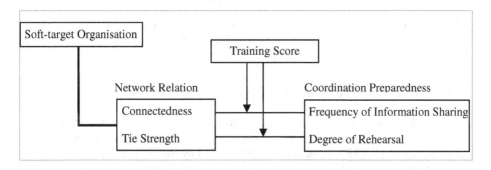

Fig. 2. A model for assessing Coordination Preparedness

We use *connectedness* and *tie strength* as independent variables in our model to measure *network relation*. *Network connectedness* or simply *connectedness* defines the number as well as nature of inter-organisational relationships such as mutual participation to achieve a common goal. It has been defined as interdependency among organisations and their network roles [17]. The second variable for network relationship is *tie strength* which is taken from the research of Kuti [12]. It defines the strength of network relationship as a source of coordinating activities such as security staff training with public emergencies agencies.

In order to assess network relationship against coordination preparedness, we define two dependent variables which form the basis of our coordination preparedness measure. *Frequency of information sharing* depicts how often actor exchange key information regarding only security intelligence. It does not include normal behavioral organisational information sharing with other organisations. The variable *degree of rehearsal* refers to all neighbors in the network, an actor rehearse its emergency preparedness plan. As a *STO* is always in the centre of a star network, this variable depicts the number of emergency agencies that a STO rehearses its emergency preparedness plan with them.

3.2 Research Hypothesis

Based on the review of literature and in alignment with our model, we propose the following hypothesis:

H1: There is a significant relationship between network involvement and coordination preparedness of an actor, where higher level of network relation produces an increase in coordination preparedness.

To assess this hypothesis, we present another four sub-hypotheses (*sH*) to evaluate and test our principle theory. They are:

- (*sH1*) *Connectedness* correlates to *Frequency of Information Sharing*
- (*sH2*) *Connectedness* correlates to *Degree of Rehearsal*
- (*sH3*) *Tie Strength* correlates to *Frequency of Information Sharing*
- (*sH4*) *Tie Strength* correlates to *Degree of Rehearsal*

H2: The relation in the H1 is mediated by the quality of security staff training. This means quality of staff training can be used to predict the strength of relation between network relation and coordination preparedness.

4   Coordination Preparedness Dataset

The dataset entitled *Preparedness of Large Retail Malls to Prevent and Respond to Terrorist Attack, 2004* is located at the Inter-University Consortium for Political and Social Research (ICPSR) website. The study funded by the United States Department of Justice and the National Institute of Justice was developed with the original purpose to assess the level of security in large indoor shopping malls as well as the associated issues of training and legislation of private security forces (Davis et al., 2006). Research investigation was carried out by Robert C. Davis of Police Foundation, Christopher Ortiz of Vera Institute of Justice, Robert Rowe of American Society for

Industrial Security, Joseph Broz of Midwest Institute of Research, George Rigakos of Carlton University, and Pam Collins of University of Eastern Kentucky.

The research agenda was to address the degree to which malls have become better prepared to respond to terrorist attacks in the aftermath 9/11 events. The framework for the collection of data involved sending letters with surveys attached to 1372 security directors across the country in 2004. The researchers also collected survey data from State Homeland Security Advisors. Furthermore, for their research purpose the researchers visited 8 shopping malls in United States and 2 malls in Israel (Table 1).

Table 1. Response rate of research sample

	No. Invited	No. Participated	Response Rate
Shopping Mall Security Advisor	1372	120	8.75%
State Homeland Security Advisor	50	33	66%
Site Visit (USA)	8	8	100%
Site Visit (Israel)	2	2	100%

The sampling technique used to invite the participants was the size of enclosed retail malls across the country. The security directors of those retail malls which were at least 250,000 square feet in size were invited to participate in the survey.

4.1 Exploring the Data

As noted on the ICPSR site, access to the research is provided by means of SPSS data files and supplementary machine-readable documents and data collection instruments. The first stage of collecting the data required a thorough exploration of the survey instrument to identify possible questions that provide relational data to assess the respondents' social network, or questions relevant to an analysis of the current perceptions of their emergency preparedness abilities. As the proposed model is for *soft-target organisation*, we were looking for all degree-based relational data of the respondent in the survey instruments.

In searching this degree-based data, three questions (1, 2, and 3 in Table 2) were found which provided information of the perceived interaction of the respondent with other agencies. The response range for question 1 is 0 to 3 organisations. For question 2 and 3, the response range is 0 to 2; where 0 indicates not at all involved and 2 indicate the strongest involvement. The scores of these three questions are combined to form the respondent's degree of connectedness with other organisations. A further investment of the survey instrument found questions to measure the respondent degree of rehearsal of emergency preparedness protocols (question 4), tie strength (question 5), and frequency of information sharing (question 6) with other agencies. Question 4 has similar response pattern as like question 1. Question 5 had response range of 0 to 2; where 0 indicates less close relation since 9/11, 1 indicates unchanged relation since 9/11 and 2 indicates closer relation since 9/11. For the question 6, the response range is 0 to 2; where 0 means never share key information, 1 means rarely share key information, and 2 indicates regularly share key information.

Table 2. Survey questions used to measure model variables

Q. No.	Degree-based Questions
1	Have emergency response plans developed to coordinate and communicate activities of security staff with local law enforcement, fire, and medical first re ponders in case of attack? If yes, with which agencies?
2	How involved has your state homeland security advisor been in planning, reviewing, or approving your security measures?
3	How involved have local or state law enforcement agencies been in planning, reviewing, or approving your security measures?
4	Have exercise been carried out to rehearse protocols with first responders? If yes, with which agencies?
5	How is your working relationship with local law enforcement since 9/11?
6	To what extent does local law enforcement informs you about key security intelligence?

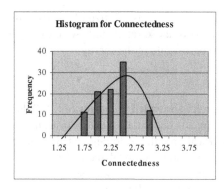
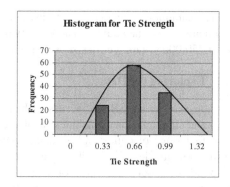

Fig. 3. Histogram for *Connectedness* and *Tie Strength*

An examination of the *connectedness*, and *tie strength* measures in Microsoft Excel reveals common distributions of both of them that follow a non-normal curve. Each graph consists of centralized score having a tapered skew to the left for *connectedness*, and a small tapered skew to the right for *tie strength* (Figure 3). These distributions are against a line indicating a non-normal and non-parametric statistical test is needed to be carried out in order to test their correlation with other variables of our model. The Spearman test is a non-parametric alternative to the Pearson test which investigates the relationships between two continuous scores.

4.2 Data Preparation

A 2-phase method for data preparation and analysis is used to assess our emergency preparedness model against the survey data. Figure 4 depicts an overview of the software used and the purpose of each phase. The first phase included importing the data files into Microsoft Excel by placing the data into columns of Microsoft Excel representing questionnaire responses. Once the data is set up correctly, variables were cleaned and invalid responses such as refusals were removed in order to prevent inaccurate statistical testing. In the second and final phase, all the variables are placed into SPSS to perform some statistical analyses for hypothesis testing as defined in our proposed model.

Data Preparation Methods		Purpose of Software
Microsoft Excel	Phase 1	Cleaning raw data file, measure variables, Out-degree centrality.
SPSS	Phase 2	Perform statistical analysis

Fig. 4. Overview of Software and phases of data preparation

5   Result and Discussion

We design both macro-level and micro-level test to validate our proposed hypotheses. At macro-level, we considered 117 datasets; exclude 3 datasets with missing values. A Spearman test is carried out to determine if there is a relationship between the continuous independent network relationship variables of *connectedness*, and *tie strength* with the continuous dependent coordination preparedness variables of *frequency of information sharing*, and *degree of rehearsal*. The result (Table 3) of this test indicates that there is a positive correlation coefficient between each independent variable with all dependent variables where an increase in the measure of any independent variable produces an increase in both dependent variables.

Table 3. Results of Spearman Correlation test (macro-level)

	Connectedness	Tie Strength	Freq. of Info. Sharing	Deg. of Rehearsal
Connectedness	1	X	X	X
Tie Strength	X	1	X	X
Freq. of Info. Sharing	0.267^{**}	0.345^{**}	1	X
Degree of Rehearsal	0.308^{**}	0.275^{**}	X	1
Note: X denotes unnecessary or out of scope testing **. Correlation is significant at the 0.01 level (2-tailed).				

From the results of the Spearman test, we find that there is a positive correlation coefficient between *connectedness* and each of the two coordination preparedness variables, where increased *connectedness* correlated to:

- *(sH1)* increased *frequency of information sharing*

We find from testing the data that the number of maintained relationships displayed by an actor have an effect on its information sharing frequency with other actors in the network.

- *(sH2)* increased *degree of rehearsal*

Our testing of this sub-hypothesis also provides evidence that the number of well maintained relationships displayed by an actor is a contributing factor in determining with how many neighbors an actor rehearse its emergency plan.

The relationship between the two dependent coordination preparedness variables against *tie strength* also produces a positive correlation where an increase in *tie strength* correlates to:

- *(sH3)* increased *frequency of information sharing*

The Spearman correlation also shows a positive result for this sub-hypothesis that by increasing the strength of relation an actor has over other actors in the network, the more frequently it can share information with others.

- *(sH4)* increased *degree of rehearsal*

Results indicate a positive correlation for *tie strength* that by increasing the strength of relationship, an actor can rehearse it coordination preparedness plans with more neighbor actors in the network.

A subsequent micro-level test for correlation is carried out to analyze our second hypothesis and also to provide support evidence of the relationship as in the first hypothesis. Well-trained security staff is one of the most important requirements for the prevention and respond to any kind of crisis for *STO*. According to the survey on state homeland security advisors, most of them endorsed improved training for security staff and emergency responders as the most important measure *STO* could take in order to better prepare against terrorist [5]. We cluster our datasets in three groups on the basis of *training score*. The questions from survey instrument like "How many hours of training does new staff receive?", "Do employee receive special training on preventing and responding to terrorism?" are taken to calculate *training score*. The range for training score is between 0 and 2.40 inclusive. Table 4 shows the training score range for each cluster. A very small difference (0.03) of *average training scores* between two consecutive clusters (0.54 and 0.51) implies a proper distribution of *training score* among all clusters. In our datasets, there are few actors having low training score; however, showing strong relation between network relationship and emergency preparedness in our proposed model. This is due to the lower number of full time security staff they have, and more dependency on contract or casual fully trained security staff. To avoid this, we consider 0.25 as our minimum *training score* for cluster 1. After eliminate all missing values we find 89 training scores out of 120.

Table 4. Training score range for each cluster

Cluster Number	Training Score Range	Avg. Training Score (base on all cluster members)	Difference
Cluster 1	0.25 - 0.75	0.58	
Cluster 2	0.76 – 1.25	1.12	0.54
Cluster 3	1.26 – 2.40	1.63	0.51

The micro-level results also support our second hypothesis and findings in the macro level. In the micro-level results (Table 5) we find that with the increase in cluster number i.e. increase in training score, there is an increase in the correlation values between the all the combination of independent and dependent variables. For example, the correlation values between connectedness and *frequency of information sharing* are 0.221, 0.289, and 0.396 for Cluster 1, Cluster 2, and cluster 3 respectively, which provide strong support for our second hypothesis. We see that there a strong positive relation (correlation coefficient score 0.623) between *tie* strength and *degree of rehearsal* for cluster 3. This is due to the way we define *training score* and cluster. We consider *'special training'* on emergency with other emergency agencies in measuring actor training score.

Table 5. Results of Spearman Correlation test for all clusters (micro-level)

		Connectedness	Tie Strength	Freq. Info. Sharing	Degree of Rehearsal
Cluster 1 N = 46	Connectedness	1	X	X	X
	Tie Strength	X	1	X	X
	Freq. Info. Sharing	0.221**	0.302**	1	X
	Degree of Rehearsal	0.267**	0.208**	X	1
Cluster 2 N = 31	Connectedness	1	X	X	X
	Tie Strength	X	1	X	X
	Freq. Info. Sharing	0.289**	0.330**	1	X
	Degree of Rehearsal	0.314**	0.342**	X	1
Cluster 3 N = 12	Connectedness	1	X	X	X
	Tie Strength	X	1	X	X
	Freq. Info. Sharing	0.396**	0.623**	1	X
	Degree of Rehearsal	0.349**	0.354**	X	1

Note: X denotes unnecessary or out of scope testing
  **. Correlation is significant at the 0.01 level (2-tailed).
  N indicates number of training score on that cluster

6   Conclusion

In this paper, we measure coordination preparedness using degree centrality of SNA technique for the central actor (*STO*) of an emergency network, which maintain a star or wheel network structure. We present a model for coordination preparedness based on network relationship. Using this model, an organisation can be reviewed in order to find its current state of coordination readiness and therefore, be judged for its potential to response to an actual emergency. Our research suggests that there is indeed a positive correlation between network relation and coordination preparedness such that by increasing an actor's involvement within the network, it is likely the ability of that actor to coordination in emergency will also increase. The results from both at micro-level and macro-level seem to complement each other and provide a stronger support for our proposed hypothesis.

References

1. Baligh, H.H.: Decision rules and transactions, organisations, and markets. Management Science 32, 1480–1491 (1986)
2. Beaumont, P., Chaib-draa, B.: Multi-Platform Coordination in Command and Control. National Science and Engineering Research Council of Canada (2005)
3. Brandes, U., Fleischer, D.: Centrality Measures Based on Current Flow. In: Diekert, V., Durand, B. (eds.) STACS 2005. LNCS, vol. 3404, pp. 533–544. Springer, Heidelberg (2005)
4. Comfort, L., Kapucu, N.: Inter-organisational coordination in extreme events: The World Trade Center attacks, September 11, 2001. Natural Hazards, 309–327 (2003)
5. Davis, R.C., Ortiz, C., Rowe, R., Broz, J., Rigakos, G., Collins, P.: An Assessment of the Preparedness of Large Retail Malls to Prevent and Respond to Terrorist Attack, A report submitted to U.S. Department of Justice (2006)
6. Donini, A., Niland, N.R.: Lessons Learned, A Report on the Coordination of Humanitarian Activities. United Nations Department of Humanitarian Affairs, New York (1994)
7. Freeman, L.C.: Centrality in Social Networks: Conceptual Classification. Social Networks, 215–239 (1978)
8. Kapucu, N.: Inter-organisational Coordination in Dynamic Context: Network in Emergency Response Managements. Connections, 33–48 (2005)
9. Kirn, S., Gasser, L.: Organisational Approaches to Coordination in Multi-Agent Systems. National Science Foundation, Arlington (1998)
10. Krugman, P.: A Can't-Do Government, The New York Times, published on September 2 (2005)
11. Kruke, B.I., Olsen, O.E.: Reliability-seeking network in complex emergencies. Int. J. Emergency Management 2(4), 275–291 (2005)
12. Kuti, M.: Cordnet – Towards a distributed behavioral model for emergency response coordination, A thesis submitted to the Faculty of the University of Sydney (2007)
13. Malone, T.W.: Modeling coordination in organizations and markets. Management Science 33, 1317–1332 (1987)
14. Malone, T.W.: What is Coordination Theory? National Science Foundation Coordination Theory Workshop, Massachusetts Institute of Technology, Cambridge, USA (1988)
15. Malone, T.W., Crowston, K.: The Interdisciplinary Study of Coordination. ACM Computing Surveys 26(1) (1994)
16. Mullen, B., Johnson, C., Salas, E.: Effects of communication network structures: Components of positional centrality. Social Networks 13, 169–186 (1991)
17. Rathnam, S., Mahajan, V., Whinston, A.B.: Facilitating Coordination in Customer Support Teams: A Framework and Its Implications for the Design of Information Technology. Management Science 41(12), 1900–1921 (1995)
18. Riley, K.J., Hoffman, B.: Domestic Terrorism, A National Assessment of State and Local Preparedness. RAND (1995)
19. Wasserman, S., Faust, K.: Social Network Analysis: Methods and Applications. Cambridge University Press, New York (1994); Appendix: Springer-Author Discount

Transforming Crisis Management: Field Studies on the Efforts to Migrate from System-Centric to Network-Centric Operations

Nitesh Bharosa, Bart van Zanten, Marijn Janssen, and Martijn Groenleer

Delft University of Technology, Jaffalaan 5, 2628 BX Delft, the Netherlands
{n.bharosa,b.vanzanten,m.f.w.h.a.janssen,
m.l.p.groenleer}@tudelft.nl

Abstract. Governments are searching for ways to improve information sharing between autonomous agencies. During crises, information demand and supply are often unbalanced, leading to situations in which relief workers are faced with incorrect, outdated or incomplete information. To address such challenges, network-centric operations (NCO), which involves information sharing with the socio-technical network as the central enabling mechanism, has been proposed. Yet, NCO is ill-understood and it is unclear whether the promised benefits can be realized in practice. In this paper we address the gap between the concept and reality of NCO. The necessary capabilities for NCO are identified using literature research and potential benefits are analyzed using field research. We found that NCO is not a silver bullet for overcoming the inherent problems of crisis management and could even reinforce existing problems. Our findings suggest that NCO is difficult to implement and needs to be complemented with capability development in the information and cognitive domain.

Keywords: network-centric operations, capabilities, crisis management, information sharing, coordination.

1 Introduction

The occurrence of major crises such as the 9/11 terrorist attacks in 2001, the 2004 SARS outbreak and the Asian tsunami have challenged governments to rethink information sharing between governmental agencies [e.g., 1, 2]. On several occasions government officials and commanders of relief agencies in the Netherlands concluded that especially the coordination of information sharing is still a major problem [e.g., 3, 4]. Evaluation studies on crisis management efforts around the world have reported similar conclusions.

In order to counter information sharing and coordination problems during crises, many governments seem to believe in the potential of network-centric operations (NCO) [e.g., 3, 5]. NCO involves sharing information in an adaptive manner among diverse actors and systems with the socio-technical network as a central enabling mechanism. According to the advocates of NCO, network-centric information sharing leads to a multitude of benefits, including improved information quality, collaboration

M.A. Wimmer et al. (Eds.): EGOV 2009, LNCS 5693, pp. 65–75, 2009.

and coordination [6-8]. As to date NCO is an ill-understood concept and the claimed benefits remain unsubstantiated by scientific evidence. In addition, academic contributions and their implications on information sharing and quality in the crisis management domain are scarce [9]. As such, there is a need for investigating the concept in more detail and how its implementation would influence information sharing and during crises. Accordingly, the objective of this paper is to understand NCO and its benefits for crisis management by analyzing field exercises.

This paper proceeds with a discussion on the challenges for information sharing during crises. After a theoretical elaboration on NCO, a framework of necessary NCO capabilities for countering information sharing problems is presented. Then, using field research, an empirical analysis on the implementation of NCO and the problems countered is presented. The paper ends with a conclusion on the added value of NCO for crisis management.

2   Information Sharing during Crises

2.1   Challenges for Information Sharing

Traditionally, hierarchy is the dominant model for coordination and information sharing during crises [10]. Hierarchical structures reflect the belief that the most effective repression operations are carried out under a rigid command and control structure. Moreover, the standard administrative approach to solving complex problems has been to organize work involving multiple agents in a vertical fashion [11]. Hierarchy is used to establish control, specify tasks, allocate responsibilities and reporting procedures, and presumably gain reliability and efficiency in workflow. This approach works well in routine circumstances when there is time to plan actions, train personnel, identify problems and correct mistakes.

This model of hierarchically coordinating resources and information has been criticized for various reasons, including that it is not flexible and it does not support emergent events and processes [e.g., 12, 13]. Under the urgent and uncertain conditions of crises, such hierarchical procedures almost always fail [14]. Because of cumulative stress, hierarchical organizations tend to break down, and personnel is hindered by a lack of information, constraints on innovation and an inability to shift resources and action to meet new demands quickly. [e.g., 12, 13]Scholars [e.g., 12-15] explain this failure by looking at the characteristics of crises, which include complexity, uncertainty urgency and dynamics. For instance, Bigley and Roberts [10] state that responding to a crisis, either of a natural kind (e.g., floods, earthquakes) or human induced (e.g., terrorist attacks), is an extremely complex process in terms of the number of organizations, information systems and the interactions between actors and information systems. During the response process, multiple autonomous agencies form a response network and need to share information on the strategic, tactical and operational levels. As a crisis evolves, the state and configuration of actors and systems in the response network changes rapidly, indicating a high level of dynamics. The process of information sharing and coordination is further hampered by time pressure [15] and event uncertainty [16]. Moreover, uncertainty often leads to the unpredictability of information needs and flows [17]. Under such circumstances, we need to acknowledge that not all relevant information is known, and that previously known conditions may be in a state of flux.

Considering the characteristics of a crisis, previous research argues that information sharing challenges are prevalent in crisis response, especially when groups that are accustomed to hierarchy and a centralized way of information sharing must suddenly work in a flatter, more dynamic, and ad-hoc structure that emerges during post-crisis relief efforts [18]. Some scholars argue that a network centric approach to information sharing may help to address information sharing challenges. NCO approaches have also gained the interest of both politicians and practitioners.

2.2 Network-Centricity: A New Approach to Information System Design

Network-Centric Operations" (NCO) or "Network-Centric Warfare" originates from the U.S. Department of Defense (DoD) and was first coined by David Alberts, Art Cebrowski, and John Gartska in a series of articles starting in 1996. The original authors considered NCO at the heart of the envisioned DoD transformation in 2020 [19]. Similar terms have been introduced in other countries as well, including Network Enabled Capability (NEC) in the United Kingdom and Network Based Defense in Sweden. The original Network-Centric Warfare (NCW) hypothesis posits the following relationships between twenty-first century information technologies, information sharing, and war fighting capabilities [20]:

1. A robustly networked force improves information sharing;
2. Information sharing enhances the quality of information and shared situational awareness;
3. Shared situational awareness enables self-synchronization and enhances sustainability and speed of command;
4. These, in turn, dramatically increase mission effectiveness.

The above hypothesis, suggesting relationships among the degree of networking, information sharing, improved awareness, improved information quality, and shared situational awareness. The NCO hypothesis has not been tested and is disputable as it is very solution driven. The objective of this paper is not to test this hypothesis, but rather to understand its implications for information sharing in crisis management. In order to understand the implications, we need to focus on the concept of networking, which is the main concept in the hypothesis. In the NCO hypothesis, networking implies information-related processes and all forms of collaboration among a distributed and changing set of human participants via the technical infrastructure. The essence of the network-centric approach is that the empowerment of soldiers throughout the brigade with decision-making authority and collaboration of small and agile teams that operate autonomously lead to information superiority. "Networking the Force" entails much more than providing connectivity among force components. It involves the development of distributed collaboration processes designed to ensure that all pertinent available information is shared and that all appropriate assets can be brought to bear by commanders to employ dominant maneuver, precision engagement, full-dimensional protection, and focused logistics.

Still, in its current state, NCO is not so much a theory as it is a set of required capabilities. In order for a military force to operate as a network centric organization, Alberts and Hayes [6] suggest the development of a number of capabilities in the physical, information and cognitive domains (see Table 1).

Table 1. Required capabilities for NCO

Domain	Required capability
Physical domain	All elements of the force need the ability to be robustly networked in order to achieve secure and seamless connectivity
	Information systems that support NCO must exchange data seamlessly and act on a compatible understanding of the data's meaning
Information domain	The force needs the ability to share, access, and protect information to a degree that it can establish and maintain an information advantage over an adversary
	The force requires the ability to collaborate in the information domain, which enables a force to improve its information position through processes of correlation, fusion, and analysis
Cognitive domain	The force requires the ability to develop high quality awareness and share this situational awareness
	The force requires the ability to develop a shared knowledge of commanders' intent
	The force requires the ability to self-synchronize its operations

Table 1 summarizes a set of necessary capabilities for network-centric organizations. Alberts and Hayes [6] argue that by developing these capabilities several advantages can be achieved. Daft and Lewin [21], for instance, argue that the defining characteristics of networked organizations as new organizational forms include flatter hierarchies, decentralized decision-making, permeable internal and external boundaries, self-organizing units and self-integrating coordination mechanisms. Accordingly, these characteristics of networked organizations should lead to benefits such as a greater capacity for tolerance of ambiguity, empowerment of employees an capacity for renewal [21]. Perhaps most important, NCO utilizes a new organizational structure and a new information-centric concept of operations. An overview of expected advantages of NCO capability development for military organizations found in the literature is presented in Table 2.

In recent years NCO has been increasingly applied to the organization of crisis management. The idea is that the network-centric approach as used in the military domain could be useful in crisis response because both concern complex multi-actor situations in which there is short decision-making time. Accordingly, in the crisis management domain, the 'force' mentioned in Table 1 would refer to a crisis management organization consisting of multiple governmental agencies, including municipalities, police departments, fire departments, ambulance services and so on. We do not yet know how NCO capabilities can exactly be developed in the crisis management domain and whether the expected advantages are actually realized by using NCO. Therefore, we study crisis management operations according to the NCO approach in practice.

Table 2. Expected benefits of NCO capability development

Expected benefits	Explanation
Empowerment and user autonomy [6]	A network-centric organization has a decentralized organizational structure. Because of this decision making and responsibilities are shifted to lower levels in the organization empowering individual soldiers in their work.
Robust information sharing (Peer 2 Peer) [8]	In a network-centric organization the various units (teams) operate fairly independent of each other. This means that failure in one unit does not (necessarily) have effect in other units.
Situational awareness across multiple echelons[6]	Parts of the organization work with each other to produce actionable information (information which can be directly translated to decisions and actions), fusing many separate facts into a common picture of the battle space.
Tolerance for ambiguity and capacity for renewal [22]	Provide flexible information systems that can swiftly adapt to the information demands of a particular operational scenario. This is necessary because information needs and what user collaborations must be supported are not always known in advance.
Rapid feedback on information sent [8]	The independence and distributions of organizational units enables feedback on information sent between units.
Real time information flow support [6]	Information flow within NCO is synchronous, which means senders and receivers of information can only exchange information when both have contact with each other.
Enhanced quality of information [6]	Information superiority, which includes creating and maintaining a continuous, high quality information flow throughout the force helps to ensure a clear and common understanding of the situation.

3   A Research Design for Studying Information Sharing

To better understand NCO and its implications for information sharing in the crisis management domain, a field study was conducted using two main research instruments: 1) fifteen of semi-structured interviews and 2) twenty-four observations of several crisis response exercises. The interviews were conducted prior to the crisis management exercises in the Rotterdam-Rijnmond Safety Region in the Netherlands. We selected this region because it organizes several large scale exercises annually which aim to allow relief workers to gain experience with responding to crises and the use of information technology.

The first part of our study entailed interviewing information system architects in the safety region. Fifteen senior information system architects were interviewed to gain understanding of how they perceive and develop NCO capabilities in the information architecture of their respective agencies. According to this objective, the sampling of the respondents was selective based on three main criteria: 1) the respondents needed to have at least 5 years of experience with information sharing in crisis management, 2) they must occupy a senior position in either the development or use of information systems for crisis management and 3) combined, the sample should represent the various relief agencies in the Netherlands. Each interview was guided by a predefined and pre-tested interview protocol containing open-ended and closed questions (the protocol is available upon request). The basic set of questions included: how does your organization define NCO, which NCO capabilities are implemented in the information architecture and which benefits and limitations do you expect when following the NCO? The interviews were voice recorded on tape so as to minimize data loss due to note-taking. Shortly after each interview, the interview notes were first transcribed and emailed to the respondents that were requested to validate these within two weeks. To be able to compare the results of the various interviews, we used ATLAS.ti which can be classified as a qualitative text analysis application.

After the interviews we observed relief workers in decision-making teams during large scale crisis management exercises in the Port of Rotterdam, the Netherlands. Through close collaboration with the exercise organizers, two researchers were allowed to observe experimentation with NCO capabilities during four days of exercises in December 2008. Each day, three exercise rounds were organized and in each round a set of 15 to 18 relief workers were trained according to a script-based simulation of crisis events. Combined we have 24 observations. The objectives of the observations were to determine how the NCO capabilities were implemented in the decision-making teams and which advantages the individual NCO capabilities resulted in practice. These objectives, together with the exercise script (which we had prior to the exercises), table 1 and table 2 shaped the observation protocol which guided the field observations (the protocol is available upon request). After each exercise, we were able to take part in a plenary briefing of the relief workers, allowing us to capture more data on their experience with information sharing.

4 A Field Study of NCO in the Netherlands

4.1 Findings from the Interviews with Information System Architects

We present the findings of the interviews according to four questions: (1) what is NCO, (2) do you adopt NCO and why, (3) how do you translate NCO to changes in the current information system architecture, and (4) which arrangement need to be made to fully enable the benefits of information sharing in an NCO mode?

Regarding the first question, the interviews revealed that the various information system architects do not share the same understanding of what NCO is, what capabilities need to be developed and which advantages this approach has for crisis management. While a majority of the information architects argue that NCO could lead to improved information sharing, several of them also acknowledged that despite the appealing advantages of NCO, the implications of this concept and the measures needed to implement it are not yet clear. One respondent explains: "We are at the beginning of a transition from system-centric information system developed towards network-centric information system developed. The main problem is that we do not fully understand the implications of NCO on the organizational and informational levels". Another respondent argues that there may be more obstacles then we may think: "NCO assumes a high level of uniformity, integration and standardization on multiple levels of the response organization as is the case in the military, whereas this is often not the case in the domain of crisis response where relief agencies are both autonomous and heterogeneous in their daily operations".

Regarding the second question on the adoption of NCO and why, all the respondents acknowledge that they have adopted NCO in their design for information systems.

When asked why they have adopted NCO, the majority of respondents argue that the urgency to adopt NCO is politically shaped by the Netherlands Ministry of Internal Affairs since 2005. The Ministry advocates NCO in different ways, including workshops, project funding and national exercises.

Regarding the third question on the translation of NCO into design choices, the majority of information system architects point out CEDRIC pushed by the Ministry. This information system is a web-based application for horizontal (between the strategic, tactical and operational echelons) and vertical (between various relief agencies) information sharing. Basic functionalities of the CEDRIC information system include situation report generation, situation on the map visualization (plotting) through maps, emailing, logging, and searching through stored files in its database. In order to operate CEDRIC on the three echelons, the role of information manager has been developed. The information manager now has a formal position in decision-making teams and acts as the operator of CEDRIC.

Finally, regarding the fourth question, the respondents mentioned a range of limitations of NCO and the way it is being implemented in practice. Overall the respondents were somewhat reluctant to acknowledge the claim that CEDRIC, despite its functionalities, truly enables network-centric information sharing. One respondent explains: "NCO suggests that information is available to everyone involved in a specific crisis situation and that the involved actors are able to filter their own relevant information and make decisions based on this information. This, however, requires more than just CEDRIC". Moreover, a key concern CEDRIC is unable to deal with is the filtering of information beyond an integrated search engine. "We need to develop both automated and human filters in the decision-making team in order to quickly display relevant information".

Another respondent suggests that to be truly NCO, the current technical capabilities need to be extended beyond the interoperability and integration debate, "a huge problem is access to third party/secured information. If the information manager needs to be able actively collect information from private business databases using for instance using web services, this would only work if the appropriate institutional arrangements such as contracts and service level agreements are in place". From this quote we can conclude that the shift from system-centric to network centric requires arrangements beyond the physical, information and cognitive domains are necessary. One respondent provided a comprehensive statement which summarizes the necessary changes in the current information system architectures: "developing NCO capabilities require changes in all levels of the information system architecture, including changes in process sequences, information flows, task structures, and coordination approaches". He continues: "These are enabled by (1) the skills and expertise of the individual relief workers, (2) the availability of high quality information, and (3) the capabilities of the various information systems".

4.2 Findings from the Observations of the Crisis Response Exercises

The interviews concluded that NCO was adopted in two ways: (1) the introduction of CEDRIC for cross-echelon and multi-agency information sharing and (2) the introduction of the role of information manager (as operator of CEDRIC) in decision-making teams on the three echelons. The main goal of the observations was to determine if

NCO, as implemented via CEDRIC and the role of information managers, allowed for the creation of the benefits which were expected according to literature (see table 2). Hence, the units of observation were CEDRIC and the information managers.

Overall, the observations show that despite CEDRIC and the role of the information manager were used in the information sharing and coordination process, they did not generate the expected benefits as listed in table 2. There are several reasons for this.

Table 3. Observed NCO capabilities in practice

Domain	NCO capability	Capability in practice
Physical domain	Team members need the ability to be robustly networked in order to achieve secure and seamless connectivity.	Via CEDRIC, robustness in sharing information is only partly realized due to the fixed set of information sources, destination and flows. Often, connectivity was hampered by the failing technical infrastructure.
Information domain	Team members need the ability to share, access, and protect information.	Information sharing (via both geographical situation plots and situation reports) was possible via CEDRIC. However, access to private (business) information was not possible.
Information domain	Team members require the ability to collaborate in the information domain.	Members experienced difficulty with determining which information would be useful on multidisciplinary level and which information just on mono-disciplinary level.
Cognitive domain	Team members require the ability to develop high quality awareness and share this situational awareness.	Both situation plots and report were used to create a common operational picture; however, there was often ambiguity regarding the information in the situation reports.
Cognitive domain	Team members require the ability to develop a shared knowledge of commanders' intent.	In each team, the leader used the whiteboard to draw situation plots as he pulled information through talks with the individual team members. However, the drawings were often ad-hoc and difficult to exchange with the other echelons.
Cognitive domain	Team members require the ability to self-synchronize their operations.	Active participation of the information manager proved very important in synchronizing situational overviews and the joint operational picture. However, not all information managers participated actively as they were often busy with typing situation reports based on the meetings.

First of all, NCO was implemented in the decision-making units as just a technology (CEDRIC) with a role (information manager) which combined, should have allowed information to be shared quickly and appropriately between agencies and across echelons. As observers, we noted that there was a clear mismatch in the capabilities NCO provided (in the implemented form) and the information sharing and coordination process in the decision-making unit. The information sharing process, which started out the rational (according to a structure) quickly changed into a more naturalistic (ad-hoc depending on who has information) mode, reflecting the decision-making process in the teams. As CEDRIC and the information manager were focused on information sharing between agencies and across echelons, this combination (read information system) was unable to adapt to the changed decision-making mode in the decision-making unit. As a result, the information manager was often waiting for information being brought into the team (reactive) instead of proactively searching for high quality information within and outside the team.

During the exercises we observed that NCO was reduced to a tool (CEDRIC) with an operator (the information manager). The information manager used CEDRIC for generating a situational report which is shared with the control room and the higher level echelon. Accordingly, many information managers we observed were pre-occupied with listening and typing situation report forms in CEDRIC.

Finally, we observed that many exercise participants were not even aware of what CEDRIC was capable of when it comes to providing and sharing this information. The explanation for this is that the relief workers from different agencies do not know each other and CEDRIC is not used during none-crises. Hence, capabilities such as sharing a situational plot were, in spite of the necessity, hardly used during the exercises. In Table 3 the implemented NCO capabilities are listed followed by the advantages that were realized in Table 4.

In table 3 the gap between the capabilities required for NCO and the capabilities developed in practice are summarized. The following table summarizes the gaps between the expected and the realized benefits of NCO.

Table 4. Gap between expected and realized benefits of NCO

Expected benefits	Realization of benefits (expressed as full, partial or not realized)
Empowerment and autonomy	Not realized. Even though the information manager had the capability with CEDRIC allowing him to search for information outside of the decision-making team, this capability did not empower the decision-making team was not empowered by this capability.
Robust information sharing	Partially realized. The various teams did operate fairly independent of each other in terms of decision-making and action. However, in terms of information sharing, the teams on the different echelons dependent on the information in the situation reports.
Shared situational awareness within and across multiple echelons	Partially realized. The exchanged situation reports and situation plots in CEDRIC did help in establishing a shared situational awareness. However, due to the poor documentation and lack of reporting and plotting standards, there were still a lot of discussions pertaining the situation which in turn delayed decision-making and action.
Tolerance for ambiguity and capacity for renewal	Not realized. Combined in an information system, CEDRIC and the information manager were unable to adapt to the information demands of team members as the information sharing process shifted from structured (protocol driven) to event driven.
Rapid feedback on information sent	Partially realized. Despite the fact the situation reports and plots were shared quickly with the other echelons, feedback via CEDRIC (via email) often took several minutes, which is too long for some information object (e.g., victim information).
Real time information flow support	Partly realized. Information flows through CEDRIC were both synchronous (dynamic situation plots using geographic maps) and a-synchronous (situation reports sent via email).
Enhanced quality of information	Not realized. CEDRIC did not have any means of checking information correctness, consistency, timeless or relevancy.

Table 3 illustrates that the implemented NCO capabilities (via CEDRIC and the information manager) often only partially or do not enable the achievement of expected benefits. Hence, we found that there is a gap between both the capabilities and benefits of NCO in theory and in practice. We discuss some implications of our findings in the next section.

5 Discussion and Recommendations

The goal of this research was to better understand NCO and its potential benefits for information sharing during crisis management. NCO can be viewed as a set of required capabilities that, if implemented, realize various benefits for relief workers in crisis management networks. Our interviews with information system architects reveal that there is no agreement on what constitutes NCO, which capabilities need to be developed and which advantages can be realized. The architects do however agree that the current, system-centric approach to the development of information systems, reflecting a single-program, stove-piped view is a major obstacle for improving information sharing between agencies. The majority of architects do agree that the development and implementation of a cross-organizational and cross-echelon information system such as CEDRIC is a first step towards NCO.

Our field observations, however, show that CEDRIC embodies only a limited set of the required NCO capabilities and that most of the expected benefits are only partially realized. Although proponents of NCO might argue that these shortcomings cannot be attributed to the implementation of NCO, the fact remains that the implementation of NCO resulted in some shortcomings and the NCO descriptions provide no guidance or support to overcome them. NCO might even reinforce certain problems as even more information overload and make the selection and validation of the quality of information even more difficult.

In addition, we found that technology is a considerable step but its effectiveness depends on the development of new organizational policies and roles regarding information sharing. Hence, in order to unleash the potential benefits of NCO, we recommend that information system architects take into consideration what kind of capabilities need to be developed in the informational and cognitive domains in conjunction with the capabilities developed in the physical domain and focus on aligning the capabilities between the domains. In the information domain this would for instance require the development of capabilities for information quality assurance, while in the cognitive domain, it would for instance require the education and training of relief workers specifically with regard to proactively sharing information.

In general, further research needs to investigate the NCO and the implementation thereof in practice (considered in the broader context of technology and users) as well as to gain more knowledge on the benefits and disadvantages of NCO and the capabilities. More specifically, further research needs to at least address three questions: 1) how do we bridge the gap between system-centric versus network-centric information system design, 2) which policies, roles and capabilities need to be developed in order to orchestrate information sharing in a network of heterogeneous agencies and 3) which architectural mechanisms need to be in place to assure high information quality in a network-centric setting.

References

1. De Bruijn, H.: One Fight, One Team: The 9/11 Commision Report on Intelligence, Fragmentation and Information. Public Administration 84, 267–287 (2006)
2. Pan, S., Pan, G., Devadoss, P.: E-Government Capabilities and Crisis Management: Lessons From Combating SARS in Singapore. MIS Quarterly Executive 4, 385–397 (2005)
3. ASE: Alle Hens on Deck: ASE Veiligheid. In: Relations, I.A.a.K. (ed.). Capgemini (2008)
4. Kouzmin, A., Jarman, M., Rosenthal, U.: Inter-organizational Policy Processes in Disaster Management. Journal of Disaster Prevention and Management 4, 20–37 (1995)
5. National Research Council: Improving Disaster Management: The Role of IT in Mitigation, Preparedness, Response and Recovery. National Academic Press, Washington, DC (2007)
6. Alberts, D., Hayes, R.: Planning: complex endeavors. DoD Command and Control Research Program, Washington, DC (2007)
7. Aarholt, E., Berg, O.: Network Centric Information Structure - Crisis Information Management. Teleplan AS, Lysaker, Norway (2004)
8. Gonzales, D., Johnson, M., McEver, J., Leedom, D., Kingston, G., Tseng, M.: Network-Centric Operations Case Study. The Stryker Brigade Combat Team. RAND National Defense Research Insititute (2005)
9. Van de Ven, J., Van Rijk, R., Essens, P., Frinking, E.: Network Centric Operations in Crisis Management. In: Fiedrich, F., Van de Walle, B. (eds.) 5th International ISCRAM Conference, Washington, DC, USA (2008)
10. Bigley, G.A., Roberts, K.H.: The incident command system: High reliability organizing for complex and volatile task environments. Academy of Management 44, 1281–1300 (2001)
11. Simon, H.A.: The Sciences of the Artificial. MIT Press, Cambridge (1996)
12. Drabek, T., McEntire, D.: Emergent phenomena and the sociology of disaster: lessons, trends and opportunities from the research literature. Disaster Prevention and Management 12, 97–112 (2003)
13. t' Hart, P., Rosenthal, U., Kouzmin, A.: Crisis Decision Making: The Centralization Thesis Revisited. Administration & Society 25, 12–45 (1993)
14. Comfort, L., Kapucu, N.: Inter-organizational coordination in extreme events: The World Trade Center attacks, September 11, 2001. Natural Hazards 39, 309–327 (2006)
15. Smith, C., Hayne, S.: Decision making under time pressure. Management Communication Quarterly 11, 97–126 (1997)
16. Argote, L.: Input Uncertainty and Organizational Coordination in Hospital Emergency Units. Administrative Science Quarterly 27, 420–434 (1982)
17. Longstaff, P.H.: Security, Resilience, and Communication in Unpredictable Environments Such as Terrorism, Natural Disasters, and Complex Technology. Harvard University (2005)
18. Manoj, B.S., Hubenko, A.H.: Communication Challenges in Emergency Response. Communications of the ACM 50, 51–53 (2007)
19. Cebrowski, A., Garstka, J.: Network-Centric Warfare: Its Origin and Future. United States Naval Institute (1998)
20. Alberts, D.S., Garstka, J.J., Stein, F.P.: Network-Centric Warfare: Developing and Leveraging Information Superiority, vol. 2. CCRP Publication Series (2002)
21. Daft, R.L., Lewin, A.Y.: Where Are the Theories for the "New" Organizational Forms? An Editorial Essay. Organization Science 4, i–iv (1993)
22. NESI: Net-Centric Implementation Framework. Net-Centric Enterprise Solutions for Interoperability (2008)

Joined–Up E–Government – Needs and Options in Local Governments

Anders Persson and Göran Goldkuhl

Dept. of Management and Engineering,
Linköping University,
581 83 Linköping, Sweden
{Anders.Persson,Goran.Goldkuhl}@liu.se

Abstract. In this paper a study on the pre-requisites for joined-up eGovernment in municipalities is reported. The purpose of the paper is to explore possibilities and restrictions of ICT for promoting joined-up government. The need for eGovernment and joined-up government research to merge is discussed as is the needs and options of government change in relation to eGovernment and joined-up government. Four themes concerning change is identified in the paper and related to information systems (IS) and organizational change.

Keywords: Joined-up government, eGovernment, citizen centricity .

1 Introduction

The horizontal coordination of activities across functional and jurisdictional bounda-ries is often described as one of the eternal problems occupying managers and re-searchers in public administration [1]. The end of the last millennium saw the rise of joined-up government [2] and eGovernment as two perspectives aiming at bringing new solutions to this problem and to other problems as well. Joined-up government and eGovernment are both originating in practical application and problem solving. Neither the strive for horizontal coordination [3] nor technology in government are new issues but both these were refocused and highlighted approaches towards the end of the millennium and onwards. As a new public policy joined-up government emerged in the UK with a focus on how to achieve vertical and horizontal coordina-tion [2]. At the same time eGovernment emerged as an articulated field in practice and research bringing solutions to the external face of public administration as well as offering the possibility that ICT could alter the operations inside the agencies. This development also fostered integration in a more citizen centric fashion across functional boundaries [4]. Although the integration theme is a frequent claim by eGovernment researchers and practitioners, the obvious connections to joined-up government has not until recently been explored. This is especially true as regard to the research domain of one-stop government within the eGovernment. This field has clear connections with joined-up government although not fully exploring its enrich-ment potential. Joined-up government is considerably weak when it comes to the potential of ICT for joining up on as well the national as the local level. ICT is mainly treated as a background phenomenon and a tool rather than a facilitator.

M.A. Wimmer et al. (Eds.): EGOV 2009, LNCS 5693, pp. 76–87, 2009.

Thus the purpose of this paper is to explore the possibilities and restrictions of ICT as means of promoting a balanced joined-up government spanning across functional- and jurisdictional boundaries in municipalities. This means to take steps towards an integration of these two types of public administration policies which we will call joined-up eGovernment. The main empirical foundation of the paper is a case study in four municipalities concerning the establishment of new companies in a local presence. The process of establishing a business is a complex, highly uncoordinated process of services, permits and projects concerning alterations in the surrounding infrastructure or local adaptations and additions. Positive results from these sub processes need to be in place in order to start up the operation of the company. From the company's point of view these services and permits are all part of one integrated joint process where the different parts of the municipality play a crucial part in realizing the needed result. This complex situation spans across functional and jurisdictional boundaries as well as boundaries created by information systems (IS). The paper is organized according to the following structure; this section is followed by a section on the research design. The next section outlines the theoretical frame of reference ending in a synthesis on the need for discussing joined-up eGovernment. The fourth section introduces the case study. The fifth section covers the empirically-based analysis of needs and options for joined-up eGovernment within a local government context. The last section draws the conclusions of the paper.

2   Research Design

The paper is based on a case study covering the area of company localization and development in municipalities. The study covers four Swedish municipalities in a research project called PROFET granted by the research council Vinnova.

The research project can be characterized as a practical inquiry [5,6] with several purposes. 1) It aimed, in action research manners [7], to contribute to the development of workpractices and information systems in particular municipalities. It aimed also to an improved abstract understanding (through theorizing) of problems and options of joined-up government and eGovernment. This developed knowledge should be abstracted beyond these particular cases. It should contribute both to 2) the scientific body of knowledge and to 3) practical management of such issues in public administration (i.e. a general practice contribution). The practical inquiry comprises interviews and the study of documents (laws, regulations, municipal policies etc) and existing information systems. The practical inquiry also comprised a participatory design of an information system for process and case handling. Two researchers (the authors) worked together with public administrators from the four municipalities (which represented different functional areas) in eliciting requirements for a new IS. The main purpose of this new IS was to facilitate coordination of case handling concerning companies' establishment processes. The empirical data from the inquiry have been analyzed in a qualitative, interpretive way [8]. We have also reported and discussed our results with the practitioners in the project, in order to validate our findings and make them articulated in a comprehensive and meaningful way. The practical inquiry approach makes it possible to report findings from the project although it is still on-going. The project started with large scale problem inquiries in the four municipalities leading up to the identified needs and options for joined up eGovernment in the studied municipalities. This work consisted of more than 100 interviews with case-handling officers and managers in the municipalities as well as companies that had located to one of the municipalities prior to the study.

3 Perspectives on Joining Up

3.1 Joined-Up Government

In public administration of the 80s and 90s New Public Management (NPM) [9,10] emerged as the core management strategy. But alongside the client [11] and results focus [12] the NPM strategy brought the dysfunction of fragmentation [13]. The Blair government coined the now famous phrase: "Joined-up problems need joined-up solutions" [2]. This marked a shift in focus from the NPM era towards needs-based holism [13] focusing primarily on the needs of clients rather than the efficiency of government. In public administration research and practice this fostered the research area of joined-up government (JUG) [1,2]. Today when studying government institutions the eternal problem of lacking coordination constitute a core focus [1]. Pressman & Wildawsky [14] draw similar conclusions when stating that lacking coordination is one of the most commonly expressed dysfunctions of bureaucracy and a highly regarded agenda for reform. Joined-up government is described as a way of achieving vertically and horizontally coordinated action within government [3]. As such joined-up government constitutes a way to work across jurisdictions, budget areas and functions in order to foster collaboration and a more holistic view on the different policy domains of government [3]. According to Pollitt [4] the following four characteristics can be handled with joined-up thinking; (1) Situations with undermining policies can be eliminated; (2) Scarce resources handled better; (3) Synergies created with stakeholder networks; (4) Allowing seamless rather than fragmented services. According to Mulgan [15] this problem of joined-up government is twofold. Firstly it is a problem of coordination and secondly it is a problem of integration and organization. The first is a problem of encouraging the involved agencies to work on broadly the same agenda and the latter is a problem of aligning structures, incentives and cultures to fit inter-organizational tasks. Core aspects of importance in JUG are the focus on achieving vertically and horizontally coordinated thinking and action [3]. The JUG implementation in the UK has mainly focused on high level policy and through joining up agencies and other actors into cross functional holistic structures [2]. The discussions on joined-up government, horizontal management or whatever term used commonly focus on organizational and institutional issues other than ICT in government. For example Mulgan [15] stresses that ICT-strategies in government is one key area where it is important to use joined-up thinking in order to achieve results but do not stress ICT-in government as a corner solution to the coordination problems of government in other areas. As predominantly focused and associated with issues in contemporary public administration JUG also lacks the perspective on what ICT could mean in the process of transforming public administration [16]. Margetts [16] criticizes how ICT has been neglected within public administration research. When JUG is discussed several associated problems are stressed. James [17] stresses the accountability problems of JUG and horizontal joining of agencies and functions. Pollitt [3] stresses that silos and functional and jurisdictional boundaries are not obsolete thinking. These are in fact the cornerstones of current accountability arrangements and also important foundations for professionalism and technical, institutional and intellectual capital.

3.2 EGovernment

Since the turn of the millennium governments around the world have focused on ICT as a means of transforming the external face of government services [16]. Concerning ICT in public administration different researchers come to different conclusions. Bovens & Zouridis [18] draw conclusions from what the latter authors call decision-making factories and claim that ICT strengthen bureaucratic values and limit the discretion of street-level bureaucrats. Welch & Pandey [19] study Intranet implementation as a means of reducing red tape by limiting the effects of stove piped structures and thus bureaucratic dysfunctions. Stage-models covering eGovernment commonly include an integration stage that focus on network administration and integration [20,21], vertical and horizontal integration [20] and thus focus on ICT a as a means of limiting the effects from stove piped structures. Prior to this development ICT was important but mainly seen as something bringing internal possibilities to the public administration. Researchers [22,23] identified the effects of ICT as a means of strengthening the bureaucratic values of the Weberian bureaucracy within the stove-pipes of governmental organizations. This conclusion was drawn from the possibility to automate government actions in order to ease the dysfunctions of bureaucratic discretion. In the IS community the opposite frequently occurs as eGovernment is discussed as a technological issue and often from the supply side [24] with no weak connections to public sector core values and management regimes [25,20,21]. The eGovernment counterpart to JUG, one-stop government, has been used to study and implement citizen-focused integration of services [4].

The counterparts in one-stop government are the focus on the needs of the citizen in creating jointly located or integrated technology mediated services [4]. Other researchers not associated with one-stop government as a concept stress the same when focusing on integration and cross functional information flows [20,21]. This body of research however commonly covers integration from a supply oriented perspective focused on providing what citizen wants and less focused on what is *good governance*. This latter aspect of focusing on the problematic and unsolved side of eGovernment is crucial for the successful deployment of ICT in joining up functions and agencies. This is also a theme that has been stated in critical research on the shortcomings of eGovernment as an overoptimistic approach to technology [26].

3.3 IT as an Instrument for Joined-Up Government

JUG as described in research literature is mainly focused on top down steering of government agencies [15]. The concepts of joined-up government and eGovernment need to move closer together. Joined-up policymaking and steering need to be implemented and ICT have to be further highlighted and identified as an important instrument in order to reach these effects. An example of this is that the Swedish National

Auditing Office has evaluated the policy of improved electronic government in one report focusing on technology for better government and how effective the implementation of the eGovernment policy actually is [27]. When evaluating other branches of government ICT usage is not commonly focused. Thus eGovernment is treated as an island of its own and not as a critical factor for government efficiency.

In the joined-up government body of literature ICT is treated somewhat sparse. The other way around is true for the eGovernment body of literature. While JUG is treated mainly as a source for strategic renewal and renewal of leadership in public administration on strategic and policy level eGovernment research and practice is in a sense more orientated towards better implementation and more citizen centric services [28]. This can be seen as eGovernment being oriented towards the administrative layer of government and towards good implementation. Thus JUG is mainly focused on policy level issues of governance and thus neglecting solutions such as eGovernment for aiding the implementation of joined-up policies. It is our belief a subdivision of the government reformation that damage progress. In eGovernment there is a need to look beyond technology and implementation and towards policy issues such as accountability, specialization and other core values. In accordance to this view JUG needs to focus more on how implementation of joined up policies and concepts can be aided in implementation by ICT. Altogether the areas of joined-up government and eGovernment, whether it is in terms of one-stop government or as part of the more common integration theme, are parts of a similar movement with similar goals. There is common criticism of eGovernment research as being descriptive in its technologically and supply oriented case study orientation that can be associated with the lacking theoretical foundations [26] to why and how to join up government services and what it costs. Issues well discussed within the JUG agenda, as problems of accountability, specialization and silo structures are not commonly double sided issues in eGovernment research. ICT is commonly seen as a breaker of organizational boundaries [19]. That is not contested in this paper but the issue of what can be done with ICT cannot be discussed alone. The question why it should be done and in accordance to what governing principles is even more important and not commonly discussed within the IS community.

3.4 Case Study Introduction: Business Development and Localization in Local Government

In the municipalities studied, information systems strengthen the silos and lock information inside the functional and jurisdictional boundaries rather than open up information flows and facilitate information sharing across jurisdictions. In addition to this the stove pipes all have different stakeholders besides the establishing company and thus an obligation to balance stakeholders' interests. Establishing a new company in one municipality brings the need for several services from the municipality administration as well as from other branches of government. These services cover a properly planned property and permits for the buildings and construction process as well as permits for the business operations. The business also needs to have the property provided with local infrastructure such as water and electricity and general infrastructure such as suitable and adapted roads, parking lots and public transportation. Through the eyes of the establishing company this is one joint project leading to the fully operational business. However through the eyes of the different branches and functions of the municipality this company establishing is based upon several different cases that need to be handled separately. This view leaves the coordination and initiation of the different cases totally in the hands of the companies with little or no support from the municipality for coordination. This is a mismatch in expectations and undermines the legitimacy of the municipality administration and promoting the view that the municipalities are business unfriendly.

A company that desire to establish its business in a municipality needs a property that is properly planned and allocated to the type of business. Depending on the type of business several other permits needs to be in place in order for the company to run its business. This covers alongside the planned property and depending on the business type building permits, construction compliance permit, and environmental permits for preparing, holding and releasing emissions harmful to the environment. In cases of preparing food and serving food and alcohol to the public the company needs permits for the processing and serving of food as well as a permit for serving alcohol. In addition to this new companies in virgin premises need infrastructure in order to be able to function. This calls for municipality projects for building roads, junctions and bringing infrastructure such as water, sewer and electricity to the premise. In all, this is a grand undertaking covering a vast number of jurisdictions and municipal agencies. This complex situation is today highly uncoordinated between different municipality actors. The result is that the municipalities are conceived as business unfriendly. Companies locating in the municipality have the main responsibility for the coordination of permits and applications. Because of the complex nature and vast number of permits this process is difficult and many companies lack the knowledge concerning what permits that are needed and applicable to their situation. Alongside this problem the companies rarely have established contacts with the functions of the municipality and thus also lack knowledge concerning how the municipality is organized. The sum of this is that the process for many businesses can properly be characterized as a process of discovering what permits and what municipality functions that needs to be addressed.

Alongside the focus of citizen centricity in government these municipalities are in the process of transforming into a more business focused administration. In order to reach this goal the responsibilities for coordination of permits and gaining knowledge about the municipality organization need to be shifted from the client company to joined-up thinking in the municipalities.

3.5   Case Study Analysis: Needs and Options for Joined-Up eGovernment

The stove piped structure of the municipality creates fragmentation across different dimensions. These are the jurisdictions, political superstructure, organizational and administrational divisions. The last dimension is how information is locked inside the stove piped structure in separate information systems. These different aspects of the stove piped structure in municipalities cause different dysfunctions in the handling of case processes. The dysfunctions are below expressed and condensed in needs that also form prerequisites for joined-up government in the municipalities that correspond to the demands and expectations from client businesses. The basis for the discussion is a twofold incentive. The first is the demand side corresponding to the expectation of how the relation with the municipality should be. The other is the supply side where governments across the world as well as in this context focus on joined-up government, coordinated eGovernment and one-stop shops. The following discussion is based on these core prerequisites and ideals for joined-up government.

3.5.1   Joined-Up Handling of Client Assignments/Applications

As stated earlier establishing a business is seen as one process conducted by the client companies. The companies have expectations of joint-up behavior from the municipality which is seen and treated as one joint actor. Companies expect the process of establishing as a joint process covering different applications, permits and projects. Thus there is an expectation gap between companies and municipality concerning how the municipality should act. This dysfunction is further deepened by the fact that many case handling officers do not view coordinated actions as their responsibility. When it comes to applications, initiating a case process and handling a case process the need for a holistic view is crucial. Frequently the start of a process through initiation of an application or a discussion is conducted at the wrong municipality actor or jurisdiction and thus the initiation of the processes need to be rearranged. Another aspect is the problem of coordination of the different applications. The permits build on each other and can be seen as a process of refinement. The coordination of when and how the next case should be initiated is currently managed by the actor with the least knowledge (i.e. the company). The complete knowledge of the process is something that is evolving within the client sphere and commonly unassisted by the municipality actors.

- Internally coordinated action among municipality actors
- Municipality functions acting as one joined-up actor
- Handling applications as parts of a process rather than fragmented actions

A more joined-up handling of the case processes is needed both for aiding the client but also for the aspects and quality and resource effectiveness in the municipality. The lacking planning of the required applications as a process results in waste of resources on both the client and municipality side. In order for the process as a whole to be more predictable and managed on the client side as well as on the municipality side the need for a whole of approach to cross functional aggregated cases is needed. This also calls for lifting accountability for separated sub processes to accountability for joined-up processes covering all applications and permits. One major obstacle in this respect is the existing information systems present in several of the functions. These are built to support the specific work from the view of a particular jurisdiction. This makes the aspect of integrating information and adding a process dimension to this information systems environment a huge undertaking. This is inherited from of the fact that the information systems add a dimension of information structure to the stove pipes of jurisdictions and organization.

- Creating accountability standards for joined-up processes in addition to accountability for sub processes.
- Redesigning current information systems and providing access to other judicial branches of the municipality in order to bridge rather than enforce stove pipes concerning information sharing.

- Designing information systems support for handling case processes on an aggregated rather than a fragmented level.

3.5.2 Joined-Up Handling of Contacts and Questions from Clients

Most municipality functions and departments use the formal application as initiation of the case. This means that earlier than at this point the knowledge concerning the business locating to the municipality is mainly personal information that is not documented and not shared between departments. This leads to lacking knowledge about the case processes to be initiated in the future and thus this will cause unwanted bottlenecks. Further on, this is crucial strategic knowledge concerning how the demand for exploitable and properly planned properties and also the demand for permits in the future. Thus the future beyond received applications is unknown to the municipality leading to a very short planning horizon. The fact that one hand doesn't know what the other is doing is a common dysfunction of lacking coordination. In this case the fact that one part of the municipality can say yes to the company and another can say no without knowing of what each other is saying is hurting the legitimacy of the municipality.

- Contacts and needs of businesses need to be general knowledge potentially shared among municipality officers
- Documentation needs to be based on contacts rather than formal applications.
- Planning of forthcoming case processes needs to be initiated based on contact information rather than formal applications.
- Decisions and offers need to be based on coordinated assessments of whole processes rather than fragmented decisions based on sub processes.

The existing information systems are based on the fact that a formal application is the basis of a logged entry concerning a particular client company. All the existing information systems, except for one, cannot log contact data without entering a formal application thus these systems do not provide the needed functionality of entering and sharing contact data. What is needed is that all that's said and done regarding a company must be logged and shared in order for the municipality to function as a joint actor rather than a fragmented set of actors that are not communicating actions toward a particular client.

- Shared information among all functions concerning contacts with clients.
- Information systems arranged to document and support offers to clients based on joined-up assessments of contact stage information and needs.

3.5.3 Joined-Up Documentation and Handling of Basic Data

Documentation developed within different functions and documentation and applications provided by client companies are in the current situation dysfunctional aspects of wasting possibly multi functional information. The applications can fulfill a shared value if handled jointly. Building plans can cover several purposes such as describing kitchen layout, construction plans, building permit basic data, fire exits, but is not treated as such. A typical client thus prepares several layout plans throughout the process that could easily be covered in one or two plans with a joined-up perspective on what documentation is required. This is however true on the back office side of government where shared documentation and information could easily be multifunctional if shared over the boundaries of jurisdictions. Thus the following needs can be extracted. The basic data used for handling the different sub cases that constitute the joined-up case on aggregate level are in many cases the same. The data about the establishing company and the information about the business operation and needs are general information that most municipality functions and departments need. This information is despite this not collected generally and not gathered with other perspectives than that of the gathering institution. Thus the client company has to leave the same bits of information to multiple actors within the municipality.

- Demand and development of documentation needs to be altered from stove piped function centered to multifunctional addressing of joined-up needs.
- Documentation needs has to be addressed pre-emptively as prerequisites for a case process rather than being discovered in an evolutionary fashion.
- Basic data concerning the client business needs to be handled jointly in order to reduce the dysfunction of leaving information on multiple instances,

This however also demands a joined-up approach to how documentation is viewed upon in the municipality. The whole processes of conducting case handling and demanding information and documentation from clients has to be rearranged. This implies a changing focus from stove piped information gathering and case handling to joined-up case handling and information gathering and retrieval. Thus the process (and its different cases) can be handled jointly and multifunctional application data and documentation can be gathered and shared among functions. In terms of legislation it is questionable if this is fully allowed today. Current information structure and information systems are not supporting such a joined-up approach. The legal aspect of data sharing and common documentation is reviewed on higher levels in government in order to allow joined-up government. Thus this problem is transitory. On the information systems side the problem is more severe. As stated earlier most data is either locked in separate information systems that do not allow sharing information or is 'personal' data stored by case handling officers locally. Thus a complete revision of the information systems infrastructure is both needed and crucial for a more joined-up approach to evolve. Concerning documentation the basic data are seriously fragmented today. The departments with dedicated information systems have portions of the aggregated need for information stored for use by the case handling officers in each separate department. In the departments with office equipment and personal IS usage the basic data is 'privately' stored and used information.

- The view on how, where and why clients and functions create documentation can be altered from stove pipe based to multifunctional.
- For joined-up action the information systems environment can be altered to supporting joined-up documentation gathering and retrieval.
- For joined-up eGovernment to emerge information systems can add an aggregated information layer concerning general and specific multifunctional data and documentation.
- Basic data concerning the client business and contact information to company actors is crucial to store and retrieve jointly in a central client database.

3.5.4 Joined-Up Client Identities

Also important is how the client business is identified. The current situation implies that there is no common identification of the company. Businesses are reduced in complexity from whole of processes and needs to the complexity of the stove piped function. Thus the business establishment process is reduced from the business case to a building permit case. In this process the business is lost and reduced to a case identification number or other identification entities not including the natural business identity. Thus the different permits, applications and infrastructure parts of the business localization are treated as separated islands without a common identity. Examples are that a building permit is identified and associated with a place and an applicant that can be the entrepreneur, a consultant or any person or organization in the service of the business. The typical building permit is not associated with the company as such. An environmental permit for the company is on the other hand associated with a place and what is intended to be manufactured or stored there. A company serving alcohol or food to the public is associated with the responsible head of business and not the business as such.

- Joined-up government needs to be based on whole clients and not fragments.
- The municipality must change how clients are thought of and handled for joined-up eGovernment to occur regardless of how information systems are designed.

This is an important downside regarding the efforts to coordinate and identify the different municipal agencies efforts in the process of providing the necessary permits for the company. This dysfunction enforces the previously identified dysfunctions of lacking coordination and joined-up handling of what is associated as a process by the businesses. Another issue here is that large corporations are treated jointly through informal associations that are nonexistent in the current information systems and thus a manual or verbal association in the minds of case handling officers. Small companies are rarely handled with these informal identifications and the company as such is not a subject.

- Information systems can support joined-up handling of whole clients jointly by adding the company as a formal entity in thought as well as documentation and data.

4 Conclusions

To conclude this paper we need to readdress the purpose. We set out to explore the possibilities and restrictions of ICT as a means of promoting joined-up government in municipalities. In the paper four themes concerning joined-up thinking and action has been identified: (1) Joined-up handling of client assignments/applications, (2) joined-up handling of contacts and questions from clients, (3) joined-up documentation and handling of basic data, (4) joined-up client identities. All these themes are concluded as needed in order to change the municipality in a direction of joined-up government behavior. Another core aspect of the paper was to discuss the need for public administration research and eGovernment research to merge as these both have founding aspects of how to achieve coordinated joined-up eGovernment. As the discussion suggests this is important. It is clear that eGovernment information systems for support of joined-up behavior are possible and plausible solutions to important dysfunctions in municipalities. Despite this conclusion the cornerstones does not lie within the technical solutions. Holding the municipality accountable for joined-up behavior and redefining the client from stove piped case fragments to identified and jointly handled entities are important prerequisites for joined-up government. Thus joined-up government can be achieved and handled without information systems support but can be enforced and bettered with redesigned handling of information and data gathering. Joined-up eGovernment cannot in this respect exist without a redefined municipality. eGovernment solutions can help the clients of the municipality without redesigned thinking and action but will in the municipality of today aid the stove piped structure if this is not redesigned.

References

1. 6, P.: Joined-up government in the western world in comparative perspective: a preliminary literature review and exploration. Journal of Public Administration Research and Theory 14(1), 103–138 (2004)
2. Bogdanor, V.: Joined-up Government. Oxford University Press, Oxford (2005)
3. Pollitt, C.: Joined-up Government: a Survey. Political Studies Review 1(1), 34–49 (2003)
4. Kubicek, H., Hagen, M.: One Stop Government in Europe: An Overview. In: Hagen, M., Kubicek, H. (eds.) One Stop Government in Europe, pp. 1–36. Results from 11 National Surveys, University of Bremen, Bremen (2000)
5. Cronen, V.: Practical theory, practical art, and the pragmatic-systemic account of inquiry. CommunicationTheory 11(1), 14–35 (2001)
6. Goldkuhl, G.: Practical inquiry as action research and beyond. In: Proceedings of the 16th European Conference on Information Systems, Galway (2008)
7. Baskerville, R., Wood-Harper, A.T.: A critical perspective on action research as a method for information systems research. Journal of Information Technology 11(3), 235–246 (1996)
8. Walsham, G.: Interpretive case studies in IS research: nature and method. European Journal of Information Systems (4), 74–81 (1995)
9. Osborne, D., Gaebler, T.: Reinventing Government. Addison-Wesley, Reading (1992)
10. Hood, C.: Economic rationalism in public management. Open University Press, Buckingham (1994)
11. Kettl, D.: Public Administration at the Millennium: The State of the Field. Journal of Public Administration Research and Theory 10(1), 7–34 (2000)
12. Kickert, W.: Public governance in the Netherlands: An alternative to anglo-american managerialism. Public administration 4(75), 731–753 (1997)
13. Dunleavy, P., Margetts, H., Bastow, S., Tinkler, J.: The new public management is dead; Long live digital era governance. Journal of Public Administration Research and Theory 16(3), 467–494 (2005)
14. Pressman, J., Wildavsky, A.: Implementation. University of California Press, Ltd., London (1984)
15. Mulgan, G.: Joined up government: Past, present and future. In: Bogdanor, V. (ed.) Joined-up government. Oxford University Press, Oxford (2005)
16. Margetts, H.: Electronic government: A revolution? In: Peters, B.G., Pierre, J. (eds.) The handbook of Public Administration. Sage, London (2003)

17. James, O.: The UK Core Executive's Use of Public Service Agreements as a Tool of Governance. Public Administration 82(2), 397–419 (2004)
18. Bovens, M., Zouridis, S.: From street-level to system-level bureaucracies: How information and Communication technology is transforming administrative discretion and constitutional control. Public Administration Review 62(2), 174–184 (2002)
19. Welch, E., Pandey, S.: E-Government and Bureaucracy: Toward a Better Understanding of Intranet Implementation and Its Effect on Red Tape. Journal of Public Administration Research and Theory 17(3), 379–404 (2006)
20. Layne, K., Lee, J.: Developing fully functional e-government: A four stage model. Government Information Quarterly 18(2), 122–136 (2001)
21. Hiller, J., Bélanger, F.: Privacy strategies for electronic government. PriceWaterhouse Coopers Endowment for the business of Government E-government series, Arlington (2001)
22. Snellen, I.: Street level bureaucracy in an information age. In: Snellen, I., van de Donk, W. (eds.) Public administration in an information age, pp. 497–505. IOS Press, Amsterdam (1998b)
23. Homburg, V., Bekkers, V.: E-government and NPM: A perfect marriage? In: Bekkers, V., Homburg, V. (eds.) The Information Ecology of e-government: E-government as Institutional and Technological Innovation in Public Administration. IOS Press, Amsterdam (2005)
24. Reddick, C.: Citizen interaction with e-Government: From the streets to servers? Government Information Quarterly 22(1), 38–57 (2005)
25. Kumar, V., Mukerji, B., Butt, I., Persaud, A.: Factors for Successful e-Government Adoption: a Conceptual Framework. The Electronic Journal of e-Government 5(1), 63–76 (2007)
26. Heeks, R., Bailur, S.: Analyzing e-government research: Perspectives, philosophies, theories, methods and practice. Government Information Quarterly 24(2), 243–265 (2007)
27. Riksrevisionen: Vem styr den elektroniska förvaltningen? Riksrevisionen, Stockholm (2004)
28. van Duivenboden, H.: Citizen Participation in Public Administration The Impact of Citizen Oriented Public Services on Government and Citizen, OECD E-Government Project, OECD, Paris (2002)

Can ICT Reform Public Agencies?

Arild Jansen [1] and Einar Løvdal [2]

[1] Department of e-government studies, University of Oslo
[2] The Universities and Colleges Admission systems
Arildj@jus.uio.no, e.s.lovdal@usit.uio.no

Abstract. This study examines the reorganisation of the administration of admission to higher education in Norway, which has also included the development of a nationwide, ICT-based case handling system. This reform process was initiated out of the need to provide politicians with information for control and regulatory purposes, and the reform resulted in a centralised management information system. This system, however, has evolved into a coordinated but also partly locally delegated decision-making instrument which processes most of the applications for admission to higher education in Norway.

Our analysis aims at identifying the driving forces and mechanisms that have motivated this long-term and complex development process. We ask to what extent we may claim that management interests have been the key factor in these reform processes? Or, has the development been impelled instead by advances in new information and communication technologies?

Our conclusion is that neither of these hypotheses can fully explain these processes. It is indisputable that political and central management priorities have been crucially important in this reform. At the same time, we cannot neglect the dynamics related to the visions that technological developments have created. Such visions, implemented through collaborative processes and including a central project team and support staff in the various local institutions, seem to have created an environment for innovative technical and administrative solutions.

Keywords: Administrative reform, legislative reform, automated decision making, organizational changes, ICT.

1 Introduction

The Norwegian government is able to celebrate 50 years of computer use in public administration, since an IBM 360 was put into operation in spring 1958 for calculating public taxes. At the same time, but rather incidentally, the question was raised as to whether computers will bring about significant organisational change. In a classic 1958 Harvard Business review article, *Management in the1980s*, Leavitt and Whisler predicted that "IT would replace the traditional pyramidal hierarchy in organisations with a lean structure resembling an hourglass, and productivity would sour through the elimination of most middle managers". Since that time, it has been commonplace to assume that ICT has the potential to bring about administrative reform. K. Laudon

M.A. Wimmer et al. (Eds.): EGOV 2009, LNCS 5693, pp. 88–102, 2009.

(1974) posed the question of administrative reform specifically with respect to local government. Similarly, Fountain (2002, p 45) states that "Technology is a catalyst for social, economic and political change at the levels of individual, group, organizational and institutions".

Others, however, argue that ICT (on its own) does not tend to produce reforms and that it is implausible that ICT has been an instrument for administrative reforms (King and Kraemer 1985, George and King 1991). In a more recent paper, Kraemer and King (2008) claim, based on a number of studies of ICT in US government agencies, that ICT has instead been used to reinforce already existing administrative and political structures.

The aim of this paper is to contribute to the discussion by examining the extent to which ICT has been an instrument for administrative reform in the public sector in Norway. The case for this study is the development of NUCAS[1] (The Norwegian Universities and Colleges Admission Service), which coordinates admissions to regular undergraduate studies at all the universities, university colleges, state colleges, and some private colleges in Norway. This development started out as a technical project aiming at providing adequate information to the central government about applications for admission, student statistics, etc. After more than 15 years of development and supported by important changes in the legal framework[2], the result is a web-based, nearly automated admission service, as well as the building of a new organisation.

However, in terms of governmental changes, one might ask what the primary driving forces behind this development have been? Is it justified to claim that this administrative reform first and foremost is the result of innovative applications of new technology? Or is the reform merely another example of the use of new technologies to make public services more efficient and user oriented, in a context where changes in government organisations have been planned and controlled? This study aims to answer these questions by analysing the various stages of the development. We seek to identify the types of changes which have taken place and the effects of these changes for the ministry, for the individual institutions involved, for the students and for the educational sector as a whole.

This paper is structured as follows. In the first section we present our theoretical framework, followed by an analysis of the different phases in NUCAS development processes. In the second section we discuss our findings compared with previous research in the field.

2 Theoretical Perspectives

Although computers have been in use in public administration for several decades, the term electronic government (e-government) was coined rather recently. Today governments at all levels across the globe have adopted e-government systems in ways that have apparently changed their internal organisation as well as their interaction with their environment. Furthermore, it appears to have become commonly accepted practice to view e-government as a way by which to reform public administration, not least from a political point of view (se e.g. Fountain 2001, Grønlund 2003, Coleman 2008, Davis 2008).

---

[1] The designation in Norwegian is Samordna Opptak (SO). See http://info.samordnaopptak.no/

[2] NUCAS has been awarded several prizes, e.g. the eNorge-award in 2004.

Fig. 1. Elements in an administrative reform process (based on Schartum 2008)

By *administrative reform* we understand the term to entail "an effort to bring about dramatic change or transformation in government, such as a more responsive administrative structure, greater rationality and efficiency or better service delivery to citizens" (Kraemer and King (2008, p 2). Although this definition does not include the use of new technology, one could scarcely entertain the notion of reforming public (or private) institutions today without extensive use of ICT.

E-Government research is not yet a distinct research domain. It is also being questioned whether it should be a separate domain. Scholl (2008) claims that e-Government research is at best multidisciplinary, in that it involves multiple disciplinary communities and attempts to approach the phenomenon from the perspectives of different disciplines. E-government has traditionally been seen as including computer and information system research along with public administration and political science. However, as the structure and function of the public sector is to a large extent regulated by statutes and regulations, reforms will most likely involve (or even depart from) changes in legal arrangements. We see that such reforms will include technical developments and changes in organisational structures, as well as legislative reforms. [See for example, Fountain (2001) and Grønlund (2003)]. Figure 1 illustrates the relationship. We emphasize the close interrelationship between the three elements: new technical solutions require changes in legislation as well as a new organisational pattern, and vice versa (see e.g. Jansen and Schartum 2007). The direction of impact, however, is not unambiguous; new legislation may lead to organisational changes that are supported by new ICT systems (Sjøberg 2006), or the other way around (Johnssen 2006). Therefore, we need to identify the different patterns.

Hovy (2008) claims that since eGovernment research is interdisciplinary, it should include *normative* perspectives (such as analyses of political goals and values, legislation etc.), *technological* elements (such as discussions about construction and implementation issues etc.) and *evaluative* elements (such as, for example, studies on the effects of introducing new technical solutions and organisational patterns). The approach of this paper is to include all three perspectives. We examine how changes in policies and legislation initiated by politicians have caused the development of new technical solutions and organisational changes along with revisions of laws and regulations. At the same time, we investigate whether this drive towards using modern technology has actually been the catalyst for some of these changes.

2.1 To What Extent Does Technology Matter?

Through an extensive review of the literature on ICT and government, Kraemer and King (2008) have examined whether ICT has been an instrument of administrative reform in the U.S. They conclude that this has not been the case in the history of ICT and government in the US. They claim that ICT, rather than being an instrument of reform, "has served the interest of those in power and has supported existing administrative and political structures". In their analysis, they have listed four reform propositions as key components of their hypothesis, and which may be fruitful to test. Their propositions are[3]:

Reform Prop.1: **Computers have the potential to reform public administration and their relations to their environments**

Kraemer and King's findings were: *"Experience with information technology and administrative reform has shown technology to be useful in some cases of administrative reform, but only in cases where expectations for reform are already well established. ICT applications do not cause reform and cannot encourage it where the political will to pursue the reform does not exist* (op cit. page 6).

In order to test this proposition, we have to identify whether reforms have taken place, and if so, how and why they have been implemented.

Reform Prop. 2: **Information technologies can change organisational structures and, thus, is a powerful tool for reform**

The question is whether new IT solutions have contributed to reforms other than those planned, for example whether "bottom-up" forces have influenced organisational structure and division of labour. Kraemer and King make the claim based on vast empirical evidence that the main impact of IT applications has been to reinforce existing structures of communication, authority and power in organisations, whether centralised or decentralised. Their findings are: *IT applications have brought relatively little change to organisational structures and seem to reinforce existing structures* (op cit. p 8).

Reform Prop. 3: **Properly used, IT will be beneficial for administrators, staff, citizens and public administration as a whole**

Kraemer and King claim that empirical evidence suggests that those who control IT deployment and applications determine whose interests are served by the technology. Their findings are: *the benefits of IT have not been distributed evenly within the government organizational functions. The primary beneficiaries have been functions favoured by the dominant political-administrative coalitions in public administrations and not of those of technical elites, middle managers, clerical staff and ordinary citizens.*

This implies that we must analyse the intents and purposes for which the technical solutions have been developed, and whose interests they might serve.

---

[3] In the present version of the paper, we will discuss the three first propositions.

3 Research Approach

Our research is based on an interpretative case study in which we have analysed the history of the development process in the NUCAS project, spanning a period of more than 15 years. The empirical data were collected from various project reports describing the development phases along with white papers, budget propositions, statutory acts as well as regulations and parliamentary committee recommendations. In addition, interviews were conducted with stakeholders in the ministry and the educational institutions, as well as with students. Other important sources are accounts related by participants involved in these processes.

This method of data collection entails challenges in terms of reliability since one of the main informants[4] has been closely related to the project, which in turn implies a degree of uncertainty related to the bias and correctness of the data. The data have also been collected a long time after the end of early phases of the project. Consequently, important facts or viewpoints may have been forgotten, or the significance of conflicts may be underestimated. The strength of these sources, however, is their proximity to the case in question, presumably making the data highly valid.

Our analysis is based on a straightforward interpretation of the relevant documents describing the stages in development and is aimed at identifying the type of changes that have taken place and the effects these changes have had on the institutions and participants involved.

4 NUCAS and the Norwegian Educational System

Today NUCAS coordinates admissions to regular undergraduate studies in Norway. However, this has not always been the case. The present organisation and administrative routines are the result of more than 40 years of development, although the past 16-17 years have been the most important in the context of our analysis. It is thus important to view the NUCAS process as the continuation of a long line of reforms beginning in the 1960s and coinciding with the growth of the regional universities and state colleges in Norway. The process resulted in more than 100 educational institutions being distributed throughout Norway. The consequence was a massive educational revolution in Norway, resulting in an increase from about 10,000 students in 1960 to 41,000 students enrolled in 1988. However, the application and admission routines at the time were fully decentralised. Each student had to submit his/her application to the individual institutions, and there was no central registration system that could provide the central authorities with necessary information in order to survey and control application and admission systems.

This perceived crisis in our higher education caused radical changes in the entire educational sector in Norway through a number of reforms. One change was a reduction in the number of colleges and the foundation of a Norwegian Educational network ("Norgesnettet") between the universities, university colleges and regional college centres. Another very important element was the harmonising of regulations for universities and regional colleges, resulting in a single, unified law applying to the entire sector. This law became essential for the development of the admission

---

[4] One of the authors has been head of the development project from 1991 and up until the present time, while the other author has worked in the field of IT policy for the government for several years.

handling system. Prior to this law, the regulations for admission were decentralised, whereas the new law authorised the Ministry to adopt common regulations defining uniform qualification requirements for entrance to higher education.[5] Furthermore, this regulation was intended to establish a set of common, standardised and formalized rules which would ensure a decentralised, fair and predictable admission process which could also be supported by a computer-based decision-making system.

New reforms were to follow. In the context of this paper, the "Quality reform"[6] from 2003 was essential, as it defined a completely harmonised framework for the entire sector, based on 3-year bachelor and 2-year master programs. Various administrative systems have been developed to support the implementation of this reform, resulting in the formalisation and bureaucratisation of routines and functions in the administration of students' records at the individual institutions. This, however, was one of the objectives of the reform: on the one hand to publicly specify the rights of students and at the same time to implement a more rigorous follow-up of their progress[7]. These reforms, as we will see, have had a decisive impact on the processing of applications and on the admission system itself, in terms of the entrance requirements, the structure of the various educational programs and the professionalization of administrative routines in the different institutions.

4.1 The NUCAS Development Process

This revolution (or perhaps evolution) of the admission system originated from a rather chaotic situation in about 1990, when all handling of cases was fully decentralised and when no one was able to determine the actual number of applicants in any given year, since the applicants had to submit an individual application to each institution to which they applied. A committee was appointed and submitted its report in December 1990. As one result, the NUCAS-project was established. A brief chronological overview of the milestones in the development process is presented in Table 1:

Table 1. Milestones in the NUCAS development project

1991	The NUCAS-project established
•	The development of an IS for central registration of all applicants to higher education in Norway
1992 -94	Pilot projects based on a new coordinated, distributed model for admission handling
•	Selected case handling, NUCAS-project responsible for the coordination of central services
•	A new, co-ordinated regulation of rankings for colleges, replacing 17 older ones
1995	A common law for universities and university colleges
•	Generel competence requirements as the basis for admission to higher education
1996-97	Implementation of the National coordinated Admission Model (NOM)
•	Nationally available electronic application handling and admission services available to all
2000	Implementation of automatic case handling based on electronic diplomas
•	Full case handling throughout the university and college sector from 2000
2000	First year enabling submissions of applications etc. via Internet ("søkerveven")
2001	The *Competence* reform is implemented
2002	The SO organisation takes over operations and maintenance of the National Diploma database
2003	Quality reform, a number of new bachelor and master studies were initiated
2003 –	The NUCAS-project becomes formalised as a permanent administrative agency

---

[5] Ot. prp.58 (1999-2000). Http://www.regjeringen.no/Rpub/OTP/19992000/058/PDFA/ OTP199920000058000DDDPDFA.pdf

[6] St.meld. nr. 27 (2000–2001) Gjør din plikt – Krev din rett Kvalitetsreform av høyere utdanning.

[7] See e.g. St. mld. 27 (2000-2001), sect. 5.3.1, p. 27-29. See also Stensaker (2006).

The goal of project was to develop a completely new administrative system that was given the mandate to

- Establish a national information system able to supply statistics for use in assessing the demands for higher education.
- Establish a nationwide computer network (UNINETT) interconnecting all institutions.
- Begin developing pilot projects for an ICT-based admission system that would help to correct the deficiencies of the existing decentralized system, as well as its, uncoordinated routines in processing applications.

A crucial step of this development process was the design of the NOM[8] model, which is a combination of central coordination and service provision along with local responsibilities at each individual institution. This model, allowing the individual local institution to process applications to other institutions, requires close co-operation between them, as well as standardised rules pertaining to admission.

The importance of the development of an ICT-based infrastructure for communication and exchange of data between the co-operating institutions should not be underestimated. The UNINETT was built as an advanced computer network to provide important services such as electronic mail and file transfer, replacing the physical transport of floppy diskettes.

The later stages in the development were to include

- Elimination of paper communication and the need to send hard-copy documentation for the great majority of applicants. This was made possible through the introduction of electronic diplomas.
- Fully automated case handling for the great majority of applicants. Manual case handling was to be eliminated.
- Immediate admission offer or admission guarantee for those fulfilling admission criteria.
- A simplification and revision of admission regulations – planned to be implemented by the end of 2009.

Thus, there was an urgent need for a standardised, publically available, electronic signature that can ensure electronic authentication and signature, which still (in June 2009) is not in place.

4.2 The Structure of the NUCAS Electronic System

The data on the applicants are collected from various databases, among them a register containing electronic diplomas from secondary schools. These data are exported to the local administrative systems at the individual sites, and are further used by the Norwegian State Educational Loan Fund in their handling of applications for financial support. In this respect, the NUCAS admission machine may be seen as a *hub* for many other administrative systems in the educational sector.

---

[8] NOM is the abbreviation for "Norsk Opptaks Modell", (National Admission Model).

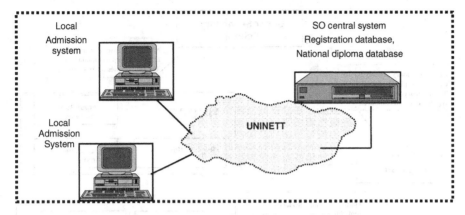

Fig. 2. The National Admission Model

A basic building block for this system was the development of a new *data model*, containing a formalised and codified representation of all existing rules and regulations related to the admission procedures, including competence and ranking data bases (with formalised representation of all competences related to admission and the algorithms for ranking the applicants at the individual institution for all types of educational programs). [9] This data model has been instrumental in supporting the local application and admission handling systems. Another challenge was clearly the development of *electronic diplomas*, which entailed the formalisation of a very complex set of rules along with a large number of programs in secondary schools. [10]

This information system, the NUCAS "admission machine" is illustrated in Figure 3:

4.3 Stakeholder Involvement

Seen from the viewpoint of the NUCAS-project participants, there has been a well-defined division of work and responsibilities between the Ministry of Education and Research, the NUCAS central service and the institutions of higher education. The Ministry has played an instrumental role in funding the NUCAS central service and in implementing the necessary revisions in legislation and other regulations covering application procedures and admission criteria. In this respect, we may say that he project has been mandated and controlled by the central authorities, pursuant to political decisions made by the parliament. Moreover, according to our informants, there has been a fruitful co-operation between the various actors in this project. [11]

---

[9] The robustness of this database was illustrated when the Parliament (Stortinget) in the late spring 1999 revised the admission rules to include credits for having completed military service. This change was easily implemented in the admission "machine" early in July same year, thus into effect almost immediately.

[10] The reform 94 included more than 200 different "programs", that is legal combinations of courses at secondary schools.

[11] This is emphasised by the representatives of the local admission offices.

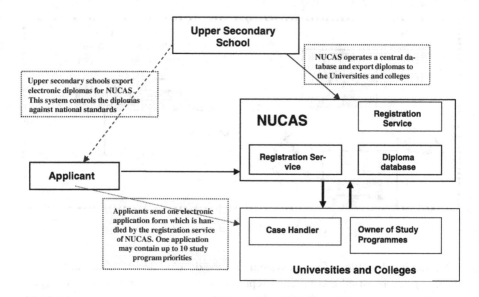

Fig. 3. The NUCAS admission machine

An important feature of NUCAS system is the solid coordination of all phases of the admission process:

- *One application form* per applicant, even when applying for admission to study programs at different universities and colleges.
- *One case handling institution* per applicant, thereby eliminating duplicate work even when the application contains study programs at several institutions.
- *One final admission offer* per applicant, to the highest prioritized study program for which the applicant meets admission criteria.
- Coordinated *centralised registration* of application in combination with *decentralised case handling* and final *centralised selection procedures* (the NOM model).

While the 3 first features were included in the original proposal from 1991, the last feature, the realisation of the NOM model, was made possible only through the design and implementation of the rather sophisticated technical solution that grew out of the pilot projects from 1993-1996.

These are the achievements;

- No duplicate evaluation work – as the average number of institutions involved in admission work per applicant dropped from 3.5 before 1995 to currently less than 1.1.
- 84% of students entering higher education receive their admission offer in the first round of the national selection, while 97% receive it before mid-August.

- Case handling is semi-automatic by means of electronic diplomas, covering 66% of qualified applicants
- The collection system for electronic diplomas now annually covers 97% of pupils finishing secondary school.
- Improved service levels and quality both for the applicants, for the universities and colleges, and for the public authorities.
- Lowered costs for admission work at all levels.
- Achieved efficiency by use of Internet services and semi-automated case handling

For *central management,* the system ensures updated statistics on the number of applicants and admission to each program. It is even possible to analyse the effects of specific regulation measures, and therefore to fine-tune the admission criteria in a number of different ways.

For the *local institutions* the new system has reduced and simplified the admission process. It is also important that within a short time after the application deadline administrators will know how many students have applied for admission to each program. Consequently, they may initiate additional recruitment actions as needed. They also have the opportunity to promote their specific programs to targeted student groups. Schools with specific admission requirements are also allowed to manage these autonomously.

For *the student* the system offers a much simpler and quicker admission process. They can retrieve updated information on all study programs as needed; they will have access to all admissions rules and procedures, and they may check the probability of being admitted to the selected program based on statistics from previous years. The admission procedure is fairer, as the best ranked students cannot book additional programs, since they are required to choose a single first priority.

The combination of centralised and decentralized case handling offers opportunities for better quality control of data. It is also much more difficult to cheat the system, as electronic diplomas are collected automatically from the upper secondary schools and are sent to the local institutions. For both the ministry/ directorate and the institutions, this has contributed to greater efficiency and fewer errors.

5 Analysis and Discussion

What are the main elements of this reform process? From the review of the development processes above we have seen how the growth in the number of applications to higher education in Norway created an unmanageable situation. This led to the establishment of the NUCAS-project as a political response, mandated to be developed in an MIS-system. The improved general outlook influenced further development, and along with various reforms, a new national admission system was implemented, finally as a decision-making system. One way of illustrating these processes is the following chronological overview:

Table 2. The development of NUCAS: important political, organisational and technical actions

Time period	Situation in the educational sector	Political changes in regulations	Administrative and organisational actions	Milestones in technical developments
1970-90	Increasing growth and complexity Uncontrolled and unmanageable rush of student applicants	End of college expansion The Hernes committee was appointed in 1988	A task force was mandated to propose measures for more regulation and control	Development of local administrative systems – no interaction between these systems
1990-91		Implementation of the Hernes proposals	Establishment of the NUCAS-project. Introduction of one admission deadline across the sector	UNINETT in operation Development of a management Information system
1992-1994	Focus on structure: More Collaboration and cooperation in the sector	Norgesnettet and the college reform	Development of the NOM-model as basis for the reform work	Pilot projects were carried out
1995-99		A unified law for all higher education. Harmonisation of admission& ranking procedures	Consolidating NUCAS-project and local admission offices	Implementation of a new data model and a admission machine Pilot version of web-based system
2000-02	Focus on content in the education : Increased quality and efficiency	Competence reform	Implementation of new rules for admission etc.	Full electronic coordination of admission handling. Web-based application system National diploma data base
2003-		Quality reform	SO becomes an permanent organization	Application and admission handling is 90% automated

This table may appear to indicate that the organisational and administrative changes, supported by adequate technical solutions, have been the result of overall planned actions. However, when looking closer into this chronology of development, it seems evident that the technical achievements along with local initiatives have been influential in the implementation of the reform process and that the results are somewhat different from what was originally planned, e.g. the NOM (National Admission Model) combined central coordination and service provision with local responsibilities in the handling of the admission. The latter was not part of the original proposal, but grew partly out of the development work.

It is therefore important to understand how all three factors (political goals, organisational settings and technical achievements) have influenced the development and reform processes in various ways. Although the ministry and the political system have had an overall plan, the technically-oriented initiatives as well as the local institutions, including the administrative staffs, have been instrumental in the processes. While the central authorities mandated the NUCAS-project and defined the general framework for the development and implemented the necessary changes in laws and regulations, it is apparent that the technical project along with the institutions have influenced both the revisions in regulations (through the work with the new data model) as well as the establishment of NUCAS as a government agency.[12] In particular the design and development of the admission machine and web-based application handling routines have been important in the implementation of the overall solution.

6 Results

We have found that the goals that were defined for the project have been fulfilled. It is relevant, however, to ask: Who actually benefited from this reform? - the ministry, the institutions, the students or society at large? As we have seen, the NUCAS-project, initiated in order to provide a management information system for the central authorities, has turned out to be a nearly automated decision-making system, however partially delegated to local institutions for processing and decision-making. This process of technical development has been enabled by necessary changes in legislation. We do not claim that these legal reforms were caused by the (technical) development work; the new laws implemented in 1995, 2001 and 2003 (see Table 1 above) were the result of deliberated political processes. But in the writing of the detailed regulations, some consideration of the automation of the admission process was also taken.

Another important step was the establishment of NUCAS as a central agency. This would not have been an option without the success of the technical development and implementation work, including support from the local admission offices. The introduction of the Competence reform (2001) as well as the Quality reform (2003) entailed new requirements to the project. However, the robustness and flexibility of the system, in that it has been able to implement these reforms in effective ways, has consolidated NUCAS as an organisation. It seems that NUCAS, at least partly, supports the techno-bureaucratic management and control of the students. On the other hand, these reforms have also been beneficial for the individual institutions and for the students.

Our findings are summarized in the table below.

Table 3. Goal, benefits and effects of the NUCAS system for different actor groups

Actor groups Effects etc.	Central government	Local institutions	Students /others
Management tool	The MIS provided a adequate tool for their management of the whole educational sector	The MIS turned out to be useful at a local level. It supports local case handling based on standard criteria	The Web-based information system is perceived as useful in their application process as they can get all information they need.
Regulation and control	The admission machine supports the implementation of changes in ranking and priorities in a flexible way	The data from NUCAS is being used in administering and controlling the students	The negative side is that their flexibility is reduced, and it is difficult to circumvent/"fool" the system
Efficiency and effectiveness	Administrative work has become less demanding	Less resources used for application handling admission management	The application and admission process is much simpler and demands less effort
Other benefits	The use of advanced technology is viewed as goal on its own in an eGovernment perspective	This system is also useful in attracting new students as it allows for local marketing	It can also help the students in claiming their rights

---

[12] The source is an oral report from a meeting between the NUCAS-project and the Ministry of Education. This claim was confirmed by the Deputy Secretary General in the Ministry of Education in a meeting in December 2008.

7 Concluding Discussion

Do our findings conform to the propositions that were formulated by Kraemer and King?

Prop.1. Computers have the potential to reform public administration and their relations to their environments

Our analysis has shown that the reform processes were initiated and actively supported by the ministry, based on political decisions. To a large extent, the results of these reforms are as planned. The NUCAS system, along with other systems has strengthened the ministry and central management's capabilities for control and regulation. However, there are clearly effects that go beyond the primary goals and can be attributed to the application of new technology. We cannot, however claim the new technologies have driven this reform on their own. We may therefore conclude that the proposition is partly supported, and that our findings are not fully in accordance with Kraemer and King's findings that "ICT applications do not cause reform and cannot encourage it where the political will to pursue the reform does not exist" (p. 2).

Prop. 2. *Information technologies can change organisational structures and, thus, is a powerful tool for reform*

Our analysis has shown that some organisational changes have been planned by the ministry. On the other hand, the NOM model and even the NUCAS organisation seem to be the result of successful ICT-based innovation supported by local interests, and would not have been feasible without these technical and organisational achievements. The proposition appears at least to be supported, which implies that we disagree to a certain extent with Kraemer and King's finding that "IT applications have brought relatively little change to organisational structures and seem to reinforce existing structures".

Prop.3 **Properly used, IT will be beneficial for administrators, staff, citizens and public administration as a whole**

Our findings as summarized in Table II show that NUCAS has been beneficial for central governmental management, for the staff at local institutions, for students, and even for society at large. Even though the system allows for efficient supervision and control, it also serves other interests. Proposition 3 is supported, while we (at least partly) disagree with Kraemer and King's claim that "the primary beneficiaries have been functions favoured by the dominant political-administrative coalitions in public administrations and not of those of technical elites, middle managers, clerical staff and ordinary citizens"

Our main conclusion is that there is no clear rejection of any of the propositions, but rather the contrary, that they are at least partially supported. We do, not claim, however, that these propositions can fully explain the reform processes in the NUCAS developments. On the one hand, there is no doubt that political and central management priorities have been decisive in this reform. At the same time, we have to acknowledge the power inherent in the vision that technological developments creates. Such visions, combined with successful development work and supportive managers in the various local institutions seem to have created an environment for innovative technical and administrative solutions.

To what extent can these findings be generalized? Our case is unique in the sense that it applies to the development of a new, specific system. It has been selected for this study because it succeeded in fulfilling a political goal (indeed, even goals that were not defined at the outset). One may say that a total match has occurred between technical achievements, organisational developments and political ambitions. The creation of a new organisation may be an "easier" administrative reform process, even though it also entailed more substantial changes in existing rules and procedures, than it would be to implement radical changes in an existing organisation. We believe that another, very important factor for the success has been that all government agencies involved in this reform process are subordinate to the same minister, who has the authority to enact necessary revisions of laws and regulations without negotiating with other members of the government. This implies that it has been an inter-organisational reform, and not a cross-sectoral one. The latter is much harder to accomplish (see for example Coleman 2008). Thus, our findings cannot be generalized without taking into consideration the specific context of this reform.

There are a number of lessons to be learned concerning how to carry out this type of technical development and administrative reform in general. One lesson learned is found in the step-by-step, chronological history of development, in which each goal was linked to political priorities. A second lesson is that there is a need to build a technical and organisational infrastructure that supports the reform process. A third lesson is the understanding of the mutual relationship between technical achievements, changes in legislation and organisational developments, as illustrated in Figure 1 above. We believe these lessons may be useful to others, too.

References

Coleman, S.: Foundations of Digital Government. In: Chen, et al. (eds.) E-government research, case studies and Implementations. Springer, New York (2008)

Davis, S.: Introduction to digital government research in Public policy and management. In: Digital Government. E-government research, case studies and Implementations. Springer, New York (2008)

Fountain, J.: Building the Virtual State Information Technology and Institutional Change. Brookings Institutions Press, Washington (2001)

Fountain, J.: Information, Institution and Governance Cambridge. Harvard University (2002)

George, J.F., King, J.L.: Examining the computing and centralization debate. Communication of the ACM 34(7), 63–72 (1991)

Grønlund, Å. (ed.): Electronic Government: Design Visions and Management. Idea Group Publ. (2002)

Hovy, E.: An outline for the Foundation of Digital Government Research. In: Chen, et al. (eds.) Digital Government. E-government research, case studies and Implementations. Springer, New York (2008)

Johnssen, G.: E-forvaltning och lagstiftning i Sverige 2000-2006. In: Schartum (ed.) Elektronisk forvaltning I Norden. Fagbokforlaget (2006)

King, J.L., Kraemer, K.L.: The dynamics of computing New York. Columbia Uni. Press (1985)

Kraemer, K., King, J.L.: Information Technology and Administrative reform. Will Government be Different? In: Norris (ed.) E-Government Research. Policy and Management. IGI Publishing, Hershey (2008)

Leavitt, H., Whisler, T.L.: Management in the 1980s. Harvard Business Rev. 36, 41–48 (1958)

Laudon, K.: Computers and bureaucratic reforms. John Wiley & Sons, New York (1974)

Løvdal, E.: Samordna opptak: Norge samlet til ett utdanningsrike. In: Jansen, I.A., Schartum, D.W. (eds.) Elektronisk forvaltning på Norsk. Fagbokforlaget, Bergen (2008)

Ot. prp.58 (1999-2000), http://www.regjeringen.no/Rpub/OTP/19992000/058/PDFA/OTP19992 0000058000DDDPDFA.pdf

Schartum, D.W. (ed.): Elektronisk forvaltning i Norden. Praksis, lovgivning og rettslige utfordringer. Fagbokforlaget (2007) ISBN: 978-82-450-0554-7

Schartum, D.W.: Designing and formulating data protection law. International Journal of Law and Information Technology (2008)

Stensaker, B.: Institusjonelle kvalitetssystemer i høyere utdanning – vil de bidra til bedre kvalitet? Evaluering av kvalitetsreformen: Delrapp.2, NIFU Oslo (2006)

Scholl, H.J.: Discipline or Interdisciplinary Study Domain. Challenges and Promises in Electronic Government research. In: Chen, et al. (eds.) Digital Government. E-government research, case studies and Implementations. Springer, New York (2008)

Sjøberg, C.M.: Rätt rättsinformasjon i e-forvaltningen. In: Schartum (ed.) Elektronisk forvaltning I Norden. Fagbokforlaget (2006)

Time to Give in: Firm Belief in Administrative Reform as a Driver for Delivering Benefits from IT

Jeppe Agger Nielsen[1], Rony Medaglia[2], and Kim Normann Andersen[2]

[1] Aalborg University, Department of Economics, Politics and Public Administration,
Fibigerstræde 1, DK-9220, Aalborg, Denmark
agger@epa.aau.dk
[2] Copenhagen Business School, Center for Applied ICT, Howitzvej 60, DK-2000,
Frederiksberg, Denmark
{rm.caict,andersen}@cbs.dk

Abstract. This paper presents the results of a survey on the opinions of Danish local government managers on the future use of IT after the merger of 271 municipalities into 100. Findings show that the highest expectations on the outcome of IT implementation are related to increased efficiency and to new and better ways to solve tasks. However, the high hopes are contrasted by the respondents' experiences with the use of IT thus far. Managers are not optimistic about the possibility that IT can lead to a strengthening of local democracy and citizen involvement. Overall, findings show that the municipalities' visions on the use of IT support a company-oriented way of thinking that mainly focuses on management and effective operation.

Keywords: IT adoption, local government, administrative reform.

1 Introduction

In 2007, the municipalities in Denmark were restructured by merging 271 into 100 municipalities, and also by merging 13 regions into 5. In parallel to this merger process, the division of work between local and central government was reconfigured substantially. There is nothing as rigid and slow to change as governmental structures and division of labour in government. Whereas this statement perhaps is true, the administrative reform in Denmark can be argued to be an example of the opposite.

But how do the new municipalities view the prospects of digitalization, and where do they see possible obstacles? What does the actual reform mean for their use of IT? Are there special areas where the municipalities wish to provide extra effort? Is internal efficiency the issue that has the highest priority? Or is it rather service and online self-service solutions? And how do the municipalities look at the possibilities for involving citizens and developing local democracy by using IT?

The local government administrative reform in Denmark has repeatedly been emphasized as a lever for IT adoption in municipalities (e.g. [1], [2]). Among political decision-makers in the National Parliament, special interest organisations, and consultancy companies, there is widespread agreement that the adoption of IT in the new municipalities will lead to added efficiency, improved public service, and more involvement of people in the democratic processes.

M.A. Wimmer et al. (Eds.): EGOV 2009, LNCS 5693, pp. 103–114, 2009.

However, digitalization enthusiasm seems to be partly in contrast with existing research results on adoption and benefits from use of IT [3], [4], [5]. Research has shown that IT can have a contradictory role in organizational transformation [6] and that workers in government have a certain degree of inertia in their initial use of IT and work around system constraints in unintended ways (reinvention) [7]. Even though there is no exact agreement about what the extensive digitalization efforts have led to, a large number of studies indicate that there is a wide gap between the actual results and the enthusiastic rhetoric that has influenced the debate about the potentials of digital administration. Empirical studies had some difficulty in showing that massive IT investments have led to corresponding savings in administrative and staff-related expenses (see e.g., [8], [9], [10], [11], [12], [13], [14]). Similarly, a number of attempts at increasing citizen participation in democratic processes via the Internet (e.g., in the Danish municipalities of Hals and Søllerød) [15], [16] resulted in only a limited democratic increase, and has not lived up to the expectations that were stated in the project descriptions. Moreover, the demand from the citizen side – with a few exceptions – has also been very scarce [17].

This paper begins with an insight into the survey database and a specification of the investigation dimensions. Next, the municipal managers' visions on the use of IT in the new municipalities are presented and discussed. The internal task management is then focused on, followed by external relations and the issue of services and citizen involvement. As a result, we identify which perspective dominates the use of IT in the new municipalities – the efficiency-oriented, the service-oriented, or the democracy-oriented. The paper ends with conclusions, and outlines some scenarios for the future use of IT.

2   Framework and Collection of Data

According to Heeks [18] e-government can be considered as "all use of information technology in the public sector". E-government takes place in the public sector and includes the internal administrative case handling, but also the externally-oriented information and communication with companies, citizens and other society players [19]. Figure 1 shows a wide perspective (including both the internal work processes and the external relations) on the use of IT in municipalities, which is the core focus of this paper.

Internal work processes	External relations
- Changes in working routines	- Services (self-service solutions etc.)
- New ways to solve tasks	- Democracy and citizen involvement
- More effective task management	
- Control and management	

Fig. 1. Dimensions of analysis

First, when we look "inside" the municipal organization, the issue is the *practical work routine*, including the extent to which the municipalities expect that IT leads to new ways of solving tasks and to more effective task management, etc. Second, the issue is about the perspectives for better political-administrative *control and co-ordination* through IT. When we look "outwards" two dimensions are essential: 1) the extent to which the municipalities invest in electronic services in the relationship with citizens and companies through self-service solutions, among other things; 2) their efforts in involving citizens in the decision-making process and in strengthening the local democracy.

The analysis carried out draws on data from different sources. First, an extensive survey on the municipal managers in the 98 new municipalities was conducted. The questionnaire was submitted electronically with the help of the Rambøll Management product Survey Xact ®. The municipal managers were sent an email in which they were informed about the investigation, and were provided with a link to the online survey. In order to carry out data processing, the collected data were transferred to the statistics software SPSS.

Table 1. Survey data

	N	%
Total number of questionnaires submitted	98	100
Wishes not to participate – by phone or in written form	7	7
Unreturned questionnaires	26	27
Total number of completed questionnaires	65	66

As evident in Table 1, 65 out of 98 municipal managers answered the question-naire, resulting in a response rate of 66%. Of the 66 merged municipalities, we received 47 responses, equivalent to 71%. The response rate was a little lower for the 32 non-merged municipalities, that is, 18 responded, equivalent to 56%. Overall, the response rate can be said to be satisfactory – given the municipalities' "busy" time during the submission of the survey.

The data does not contain systematic imbalances regarding population size and geographical position, with the exception of a slight over-representation of the few small island municipalities, and of an under-representation of suburban municipalities that are not part of greater Copenhagen. About 50 out of the 98 municipal managers answered the questions about IT use that is investigated in this paper. Even though the answers do not point to systematic imbalances concerning population size and geo-graphical position, the rather low response rate suggests that the results are to be interpreted with caution.

We collected valuable information about the municipalities' choices and priorities concerning the political and administrative organization, as well as the expectations on the municipalities' communication and digitalization efforts.

The municipal managers, who had been key figures in the change-over process, were considered to be key informants with regards to such questions. Since the survey was administered only to the top administrative management, the resulting data provides a specific "picture" of the organization and control conditions. The answers to a number of questions would have been different if we had involved people further down in the administrative organization.

Finally, it is to be noted that the results of the survey provide only a "snapshot" of the conditions in the new municipalities. The municipal organization and control conditions are still going through adjustments, development and change. The ongoing developments and changes following the formation of the new municipalities in January 2007 are not covered in this study. However, the trend of the transformations is deemed to be revealed by the "snapshot" provided by this study. Second, as a supplement to the municipal managers' information and assessments, the following data was collected: relevant documentary material, communication strategies, IT strategies.

3 Findings

We start by looking at the municipal managers' expectations on a number of different aspects of the municipalities' IT use.

Table 2. Expectations on the IT development by municipality managers (%)

To what extent do you expect that...	To a high degree	To some extent	Only to a small degree	Not at all	I don't know	N
The use of IT will result in changes in working routines and create new ways to solve tasks?	73	25	2	0	0	51
Internal digitalization tools (ESDH, Intranets etc.) will contribute to a more effective task management?	69	29	2	0	0	51
IT will stimulate opportunities for cooperation between the local authority's units?	63	31	6	0	0	51
IT will contribute to improving the general control in the local authority?	57	41	2	0	0	51
External digitalization tools (self-service solutions etc.) will contribute to a more effective task management?	53	33	14	0	0	51
IT will lead to a strengthening of the local democracy?	20	31	33	8	8	51

As Table 2 shows, the municipal managers have high expectations and certainty on almost all dimensions. It is to be noted that the answer categories "not at all" and "I don't know" are mostly close to zero. Internal efficiency gains appear to be prioritized.

There is an overwhelming majority (about 70%) indicating, for instance, that the use of IT will contribute to creating new ways of solving tasks and will ensure a more effective internal task management to a high degree. Similarly, there is a large majority that is of the opinion that IT will stimulate opportunities of cooperation across the local authority's units.

When the focus is on the possibility of improving the general political and administrative control, the municipal managers completely agree on the potentials of technology. Only one respondent in the survey answered that IT will result in improved control only to a small degree (Table 2).

Table 3. The weight of the management functions in relation to e-government (%)

	N	%
Big weight	43	78
Unchanged weight	11	20
Less weight	1	2
Total	55	100

As shown in Table 3, almost 80% of the municipal managers expect that e-government will gain a larger weight management-wise. The increased weight of management in connection with e-government is, together with larger weight on developmental and change management and communication, the highest value among all the management functions that we investigated (management, finance control, developmental and change management, personnel administration, network management, communication and digital administration).

When we focus on the "outwards" dimensions of the municipal service – self-service solutions, etc. – the municipal managers also see great prospects in Information and Communication Technology. Despite the positive trend being hardly impressive compared with the perspectives for the internal streamlining, 53% thinks to a high degree that the further development of the external digitalization for communicating with citizens and companies leads to a more effective task management. A smaller group of 14% thinks that this is the case only to a small degree (Table 2). The overall large confidence in the external digitalization tools is somewhat surprising.

In any case, the electronic channel for communicating with public bodies is not the preferred method by citizens. A survey carried out in 2006 shows that citizens in all age groups (particularly the elderly) prefer personal service to the electronic one [20].

Table 4. Barriers for contact with public bodies via the Internet (2006)

	%
Lack of personal contact	50
Lack of direct answers	39
Concerns regarding protection and safety of my personal data	32
The service I need is not available online or difficult to find	16
Use of the Internet is too complex	16
Other	29

Note. % of respondents online in the last month. Source: [21]

Similarly, data from Statistics Denmark show (see Table 4) that lack of personal contact is the main barrier in the use of the Internet to get in touch with public bodies. However, data also reveals that the number of citizens that search for information on public authority homepages, download forms and send in forms electronically, has grown considerably since 2003-2006 [22]. It is mainly in relation to tax filing (advance income estimate statements, income tax forms, etc.) that the citizen use of the self-service solutions is seriously becoming a trend.

Under municipal support, the use of electronic self-service solutions (e.g., notification of moving, revaluation for childcare, meter reading, etc.) has so far been rather scarce. In fact, more than half of the municipalities estimate that citizens have used the electronic forms only to a little extent [21]. However, the municipal managers' optimism regarding IT does not concern all the aspects that we have investigated. There is particularly one area where confidence is not as strong. "Only" 20% think that the use of IT can, to a high degree, lead to a strengthening of local democracy; a further 33% think that this is the case only to a small degree; and 8% think that this not the case at all (Table 2).

This shows that it is not the issue of digital democracy that attracts big attention from the new municipalities. When asked about where they see the main challenges for IT use in municipalities, municipal managers do not see the strengthening of local democracy as a central challenge, in comparison to a number of other challenges (Table 5). According to municipal managers, the main challenge is to improve political and administrative control and, to a higher degree, to advance the use of IT in strategic management. Gaining a more effective task management is also a central challenge. This is probably because, thus far, harvesting the prospective streamlining profits and disengaging resources has been difficult. Generally, the development of control aspects and of efficiency – both within and outside the IT area – ranks higher on the agenda than the development of democracy. This is probably also connected with the budget pressures that, among other things, the municipalities have to cope with as a consequence of the current tax freeze in Denmark.

Table 5. Main challenges for IT use in municipalities (%) N=51

	%	Rank
IT as a general means of control for the political and administrative management	73	1
IT as a means to ensure a more effective task management	67	2
IT as a means to create new ways to solve tasks	59	3
IT as a means to create new forms of external interaction and communication (with citizens, companies etc.)	53	4
IT as a means of to create new forms of interaction and communication internally in the municipality	47	5
IT as a means to strengthen local democracy	12	6

The municipal managers' priorities are not to be interpreted as that the municipalities distance themselves from using IT tools in the development of local democracy. A question directly aimed at the municipalities that have developed a democratization strategy shows that 21 out of 29 municipal managers included the use of IT as an essential element in relation to the local authority's democratization strategy. There are municipalities that seem to invest rather strongly on digital democracy and citizen involvement. Silkeborg municipality, for instance, has claimed that they wish to become "Denmark's best local democracy" by actively exploiting technology [23]. However, when we look at the larger picture, it is not here where the biggest investments lie. When the municipal managers are asked to give priority to, and estimate, where the expectations and challenges for the use of IT are, its use as a means for strengthening the local democracy is at the bottom of the list.

The overall picture shows that the use of IT in the new municipalities is dominated by an efficiency perspective with a focus on effective operation and control. Even though optimism is scarcely voiced, there is a large trust in prospects related to digital services. Conversely, the expectation that IT can strengthen local democracy and citizen involvement is far from being of the same extent. The municipal managers' perspectives are pretty much in line with the municipalities' choices and visions on administrative organization and control. Moreover, the municipalities are considered to be dominated by business logic, where the question about effective and coordinated operation plays a decisive part.

However, the fact that efficiency and service aspects are generally given a higher priority than the democracy aspects is well known. According to Torpe and Nielsen [24], both the State and the municipalities are more interested in digital administration than in digital democracy. Local Government Denmark (KL) has stated that digital administration, and not digital democracy, is a top priority [25]. The actual reform, in fact, is considered to be strengthening the municipalities' use of IT. We have investigated at the municipal manager's level regarding the mergers of municipalities, and there is great agreement. 34 out of 35 of the municipal managers who responded think that the actual reform to a high extent or to some degree helps to strengthen the need for tools of electronic control. 31 out of 34 of them point out that the reform to a high extent or to some degree gives occasion to exploit IT in the solution of new tasks.

The possibility of optimizing the advantages of technological change in the internal work processes, and minimizing the negative consequences, will depend on a high level of appropriate training of the employees [26]. We have therefore asked the municipal managers to what degree they think their staff had the necessary IT technical competences to fulfill the local authority's IT objectives.

Table 6. Do staff have the necessary IT technical competences to fulfil the local authority's IT objectives?

	N	%
To a high degree	5	10
To some degree	43	86
Only to a small degree	2	4
Not at all	0	0
Total	50	100

As indicated in Table 6, 10% of the municipal managers estimate that the staff is to a high degree in possession of the necessary IT technical competences to fulfill the local authority's objectives, while a surprising 86% estimate that it is so to some extent. 4% point out that staff have the necessary competences only to a small degree.

There are fairly few among the municipal managers who can be considered to be either "optimists" or "pessimists" – almost all take a pragmatic position and point out that the employees "to some extent have the necessary competences". The municipal managers' confident visions of the staff's IT competences have possibly been a little overestimated. In any case, regarding staff in the public sector, it has been stated "that it is a widespread myth that the staff is good at using technology and that the staff will be qualified on the Internet technological competences" [26]. Therefore, there are probably good reasons to invest in further IT training for employees (and leaders) in the new municipalities in order to be able to better exploit the advantages of technology. The need for additional IT qualification is not a new observation, but it is, nevertheless, important – also in the new municipalities.

The potentials of Information and Communication Technology are also concerned with the extent to which technology can replace existing channels in the relationships with citizens and companies. As we have seen before, electronic opportunities, despite a rising offer of digital services in the municipalities [27], have not replaced traditional channels, i.e., mail, telephone and personal service. Such a picture is also in line with a number of earlier research results, suggesting that digital channels are not considered as a replacement, but rather as complementing existing forms of contact and communication (see e.g., [28], [29], [30]). If we also look at the communication channels that the municipalities have adopted in relation to the merging process, we can see a corresponding pattern.

Table 7. Overview of the municipalities' communication forms in the merging process. N=49 (merged municipalities).

Communication forms	%
Homepage	98
Intranet	61
Newsletters/staff letters for employees	80
Staff/information meetings for the staff	82
Newsletters etc. for the citizens	63
Citizen meetings	69
The press	94

An analysis of the communication strategies of the merged municipalities shows that the municipalities have used both electronic and traditional channels in both internal and external contact and communication (see Table 7). For external communication/ contact, it is not only homepages and discussion forums that are used (and, in some municipalities, electronic citizen panels), but also physical citizen meetings, press releases in local newspapers, radio spots, distributed "citizen newspapers", etc. For internal communication/ contact, among other things, Intranet solutions and electronic newsletters are used, but also newsletters in paper format, traditional personnel magazines, meetings, etc. And this multiple strategy is taken into account. As it is stated in the strategy of the municipality of Mariagerfjord, for instance: *"It is important to emphasize that one cannot be content with electronic newsletters. The largest part of the employees still "works out there in the field" and does not have access to a PC in the workplace on a daily basis. All experiences also how that not all PC users can be reached with electronic newsletters"*.

Another example from the communication strategy of the municipality of Roskilde points in the same direction: *"The internet-based media can play a key role when new information has to be communicated quickly and effectively to the staff. But we will not be able to reach all employees in the three municipalities through the net, therefore this communication form must be combined to a necessary extent with meetings and newsletters"*. This shows that the municipalities in a complex municipal reform process have chosen a "both" strategy.

In spite of the fact that the new technological possibilities have not replaced the "old" channels, there still are municipalities that focus more radically on technology. The communication strategy of the municipality of Hørsholm reads, among other things: *"The website and the Intranet are the municipalities' main information channels"*. Generally, it has to be observed that today the website in particular is considered to be very crucial in the relationship between the local authority and the citizens, the business world, etc. (see Table 7). For instance, in regards to the creation of the Ny Middelfart municipality, it is stated: *"A shared homepage (www.nymiddelfart.dk) is established, where all municipality processes can be followed at any time. Approved minutes from steering committees, work groups etc. will regularly be forwarded. The homepage will become the central meeting place for all partners who are searching for knowledge and insight about the new Northwestern Fuen municipality"*. Homepages have, to a high degree, become the municipalities' interaction platform [31], and a number of studies from Statistics Denmark, among others, also indicate that citizens increasingly use public authority homepages. However, the municipal homepages thus far have shown their value particularly as an information channel.

As mentioned, self-service solutions act only to a small degree as a supplement to the personal contact and – with few exceptions – it has proved difficult to find examples of electronic debates "that have effect" as a forum for democratic dialogue [16].

However, despite the municipal managers' limited belief that IT can strengthen local democracy, the analysis of the communication strategies shows that IT is used actively to ensure better conditions for communication with citizens and companies, etc.

4 Conclusions

In this paper we have mapped the visions of the new municipalities on the future use of IT. The ambition level is on the top in almost all areas. Not the least is the efficiency-oriented perspective that seems to have a high priority. The highest expectations are related to increased efficiency, new and better ways to solve tasks, and improved political and administrative control. This is possibly not so surprising. These findings are fairly in line with the statements that the municipal managers had in the "old" municipalities as digital administration [32].

However, there is widespread agreement that the local government administrative reform pushes on the ongoing development. The high expectations are more than intact, and management-wise, the issue of e-government, according to the municipal managers, will be given a higher priority in the years to come.

In spite of the huge expectations, the municipal managers do not believe that a more effective and coordinated operation automatically follows the increase in IT effort. Together with the question about improving the political and administrative control, these are the main challenges that the municipal managers see. And there are understandable reasons for them. Previous investigations have shown that it has been very difficult to prove appreciable financial savings, reduction by staff, etc., in connection with the introduction of IT.

However, it seems that it is not the IT competences of the staff that constitute the great barrier. Rather few municipal managers think ('only to a small degree' or 'not at all') that their staff has the necessary competences to fulfill the local authority's IT objectives, and that they are rather confident about IT. The study also indicates that the municipal managers have ample confidence in the use of electronic services.

About 85% of the municipal managers think that self-service solutions, etc., ('to a high degree' or 'to some degree') will lead to more effective task management. However, the widespread optimism can appear paradoxical – citizens of all age groups actually prefer personal contact rather than electronic service.

In spite of general technology optimism, there are still areas where the expectations are less present. There is particularly one area, local democracy and citizen involvement, where confidence is not as strong. The managers' visions on IT use support a company-oriented way of thinking that focuses on management and effective operation.

However, this does not mean that the municipalities do not use IT in their communications with citizens. This emerges from an analysis of the communication strategies of the merged municipalities. The discussion also shows that the electronic channels are not used as a replacement of the analog contact – they are rather seen as supplementing and reinforcing. The communication strategies of the municipalities are characterized by a "multiple" strategy, concerning both internal and external communication. That said, websites play a crucial role in the relationship with citizens and companies, just as Intranets seem to have greater importance in internal communication. The palette of service and communication channels has been extended, but that has not led to closing down the analog channels.

It will be interesting to see whether the municipal reform will become the future catalyst for the catching up on possible profits. Given the previous experience, there is room for doubt. However, it seems rather unthinkable that, as a leading modern public organization today, one can have a negative view on the possibilities of technology. The truth of administration digitalization is rarely questioned, and there are few (if any) in Denmark who in recent years have dared to say that e-government is not the road forward.

With this in mind, the perspectives and expectations of municipal managers are probably to be interpreted not only as a question of gaining added efficiency and better service, but also as a question of securing external legitimacy, to be seen as being a modern organization/ company. Another scenario is that the high hopes of municipal managers will actually be fulfilled with time. In this case, the assumption would be that the technologies (and the technology use) will eventually mature to the extent that securing profits will then be possible. And even though this is not the general picture, new figures show that IT has actually been a success to a high degree in reducing the costs, as a consequence of digital administration, in just under 10% of the municipalities (according to their own information) [33].

References

1. Regeringen, K.L., Amtsrådsforeningen, et al.: Strategi for digital forvaltning 2004-2006 (2004)
2. Rambøll Management: IT i praksis 2006. Strategi, trends og erfaringer i danske virksomheder. Rambøll Management A/S (2006)
3. van Deursen, A., van Dijk, J., Ebbers, W.: Why E-government usage lags behind: Explaining the gap between potential and actual usage of electronic public services in the netherlands. In: Wimmer, M.A., Scholl, H.J., Grönlund, Å., Andersen, K.V. (eds.) EGOV 2006. LNCS, vol. 4084, pp. 269–280. Springer, Heidelberg (2006)
4. Attour-Oueslati, A., Dufresne, D., Longhi, C.: The development of the local E-administration: Empirical evidences from the french case. In: Wimmer, M.A., Scholl, J., Grönlund, Å. (eds.) EGOV. LNCS, vol. 4656, pp. 412–423. Springer, Heidelberg (2007)
5. Arendsen, R., van Engers, T.M., Schurink, W.: Adoption of high impact governmental eServices: Seduce or enforce? In: Wimmer, M.A., Scholl, H.J., Ferro, E. (eds.) EGOV 2008. LNCS, vol. 5184, pp. 73–84. Springer, Heidelberg (2008)
6. Robey, D., Boudreau, M.-C.: Accounting for the Contradictory Organizational Consequences of Information Technology: Theoretical Directions and Methodological Implications. Information Systems Research 10(2), 167–185 (1999)
7. Boudreau, M.C., Robey, D.: Enacting Integrated Information Technology: A Human Agency Perspective. Organization Science 16(1), 3–18 (2005)
8. Heeks, R. (ed.): Reinventing Government in the Information Age. International practice in IT-enabled public sector reform. Routledge, London (1999)
9. Heeks, R.: Implementing and Managing eGovernment. An international Text. SAGE, London (2006)
10. Moon, J.M.: The Evolution of E-Government among Municipalities: Rhetoric or Reality? Public Administration Review 62(4), 424–433 (2002)
11. Andersen, K.V.: E-government and Public Sector Process Rebuilding (PPR): Dilettantes, Wheelbarrows and Diamonds. Kluwer Academic Publishers, Amsterdam (2004)
12. Remmen, A., Larsen, T., Mosgaard, M.: Digital forvaltning – erfaringer fra Det Digitale Nordjylland. In: Holmfeld, L., Dalum, B., Ulrich, J., et al. (eds.) Det Digitale Nordjylland – ikt og omstilling til netværkssamfundet?, Aalborg Universitetsforlag, Aalborg (2004)
13. Østergaard, M., Olesen, J.D.: Digital forkalkning – en debatbog om digital forvaltning. Dafolo Forlag, Frederikshavn, Denmark (2004)
14. Saxena, K.B.C.: Towards excellence in e-Governance. In: Towards E-Government: Management Challenges, pp. 26–34. Tata McGraw-Hill, New Delhi (2004)
15. Torpe, L.: Demokrati på nettet. Status og perspektiver i danske kommuner. In: Hoff, J. (ed.) Danmark som informationssamfund. Muligheder og barrierer for politik og demokrati. Aarhus Universitetsforlag, Aarhus (2004)
16. Torpe, L., Agger Nielsen, J., Ulrich, J.: Demokrati på nettet. Offentlighed, deltagelse og digital kommunikation. Aalborg Universitetsforlag, Aarhus (2005)
17. Andersen, K.V.: Den brugerdrevne forvaltning. Muligheder og grænser for digitalisering. Jurist- og Økonomforbundets Forlag, Copenhagen (2007)

18. Heeks, R.: Implementing and Managing eGovernment. An international Text, p. 1. SAGE, London (2006)
19. Jæger, B.: Kommuner på nettet. Roller i den digitale forvaltning, p. 50. Jurist- og økonomiforbundets Forlag, Copenhagen (2003)
20. Rambøll Management: IT i praksis 2006. Strategi, trends og erfaringer i danske virksomheder. Rambøll Management A/S, p. 92 (2006)
21. Danmarks Statistik og IT og Telestyrelsen: Informationssamfundet Danmark. It status 2006. Danmarks Statistik, Copenhagen, p. 82 (2006)
22. Andersen, K.V.: Den brugerdrevne forvaltning. Muligheder og grænser for digitalisering, p. 17. Jurist- og Økonomforbundets Forlag, Copenhagen (2007)
23. Ny Silkeborg Kommune: Digitalt demokrati og nye dialogformer. Topmøde om teknologien i nærdemokratiet tjeneste. Ny Silkeborg Kommune (2005)
24. Torpe, L., Nielsen, J.: Digital communication between citizens and local authorities in Denmark. Local Government Studies 30(2), 191 (2004)
25. KL: Digital forvaltning – mål og strategi. E-demokrati skrivelse. KL (2001)
26. Andersen, K.V.: Den brugerdrevne forvaltning. Muligheder og grænser for digitalisering, p. 67. Jurist- og Økonomforbundets Forlag, Copenhagen (2007)
27. Danmarks Statistik og IT og Telestyrelsen: Informationssamfundet Danmark. It status 2006. Danmarks Statistik, Copenhagen (2006)
28. Ulrich, J.: Den demokratiske samtale på nettet – en kvalitativ analyse af debatten på hals.dk. In: Torpe, L., Agger Nielsen, J., Ulrich, J. (eds.) Demokrati på nettet. Offentlighed, deltagelse og digital kommunikation. Aalborg Universitetsforlag, Aalborg (2005)
29. Torpe, L.: Local Political Deliberation on the Internet. In: Kanstrup, A., Nyvang, T., Sørensen, E. (eds.) Perspectives on e-Government. Technology & infrastructure, Politics & Organisation, Interaction & Communication, p. 127. Aalborg University Press (2007)
30. Andersen, K.V.: Den brugerdrevne forvaltning. Muligheder og grænser for digitalisering, p. 63. Jurist- og Økonomforbundets Forlag, Copenhagen (2007)
31. Torpe, L., Nielsen, J.: Digital communication between citizens and local authorities in Denmark. Local Government Studies 30(2), 230–244 (2004)
32. Monrad-Gylling, L.: Klare mål i det offentlige skal sikre effekten ved digitaliseringen. In: Nye veje – en antologi om ledelse. Hildebrandt Consulting (2004)
33. Rambøll Management: IT i praksis 2006. Strategi, trends og erfaringer i danske virksomheder. Rambøll Management A/S, p. 95 (2006)

Shared Service Center vs. Shared Service Network: A Multiple Case Study Analysis of Factors Impacting on Shared Service Configurations

Jörg Becker, Björn Niehaves, and Andreas Krause

European Research Center for Information Systems, Germany
{becker,bjoern.niehaves,andreas.krause}@ercis.uni-muenster.de

Abstract. Shared services have proven to be a key element when it comes to increasing government efficiency by collaboration. Here, we seek to investigate into the shared services phenomenon in the context of government reforms. For this purpose, an interview and document analysis-based multiple case study has been conducted in Germany. The qualitative analysis covers two shared service implementations on the local government level and identifies important preconditions for shared service emergence, namely cost pressure as motive, the existence of key actors promoting the topic and the existence of prior cooperation. Moreover, it is shown that the structure of such previous cooperation determines, if shared services are being organised in a centralised (shared service centre) or decentralised format (shared service network).

Keywords: Shared Services, Networks, Public Sector Reform, E-Government, Qualitative Study.

1 Introduction

The emergence of public sector shared services is a core element of public sector reform. Shared services, a strategy relatively new to public administrations, integrate the analysis of technical as well as organisational issues. Up to now, they have yet only been of minor importance for researchers. A literature review shows that scientific interest in information systems outsourcing for public administrations [1] or public sector shared services [2] has been limited. Nonetheless, it is apparent that collaborative projects are becoming increasingly important for public administration theory and practice [3]. As shared services are a way of realising efficient government collaboratively, this highly relevant phenomenon needs greater scientific attention. Our study therefore aims at gaining a deeper insight into this topic, seeking to answer the following research question: *What are major preconditions for the emergence and configuration of shared service cooperation on the local government level?*

In order to elaborate on this question, our paper is structured as follows: First we will discuss related work, dealing especially with the basic terms of shared services. Subsequently, we develop a research model for our study. After describing the research methodology applied in the study, the case data – gathered from two case studies conducted in Germany – will be presented. This includes a brief case description

M.A. Wimmer et al. (Eds.): EGOV 2009, LNCS 5693, pp. 115–126, 2009.

as well as major findings regarding the variables under analysis. Consequently, the results are discussed and interpreted against the theoretical model. The paper concludes with a summary of major results, the discussion of limitations and a brief outlook on potentially fruitful avenues for future research.

2   Related Work

2.1   Shared Services

The term 'shared services' might be defined as the concentration of company resources performing activities in order to service multiple internal partners [4], which comes along with the standardisation and consolidation of redundant information processes [5]. In a public sector context, this includes centralising administrative service delivery at a certain place [6]. Processes that have been carried out multiple times by several organisational units become executed only once in the shared service organisation. In this respect, shared services constitute a form of government collaboration which is defined as a voluntary agreement between two or more distinct public sector agencies to deliver government services [7]. The main reason for establishing shared services is achieving more efficient service delivery, reflected in cost advantages as well as in higher quality [8]. Administrations should be relieved from routine jobs so that they can use more resources for individually serving their clients 'at the front-line' [9]. Therefore, shared services can especially be applicable for supporting processes like wage and salary administration, human resources, IT-infrastructure, procurement or facility management [10].

The concept of shared services thus constitutes a specific form of outsourcing. Here, two structural types of shared service organisation can be differentiated from one another, referring to its degree of (de)centrality and its constellation of service providing units (SPU) and service receiving units (SRU, see Figure 1). 1) A shared service centre represents the centralised organisational format. In this case, certain

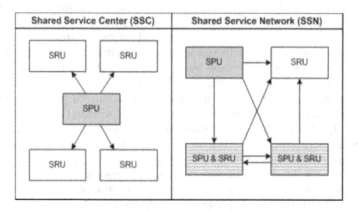

Fig. 1. Ideal types of centralised and decentralised shared service organisations

business functions are concentrated into one single place [11] and provided to several other administrative units (i.e. administrations as a whole, departments or smaller parts of them). These units might belong to the same municipality as the service providing unit, so that services are only provided internally. If they belong to different ones, the SSC realises a form of inter-municipal cooperation [12], [13]. 2) The second type of shared service organisation comprises more than one service providing unit [14] and is therefore called shared service network (SSN). In this case, there are several units, which can be located in different municipalities, providing at least one service to others. At the same time, several service receiving units exist in all municipalities involved, including the service providing units which may also receive services among themselves. Basically, a shared service network consists of at least two shared service centres with their associated service receiving units.

2.2 Research Model

Based on a comprehensive literature review, we examine key (independent) variables for their potential impact on shared service strategies:

Cost pressure: The underlying motives for the emergence of shared services are examined because of their special importance for such a project. An administration can have different reasons for establishing shared services as mentioned above. However, one of the most important reasons will be of financial nature. In times where administrations are short of money, possibilities to reduce costs are very attractive and often required [15], [16]. It has become apparent that the reduction of costs is a main driving force for IT outsourcing in general (e.g. [17]) and for e-Government projects in particular [18]. Consequently, this fact could be adapted as an important motive to shared service implementations.

Key actors: Another relevant aspect for the success of e-Government projects is the impact of key actors [3]. The introduction and acceptance of IT in the public sector generally depends on the people involved and their social interaction [19]. As management support and leadership are crucial success factors for the implementation of shared service and e-Government projects [2], [20], [21], the role of such key actors has to be taken into account when examining the emergence of shared services. The personal commitment of individual key actors is necessary to promote the topic in order to improve service delivery.

Prior cooperation: E-Government research has produced several findings concerning the necessity for collaboration and cooperation between administrations. Several authors have described that intensive cooperation is needed for successful e-Government projects and that such implementations should be accompanied by collaborative communication (e.g. [22] or [23]). Furthermore, Layne and Lee [24] presented a four-stage model for e-Government development, in which horizontal and vertical system integration form an essential part that is not realisable without cooperation between government agencies. Such system integration is strongly related to the establishment of shared services. It has also been stated that collaborative decision-making is important for initiating shared service arrangements [25]. Thus, the existence of previous cooperations seems to have special relevance for e-Government projects in general and therefore also for shared service projects. It is assumed that an emergence of shared services depends on whether certain forms of cooperation existed already before. Referring to the reasoning of path dependency [26], municipalities have to know each other from at least punctual common projects in order to have the necessary basis for a trustful cooperation during shared service delivery.

Prior structures and shared service configuration: Besides these points, several models of shared service implementation exist [2], implying that different configurations exist for cooperation between administrations, e.g. shared service centres. These configurations are important for the adoption of the shared services idea, but have so far not been discussed in detail in the public context [27]. In this study, the two structural types of shared service centres and shared service networks are differentiated and examined. It is basically assumed that the organisation of shared services corresponds to the organisation of the prior existing network to a large extent. If the preceding cooperation has central structures in terms of one partner playing a more important role than others, then the shared services will be organized centrally likewise in form of a SSC. On the other hand, decentralised structures of prior cooperation, where all partners play an equal role, rather lead to shared service networks (SSN).

3 Research Methodology

Research Method and Selection Criteria: The usage of multiple case studies is a core method within qualitative research. It is favourable when contemporary events are investigated over which the investigator has no control [28]. This is due to the fact that case studies, in contrast to experiments, for example, do not affect developments or behaviours. Thus, case studies are especially useful for examining temporal, organisational developments, which is the aim here when dealing with the emergence of shared service cooperation.

Multiple Case Study Design and Method of Reasoning: When conducting case studies, a case represents a well-defined unit of investigation for examining the interaction between dependent and independent variables [29]. The selection of cases should ensure that this interaction can be explained, but also that possible covariates are kept under control. To achieve this, the method of agreement, based on John Stuart Mill [30], has been applied. Selected cases should be equal regarding their outcome, but should differ significantly regarding other aspects (i.e. the independent variables). Among these different variables, the one which is just equal in all cases explains the equal outcome. According to this design, we have chosen cases for our investigation, in which the same outcome – the emergence of shared services – occurred, but that were heterogeneous regarding other aspects like shared services content, legal form of cooperation, location, size, and number of participants.

Case Selection and Analysis: According to the described research design, we have chosen the following two cases of inter-municipal cooperation in Germany: the central IT-procurement in Aachen (case A) and the pilot project shared services in North-Rhine Westphalia (case B). With these successful implementations of shared services, findings could be derived. We conducted seven expert interviews with persons involved in the development of the projects during a timeframe from June 2007 to July 2008. The experts interviewed were heads of IT departments, CEOs, shared service project managers, or mayors. All interviews were conducted in a semi-structured way. This included a free part for the experts to report on current content and organisation of the shared services, questions addressing environmental, organisational and individual preconditions for the shared services and an open discussion about related aspects brought up during the interview. The interviews have been complemented by analysing related documents including project documentations, meeting minutes, presentations and websites. The method for analysing the data gathered was qualitative content analysis [31].

4 Data

4.1 Case A: Aachen

IT-Procurement for local administrations and other public institutions is organised centrally in the region of Aachen since the beginning of 2004. It is operated by a company in public ownership which acts as a regional IT service provider for administrations and other organisations since 2003. The central procurement of standard hardware and software is offered as a shared service for the city of Aachen and all nineteen municipalities of the districts Aachen and Heinsberg. Here, findings include:

1. Cost pressure: In a first step, the expectation of cost-savings could be identified as crucial factor and sole motive for centralising the procurement. The municipalities could, on the one hand, save the effort for own tendering processes and additionally could achieve more favourable conditions through bundling their orders. This purpose was explained by two interviewed experts:

"The reason for organising the procurement centrally was simply the reduction of costs by doing one tendering procedure for all so that the municipalities could save their own efforts." (Manager responsible for central procurement).

"All of our e-Government processes are aligned with the claim for efficiency. [...] Managing business processes contains optimising our workflows." (Head of IT department).

2. Key Actors: In this case, important actors were the political representatives from Aachen, who planned to establish a central procurement already at the foundation of the public IT service provider. This was expressed by the provider's manager:

"The administrations were obviously interested in this service already when founding [the company] in 2003, as it was already envisaged at that time."

3. Prior Cooperation: Regarding the existence of a prior cooperation, previously centralised services have to be mentioned. Most municipalities had already received other services from the IT area by the service provider or its predecessors respectively. Already in 1975, the "common local data processing centre (GKDVZ)" Aachen was founded as cooperation between the districts Aachen and Heinsberg and the city of Aachen. The municipalities of the region were provided with information technology and mainframe services by this centre. These tasks were devolved to the newly established service provider in 2003. The municipalities therefore could already use numerous services centrally before the central procurement was established,

like development, integration and customization of applications, IT-consulting and - training, data centre-operation or mass printing and enveloping. The responsible manager stated:

> *"The administrations already cooperated before in this respect that they made use of services by [our company] and its predecessors respectively."*

Further cooperation also existed in other areas, e.g. the StaedteRegion Aachen, which leads to a political union and will become legal successor of the district Aachen. Altogether, a long-time cooperation of the municipalities has to be stated on a functional as well as on a political level.

4. Prior structures & Shared service configuration: The prior organisational network-structures can be characterized as central. The respective municipalities received several services from their IT service provider. In this respect, the company played a special role, acting as the main hub in the cooperation network of the partners involved. The current shared services are organized centrally as well (see Figure 2). In the same way as in the previously existing network, the involved municipalities and other institutions receive services from the company. The only difference is the service content, being enlarged to IT procurement.

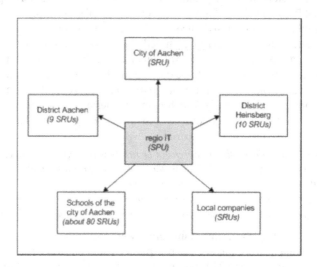

Fig. 2. Organisation of shared services Case A

4.2   Case B: North-Rhine Westphalia

In 2007 a pilot project for establishing a shared service organisation has been initiated in North Rhine-Westphalia. The four towns of Radevormwald, Hueckeswagen, Wipperfuerth and Marienheide are involved by developing solutions for a closer collaboration in the form of shared services. The towns are all located in the north of their district "Oberbergischer Kreis", from the rest of which they are explicitly separated as it expands very much in north-south direction. This has led to a strong cohesion between the four towns and the administrations as well. With the pilot project, the involved administrations aim at scrutinizing the possible applications of shared services, and exploiting the resultant advantages. For this purpose, the extent is examined to which cooperative service delivery is possible and efficient for several administrative areas. The financing is taken over by the federal state of North Rhine-Westphalia, which expects to transfer the results of the project to other intermuniciple cooperations. The official kickoff to the project took place in April 2007 by starting with analysing three administrative areas to find out if they are suitable for shared services. These areas were procurement, property management and organisation of the building yards. In mid-2008 the analysis was completed and concepts have been worked out to implement the solutions found. The related implementation is planned for the second half of the year 2008. In a next step, further administrative areas shall be analysed, including financial accounting, human resources and building supervision. Here, findings include (see Figure 3):

1. Cost pressure: Just like in the other cases, the outstanding and crucial motive for the shared service cooperation was the opportunity to reduce costs. All four municipalities have severe financial problems; therefore this aspect was of special importance to them. A member of the project steering team stated:

"[...] mainly due to financial reasons. Against the background that all four municipalities have budget deficits, ideas have to be developed to compete with this. Our idea is to save money by cooperating."

2. Key Actors: The four mayors could be identified as important key actors in this case. Although none of them was solely responsible for pushing forward the establishment of the shared services, their openness to innovative solutions and their will to cooperate enabled the project in the first place.

"A first exchange between the four mayors took place in the year 2000, termed playfully as 'Northern Alliance'. [...] So it started with informal meetings [and several years later] the idea for shared services was born in this context. [...] Without the mayors, it probably wouldn't have worked." (Project leader)

3. Prior Cooperation: There has been a series of prior cooperations between the four municipalities involved already before the beginning of the shared services project. Among these, the regular exchange between the mayors has to be pointed out, which was initiated in the year 2000 already. Based on this exchange, several cooperation projects were started. One of the mayors commented on this:

"We [the 4 mayors] have therefore joined forces some years ago to meet regularly and to agree upon bringing things forward together. Since then we have launched quite a number of projects."

Altogether the four municipalities try to act as a closed unit in their appearance to other public authorities, which has led to a clearly improved outward perception and was described by the mayor as well:

"We have combined our energies to appear jointly to others. [...] Such a meanwhile long lasting cooperation leads to a unified outward perception with a perceived value that we didn't have before." (Mayor)

4. Prior structures & Shared service configuration: The essential part of prior cooperation structures before the pilot project was the subject-oriented cooperation of the four mayors. This can be described as decentralised because each participant played an equal role in the project. The furthermore existing selective functional cooperations also have a decentralised character, since they include different single projects, that partly are executed only between some of the municipalities, partly however also between all four of them.

The current organisational network is characterized by intensive cooperation between the four municipalities. Although the project is not finished yet, all partners involved seek to take over their part and deliver services to the others. This is accompanied again by establishing the cooperation as an equal partnership, which was regarded as essential for the cooperation in the shared service project by the interviewed mayor:

"It is certainly necessary to respect an equal partnership. We, the four mayors, regard ourselves as equal, with everyone taking over his part, [...]".

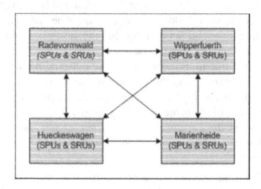

Fig. 3. Organisation of shared services Case B

5 Interpretation

In order to derive results from the interview data described above, the examined variables from both cases will be compared with each other in the next step. This leads to the variables' impact on the outcome of our case study analysis. Table 1 summarizes the findings from the case data.

Table 1. Summary of findings

	Case A	Case B
Main rationale: cost pressure *(independent variable)*	Cost savings through omission of tendering and more favourable conditions.	Primarily cost savings, secondary will to establish a joined building supervision.
Existence of key actors *(independent variable)*	Political representatives from Aachen.	Group of mayors.
Existence of prior cooperation *(independent variable)*	Administrations already used other central services. Additionally political cooperation.	Intensive exchange between mayors, several cooperative projects.
Prior structures *(independent variable)*	Centralised. Several municipalities associated with central service provider.	Decentralised. Equal partnership between mayors and municipalities, selective cooperation.
Structure of shared services *(dependent variable)*	Centralised.	Decentralised.

1. In both cases the main rationale for establishing shared services was the saving of costs. Besides, there were sometimes also further reasons, like for example certain political intentions, but the financial aspect was crucial for each case. Hence it shows that administrations primarily focus on the savings potential and disregard other possible advantages, like an improved quality of service delivery. We assumed that reduction of costs is the crucial motive for establishing a shared service organisation. This could therefore be confirmed clearly. Financial incentives are apparently the most important reason for administrations to deal with cooperation in the form of shared services.

2. Central persons, who take the role of key actors, were of special importance for the emergence in every case. Without these promoters shared services implementation would have been unlikely. It is important to note that all of these key actors had no special functional importance, but held political functions in their municipalities. We expected that particularly central actors must be present in the developing network, so that shared services can emerge. This can be confirmed by the two cases as well. The role of certain key actors and their presence as central promoters, thus, appears to be particularly important for the emergence of shared services.

3. Likewise previous cooperation existed in both cases, however, in different formats. In case A, all municipalities already made use of the central IT-provider before. In case B, a long-time cooperation on mayor level, as well as individual functional cooperation existed. Thus, it has to be assumed that previous cooperations can create the preconditions for the emergence of shared services. We stated that preceding cooperations on a functional level could be necessary, before a shared service can develop. This assumption could be confirmed, since cooperation on a functional level existed in all cases.

4. The prior structures of the developing networks were associated with the later shared service structures in every case. The previous cooperation of the central IT-procurement in Aachen was organized centrally just like today's structure - with the central provider and the municipalities as its customers. In the other case the previous cooperation was decentralised, and from that origin a decentralised shared service network developed as well. We assumed that prior existing structures determine the later shared service configuration. The two cases support this. A shared service centre emerged out of a central structure, a shared service network developed from decentralised structures. These research results lead to important findings regarding the emergence and configuration of shared services (see Figure 4).

It showed that two conditions are crucial for the emergence of a shared service cooperation. This is on the one hand the existence of a preceding cooperation, on the other hand the presence of certain key actors. They ensure that an idea of establishing shared services is actually put into practice. Thus, one main finding is that shared services emerge especially if these two conditions are given. However, a sufficient condition must still be present, since shared services are not implemented as an end in itself. It could be found that the expectation of cost savings seems to be this sufficient condition. Administrations obviously seek improvements of the financial situation in the first place. Other motives play only a subordinated role, if they exist at all. Regarding the shared service configuration, the results suggest the following relationship: The structures of prior existing cooperations can determine the subsequent shared service structure - central shared service centres seem to develop from a central structure, decentralised shared service networks seem to develop from decentralised cooperations.

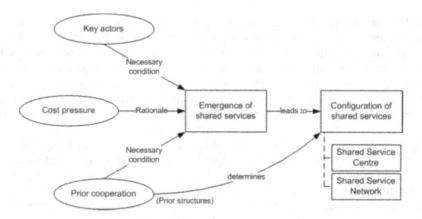

Fig. 4. Causal relationships derived from the multiple case study

6 Conclusion

Shared services are a central means for collaboration and public sector reform, addressing technical and organisational issues as well. The importance of such cooperation is undoubted, yet little research has been conducted with regard to this topic. With our study, we try to give insights especially into the preconditions under which shared service cooperation emerges and is being shaped. An explanatory, multiple-case study analysis based on two shared service projects from Germany contributes new findings to the research topic. First of all, cost pressure could be identified as a main rationale for starting a shared service project. Besides such a motive, two other preconditions support the emergence of shared services. On the one hand, the presence of certain key actors, especially from the political and management level, is helpful in order to promote the topic. On the other hand, prior cooperation between the municipalities involved is important for building the shared service cooperation on a trustful relationship. Additionally, the structure of such previous cooperation determines the structure of the emerging shared services. Centralised prior cooperation structures lead to shared service centre structures, while shared service networks emerge from cooperation with a decentralised character.

Practical implications from these points refer to the managerial actions needed when building up shared services. Responsible actors from local government especially have to take into account that relying on a previous cooperation and appointing key actors to promote the project is fundamental. Moreover, prior existing structures have to be considered by project leaders and decision makers when it comes to choosing an organisational format for the shared services.

The case selection is a possible limitation of the presented study. Generalisability of the results could be improved by examining more cases. Studies from other countries, which have to deal with the same issues of government reforms, might overcome the regional limitation of the study and generate other important aspects. Furthermore, such cases could be examined where other forms of cooperation have emerged. Here, findings could be related to the preconditions examined, providing a sharper view on the circumstances of public sector cooperation.

References

1. Marco-Sima, J., Macau-Nadal, R., Pastor-Collado, J.: Information Systems Outsourcing in Public Administration: an Emergent Research Topic. In: European and Mediterranean Conference on Information Systems (EMCIS), Valencia, Spain, June 24-26 (2007)
2. Walsh, P., McGregor-Lowndes, M., Newton, C.J.: Shared Services: Lessons from the public and private sectors for the nonprofit sector. The Australian Journal of Public Administration 67(2), 200–212 (2008)
3. Gil-Garcia, J.R., Chengalur-Smith, I., Duchessi, P.: Collaborative e-Government: impediments and benefits of information-sharing projects in the public sector. European Journal of Information Systems 16(2), 121–133 (2007)
4. Schulman, D.S., Dunleavy, J.R., Harmer, M.J., Lusk, J.S.: Shared Services: Adding Value to the Business Units. Wiley, New York (1999)
5. Wang, S., Wang, H.: Shared services beyond sourcing the back offices: Organizational design. Human Systems Management 26(4), 281–290 (2007)
6. Habbel, F.R., Prodoehl, H.G.: "Rakeling" oder die Reform der öffentlichen Verwaltung in Deutschland durch Shared Services. Winkler & Stenzel, Burgwedel (2006)
7. Dawes, S., Préfontaine, L.: Understanding new models of collaboration for delivering government services. Communications of the ACM 46(1), 40–42 (2003)
8. Triplett, A., Scheumann, J.: Managing shared services with ABM. Strategic Finance 81(8), 40–45 (2000)
9. CIO council: Shared Services (2008),
   `http://www.cio.gov.uk/shared_services/introduction/`
10. Wegener, A.: Kommunale Dienstleistungspartnerschaften. Mit Shared Services zu einer effektiveren Verwaltung. Bertelsmann, Gütersloh (2007)
11. Bergeron, B.: Essentials of Shared Services. Wiley, Hoboken (2003)
12. Sorrentino, M., Ferro, E.: Does the Answer to eGovernment Lie in Intermunicipal Collaboration? An Exploratory Italian Case Study. In: Wimmer, M.A., Scholl, H.J., Ferro, E. (eds.) EGOV 2008. LNCS, vol. 5184, pp. 1–12. Springer, Heidelberg (2008)
13. De Vries, W.: Unity in Diversity: An Analysis of Inter-governmental Cooperation in the Field of geoICT. In: Wimmer, M.A., Scholl, H.J., Ferro, E. (eds.) EGOV 2008. LNCS, vol. 5184, pp. 172–183. Springer, Heidelberg (2008)
14. Janssen, M., Joha, A.: Emerging shared service organisations and the service-oriented enterprise: Critical management issues. Strategic Outsourcing: An International Journal 1(1), 35–49 (2008)
15. Eyob, E.: E-government: Breaking the frontiers of inefficiencies in the public sector. Electronic Government 1(1), 107–114 (2004)
16. UNDESA: United Nations e-Government Survey 2008. From e-Government to Connected Government. UN Department of Economic and Social Affairs, New York (2008)
17. Smith, M.A., Mitra, S., Narasimhan, S.: Information Systems Outsourcing: A Study of Pre-Event Firm Characteristics. Journal of Management Information Systems 15(2), 61–93 (1998)
18. Huang, Z., Bwoma, P.O.: An overview of critical issues of E-government. Issues of Informational Systems 4(1), 27–30 (2003)
19. Horton, K.S., Wood-Harper, T.A.: The shaping of I.T. trajectories: evidence from the U.K. public sector. European Journal of Information Systems 15(2), 214–224 (2006)
20. Ang, C.L., Davies, M.A., Finlay, P.N.: An empirical model of IT usage in the Malaysian public sector. Journal of Strategic Information Systems 10(2), 159–174 (2001)

21. Ke, W., Wei, K.K.: Successful E-Government in Singapore. Communications of the ACM 47(6), 95–99 (2004)
22. Strejcek, G., Theil, M.: Technology push, legislation pull. E-government in the European Union. Decision Support Systems 34(3), 305–313 (2002)
23. Tan, C.W., Pan, S.L.: Managing e-transformation in the public sector: an e-government study of the Inland Revenue Authority of Singapore (IRAS). European Journal of Information Systems 12(4), 269–281 (2003)
24. Layne, K., Lee, J.: Developing fully functional E-Government: A four stage model. Government Information Quarterly 18(2), 122–136 (2001)
25. Janssen, M., Joha, A., Weerakkody, V.: Exploring relationships of shared service arrangements in local government. Transforming Government 1(3), 271–284 (2007)
26. Pierson, P.: Increasing Returns, Path Dependence and the Study of Politics. The American Political Science Review 94(2), 251–267 (2000)
27. Ulbrich, F.: The Adoption of IT-Enabled Management Ideas. Insights from Shared Services in Government Agencies. EFI, Stockholm (2008)
28. Yin, R.: Case Study Research: Design and Methods. Sage, Thousand Oaks (2003)
29. Barrios, H.: Qualitative Methoden des Vergleichs in der Politikwissenschaft. In: Barrios, H., Stefes, C. (eds.) Einführung in die Comparative Politics, pp. 29–51. Oldenbourg, Munich (2006)
30. Mill, J.S.: A System of Logic, New York. Ratiocinative and Inductive (1846)
31. Mayring, P.: Qualitative Inhaltsanalyse. Grundlagen und Techniken. Deutscher Studien Verlag, Weinheim (2000)

E-Government Implementation Evaluation: Opening the Black Box

Maddalena Sorrentino[1], Raffaella Naggi[2], and Pietro Luca Agostini[3]

[1] Università degli Studi di Milano, Dip. di Scienze Economiche, Aziendali e Statistiche,
Via Conservatorio 7, 20122 Milano, Italia
maddalena.sorrentino@unimi.it
[2] Luiss Guido Carli, Viale Romania 32, 00197 Roma, Italia
rnaggi@luiss.it
[3] Università Cattolica del Sacro Cuore, Dip. di Scienze dell'Economia e della Gestione
Aziendale, Via Necchi 7, 20123 Milano, Italia
pietroluca.agostini@unicatt.it

Abstract. This paper perceives e-government evaluation as a research field that can produce the cognitive input to help us understand the causal nexus that should attribute the effects of an e-government programme to its implementation and transform this learning into an effective intervention tool. Drawing on contributions from Organization Theory and Policy Studies, we propose an interpretive key that assigns a dual role to e-government evaluation: valuable cognitive resource and tool of accountability for the policymakers. The reflections offered here are based on an exploratory case study of a City of Milan project and aim to provide further insights for e-government research and help better inform managerial praxis.

Keywords: e-government, Evaluation, Implementation, Interdisciplinary Approach, Policy Studies, Organization Theory.

1 Introduction

Policy makers, policy advisers and practitioners need to be better informed about the costs, benefits, risks and outcomes associated with e-government [1]. Unfortunately, at present, although e-government initiatives have been credited as engines of government reform, empirical evidence is insufficient to determine their effects on public sector performance [2].

Why do we talk so much but discover so little about the effects of e-government? The intentions, the expectations and the economic resources of the local public administrations or national governments are widely known. But, generally, we know little about the effects (desired or not) on the direct recipients and on the broader social system [3]. Paradoxically, even less is known about the implementation processes of the e-services and ICT platforms. In other words, we continue to think as if the outputs, outcomes and impacts of e-government were divorced from the organizational processes that generated them.

M.A. Wimmer et al. (Eds.): EGOV 2009, LNCS 5693, pp. 127–138, 2009.

In this paper, the term 'e-government' signifies the use of information and communication technologies (ICT), and in particular the Internet, as a tool to accomplish better government [4:11]. The OECD explicitly associates the general objective 'better government' with the achievement of: 'better policy outcomes (...) and other key outputs identified' [4:11]. Unfortunately, the current discourse tends to neglect the relationship that, according to the OECD, exists between e-government and policymaking, with the result that the implementation of a public programme launched via the development of e-services and related platforms continues to be a "black box" for the external observers and the decision-makers themselves. An opacity that raises significant barriers when it comes to evaluating the e-government results.

The paper seeks to shed light on precisely those processes, indicating in the organisational dimension one of the interpretive keys needed to set and evaluate e-government correctly, that is, in a non-rhetorical and a non-ritual way. In particular, our focus will be on implementation, meant as the "moment of truth" in which the public policies are translated into goods, services and technological solutions. According to Majone and Wildavsky [5:175], 'implementation is the continuation of politics by other means'.

Our discussion takes the cognitive stance of an external analyst seeking to offer a scientifically founded opinion on the Ecopass pollution charge implemented by the City of Milan. We plan to use this case to verify the practicability of an evaluation approach that factors in the organizational perspective. This paper does not discuss the effectiveness of the Ecopass regulation in meeting its goals. We will use the analytical tools of Policy Studies and Organization Theory as our main interpretive keys.

The case is presented in the form of an exploratory study, the goal of which is to develop pertinent hypotheses and propositions for further enquiry [6], [7]. Our methodological choice was spurred by the fact that the analysis focuses on a pilot scheme. Initially, the City of Milan implemented Ecopass for a 12-month trial period, but recently extended it for another year. The informative base for our analysis has been built from a number of sources: the authors' experience in the field of organisational analysis; and an in-depth examination of documents, such as announcements, presentations, news releases, articles that have appeared both in the press and on official websites, and the independent blogs and websites that mushroomed after the Ecopass launched. We have made a systematic review of these documents since July 2007. In parallel, we carefully examined the international literature.

The results of our work are presented as follows: Section 2 illustrates the guiding framework for our analysis. Section 3 reviews the literature that has approached the theme of the evaluation of public policies. Section 4 describes the key points of the Ecopass project, while Section 5 comments on the case and proposes an interdisciplinary touchpoint for interpreting the main findings of the study. Section 6 discusses some of the possible implications stemming from the use of an organization-aware toolbox for the research and practice of e-government evaluation and offers final remarks.

2   Analysis Framework

Evaluation is needed 'to argue the case for new projects and expenditure, to justify continuing with initiatives, to allocate additional IT funds, to assess progress towards programme goals and to understand impacts' [4:134]. We believe that, by nature, the evaluation effort must be oriented to forming an opinion on the processes *and* results of public programmes. It seeks to broaden the cognitive scope of the policymakers and the administrations [8], [9]. The evaluator relies on a toolbox (conceptual, theoretical, methodological, technical) to ascertain – data in hand – whether the intervention has or hasn't changed "the world" compared with the initial plan.

The evaluation can be of (Fig. 1): a) the immediate products (outputs) or the effects triggered by the public policy (i.e. outcomes and impacts); b) the implementation, i.e. the operational launch of the services; or, c) the phase in which the agenda is defined (known as the issue-making and decision-making phase). This is how the ex-post evaluation of all the activities that retrospectively analyze the outputs, the outcomes, and the impacts of a public policy is defined. The ongoing (or in itinere) evaluation is defined as all those techniques used to analyze performance during the implementation process. Ultimately, the ex-ante evaluation is defined as the retrospective analysis of the decisions taken before the launch of the implementation phase.

The three types of evaluation meet diverse cognitive needs. The ex-ante and ex-post evaluation confirm or revoke the decisions already taken. Vice versa, the ongoing evaluation – which generally responds to a more advanced cognitive question – accompanies the decision-makers during the actual implementation of the services, accounting and reporting on the situation as it unfolds. Because the ex-ante evaluation has no bearing on the aims of this paper, from hereon we will discuss prevalently the other two categories. As mentioned in the Introduction, this paper is interested in analyzing the organizational processes and decisions that precede the production of the outputs, outcomes and impacts. Fig. 1, below, which refers to and has been adapted from the diagram developed by Lippi [9:77], shows the specific object of our analysis in the box with the bold border.

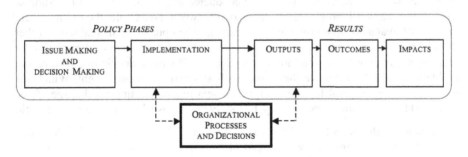

Fig. 1. Policy phases and results (adapted from Lippi [9:77])

3 Literature Review: Policy Evaluation vs. Policy Inquiry

Evaluation is not a generic study of social change, but, to the contrary, addresses a *specific* intervention ([9], our italics) launched on the initiative of an individual or collective client (policymaker, programme executives, public-sector managers, interest groups). The analysis is underpinned by five basic questions that enable us to chart a research pathway in a Policy Evaluation perspective: When? Where? For whom?

What? Why? [10:206]. For example, in responding to the first question (When?), the evaluation must establish whether it is appropriate to conduct a retrospective evalua-tion (ex-post), an ongoing (in itinere) evaluation, or to analyze the programme before it is implemented (ex ante). The second question (Where?) concerns the choice of settings to examine, for example, the implementer agency or another organizational body or even a specific target population. Responsibility to a controlling institution or the need to lend support to critics or to a specific interest group orient the identifica-tion to the recipients of the research (For whom?). The reply to the question 'What?' means identifying the "object" on which to focus (e.g., the project, the programme, the service) and to ask "how does this change the status quo?" [11]. Finally, the rea-sons (as understood by the client) for making the evaluation study are summed up in the question 'Why?'. The evaluation is either formative or summative [12] depending on whether the object is to guide the structural improvement of the programme or to furnish a summary opinion on its specific aspects.

Policy Evaluation owes the clarity of its assumptions to its primary merit. Design-ing an evaluation based on this linear approach must be specified beforehand and, once accepted, be conducted rigorously. In addition, Policy Evaluation makes a marked distinction between policymakers (politicians and senior officials) and ana-lysts, drawing a clear line that reassures both parties: to the former, the division of tasks, to the latter the identification of the best means to realize them [12:235]. The most orthodox version of Policy Evaluation is the target for a number of theoretical proposals (grouped under the name of Policy Inquiry) that advance strong doubts on both the assumptions that underpin it and its practicality. The studies offered by the Policy Inquiry school of thought are actually variegated in terms of the concepts and methods. As a result, we will cite a few common aspects useful for our proposed discussion.

When and Where. The evaluation can be conducted at any time and can be "summa-tive" or ongoing [10], however, the distinction between the ex ante, the in itinere, and the ex post evaluation can prove to be unrealistic when put to the factual test. Further, the analysis of a problem does not always precede the identification of the solution but vice versa, given that it is common knowledge that PA often decide to intervene in a problem because they believe they have the best solutions to put it right. Which, de-pending on the temporal horizon and the context examined, implies that the effects attributed to a programme can overlap, be barely distinguishable, or even incompatible.

For whom. As Regonini [11:382] observes, frequently "the problems to be dealt with have the power to attract actors" instead of the other way around. Social conditions are indispensable factors in determining the value of a public policy [9]. The results of the evaluation acquire meaning only in relation to the responses expected by the dif-ferent stakeholders. Given that each stakeholder category has a different agenda [13], the evaluation thus needs to unravel the following knots: which are the most impor-tant criteria of opinion? Those of the politicians? Those of the direct beneficiaries of an intervention? Those of the agency paying for it?

What. Policy evaluation assumes that the purposes and the objectives of the policies are a given and, therefore, that these can be easily deduced from official texts and documents. Taking into account that the political arena (like that in Italy) is often characterized by the vagueness of the legislative definition [14:30], the question then becomes: must the evaluation be restricted to analyzing the explicit official objectives of the intervention or is it more opportune to also analyze the unexpected effects and the unforeseen consequences? Is it possible – ask Pressman and Wildavsky [8] – to express an opinion disregarding such effects?

Why. Rossi, Freeman and Lipsey [15] underscore the difficulty of clearly defining the evaluation goals, especially as the programmes are diffused in nature and produce the expected results in the longer term or in an undefined timeframe. We then need to consider that, in most cases, the politicians and programme management are unable to draw on information attesting to current performance or on the methods to enhance that performance. As a consequence, the top administrators tend to assign a fairly low priority to improving the performance of the agencies under their responsibility. Business literature also highlights the ambiguity of the notion of performance in the public sector. Therefore, any kind of measuring system is bound, fatally, to be put to the debate [16].

In brief, Policy Evaluation seeks mainly to identify the conditions that enable the adoption of the best solutions and the setting up of data reporting systems for monitoring the results [11]. Therefore, an efficacious project is believed the precondition for ensuring good performance. The main limitation of these studies is their inability to realistically capture the social dimension of the policies, their often 'tortuous' dynamic, the fruit of a slew of conflicting interests, and strategic games between 'partisan actors' [17].

Research inspired by Policy Inquiry seek – unlike the linearity of the mainstream approach – to shed light on the social interactions that are brought into play when a public policy is implemented. This current of study starts with the observation that any policy is a "polyhedron with a great many faces" [11:371]. Consequently, the possibility of adopting a rational design approach to evaluation is denied [18] and that is obviously a limitation. The effects of the programmes, according to the Policy Inquiry studies, lie exclusively in the stakeholders' recognition: the evaluation is a process that creates "the reality" [18:141]. It is precisely because of the unpredictability of the implementation processes that implementation is called the "black box" of policymaking [19].

In essence, the clashing and polarized positions make it hard to interpret the concrete situations that the evaluation practice must address. Of course, each of these efforts has improved our understanding of policy implementation, but we now need to make the next leap forward. First, by "opening the black box", that is, developing the tools needed to understand the causal nexus that should "enable the attribution of the effects to the realization of the programme itself" [20:xiv]. Second, by translating the theoretical proposals into operational terms ("transform this learning into an appropriate intervention tool" [11:184]).

4 The Milan Ecopass Project

In July 2007 the City of Milan decided to introduce a vehicle entry charge (called the Ecopass), aimed at restricting access to polluting vehicles. The regulation (the first of its kind in Italy) came into force in trial form in January 2008 and has been confirmed for 2009. The initiative aims to improve the levels of air quality in line with the parameters set by various EU Directives (now merged into Directive 2008/50/EC [21], [22]) and by the subsequent national and regional laws on the matter.

The Ecopass regulation involved a broad spectrum of interventions to the viability, technological platforms, administrative procedures, personnel training practices and citizen communication. Although the project has the primary goal of fighting pollution, it can nevertheless be framed within the e-government context. According to Fountain [23:241] "a useful way to think about e-government operations is to distinguish among three sets of relationships": government-to-citizen (G2C), i.e. the flows of information and services between the government and its citizens; government-to-business (G2B), i.e. all transactions between the Public Administration and the private sector; and government-to-government (G2G), i.e. inter-agency and inter-governmental linkages. All three of these relationships characterize the Ecopass project and can be identified by analysing the reconfigurations involved in the implementation of the "pollution charge".

From a *technological* viewpoint the Ecopass implementation required several changes to the City of Milan's legacy IS, including a newly established intergovernmental (G2G) network between the (local) Milan system and some of the (central) archives kept by Italy's Ministry for Transport. Also, the area affected by the regulation (8.2sq km) entailed hefty investments in, among other things, the installation of 43 access points monitored by CCTV and other remote control devices, so that vehicle number plates can be checked against the data contained in the national motor registry. This sharing of *information* created a joint inter-agency resource [24] that could be used by the system for verifying the vehicle category, its pollution level and the corresponding cost of the entry permit.

Also the *channels* businesses and citizens can use to access information about and purchase the pass were enhanced through ICT-based services (G2B and G2C interactions): besides the traditional information desks, newsstands and shops, they in fact include the City of Milan web portal, a dedicated call centre, bank ATMs and an SMS-based service. All the channels are connected to the central control room via computer-network.

Another aspect to highlight is that the initiative foresees new "forms of citizen consultation" for the whole Ecopass initiative, therefore calling for *e-participation* [25] and greater engagement with citizens [26]. So the project's ICT component is seen – at least in official statements – as an instrument for not only conveying the new service and enabling the actual technical implementation of Ecopass, but also for enhancing two-way communication between the Milan municipality and its citizens.

The Ecopass project has been controversial since the early phases of its formulation. Not only did it raise vociferous protests from local traders and residents, but it also sparked an intense debate across various institutional and political levels (e.g. the administrations of the City and Province of Milan, and the Regione Lombardia) and among a host of technicians from several disciplinary spheres. The controversy heated up also due to a slew of malfunctions and delays in the electronic payment systems. The shifting of the blame between the implementers and the critics of the procedures adopted for purchasing the technologies exacerbated the disputes between Ecopass supporters and opponents, but did not lead to its modification. In the months after the project launched, most of the technological glitches were remedied.

As mentioned above, the Ecopass initiative calls for promoting forms of informed participation among citizens, combined with the 'monitoring of the regulation's impact from the environmental, socio-economic, and vehicle traffic viewpoints'. However, as yet, the City of Milan – through its "Mobility Agency" – has limited itself to the systematic diffusion on its website of periodical technical reports ensuing from the monitoring of traffic flows and air quality in the town centre. As far as we know, the PA has not made an organic evaluation that goes beyond the immediate outputs of the project and takes into account the organizational processes. We will try to bridge this gap by proposing a revised evaluation framework.

5 Discussion

A controversial regulation, such as that just described, puts the evaluator in a tough position. The role of the evaluation is to furnish interested parties with a founded and constructive opinion from a different cognitive position. Basically, evaluation means connecting the "context and content of what is implemented" [8].

Taking different cognitive positions leads to different opinions [9:21]. The most diffused cognitive position is that of common sense. A common sense opinion, as expressed by the man on the street, translates into the approval or disapproval of the conduct of the administrators in respect of a specific service or on the principles guiding the action, which neither provides an evaluation of its merit nor serves to understand the reasons for its success or lack of success. An example of the *zero level* evaluation is the intense debate – reported also in Italy's leading newspapers – that has involved the various layers of public opinion on the Ecopass project.

Apart from the common sense-derived opinion, we have the cognitive opinion of the expert, i.e. opinions founded on direct experience or competence. The opinion of the stakeholders is, by definition, partisan [27]. Therefore, if a stakeholder is a political body, the evaluation will be guided, above all, by its ideological orientation and interests. This latter – in the policymaking arena – is positioned at evaluation *level one*. The past few months have seen a great many representatives of local and governmental institutions intervene in the Ecopass debate. Citizen committees and delegates of the various categories (e.g. craftsmen, retailers, professionals, companies based in the suburbs) have all "pleaded" their case.

The opinion above that of level one comes from outside the policymaking arena, i.e., it is not influenced by vested party interests. This type of view stems from an extraneous cognitive position, which we can class as evaluation *level two*. This is an ideal position as it not only enables the policymakers to enrich their knowledge, but also raises the degree of accountability to the citizen-voters. In that sense, the evaluation helps to shed a new and different light on the problems in question. The extent to which the goals of the Ecopass project have been achieved will be verified in the upcoming months (given that the trial period expired at the end of 2008). At the date of this report, no external evaluation had been conducted on this initiative, at least to our knowledge.

The Ecopass is a case in the public domain that, as such, presents conceptual challenges that are well known to scholars, policymakers, and public administrators alike.

How has the evaluation puzzle been addressed in the sphere of the Ecopass project? Adopting Lippi's proposal [9], the opinions offered by the diverse parties in question have stopped at level zero and level one, while the assessment activities undertaken by the City have been conducted in a fairly de-contextualized way compared with the internal dynamics and decision-making processes. For example, July 2008 saw the city councillors publish a document that purports to show a correlation between the Ecopass implementation and the data related to the level of hospital admittances of town-centre residents. Other data disclosed by the City of Milan for January-September 2008 indicate a reduction in airborne micro-particles, fewer road accidents in the traffic-restricted area and an increase in the number of passengers using public transportation.

The Policy Evaluation framework reveals that the City of Milan wanted to show the effectiveness of the regulation by presenting limited data on its output (that is, the products of the activities implemented) and on its outcome (that is, the results on the recipients as a direct consequence of the policies adopted [11]). However, the city administrators made no attempt to analyze the impact, the trickiest evaluation because it aims to determine whether the programme has influenced the situation-problem in the way expected [28].

Interpreting the case in line with Policy Inquiry [11] suggests that the logic of delivery benchmarking has prevailed in Milan, that is, the public administrators have concentrated solely on reporting systems based on data and information that mostly exist within the institution already. Without going into either the merit of the criteria chosen by the City to show that it has achieved the results expected from Ecopass or the cause-effect relation on which these are built (the slogan chosen by the City of Milan is "Less Traffic, Cleaner Air"), we believe we are looking at an evaluation attempt that has been kept wholly within the perimeter of the policymaking arena and that basically consists of a selective documentation (i.e. 'without evidence of lack of success', [29:93]) of the results obtained in the timeframe in question. According to Rebora [14:40], in these cases, it is more appropriate to talk about 'pre-evaluation methods'.

To move forward in our reflection, we might be better drawing on the analytical tools offered by Organization Theory. This is not an antithetical choice over other disciplinary areas that have approached the evaluation theme, but, to the contrary, is complementary. Nevertheless, there can be no doubt that organizational theory presides over the process logic that structures the technical goals and technical actions in organizational settings.

A theoretical perspective founded on organizational action [30], [31] shifts the evaluation focus to processes of action and decision, to the intentional and bounded rationality that has led to the implementation of Ecopass. That approach traces the effects of the interventions launched in the technical area back to the organizational processes of: *design* (i.e. the decisions on the architecture and technical standards); *adoption* (i.e. the decisions of integrating the artefacts in the activities); and *use* (i.e., of appropriation in the daily practices of the users) of ICT platforms.

The Ecopass case highlights this complex interweave of decisional processes at diverse levels, distinguishable only from the analytical standpoint, in which time plays a key role. For example, it is precisely due to the very short-term deadlines that the IS department of the City of Milan had to adopt a "big bang" approach (in which the transition to the new system was implemented in a reduced timeframe); the decision deemed the most risky by the relevant literature (see, for example, [32], [33]) because irreversible. During the first few weeks of implementing Ecopass, a malfunction in the system that automatically reads the number plates caused about 160,000 fines to be issued to motorists unaware that they had infringed the new regulations for driving into Milan town centre. The ensuing requests for clarification from the motorists sent the municipal offices and the call centre into turmoil, while the justices of the peace and the prefectures were swamped with appeals.

Time also influenced the decisions on personnel training/instruction and internal communication. The new system was a bearer of constraints and opportunities: it enabled the decision-makers to produce new forms of regulation that, in turn, had an impact on the informative assumptions of the various subjects. For example, the January-September 2008 experience revealed the existence of a substantial cognitive gap between the actors involved, some of whom had no idea of the work done by the others, even though the implementers (traffic police, municipal transport company, IS department, councillors) report to one and the same institutional subject: the City of Milan.

Most of the technological glitches encountered were eventually remedied, therefore, we could say that the ICT infrastructure set up for the Ecopass project ultimately "held". Retrospective reconstruction of the practice highlights a sometimes tortuous unravelling of decisions and objectives, which partly changed along the way in conjunction with the players' awareness of the opportunities for change. Primarily, the automatic control system of the central access points enables the Milan municipality to gather a significant quantity of information on vehicle circulation. This seems especially useful for designing future interventions in the local urban area as it provides a cognitive base – which, in turn, can be analyzed through ICT tools – that didn't exist prior to Ecopass. The second opportunity lies in the upgrading of the applications portfolio, which delivered some new front-end services to all the citizens via the City of Milan's website.

The Ecopass case is a particularly fast-paced example of a process of organizational change with a major impact on the citizens, whereby the adoption of new ICT-based solutions, despite being an important objective, is not on its own an element capable of determining the results. ICT artefacts are organisationally relevant because they introduce new rules into the various processes (analytically identified) and impose them on others. The analysis of the secondary data sources available does not yet enable us to identify in what way the constraints and opportunities - stemming from the choices of the design, adoption, and use of the ICT-based services and artefacts - have influenced the generation of Ecopass outputs, outcomes and impacts. However, we can reasonably assume that the origins of the problems dogging the project were also due to an underestimation of the organizational effort.

Finally, we underscore that in a perspective such as that proposed here, also the evaluation takes on a different role. Above all, the evaluation is an integral part of the organizational action and is itself a process. As a consequence, the evaluation cannot be de-contextualized, given that it necessarily appears within a specific organizational setting and involves a number of plans (technical, structural, institutional).

6 Implications and Final Remarks

This paper has sought to address e-government implementation evaluation from a more advanced and interdisciplinary cognitive level. Policy studies help us to wipe the slate clean of the assumption that e-government is neutral. In addition, these admit from the start that shifts and swings exist compared with the initial plan, so we must perforce consider the results on the recipients (demand side) of the regulations, not the regulations as such. On the other hand, organizational analysis can help throw light on another front (the supply side), i.e. on the processes of action and decision that have led to specific effects.

Bounded rationality guides the organizational action and enables its evaluation. Further, the evaluation itself is understood to be a process intrinsic to the organizational action. That means we can exclude *a priori* the possibility of successfully maximizing the results (and thus evaluating these in terms of efficiency), because it would be like saying that the relationship between the *means* – i.e. the technical knowledge, the software programmes, the operating practices, and the ICT platforms developed and deployed - and the *ends* - or the problem that lies at the root of the e-government programme - is optimal. Unlike other kinds of assessment, the organizational evaluation can always be carried out. It is an evaluation of the organization's 'fitness for the future' [29:84] and consists of evaluating the goals of the action, the process relationships and the reciprocal congruency of all these dimensions.

But what are the advantages of adding the organizational dimension to the evaluator's conceptual 'toolbox'? We cite only a few of the aspects worthy of attention. First, the organisational perspective enables us to put into practice the principle according to which every public service organization 'must focus on both the content of the intended programmes *and* how to establish and maintain a viable organization to implement the programme' [34:63-64] (italics in the original). We must not forget that 'too often, organizational aspects are not planned (...) or worse (...) project leaders try to avoid thinking about these components entirely' [34:64].

Second, placing the organizational processes of action and decision at the centre of the analysis means considering time a key variable. This is compatible with the assumptions of the ongoing (or level two) evaluation, i.e. that which offers the policy-makers and managers the highest cognitive input for correcting or reorienting the public objectives and strategies.

Third, and as a consequence of the preceding point, shedding light on the processes helps increase the body of common knowledge available on the organization and its relationships with the environments with which it interacts. Enlightenment, in turn, is a stride forward in improving organizational learning and creates the conditions that favour further assimilation of a culture oriented to external accountability. As underscored also by Scheirer [35:188], the assessments made at the implementation stage have a strong impact on the future diffusion and institutionalization of the new solution or programme.

Fourth, the processual vision of organizational phenomena enables us to analyze situations in which the change goes beyond the "boundaries" of a specific institution. This possibility is especially significant, given that e-government is rarely implemented by one public administration alone: see, for example, the trend of sharing the delivery of e-services via intermunicipal agreements [36].

Our contribution to the reflection pauses here for now. Although the paper presents only an initial (and therefore limited) exploration of the direction indicated, we believe it offers a useful contribution, also in a public management perspective: as Roberts-Gray et al. [37:63] put it, by analyzing the congruence "between programme and environment at macro, intermediate, and micro levels" evaluators provide programme managers with an instrument for deciding where and how to change implementation processes, so that the intended benefits are actually produced. The Ecopass project is still a work in progress and can be interpreted using several keys, although most certainly the organisational approach augments the significance of evaluation research.

References

1. Foley, P.: The Real Benefits, Beneficiaries and Value of E-Government. Public Money & Management 25, 4–6 (2005)
2. Lim, J.H., Tang, S.-Y.: Urban E-Government Initiatives and Environmental Decision Performance in Korea. Journal of Public Administration Research and Theory 18, 109–138 (2008)
3. Weiss, C.H.: Evaluation: Methods for Studying Programs and Policies. Prentice Hall, Englewood Cliffs (1998)
4. OECD: The e-Government Imperative. OECD, Paris (2004)
5. Majone, G., Wildavsky, A.B.: Implementation as Evolution. In: Pressman, J.L., Wildavsky, A.B. (eds.) Implementation. University of California Press, Berkeley (1984)
6. Yin, R.K.: Case Study Research: Design and Methods. Sage, Thousand Oaks (2003)
7. Darke, P., Shanks, G., Broadbent, M.: Successfully Completing Case Study Research: Combining Rigour, Relevance and Pragmatism. Information Systems Journal 8, 273–289 (1998)
8. Pressman, J.L., Wildavsky, A.B.: Implementation, 3rd edn. University of California Press, Berkeley (1984)
9. Lippi, A.: La valutazione delle politiche pubbliche. Il Mulino, Bologna (2007)
10. Browne, A., Wildavsky, A.B.: What Should Evaluation Mean to Implementation? In: Pressman, J.L., Wildavsky, A.B. (eds.) Implementation, 3rd edn. University of California Press, Berkley (1984)
11. Regonini, G.: Capire le politiche pubbliche. Il Mulino, Bologna (2001)
12. Scriven, M.: Evaluation Thesaurus. Sage, Newbury Park (1991)
13. Gregory, D., Martin, S.: Crafting Evaluation Research in the Public Sector: Reconciling Rigour and Relevance. British Journal of Management 5, 43 (1994)
14. Rebora, G.: La valutazione dei risultati nelle amministrazioni pubbliche: proposte operative e di metodo. Guerini e Associati, Milano (1999)
15. Rossi, P.H., Freeman, H.E., Lipsey, M.W.: Evaluation, a Systematic Approach. Sage, Thousands Oaks (1999)
16. Stewart, J., Walsh, K.: Performance Measurement: When Performance Can Never Be Finally Defined. Public Money & Management 14, 45–49 (1994)
17. Lindblom, C.E.: The Science of 'Muddling' Through. Public Administration Review 19, 79–88 (1959)
18. Guba, E.G., Lincoln, Y.S.: Fourth Generation Evaluation. Sage, Newbury Park (1989)
19. Barrett, S., Fudge, C.: Policy and Action: Essays on the Implementation of Public Policy. Routledge, London (1981)
20. Stame, N.: Classici della valutazione. FrancoAngeli, Milano (2007)

21. Directive 2008/50/EC of the European Parliament and of the Council of 21 May 2008 on Ambient Air Quality and Cleaner Air for Europe, http://eur-lex.europa.eu
22. European Environment Agency, http://www.eea.europa.eu
23. Fountain, J.E.: The Virtual State: Transforming American Government? National Civic Review 90, 241–252 (2001)
24. Mayer-Schönberger, V., Lazer, D.: E-Gov and the Coming Revolution of Information Government. Working Paper, Belfer Center for Science and International Affairs (2008)
25. Macintosh, A., Whyte, A.: Evaluating how eParticipation Changes Local Democracy. In: Irani, Z., Ghoneim, A. (eds.) Proceedings of the eGovernment Workshop, eGov 2006, pp. 1–16. Brunel University, London (2006)
26. Fountain, J.: Paradoxes of Public Sector Customer Service. Governance: An International Journal of Policy and Administration 14, 55–73 (2001)
27. Lindblom, C.E.: The Intelligence of Democracy: Decision Making Through Mutual Adjustment. The Free Press, New York (1965)
28. Dente, B., Vecchi, G.: La valutazione e il controllo strategico. In: Azzone, G., Dente, B. (eds.) Valutare per governare. Etas, Milano (1999)
29. Thompson, J.D.: Organizations in Action. McGraw-Hill, New York (1967)
30. Maggi, B.: Razionalità e benessere: studio interdisciplinare dell'organizzazione. Etas, Milano (1990)
31. Maggi, B.: De l'agir organisationnel: un point de vue sur le travail, le bien-être, l'apprentissage. Octarès, Toulouse (2003)
32. Alter, S.L.: Information Systems: A Management Perspective. Benjamin-Cummings Publishing, Redwood City (1995)
33. Veryard, R.: The Economics of Information Systems and Software. Butterworth-Heinemann, Oxford (1991)
34. Scheirer, M.A.: A Template for Assessing the Organizational Base for Program Implementation. New Directions for Program Evaluation 1996, 61–79 (1996)
35. Scheirer, M.: Approaches to the Study of Implementation. IEEE Transactions on Engineering Management 30, 76–82 (1983)
36. Sorrentino, M., Ferro, E.: Does the Answer to eGovernment Lie in Intermunicipal Collaboration? An Exploratory Italian Case Study. In: Wimmer, M.A., Scholl, H.J., Ferro, E. (eds.) EGOV 2008. LNCS, vol. 5184, pp. 1–12. Springer, Heidelberg (2008)
37. Roberts-Gray, C., Scheirer, M.A.: Checking the Congruence between a Program and its Organizational Environment. New Directions for Program Evaluation 1988, 63–82 (1988)

Refinement, Validation and Benchmarking of a Model for E-Government Service Quality

Babis Magoutas and Gregoris Mentzas

Technical University of Athens, 9 Iroon Polytechniou str., 15780 Zografou, Greece
{elbabmag,gmentzas}@mail.ntua.gr

Abstract. This paper presents the refinement and validation of a model for Quality of e-Government Services (QeGS). We built upon our previous work where a conceptualized model was identified and put focus on the confirmatory phase of the model development process, in order to come up with a valid and reliable QeGS model. The validated model, which was benchmarked with very positive results with similar models found in the literature, can be used for measuring the QeGS in a reliable and valid manner. This will form the basis for a continuous quality improvement process, unleashing the full potential of e-government services for both citizens and public administrations.

Keywords: quality model, validation, refinement, eGovernment, benchmarking.

1 Introduction

Europe continues to make sound progress on the supply of online public services [5]. During the recent years the focus of e-government research and development has evolved from "bringing public services online" to a concept of effective and user centric service delivery. Citizens expect a significant increase of service quality through the internet channel, compared to traditional channels [21]. So, the quality of public e-services and portals is in the center of the user centric e-service delivery concept. The public administrations should put emphasis on the improvement of service and portal quality in order to satisfy citizens and thus leverage the move of the demand size of public services from traditional to online channels. With this way the full potential of e-government will be unleashed, as on the one hand citizens will be provided with highly effective and user-friendly services, while on the other hand the public administrations will be able to take advantage of the enormous cost reduction and re-organization possibilities that are created.

Monitoring of e-government service and portal quality forms the basis for improving the quality of public e-services. Measurement of intangible concepts, like quality, attitudes, behaviors, emotions, is commonly done by using instruments like surveys, interviews, assessments etc., as these concepts cannot be measured directly. Models are instruments that attempt to quantify constructs which are not directly measurable. Thus a quality model attempts to quantify the quality construct; in other words it is responsible for providing an answer to the question about what to measure, as far as the quality is concerned. Quality of public services is a complex aspect, as it depends

M.A. Wimmer et al. (Eds.): EGOV 2009, LNCS 5693, pp. 139–150, 2009.

on the characteristics of several quality areas of the e-government portal and the back-end system. These characteristics and quality areas should be taken into account by the quality model.

It is stressed by several researchers that it is very important to use standardized instruments and models for measuring user satisfaction [10]. The process of developing a standardized model involves two major phases [18]: (i) the exploratory phase, where the hypothesized measurement dimensions are developed and (ii) the confirmatory phase, where the hypothesized dimensions are tested and validated empirically. In other words the purpose of the confirmatory phase is to test the a priori model developed in the exploratory phase.

In this paper we present the refinement and validation of a model for Quality of e-Government Services (QeGS) [16], which includes a set of quality dimensions and factors, i.e. a set of quality aspects, affecting citizens' perception about the quality of the e-government portal and its services. We built upon our previous work [16] [20], where a conceptualized model was identified and put focus on the confirmatory phase, in order to develop a valid and reliable QeGS model. The validated model, which was benchmarked with very positive results with similar models found in the literature, can be used for measuring the QeGS in a reliable and valid manner.

The paper is structured as follows. After this introduction, in section 2 we provide an overview of the initial QeGS model, as conceptualized in the exploratory phase of the development process, and we identify the major risks and concerns that reveal the need for validating it. The methodology followed for validating and refining the model is described in section 3, while section 4 includes the validation results and the developed refined model. In section 5 we present the benchmarking results, while section 6 contains our conclusions and recommendations for future work.

2 The QeGS Model and the Need for Validation

The development of a quality model for the domain of e-government is challenging, due to the complexity and number of parameters that must be taken into account. As already said the model development process starts with an exploratory phase, where the hypothesized measurement dimensions are developed. This includes the identification of salient attributes and dimensions of the construct of interest, which in our case is QeGS. Such a conceptualization of dimensions addresses the question what is included and/or excluded in the definition of QeGS. The state of the art is a very valuable source of information for choosing which dimensions should be included in the construct and which shouldn't. This is stressed by the authors of [7], who state that it is imperative that researchers consult the literature when conceptualizing constructs and specifying domains. In this way the domain of the construct of interest is specified in a complete manner and the conceptualized dimensions incorporate various facets of the construct.

We consulted the state of the art in the area of QeGS and after investigating and synthesizing the dimensions derived, we came up with the initial conceptualized model [16], which is depicted in Table 1. The initial version of the QeGS model, which has a hierarchical structure, includes 33 quality dimensions, incorporating various facets of e-government service and portal quality. It was designed to capture six quality factors of e-government services. Factor and dimensions are both quality aspects of a portal and its e-services as perceived by citizens, but they examine quality in different levels of detail. Quality factors focus on high level aspects such as the usability of the portal/web site, the quality of information, etc., while quality dimensions examine in more detail each quality factor.

The forms interaction factor deals mainly with the attributes of interaction with the e-government portal using forms (e.g. on-line help in forms, automatic calculation of form fields). Service reliability is related to the ability of the e-government portal to deliver public e-services in a sufficient and adequate way or even better. Support mechanisms are related to the process that is followed in order to provide support to the portal's users. Information quality represents the quality of information presented on the portal, and it is related to data accuracy, freshness, completeness, relevancy etc. Portal's usability deals with issues like the web site's structure, its design and appearance, the quality and effectiveness of search facilities and so on. The security that the portal provides to its users is represented by dimensions grouped under this quality factor. Examples of issues addressed, include the procedure of username and password acquisition and the secure archiving of personal data.

Table 1. The Initial QeGS Model. * Dimension deleted in the refined QeGS model, ** Dimension moved to reliability factor in the refined QeGS model.

Forms Interaction	Service Reliability	Support mechanisms
➤ Form download speed **	➤ Ability to perform the promised service accurately	➤ Problem solving
➤ Existence of on-line help in forms	➤ In time service delivery	➤ Prompt reply to customer inquiries
➤ Sufficient data recalling	➤ Accessibility of site	➤ Knowledge of employees
➤ Automatic calculation of forms	➤ Browser-system compatibility	➤ Courtesy of employees
➤ Adequate response format *	➤ Download speed	➤ Ability of employees to convey trust and confidence
		➤ 'Frequently Asked Questions' in site *
		➤ Existence of contact info *

Portal's Usability	Quality of Information
➤ Web site's structure	➤ Data completeness
➤ Web site's appearance	➤ Data accuracy and conciseness
➤ Easy to remember URL *	➤ Information freshness
➤ The existence of search facilities	➤ Number & quality of links *
➤ Site-map	➤ Relevancy of information provided
➤ Ability of customization	➤ Ease of understanding/ Interpretable

Security
➤ Procedure of acquiring username and password
➤ Necessity of personal data provided
➤ Secure archiving of personal data
➤ Use of personal data

Although the initial QeGS model was the result of a thorough and complete investigation of the relevant literature, it needs to be validated. Measurement of intangible constructs is neither simple nor straightforward [23]. A difficulty in using any method to measure a phenomenon of social science is that one never knows for certain whether he/she is measuring what he/she wants to measure, or whether he/she is measuring it the right way. Inaccuracies of measurement, applicability of the measuring instrument and the research method utilized are some aspects that must be taken into account during instrument validation [22]. In our case the QeGS model examines and integrates factors and dimensions that capture QeGS, which is an intangible concept. By taking into account the aforementioned difficulties of measuring an intangible concept, we can identify three major categories of concerns and risks, which reveal the need for validating the QeGS model:

- Concerns and risks related to the <u>validity</u> of the model [23]. This involves the questions whether the QeGS model conceptualizes what it was designed to measure, whether important aspects of QeGS are omitted, or whether the selected dimensions are true indicators of QeGS.
- Concerns and risks related to the <u>reliability</u> of the QeGS model [9]. This involves the extent to which the measurements made using the model remain consistent over repeated tests of the same subject under identical conditions. In other words this risk is related to the extent to which an individual juror could assess the same quality dimension the same way each time.
- Concerns and risks related to the <u>dimensionality</u> of the model [7], i.e. to the correctness of the various groupings of quality dimensions under quality factors.

3   Methodology for Validation and Refinement

Measures and metrics are the sine qua non of solid, scientific research [24]. The conceptualized QeGS model, depicted in Table 1, identifies specific quality measures (factors and dimensions), which define customer/citizen satisfaction with e-government portals and services. As described in the previous section, it needs to be validated that the dimensions derived are actually capturing the six factors assumed in the initial QeGS model and that it is valid and reliable. This is part of the confirmatory phase of the model development process, where the hypothesized dimensions are tested and validated empirically.

Fig. 1 depicts schematically the methodology followed for testing and validating the a priori QeGS model of Table 1, which results in the development of a refined version that addresses the concerns and risks introduced in section 2. As can be seen in Fig. 1, the methodology, which is based on the idea of the two-phased model development process, consists of four major steps and two feedback transitions between steps. The first step concerns the conceptualization of dimensions realized in the initial QeGS model, and was covered in section 2. The next steps are followed in order to produce the refined version of the QeGS model and include the collection of data, the empirical validation of the model by using the collected data and the development of refined versions in an iterative process. In the next sections we discuss in detail the various steps.

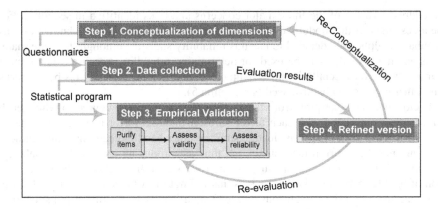

Fig. 1. Methodology for Validating and Refining the Initial QeGS Model

3.1 Data Collection

In an effort to test empirically the suggested dimensions of the construct of interest, it is important to find a real-world application domain. In our case an appropriate application domain is the e-government portal of a public authority that offers public e-services to citizens. In this step we collect citizen feedback, which is used later for validating empirically the initial QeGS model. This is achieved by using a survey in order to collect data from a sample of real citizens concerning their ratings of all the construct's attributes and dimensions.

So we developed an online questionnaire constituted of statements that concern the quality characteristics of the portal and its public e-services, and that represent the quality dimensions of the initial QeGS model. The relation between statements and quality dimensions/factors is one by one, meaning that for each quality dimension/factor, one relevant statement has been added to the questionnaire. In this way the questionnaire operationalized the 33 dimensions and 6 factors of the QeGS model. Special attention was given to the wording of statements, so that each statement represents the relevant quality dimensions and factors as precisely as possible. This questionnaire has been integrated with the e-government portal of the Greek Ministry of Interior [8] and citizen respondents have been asked to complete it, by rating their perceptions of each of the dimensions/factors using a 1 to 5 scale, in which the anchor for 1 was "strongly disagree" and for 5 "strongly agree".

3.2 Empirical Validation and Refinement

The data collected were used in order to validate empirically the categorization of quality dimensions into relevant quality factors, i.e. model's dimensionality, as well as its validity and reliability. This was done by using statistical methods. Initially preliminary item purification was carried out, as described in [7], to identify and purify any cases that can affect the correctness of the aforementioned statistical methods.

For the assessment of model's validity we used factor analysis, which has enjoyed widespread use as a statistical method of measuring construct validity [26], [11]. By using factor analysis in order to assess the validity and dimensionality of the model, we address two out of the three major concerns and risks identified in section 2. For the assessment of the model's reliability we used coefficient alpha [9], known also as Cronbach's alpha. We decided to use this reliability statistic, although there are many statistical methods that can be used for determining reliability, because it is the most commonly used, especially in the domain of quality monitoring, and thus benchmarks with other models can be produced (see section 5).

Factor loadings emerging from the factor analysis show the degree to which each dimension is correlated with each factor. Greater than 0.5 factor loadings are considered significant [12], [15]. Low loadings on the other hand indicate that some dimensions are not drawn from the domain and thus are producing error and unreliability. To this end, factor loadings can suggest the following refinements to the initial version of the QeGS model: (i) Dimensions that did not meet the loading cut-off for any factor are removed; (ii) Dimensions that load significantly with a different factor from the one initially conceptualized, are moved to the new factor.

On the other hand, alpha coefficients are estimators of reliability on the factor level as well as on the model level. Several scales have been developed to serve as a benchmark to determine model reliability, using alpha coefficient, like the scales developed by Landis and Koch [17] and George and Mallery [14]. The general accepted cut off value for a model to be considered reliable and rigorous is 0.8 [12]. The reliability of models that don't meet this cut off value is questionable. At a finer-grained level of detail, a low coefficient alpha for a factor is an indication that the specific factor is not reliable.

By taking into account the suggestions produced by the purification, validity and reliability statistical methods, and after implementing the changes proposed, a new refined version of the model is made available, which is subject to a new evaluation. This kind of evaluation in several rounds is stressed in [7] and has been followed for the evaluation of several quality models that we have reviewed in the context of the literature review. The process of iterative evaluation continues, until significant levels of validity and reliability are achieved. Generally, there are three possible scenarios depending on the results of the initial evaluation:

- The evaluation shows satisfactory coefficient alphas and the dimensions agree with those conceptualized. This is the most desirable scenario. The interpretation of such results is that the model shows significant levels of validity and reliability and furthermore that the dimensionality and groupings hypothesized are confirmed. In this extreme case there is no need for any iteration, as the refined version of the model is identical to the initial version and hence the "refined version" step of Fig. 1 is skipped.
- Dimensions which were conceptualized as independent clearly overlap. In this case new groupings of dimensions should be defined, by moving dimensions from one factor to another, according to the suggestions of the factor analysis. The refined version of the model that is produced in this way should be checked again concerning its validity and reliability.
- The alpha coefficients and factor loadings are too low. This is the least desirable scenario. The interpretation of such results is that perhaps the dimension pool of the conceptualization phase did not cover all aspects of the domain. The appropriate strategy in this case is to loop back to step 1 and redo the conceptualization.

4 Model Validation and Refinement

The questionnaire was available online for the period February - June 2007. In all, 634 completed and usable responses were received, each of which evaluated the e-government portal of the Greek Ministry of Interior [8] and the public e-services delivered through it. The body of responses came from a range of ages and educational backgrounds. The responses came mainly from people in the age group between 26 and 45, something which is expected as it is the age group that is mainly using the internet in Greece and also needs to interact with government services. For ages less than 26, although they use the internet a lot, they are in an age group that does not need to interact yet with government services. On the other hand users older than 46 do not use the internet so much, and thus do not use e-government services, as reported in [19]. Concerning the respondents' educational level, the bigger percentage of them has a higher education degree. This is consistent with the findings of [19], that higher educated people tend to use the internet more for interacting with the Greek government. Hence the composition of our sample is in line with the general demographic characteristics of e-Government users in Greece.

The answers collected were transferred to the Statistical Package for the Social Sciences (SPSS) [14] for further analysis. By using this statistical software, we ran the statistical methods described in section 3.2, in order to confirm that the model captures the 6 factors initially conceptualized (Forms Interaction, Reliability, Support Mechanisms, Information, Usability, and Security) and to assess its validity and reliability. By following the process defined in section 3, and after three iterations we came up with the refined version of the model (see Table 1). The process confirmed the existence in the model of the six factors using the dimensions which were conceptualized in the exploratory phase. This process though, suggested that five dimensions (number & quality of links, FAQ, easy to remember URL, adequate response format, existence of contact information) do not load adequately to any of the factors and also that there is one dimension (form download speed) that loads in a different factor from the one it was assigned to in the exploratory phase[1]. Looking more carefully at these suggestions we can intuitively identify the reasons for the changes proposed– i.e. removing the five dimensions from the initial version of the model and moving one dimension to the factor that loads more.

- The number & quality of links dimension which is stated as "This portal offers enough and of high quality hyperlinks", does not imply so strong a relation to the "Information" quality factor and this is because (as it appears from the factor analysis), it has been perceived more as a reliability attribute (loads more in the "Reliability" factor), but still not enough to remain in the model.
- The FAQ dimension, "The FAQ section of this portal covered completely the topic that you were interested in", appears in the factor analysis to load more on the "Information" factor, than on the "Support Mechanisms" one, although not enough to remain in the model. A possible explanation is that the FAQ pages actually contain information, while all the other support dimensions involve the participation of an employee from the portal.

---

[1] The detailed results of validity analysis are available upon request.

- The easy to remember URL dimension, "This portal's URL is easy to remember", is not very relevant either to the "Usability" of a web site or to any other factor in the model, thus its factor loadings are low for all factors. It seems that the initial conceptualization of this dimension was wrong.
- The adequate response format dimension, "Submitted requests or results of their elaboration are easy to be stored locally or printed", although is loading in the "Forms Interaction" factor, it is not loading enough to remain in the model. Intuitively it happens because this dimension is referring to a slightly different function of the e-government portal, compared to the other "Interaction" dimensions that refer mainly to interaction with online forms. A possible reason explaining this result is that the e-government portal of the Greek Ministry of Interior doesn't offer the functionalities that this dimension is referring to.
- The form download speed dimension, "Forms in this portal are downloaded in short time", has a strong element of speed in it, which is more a "Reliability" attribute than a "Forms Interaction" attribute. So the results of the analysis that categorize this dimension under the "Reliability" factor are intuitively correct.
- Finally it seems that the existence of contact information, "This portal provides contact information", doesn't contribute so much to QeGS.

The reliability analysis was conducted on the model level by calculating the alpha coefficient for the total questionnaire, as well as on the factor level by calculating the coefficient for each factor individually [12]. The test on the model level resulted in an alpha coefficient score of 0.97, suggesting that the scale is in fact very reliable. Furthermore the reliability tests resulted in alpha coefficient scores greater than 0.8 for all factors, suggesting that the scales by factor are also very reliable. More specifically the alpha coefficients per factor are: (Usability Factor: 0.848; Information Factor: 0.853; Forms Interaction Factor: 0.870; Reliability Factor: 0.894; Support Mechanism Factor: 0.925; Security Factor: 0.900).

5 Benchmarks of the QeGS Model

This section covers benchmarks of the refined QeGS model with other quality models from the literature. The purpose of the comparison with other models is to provide a bird's eye view of the reliability of our model compared to the state of the art, and not to give a rigorous benchmark, as the latter is not feasible for models that have been developed for different purposes and don't measure exactly the same concept.

In order to select the quality models that will be used for comparison, we researched the literature approaches used as the basis for conceptualizing the initial QeGS model [16], [20]. We selected those quality models that have been validated and whose reliability is reported. Only 8 out of the 30 approaches that concern quality of e-services and e-government services report reliability results. This finding is in line with the results of [4], according to which the proportion of researchers in IS research that validate their instruments is small. For each one of the 8 models selected, the overall Cronbach's alpha, as well as the number of dimensions used in order to conceptualize quality, have been collected. We should note that each one of these models doesn't measure the same attributes of quality. For this reason the validity is not used as a criterion for the comparison between models, as it is strongly related to the concept that is conceptualized by each model (e.g. e-government service quality, human-computer interaction quality, e-commerce site quality, etc.). On the other hand, reliability is a more general concept of model performance, since comparisons of reliability can be done at a coarse-grained level of detail.

Another important note is that the reliability of a model is a function of the number of dimensions examined by it. The more parsimonious a model is the more realistic the estimation of the fit of the model to the collected data is, for a given level of reliability [26]. In other words, if we take a given model with a given reliability and remove some dimensions, then the reliability of the new model will decrease. For this reason we have added a second axis of benchmarking analysis, the number of dimensions, in addition to the model reliability axis. The results of the benchmarking in terms of reliability are reported in Table 2.

Table 2. Comparison of Quality Models in Terms of Reliability

Model	ID	Cronbach's α	Dimensions
Initial QeGS Model [16]	1)	0.974	33
Refined QeGS model	2)	0.970	28
E-Qual [2]	3)	0.960	27
HCI Satisfaction [6]	4)	0.939	27
Public e-Services Satisfaction [13]	5)	0.930	29
Nursing Website Quality [27]	6)	0.930	32
e-Commerce quality [29]	7)	0.930	38
User-perceived web quality [1]	8)	0.910	25
E-S-QUAL [3]	9)	0.900	22
e-government in Thai [25]	10)	0.874	20

As can be seen in the table, where the models have been sorted according to their reliability, the refined version of the QeGS model surpasses all of the eight models drawn from the relevant literature, in terms of reliability. On the other hand the initial version comes ahead of the refined. This is attributed to the purification of some dimensions which had as a result the increase of the model's validity, but at the cost of a slight decrease of its reliability. Nevertheless the overall reliability of the model remains very high; it is considered "excellent" and "almost perfect" according to George and Mallery [14] and Landis and Koch [17] reliability scales, respectively.

As mentioned before, safe conclusions about the ranking of the refined QeGS model compared to competitive models, regarding their reliability, can be drawn only if we take into account the second axis of benchmarking introduced above. If we look at the table closely we can conclude safely that the refined version of our model is better than models with IDs 5, 6 and 7, because these models report lower reliability (0.930) and the target concept of interest has been conceptualized using more dimensions than our model (29, 32 and 38 respectively).

Models 3, 4, 8, 9 and 10 on the other hand, although they report lower reliability (0.960, 0.939, 0.910, 0.900 and 0.874), also use fewer dimensions (27, 27, 25, 22 and 20). In order to enable a safe comparison with these models, we have depicted each model's pair of (reliability, number of dimensions) in the Reliability-Dimensions space. This graphical representation can be seen in Fig. 2. The X-axis corresponds to the reliability axis, while the Y-axis corresponds to the number of dimensions. The vertical and horizontal position of each model in this two-dimensional space is displayed with a data label and a number indicating the model's ID (see Table 2). Ideally, a model should have a reliability coefficient close to 1.00, and should contain as few dimensions as possible (a perfectly reliable and very parsimonious model). This means that the models that are closer to the lower-right corner of Fig. 2 are better.

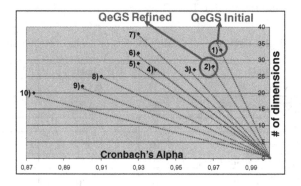

Fig. 2. Quality Models in the Reliability-Dimensions Space

By observing the figure we can conclude that the refined version of the QeGS model has achieved a better combination of reliability and parsimony than models 4, 8, 9, 10 and the initial QeGS model, because it is closer to the lower-right corner, compared to the aforementioned models. The only competitive model that is very close to ours, in terms of performance, is the model with ID 3, the E-Qual model.

These very good results are attributed to the thorough and complete investigation of the state of the art which formed the basis for the development of the QeGS model. These results show that the QeGS model is rigorous, as it has been conceptualized with a significant level of accuracy.

6   Conclusions and Future Work

In developing the QeGS model, we have paid attention to creating a model that has validity in measuring perceived quality of e-government services and portals. In terms of content, we believe that the model is relatively balanced, drawing on an analysis and integration of items relating to service quality, content quality and system-interaction considerations. Thus, in terms of correspondence between modeling and reality, this adds a high degree of validity. This was also proved empirically, by validating the conceptualized model.

We believe that a validated quality model and instrument[2] specifically developed for e-government will provide e-government researchers a tool to identify favorable e-government features that would stimulate positive evaluation and use experience. It will be useful for synthesizing and comparing results of similar case studies and accumulating knowledge in evaluations of e-government portals and services. Results of such studies will help public administrations to provide better services and to enhance citizens' satisfaction.

While the refined QeGS model was developed using a large sample gathered in Greece, a cross-country validation using another large sample gathered elsewhere is required for its greater generalization. We plan to perform such a cross-country validation as part of our future work. Furthermore the QeGS model presented in this paper has been developed in such a way so it can be applied to e-government portals possessing the fifth level of online sophistication [5]. This is currently the maximum level of sophistication an e-government portal can possess. In case advancements in the state of the art of e-government portals and services occur, we plan to keep the model up to date by incorporating the new quality dimensions that may arise in a new conceptualization phase, followed by a confirmatory phase where the updated model will be validated according to the methodology presented in this paper.

Acknowledgments. Research reported in this paper has been partially financed by the European Commission in the IST project FIT (Contract no.: 27090).

References

1. Aladwani, A.M., Prashant, C.P.: Developing and validating an instrument for measuring user-perceived web quality. J. Information & Management 39(6), 467–476 (2002)
2. Barnes, S.J., Vidgen, R.T.: Assessing the quality of auction web sites. In: 34th Hawaii International Conference on Systems Sciences, Maui, Hawaii (2001)
3. Boshoff, C.: A Psychometric Assessment of E-S-Qual: A Scale to Measure Electronic Service Quality. J. Electronic Commerce Research 8(1), 101–114 (2007)
4. Boudreau, M., Gefen, D., Straub, D.: Validation in IS research: A state-of-the-art assessment. MIS Quart. 25(1), 1–24 (2001)
5. Cap Gemini: The User Challenge Benchmarking the Supply of Online Public Services. Report of the Seventh Measurement (2007)
6. Chin, J.P., Diehl, V.A., Norman, K.L.: Development of a Tool Measuring User Satisfaction of the Human-Computer Interface. In: CHI 1988 Conference: Human Factors in Computing Systems, pp. 213–218 (1988)
7. Churchill Jr., G.A.: A Paradigm for Developing Better Measures of Marketing Constructs. J. Marketing Research 16(1), 64–73 (1979)
8. Citizen Service Centres' e-government portal, http://www.kep.gov.gr
9. Cronbach, L.J.: Coefficient alpha and the internal structure of tests. J. Psychometrika 16(3), 297–334 (1951)
10. Doll, W.J., Xia, W., Torkzadeh, G.: A Confirmatory Factor Analysis of the End-User Computing Satisfaction Instrument. MIS Quarterly 18(4), 453–461 (1951)

---

[2] The questionnaires corresponding to the refined QeGS model are available upon request.

11. Eysenck, H.J.: Criterion analysis: an application of the hypothetico-deductive method in factor analysis. J. Psychol. Rev. 57, 38–53 (1950)
12. Field, A.P.: Discovering statistics using SPSS. Sage Publications, London (2005)
13. Galan, J.P., Sabadie, W.: Construction of a measurement tool to evaluate the satisfaction of public service web sites users. In: 7th int. research seminar in service management (2002)
14. George, D., Mallery, P.: SPSS for Windows step by step: A simple guide and reference, 4th edn. Allyn & Bacon, Boston (2003)
15. Hair, J.F., Anderson, R.E., Tatham, R.L., Black, W.C.: Multivariate Data Analysis with Readings. Prentice-Hall, Englewood Cliffs (1995)
16. Halaris, C., Magoutas, B., Papadomichelaki, X., Mentzas, G.: Classification and Synthesis of Quality Approaches in E-government Services. J. Internet Research: Electronic Networking Applications and Policy 17(4), 378–401 (2007)
17. Landis, J.R., Koch, G.: The measurement of observer agreement for categorical data. J. Biometrics 33, 159–174 (1977)
18. Mackenzie, K.D., House, R.: Paradigm Development in the social sciences. In: Research organizations: Issues and controversies. Goodyear Publishing, Santa Monica (1979)
19. Observatory for the Greek Information Society: Online Statistics of the eEurope Indicators Survey, http://stats.observatory.gr
20. Papadomichelaki, X., Magoutas, B., Halaris, C., Apostolou, D., Mentzas, G.: A Review of Quality Dimensions in E-government Services. In: Wimmer, M.A., Scholl, H.J., Grönlund, Å., Andersen, K.V. (eds.) EGOV 2006. LNCS, vol. 4084, pp. 128–138. Springer, Heidelberg (2006)
21. Schellong, A., Mans, D.: Citizens preferences towards one-stop government. In: The 2004 annual national conference on Digital Government research, Seattle, WA. ACM International Conference Proceeding Series (2004)
22. Sedera, D., Gable, G., Chan, T.: Measuring Enterprise Systems Success: A Preliminary Model. In: Proceedings of the 9th AMCIS, pp. 576–591. Tampa, Florida (2003)
23. Straub, D.W.: Validating instruments in MIS research. MIS Quarterly (1989)
24. Straub, D.W., Hoffman, D., Weber, B., Steinfield, C.: Toward new metrics for net-enhanced organizations. J. Information Systems Research 13(3), 227–238 (2002)
25. Sukasame, N.: The development of e-service in Thai government. BU Academic Review 3(1), 17–24 (2004)
26. Thompson, B., Daniel, L.G.: Factor Analytic Evidence for the Construct Validity of Scores: A Historical Overview and Some Guidelines. J. Educational and Psychological Measurement 56, 197–208 (1996)
27. Tsai, S.L., Chai, S.K.: Developing and validating a nursing website evaluation questionnaire. J. Advanced Nursing 49(4), 406–413 (2005)
28. Walrad, C., Moss, E.: Measurement: the key to application development quality. J. IBM Systems 32(3), 445–460 (1993)
29. Wang, Y.S., Tang, T.I., Tang, J.T.E.: An Instrument for Measuring Customer Satisfaction Toward Web Sites That Market Digital Products and Services. J. Electronic Commerce Research 2(3), 89–102 (2001)

Identifying Weaknesses for Chilean E-Government Implementation in Public Agencies with Maturity Model

Mauricio Solar, Hernán Astudillo, Gonzalo Valdes, Marcelo Iribarren,
and Gastón Concha

Universidad Técnica Federico Santa María (UTFSM), Chile
{msolar,hernan,gvaldes,miribarren,gconcha}@inf.utfsm.cl

Abstract. Evaluating readiness of individual public agencies to execute specific e-Government programs and directives is a key ingredient for wider e-Government deployment and success. This article describes how the eGov-MM model was used to over 30 many Chilean public agencies and to identify specific areas in which each of them should focus improvement efforts. eGov-MM is a capability maturity model, patterned on similar models from the IT and organizational domains; it recognizes 4 leverage domains, 17 key domain areas (KDA) and 54 critical variables, identifies capability levels for each critical variable and KDA and proposes a synthetic maturity level for institutions. The 9-agencies pilot study and the 30-agencies massive study indicate that, in Chile today, the best developed areas are IT-related and mirror exactly those that are pre-requisites for the goals of the 5-years Digital Strategy, and the least evaluated are related to internal processes and human capital management.

Keywords: e-government, roadmap, capability, maturity model.

1 Introduction

The eGov-MM model (e-Government Maturity Model) [1] resulted from a project to build and apply a model to measure public institutions readiness to manage and implement e-Government. The project was executed by the Informatics Department of Universidad Técnica Federico Santa Maria (Chile) for the Executive Secretariat of Digital Strategy of the Ministry of Economy of the national Chilean government.

eGov-MM allows evaluating a public institution against the best international practices in the area of eGov, including formulation of organizational strategies, management of Information and Communication Technologies (ICT), operative management, and capabilities of the organization and its human resources. It also proposes concrete roadmaps for capability improvement, i.e. directives about where the organization financial and human resources should be canalized to improve its capability to carry out eGov initiatives.

The eGov-MM model [1] considered several information sources in its initial formulation:

- Models that provide the standard structure of CMM [2, 3].
- Models that show scopes and levels for maturity and capability [4] directly related to eGov (e.g., interoperability and financial analysis of ICT investments in the public sector) [5].

M.A. Wimmer et al. (Eds.): EGOV 2009, LNCS 5693, pp. 151–162, 2009.

- Models of specific intention that provide scopes and levels of maturity and capacity on subjects related to eGov (e.g., enterprise IT governability and architectures) [6, 7].
- Best eGov practices (for implementation, measurement and evaluation) identified from the growing presence of national state-of-the-art experiences and international experiences (namely, from UK, the USA, Australia, Canada, Sweden, Denmark, Korea, Ireland, New Zealand and Brazil) [8].

The model was piloted with seven (initially 9) public agencies, and a tuned version was generated that incorporates the participants' feedback and an eGov implementation roadmap for each evaluated public agency. An associated self-assessment Web tool was also built and similarly validated. The refined model was then used to evaluate thirty public agencies; this sample was chosen with systematic random sampling modified to include public agencies of all maturity levels, sizes, and coverage.

Section 2 describes the eGov-MM and its main characteristics, objectives and benefits; Section 3 explains how an organization maturity is evaluated; Section 4 presents the pilot results; Section 5 presents the validation via massive application to 30 public agencies; and Section 6 summarizes and concludes.

2   General Structure of the eGov-MM

The eGov-MM is structured around three main elements: Information Criteria, ICT Resources, and Leverage Domains. There are four leverage domains, which group 17 Key Domain Areas (KDA) and 54 Critical Variables (see Fig 1).

2.1   Capability and Maturity Levels

Capability Level (CL): The capability is a measurement of the state of each KDA that contributes to support the organization development. The capability of a KDA is determined using the CL of each of its Critical Variables, i.e. what is really evaluated it is the capability of these variables to satisfy certain requirements. The capabilities of the critical variables are weighed according to their importance to give a final KDA CL.

Maturity Levels (ML): The CL of a KDA and its critical variables determine the organizational ML. The ML is a property of the organization as a whole; each ML corresponds to a predetermined configuration of KDAs in predefined CLs. The model allows, once the current ML is assessed, to identify the states required to advance to a higher level and propose a "roadmap" to improve the organization.

2.2   Model Contributions and Benefits

The model is a diagnosis element for public agencies, with several purposes:

- **Identify** the fundamental areas in the development of an eGov strategy.
- **Establish** the technological CL in scopes relevant to the delivery of services to citizens.
- **Determine** the ML of the organization's technology management.
- **Articulate** a development strategy of its capabilities for continuous improvement of its maturity degree (roadmap).

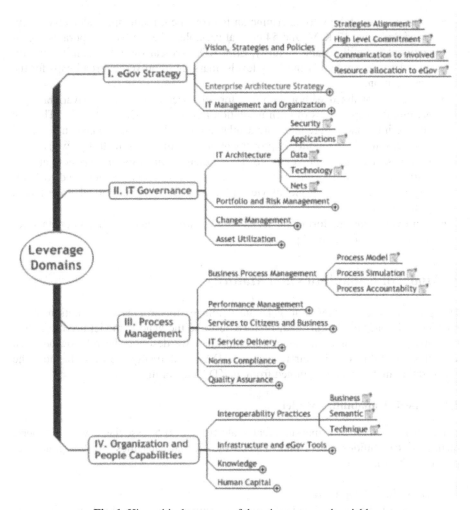

Fig. 1. Hierarchical structure of domains, areas and variables

The main benefits already identified in the eGov-MM model application are:

- It is a reference framework to identify the areas that support an eGov strategy, based on internationally recognized best practices for IT management (as summarized in a state-of-the-art [8] executed as part of the same project). Additionally, the model incorporates locally arisen best practices, and combines ideas and knowledge of eGov development specialists.

- It can be applied to improve both interoperability practices and technology management capabilities. Having an ordered set of good practices and an evaluation methodology yield a support tool for strategic and tactical management. The eGov-MM incorporates the business requirements and the information to support, which themselves demand associated IT resources that, when applied to the "Leverage Domains", should give necessary criteria to fulfill the business goals.

- It has a methodology to determine an improvement roadmap; besides the 4 leverage domains, 17 KDA and 54 critical variables, the model incorporates organizational capabilities and maturity. Each KDA critical variable has minimum required values for higher maturity levels, marking improvement roadmaps for the organization.
- It is operationalized with a Web tool for self-assessment of critical variables, regarding the capabilities of each institution to carry out eGov initiatives. The tool and the information it requires are available for public agencies, and can be evaluated periodically to monitor improvement of capabilities and maturity levels.
- It allows integrating the key issues for efficient technology management at each institution, combining the organizational, process, human capital, and technology domains, to get a global view of eGov development for all government agencies.
- It provides data to formulate technological projects and to base budgetary requests on an institutional perspective.

3 Model of Capabilities and Maturity

One goal of the eGov-MM is to generate roadmaps for progressive evolution of capacities and maturity. To this end, first we describe the generic model used to define the capacity levels for each model variable; then we describe the relation between variables capabilities and their respective KDAs; and finally we describe how the organization maturity is determined from its KDA capabilities.

3.1 Generic Capabilities Model

For each KDA there is a measurement scale from 1 to 5, associated with a generic qualitative capabilities model that ranges from "initial capacities" to "integrated capacities"; the values are:

Level 1: Initial capacities
- The KDA is approached *ad-hoc* and reactively, and individually case by case.
- There is evidence that KDA has been recognized and needs to be approached.

Level 2: Developing capacities (repeatable but intuitive)

- A regular intuitive pattern is followed itself to approach the KDA; different people use similar procedures for the same task.
- There is no formal training or procedures spreading, and the responsibility to follow them falls to each individual.

Level 3: Defined capacities

- Procedures related to the KDA are defined, documented and communicated.
- There is informal training to support particular initiatives related to the KDA.
- The procedures are not sophisticated, but are the formalization of existing practices.

Level 4: Managed capacities

- It is possible to monitor and measure fulfillment of procedures, and to take action when the KDA apparently is not working properly.
- Established standards and norms are applied through the organization.
- Tools are mainly automated.

Level 5: Integrated capacities (Optimized)

- Procedures have become best practices, and continuous improvement is applied.
- ICT is used in an integrated manner to optimize the KDA.
- Use of standard or world-wide tools helps to optimize the KDA.

The capacity levels of each KDA are built from the levels of their variables. For each level, several aspects are considered (incrementally in each level): awareness; human capital training; communication; procedures and practices; compliance of standards and norms; tools and automation; and involvement and responsibility.

3.2 Relationship between Capability Variables and KDAs

The capability level (CL) of a KDA is generally the average of the CLs of its critical variables. To accommodate eGov strategies or country development levels with different variables relevance, weights are used for each variable group. Thus, the CL of a KDA is the *weighted average* of the CLs of its variables *Vi* (see Eq. 1).

$$CL_{KDA} = Average[CAP(V_1)*P_1, CAP(V_2)*P_2,\dots,CAP(V_n)*P_n] \qquad \text{(Eq. 1)}$$

The weights P_i used in the first model applications (pilot and initial massive application) are shown in Table 1.

3.3 Organizational Maturity Model

Maturity is a property of the organizational unit as a whole, and the maturity level (ML) is obtained from the KDA capacity levels that the unit has. Thus, each ML:

- Frames a set of KDAs for a given CL.
- Establishes equivalence among eGov implementation maturity of units.

There are several options to determine an organization maturity, namely:

1. Minimum CL among all KDAs
2. Average CL of all KDAs
3. Predetermined KDA configuration, using a set of values for all KDAs in model.
4. Configuration of high-priority KDAs, using a set of *minimum* values for all KDAs in the model.

The last criterion (Configuration of high-priority KDAs) was adopted in eGov-MM. The organization ML is determined (Eq. 2) by a set of values for all KDAs in the model (see Table 2).

Table 1. Variable weights of the "eGov Strategy" KDA

KDA	Variable	Weight
Vision, Strategies and Policies	Strategy Alignment	15
	High Level Commitment	30
	Communication to involved	25
	Resource allocation to eGov	30
		100
Enterprise Architecture Strategy	Definition of Implementation Strategy	30
	Alignment with Reference Models	20
	Strategy of Services Reuse	20
	Business Architecture	30
		100
IT Management and Organization	IT Organization Planning	15
	IT Infrastructure Planning	25
	Organizational Structure Definition	30
	IT Processes Map	30
		100

$$ML1 = Conf1(CAP(KDA1), \dots , CAP(KDAi)) \qquad (Eq.\ 2)$$

$$ML5 = Conf5(CAP(KDA1), \dots , CAP(KDAk))$$

This mechanism was selected for eGov-MM for its flexibility to allow graduating progress according to specific eGov strategies, since it only requires to fix a minimum set of KDAs that are important for a given ML; development criteria and rates for other KDAs are left to the organization. The actual criteria to use can be extracted from domain specialists or agencies leaderships; e.g. from phrases such as:

- "Maintaining enterprise architecture is an advanced issue, which allows aligning business objectives and computer networks … and thus should not be requiring nor evaluating for lower MLs…"
- "It is very important to start by aligning the IT, eGov and of business strategies … this should be required even for lower MLs".

4 eGov-MM Pilot Study

This section presents the results of applying the eGov-MM and its self-evaluation tool to a small set of public agencies as a validation mechanism; it describes the main sample characteristics, the pilot methodology used, the results of capacity measurement for the sample, and the relevance of the variables.

4.1 Sample and Pilot Study Methodology

Nine public agencies were initially selected for the pilot study, using three criteria:

1. It should include institutions at maturity level 3, as estimated by their capabilities in two easily-verifiable areas: basic infrastructure (connectivity, processing infrastructure, security), and online services implementation.

Table 2. Example of organizational ML with a set of high-priority KDAs

KDA	Variable	ML1	ML2	ML3	ML4	ML5
eGov Strategy	Vision, Strategies and Policies		2	3	3	3
	Enterprise Architecture Strategy				2	3
	IT Management and Organization		2	3	4	5
IT Governance	IT Architecture				2	3
	Portfolio and Risk Management			3	3	3
	Change Management				3	3
	Asset Utilization			3	3	3
Processes	Business Processes Management			3	3	3
Management	Performance Management			3	3	3
	Services to Citizens and Business		2	3	4	5
	IT Service Delivery		2	3	4	5
	Norms Compliance		2	3	4	5
	Quality Assurance			3	3	3
Organization	Interoperability Practices		2	3	4	5
and People	Infrastructure and e-Gov Tools		2	3	4	5
Capabilities	Knowledge				3	3
	Human Capital				3	3

2. It should have at least 3 public agencies per level.
3. A maturity level should be chosen that allowed to validate that the model can predicted the real situation, even if it included additional areas and indicators.

Of the nine selected agencies, one declined to participate, and another one accepted but did not send any representatives to the assessment workshops.

To maximize participation and yet simplify execution, the assessment was supported with upper management involvement, conducted as a guided self-assessment, and prepared with qualification workshops segmented by knowledge area, to limit KDA subgroups for each audience. Three profiles were defined for the institutions' representatives: (1) Operational Management (Director or Assistant director); (2) IT Management (Assistant director or IT Unit Head); and (3) Human Resources Management (HR Head).

4.2 Pilot Study Results

At the workshops guided self-assessment, participants responded questionnaires for their specific knowledge areas, and gave the results shown in Tables 3 and 4.

Capabilities: Table 3 shows the KDA capability values for each participant institution. Six of the participants evaluated all 3 profiles (but one gave incomplete answers). Two issues deserve comment:

- The highest average capability values (shaded soft) are for "IT Architecture" and "Interoperability Practices". Since this contradicts our (admittedly impressionistic) field observations, we surmise that the capability concept was not fully understood and/or the questions did not cover well the capability level.

- The lower capability levels (shaded dark) are "Performance Management", "Services to Citizens and Business", "Norms Compliance" and "Human Capital". These values seem realistic, again based on our field observations.

Table 3. Capabilities of Key Areas for the pilot public agencies

Areas	MIN VU	TGR	INP	SEN CE	SERC OTEC	SAG	ISP	Average
eGov Strategy								
Vision, Strategies and Policies	3	3	2		1	3	2	**2.3**
Enterprise Architecture Strategy	1	4	2		1	2	3	**2.2**
IT Management and Organization	3	3	2	3	4	2	2	**2.7**
	2.3	3.3	2.0		2.0	2.3	2.3	
IT Governance								
IT Architecture	5	3	2	3	3	2	3	**3.0**
Portfolio and Risk Management	3	2	2	1	2	2	2	**2.0**
Change Management	2	3	2	2	2	3	2	**2.3**
Asset Utilization	4	2	2	2	1	2	2	**2.1**
	3.5	2.5	2.0		2.0	2.3	2.3	
Processes Management								
Business Processes Management	3	4	1		1	3	2	**2.3**
Performance Management	1	1	3		3	2	1	**1.8**
Services to Citizens and Business	3	2	1		1	2	2	**1.8**
IT Service Delivery	3	1	2	3	2	1	3	**2.1**
Norms Compliance	2	3	1	1	1	3	2	**1.9**
Quality Assurance	2	2	3		3	3	3	**2.7**
	2.3	2.2	1.8		1.8	2.3	2.2	
Organization and People Capabilities								
Interoperability Practices	5	4	4	4	4	3	3	**3.9**
Infrastructure and e-Gov Tools	3	2	1	2	4	3	1	**2.3**
Knowledge	3	3	3	2	3	1	1	**2.3**
Human Capital	2	4	2	2	1	1	1	**1.9**
	3.3	3.3	2.5	2.5	3.0	2.0	1.5	
Average per Organization	**2.3**	**2.3**	**1.7**	**1.3**	**1.8**	**1.8**	**1.7**	

Table 4. Relevance of variables per area according to pilot-participating experts

		Frequency Relevance Level			
		1	2	3	4
Operational	Total	5	17	36	66
Management	Percentage	4%	14%	29%	53%
	% answer 3 & 4				82%
IT Management	Total	1	4	30	99
ment	Percentage	1%	3%	22%	74%
	% answer 3 & 4				96%
Human	Total	3	5	6	27
Resources	Percentage	7%	12%	15%	66%
	% answer 3 & 4				80%
	Weighted Total				**89%**

Relevance of Variables: Besides the guided self-assessment, a survey was conducted to determine the relevance level of the variables included in the model. The results (see Table 4) show that, on average, 80% of the variables were considered as of high or very high relevance (levels 3 and 4). If a weighted average is used that considers the percentage of variable presents in each of the 3 scopes, this value grows to 89%. Most remarkable is the case of the "IT Management" scope, where only IT Unit Heads participated and who gave a relevance perception of 96%.

5 Larger Study Results

The eGov-MM was refined with the pilot study results, and was validated with a larger set of 30 public agencies. Table 5 ranks the evaluated institutions. Fully half of them are at maturity level 2, and only a single leading agency is at level 3.

5.1 Ranking of Public Agencies

An organization maturity level is determined by the KDA with smaller capacity; e.g. an institution with 16 of 17 KDAs with a good capacity level but one KDA with level 1, has a maturity level of 1. To allow readers to identify these situations, Table 5 has an extra column with the "percentage maturity", the sum of all its KDA capabilities divided by its total capability.

Table 5 also shows that the groups with maturity 1 and 2 are institutions that with little additional work can increase their organizational maturity; e.g. INP and Customs are about to reach level 2, and Housing Sub-ministry is close to level 3.

5.2 Analysis of Key Areas

Table 6 indicates the average capacity value of each KDA in the sample of public agencies that participated in the larger study. The mean level of organizational maturity of the evaluated public agencies was 2 (of a maximum of 5). A key finding was that the average value in 16 of the 17 key domain areas is below level 3.

The best developed areas are:

- *Interoperability Practices and IT Architecture*, which are explained by the emphasis of the Chilean Digital Strategy in the last few years, whose goals are to advance towards integrated eGov and to generate norms for its implementation.
- *Services to Citizens and Business,* which are explained because eGov strategy has privileged putting public agencies and transactions online, and hence the development of technological channels to serve citizens' services requests.
  The least developed areas are:
- *Business Process Management*, a subject that has been insufficient and unequally developed, depending on each agency modernization strategy. Only in the last few years has been emphasis on improvement of the management processes themselves, via legal initiatives about IT incorporation in administrative processes.

- *Knowledge*, which is an important challenge eGov development field. Currently there are only embryonic initiatives to use systems that empower collaborative work and knowledge transfer; major advances are required.
- *Human Capital*, with a need to incorporate, train and formally develop both people and competences, required for sustainable systemic, processes and technological management of the complexity level required for integrated eGov.

Table 5. Maturity ranking for the sample

Institution	Maturity	
	Percentage	Absolute
SII (Tax service)	74%	3
Housing	58%	2
TGR	55%	2
AGCI	54%	2
SAG (Agriculture)	53%	2
SERNAC	53%	2
Navy Ministry	53%	2
FONASA	52%	2
SSMSO	52%	2
CSE	51%	2
ISP	49%	2
SML	49%	2
JUNAEB	48%	2
SUBTEL	47%	2
SEC	45%	2
SUSESO	42%	2
SENCE	54%	1
INP	51%	1
Customs	49%	1
DGAC	48%	1
SERCOTEC	46%	1
ONEMI	44%	1
CNE	41%	1
Sernapesca (fishing)	40%	1
Airports	39%	1
Labor Ministry	39%	1
Gendarmería	38%	1
Subs. RR.EE.	38%	1
Planning Ministry	36%	1
SUBDERE	33%	1
Average	**48%**	

Table 6. Average capability of Key Areas

KDA	Average capability
Interoperability Practices	3.10
Services to Citizens and Business	2.70
IT Architecture	2.67
IT Service Delivery	2.63
Infrastructure and eGov Tools	2.60
IT Management and Organization	2.47
Performance Management	2.43
Asset Utilization	2.37
Norms Compliance	2.33
Quality Assurance	2.30
Change Management	2.30
Vision, Strategies and Policies	2.23
Enterprise Architecture Strategy	2.20
Portfolio and Risk Management	2.20
Knowledge	2.10
Business Process Management	2.07
Human Capital	1.83

6 Conclusions

The eGov-MM was initially deployed with a pilot study, and its results were used to refine the model and associated assessment Web tool. An associated survey found that 80% of the used variables were considered highly or very highly relevant, a level that rose to 96% for IT Management.

The refined model was applied to 30 public agencies. It found that all but one of the 30 agencies are at level 1 or 2, and that the most developed KDAs are "Interoperability Practices", "Services to Citizens and Business", and "IT Architecture"; the less developed are "Knowledge", "Business Process Management", and "Human Capital".

An explanation for these findings is that, for the last 5 years, the Chilean Digital Strategy has emphasized Web presence and online services, both issues that demand improvement in IT infrastructure but not necessarily in underlying processes. Clearly, efforts to introduce IT in business processes have not been coupled with efforts to formalize internal processes and to develop the required human capital. This result is perhaps country-specific, but nonetheless illuminating on the model measurement power and of the real effects of government policies and priorities.

Another finding was that several agencies (e.g. INP, Customs, and Housing) are quite close to reach a higher maturity level, and are being held down only by isolated and (now) well identified areas, which can (now) be targeted for improvement.

Thus, eGov-MM is not only a diagnostic tool, but also a generator of improvement roadmaps. Government has a methodological and technological tool to measure status and improvement of eGov implementation by specific public agencies.

References

1. Iribarren, M., Concha, G., Valdes, G., Solar, M., Villarroel, M., Gutiérrez, P., Vásquez, A.: Capability Maturity Framework for e-Government: A Multi-dimensional Model and Assessing Tool. In: Wimmer, M.A., Scholl, H.J., Ferro, E. (eds.) EGOV 2008. LNCS, vol. 5184, pp. 136–147. Springer, Heidelberg (2008)
2. Software Engineering Institute: CMMI for Development v1.2. USA (2006)
3. Andersen, K.V., Henriksen, Z.H.: E-government Maturity Models: Extension of the Layne and Lee Model. Government Information Quarterly 23, 236–248 (2006)
4. Cresswell, A., Pardo, T., Canestarro, D.: Digital Capability Assessment for e-Government: A Multidimensional Approach. In: Wimmer, M.A., Scholl, H.J., Grönlund, Å., Andersen, K.V. (eds.) EGOV 2006. LNCS, vol. 4084, pp. 293–304. Springer, Heidelberg (2006)
5. Layne, K., Lee, J.: Developing Fully Functional e-Government: A Four Stage Model. Government Information Quarterly 18, 122–136 (2001)
6. Wimmer, M.A., Tambouris, E.: Online One-Stop Government: A Working Framework and Requirements. In: Proc. of the 17th IFIP World Computer Congress, pp. 117–130. Kluwer Academic Publishers, Boston (2002)
7. Esteves, J., Joseph, R.: A Comprehensive Framework for the Assessment of e-Government Projects. Government Information Quarterly 25, 118–132 (2008)
8. Valdes, G., Iribarren, M., Concha, G., Solar, M., Visconti, M., Astudillo, H., Villarroel, M., Gutiérrez, P., Vásquez, A.: Identifying relevant National e-Government Implementations for an Emerging Country: A Selective Survey. In: Wimmer, M.A., Scholl, H.J., Ferro, E. (eds.) EGOV 2008. LNCS, vol. 5184, pp. 141–149. Springer, Heidelberg (2008)

A Multiple-Item Scale for Assessing E-Government Service Quality

Xenia Papadomichelaki[1] and Gregoris Mentzas[2]

[1] Information Management Unit,
Institute of Communication and Computer Systems School of Electrical & Computer
Engineering, National Technical University of Athens, Zografou Campus,
157 80 Zografou, Athens, Greece
xpg@central.ntua.gr
[2] Information Management Unit, Institute of Communication and Computer Systems
School of Electrical & Computer Engineering, National Technical University of Athens,
Zografou Campus, 157 80 Zografou, Athens, Greece
gmentzas@mail.ntua.gr

Abstract. A critical element in the evolution of e-governmental services is the development of sites that better serve the citizens' needs. To deliver superior service quality, we must first understand how citizens perceive and evaluate online citizen service. This involves defining what e-government service quality is, identifying its underlying dimensions, and determining how it can be conceptualized and measured. In this article we conceptualise an e-government service quality model (e-GovQual) and then we develop, refine, validate, confirm and test a multiple-item scale for measuring e-government service quality for public administration sites where citizens seek either information or services.

Keywords: e-government, service, quality, measurement, instrument.

1 Introduction

The subject of e-service and Web site quality is very rich in context of definitions, models and measurement instruments. Nevertheless, different dimensions have been proposed and there is no consensus on the component dimensions. Collectively, the extant literature suggests that e-service quality is a multidimensional construct although the content of what constitutes e-service quality varies across studies [1].

The quality of e-services approaches focuses on the quality of the service itself as delivered. Emphasis is put on the way the client receives the services from the front office-web site. It is a customer oriented approach since it is motivated by the customer's needs. Quality dimensions of these approaches are related to the delivered service (availability, usability, security etc. of the service) and/or input from the receivers of the service (customers' priorities and needs). Also there is research work reported on E-Commerce website quality, online service quality approaches and B2C e-commerce web site quality. A detailed summary and classification of the existing literature in the field of quality of service for e-government is available [2].

M.A. Wimmer et al. (Eds.): EGOV 2009, LNCS 5693, pp. 163–175, 2009.

Research on e-government service quality is mostly descriptive and only discusses some of the aspects inherent in service quality. Some research has been conducted for e-government by collecting users' opinions about the factors that characterize the quality of an e-government web page [3], [4], efforts that try to benchmark the actual status of e-government implementation [5] and finally by evolving an instrument that was developed originally for assessing user perceptions of the quality of e-commerce Web sites [6], [7] or identifying evaluation criteria and assessing user perceptions for the quality of e-Commerce Web sites [8], [9], [10].

The objective of this paper is to develop and validate an instrument to measure citizen perceived service quality from e-government sites or portals. Throughout this article we describe the development, refinement, psychometric evaluation, potential applications and limitations of a multiple-item scale for measuring e-government service quality (e-GovQual) of government sites, where citizens seek either information or service. After an extensive literature review as mentioned throughout the paper we classified 33 e-government quality attributes under six main quality dimensions: Ease of Use, Trust, Functionality of the Interaction Environment, Reliability, Content and Appearance of Information, and finally Citizen Support.

After creating the conceptual model there was a need to confirm whether the sample of items depicted, capture the construct of e-government service quality. As a next step we designed a questionnaire based on these criteria in order to elicit and assess information on preferences of the citizens when evaluating e-government service and governmental web sites. The scale was produced following guidelines for measurement development proposed by Churchill [11]. In order to refine and evaluate the scale to measure e-Government quality an online survey took place that collected 630 responses. The scale was refined; we tested its reliability and looked for a stable factor structure that resulted in 25 quality attributes classified under 4 quality dimensions: Reliability, Efficiency, Citizen Support and Trust. This instrument developed under the above process would be valuable to researchers and practitioners interested in designing, implementing, and managing governmental web sites.

The paper consists five sections. The next section identifies the variables that capture e-government service quality and describes the development of the conceptual model relating six essential factors of e-government service quality to citizens' perceptions, while the third section describes the data collection and the steps involved in scale development-preliminary scale, refinement through qualitative research (collection/ combination of sector experts' experiences). The forth section discusses applications of the proposed scale, limitations of the current study and directions of future research, while the paper ends with the conclusions.

2   Development of an E-Gov Quality Model

Our goal was to develop a measure which has desirable reliability and validity properties. Firstly we defined the universe of content and then we wanted to show that the test items are a sample of that universe. Content validity is ordinarily to be established deductively since we sampled systematically within that universe to establish the test [12]. In other words, after an extensive literature survey and critical screening of the existing approaches on Web site quality, portal quality, e-service quality, e-government and quality measurements (previously validated scales), the boundaries of the research were defined and we identified an exhaustive candidate list of items from the domain of all possible items consisting the quality construct of e-government service. Thus, a multitude of quality attributes of different approaches was identified. Some of them are E-S-QUAL [1], [13], User-perceived web quality [14], E-Qual [15], Web-Qual™ [16], SITEQUAL [17], IP-Portals [18] etc.

For a better insight at the phenomenon, the Delphi method was used to initially assess sample items in order to provide input for developing a conceptual model of e-government service quality. After two evaluation rounds 33 e-government quality attributes remained in the list classified under six main criteria determined as the e-government service quality dimensions: Ease of Use (navigation, personalization, technical efficiency), Trust (privacy, security), Functionality of the Interaction Environment (support in completing forms), Reliability (accessibility, availability), Content and Appearance of Information and Citizen Support (Interactivity), (table 1).

Table 1. E-GovQual dimensions/attributes

Ease of Use	Trust
• Web site's structure/ Site-map	• Secure archiving of personal data
• Customized search functions	• Non repudiation by authenticating the parties involved
• Set up links with search engines	• Procedure of acquiring username and password
• Easy to remember URL	
• Personalization of information	• Correct transaction, Encrypting messages
• Ability of customization	• Digital Signatures, Access control
Functionality of the interaction environm.	**Reliability**
	• Ability to perform the promised service accurately
• Existence of on-line help in forms	
• Reuse of citizen information to facilitate future interaction	• In time service delivery
	• Accessibility of site
• Automatic calculation of forms	• Browser-system compatibility
• Adequate response format	• Loading/transaction speed
Content & Appearance of Information	**Citizen Support (Interactivity)**
• Data completeness	• User friendly guidelines
• Data accuracy and conciseness	• Help pages, Frequently Asked Questions
• Data relevancy	• Transaction tracking facility
• Updated information	• The existence of contact information
• Linkage	• Problem solving
• Ease of understanding/ Interpretable Data	• Prompt reply to customer inquiries
	• Knowledge/Courtesy of employees
• Colours, Graphics, Animation	• Employees who convey trust,/confidence
• Size of Web pages	

The dimensions are discussed below:

Ease of Use (navigation, personalization, technical efficiency). Ease of use is defined as how easy the Web site is for citizens to interact with. The importance of this dimension has also been noted by other researchers [19]; [20].

The use of set-up links with major search engines and an easy to remember and concise URL can facilitate citizens in finding the Web site on the worldwide Web. Moreover, internal navigation can be greatly assisted by a consistent web site structure, by including a site-map in the site that allows users to skip sessions that are of no interest or by customized search functions where the citizens are allowed to search within the site by transactions, by public agencies or by keywords. Other supplementary tools for navigation include menus, directories, buttons, subject trees, image maps, and colors [21], [22] found out in their research that for the Governmental domain "easy to navigate" is the most important feature with "clear layout of info", "up-to-date info", "search tool" and "accuracy of info" following.

Furthermore, personalization of information - how much and how easily the site can be tailored to individual customers' preferences, for example communicating with the citizens in language they can understand and offering choices of languages other than the official language of the country or providing choices that aid people with disabilities to use the site, can improve the easiness of use of a governmental site. Finally, the ability of customization-so that the system recognizes the user and displays in the first page links that the user frequently uses or remembers the settings concerning the preferred language and display can aid citizens that repeatedly use the Web site. Previous research has shown that government Web sites are well designed and easy to use [19].

Trust (Privacy/Security). Trust consists of privacy and security and is defined as the citizen's confidence towards the Web site concerning freedom of danger risk or doubt during the e-service process. The importance of trust as a critical aspect of e-service has already been stressed in other studies [20].

Privacy consists of the protection of personal information, not sharing personal information with others, protecting anonymity, secure archiving of personal data and providing informed consent. Security is defined mainly as protecting users from the risk of fraud and financial loss from the use of their credit card or other financial information but also by ensuring that the whole transaction is carried on the way it was supposed to. Security can be enhanced by encrypting, by access control, by digital signatures and by having procedures of acquiring username and password.

Functionality of the interaction environment (support in completing forms) Forms play an integral role on e-government in allowing users to communicate and interact with the public administrations, allowing the collection of required information. Especially for e-government services of maturity level 3 or greater, forms are used as the major medium for submitting information online. Thus, quality characteristics of online forms are of high importance for citizens during their interaction with e-government portal and influence significantly the qualitative result of the delivered service.

During the on-line filling of forms the ability of the system to recall previously submitted information, the ability of the system to fill certain fields as a result of internal calculations on other fields or previously submitted information, the ability of the system to provide several alternative choices to the user concerning what he can do with a form he has filled in (submit, print, save, e.t.c.), or finally the automatic presentation of help text in form fields which aids users to fill in the form, facilitates the on-line interaction of the citizen with the public sector.

Reliability. Reliability is defined as the citizen's confidence towards the e-government site concerning correct and in time delivery of the service. Reliability refers to the ability to perform the promised service accurately, consistently and in time. The term includes correct technical functioning (accessibility and availability) and accuracy of service promises. Accessibility is a general term used to describe the degree to which a system is usable by as many people as possible without modification. It is not to be confused with usability which is used to describe how easily a thing can be used by any type of user. Also, the capability of the system to be displayed and used independently of the web browser used enhances its accessibility. Availability refers to the degree to which a system suffers degradation or interruption in its service to the citizen as a consequence of failures of one or more of its parts. It represents the probability that a service is available. The availability of a site can also be enhanced by ensuring the 24/7 accessibility to it, and a high loading and transaction speed.

Content & Appearance of Information. This dimension refers to the quality of the information itself as well as to the presentation and layout of it i.e. proper use of color, graphics and size of web pages.

As far as the quality of information is concerned characteristics as completeness, accuracy, conciseness and relevancy are considered as positive while too much or too little information are both considered to be negative elements. Timeliness of information is also a crucial factor since previous work has shown that government Web sites are not updated regularly [19]. Linkage is defined as the number and quality of hyperlinks a site offers. The correct links supplement the information a site offers so it is important to select and maintain the proper links. Moreover, avoiding broken links by regular checking is essential. The easiness of understanding and information that is interpretable is crucial since especially in governmental documents where there is too much terminology and the language used is too formal. Last but not least is the site aesthetics with characteristics such as the colors used, the graphics, the animation and the size of web pages.

Citizen Support (Interactivity). Citizen Support refers to the help provided by the organization to assist citizens in their quest of information or during their transactions.

This help may consist of user friendly guidelines, help pages and Frequently Asked Questions in site as well as tailored communication availability. For occasions that the above are insufficient the existence of contact information - so that personal advice can be offered either through e-mail or through a traditional channel such as the telephone, fax or postal mail - is required. In cases of interaction between the citizen and the organization's employees, quality dimensions of service quality literature [23] may apply - such as prompt reply to customer inquiries, knowledge of the employees, courtesy of the employees, ability of employees to convey trust and confidence and problem solving. The latter attributes suggest the need for interaction and not only visiting a Web site. Finally the ability to track the progress and the status of a transaction is considered positive. Nevertheless as mentioned in the literature the Citizen Support dimension applies only when citizens experience problems [1].

The above discussed are reflected in the model Figure 1.

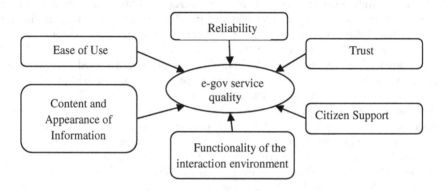

Fig. 1. E-GovQual: Conceptual model for e-gov service quality

3   Research Method

3.1 Preliminary Scale development

After creating the conceptual model there was a need to confirm whether the sample of items depicted there, capture the construct of e-gov service quality. As a next step, a questionnaire based on these criteria has been designed to elicit and assess information on preferences of the citizens when evaluating e-government services and governmental Web sites.

First we arranged the attributes chosen in a questionnaire phrased in SERVQUAL's format [23]. Each statement was reviewed so that its wording would be as precise as possible. Each item was measured using a five point Likert scale relating to the citizen's feelings about the site under assessment. The extent to which the citizen believed the site had the feature described by the statement was ranging from (1) "strongly disagree" that the portal has the feature to (5) "strongly agree". There were also two more general sets of questions, with each statement inspecting the citizen's feelings for the six constructs, once for the site under examination and once for an ideal site. Another question asked the citizens a total rate of the site under evaluation and of course some demographic questions. The scale items of the above described questionnaire are available by the authors upon request.

3.2 Data Collection

In order to refine and evaluate the scale to measure e-GovQual, an online survey took place. Data collection was web-based and respondents were notified about the survey along with the link to the Web site from KEP's home-page (www.kep.gov.gr). KEP is a Greek governmental site which has been designed and developed for citizens' electronic information and service as well as for facilitating KEP's employees in their every-day work by seeking information on their work or even submitting an online application on behalf of a citizen. The site's information covers the entire scope of the Public Sector and dealings with Public Administration. In addition, it gives the ability to submit electronic applications to KEP for a series of administrative documents, implementing a substantial step toward electronic management in Greece. A total of 630 respondents that comprised of citizens along with KEP's employees, answered the online survey between 6th of February 2007 and 19th of June 2007. The demographic profile of survey respondents indicated a mature group of Internet users who were very familiar with both web-usage and e-government transactions. Among the 630 respondents 77.8% was working for KEP and public sector. Ages of respondents varied, but were generally older than student-based surveys with 8.1% of the respondents being under the age of 25, 57.9% ranging from 26 to 35; 28.3% were ages 36-45 and 5.6% were over age 46. A large portion, 70.1% of the respondents had at least college education. Use of the Internet was rather heavy among the participants with 60.7% of the respondents surfing in Internet more than 10 hours per week; while the high familiarity of the sample with KEP's site (71.5% had daily usage) was considered very positive in our research. The characteristics of the respondents were similar to Internet user profiles gathered in other studies. Finally no monetary or bonus was given to the respondents, while the responses were purely voluntary.

3.3 Data Analysis-Scale Reduction

During data analysis and purification we conducted reliability analysis by grouping the items to the six conceptual dimensions from which they were derived. The most widely used reliability coefficient is Cronbach's coefficient alpha with acceptance level at least 0.7. The coefficient alpha values ranged from 0.84 to 0.92, exceeding the conventional minimum of 0.7 and demonstrating high internal consistency and hence reliability of each dimension.

We refined the instrument (by reducing the list of items within each dimension) by examining corrected item to total correlations and discarding items whose elimination improved reliability or in other words Cronbach's coefficient alpha, until no item's removal increased a construct's overall alpha. The result was the removal of two items. Prior to any removal we ensured that the particular item could not be viewed as representing a distinct additional construct.

In an attempt to identify internal consistency problems and improve reliability levels, all items were screened along Churchill's recommendations [11] to make sure that no items possess low correlations (less than 0.4) with similar traits.

We next conducted exploratory factor analysis to examine the dimensionality of the scale.

With 55 questions in the initial questionnaire and a rule of thumb for factor analysis of at least five times as many observations as there are variables to be analyzed [24], at least 275 subjects were required. The 630 respondents of our survey quite exceeded the mentioned limit.

In our quest for a stable factor structure, we used principal components analysis as the extraction method and Promax rotation method with Kaiser normalization. The criterion to determine the initial number of factors to retain was that the eigenvalues be greater than 1, but also taking the scree plot under consideration.

The initial factor analysis extracted four factors that were evident on the scree plot and had an eigenvalue grater than one. Then we eliminated 'crossloading' items (items that load at 0.32 or higher on two or more factors). In this step three items were deleted.

Item loadings >0.3 are considered significant, item loadings >0.4 are more important and item loadings >0.5 are considered very significant. There are no accepted absolute standards for the cut-offs while the choice is based on judgment, purpose of the study and prior studies. Our goal is to examine the most significant loadings in interpreting the factor solution so we decided to eliminate items with loadings smaller than 0.5. Under these criteria three items were eliminated while another one item revealed its connection to a different factor than the one it was appointed to, in the first place. Before any item was deleted it was screened to make sure it could not be viewed as representing a possible additional construct, while the item that was moved from its intended construct to a different construct it correlated more highly, was screened in order to ensure that it has conceptual relation with its new construct. We then resubmitted the remaining items to a second round of factor analysis where we reached a meaningful factor structure where each item was found to load strongly on only one factor (Table 2).

The factor analysis revealed four factors with eigenvalues >1, while the scree test concurred with a four factor solution, not six as proposed initially by the authors. The four factors emerged from the factor analysis account for 70% of the variance with most factor loadings above 0.60.

Items derived from the factors 'Ease of Use', 'Functionality of the interaction environment' and 'Content & Appearance of Information' loaded on the same factor which was renamed 'Efficiency' reflecting the ease of using the site and the quality of information it provides.

The outcome of the above process was the final e-GovQual Scale, consisting of 25 items, loading strongly on the following four dimensions:

•Reliability: The feasibility and speed of accessing, using and receiving services of the site (6 items)
•Efficiency: The ease of using the site and the quality of information it provides (11 items)
•Citizen Support: The ability to get help when needed (4 items)
•Trust: The degree to which the citizen believes the site is safe from intrusion and protects personal information (4 items)

The scale items of the e-GovQual scale are available on request

Table 2. Principal Components Analysis

Factor Analysis' Items' Loadings			
	Components		
	Factor 1 - Efficiency	Factor 2 - Reliability	Factor 3 - Citizen Support	Factor 4 – Trust
Ease of Use			
Site Structure	.768		
Search Engine	.721		
Site Map	.777		
Customization	.883		
Content & Appearance of Information			
Detailed Information	.873		
Precise Information	.744		
Up2Date Information	.543		
Relevant Information	.729		
Functionality of the interaction environment			
Form Fast Download		.687	
Form Pre-Filling	.616		
Form Auto Calculation	.648		
Form Help	.669		
Reliability			
Site Availability		.683	
Successful Service Delivery		.699	
Service Offered In-Time		.595	
Pages Fast Download		.909	
Site Browser Compatibility		.783	
Citizen Support			
Help Desk Employees Interested			.830
Knowledgeable HD Employees			.888
Polite Help Desk Employees			.972
Trustful Help Desk Employees			.873
Trust			
Secure Acquisition Username & Password				.760
Provision of Min Personal Data				.892
Personal Data Security				.782
Usage of Personal Data				.788

Extraction Method: Principal Component Analysis.
Rotation Method: Promax with Kaiser Normalization.
Rotation converged in 6 iterations.
Total variance explained by the four factors: 69.066%
Loadings<.30 not shown
The above results derived by SPSS software package

4 Discussion

Informed by insights from the extant literature, we set out to conceptualize, construct, refine, and test a multiple-item scale (e-GovQual) for measuring the service quality delivered by governmental web sites. E-GovQual is a four-dimensional, 25 item scale. We hope that it will assist practitioners in systematically assessing and improving the service quality provided by qovernmental web sites. We next offer directions for further research on the field and discuss practical implications of our findings.

The scale demonstrates good psychometric properties based on findings from a variety of reliability and validity tests. However the e-GovQual scale should be viewed as a preliminary scale and a confirmatory phase with broad samples of citizens should follow. E-GovQual's development was based on the responses of citizens that actually use governmetal sites. While the citizens, participating in the survey, are typical users of e-government sites their preferences do not necessarily represent the preferences of the non users of e-government sites as well. So, further research with samples of citizens that are potential users of e-government sites should follow in order to reveal their reservations in using the web, for their transactions with the state. In addition the participants in this study may possess attributes and behaviors that differ from those in other parts of the world. Another point worth mentioning is that although the chosen site enjoyed high frequency of visits there is a need to examine the reliability

Table 3. E-Gov sites area of concern and recommended actions

Area of concern	Recommended action
Reliability	Have sufficient hardware and software and communications capacity to meet peak demand. Develop a system that can be displayed and used independently of the web browser used.
Efficiency	Design pages that are easy to read and understand with detailed, up-to-date and reliable information. Any limitations in the accuracy and currency of the information should be made clear. Update and review dates should be clearly stated on all pages. When information on the website is converted from print publications, attention should be paid to restructuring the information for the hypertext environment. Develop an efficient navigation system and sufficient orientation information. Develop a system capable to provide tailored information. Use text, colors and graphics that are pleasing to citizen's eye. Designers should take account of guidelines for making pages accessible to users with disabilities
Citizen Support	Assist citizens in their quest for information or during their transactions by user friendly guidelines, help pages, FAQ, or even personal advice. Contact details (electronic and conventional) for the entity should be easy to find on the website especially for the case that citizens experience problems.
Trust	Adopt and promote security and privacy policies and procedures that make citizens feel secure in dealing with the organization. There should be a statement informing citizens about the organization's policy on the privacy and security of their interactions with the site.

of e-GovQual in the context of more diverse web sites and to refine the scale if necessary. Finally further research should be conducted in more mature sites that can fulfill a request electronically while with the site that we chose only submission of a request takes place.

As the discussion above illustrates there is a need for further research to deepen our understanding of the assessment, antecedents and consequences of the quality of electronic service delivery. However, the findings of the present study have several important, even if broad, implications for practitioners. Therefore we provide a list of recommended actions for each area of concern detected by e-GovQual (Table 3). Although the recommended actions in some cases might appear obvious and may also hold true for other websites, for completeness we provide a full list.

5 Conclusions

The development of high quality e-government information products and services is an important issue addressed through the development of a model for understanding citizen perceptions and expectations that lays the foundation for the development of a validated measurement instrument. Identification of the quality factors that affect citizen satisfaction may be used to better understand use requirements, aid in the development of government to citizens systems specifications, focus testing efforts, and evaluate potential modifications to existing e-government web site designs and operations.

The model presented in this paper focuses future research on extending the knowledge of quality dimensions affecting e-government web sites in order to more fully develop guidelines for governmetal site development and provides both researchers and practitioners with a tool to aid both research and the construction of e-government sites.

The present study employed a rigorous scale development procedure to establish an instrument (e-GovQual) that measures users' perceived service quality of e-government sites. Within E-GovQual four factors are used: reliability, efficiency, citizen support and trust. Each of the four factors had a significant impact on overall service quality. Through understanding the service quality dimensions for governmental sites, an organization will stand a much better chance of gaining and serving much more citizens. For practitioners, the 25 items across four factors can serve a useful diagnostic purpose. They can use the validated scale to measure and improve service delivery. Furthermore, the four-dimension measurement scale adds to extant literature by establishing a basis for further theoretical advances on service quality related to the electronic service provision to the citizens.

References

1. Zeithaml, V.A., Parasuraman, A., Malhorta, A.: Service Quality Delivery Through Web Sites: A Critical Review of Extant Knowledge. Journal of the Academy of Marketing Science 30(4), 362–375 (2002)
2. Halaris, C., Magoutas, B., Papadomichelaki, X., Mentzas, G.: Classification and Synthesis of Quality Approaches in E-government Services. Internet Research: Electronic Networking Applications and Policy 17(4), 378–401 (2007)

3. Eschenfelder, K.R.: Behind the Web site: An inside look at the production of Web-based textual government information. Government Inf. Quarterly. 21, 337–358 (2004)
4. Brebner, M., Parkinson, M.: The accessibility of New Zealand public library Web sites to people who are blind or vision impaired. In: LIANZA Conference, Wellington, New Zealand (2006)
5. Kaylor, C., Deshazo, R., Van Eck: Gauging e-government: A report on implementing services among American cities. Government Inf. Quarterly 18, 293–307 (2001)
6. Barnes, S.J., Vidgen, R.: Interactive E-Government: Evaluating the Web Site of the UK Inland Revenue. Journal of Electronic Commerce in Organisations 2(1), 42–63 (2003)
7. Barnes, S.J., Vidgen, R.: Data Triangulation and Web Quality Metrics: A Case Study in E-Government. Information & Management 43(6), 767–777 (2006)
8. Korsten, H., Bothma, T.: Evaluating South African government Web sites: methods, findings and recommendations (Part 1). South African Journal of Information Management 7(2) (2005)
9. Horan, T.A., Abhichandani, T., Rayalu, R.: Assessing User Satisfaction of E-Government Services: Development and Testing of Quality-in-Use Satisfaction with Advanced Traveler Information Systems (ATIS). In: HICSS 2006, Proceedings of the 39th Annual Hawaii International Conference on System Sciences, vol. 4, p. 83b (2006)
10. Smith, A.G.: Applying evaluation criteria to New Zealand government websites. International Journal of Information Management 21, 137–149 (2001)
11. Churchill, G.A.: A Paradigm for Developing Better Measures of Marketing Constructs. Journal of Marketing Research XVI, 64–73 (1979)
12. Cronbach, L.J.: Test Validation. R. L. Thorndike, Educational Measurement, American Council on Education, Washington, DC (1971)
13. Parasuraman, A., Zeithaml, V.A., Malhotra, A.: E-S-QUAL: A Multiple-Item Scale for Assessing Electronic Service Quality. Journal of Service Research 7, 213–234 (2005)
14. Aladwani, A.M., Palviab, P.C.: Developing and validating an instrument for measuring user-perceived web quality. Information and Management 39, 467–476 (2002)
15. Barnes, S.J., Liu, K., Vidgen, R.T.: Evaluating WAP news sites: the WEBQUAL/M approach, in global cooperation in the new millennium. In: Proceedings of the Ninth European Conference on Information Systems, Bled, Slovenia (2001)
16. Loiacono, E.T., Watson, R.T., Goodhue, D.L.: WebQual™: A Website Quality Instrument. Working Paper 2000-126-0, University of Georgia (2000)
17. Webb, H.W., Webb, L.A.: Sitequal: an integrated measure of web site quality. Journal of Enterprise Information Management 17(6), 430–440 (2004)
18. Yang, Z., Cai, S., Zhou, Z., Zhou, N.: Development and Validation of an Instrument to measure user perceived service quality of information presenting Web portals. Information & Management 42, 575–589 (2005)
19. Santos, J.: E-service quality: a model of virtual service quality dimensions. Managing Service Quality 13(3), 233–246 (2003)
20. Gefen, D., Karahanna, E., Straub, D.: Trust and TAM in online shopping: an integrated model. MIS Quarterly 27(1), 51–90 (2003)
21. Clyde, A.L.: Library and the web: a strategic planning approach to web site Management. The Electronic Library 18(2), 97–108 (2000)
22. Zhang, P., Von Dran, G.: Expectations and Rankings of Website Quality Features: Results of Two Studies on User Perceptions. In: 34th Hawaii International Conference on System Sciences, Hawaii, USA (2001)

23. Parasuraman, A., Zeithaml, V., Berry, L.: SERVQUAL:a multiple-item scale for measuring consumer perceptions of service quality. Journal of retailing 64, 12–40 (1988)
24. Hair, J.F., Anderson, R.E., Tatham, R.L., Black, W.C.: Multivariate Data Analysis, Upper Saddle River, NJ, p. 730 (1998)

Process-Based Governance in Public Administrations Using Activity-Based Costing

Jörg Becker, Philipp Bergener, and Michael Räckers

European Research Center for Information Systems, University of Muenster,
Leonardo-Campus 3, 48149 Muenster, Germany
{Becker,Philipp.Bergener,Michael.Raeckers}@ercis.uni-muenster.de

Abstract. Decision- and policy-makers in public administrations currently lack on missing relevant information for sufficient governance. In Germany the introduction of New Public Management and double-entry accounting enable public administrations to get the opportunity to use cost-centered accounting mechanisms to establish new governance mechanisms. Process modelling in this case can be a useful instrument to help the public administrations decision- and policy-makers to structure their activities and capture relevant information. In combination with approaches like Activity-Based Costing, higher management level can be supported with a reasonable data base for fruitful and reasonable governance approaches. Therefore, the aim of this article is combining the public sector domain specific process modelling method PICTURE and concept of activity-based costing for supporting Public Administrations in process-based Governance.

Keywords: E-Government, Domain Specific Process Modelling, PICTURE, Activity-Based Costing, Process-Based Governance.

1 Introduction

Governance in public administrations is confronted with new challenges. The chance from the classical input orientation to output orientation significantly changes the data basis for the public leadership. At the same time, the demand for service quality by customers is increasing [1] while tax revenues are decreasing. This leads to a situation where cities and municipalities in Europe have to thing about improving and redesigning there business processes [2, 3]. Therefore, decision makers in public administrations need new tools to supply them with relevant governance information especially about processes costs and efficiency and possible influences of IT technologies like document management systems or workflow management systems.

Through New Public Management (NPM) new possibilities of cost control for public administrations arise. With NPM the way of accounting in German public administrations changes from the classical fiscal accounting to double-entry accounting as known from the private sector [4]. Based on this new accounting approach, administrations have the possibility to introduce an almost complete resource usage concept [5]. Elements like target agreements concerning products and contract management with the employees are essential constituents of this reformation.

M.A. Wimmer et al. (Eds.): EGOV 2009, LNCS 5693, pp. 176–187, 2009.

Activity-based costing is a useful assessment instrument for public administrations. Public administrations, as an overhead intensive service sector, are suited particularly well in this case. NPM offers relevant data basis for activity-based costing. It allows for assessing administration processes from a cost perspective in different overhead areas and so delivers fruitful information for higher management level. The obtained cost rates can be used for cost control as well as for comparing administrations, comparing as-is and to-be costs, decide on reorganization projects, or IT-investments [5, 6].

Process models are an appropriate measure for supporting activity-based costing. The process models are used for transparency issues concerning the knowledge of activity flows and for documenting the often implicit process knowledge of the employees. Thus, process modelling provides a qualitative description of activities, providing in depth-understanding and thereby a starting point for governance related decisions in organizations. However, detailed concepts how to combine activity-based costing and process modelling are still very rare [7, 8].

Business process modelling public administrations face specific challenges. Their highly diversified product portfolio often contains more than 1,000 processes [9]. This big amount of business processes also shows the demand for holistic governance mechanisms especially for decision and policy makers in public sector. In this situation, generic modelling languages like event-driven process chains [10] or BPMN [11] often turns out to be very difficult due to the large amount of processes [12]. The modelling method PICTURE, which has exclusively been developed for the needs of public administrations, has proved to be adequate for this field of application. It has been successfully used for modelling and analyzing by now more than 1,000 processes in public administrations [13].

The contribution of this article is the combination of the domain-specific modelling method PICTURE and the concept of activity-based costing. This integration enables public administrations decision- and policy makers to get a sufficient data base for governance related decisions. Based on the fast and easily process modelling, data sourcing and maintenance can be arranged continuously and so decision- and policy makers can resort to always up to date data.

The following chapter explains the basic concepts of activity-based costing and its applicability to public administrations. Afterwards the PICTURE method is presented as a domain specific modelling method especially developed for the public sector. In the fourth chapter both concepts are compared, a connection is set up and illustrated using an example. This article concludes with a summary and an outlook to future research areas.

2 Activity-Based Costing in Public Administrations

The central idea of activity-based costing is to change the way of breaking down overhead costs on outputs like products or services. Instead of distributing the overhead as a fixed percentage of direct costs, activity-based costing assigns costs according to the resources used for producing the outputs. The resource consumption by the outputs is measured through their usage of certain activities or processes. Activities are tasks performed by an organization's employee which consumes resources. In turn the activities are needed to create the outputs. The frequency of execution for an activity is determined by the cost driver, an "event associated with an activity that results in the consumption of [...] resources" [14]. To calculate the activity cost driver rate – the cost rate for a single execution of an activity – the total costs for caused by the activity are divided by the cost driver. The total costs of an activity result from the share of the activity to the overall capacity of the resource. Sometimes, the factor allocation resources costs to activities are called resource drivers [15, 16].

Due to these properties activity-based costing is especially suitable for application areas with a high overhead fraction. That is mainly the case in personnel intensive areas like the service sector. In service companies basically all benefit processes can be included in the activity-based costing. Activity-based costing is therefore a well suited and useful costing instrument for the service sector [17]. Public administrations mainly provide services, too. Hence, personnel costs often are the dominating cost factor in this sector. At the same time, departments often offer multiple services at once in an administration and often several departments are involved in providing a service. Activity-based costing can help to allocate this large amount of overhead costs to the services of the public administrations better than simple measures like the number of employees of a organizational unit or their share of budget [6].

To actually implement activity-based costing, public administrations need cost rates to measure the resource consumption in monetary terms. For the majority of costs, the personnel costs, those data are well known to public administrations. For other data like e.g. printing costs, public administrations can revert to existing studies [18].

Furthermore, the execution of activity-based costing requires identification, structuring and recording of the relevant activities or processes. A method that has turned out to be very useful for recording, documenting and also analyzing processes is process modelling [19, 20]. That is why it is not surprising that also in literature respective approaches to integrate the two instruments have been discussed [7, 8]. However, a more detailed examination of the conceptual fit between different approaches is still missing.

3   Picture Method

PICTURE is a domain specific modelling method [21-23] which has been developed specifically for public administrations. The target when developing the PICTURE method was on the one hand to represent preferably the complete process landscape of an administration with justifiable effort and on the other hand to create process models which can be used for further semi-automatic analysis. For a more profound introduction to PICTURE cf. [24, 25]. Like many other modelling approaches PICTURE differentiates several views on the modelling object for reducing complexity when modelling. PICTURE distinguishes four views:

Process View
The process view describes the operational structure of the administration in the form of single activities and the hence evolving processes. At the same time the process view integrates all other views by recording "who" carries out single activities, "with what" they are carried out and "what" is edited respectively produced. The central element of the PICTURE method and thus also of the process view are the process

building blocks. Each process building block represents a typical activity in the sequence of work of public administrations. This strictly defined language construct facilitates modelling because it refers to the known vocabulary of the domain. An overview of the building blocks is presented in Fig. 1.

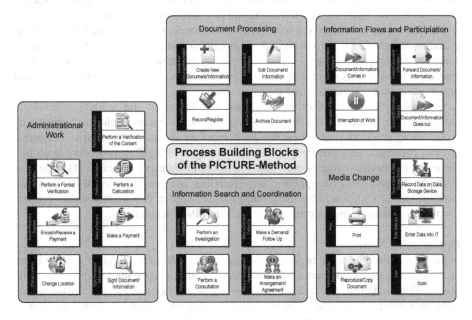

Fig. 1. PICTURE Process Building Blocks

For describing the details of an activity execution more closely and for recording properties which are necessary for subsequent evaluations the PICTURE building blocks are specified in more detail by attributes. For example, for the building block *Document/Information comes in* attributes like *Input Channels*, *Received Document* or *Used Information Systems* and the *Sending Organizational Unit* are recorded. The attribute *Input Channels* is an example for an attribute which requires multiple entries which have to be weighted. In PICTURE this is presented by a percentage distribution. Another important attribute also with regard to supporting activity-based costing is the *required processing time* which can be found in many building blocks like e.g. *Enter data into IT*.

At the next structural level building blocks are composed to sub processes. Thereby a sub process is understood as a sequence of activities (process building blocks) which are carried out within one organizational unit by one administrative employee and which contribute to the performance of a task of the complete process. Sub processes contain attributes, too. Here it is for instance recorded how often the sub process is carried out per year (*number of cases*) and who is responsible for its execution.

Within sub processes the modelling of process building blocks is done strictly sequential. This is due to the reason that one sub process only comprises those activities which one single administrative employee carries out. Therefore, it is assumed that he can only do one task at a time. Furthermore, it is possible that for one sub process several alternative operational variants exist, e.g. due to a decision (acceptance respectively rejection). For representing such a situation PICTURE offers two different constructs. One the one hand, attributes can be used, like the above described attribute *Input Channels*, where different cases can be represented by entering percentages. On the other hand, it is possible to define sub process variants. Such a sub process variant describes the alternative execution of the sub process from start to finish.

Sub processes are composed to processes. A process is characterised by providing exactly one benefit for the customers of an administration. Examples for such processes are *Moving an identity card* or *Extending the parking permit*. In the simplest case a process consists of exactly one sub process; processes passing through several organisation units consist of more than one sub process.

Besides the differentiation regarding the refinement of the modelling levels to processes, sub processes, variants and finally process building blocks, aggregating processes to products is also possible by combining processes to groups or superior groups. These groups represent products, product groups etc. The procedure leads to a hierarchy of services which opens out into a comprehensive product catalogue. For example, the processes for applying for, extending and giving notice of the loss of a passport can be combined into the group *Passport affairs*. A potential superior group for processes concerning identity cards would be "Pass documents".

Organisation View

In the organisation view the organisational structure of the administration is represented in a hierarchical composition of the different organisational units and positions. The organisational units are the basic elements of the organisation view. The organisational units are responsible for the execution of process aspects within the processes. That is why in PICTURE sub processes are assigned to organisational units.

Besides the organisational units, positions and administrative employees are also to be maintained in this view. This is of special importance regarding the determination of personnel costs. Different position types and according properties like cost rates and capacities are specified for the positions. This allows for recording the relevant costs for employees as they are assigned during the modelling with PICTURE to the respective position. This is relevant for a subsequent automated analysis. Besides the mere storage of cost rates it is also important to state here to which process building block attributes these cost rates will be assigned (i. e. specifying the resource drivers for the cost rates). In the field of personnel cost this are mainly time attributes like processing time.

Business Object View

The business object view contains information concerning the necessary input (e.g. applications) and the corresponding produced output or possible intermediate products (e.g. statements or notifications) of an administrative process. Here, all services including internal support processes for customer related services which can provide an assessable input or output are important because cost can and should be assigned to all these elements. It does not matter from a modelling perspective whether the input was created within the administration or whether it was given from the outside. An internal input has to be the output of another sector and thus can be quantified. This can be internal order documents or information. An external input normally does not cause costs until it arrives. These costs are measured and operationalised via the process view.

Resource View
The resource view shows which work equipment is needed for providing an administrative service. That is, for example, software applications like MS Office or specialised procedures as well as hardware (printer, scanner) or judicial information like laws. The resource view contains element types for representing these non-organisational work supporters as well as *sources* and *targets* of the business objects. In their roles as work supporters resources can be compared to the already mentioned element types of the organisation view. In their roles as *sources* or *targets* of business objects they determine where business objects – especially documents and information – come from and where they are stored like e.g. in specialised procedures. In the context of activity-based costing the resource modelling serves for adding these cost types like printing or archiving costs to the activities in which they are used. Thus, a product-centred addition of the respective costs will be possible if the required cost rates are stored with the resources in the PICTURE method. Thereby the corresponding attributes from the method have to be assigned to the resources like e.g. the attribute "printed pages" to a printer.

4 Integration of Activity-Based Costing and PICTURE

To integrate activity-based costing and the PICTURE method, the constructs of both instruments have to be compared and assigned to each other. Our aim is to show, that activity-based costing elements can all be mapped on corresponding PICTURE-Elements. Furthermore, we will expand the elements of ABC with constructs representing processes and process structures dwelling on the German version of ABC, the process costing (Prozesskostenrechnung) [26].

We will argue that this allows for process oriented implementation of activity based costing in the domain of public administrations. This will enable a more in-depth reflection of reasons for inefficiencies and reorganisation potentials in business processes and thereby support efficient governance in public administrations.

Output: Activity-based costing is applied to allocate costs to outputs. In general these could be for example products or services. In the context of public administrations as an information processing organisation, the suitable outputs are the administration's services as they do normally not produce material goods. This corresponds to the concept of a product in PICTURE which is allocated above the processes level. PICTURE structures these products in a hierarchical way, thus enabling an aggregation of cost data along this hierarchy.

Primary process and Subprocess: PICTURE uses different levels to structure the activities needed to deliver a service. The top level - the processes - encapsulates all activities needed to deliver a process while a sub-process depicts activities within a certain organizational unit. Process building blocks finally are the atomic level to describe activities in PICTURE. In contrast, activity-based costing does only have the concept of activities which are not further structured. The examples in the literature show activities on a quite high level of abstraction like "process orders"[27] or "disbursing Materials" [28]. These examples seem to be similar to a sub-process in PICTURE, as activities in activity-based costing are used to distribute resource costs which are normally associated with single organisational units. However, the concepts of processes and process building blocks can be easily integrated in activity-based costing. This is e.g. the case for the German process costing. Processes allow for an accumulation of the costs of several activities conducted while delivering a service, while the detailed level of process building blocks can help to break down activities further and therefore makes it easier to capture the resources used by an activity through the attributes of the process building blocks.

Table 1. Comparison of Elements of Activity-Based-Costing/PICTURE

Activity-Based Costing	PICTURE
output	product
primary process	process
sub-process	sub-process
activity	process building block
	building block attribute
cost driver	business object
ressource	ressource
	position

Cost driver: Cost drivers in activity-based costing denote the determining factors (e.g. amount of building applications) that are responsible for the execution frequency of a main process. Such inputs or outputs can be represented in PICTURE by means of the processed object view. The respective amount of process and sub-process executions per year is recorded in form of an attribute on the process level and sub-process level, respectively.

Resource: The resources, respectively the resource consumptions, determine which costs are produced by activities. The most important resource in this context is the labour utilisation. The resource labour is modelled with the aid of the organisation view. In this view it is possible to deposit the payment and the (annual) labour time of a certain position. On the basis of these data the minute-by-minute wage rate can be calculated. The other resources are recorded in the resource model. The allocation of resources to activities happens by annotating the resources to the according process building block.

Table 1 summarizes the above mentioned considerations in tabular form. The conducted mapping between central elements of both approaches show, that easy linkage is possible. This supports the assumption that business process modelling enables implementation and information gathering for activity based costing in a certain application domain.

5 Activity-Based Costing in PICTURE – An Example

To conduct activity-based costing in PICTURE the relevant services and activities have to be identified in accordance to the activity-based costing approach. For this purpose the definition of a process in PICTURE, which is geared to the external services of the public administration, can provide assistance. In the presented example this is the process "Modification of an income tax card" which in turn consists of the sub process "Modify income tax card".

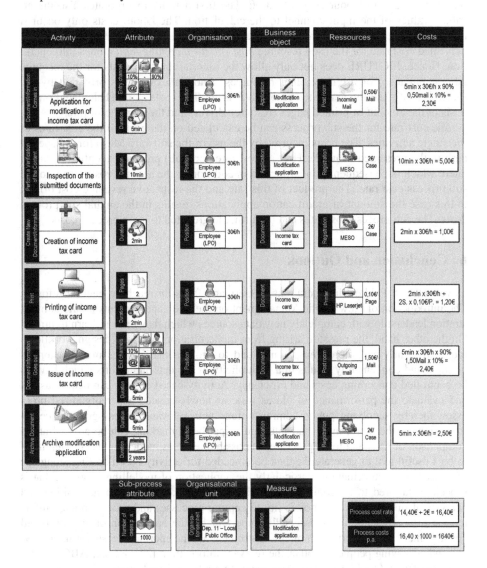

Fig. 2. Exemplary process "Modify income tax card"

The identified processes have to be modelled subsequently with the PICTURE method. Thereby the attributes which are relevant for the activity-based costing, especially the used resources and the personnel in charge, have to be recorded. The sub process "Modify income tax card" is depicted in Fig. 2.

The respective partial cost rate can be calculated if the corresponding cost information is deposited in the organisation model and in the resource model. In the example of Figure 2 the deposited cost rate of an employee of the Local Public Office amounts to 30€ per hour. The second activity, the inspection of the submitted documents, therefore results in labour costs of 5.00€. The first activity incorporates also the attribute values of the input channel to the calculation. The labour costs only occur if the application is submitted in person by a citizen. In case of a postal submission, the deposited cost rate for the used resource *post room - incoming mail* comes into operation. Hence, PICTURE does not only allow the ascertainment of costs for the resource labour, but also for arbitrary other resources. Another example is provided by the fourth activity and the annotated resource *Printer*. The costs can be calculated on the basis of the amount of printed pages (resource driver) and the stored cost rate.

The cost rate for the sub process can be calculated on the basis of the cost rates of the single activities. The costs incurred by the use of the software Meso form a special case in the presented example. Here, a cost rate per (sub) process execution is calculated, which is consequently incorporated in addition to the activity cost rates into the sub process cost rate. The product of this rate and the respective resource cost driver, in this case the amount of modification applications, results in the annual sub process costs. The sub process cost rates can be further aggregated to main process costs.

6   Conclusion and Outlook

Governance in Public administrations in Germany faces far reaching internal reforms. The introduction of New Public Management on the one hand presents public administration leadership with completely new data sources which they have to learn to utilize. On the other hand, the pressure arising from modernisation efforts to design workflows more efficiently and more transparently and to provide the services more customer-oriented and conveniently results in a multiplicity of projects and efforts which have to be controlled concerning costs and efficiency. Activity-based costing can help to assess and evaluate the performance of old as wele as newly created and reorganized processes, thereby supplying public administrations with relevant process governance information Furthermore, intra- and inter-municipal benchmarking can be applied and a comparison of as-is and to-be processes is possible. Process modelling has proven itself to be a useful tool to generate the data pool needed for activity-based costing alongside with accounting information. Particularly the application of modelling approach that is especially tailored to a certain domain leads to a quicker and easier acquisition and analysis of information. The possibility to capture processes and process-related information in a efficient way is especially important for the application of activity-based costing since the main criticism on this instrument are the enormous costs for interviewing and surveying people to gather the relevant information [27]. Hence, ABC can become an efficient tool for process governance in public administrations.

The present article underlines how the domain specific modelling approach PIC-TURE and the concept of activity-based costing can be combined to support the governance of business processes in public administrations. The example shows that the information gained during the phase of modelling suffice to make consolidated statements about the process costs accounting for personnel costs as well as other types of resource consumption. This information can be aggregates and thus enable public decision makers in controlling there processes and deciding e.g. on IT-investments or organisational changes.

Through the introduction of a cost-based evaluation of public administrations work and an assessment of services offered by administrations based on a process oriented view, the organisations get enabled to benchmark their services not only based on KPIs but on service descriptions. The essential advantage of this approach is an activity-oriented and not only a result-oriented comparison of public services. Hence, the application of PICTURE to realize ABC in public administrations bears the potential to bring public administrations closer to a holistic governance of their business processes.

Based on these findings, further research activities should particularly concentrate on the development of a procedure model that standardizes the application of process oriented activity-based costing in the area of public administrations. Our work led to the conclusion that this would be a promising approach. Following this, empirical evaluation of activity-based costing with the use of the PICTURE method is a close next step.

Acknowledgements

The work published in this paper is partly funded by the European Commission through the STREP PICTURE. It does not represent the view of European Commission or the PICTURE consortium, and the authors are solely responsible for the paper's content.

References

1. Janssen, M.: Modeling for Accountability: The Case of the Virtual Business Counter. In: Proc. 11th Americas Conference on Information Systems (AMCIS 2005), pp. 2021–2029 (2005)
2. Becker, J., Niehaves, B., Algermissen, L., Delfmann, P., Falk, T.: eGovernment Success Factors. In: Traunmüller, R. (ed.) EGOV 2004. LNCS, vol. 3183, pp. 503–506. Springer, Heidelberg (2004)
3. Gronlund, A.: Electronic Government - Design, Applications and Management. Idea Group Publishing, Hershey (2002)
4. Hood, C.: The 'New Public Management' in the 1980s: Variations on a Theme. Accounting, Organizations and Society 20, 93–109 (1995)
5. Jackson, A., Lapsley, I.: The diffusion of accounting practices in the new "managerial" public sector. The International Journal of Public Sector Management 16, 359–372 (2003)

6. Brown, R.E., Myring, M.J., Gard, C.G.: Activity-Based Costing in Government: Possibilities and Pitfalls. Public Budgeting and Finance 19, 3–21 (1999)
7. Tatsiopoulos, I.P., Panayioto, N.: The integration of activity based costing and enterprise modeling for reengineering purposes. International Journal of Production Economics 66, 33–44 (2000)
8. Tornberg, K., Jämsen, M., Parakno, J.: Activity-based costing and process modeling for cost-conscious product design: A case study in a manufacturing company. International Journal of Production Economics 79, 75–82 (2002)
9. Algermissen, L., Delfmann, P., Niehaves, B.: Experiences in Process-oriented Reorganisation through Reference Modelling in Public Administrations - The Case Study Regio@KomM. In: Proc. 13th European Conference on Information Systems (ECIS 2005) (2005)
10. Scheer, A.-W.: ARIS - Business Process Modeling, 3rd edn. Springer Publishing, Heidelberg (2000)
11. Object Management Group. Business Process Modeling Notation, V1.1., http://www.bpmn.org/Documents/BPMN%201-1%20Specification.pdf
12. Becker, J., Algermissen, L., Falk, T.: Prozessorientierte Verwaltungsmodernisierung - Prozessmanagement im Zeitalter von E-Government und New Public Management. Springer, Berlin (2007)
13. Pfeiffer, D.: Semantic Business Process Analysis - Building Block-based Construction of Automatically Analyzable Business Process Models. Münster (2008)
14. Babad, Y.M., Balachandran, B.V.: Cost driver optimization in activity-based costing. The Accounting Review 68, 563–564 (1993)
15. Cokins, G., Stratton, A., Helbling, J.: An ABC manager's primer. Irwin Publishing, Chicago (1993)
16. Gupta, M., Galloway, K.: Activity-based costing/management and its implications for operations management. Technovation 23, 131–138 (2003)
17. Ruhl, J.M., Hartman, B.P.: Activity-Based Costing in the Service Sector. Advances in Management Accounting, 147–161 (1998)
18. KGSt: Kosten eines Arbeitsplatzes (Stand 2007/2008). Kommunale Gemeinschaftsstelle für Verwaltungsmanagement, Cologne, Germany (2007)
19. Green, P.F., Rosemann, M.: Integrated Process Modeling: An Ontological Evaluation. Information Systems 25, 73–87 (2000)
20. Shanks, G., Tansley, E., Weber, R.: Using ontology to validate conceptual models. Communications of the ACM 46, 85–89 (2003)
21. Guizzardi, G., Pires, L.F., Sinderen, M.J.v.: On the role of Domain Ontologies in the design of Domain-Specific Visual Modeling Languages. In: Proc. 2nd Workshop on Domain-Specific Visual Languages, 17th ACM Conference on Object-Oriented Programming, Systems, Languages and Applications (OOPSLA 2002) (2002)
22. Luoma, J., Kelly, S., Tolvanen, J.-P.: Defining Domain-Specific Modeling Languages - Collected Experiences. In: Proc. 4th Object-Oriented Programming Systems, Languages, and Applications Workshop on Domain-Specific Modeling (OOPSLA 2004) (2004)
23. van Deursen, A., Klint, P., Visser, J.: Domain-Specific Languages: An Annotated Bibliography. SIGPLAN Notices 35, 26–36 (2000)
24. Becker, J., Bergener, P., Kleist, S., Pfeiffer, D., Räckers, M.: Model-based Evaluation of ICT Investments in Public Administrations. In: Proc. 14th Americas Conference on Information Systems (AMCIS 2008), pp. 1–10 (2008)

25. Becker, J., Pfeiffer, D., Räckers, M.: Domain Specific Process Modelling in Public Administrations – The PICTURE-Approach. In: Wimmer, M.A., Scholl, J., Grönlund, Å. (eds.) EGOV 2007. LNCS, vol. 4656, pp. 68–79. Springer, Heidelberg (2007)
26. Mayer, R.: Prozesskostenrechnung - State of the Art. In: GmbH, H.P. (ed.) Prozesskostenmanagement, pp. 3–27. Franz Vahlen (1998)
27. Anderson, S.R., Kaplan, R.S.: Time-Driven Activity-Based Costing. Harvard Business Review 82 (2003)
28. Cooper, R., Kaplan, R.S.: Measure Cost Right: Make the Right Decision. Harvard Business Review 66, 96–105 (1998)

Survey of E-Government Portals
in European Capitals and Large Cities:
A Benchmarking Study of G2B-Services

Frank Hogrebe, Nadine Blinn, and Markus Nüttgens

University of Hamburg
Faculty of Economics and Social Sciences
Information Systems, Hamburg, Germany
Von-Melle-Park 9, D-20146 Hamburg
{frank.hogrebe,nadine.blinn,
markus.nuettgens}@wiso.uni-hamburg.de

Abstract. To fulfil the requirements of the EU Services Directive, suppliers of public services have to realign their product and process organisation. At present, a summary on the implementation status does not exist for European capitals and large cities. Thus, the paper presents the status quo by illustrating the results of a benchmarking survey. The survey analyses the offer of G2B eServices in all 27 European capitals and all European cities with more than 500.000 inhabitants and it was done in 21 first EU-languages and in English as second language. The findings of the survey address academic research as well as administration practice in the context of eGovernment.

Keywords: Benchmarking study, municipal portals, G2B-Services, mystery user approach, maturity model.

1 Motivation

With the Directive on services in the internal market - also named as EU Services Directive - [EU06] in mind, municipalities have to intensify their offer of eServices. First and foremost, formalities as well as procedures to start up and exercise a business must be reachable by electronic means and "from a distance". Hence, aspects such as optimisation of administrative processes, cost savings for the business in question and reduction in bureaucracy are challenges for eGovernment resulting from these requirements. Up to the time of executing this survey, the status quo of the implementation of municipal Government-to-Business (G2B) eServices in Europe has not yet been analysed. This paper is bridging this gap by giving a structured overview on G2B eServices offered by European capitals and large cities. The survey is conducted by the following working hypothesis:

- G2B eServices are limited to core services (e.g. registration of a business, E-Tendering).
- Advanced services (e.g. meta-services for forms, geographic information systems data [GIS]) are not yet extensively offered.

M.A. Wimmer et al. (Eds.): EGOV 2009, LNCS 5693, pp. 188–197, 2009.

The paper is structured as follows: First we sum up benchmarking approaches in eGovernment. Additionally, we give an overview of existing studies concerning benchmarking eGovernment (Section 2). Then we give a detailed description of our methodological approach and research design (Section 3). Subsequently, the results of our research are presented and discussed (Section 4). The paper closes with a summary and a discussion of further research questions.

2 Benchmarking Requirements and Related Studies

Public authorities are requested to align their organisation and processes concerning eServices according to the Directive. EU Member States are requested to implement laws and administrative instructions by the end of 2009 in order to fulfil the requirements of the EU Services Directive. The implementation of the directive aims at

Table 1. Benchmarking studies on eGovernment

Year	Title / Title Translation	Organisation/ Author	Thematic focus	Reference field (geogr.)	G2B
2007	Evaluation and Optimisation of municipal e-Government processes (in German)	Hach [Ha07]	Process systematisation and benefit analysis	National (Germany)	yes
2007	eGovernment – Opportunities for small and medium – sized businesses? (in German)	Slapio et al. [SKL07]	Business-related eGovernment processes from the point of view of the German Chamber of Industry and Commerce	National (Germany)	yes
2006	Europe-wide increasing availability of public e-Services (in German)	Capgemini [Ca06]	Europe-wide comparison of e-Services; 20 services as benchmarking criteria, analysis towards service categories and maturity levels	International (Europe)	yes
2003	Benchmarking E-Government in Europe and the US	Graafland-Essers, Ettedgui [GE03]	User Survey	Inter-/ National (Europe)	yes
2003	E-Government for businesses: Survey on the implementation of business-oriented e-Government services in Baden-Württemberg 2003 (German)	Fraunhofer Institut [FIS03]	Focus on business-related eGovernment services (The implementation is measured by 4 complexity levels)	National (Germany)	yes
2003	E-Government in municipalities (in German)	Kubicek, H, Wind, D. [KW03]	The authors do not accomplish a study, they overview studies from other sources concerning Nordrhein-Westfalen	National (Germany)	no
2002	BEGIX: Balanced E-Government-Index (in German)	Bertelsmann Stiftung [BS02]	Focus on self-entry and assessment of eGovernment services (reference index; level of implementation is measured by 5 categories)	National (Germany)	yes

creating a single market for services within the EU. To analyse the municipal portals for G2B eServices, the benchmarking method is applied. Benchmarking methods belong to the so-called accompanying evaluation methods. In the context of eGovernment we follow the benchmarking definition of [He06]: „eGovernment benchmarking means undertaking a review of comparative performance of e-government between nations or agencies".

In summary, our study is a qualitative approach focusing ePublic Services for businesses. As our focus is on the analysis of administrations in European Capitals and large cities, the comparison is accomplished externally on a horizontal basis. Due to similar processes and products in the public administration area, a high comparableness is set [BHL08]. In the field of benchmarking e-Government services, national as well as international studies exist focusing on different aspects of e-Government. Table 1 gives a structured overview.

Moreover, SCHUSTER [Sc03] overviews national and international surveys and studies on municipal services. At present, a Europe-wide comparative study on the implementation of G2B eServices does not exist. The study presented in this paper aims to bridge this gap.

3 Methodological Approach

The benchmarking study is accomplished methodologically according to the "Procedural model for the Benchmarking of Services" – DIN PAS 1014 [DIN01]. The accomplishment of the benchmarking study follows two methods of "Third-party Web Assessment" [He06], whereas the approach "mystery user" is applied in a first step. In a second step, another approach belonging to the "Third-Party Web Assessment" is applied: we use the "categorisation" according to HEEKS, firstly, to analyse presence and absence of defined services and web portal characteristics, and, secondly to do a classification according to a stage model rating [He06]. The study was accomplished analysing 25 criteria divided into five categories:

- Category 1: Search functionalities for G2B eServices
- Category 2: Clarity of eServices offered to businesses (overall view)
- Category 3: Contact partner services for businesses
- Category 4: Form services for businesses
- Category 5: Municipal G2B eServices

The choice of criteria is based on results of expert interviews as well as business interviews. Table 2 gives a detailed overview of the municipal G2B eServices.

As Category 5 consists of municipal G2B services, we give a short description of the particular services:

- Industrial real estate and commercial property: Industrial real estates and commercial properties comprise estates and buildings (including equipment) for commercial use. According to this, departments for communal business development provide municipal offers and information services for businesses.

Table 2. Criteria Catalogue for G2B eServices

No.	criteria	measurement units
1.	Industrial real estate and commercial property - in which complexity level these are available on the business portal?	complexity level
2.	Services for founders of new businesses - in which complexity level these are available on the business portal?	complexity level
3.	Registration of a business - in which complexity level these are available on the business portal?	complexity level
4.	E-Tendering - in which complexity level available on the business portal?	complexity level
5.	Other municipal business-oriented services - in which complexity level these are available on the business portal?	complexity level

- Services for founders of new businesses: Founding of new business means the realisation of self-employment. The founding of a new business starts with the entry in business operations and because of legislation with the registration of a business. Services for founders comprise: consulting, support programms, official registrations etc.
- Registration of a business: The registration of a business means the official registration of self-employment with the relevant authority.
- E-Tendering: Public tendering is part of the procedure to allocate assignments. Hence, potential tenderers are invited to submit offers. These procedures are usually strictly standardised by legal frameworks.

Selected criteria are rated according to complexity levels [BM00], [FIS03], whereas the following specifications are possible:

- Complexity Level 0:   no *eServices* (for the service selected)
- Complexity Level 1:   *Information* (on the selected service is available online)
- Complexity Level 2:   *Interaction* (downloading of files is possible)
- Complexity Level 3:   *two-way interaction* (editing of forms and authentication is available)
- Complexity Level 4:   *online-tracking* (presentation of current time perspective and status of the proceedings or open steps until a process is completed)
- Complexity Level 5:   *Transaction* (complete online processing – permits and payment included)

Points were given according to the complexity level, e.g. a service in complexity level 4 is calculated with 4 points for the city in question. The points were transferred to an evaluation matrix. Hence, after rating and weighting the criteria, the total points for each city can be calculated. During the time period of the study the city with the highest number of points has the best online portal with regard to quantity and quality of G2B eServices.

4 Results of the Study

The research and analysis method described above was applied to all European capitals and all European cities with more than 500.000 inhabitants [EU08] in October 2008. According to this, the main unit for the study comprises 27 European capitals and additionally 36 large cities, in total 63 cities. Some of the capitals have more than 500.000 inhabitants. The selection of cities was carried out keeping in mind that businesses tend to locate in capitals and large cities rather than in rural areas [MP07]. So, the G2B eServices in a large number of businesses are analysed in this study. The starting point for each analysis was the main portal of a municipality, visited via {name of city}.countrycode (main page). On the basis of the criteria catalogue, free accessible city portals were analysed. To avoid misunderstandings because of language problems,

```
Overview of first languages:

 1. language  Bulgarian    1 portal
 2. language  Danish       1 portal
 3. language  German      12 portals
 4. language  English      7 portals
 5. language  Estonian     1 portal
 6. language  Finnish      1 portal
 7. language  French      10 portals
 8. language  Greek        2 portals
 9. language  Dutch        2 portals
10. language  Italian      6 portals
11. language  Letvian      1 portal
12. language  Lithuanian   1 portal
13. language  Polish       5 portals
14. language  Portuguese   1 portal
15. language  Romanian     1 portal
16. language  Swedish      1 portal
17. language  Slovakian    1 portal
18. language  Slovenian    1 portal
19. language  Spanish      6 portals
20. language  Czech        1 portal
21. language  Hungarian    1 portal
              total       63 portals

Qualification of portal analysts:native speakers
and sworn graduated interpreters and translators
```

Fig. 1. Overview of first languages in the sample

the studies for the different cities were accomplished by native speakers and sworn graduated interpreters and translators in all 21 different languages. Figure 1 shows the distribution of the different languages to the portals analysed:

The EU Services Directive in mind, we also analysed, if municipalities also offer the same range of eServices in more languages than the mother tongue. While we identified a heterogeneous field, firstly, of the quantity of second languages offered, and secondly, the quality of the eServices offered in second languages, we were able to identify 38 cities offering their services in English as a second language.

According to the principles of the "third party web assessment" method, no contact with the municipalities by telephone or by mail was carries out, so as to guarantee objectivity. So, only those portals offering services that were freely accessible to businesses were considered.

For the municipal G2B eServices we can assume that 27, 94% of the portals (67, 89% in second language) do not offer information services as required by the EU Services Directive. Complexity Level 2 (Download) is only fulfilled by 34, 92% of the portals (10% in second language). Interaction is only available in 7, 94% of the

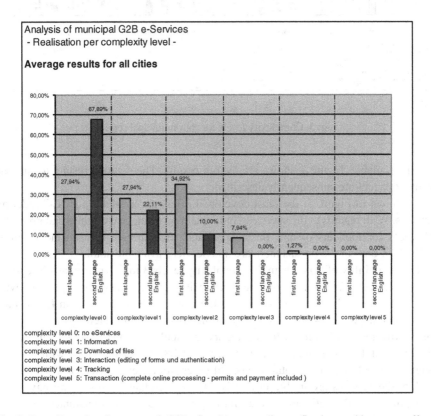

Fig. 2. Overall results of category 5: G2B eServices according to first/ second language offers

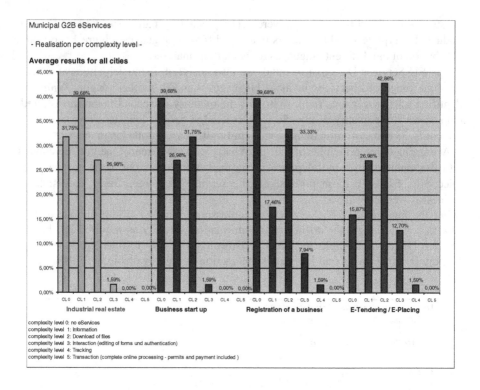

Fig. 3. Complexity levels for four municipal services

portals available. Figure 2 shows the overall results. The detailed results for the municipal services are subsequently described.

As shown in Figure 3, the most developed offers are available for "E-Tendering" services. With regards to the services "Industrial real estate and commercial property", "Services for founders of new businesses" and "Registration of a business", in 31, 75% to 39, 68% of the portals there are no eServices available at all.

The availability of services in the complexity levels 3 to 5 is marginal. Exceptional are the services "Registration of a business" with 7, 94% offers in complexity level 3 and "E-Tendering" offered on 12, 7% of the portals. The best portal in English as a second language has 54 points, i.e. 36% of the possible points. Here, there is potential for improvements in every criteria category, particularly in the development of complexity level 1-5 of municipal services. Even if 88, 4% of the cities with a second language or 60, 3% of the total number of cities offer their services in English, only 36% of the services are usable in English. If we correlate the result, we have to assume, that a good positioning in the first language offer is not a guarantee for a good positioning in the second language offer (cp. Figure 4):

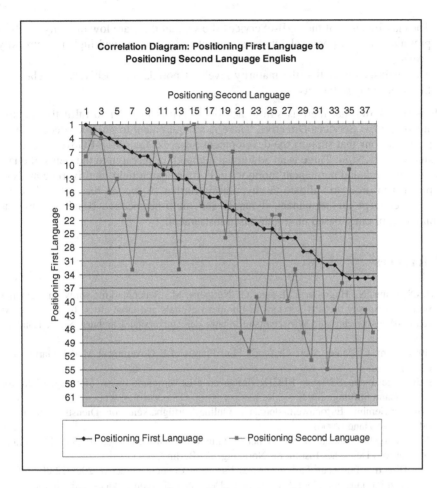

Fig. 4. Correlation diagram for first and second language offers

5   Summary and Further Research

This report presents the findings of a G2B eServices survey. The survey was accomplished in European capitals and large cities (with more than 500.000 inhabitants) by a "third party web assessment" method. The survey was carried out in all 21 first languages and in English as a second language. With the requirements of the EU Services Directive in mind, the report provides an overview of the services implemented and of the state-of- the-art of maturity levels for the portals focused on. Based on the "Procedural model for the Benchmarking of Services" – DIN PAS 1014 and conducted by the "Mystery User" approach, the study was accomplished objectively and as close to a real-life situation as possible. The validation of the working hypothesis leads to the following core findings:

- The classification of the G2B-eServices shows, that there are low maturity levels at present. There is potential for development so as to achieved higher complexity levels.
- The analysis shows that the maturity levels of portals are positively correlated to the positioning of the city.

The study shows that there is still a lack of eServices in order to fulfil the requirements of the EU Services Directive. There is a requirement to provide adequate ICT-implementations that support the development towards "One-Stop-EGovernment" for businesses [HKN08]. There is an additional demand for research in the fields of quantitative research and permanent monitoring. For a research field, multivariate analysis is planned in order to validate the hypothesis further. A second research field comprises a concept for permanent, dynamic and multi-perspective benchmarking and monitoring of cities based on a web-based instrument.

References

[BHL08] Blinn, N., Hogrebe, F., Lange, G., Nüttgens, M.: Benchmarking study on municipal portals: A Survey of G2B-Services in European capitals and large cities. In: Nüttgens, M. (ed.) Arbeitsberichte zur Wirtschaftsinformatik der Universität Hamburg Nr. 4, Hamburg (2008)

[BM00] Baum, C., Maio, A.D.: Gartner's Four Phases of E-Government Model. Gartner Inc. (2000)

[BS02] Bertelsmann Stiftung: BEGIX: Balanced e-Government Index. Herausgegeben von Bertelsmann Stiftung (2002)

[Ca06] CapGemini: Europaweit steigende Online-Verfügbarkeit von Dienstleistungen der öffentlichen Hand (2006)

[DIN01] Vorgehensmodell für das Benchmarking von Dienstleistungen. PAS 1014. Herausgegeben von Deutsches Institut für Normung e.V. Berlin (2001)

[EU06] Directive European Parliament and European Council: Directive 2006/123/EC of the European Parliament and the Council of 12 December 2006 on services in the internal market. EU Services Directive (2006)

[EU08] Urban Audit. Edited by Eurostat (2008)

[FIS03] Fraunhofer Institut Systemtechnik und Innovationsforschung ISI: E-Government für Unternehmen: Untersuchung zur Umsetzung unternehmensbezogener E-Government-Dienste in Baden-Württemberg (2003)

[GE03] Graafland-Essers, I., Ettedgiu, E.: Benchmarking e-Government in Europe and the US. Santa Monica, Calif. RAND (2003)

[Ha07] Hach, H.: Evaluation und Optimierung kommunaler E-Government-Prozesse. 1. Aufl. Baden-Baden: Nomos Verl.-Ges (2007)

[He06] Heeks, R.: Benchmarking eGovernment. Improving the National and International Measurement, Evaluation and Comparison of eGovernment. Development Informatics Group. Institute for Development Policy and Management (2006)

[HKN08] Hogrebe, F., Kruse, W., Nüttgens, M.: One-Stop-eGovernment für Unternehmen: Ein Bezugsrahmen zur Virtualisierung und Bündelung öffentlicher Dienstleistungen am Beispiel der Landeshauptstadt Düsseldorf. In: Bichler, M., Hess, T., Krcmar, H., Lechner, U., Matthes, F., Picot, A., Speitkamp, B., Wolf, P. (eds.) Multikonferenz Wirtschaftsinformatik, MKWI 2008, München, 26.2.2008 - 28.2.2008, Proceedings. GITO-Verlag, Berlin (2008)

[KW03] Kubicek, H., Wind, M.: E-Government in Kommunen. Studie für die Enquetekommission "Zukunft der Städte in NRW" des Landtags Nordrhein Westfalen (2003)
[MP07] Moldinger, P., Philipp, K.: Erweiterte Auswertungen mit dem Unternehmensregister. Herausgegeben von Statistisches Bundesamt (2007)
[PS07] Palvia Jain, S.M., Sharma, S.: E-Government and E-Governance: Definitions/Domain Framework and Status around the World. In: Agarwal, A., Venkate Ramana, V. (hg.) Foundations of E-government. 5th international conference on E-Governance, Hyderabad, India
[Sc03] Schuster, F.: Der interkommunale Leistungsvergleich als Wettbewerbssurrogat. Verl. für Wirtschaftskommunikation, Berlin (2003)
[Sc04] Benchmarking Electronic Government. Ein Selbstbewertungsmodell für kommunale Electronic Government-Aktivitäten ("eLoGoAssess"). Universitätsverlag Potsdam, Potsdam (KWI-Projektberichte, 8)
[SKL07] Slapio, E., Kurten, D., Linden, A.: Electronic Government - Chancen für den Mittelstand, Köln (2007)

Assessment of Website Quality: Scandinavian Web Awards Right on Track?

Hanne Sørum[1], Rony Medaglia[2], and Kim Normann Andersen[2]

[1] Norwegian School of Information Technology, Schweigaardsgate 14, Oslo, 0185, Norway
{hanne.sorum@nith.no}
[2] Copenhagen Business School, Center for Applied ICT (CAICT), Howitzvej 60,
Frederiksberg, 2000, Denmark
{andersen,rm.caict}@cbs.dk

Abstract. This paper maps the criteria used for measuring website quality in a range of Scandinavian web awards. In order to categorize the evaluation criteria we have used the DeLone and McLean Model, and findings show that there is a heterogeneous pattern of methods and criteria used. System quality aspects are mainly assessed by usability criteria, while the rest of the criteria are evenly divided between information quality and service quality. The remaining evaluation criteria mapped, such as innovation and creativity, fall out of the model. Our analysis also reveals that the assessments are rarely grounded on standardized and objective measures, and that the actual user opinions are ignored in the evaluation process.

Keywords: Web awards, website evaluation, DeLone and McLean Model, system quality, information quality, service quality.

1 Introduction

Quality assessments in a web award context have become regular events in many countries, and show that honouring excellence on the web is a growing phenomenon. Even though there is a gap between the Oscar movie awards and web awards, the concept of showing beauty is the key. Various EU projects, such as eGovMoNet[1] and EU-supported awards, as well as various researchers, are addressing how to approach evaluation of website quality (e.g. [1], [2]). Private consulting companies are also increasingly tackling the issue of website quality evaluation (e.g. [3]). The question about having a high quality website is now probably more important than ever and requires that governments today present effective websites with their clear mission. Quality assessment is therefore a critical part in order to satisfy the users' needs and requirements, and make them achieve their goal.

---

[1] eGovMoNet is a Thematic Network co-funded by the European Commission (CIP project number 224998, Project period: 01-05-2008 – 01-05-2010) to establish a community to review national eGovernment measurement frameworks.

M.A. Wimmer et al. (Eds.): EGOV 2009, LNCS 5693, pp. 198–209, 2009.

We bring the DeLone and McLean model [4] which captures information quality, system quality, and service quality, into an eGovernment context, and through this we map the use of evaluation criteria in ten Scandinavian web awards. We choose to focus on a sample of web awards in Scandinavia given the well-established record of adoption of Information Technology in the public sector that characterizes Scandinavian countries. Our analysis may give us some insight into to what extent the model features shortcomings as far as public sector use in this context is concerned.

In this paper, web awards are defined as national awards in which the aim is to evaluate a number of websites drawing on shared evaluation criteria, and in which winners are chosen by a jury on the grounds of the outcome of an evaluation process. In some of the awards the participants have to sign up for participation, while in others the websites are signed up automatically. These latter are usually the ones organized by the government and where the participants belong to the public sector (e.g. municipalities and government websites). Both public and private websites today are very complex, and to some extent it is difficult, and probably even not equitable, to evaluate all websites following the same set of criteria. Therefore, the use of evaluation criteria varies among the awards.

Drawing on these considerations, we address the following research question: *Through which criteria is website quality measured in national website awards?* This research question will be tackled by looking at two key aspects of web awards: (1) the use of system-, information-, and service quality criteria; (2) the use of objective versus subjective evaluation criteria.

The paper is divided into six sections. The next section deals with background and prior research of website quality assessment. Section three presents the research framework, based on the DeLone and McLean Model of IS success, and the fourth section describes the research methods used. Findings are reported in section five, distinguishing between the two key aspects addressed by the research question. Finally, we sum up the contribution of the paper and indicate two propositions for further research on the topic area.

2 Website Quality Assessment – Background and Prior Research

Web awards have become regular events in Norway, Sweden and Denmark, as well as in other countries. The type of feedback and the evaluation processes vary among the awards. In private web awards the type of feedback often depends on the price for participation, the time spent on the evaluation process, as well as on the context and purposes of the individual award. In awards organized by the government, the feedback to the participants seems to be more detailed and informative in order to satisfy political intentions and goals. The process of quality assessment of public websites in Norway started in 2001 and has since been carried out annually with an increased number from around 550 to 700 websites. The project has had quite an impact on eGovernment development in Norway and is used by the government to monitor the fulfillment of the objectives stated in the national eGovernment plan eNorway 2009. Denmark is the only country that has been doing similar work and to the same extent since 2001, with the project named *Bedst på Nettet* ("Best on the Net") [5]. In 2008 the Danish award assessed around 600 websites on criteria pertaining to user-friendliness, advances in e-government, utility, openness and technical accessibility. Every year awards are given for the best public website, based on benchmarking and outcomes of the evaluation. To a certain extent, one Swedish award carries out a similar type of evaluation as Norway and Denmark, primarily focusing on public websites and innovation in e-services, where the target group is citizens and business. The use of measurement scales varies across different awards. However, there are overlaps and heterogeneous patterns. Due to the quality assessment process, this type of evaluation commonly distinguishes between technical and manual assessment. Technical assessment is often used to evaluate technical aspects of the websites such as, for instance, the total size (in kb) of the websites and the presence of broken links. Manual assessment is primarily based on visual checks of the structure and the information presented, done by an evaluator. Both types of tests could be repeated, by another evaluator, with almost the same results.

The term website quality is widely used, both in practice and in the research literature, and therefore its meaning needs to be defined for each individual study. There are differences regarding which aspects of websites are deemed to contribute to high quality, as well as regarding the purpose and aim of the measurement [6], [7], [8]. In the public sector in Norway and Denmark, for instance, central guidelines for quality indicators have been launched. According to the quality assessment of public websites in Norway (done by The Agency for Public Management and eGovernment), the following definition of website quality has been used: "The quality of websites is defined as that public information and services on the Internet must meet a predefined standard or level that can satisfy some central user needs" [5]. In the research literature, website quality is not a consistently defined term either, even though it is often used to report or evaluate websites [9], [10], [11], [12]. A number of frameworks of website quality have been developed [13], [14], but they do not lead to a standard measure that is universally accepted. DeLone and McLean [4] in their updated IS success model demonstrate that quality requires an understanding of the users and of user satisfaction. However, Sharkey et al. [15] address difficulties in measuring e-commerce success by implementing the DeLone and McLean model, and consider the influence of quality on e-commerce. Methods used in the evaluation process commonly are: observing users, asking users, asking experts, user testing, inspections and modeling users' performance [16], [17]. Automated tests are also regularly used, especially when it comes to technical assessments like, for instance, accessibility requirements [18], [19]. Returning to the quality assessment in web awards, these are always done as analytical evaluation. The common way is to evaluate all the websites on the basis of the same set of criteria, and having the most highly ranked companies eventually judged by a jury (an expert group).

3   Research Framework

The original DeLone and McLean IS Success Model published in 1992 provided a comprehensive framework for measuring IS success as a result of the performance of Information Systems [20]. This framework was based on theoretical and empirical Information System research conducted by a number of researchers in the 1970-80s. A decade after, the authors published an updated model capturing three website quality aspects: system quality (adaptability, availability, reliability, response time, usability), information quality (completeness, ease of understanding, personalization, relevance, security), and service quality (assurance, empathy, responsiveness). In this framework, system quality is related to the Internet environment, measuring the desired character-istics of a website. Information quality captures the content issue, while service quality is the overall support delivered by the service provider. Its importance is most likely greater than previously estimated since the users are now customers, and poor user support will translate into lost customers and lost sales. Service quality is relevant for public websites that need to serve the citizens, and meet their expectations and re-quirements. The model from DeLone and McLean is widely used in the research litera-ture to measure IS success [21], [22], [23], [24]. Each of the website quality aspects is measured by underlying dimensions. According to previous research, there are differ-ent ways of measuring website quality, and in this study the evaluation criteria from the awards could be mapped in several ways. In order to categorize definitions of web-site quality aspects, we use the three website quality aspects (system quality, informa-tion quality, service quality) of the IS Success Model from DeLone and McLean as a framework. Even if this is a general framework that is used to define information sys-tem success, we still find it appropriate for use in this study. Many of the same aspects are relevant for a website presentation, and the framework provides an operationaliza-tion of each of the three quality aspects presented.

4 Methodology

In this paper we look at ten web awards in the Scandinavian countries, Norway, Denmark and Sweden. During the mapping process there were some challenges in fitting into the DeLone and McLean Model. Therefore, we extended the table with the category of "other aspects". As the study adopts an exploratory perspective to a field that still is relatively uninvestigated, we do not aim at providing an exhaustive cover-age of all web awards in Scandinavia. In order to collect data, the presentations on the awards homepages (or related sites) were analyzed, resulting in the following web awards from Scandinavia being selected.

There is a huge difference between the awards website presentations, ranging from those with rich and with detailed information, to those featuring almost nothing. Some of the awards have also changed their websites during the data collection period; thus, information from the last available version or last search in databases was used. The final search was completed in the middle of November 2008. The data collected was translated into English for use in this paper. In order to categorize the evaluation criteria in the web awards, we mapped the categories on the basis of the website quality aspect of the DeLone and McLean IS Success Model. First, we collected the data regarding the evaluation criteria; second, we mapped the criteria based on the model; finally, we ana-lyzed the contribution to each of the quality aspects. There are three limitations that we need to point out: (1) the criteria we map are the high level criteria (only the criteria naming is used in the categorization), which means that the operationalization of the criteria is not taken into consideration in this study, as is in some of the awards it is unknown to the researchers; (2) the mapping has been done according to the researchers' own interpretation of the evaluation criteria in the DeLone and McLean Model; (3) the researchers have only used the information presented at the organizers' websites.

Table 1. Web awards from 2008 included in this paper

Country	Web Award	Organizer of the Award	Assessing public websites	Assessing private websites
Norway	Norge.no	The Agency for Public Management and eGovernment	X	
	Farmandprisen Beste Nettsted	Farmand Activum	X	X
	Årets nettsted	The Norwegian Communication Association	X	X
	Rosingprisen	The Norwegian Computer Society	X	X
	Gulltaggen	The organization for interactive marketing	X	X
Sweden	Guldlänken	Vinnova and the Swedish Association of Local Authorities and Regions	X	
	Web Topp 100	IDG Internetworld	X	X
Denmark	Bedst på Nettet	The National Danish IT and Telecom Agency	X	
	E-handelsprisen	The Danish Distance Selling and E-business	X	X
	Digitaliseringsprisen	Rambøll Management Consulting	X	

In addition to the mapping, we interviewed the organizers of a web award in Norway assessing public websites (The Agency for Public Management and eGovernment). The purpose was to get insights from a project manager's perspective. Two explorative interviews with open-ended questions with participants in the Danish award *Bedst på Nettet* were also carried out. The participants were randomly selected among winners during the last years and interviews were carried out at the one-day award conference in Denmark in 2008. The statements from the interviews were driven by an unstructured approach where the goal was to understand how the participants found the award important in order to improve the quality of the website.

5 Findings

5.1 System-, Information-, and Service Quality Criteria

Using the DeLone and McLean IS Success Model [4] we mapped the evaluation criteria from the web awards in 2008 in three categories, system quality, information quality and service quality. Drawing on this model we have the opportunity to present the importance of each of the three quality aspects in a Scandinavian web award context. Some of the evaluation criteria in these awards measure one or more quality aspects, and in some of the awards the criteria stand outside any of the measures; we have therefore added a fourth category to capture these ("other aspects"). Each of the evaluation criteria has been named under only one website quality aspect (either system-, information-, or service quality) or "other aspects", even if some of the criteria could have been marked under two aspects. By this we mean that some of the evaluation criteria could fit into e.g. both system- and service quality.

The findings in Table 2 show that when we map the evaluation criteria by using the three quality aspects (system-, information- and service quality), system quality is the most frequently used quality aspect in the Scandinavian awards. However, the criteria vary from technical design features to user-friendliness. Moreover, usability is a keyword in this quality dimension that refers to how easy it is to find information and services on the website. Unsurprisingly, the quality of use is very important – but the user's subjective view seems to be left out in the evaluation process. More precisely, most of the awards ignore the actual use and therefore they can only be used at best for improvements of trivial features of the website quality.

Secondly, when it comes to measurement of information quality – which captures the content issue, including the text presented and the quality of content in general – this also seems to be important. There is agreement in the literature [25] that the main reasons why people return to a website are ease of understanding, completeness, personalization and security. These are important aspects both for public and private websites. However, we propose that information quality is not measured very broadly, and that it is mostly related to e.g. the extent to which contact information is presented and the website provides updated news. One reason for this absence in the awards may be that information quality is time consuming to measure. Service quality refers to the overall support delivered, measured by assurance, empathy and responsiveness [4].

In our mapping the quality of services also refers to digital self-services and the provision of services to the users in general. To a certain extent, this is also related to system quality, since the system needs to arrange for the technical requirements. In the column named "other aspects" we presented the evaluation criteria that are difficult to map in any of the three quality aspects from the DeLone and McLean Model. However, measurement of assurance, empathy and responsiveness seems to not be directly measured, through e.g. contacting the service provider in order to assess the service level. Summarizing, these findings show that measures as innovation and creativity are widely used when it comes to awards organized by private companies or organizations, even though they are not captured by the model.

Table 2. Evaluation criteria from the awards categorized by using the DeLone and McLean model

Country	Web Award	System Quality	Information Quality	Service Quality	Other Aspects
Norway	Norge.no	Accessibility, user-adoption	Useful content		
	Farmandprisen Beste Nettsted	Ease of use	Content		Made-for-the-medium, promotion, emotion
	Årets nettsted	Accessibility, navigation and interaction, internal search, external search	Text and communication		Concept and design, target group, key lfunctions, innovation and complexity
	Rosingprisen	User-friendliness, functionality, technology and design			Innovation
	Gulltaggen	Navigation			Interactivity, reactivity, innovation, usefulness
Sweden	Guldlänken	Efficiency, layout, interaction design	Use of language and pictures	Exchange of services, follow up and administration	Innovation, overall experience
	Web Topp 100	Structure and navigation, functional design	Content quality		Creativity and innovation of the use of the Internet, development during the last year
Denmark	Bedst på Nettet	Navigation, user-friendliness technical accessibility	Web communicationopenness and usefulness	Digital self- service	
	E-handelsprisen	Accessibility	Openness and usefulness	Digital self- service	
	Digitaliseringsprisen			Digital services	Digital collaboration, innovation, measurable benefits in digital projects and the capability on focusing on the user's needs

5.2 Objective versus Subjective Evaluation Criteria

Measurement of website quality can be done in various ways. According to Ølnes [5] evaluations of websites can be divided into four groups, (1) self-evaluation, (2) expert evaluations, (3) user tests and user surveys and (4) automated tests, mainly of technical characteristics. Different methods may not necessarily lead to the same results and Ølnes [5] reported that, in relation to the award *Bedst på Nettet* in Denmark, "results showed that the expert evaluations were not necessarily correlated with the user test of the same website". Among these methods, expert evaluation is widely used in a web award where the evaluation criteria are based on a standard set of measures and guidelines. This means that the assessment of the same website could be repeated (by another evaluator) with the same results. These types of measures often consist of (1) visual checks of the navigation structure and details of the information presented, and (2) technical assessments of e.g. download time, the coding and number of broken links. The use of measurement scales typical consists of text alternatives where the evaluator chooses the most suitable answer. Subjective aspects are related to the "look and feelings" aspect and seem to be left out in the evaluation process that all the participants (websites) go through. Moreover, the user's interest from a subjective point of view, which could be the evaluation of the extent to which users actually can complete typical tasks, is also left out in this process.

Table 3. Jury comments on three of the winners of Bedst på Nettet 2008 in Denmark

Winning website	Comments from the Jury
www.frederiksberg.dk	This website provide us with logic and intuitive division in three main entrances to the content of the website, simple design with a great balance between pictures and text, consistent navigation. The information on the website is easy to understand.
http://bibliotek.stevns.dk	In order to meet the user's requirements the website presents pictures and icons that communicate the content and makes it intuitive to navigate on the website. The website has a clear focus about the target group, and the site is optimized in order to provide the users with personalized information.
http://www.kts.dk	Technique does not have to be unsexy! And this is a splendid example. The website is designed for the target group and the main page presents lots of opportunities without losing the overview, and gives the users fast access to relevant information. The users can also check their e-mail by using the mobile phone. The web design is good with a balance between text and pictures.

After the objective evaluation process has taken place, the websites get ranked by score and those with the highest score are nominated for winning a prize for best website. At this stage the role of the jury is important. Moreover, when the jury finally chooses a winner for each of the award categories (e.g. best design or most innovative website), the comments and justification are not primarily grounded on objective, but rather on subjective measures seen from an expert point of view. The jury is typically a mix of web practitioners, business people and academic staff. The extent to which the jury has any guidelines in this final phase is still unexplored. Table 3 provides an example of some of the comments to the winners in the Danish awards *Bedst på Nettet* in 2008. Here we can find some interesting arguments for why the jury actually chose the winners.

The use of evaluation criteria in these web awards, and the extent to which they lead to website quality improvements, are objects of debate. One of the winners of the Danish award *Bedst på Nettet* in 2008 points out: *"We spend a lot of effort in order to fulfill the criteria, but we think there is too much focus on accessibility, even if it is important"*. Another one said: *"If a website wins a prize one year there is no need to do considerable changes in order to get highly ranked the following year. There is lack of user involvement and assessment based on look and feelings. Anyway, fulfilling the criteria's is important in our work, but I think they level for receiving full score could be higher."* Standardized objective measures rather than subjective ones (e.g. opinions from real users of the websites) seem to be dominant.

As stated by the project manager of the award organized by the Norwegian Agency for Public Management and eGovernment, some participants have similar comments regarding the use of evaluation criteria: *"We received some criticism: that we measure the content of the website to a small extent, and that some of the criteria are not relevant for all the websites. We do know that there is an overload of technical criteria, but the reason is that we are dependent on an objective evaluation within a limitation of resources"*. Moreover, *"It is difficult to change the evaluation criteria, but we are in a dialogue with The Norwegian Language Council for developing criteria regarding the content presented at the website. We have also discussed about dividing the websites into categories, so we can measure relevant aspects of different types of public websites. But this change is not possible within the limitations of resources we have today"*. The methods used are less time-consuming and comprehensive compared to traditional usability testing. Summing up, in web awards expert evaluations is widely used, there are standardized objective criteria and the users' voice from a subjective point of view is ignored.

Today, more than ever, new e-services are important to meet the users' expectations for effectiveness and use. Web 2.0 is the new generation of applications where the users are highly involved, and platforms such as Facebook, Wikipedia and YouTube make it possible for users to communicate in a new way. In the web awards in Scandinavia it seems that the quality assessment in 2008 presented a lack of this dimension to get valuable feedback in the evaluation process.

6   Conclusion and Further Research

Improvement of website quality has been analyzed in this paper through the lenses of national web awards in three Scandinavian countries, Sweden, Norway, and Denmark. Using data from public and private sector awards in 2008, the award categories and variables were mapped using the DeLone and McLean Model. Limitations of the study are related to possible biases in the mapping process which was carried out, based on the authors' interpretation and on the choice of the cases for data collection through the interviews. However, the paper aims at filling a gap regarding the research area of national web awards, which is still largely under-investigated.

Returning to our research question, *"through which criteria is website quality measured in national website awards?"*, findings show that: (1) in web awards the assessment of system quality, e.g. through various usability measures, is frequently used. However, the users and the actual use of the websites seem to be ignored. Information quality is typically measured by the use of text and language, and by the extent to which they are easy to understand. When it comes to service quality, this seems to be measured by which services are actually provided. While presenting digital services is important, there is a lack of measurements related to the extent to which the organizations actually provide service quality to the users, through e.g. empathy and quality of feedback. The evaluation criteria that fall out of this model are more creative aspects as innovation and concept. Drawing on this, it seems like the feedback can be used at best only for the improvement of trivial technical requirements, which are not likely to materialize in business benefits. (2) Website quality assessments in a web award context are mainly based on standardized objective measures, which means that the evaluation process could be replicated with almost the same results. The evaluation is done by experienced evaluators. The measures are primarily related to visual checks and automated assessment measuring technical aspects of the websites. Awards arranged by the government, in particular, are detailed and informal, and provide guidelines for how to improve the quality. After all the websites have gone through a screening process, the best websites with the highest score are finally judged by a jury. The winners are commonly highlighted as best practice examples.

As far as future scenarios of research are concerned, regarding the first set of findings it is surprising that what are considered to be the traditional Scandinavian IS methods (living labs, situated practices, user involvement, etc.) are not addressed in the web awards analyzed. This calls for additional research on whether the way website quality is measured is actually just a show with no connection to how information systems are developed, or whether it could lead to benefits for businesses. Thus, using the DeLone and McLean Model, in the follow-up research we will address if and how the attention to the actual improvement of website quality leads to business benefits.

Moreover, the outlier aspects that we highlighted under "other aspects", which include some web 2.0-oriented features, could be argued to have highlighted some possible shortcomings of the DeLone and McLean approach. These shortcomings could be argued to be related to the fact that it is essentially based on a market model (citizens as consumers).

Regarding the second set of findings, we suggest that the traditional and conservative choice of variables and methods can misguide the optimization of website quality and consequently can endanger the future for institutionalized web awards. The web 2.0 technologies allow the users (and others) to form ad hoc communities to give their feedback on the websites. The possibility of factoring in this feedback (by using blog crawlers, etc.) and using this as part of the awards has been ignored thus far, but appears to be a road to explore in future research and practice regarding web awards.

References

1. Elling, S., Lentz, L., de Jong, M.: Website Evaluation Questionnaire. In: Wimmer, M.A., Scholl, J., Grönlund, Å. (eds.) EGOV 2007. LNCS, vol. 4656, pp. 293–304. Springer, Heidelberg (2007)

2. van Velsen, L., van der Geest, T., ter Hedde, M., Derks, W.: Engineering User Requirements for e-Government Services. In: Wimmer, M.A., Scholl, H.J., Ferro, E. (eds.) EGOV 2008. LNCS, vol. 5184, pp. 243–254. Springer, Heidelberg (2008)
3. Wauters, P., Nijskens, M., Tiebout, J.: The user challenge: benchmarking in the supply of online public services, Capgemini, Paris, France (2007)
4. DeLone, W.H., McLean, E.R.: The DeLone and McLean Model of Information Systems Success: A Ten-Year Update. Journal of Management Information Systems 19(4), 9–30 (2003)
5. Ølnes, S.: Accessibility of Norwegian Public Web Sites. In: Proceedings of NOKOBIT, pp. 225–236. Tapir akademiske forlag, Norway (2007)
6. Seethamraju, R.: Measurement of user-perceived web quality. In: 12th European Conference on Information Systems, Turku School of Economics and Business Administration, Turku, Finland (2004)
7. Zeithaml, V.A., Parasuraman, A., Malhotra, A.: Service quality delivery through web sites: A critical review of extant knowledge. Journal of the Academy of Marketing Science 30(4), 362–375 (2002)
8. van Iwaarden, J., van der Wiele, T., Ball, L., Millen, R.: Perceptions about the quality of web sites: a survey amongst students at Northeastern University and Erasmus University. Information & Management 41(8), 947–959 (2004)
9. Loiacono, E.T.: Webqual (tm): a web site quality instrument. University of Georgia Athens, GA, USA (2000)
10. Ruiz, J., Calero, C., Piattini, M.: A Three Dimensional Web Quality Model. Web Engineering, 469–491 (2003)
11. Calero, C., Ruiz, J., Piattini, M.: Classifying web metrics using the web quality model. Online Information Review 29(3), 227–248 (2005)
12. Calero, C., Ruiz, J., Piattini, M.: A Web Metrics Survey Using WQM. In: Koch, N., Fraternali, P., Wirsing, M. (eds.) ICWE 2004. LNCS, vol. 3140, pp. 147–160. Springer, Heidelberg (2004)
13. Barnes, S.J., Vidgen, R.: WebQual: An Exploration of Web-site Quality. In: Proceedings of the 8th European Conference on Information Systems, pp. 298–305 (2000)
14. Barnes, S., Vidgen, R.: Data triangulation in action: Using comment analysis to refine web quality metrics. In: Proceedings of the 13th European Conference on Information Systems, Regensburg, Germany (2005)
15. Sharkey, U., Scott, M., Galway, I., Acton, T.: The Influence of Quality on the Success of E-Commerce Systems. In: Proceedings of the 14th European Conference on Information Systems, pp. 1711–1722 (2006)
16. Sharp, H., Rogers, Y., Preece, J.: Interaction Design: Beyond Human-Computer Interaction, 2nd edn. Wiley, Chichester (2007)
17. Aladwani, A.M., Palvia, P.C.: Developing and validating an instrument for measuring user-perceived web quality. Information & Management 39(6), 467–476 (2002)
18. Bauer, C., Scharl, A.: Quantitative evaluation of Web site content and structure. Internet Research: Electronic Networking Applications and Policy 10(1), 31–44 (2000)
19. Olsina, L., Papa, M.F., Souto, M.E., Rossi, G.: Providing Automated Support for the Web Quality Evaluation Methodology. In: Fourth Workshop on Web Engineering, at the 10th International WWW Conference, Hong Kong, pp. 1–11 (2001)
20. DeLone, W.H., McLean, E.R.: Information Systems Success: The Quest for the Dependent Variable. Information Systems Research 3(1), 60–95 (1992)
21. Seddon, P.B.: A Respecification and Extension of the DeLone and McLean Model of IS Success. Information Systems Research 8(3), 240–253 (1997)

22. Seddon, P.B., Kiew, K.Y.: A partial test and development of the DeLone and McLean's model of IS success. In: Proceedings of the International Conference on Information Systems, pp. 99–110 (1994)
23. Rai, A., Lang, S.S., Welker, R.B.: Assessing the Validity of IS Success Models: An Empirical Test and Theoretical Analysis. Information Systems Research 13(1), 50–69 (2002)
24. Wang, Y., Liao, Y.: Assessing eGovernment systems success: A validation of the DeLone and McLean model of information systems success. Government Information Quarterly 25(4), 717–733 (2008)
25. Gehrke, D., Turban, E.: Determinants of Successful Website Design: Relative Importance and Recommendations for Effectiveness. In: Proceedings of the 32nd Hawaii International Conference on System Sciences, pp. 1–8 (1999)

Post Recommendation in Social Web Site

Long Wang, Justus Bross, and Christoph Meinel

Hasso Plattner Institute, University Potsdam
14482, Potsdam, Germany
{long.wang,justus.bross,christoph.meinel}@hpi.uni-potsdam.de

Abstract. Web 2.0 applications attract more and more people to express their opinions on the Web in various ways. However, the explosively increasing information in social web sites requires an effective mechanism to timely filter and summarize social common interest, and the moderator needs this mechanism as well to recommend the proper posts and guide public discussions. In this paper, we discuss the problem of recommending post in online communities: we firstly cluster the posts in groups based on their semantic relations, then filter the potential clusters by computing the cluster's support, and finally select the recommended posts as content representatives considering global and local support from each clusters. We compare different feature selections between tags, keywords and topics on cluster formation, and discuss their differences. The human judgement in our experiment shows that the recommendation based on marked tags is much more effective and concise than those on keywords and hidden topics.

Keywords: Post recommendation, Clustering, Global Support, Local Support.

1 Introduction

Web 2.0 technologies supply richer interaction possibilities for end users to compose their posts and discuss common topics in online communities. The users publish or annotate personal content without much central governance in various forms, from plain text to rich multimedia, which could generate vast amount of noisy information. Moreover, the content on social communities tends to have a shorter lifespan because much of it focuses on an ongoing real-world event or a current "hot" topic, and public interest in such content and subsides rapidly over time. A post is a basic entry in a social web site on a particular subject from textual commentary, description, to graphics or videos. Thus several ways are used to facilitate users to find the interesting posts: using an internally embedded searching engine, selecting the posts in reverse chronological order in front page, clicking the ones listed in "most favorite" or "top N rated", or making a choice by entering the target categories or tag cloud.

In this paper, we propose a method on post recommendation in online communities. Using a case study of IT-Gipfelblog (http://it-gipfelblog.hpi-web.de), which is a webblog to discuss ICT (Information & Communications Technology)

M.A. Wimmer et al. (Eds.): EGOV 2009, LNCS 5693, pp. 210–221, 2009.

related topics. The process of discovering recommended posts is briefly described in the followings: we firstly cluster the posts based on their contents; then only the clusters having a support over a defined threshold are treated as the potentials for supplying recommended posts; and finally from each potential clusters, the posts having global and local support are ranked as part of recommendation list. The clustering step guarantees the clear conceptual distance between recommended posts and the global or local support ensures the confidence on the support from users. We try using different features such as tags, keywords and topics in clustering posts and evaluate their differences on the final recommended post lists.

The rest of the paper is structured as follows: in section 2 we describe the features related with a post in social web site. Section 3 provides the methods of clustering and representative selection based on support. After that, we discuss our experiment results in section 4. Finally, conclusion and future work are given in section 5.

2   Features Related for a Post

Selecting proper features to represent every post is the necessary work in post recommendation. Here, we illustrate the related features for a post. Generally, the features are classified into two categories: content-related and usage-related.

2.1   Content-Related: Keywords, Tags and Topics

The basic methodology proposed in text modeling is to reducing each document in the corpus to a vector of real numbers, each of which represents the importance of a content feature to that document. In online communities, the features related to the content of a post can be tags, keywords or topics. Most of previous work on text modeling is keyword based. Keywords are stemmed and filtered with the weights showing their importance to a post, and the weight is usually measured by tf or $tf \times idf$ approaches.

Tag marking is a prominent feature in social web sites, by which the users annotate their personal understandings and preferences on a post. Recently, discovering tag-based social interest attracted much attraction [1,2]. [2] found user-generated tags are condense and consistent with the web content and more concise and closer to human understanding. Tags are especially indispensable to represent semantics for the posts with only videos. However, tags depend highly on the activities of users, though they have a higher-level abstraction on the content. Compared with tags, the keywords related with a post could have a large scale, but each of them owns a measurable weight.

Different from tags and keywords which are observable, the topics or contexts are latent. Latent semantic analysis (LSA) was discussed to discover the topics hidden in corpora and proven to be efficient for text modeling [3,4]. Recently LSA is used for detecting online reviews or opinions [5,6]. Topic feature has two advantages compared with tags and keywords: one is that topics are closer to the semantics of text and more closer to human understanding, and the other is the scale of topics is much smaller than tags and keywords. The basic LSA is illustrated as follows: suppose there are T topics hidden in a corpora D composing by $|D|$ documents, the probability of the observed word-document pair (d, w) can be obtained by the marginalization over the latent topics: $P(d, w) = \sum_{i=1}^{T} \theta_d(t)\varphi_t(w)$, where $\varphi_t(w)$ is the distribution of word w in latent topic t, while $\theta_d(t)$ is the distribution of topic t in document d. Probabilistic latent semantic indexing(PLSI) [4] and Latent Dirichlet Allocation (LDA) [3] are the two representatives for topics discovering. The difference between PLSI and LDA is that PLSI generates each document as a mixture of T topics, where the mixture coefficients are chosen individually for each document, while LDA generates a document by a word distribution $\varphi_t(w)$ from a prior Dirichlet distribution $Dir(\beta)$ for each latent topic and by a topic distribution $\theta_d(t)$ for a document d from the symmetrical Dirichlet distribution $Dir(\alpha)$ as well.

In this paper, we use tags, keywords and topics to represent the posts separately, and compare the difference between their clusters and recommendations.

2.2   Usage-Related: Hits, Comments and Votes

Web usage mining [7,8,9] is already widely discussed to discover the interesting usage patterns on information portal web sites: association rules [7], sequence [8] or other graphic patterns [9]. **Support** is the factor to measure the fraction of transactions that satisfy the union of items in the consequent and antecedent of a pattern[7]. And the number of hits (or clicks) is the basic parameter to measure the support of a page or a usage pattern among the web users.

In web 2.0, besides hits, the interactions between web content and users are supplemented by the comments and votes. The comments after a post are remarks from readers on the topics in the post or the other comments. Votes are the numeric evaluations from readers on the quality of one post, and a higher average vote from enough voters is the direct measurement to measure the post quality from usage side. It is reasonable to assume that the users, who gave their comments or votes for a post , are included in the users who accessed this post, however they are the small part of whole population. We found that some posts received high hits number but fewer comments and votes, while some posts having high votes and controversial comments attracted few clicks. This means that users concentrate more on the quality of the post itself than the reactions from others. So we assume that there is no strong dependency among hits, comments and votes. And we investigate how to use hits, comments and votes to measure how a post is welcomed by users.

Dedicated to a public political social web site, the recommended posts should not exclude those welcomed by small groups of users, which could represent the common interest for a stable small group of users. Based on hits, comments and votes, a post can be simply classified into four classes shown in Table 1. From this table, the posts in c1 should be recommended due to the positive reactions over a big population and those in c4 did not show their attractions to the users and should not be recommended. A post in c3 should be noticed

Table 1. Classification based on hits, comments and votes

class	hits	comments & votes	notes
c1	high	high	globally welcome
c2	high	low	need to be improved
c3	low	high	locally welcome
c4	low	low	no interest

and recommended as well, because low hits mean it has a relatively smaller group of visitors compared with the posts from c1, but high comments and votes indicate it has the interesting topics for this group. A post in c2 shows that it has the popular information, but needs to be improved due to the low votes and comments. This investigation convinces that the recommended posts are selected from c1 and c3. From usage-related features, the difference between c1 and c3 is on the number of hits (support): post in c1 has a higher hit number than that in c3. Simply, we call that the post from c1 has a "**global support**" and the one from c3 has a "**local support**". Our results thoroughly discussed in later sections show that most of recommended posts have local supports which means a minor group of users.

3 Post Recommendation

The process of post recommendation is comprised of two steps: one is post clustering, in which the posts having similar subjects are clustered; and the other is representative posts selection based on global and local support.

3.1 Posts Clustering

The mostly used algorithms for document clustering is hierarchical agglomerative clustering (HAC) [10]. This method begins by placing each document into a distinct cluster, and pairwise similarities between every two documents are computed firstly. Then two closest clusters are merged into a new cluster. This process, computing pairwise similarities and merging the closest two clusters, is repeatedly applied. For different applications, this iteration process stops when reaching one of two conditions:

1. the number of clusters reaches the predefined number;
2. all the pairwise similarities between clusters are lower than the threshold.

Depending on how the similarity between two clusters is defined, we could obtain different clustering results. Moreover, the pairwise similarities between every two posts are the basic components to compute the similarity between two clusters. Cosine similarity,

$$sim(p_1, p_2) = \frac{\sum_{i=1}^{K} w_{p_1,i} \cdot w_{p_2,i}}{\sqrt{\sum_{i=1}^{K} w_{p_1,i}^2} \cdot \sqrt{\sum_{i=1}^{K} w_{p_2,i}^2}},$$

is used when a post is represented as a vector of tf or $tf \times idf$ showing the importance of its tags or keywords, because the post-tag or post-keyword matrix are typically sparse and cosine similarity can be fast computed.

The most common methods to compute the similarities between two clusters are single linkage, complete linkage and group average linkage. To differentiate the similarity computing in afterward sections, we call this similarity as "Inner Cluster Similarity". We use group average linkage to define the inner cluster similarity.

Definition 1 (Inner Cluster Similarity). *Given two clusters C_1 and C_2 generated under the same clustering strategy, the inner cluster similarity between C_1 and C_2 is defined as:*

$$sim_I(C_1, C_2) = \frac{\sum sim(p_{1,i}, p_{2,j})}{|C_1| \times |C_2|},$$

where $p_{1,i} \in C_i$ and $p_{2,j} \in C_j$.

Now we discuss the cluster formation based on topics retrieved by LDA. Base on LDA, every post was taken as being generated from the dirichlet distribution of all topics, so the post-topic matrix is a matrix where each cell is valued by a real number. The same situation is for topic-keyword matrix. We follow the strategy in [3] to inference and estimate the values of these two matrixes. The number of topics is a huge reduction compared to tags and keywords, and it acts the same function as number of clusters based on tags or keywords. For every topic, we use the top K posts based on their posterior possibilities, which forms a post cluster for this topic related with top K' words as well. In this case, one post could appear in multiple clusters, and the same to words.

3.2   Discovering Potential Clusters and Representative Posts

Firstly we discuss how to remove the senseless clusters and select the potential clusters for recommendation. The clusters with tiny response from users are definitely not proper to recommend, though the moderator has to be ware of the reason of getting few feedback. The support of a cluster is composed by the supports of the posts it has. A threshold showing the support is used to select the potential clusters for recommendation.

Discussed in section 2.2, two kinds of posts are considered for recommendation: one is those having high hits, high comments and votes (global support), and the other is those having low hits, but high comments and votes (local support). We use P_G and P_L to represent these two kinds respectively. Due to the limited space on a web page for post recommendation, only the representative post is selected from one cluster. So the judgement between P_G and P_L is needed. The algorithm listed in following is used to find the representative posts from clusters over a post set.

4   Experiment Results and Evaluation

We implement post recommendation in a German political blogging platform: IT-Gipfelblog (gipfelblog.hpi-web.de), which was founded at June of 2006 with

Algorithm 1. Representative post selection from clusters

1: Given clusters X from post set D
2: Initialize 3 post sets P_H, P_M and P_V having maximum hits, comments and votes:
   $P_H \leftarrow \emptyset$, $P_M \leftarrow \emptyset$, $P_V \leftarrow \emptyset$
3: **for** each cluster C_i **do**
4:     Find the m posts $\{p_1, ..., p_m\}$ that were published within a defined period ($m \leq n$) in C_i
5:     Select the post $p_{i,H}$ with the maximum hits number, $P_H \leftarrow P_H \cup p_{i,H}$
6:     Select the post $p_{j,M}$ with the maximum comment number, $P_M \leftarrow p_{j,M}$
7:     Select the post $p_{k,V}$ with the maximum votes number, $P_V \leftarrow p_{k,V}$
8: **end for**
9: Posts with global support P_G: $P_H \cap (P_M \cup P_V)$
10: Posts with local support P_L: $(P_M \cup P_V) - P_H \cap (P_M \cup P_V)$

the sponsorships from German government and some big IT-companies, and now serves as a successful public political online community on IT policies. Besides every registered user can publish his/her ideas on any IT topics, most of posts are invited from the politicians and other high representatives from economy and research institutions.

4.1   Comparison among Tags, Keywords and Topics

In this section, we give the comparisons between tags, keywords and contexts on post recommendation. The post clustering is implemented over 264 posts covering most IT topics, and 953 tags were marked for these posts. After stemming and removing the common used stop words and those happening in less than 3 posts, we got 3180 keywords from 9447 stemmed words. The tags include the single words and pieces of combinations of words as well. Table 2 shows the general statistics on tags, keywords and posts.

Table 2. Max, Min and Avg number

	$\frac{Tags}{Post}$	$\frac{Keywords}{Post}$	$\frac{Posts}{Tag}$	$\frac{Posts}{Keywords}$
Max.	36	314	109	117
Min.	2	1	1	3
Avg.	12	62	4	8

After stemming the tags, we found the size of intersection between tags and keywords is 386, which means that 60% tags used are not included in the text of posts. Though both tags and keywords reflect the post content, they are generated from differen ways: the former are from the feedback of users or the metadata from moderator, while the later come from the post itself and retrieved by NLP technologies. During clustering the posts featured by tags and keywords respectively, two clusters are emerged only if their inner cluster similarity is over the predefined threshold. Under different inner cluster similarity thresholds, the log marginal likelihood is computed in every iteration process, which measures the distance between the cluster model and data set. The likelihood refereed in [11] is computed as:

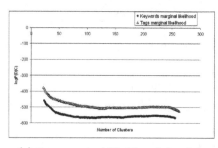

(a) Log marginal likelihood $\theta = 0.1$

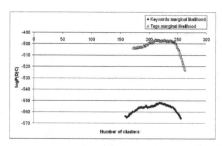

(b) Log marginal likelihood $\theta = 0.3$

Fig. 1. Clusters Tags vs. Keywords

$$L(D|C_1, ..., C_K) = \sum_{k=1}^{K} \sum_{p_i \in C_k} log P(p_i|C_k).$$

Figure 1 shows the log marginal likelihood under different inner cluster similarity thresholds based on tags and keywords. It is noted that the number of posts based on tags is larger than that on keywords, because there are some posts with only video while without text, but they are marked with tags as well. From figure 1, we explain the followings:

1. the empty areas between 0 and the starting curves in both (a) and (b) mean that no new clusters are emerged after some iterations under a inner cluster similarity threshold. Lower threshold generates more clusters than higher one.
2. with the decreasing of inner cluster similarity threshold, the maximum likelihood is caught at the stop of iterations. If similarity threshold is set 0, the maximum likelihood is got at the only one cluster including all the posts.
3. clusterings under tags and keywords generate the similar likelihoods distribution, only differs numerically, and differentiate at the points of iteration stop and maximum likelihood.
4. the reason, why there is the great shifting of the number of clusters generated at the maximum likelihood from $\theta = 0.1$ to $\theta = 0.3$ (25 vs. 200 for both tags and keywords), is the compositions of posts: some of them are highly semantically related, some are in lower similarities, and some posts are totally in uninvolved topics.
5. likelihood computed based on tags is always larger than that on keywords, this is because the dimension of tags is much smaller than that of keywords which reflects a high confidence on representing the concept of posts.

The higher inner cluster similarity threshold could generate more clusters, and lower threshold could cluster posts more compactly. However, it makes no sense to cluster all posts in one cluster by setting inner cluster similarity threshold as 0. In practice, the number of clusters formed at the maximum likelihood is even far larger than the allowed recommendation space within a web page, usually 10 and 20 at most. The dimensions of tags and keywords affect greatly selecting inner cluster similarity threshold.

Besides the similarity on general distribution of cluster numbers between tags and keywords, we investigate the difference on the composing of clusters internally. Because tags and keywords are in different scales, setting the same inner cluster similarity threshold for both is not a prerequisite. So we compare the cluster composing under the same cluster number. We use X_T and X_K to name the cluster sets based on tags and keywords under the same cluster number constraint over the post set D, note that $|X_T| = |X_K|$ and each is one division over D. If X_T and X_K are correlated, X_T and X_K likely have large overlap. Extremely, $X_T == X_K$ when $|X_T| = |X_K| = 1$ or $|X_T| = |X_K| = |D|$. Before computing the correlation between X_T and X_K, we firstly give the definition of "Outer Cluster Similarity".

Definition 2 (Outer Cluster Similarity). *Given two clusters C_1 and C_2 generated by different strategies over the same dataset, the outer cluster similarity between C_1 and C_2 is computed by Jaccard similarity:*

$$sim_O(C_1, C_2) = \frac{|C_1 \bigcap C_2|}{|C_1 \bigcup C_2|}.$$

Based on the outer cluster similarity between two clusters, we define the clustering similarity between two cluster sets over the same post set.

Definition 3 (Clustering Similarity). *Given two cluster sets X_1 and X_2 over the same post set $D = \{p_1, ..., p_n\}$, the clustering similarity between X_1 and X_2 is defined as:*

$$sim_C(X_1, X_2) = \frac{\sum_{p_1}^{p_n} S(C_{1,p_i}, C_{2,p_i})}{|D|},$$

where $C_{1,p_i} \in X_1$, $C_{2,p_i} \in X_2$, $p_i \in C_{1,p_i}$ and $p_i \in C_{2,p_i}$.

Because each post is assigned to only one cluster during any clustering strategy, this clustering similarity measures the biggest overlap between two cluster sets. The times to compute clustering similarity between X_1 and X_2 is $[\max(|X_1|, |X_2|), n]$.

HAC method merges two clusters with maximum similarity at each iteration, which means that the number of clusters based on tags and keywords reduce in the same pace during iteration process. The Figure 2 shows the clustering similarity between tags and keywords at different emerging steps under inner cluster similarity threshold $\theta = 0.0$, which means that all the posts are merged into one cluster at the last iteration step. From this figure, the clustering similarity gets its minimum value when the cluster number is 17.

Now we discuss the cluster results based on hidden topics retrieved by LDA. We tried setting different number of topics and selected the top K posts to form a post cluster for every topic. Because one post could appear in multiple clusters, for the formed clusters $X = \{C_1, ..., C_T\}$ representing T discovered topics, we compute the coverage of clusters X over the whole post set D to measure its capacity.

$$coverage(X, D) = \frac{|\bigcup_1^T C_i|}{|D|}.$$

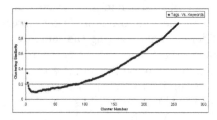
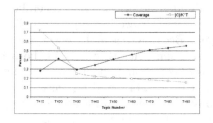

Fig. 2. Clustering Similarity: Tags vs. Keywords   **Fig. 3.** Coverage of clusters under LDA using K topics

The low coverage indicates a high overlap between post clusters, which means that the current topics can not discriminate each other. Similarly, $\frac{|\bigcup_1^T c_i|}{K*T}$ is used to measure theoretically the percentage of unique posts against the happenings of all posts in clusters. Figure 3 gives these two measurements under different topic numbers. It is noticed that with the increasing of topic number, the coverage increases in a stable tendency (when $T > 20$). However, a high number of topics is not practical in compacting the posts, and an idea number topics should have the ability to compact the posts effectively and have a high coverage as well.

Seen from Figure 3, a high coverage with a high compacting ability is reached at $T = 20$, which means that partition the posts into 20 clusters is an ideal choice. By investigating the top related stems for every topic, especially after overlooking the common stems, most of topics have their relatively clear concept boundary. For example, "topic 1" is about "working position", "topic 2" is about "energy problem" and "topic 3" is on "globalization". However, few of them have no clear topics, for example, "topic 16" is about "interview" which has no "IT" semantics and "topic 9" is about "IT company" but has no clear concept. However, the discovered topics by LDA are not so semantically intuitive as those by tags-based, and this will be further discussed in "evaluation criteria" section. The reason for this is that the quality of selected words for each posts is highly domain biased, which is the same problem to keyword-based clustering.

4.2 Evaluation Criteria

To evaluate the clustering results theatrically, routine criteria like precision and recall are usually used. These criteria are properly necessary when clustering on huge corpus in which the independency can be regarded in the generation of documents. However, in a political social web site, where the number of posts is controlled and the related topics are guided and maintained by the moderator, precision and recall criteria are not practical in the post recommendation. But it is necessary to evaluate the quality of recommended posts, especially for the discrimination between tags, keywords, contexts and users. Here we use the human reviews to approximate this goal. In our experiment, 3 moderators were asked to do the following work:

1. read through the clustering results and give the topics of every clusters
2. in every cluster, mark the posts that are not properly related with the cluster's topics

Based on the feedback of reviewers, we could evaluate the precision of different clustering strategies.

Figure 4 gives the moderators' reviews on the clusters based on tags under inner cluster similarity threshold 0.1, and 21 clusters are built. The topics every cluster is related are selected from the marked tags.

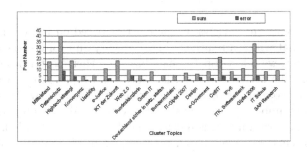

Fig. 4. Error in clustering based on tags

Figure 5 shows the reviews on the clusters based on top 10 keywords under inner cluster similarity threshold 0.1, and 36 clusters are built. The topics every cluster has are selected from the keywords. Definitely, we tried as well selecting top 20 and top 30 keywords to cluster posts. The numbers of clusters by selecting top K keywords under the same inner cluster similarity threshold are not greatly different, which is shown in Figure 7. When considering all the keywords stemmed from posts into clustering, $K > 61$ averagely, the number of clusters is 20 under similarity threshold 0.1. This means that the number of keywords (but must reach one value) are unimportant to represent the content of posts. However, the compositions of clusters are greatly different between top 10, 20 and 30 words. Moreover, it is hard to summarize the topics a cluster has when using top 20 and 30 keywords, this shows that the clustering error is very high.

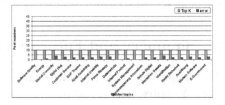

Fig. 5. Error in clustering on top 10 keywords

Fig. 6. Error in clustering on 20 topics by LDA

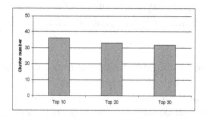   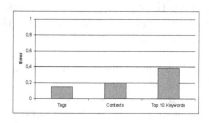

Fig. 7. Cluster numbers: top K words   **Fig. 8.** Error: tags vs. top 10 keywords

Figure 6 presents the reviews on the clusters based on LDA. The number of topics is set 20, at which a relatively high capacity and compactness is reached. For every cluster, we select top 10 posts based on their posterior possibilities.

We compare the reviews on tags, keywords and topics from two sides: error ratio and quality of cluster topics. The former is measured by the sum of posts divided by the number of posts clustered in error, and the comparison is given in Figure 8. The error on tags is much lower than those on top K keywords and contexts. The clusters topics based on tags are much human understandable than those on keywords and contexts, for example, the non semantic topics like "women", "interview", "vorstand" and "AG" are found from keywords.

Though the gap exists apparently between the "topics" marked by human reviews and retrieved automatically by clustering or LDA, clustering based on tags supplies a much intuitive and exact results than keywords and contexts based methods. It is observed that there is no difference on representative selection based on support between tags, keywords and contexts. From the final recommended posts based on tags, keywords and contexts, it is found that the number of recommended posts in global support is much less than that in local support. This shows that the users gathered into small groups based on their common interest in online community. Though clusterings based on tags, keywords and context recommend some common posts, they give different recommendation results. This is affected by the different weights of tags, keywords and contexts for a post. However, for the recommended posts in local support, clustering based on tags supplies better recommendations than contexts and keywords, which have low hits with high votes and comments. The clustering based on context plays not convincible in global support than on tags and keywords, from which the recommended posts do not have high hits than those from tags and keywords.

5   Summary and Future Work

This paper gives a methodology on post recommendation in political social web site. We solve this problem by firstly clustering the conceptual related posts based on tags, keywords and contexts separately, and secondly the potential interesting clusters are chosen based on their supports and finally the representative posts are selected from each cluster by detecting global and local support.

From the experiments, we draw the following conclusions on post recommendation in online communities:

1. Using tags is an efficient way to select representative post, because of its lower dimension and intuitive human understandability.
2. users usually gathered into small groups on common interests, and local support vs. global support is a potentially necessary policy in online communities.

However, we have to mention the limitations of our approach: one is that the data on posts and users are not enough large, we should try this recommendation mechanism on other online communities; and the other is the assumption that there is no topic drifting between one post and its comments, which assume that the comments contribute the welcomeness of a post, while in online communities it is often that the end discussion is totally different from the initially published theme.

References

1. Bateman, S., Brooks, C., McCalla, G., Brusilovsky, P.: Applying collaborative tagging to e-learning. In: Proc. Tagging and Metadata for Social Information Organization Workshop, WWW (2007)
2. Li, X., Guo, L., Zhao, Y.: Tag-based social interest discovery. In: Proc. WWW (2008)
3. Blei, D.M., Ng, A.Y., Jordan, M.I.: Latent dirichlet allocation. Journal of Machine Learning Research 3, 993–1022 (2003)
4. Hofmann, T.: Unsupervised learning by probabilistic latent semantic analysis 42(1-2), 177–196 (2001)
5. Lu, Y., Zhai, C.: Opinion integration through semi-supervised topic modeling. In: Proc. WWW (2008)
6. Titov, I., Mcdonald, R.: Modeling online reviews with multi-grain topic models. In: Proc. WWW (2008)
7. Agrawal, R., Imielinski, T.: Mining association rules between sets of items in large databases. In: Proc. SIGKDD (1993)
8. Pei, J., Han, J., Mortazavi-asl, B., Zhu, H.: Mining access pattern efficiently from web logs. In: Terano, T., Chen, A.L.P. (eds.) PAKDD 2000, vol. 1805. Springer, Heidelberg (2000)
9. Zaki, M.: Efficiently mining frequent trees in a forest. In: Proc. SIGKDD (2002)
10. Frakes, W.B., Baeza-Yates, R.A. (eds.): Information Retrieval: Data Structures & Algorithms. Prentice-Hall, Englewood Cliffs (1992)
11. Meila, M., Heckerman, D.: An experimental comparison of several clustering and initialization methods. Machine Learning (1998)

Channel Integration in Governmental Service Delivery: The Effects on Citizen Behavior and Perceptions

Willem Pieterson[1] and Marije Teerling[2]

[1] University of Twente, Center for e-Government Studies
Department of Media, Communication and Organisation
P.O. Box 217, 7500 AE Enschede, The Netherlands
w.pieterson@utwente.nl
[2] Novay, The Netherlands
Marije.Teerling@novay.nl

Abstract. Governmental agencies continuously work on the improvement of their service delivery through an array of channels. To improve service satisfaction and to reduce the cost of service delivery, channel integration gets more popular with governmental agencies. In a quasi experimental longitudinal field study, we assess how the integration of the telephone channels of three organizations affects citizens' satisfaction with government service delivery. The results show that respondents are more positive about the integration of channels after the integration took place. Further, channel integration has a positive effect on citizens' satisfaction, but does not seem to affect channel usage and channel perceptions.

Keywords: channel integration, multi-channeling, e-Government, channel management.

1 Introduction

Governmental service delivery is changing at a tremendous pace. Now that the 'new' service channels, such as websites and e-mail have reached a certain degree of maturity; new developments have arrived. New channels, such as chat and sms, are awaiting their breakthrough, but a more relevant issue appears to be the increasing popularity of multi-channel management [1]. Not withstanding the increase in use of the electronic channels, their success is not undisputable given the ongoing popularity of the traditional service channels [2, 3]. As a result government agencies are rethinking their multichannel management strategies in order to achieve both cost efficiency and customer satisfaction [4]. A key feature of this appears to be the integration of various service channels to benefit from the strengths and weaknesses of each single channel and optimize planning and data synchronization. The central governments of Canada and Australia are for example integrating all channels in one service delivery concept. Flumian and Kernaghan (2007) show that the Service Canada model is build on (1) the integration of government information systems, (2) a closer cooperation within the chain and between departments and (3) a better cooperation with private industry.

M.A. Wimmer et al. (Eds.): EGOV 2009, LNCS 5693, pp. 222–233, 2009.

Integration takes place within single organizations and as the Service Canada model shows also across organizations. Collaboration takes place across government agencies but increasingly also with private organizations. For example, the Dutch (government) car registration process takes place via the (privately owned) post offices. In the Netherlands government agencies work together in the service chain around work and income, namely municipalities, and two executive agencies (the Centre for Work and Income (CWI) and the Employees Insurance Agency (UWV). On a local level these agencies have started to integrate their service delivery process. Citizens can already access their services through one front desk for some time. The web sites and call centers from these agencies are currently being integrated.

Even though the Service Canada model is well known and cooperation amongst government organizations seems to be good practice, relatively little is know on the effects of this type of channel integration. Does integration affect citizens satisfaction levels, does it provide a better service delivery and in the end result in a decrease of channel usage – i.e., is it more efficient for the organizations to combine their service delivery?

Knowledge – beyond good practices and examples – on these effects is crucial information for government agencies to determine if channel integration and all the necessary investments are worthwhile. With this study, we increase current knowledge on these effects by presenting the findings of a two year longitudinal survey study that centered on the integration of the call centers of three separate government agencies. The main question we try to answer in this study is:

To what extent does channel integration across various organizations have an effect on citizens' behavior and service perceptions?

This main question is subdivided in four empirical research questions:

1. To what extent does channel integration lead to higher levels of service satisfaction?
2. To what extent does channel integration lead to more positive attitudes towards the integration itself?
3. To what extent does channel integration lead to changes in channel usage and channel preferences?
4. To what extent does channel integration lead to changes in channel perceptions?

First, we review relevant literature on this field; we discuss multi-channel management and earlier empirical findings on channel integration. Next, we present the research method used in the study before presenting the findings of the longitudinal study. Finally, we present the main conclusions and points for discussion.

2 Theoretical Background

The continuous technological progress and especially the rise of the Internet have resulted in numerous new service channels. Besides the well known 'traditional' channels such as the front desk, phone and (snail) mail, citizens can now access government services for instance through e-mail, websites, sms, mobile phone or chat. This plethora of new channels brings along new challenges for the management of the service delivery, which has come to be known as the field of multichannel management [e.g. 4, 5, 6]. Research on multichannel management is being executed in several areas of expertise, from government to management studies. Based on several definitions [1, 5] we conclude that multichannel management is focused on using multiple channels to deliver information and/or services to customers. In a government setting the goal of multichannel management is usually two folded. On the one hand multichannel management aims at satisfying citizens while on the other hand it should contribute to a more efficient and effective service delivery process, that is reduce the costs of the service delivery. It is this two folded goal that makes the real challenge for government organizations. Channel integration might provide part of the solution to address this challenge.

Channel integration – as perceived by the customer – implies a strong level of compatibility and a seamless interaction across the channels [7]. Or as Payne and Frow [8] indicate the structure and flow of activity in the various channels should be integrated in such a manner that they consistently deliver the value proposition in the eyes of the customer. In the marketing literature various studies indicate that channel integration results in positive effects for organizations. Firstly, it is shown that the online channels impact not only the online channel but the customer's overall satisfaction and image of the company [9-11]). Secondly, the joint effect of coordinated and consistent communications is greater than the sum of effects of single communications [12]. Hence, it is assumed that the organization provides better service delivery if channels are integrated [12-16].

At present, different strategies with respect to the management of service channels and the level of channel integration are used by government agencies. Pieterson & van Dijk [1] provide a distinction between four different service channel strategies (see Table 1). They argue that the Integrated Position is a good option for government agencies, since this strategy offers the possibilities to tailor services to different groups while not excluding service access to different groups. Further, government agencies try to steer their citizens to the channels were they are helped best at the least time this strategy also has the potential to be cost efficient and help increase satisfaction. Hence, channel integration might lead to both an increased channel satisfaction on behalf of the citizen and a cost reduction for government agencies.

Besides these four strategies, Ebbers et al. [4] suggest a model that explores what channel integration might look like at a more detailed level. This model suggests that different modes of contact should be dealt with via different channels based on the complexity and ambiguity of the task. The OECD has a similar multi-channel model based on an analysis of service delivery among different tax organizations [17], This model also relies on the integration of channels, but is focused on the integration of data in the back-offices not the front-office channels. The central idea behind this strategy is that all the data are centrally stored and used by all front-office channels. In addition the OECD approach thus holds that different channels are able to complement each other, thereby improving the quality of the service delivery.

So, whereas the first model relies on the integration of different channels with different types of services, the second model relies on integrating back-offices whereby the different front offices are fed from the integrated back-office and mid offices systems.

Table 1. Overview service channel strategies

Nr	Name	Explanation
1	Parallel positioning	Channels are positioned next to each other. Citizens are free to choose their channels and services are available through each channel.
2	Replacement positioning	Channels can replace each other. Assumption is that channels can be superior or inferior to each other. Customers would prefer to use the best channel and therefore one channel would replace another.
3	Supplemental positioning	Channels have supplemental values; each channel has its own characteristics that make it suitable for certain types of services. Therefore, governments should offer services via the best suited channels.
4	Integrated positioning	All channels are integrated in the entire service delivery process. This means that all services are offered via all channels, but that strengths and weaknesses of channels are used in their design. Citizens are guided to the 'best' channels and channels seamlessly refer to each other.

The two models of multi-channel management focus on, as we see it, one type of channel integration; integrating the different channels of one organization in one combined channel or service delivery concept. However, as we see it, a second type of channel integration exists, namely the integration of channels from different organizations in one mutual channel. One key example is the Service Canada model that offers citizens one-stop multichannel and multi-jurisdictional access to customer oriented services [18]. Canadian citizens seem to value the possibilities of free channel choice, consistent and accurate information across all channels but most of all a single government service point regardless of which organization(s) is providing the service [18]. Another example is the 311 call center from New York City in which different telephone channel of various organizations are integrated. Hence, we propose that channels can be integrated horizontally; within one organization or vertically; across different organizations. Figure 1 shows these two types of channel integration.

Overall, it seems that channel integration across one or multiple organizations might be a key factor to the improvement of public service delivery. In this study we focus on vertical channel integration and we assess how the integration of the telephone channels of three organizations affects service satisfaction, attitudes towards integration, the perceptions of the different channels and channel usage.

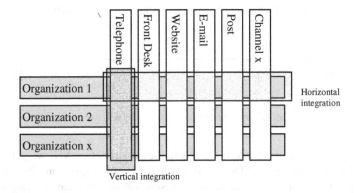

Fig. 1. A framework of different types of channel integration

3 Method

To answer the research question a close cooperation was set up with the three before mentioned government agencies responsible for carrying out legislation around work and income. Based on the case of a middle sized municipality and the efforts of these agencies to joint forces in their services delivery channels, we were able to investigate the effects of channel integration on citizen behavior and perceptions. In subsection 3.1 we discuss the background of this case and the data collection and in section 3.2 the measures used in the survey.

3.1 Case Description

In the Netherlands several government agencies are together responsible for the legislation and execution around the work and income chain. Several of those, the Centre for Work and Income (CWI), the Executive Agency for Employees' Insurances (UWV) and the municipalities have joined forces to improve work processes and joint service delivery. One of the premises of their joint multichannel service delivery vision is that the customer – i.e. citizen – should perceive the service delivery in the chain as a logical whole. In order to determine how the joint vision can be executed in 'real life', several locations are being used to test it. These test locations comprise of a joint workspace where citizens can access the services around work and income.

One of these test locations is in a large Dutch municipality (155.000 inhabitants) where the three organisations have been collaborating since 2005 to improve their services under the name "Activerium". In 2005 the organisations installed a single (physical) one stop shop and in the end of 2007 a joined telephone number was realized. The plan is to develop a web portal in the future.

To answer the research question and to see whether the integration of service channels is a success (as perceived by citizens), we conducted two survey studies at different moments in time (M1&M2). This implies that our design is that of a quasi experimental study, this quasi experimental setting allows us to draw inferences from the implementation of the channel integration. To make sure that we could address the supposed differences to the manipulation, all other aspects of the service delivery process (e.g. opening hours, number of service agents) were kept the same during the study. Figure 2 shows the changes in service delivery, and the two moments of measurement.

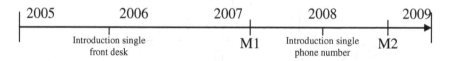

Fig. 2. Timeline channel integration Activerium

Although for this study we do not focus in the period before M1, we gathered data on channel usage from even before the introduction of the single front desk. The focus of this paper is on the change in service satisfaction due to channel integration and more specifically, the telephone integration.

For M1, we gathered data in December 2007 and January 2008. For M2, we gathered data in May / June 2008. We surveyed citizens that contacted the Activerium via the three channels (front desk, phone and web). Citizens who visited the front desk were asked to fill in the questionnaire behind a computer. Visitors of the website were redirected to the electronic questionnaire. Citizens that used the phone were surveyed via the phone. A total number of 233 respondents filled in our survey for M1; 100 citizens via the front desk, 100 via the telephone and 33 via the website. For M2; these numbers are 106, 101 and 23 (n=230). For both measurements, the number of respondents via the website is lower than anticipated. Nevertheless, the number of respondents is sufficient for statistical analysis. The characteristics of the respondents were compared to those of the population and the sample reflected the characteristics of the population sufficiently, so the data were not weighted.

3.2 Measures

Satisfaction regarding service delivery was measured using Likert scales. Since few of these measures exist, we used measures of our own that deal with a selection of service delivery aspects. These aspects used to determine satisfaction with the service are 1) opening hours (for front desk and telephone), 2) waiting (loading) time, 3) reachability, 4) completeness of the answer, 5) full answer in one attempt, 6) personalized answer, 7) clarity of the answer, 8) clarity about follow up action, and 9) friendliness. The attitude towards channel integration was measured using a number of propositions; these are listed in the table below. All propositions were measured using five point Likert scales, ranging from "totally disagree" to "totally agree". The propositions are shown below (see Table 2).

Table 2. Operationalization of attitudes towards channel integration

Nr.	Proposition
1	The service delivery improves through the introduction of one telephone number
2	The introduction of one number in stead of the existing numbers renders the service delivery more confusing
3	Service delivery will improve in the future when one website will be introduced
4	Through the introduction I will be send more often from pillar to post
5	The introduction of one telephone number meets my needs
6	The introduction of one front desk (counter) has improved service delivery
7	My impression of the service delivery through the physical one stop shop is positive
8	Through the introduction of the physical one stop shop I am sent less from pillar to post

For channel perceptions we used the same measures as [19]. These are mostly existing measures of (perceived) channel characteristics. Each perception was measured using one question. Regarding these characteristics, the respondents were asked to indicate which channel suited the characteristic best. Table 3 gives an overview of the channel characteristics and the corresponding survey questions.

Besides the channel characteristics, we asked respondents which channel they use most often for their contacts with government agencies and which channel they prefer for their government contacts.

Table 3. Operationalization of channel characteristics

Concept	Operationalization
Price	This channel is for me the cheapest.
Ease of use	This channel is the easiest to use.
Usefulness	This channel is the most useful.
Experiences	With channel I have the best experiences.
Service	This channel provides me the best service.
Contact speed	Via this channel I am in contact with the government the quickest.
Immediacy of feedback	This channel provides immediate feedback.
Multiple cues	This channel allows information to be transmitted in multiple ways.
Language variety	This channel enables to use varied language
Personalization	This channel allows me to tailor messages to my own circumstances

4 Results

In the following section we present the survey results from the longitudinal study. First, we compare M1 (2007) and M2 (2008) regarding the satisfaction with the service delivery itself, followed by the attitudes towards the channel integration, channel preference and usage and finally channel perceptions.

4.1 Service Satisfaction

We tested if the service delivery is evaluated positively in both 2007 and 2008. Using one sample t-tests, we calculated if respondents are either positive (mean>3) or negative (mean<3). For both 2007 and 2008 we see favorable attitudes towards service delivery (see Table 4).

Table 4. Service delivery perceptions in 2007 and 2008

	2007			2008		
	Mean	t	p	Mean	t	p
Opening hours*	3.91	15.479	0.000*	4.13	22.712	0.000*
Waiting (loading) time	3.09	1.192	0.000*	3.33	4.584	0.000*
Reachability	3.41	5.647	0.000*	3.53	6.955	0.000*
Completeness of the answer	3.50	7.536	0.000*	3.68	10.443	0.000*
Full answer in one attempt	3.45	7.105	0.000*	3.55	8.269	0.000*
Personalized answer	3.44	6.813	0.000*	3.66	10.379	0.000*
Clarity of the answer	3.59	9.812	0.000*	3.72	11.163	0.000*
Clarity about follow up action	3.61	10.750	0.000*	3.86	15.740	0.000*
Friendliness	3.90	15.344	0.000*	4.07	18.251	0.000*
*significant at p=.05						

Next, we analyzed the differences between 2007 and 2008 (see Table 5). We find an overall increase in satisfaction after the introduction of the integrated telephone number. We find that citizen satisfaction increases for all last chosen channels in comparable patterns as shown in Table 5. We do not find differences based on demographics (age, gender and education). Apparently, citizens are more positive regarding each aspect of the service delivery process.

Table 5. Differences in service delivery perceptions between 2007 and 2008

	Mean		t	md	df	p
	2007	2008				
Opening hours[1]	3.91	4.13	-2.74	-0.211	404	0.006*
Waiting (loading) time	3.09	3.33	-2.36	-0.239	460	0.018*
Reachability	3.41	3.53	-1.16	-0.120	460	0.247
Completeness of the answer	3.50	3.68	-1.87	-0.173	460	0.063
Full answer in one attempt	3.45	3.55	-1.08	-0.099	460	0.281
Personalized answer	3.44	3.66	-2.44	-0.221	460	0.015*
Clarity of the answer	3.59	3.72	-1.49	-0.131	460	0.138
Clarity about follow up action	3.61	3.86	-3.22	-0.253	460	0.001*
Friendliness	3.90	4.07	-2.03	-0.167	460	0.043*

*significant at p=.05
[1]Only for front desk and telephone, not for website

Since no changes in the service delivery process took place between M1 and M2, except the telephone integration, it appears that the integration itself has a positive effect on service satisfaction.

4.2 Attitudes towards Channel Integration

The second aspect of the study regards the attitudes towards channel integration. We tested if the attitudes are positive or negative. In 2007, we find that the idea of one single website is met with a positive attitude and the (past) introduction of the single front desk is evaluated positive. However, in M1, the respondents are neutral (or ambivalent) towards the introduction of the single phone number. After the introduction, we find that this form of channel integration is seen as positive (see Table 6).

Table 6. Attitudes towards channel integration

	2007			2008		
	Mean	t	p	Mean	t	p
The service delivery improves/d through the introduction of one telephone number	3.132	1.633	0.104	3.570	6.146	0.000*
The introduction of one number in stead of the existing numbers renders the service delivery more confusing	2.880	-1.462	0.145	2.296	-7.796	0.000*
Service delivery will improve in the future when one website will be introduced	3.512	6.413	0.000*	3.530	5.394	0.000*
Through the introduction of the single phone number I will be/am being send more often from pillar to post	3.097	1.259	0.209	2.661	-3.363	0.001*
The introduction of one telephone number meets/met my needs	3.013	0.174	0.862	3.465	5.037	0.000*
The introduction of one front desk (counter) has improved service delivery	3.233	3.027	0.003*	3.803	9.066	0.000*
My impression of the service delivery through the physical one stop shop is positive	3.436	6.347	0.000*	3.800	8.972	0.000*
Through the introduction of the physical one stop shop I am sent less from pillar to post	3.330	4.770	0.000*	3.543	5.572	0.000*

*significant at p=.05

Through the pairwise comparison of 2007 (M1) and 2008 (M2) (see Table 7), we find the result that attitudes have changed in a positive direction for each aspect, except for the propositions that "Service delivery will improve in the future when one website will be introduced" and "Through the introduction of the physical one stop shop I am sent less from pillar to post". Nevertheless, although attitudes haven't changed for these propositions, people are still positive regarding them. Here also, we find no differences regarding the channel through which the survey was administered and the demographic characteristics of the respondents.

Table 7. Comparison channel integration perceptions

	Mean 2007	2008	t	md	df	p
The service delivery improves/d through the introduction of one telephone number	3.13	3.57	-3.555	-0.437	448	0.000*
The introduction of one number in stead of the existing numbers renders the service delivery more confusing	2.88	2.30	4.787	0.594	450	0.000*
Service delivery will improve in the future when one website will be introduced	3.51	3.53	-0.149	-0.019	431	0.882
Through the introduction of the single phone number I will be/am being send more often from pillar to post	3.10	2.66	3.437	0.436	428	0.001*
The introduction of one telephone number meets/met my needs	3.01	3.47	-3.785	-0.452	440	0.000*
The introduction of one front desk (counter) has improved service delivery	3.23	3.80	-4.856	-0.57	443	0.000*
My impression of the service delivery through the physical one stop shop is positive	3.44	3.80	-3.239	-0.364	427	0.001*
Through the introduction of the physical one stop shop I am sent less from pillar to post	3.33	3.54	-1.782	-0.213	411	0.076

*significant at p=.05

4.3 Channel Preferences and Usage

The key question is if the integration of channels affects channel usage and channel preferences (see Table 8). This does not appear to be the case. In both 2007 and 2008, the telephone is the preferred channel, followed by the front desk. Albeit insignificant, it seems that the (past) integration of front desk and telephone have a positive effect on their usage and preferences, given the increase in percentage when comparing 2007 and 2008. It remains for the future to draw definite conclusions on this aspect.

Table 8. Channel preferences and usage

	Front Desk		Telephone		Website		E-mail		Post	
	2007	2008	2007	2008	2007	2008	2007	2008	2007	2008
Most used	26.98%	30.84%	50.70%	51.10%	11.63%	11.45%	6.51%	5.29%	4.19%	1.32%
Prefered	30.99%	36.56%	44.13%	45.81%	12.21%	10.13%	8.92%	7.05%	3.76%	0.44%

Here we find no differences between 2007 and 2008; χ^2 (4, N = 227) = 4.194, p=0.380 (for most used) and ; χ^2 (4, N = 227) = 7.892, p=0.096 (for preferred).

4.4 Channel Perceptions

It is possible that the integration of channels affects how people perceive the characteristics of the channels. For example, it might be that people find a channel more useful after its integration. We find, regarding all channel characteristics, no differences between M1 (2007) and M2 (2008) (see Table 9). This implies that the perceived (communicative) characteristics of the channels remain unchanged.

Table 9. Channel perceptions

	Chi-Square	Df	P
Personalization	3.434	4	0.488
Language Variety	2.395	4	0.663
Immediacy Feedback	3.396	4	0.494
Multiple Cues	3.833	4	0.429
Ease of Use	3.094	4	0.542
Usefulness	1.600	4	0.809
Contact Speed	3.877	4	0.423
Service	0.625	4	0.960
Price	3.994	4	0.677
Experiences	0.713	4	0.950

5 Conclusions

Multichannel management is a relatively new area of research. Whereas research has focused mostly on the electronic channels in the last decades, especially in eGovernment research, now scholars and practitioners start to realize that different channels should not be treated isolated, but that the available set of channels should be treated as a whole. We notice that this issue is of increasing importance to researchers and practitioners, given the costs associated with providing services through different channels. Even though numerous studies determine the effects of channel integration in a commercial setting, we notice a lack of empirical examination of the effects in a government multichannel setting.

We suggest two types of channel integration; horizontal integration (integration of different channels in one organization) and vertical integration (integration of a single channel across organizations). In this study, we focus on the effects of vertical channel integration. We had the unique opportunity to study the effects in a quasi experimental longitudinal setting. We studied them before and after the combination of three separate phone number in one new integrated phone service channel. The main question we answer in this study is:

To what extent does channel integration across various organizations have an effect on citizens' behavior and service perceptions?

While subdividing this main question in four empirical research questions, the aim of this study was fourfold 1) to study the effects of integration on service satisfaction and 2) attitudes towards the integration, 3) changes in channel usage and 4) changes in channel perceptions of citizens.

The results show that channel integration has a positive effect on both the service satisfaction and the attitudes towards channel integration. People are more satisfied with the process of service delivery for the majority of the service satisfaction aspects. However, we did not measure an increase in satisfaction for all aspects. Although all aspects of the service delivery process were evaluated positive and the normative satisfaction increased for all aspects, we found no significant differences between

2007 and 2008 for the reachability of the service and some aspects regarding the quality of the answer.

Regarding channel integration, we see the most important result of the study. Before the integration of the phone channels (m1), respondents were ambivalent regarding the channel integration. For example, respondents did not think that the service delivery would improve through the introduction of a single telephone number. However, in 2008, after the channel integration, respondents are positive regarding the integration. Citizens believe that the service delivery has improved significantly. This finding is important in two ways; first it shows that there is an actual effect of channel integration. Second, it shows the importance of longitudinal studies in the field. Studies such as this allow us to monitor how peoples' opinions may change over time. Had M1 been the only point of measurement, we would have been far less positive about the benefits of channel integration (at least concerning the telephone). This also has implications for the future development of eGovernment. The next step in channel integration would be to integrate the electronic channels of the different organizations. Our study shows that, over time, the attitudes are positive regarding this integration.

Third, we saw that there was no difference in channel usage and channel preference between the two points of measurement. Although channel marketing was no aim of the (quasi) experiment, the results show that channel integration does not directly affect channel behavior. To change citizens' channel behaviors other tools might be deployed, such as communication [20]. Finally, our study shows that channel perceptions remain unchanged after the channel integration. This suggests that, although citizens perceive differences in the service environment, they do not perceive the channels as different. It was to be expected that especially the amount of 'service' obtained via the telephone would increase, but this appeared not to be the case. Apparently, integration seems to affect the overall satisfaction with the service encounter but not the perceptions of channels.

Our study is the first to empirically test the effects of vertical channel integration in the public sector in a quasi experimental setting. The main conclusion we draw is that channel integration is a major contributor to the increase of citizens' satisfaction with government service delivery. However, multi-channel strategies mostly do not only aim at increasing customer satisfaction, but also on government cost efficiency [4]. Our study seems to indicate that channel integration is a useful tool to obtain both goals simultaneously. Future research should assess the costs and benefits of channel integration in more detail. Our work will continue in the observation of the electronic channels, but we foresee that scholars should also pay attention to the horizontal integration of channels and, one step further, the combination of both horizontal and vertical integration.

References

1. Pieterson, W., van Dijk, J.: Governmental Service Channel Positioning. In: Gronlund, A., Scholl, H.J., Andersen, K.V., Wimmer, M.A. (eds.) EGOV 2006. LNCS, vol. 4084. Springer, Heidelberg (2006)
2. van Dijk, J., Pieterson, W., van Deursen, A., Ebbers, W.: E-services for Citizen: The Dutch Usage Case. In: Wimmer, M.A., Scholl, J., Grönlund, Å. (eds.) EGOV 2007. LNCS, vol. 4656, pp. 155–166. Springer, Heidelberg (2007)

3. van Deursen, A., Pieterson, W.: The Internet as a service channel in the Public Sector. In: ICA Conference, Dresden, Germany (2006)
4. Ebbers, W., Pieterson, W., Noordman, H.: Electronic government: Rethinking channel management strategies. Government Information Quarterly 25, 181–201 (2008)
5. Neslin, S.A., Grewal, D., Leghorn, R., Shankar, V., Teerling, M., Thomas, J.S., Verhoef, P.C.: Challenges and Opportunities in Multichannel Customer Management. Journal of Service Research 9, 1–18 (2006)
6. Verhoef, P.C., Neslin, S.A., Vroomen, B.: Multichannel Customer Management: Understanding the Research-Shopper Phenomenon. International Journal of Research in Marketing 24, 129–148 (2007)
7. Teerling, M.L.: Determining the Cross-Channel Effects of Informational Web Sites (doctoral dissertation Rijksuniversiteit Groningen). Labyrinth Publications, Ridderkerk (2007)
8. Payne, A., Frow, P.: A Strategic Framework for Customer Relationship Management. Journal of Marketing 69, 167–176 (2005)
9. Kannan, P.K.: Introduction to the Special Issue: Marketing in the E-Channel. International Journal of Electronic Commerce 5, 3–6 (2001)
10. Porter, M.: Strategy and the Internet. Harvard Business Review 3, 63–78 (2001)
11. Sheehan, K.B., Doherty, C.: Re-Weaving the Web: Integrating Print and Online Communications. Journal of Interactive Marketing 15, 47–59 (2001)
12. Moriarty, S.E.: PR and IMC: The Benefits of Integration. Public Relations Quarterly Fall, 38–44 (1994)
13. Duncan, T., Moriarty, S.E.: A Communication-Based Marketing Model for Managing Relationships. Journal of Marketing 62, 1–13 (1998)
14. Dutta, S., Biren, B.: Business Transformation on the Internet: Results from the 2000 Study. European Management Journal 19, 449–462 (2001)
15. Katros, V.: A Note on Internet Technologies and Retail Industry Trends. Technology in Society 22, 75–81 (2000)
16. Yoon, S.-J.: Is the Internet more effective that traditional media? Factors affecting the choice of media. Journal of Advertising Research, 53–60 (2001)
17. OECD: Improving Taxpayer Service Delivery: Channel Strategy Development. OECD, Paris (2007)
18. Flumian, M., Coe, A., Kernaghan, K.: Transforming Service to Canadians: The Service Canada Model. International Review of Administrative Sciences 73, 557–568 (2007)
19. Pieterson, W., Teerling, M., Ebbers, W.: Channel Perceptions and Usage: Beyond Media Richness Factors. In: Wimmer, M.A., Scholl, H.J., Ferro, E. (eds.) EGOV 2008. LNCS, vol. 5184, pp. 219–230. Springer, Heidelberg (2008)
20. Teerling, M., Pieterson, W.: Government Multichannel Marketing; How to seduce citizens to the web channels? In: HICCS, Hawaii (2009)

Opening the Black Box: Exploring the Effect of Transformation on Online Service Delivery in Local Governments

Anne Fleur van Veenstra and Arre Zuurmond

Faculty of Technology, Policy and Management, Delft University of Technology,
Jaffalaan 5, 2628 BX Delft, the Netherlands
{a.f.e.vanveenstra,a.zuurmond}@tudelft.nl

Abstract. To enhance the quality of their online service delivery, many government organizations seek to transform their organization beyond merely setting up
a front office. This transformation includes elements such as the formation of
service delivery chains, the adoption of a management strategy supporting process
orientation and the implementation of enterprise architecture. This paper explores
whether undertaking this transformation has a positive effect on the quality of
online service delivery, using data gathered from seventy local governments. We
found that having an externally oriented management strategy in place, adopting
enterprise architecture, aligning information systems to business and sharing
activities between processes and departments are positively related to the quality
of online service delivery. We recommend that further research should be carried
out to find out whether dimensions of organizational development too have an effect on online service delivery in the long term.

Keywords: Transformational Government, Organizational transformation,
Quality of service delivery, e-Government.

1 Introduction

Over the last decades many different e-government initiatives have been introduced,
such as authentication mechanisms, electronic forms and geographic information
systems. Today, e-government is increasingly seen as an enabler of transformation of
government "that goes far beyond online service delivery" (p. 164) [1]. Instead of
merely setting up websites and information infrastructures, e-government is expected
to fundamentally change the way governments function [1-3]. In order for this new
generation of e-government initiatives to realize benefits for citizens and businesses, a
new mindset called Transformational Government is considered necessary [4]. The
service delivery of transformed governments is expected to allow for personalized and
pro-active services [5] and to enable setting up cross-agency portals [3]. To support
these advanced e-government initiatives, governments increasingly initiate organizational transformation.

Traditionally, government organizations are organized as functional hierarchies made
up of stove-piped departments supported by fragmented information technology [6].

M.A. Wimmer et al. (Eds.): EGOV 2009, LNCS 5693, pp. 234–244, 2009.

To realize online and integrated service delivery, however, multiple departments have to cooperate to perform a single service, creating a need for the formation of service delivery chains. Organizational transformation, therefore, aims for supporting these improvements in service delivery by adopting a process oriented view [7] and enabling information sharing across organizational borders [6]. According to literature on business-it alignment, the information systems and infrastructure should be attuned to this organizational transformation [8], which can be supported by the adoption of enterprise architecture [9]. Furthermore, also the management strategy deployed is likely to influence the degree to which transformational leadership is in place [10]. These are all factors expected to spur Transformational Government.

In practice, however, government organizations are still struggling to implement any of these organizational changes and little evidence is found of transformation taking place [5, 7]. Furthermore, it is yet unclear whether these transformational factors have any effect on service delivery. This research aims to fill this gap by opening the black box of transformation and exploring the relation of factors attributed to organizational transformation to the quality of online service delivery. In the Netherlands, seventy per cent of citizens' contact with the government takes place at the municipal level. Therefore, to explore these relations, we invited local governments taking part in a support program for implementing e-government initiatives to participate in this research. Surveys were sent out to around fifteen people involved in e-government development per organization. This resulted in a systematic collection of data about these transformational dimensions as well as about the quality of online service delivery of seventy local governments. These results were then analyzed to find out whether any relations can be found between transformational aspects and the quality of online service delivery.

In this paper, first, the theoretical background of Transformational Government is presented to identify factors that are expected to influence the quality of online service delivery. Secondly, the research set-up is described, followed by the analysis of the results. In section five, the findings will be discussed. Finally, we present conclusions and recommendations for further research.

2 Theoretical Background of Transformational Government

Transformational Government is concerned with realizing benefits from e-government [4]. However, as the transformational effect of information systems is complex and indirect at best [3], the need to change service delivery beyond setting up an electronic front office is felt. To enable increased effectiveness, organizational transformation is considered necessary. Seen to be a "complete change in character" (p. 15) [5], transformation is often a complex undertaking. It has been defined both as a product and as a process, referring to a paradigm shift of fundamental assumptions and to a gradual change in behavior of individuals within an organization; it is considered to be of "qualitative difference from what existed before" (p. 102) [11]. From literature, a number of factors can be identified that are expected to transform public administration beyond adopting e-government initiatives.

Government organizations are traditionally organized as functional hierarchies, in which specialized workers perform narrowly-defined tasks [6]. In these organizations 'siloed' departments, using 'stove-piped' knowledge and 'islands' of information technology, carry out their activities independently of other departments. Although this allowed departments to optimize their performance, this also resulted in customers having to deal with these departments separately instead of contacting the organization once with a service request. From a customer's perspective, however, services are often made up out of tasks carried out by multiple departments. Realizing service delivery in an integrated manner, therefore, requires departments to cooperate and to form horizontally oriented service delivery chains. The concept of a service delivery chain is closely related to the concept of a value chain. A *value chain* can be defined as invoking a number of activities to jointly create a product or deliver a service [12]. Value chains run through the entire organization, requiring changes to occur not only in the service delivering front office, but also in the back office [13].

Moreover, realizing integrated service delivery often requires multiple organizations to cooperate in order to diminish the administrative burden of citizens and businesses that no longer have to provide the same information to each organization separately. This, in turn, requires the improvement of information sharing across organizational borders [6] and the orchestration of activities in order to perform services coherently [14]. Performing services within a network, consisting of multiple departments or organizations, often leads to a redistribution of tasks, as activities are performed by the party that is best-equipped to do so. A focus on *core competencies*, which can be defined as those specific skills of an organization that set it apart from others [6], often results in the sourcing of non-core activities. This is expected to lead to the formation of shared service centers and, in time, to modular organizations [15]. Similar to the concept of a value chain, the modular organization allows activities to be divided into focused steps that can be invoked by processes. An advantage of modular organizations is increased flexibility because modules can more easily be replaced by others [16].

In order to support this organizational transformation, both management strategy and information infrastructure need to be attuned to the transformed situation. According to the *business-IT alignment* approach, the information technology employed has to be in line with the organizational strategy and business processes [2, 8]. To facilitate the creation of a common information infrastructure, enterprise architecture can be adopted to gain insight in the linkages between business and information technology [9]. Enterprise architecture can be used to ensure interoperability of information systems across departmental and organizational borders and to link technology to business processes. Furthermore, organizational transformation is not expected to take place overnight. It most likely requires a long-term process initiated by transformational leadership [10]. An innovative managerial orientation was found to be important for creating more effective e-government [17].

Transformational Government is, thus, considered to be far more invasive than implementing a service delivering front office. Instead, factors such as adopting process orientation, modularizing activities, improving information sharing across departmental and organizational borders, aligning information technology to business processes, deploying enterprise architecture and the presence of transformational leadership are also considered to have an effect on realizing better service delivery.

3   Research Set-Up

The factors identified from literature in the previous section can be broadly divided into three main dimensions of organizational transformation:

1.   Organizational development, including the formation of service delivery chains and the modularization of activities;
2.   Technology deployment, including the set-up and use of enterprise architecture, business-it alignment and the degree to which information technology is used to carry out process steps automatically; and
3.   Management strategy, including the managerial orientation and its focus on public value creation.

It is expected that organizational transformation along these three dimensions will enhance the quality of online service delivery. However, little transformation of public administration has been observed yet [5, 7]. Moreover, it is not yet well-known whether these transformational dimensions indeed have a positive effect on the quality of online service. To explore whether these dimensions influence the quality of online service delivery we set up two different surveys that were sent out to around one hundred local governments in the Netherlands.

One survey was set up for employees concerned with e-government implementation at the local level to assess the presence of these transformational dimensions within their organization. In the other survey, experts (*e-advisors*) were asked to assess the quality of online service delivery of these local governments. E-advisors are experts sponsored by the central government to guide local governments in their transformational efforts. Additionally, the Dutch government website benchmark (http://monitor.overheid.nl) was also used as a measure for the quality of local governments' online service delivery. This resulted in the conceptual model of this research presented in figure 1.

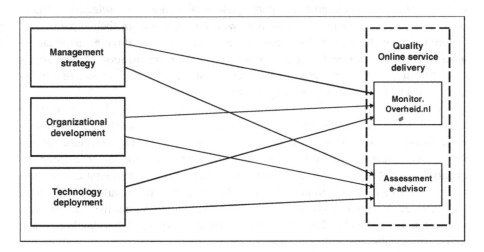

Fig. 1. Conceptual model of this research

The research was carried out among local governments involved in a program sponsored by the central government, which aims to support the implementation of e-government initiatives in Dutch municipalities. This allowed us to include both municipalities that were already undertaking transformational efforts as well as municipalities that did not yet transform. In this way, we could investigate whether the former organizations perform better in the area of online service delivery. The municipalities that are involved in this program receive funding for hiring an e-advisor. The main task of the e-advisor, who is an expert in the field of e-government, is to write an 'implementation plan' for setting up e-government initiatives in the municipality. As this requires that the e-advisors familiarize themselves with the municipal organizations and their online service delivery, they were asked to assess the quality of online service delivery. Scores ranged from 1 to 10, with 1 representing the lowest possible quality and 10 representing the highest possible quality.

An additional assessment of the local government's online service delivery quality was used in this research: the central government sponsored website benchmark (Monitor.overheid.nl). Every year, websites of all local governments are examined and ranked to establish to what extent these websites fulfill legal requirements for government's websites and to score them in terms of integrated and personalized service delivery on a scale from 0.0% to 100.0%. Comparison of the sample of local governments included in our research to the total population of Dutch municipalities showed that we included a sample that is almost perfectly representative.

On the level of the local government employees we needed to make sure that knowledgeable respondents would participate. From every municipality taking part in the support program, around fifteen employees participated in a simulation game. A simulation game is a setting in which a limited number of participants imitate a real-life situation within a short time-frame. The goal of this simulation game is to create awareness about the importance of information sharing in order to allow for the creation of service delivery chains. The participants of the game were selected by the e-advisor on the basis of their involvement with e-government in their organization. Before this game took place, these participants were asked to fill out a survey and to assess the transformational dimensions present in their organization. Again, scores ranged from 1 to 10, with 1 representing the lowest score for the presence of a transformational factor and 10 representing the highest score.

Over the course of a year, all local governments playing the simulation game were invited to participate in this research, resulting in the collection of data from the e-advisors and the employees of the same local government. Although this ensured that the persons filling out the survey were acquainted with the situation concerning the quality of online service delivery and the presence of transformational dimensions, there was also a limitation to this research. Municipalities taking part in this program have not yet undergone a complete transformation yet. Therefore, the data obtained are expected to reflect this limited and partial transformation and this should be taken into account while interpreting the data.

4 Data Analysis

Over the course of 2008, 104 local governments took part in the simulation game. All were invited to participate in this research. For 90 of these municipalities data was gathered from a total of 681 participants (an average of 7.6 participants per local government) and 70 e-advisors responded resulting in a full data set of these 70 municipalities (see table 1). In order to create an average score for each municipality, the average of the participant's scores was taken and compared to the scores that were given to service delivery.

Table 1. Number of respondents and response rates

	Number of cases (N)	Response rate
E-advisors	70	66%
Monitor.overheid.nl	443	100%*
Local government employees	681	39%
Employee aggregate – number of local governments	90	16%*
Average number of respondents per local government	7.6	

*This percentage refers to the percentage of local governments in the Netherlands that was involved in this research.

To explore if any of these transformational dimensions influence the quality of online service delivery, a Pearson correlations test was carried out to see whether the relations shown in figure 1 show a positive correlation. To find out whether questions attributed to a single dimension are related to each other, a factor analysis, using Varimax rotation, was carried out first.

4.1 Factor Analysis

To measure the *quality of online service delivery* we used two different sources: the assessment of the e-advisors and the national website benchmark (Monitor.overheid.nl) ranking all websites of local governments in the Netherlands. The benchmark assesses websites based on the overall quality of service delivery and on the quality of personalized service delivery. The e-advisors were asked different questions than those used in the benchmark, and their assessments were used to construct three variables using factor analysis: classic service delivery (SD), structured SD and advanced SD (see table 2). Using several different measures for online service delivery could strengthen the case for transformational dimensions when multiple correlations are observed.

The employees of local governments participating in this research were asked a number of questions to assess the *organizational development* of their organization. On the basis of the Varimax rotation, four variables could be constructed (see table 3). Furthermore, a fifth variable was constructed that combined the four variables: total organizational development.

Table 2. Variables constructed for quality of online service delivery

Variables constructed	Sub-variables (survey questions)
Classic SD	Presence of standard authentication mechanism.
	Pre-filling information in electronic forms.
	Online access to personal information.
Structured SD	Coherent presentation of services.
	Integration of electronic forms.
	Functional separation of front office and back office.
Advanced SD	Presence of tracking and tracing functionality.
	Allowing for online correction of personal information.
	Pro-actively approaching customers to point out their rights.
	Appointing case managers to customers.
	Ability to make an appointment with a case manager online.

Table 3. Variables constructed for organizational development

Variables constructed	Sub-variables (survey questions)
Horizontal control	Process managers have an overview of organizational processes.
	Process managers control organizational processes coherently.
Vertical control	Departments have a large degree of autonomy.*
	Different departments are managed coherently.
	Processes are managed coherently, instead of controlling dispersed activities.
	Departments coordinate business process in a centralized manner.
Tactical coordination	Departments have made service level agreements.
	Departments meet regularly to discuss business procedures.
	All necessary documents, access codes, keys, etc. are provided to new employees at the same time.
Operational coordination	Individual employees attune their activities to those of colleagues in different departments.
	Different departments cooperate on law enforcement.
Organizational development total	Horizontal control, Vertical control, Tactical coordination, Operational coordination.

* This variable correlates negatively to the other sub-variables that were used to construct the variable Vertical control.

Table 4. Variables constructed for management strategy

Variables constructed	Sub-variables (survey questions)
External management strategy	Strategies for online service delivery aim for diminishing the administrative burden of customers.
	Management is informed if a customer cannot be helped in a standard service delivery process.
Internal management strategy	Management has attention for removing bottle necks from business processes.
	Management takes time to remove bottle necks from business processes.

A Varimax rotation factor analysis was also carried out for *management strategy* and *technology deployment*. This resulted in the construction of six more transformational variables (see table 4 and 5).

Table 5. Variables constructed for technology deployment

Variables constructed	Sub-variables (survey questions)
Deployment of architecture	The organization has developed enterprise architecture.
	The architecture is well-documented.
	Management supports decisions being made on the basis to architectural principles.
	Management information is stored.
Information systems	Architecture is developed on the basis of information systems.
	Entire service delivery process can be completed online.
	Activities are performed automatically without any human interference.
Alignment to business	Control data are stored.
	Architecture development is initiated from the business side.
	Architecture is developed on the basis of business processes.
No duplication of activities	Departments share databases.
	Business processes do not perform the same activities twice.

Table 6. Pearson correlations for transformational variables constructed and quality of online service delivery (SD)

	Monitor online SD	Monitor personalized SD	Advisor classic SD	Advisor structured SD	Advisor advanced SD
Horizontal control	.154	.156	.076	.166	-.011
Vertical control	-.069	.084	.028	.094	.030
Tactical coordination	.187	.280**	.142	.173	.100
Operational coordination	.147	.189	.105	.165	.073
Organizational development total	.137	.218*	.110	.181	.059
External management strategy	.247*	.345**	.043	.245	.101
Internal management strategy	-.009	.205	-.036	-.027	-.138
Deployment of architecture	.301*	.292*	.284*	.266*	.478**
Information systems	.227	.251*	.232	.238*	.230
Alignment to business	.366**	.234	.391**	.316**	.417**
No duplication of activities	.202	.241*	.148	.391**	.461**

**. Correlation is significant at the 0.01 level (2-tailed).
*. Correlation is significant at the 0.05 level (2-tailed).

4.2 Correlations

Now five variables can be used for describing the quality of service delivery and ten more for transformational factors have been constructed, a correlation analysis was performed (see table 6).

5 Findings and Discussion

From table 6 it can be observed that a number of variables constructed from sub-variables measuring transformational efforts in local government organizations are significantly correlated to one or more of the variables attributed to the quality of online service delivery. These variables are an externally oriented management strategy aiming at realizing better service delivery for customers, deployment of architecture within the organization, the alignment of information systems to business, and the removal of duplicate activities in order for processes and departments to use the same activities and data sets if possible. This implies that adopting a management strategy targeted at better customer support and deploying technology in a way that better supports business processes have a positive impact on the quality of online service delivery in local governments. Especially the technology deployment variables are correlated to more of the measures for service delivery. Moreover, as is shown in table 6, the correlation coefficients for these variables are higher for the more complex variables of online service delivery (personalized and advanced SD), implying that these sophisticated forms of service delivery benefit more from undertaking these transformational efforts than the e-government initiatives that have been implemented over the last decades. We can, therefore, conclude that undertaking transformational efforts – especially in the dimension of technology deployment – improves online service delivery of local governments.

The other variables, however, do hardly show any significant correlations to the quality of online service delivery. Only tactical coordination is significantly correlated to personalized service delivery. This suggests that these transformational efforts do not have an effect on service delivery – at least not yet. The lack of significant correlations for this transformational dimension could be a result of this research having been carried out among local governments still in the process of implementing e-government initiatives. While organizations are still under development, it could well be possible that online service delivery does not show any significant improvements. These effects might manifest themselves only on the longer term. But as there is not enough evidence for local governments having gone through a substantial organizational development, this cannot be observed. For the variable constructed from sub-variables related to internally oriented management strategy (aimed at re-organizing business processes), a negative impact is even observed, although this negative impact is not significant. An implication could be that during the process of transforming the organization, the quality of service delivery (temporarily) decreases. Therefore, governments aiming for boosting their online service delivery on the short term could benefit from first adopting enterprise architecture to support business-it alignment, creating shared activities and facilities and adopting a management strategy that aims for creating better value for customers, before undertaking any rigorous organizational change.

Several limitations of this research should be noted. First of all, for most of the variables only indirect assessments were available as we invited experts to state their opinions on the transformational efforts and the quality of online service delivery. Furthermore, also the measure for online service delivery that was collected by the central government is not complete. Although this variable is constructed by an panel of objective researchers all using the same evaluation framework, only the outer characteristics of the websites are assessed, and, for instance, the technology supporting this website and whether the operations in the back office are performed by humans or by technology are not looked at. This was also the reason for asking a number of questions to the e-advisor, to get a clearer and more complete picture. And finally, this research was only carried out among local governments in the Netherlands. Therefore, the outcomes cannot be generalized to other government organizations or to other countries.

Based on these results and limitations, we would like to make several recommendations for further research. Firstly, we recommend that research should be carried out in organizations that have undertaken greater efforts to transform. Alternatively, this research could be carried out in local governments again in a few years' time to see whether there are any differences in outcomes. This should indicate whether the variables constructed for organizational development are also correlated to the quality of online service delivery in these organizations. Furthermore, we also recommend that further research is carried out in other government organizations besides local governments and in other countries than the Netherlands to find out whether the transformational efforts have similar impact or whether in a different organization or country other impacts can be observed on online service delivery.

6 Conclusion

This paper explores the effects of Transformational Government. Transformational efforts are defined as those efforts that aim to realize benefits for citizens and businesses. Often, however, transformation appears to be a black box, as it is unclear which factors enhance service delivery. We aim to open this black box to explore whether transformational factors have a positive effect on online service delivery of local governments. From the data collected for seventy municipalities in the Netherlands, significant positive correlations were found between the quality of online service delivery and having an externally (client) oriented management strategy in place, deploying enterprise architecture, aligning information systems to business and sharing activities between processes and departments. Moreover, these positive relations are stronger for more sophisticated initiatives such as personalized services. The absence of a significant correlation between the variables on organizational development and online service delivery suggests that organizational change in local governments does not yet have the desired effect. Instead, the results from this research imply that adopting a customer oriented service strategy and deploying technology in a way that better supports business processes have a greater impact on service delivery on the short term than the dimensions attributed to rigorous organizational change. Therefore, we recommend that further research on these transformational dimensions in more developed organizations and in other countries should be carried out to find out whether these efforts could also have any effect on the quality of service delivery over the longer term.

References

1. OECD e-Government Studies: E-Government for Better Government. OECD Publishing, Paris (2005)
2. Kim, H.J., Pan, G., Pan, S.L.: Managing IT-enabled transformation in the public sector: A case study on e-government in South Korea. Government Information Quarterly 24, 338–352 (2007)
3. Fountain, J.E.: Building the Virtual State: Information Technology and Institutional Change. Brookings Institution Press, Washington (2001)
4. Irani, Z., Elliman, T., Jackson, P.: Electronic transformation of government in the UK: a research agenda. European Journal of Information Systems 16, 327–335 (2007)
5. West, D.M.: E-Government and the Transformation of Service Delivery and Citizen Attitudes. Public Administration Review 64, 15–27 (2004)
6. Zuurmond, A., Robben, F.: We Need to Dig a New Suez Canal: How Can ICT Help Changing Compliance Costs. In: Nijsen, A., et al. (eds.) Business Regulation and Public Policy, vol. 20, pp. 229–247. Springer, Heidelberg (2009)
7. Coursey, D., Norris, D.F.: Models of E-Government: Are They Correct? An Empirical Assessment. Public Administration Review 68, 523–536 (2008)
8. Henderson, J.C., Venkatraman, N.: Strategic alignment: leveraging information technology for transforming organizations. IBM Systems Journal 38, 472–484 (1999)
9. Peristeras, V., Tarabanis, K.: Towards an enterprise architecture for public administration using a top-down approach. European Journal of Information Systems 9, 252–260 (2000)
10. Shi, W.: The Contribution of Organizational Factors in the Success of Electronic Government Commerce. International Journal of Public Administration 25, 629–657 (2002)
11. Tosey, P., Robinson, G.: When change is no longer enough: what do we mean by "transformation" in organizational change work? The TQM Magazine 14, 100–109 (2002)
12. Porter, M.E.: Competitive Advantage: Creating and Sustaining Superior Performance. The Free Press, New York (1985)
13. Beynon-Davies, P.: Models for e-government. Transforming Government: People, Process and Policy 1, 7–28 (2007)
14. Janssen, M.: Insights from the Introduction of a Supply Chain Coordinator. Business Process Management Journal. Special edition on Cyber Chain Management (edited by Ray Hackney & Janice Burn) 10, 300–310 (2004)
15. Strikwerda, J.: Na het shared service center: de modulaire organisatie. Holland Management Review 23, 45–50 (2006)
16. Baldwin, C.Y., Clark, K.B.: Design Rules. The Power of Modularity, vol. 1. MIT Press, Cambridge (2000)
17. Moon, M.J., Norris, D.F.: Does managerial orientation matter? The adoption of reinventing government and e-government at the municipal level. Information Systems Journal 15, 43–60 (2005)

Democratizing Process Innovation? On Citizen Involvement in Public Sector BPM

Björn Niehaves and Robert Malsch

European Research Center for Information Systems,
Leonardo-Campus 3, 48149 Münster, Germany
{bjoern.niehaves,robert.malsch}@ercis.uni-muenster.de

Abstract. 'Open Innovation' has been heavily discussed for product innovations; however, an information systems (IS) perspective on 'process innovation' has not yet been taken. Analyzing the example of the public sector in Germany, the paper seeks to investigate the factors that hinder and support 'open process innovation', a concept we define as the involvement of citizens in business process management (BPM) activities. With the help of a quantitative study (n=358), six factors are examined for their impact on citizen involvement in local government BPM initiatives. The results show that citizen involvement in reform processes is not primarily motivated by the aim of cost reduction, but rather related to legitimacy reasons and the intent to increase employee motivation. Based on these findings, implications for (design) theory and practice are discussed: Instead of detailed collaborative business processes modeling, the key of citizen involvement in public sector BPM lies in communication and mutual understanding.

Keywords: Business Process Management, Public Sector, Quantitative Study, Empirical Study.

1 Introduction

In recent years, local governments are under immense reform pressure. Various approaches seek to modernize, improve or restructure public administrations, be it practices in context of New Public Management [1], e-Government [2], the adoption of double-entry bookkeeping or business process management (BPM) reforms. Despite the distinct phrasing, these different approaches overlap in several elements. The central goals of local government reforms are on the one hand concerned with cost reduction [3] and the increase of efficiency [4] and, on the other hand, with customer orientation [5]. Due to the high pressure, the diversity of demands, and new areas of responsibility, local governments increasingly rely on innovation networks. Various internal and external actors are involved in reform processes, such as software and consulting companies [6], local government associations [5], or individual citizens [7]. Here, 'Open Innovation' can be regarded as a management paradigm addressing these challenges [8]. It suggests that one key to success is the access to external knowledge in order to enlarge the own pool of capabilities. The involved actors can contribute to providing distinct perspectives as well as domain specific knowledge which does not yet exist within the realms of the local government organization.

M.A. Wimmer et al. (Eds.): EGOV 2009, LNCS 5693, pp. 245–256, 2009.

Here, 'Open Process Innovation' can be regarded as a management perspective on process innovation which suggests that BPM activities are more successful when making use of potential process knowledge that lies outside of the organizational boundaries. In the public sector, this could mean that citizens were a potential contributor to the analysis and design of an administration's business processes. The majority of public services – and its underlying business processes – is highly interactive and involves several points of contact and interaction, e.g. the building application process. Thus, the involvement of citizens in public sector process management could contribute to creating a more customer-oriented administration. Moreover, involving citizens in BPM activities implies that administration staff interacts with them and gains deeper insights into the customers' perspective. These and other reasons suggest that involving citizens could potentially be beneficial to all parties involved. Nonetheless, the phenomenon is to date under-researched and – regarding the combination of open innovation and BPM perspectives – not yet to be found in IS literature. Against this background, the research question of this paper is:

What are factors that support and factors that hinder the involvement of citizens in public sector business process management activities?

In order to answer the research question we conducted a comprehensive quantitative analysis in the public sector, taking the example of local governments in Germany. The quantitative approach – as presented in the paper – is embedded in a multi-methodological study and chronologically followed a series of 24 expert interviews (for the results of the prior qualitative study see [9]). A number of 358 public administrations are included in the analysis which represents more than 3% of all German local public administrations.

The remainder of the paper is structured as follows: Section 2 builds the theoretical foundation of our analysis, presents the research model applied, and discusses six hypotheses to be examined. Subsequently, the research methodology (Section 3) consisting of a brief data collection and analysis description, is discussed, followed by a presentation of the results achieved (Section 4). In Section 5, the results are discussed, implications for theory as well as for practice are derived, and limitations of the study and potentially fruitful avenues for future research are presented. The paper concludes with a brief summary of our arguments.

2 Theoretical Foundation

2.1 Business Process Management

Business Process Management (BPM) describes the efforts of an organization to manage its processes, i.e. to monitor, analyze and optimize them. BPM can be defined as "Supporting business processes using methods, techniques, and software to design, enact, control, and analyze operational processes involving humans, organizations, applications, documents and other sources of information" [10]. The objective of the technological view on BPM is to automate business processes. The holistic management approach aims at analysis and improvement of processes as well as the management of continuous improvement. In addition, a cultural change is intended [11].

Not anymore shall the structure, defined by functions and hierarchies, determine processes, but the organization shall be aligned with the given processes – if possible, in an integrated view that considers both the structure and the processes equally [12]. Another approach focuses on the coordination of man and data in IT systems. In particular, this regards the supply of the staff that is involved in processes with contextual information to support decision-making [13]. Innovation and reengineering are synonym for radical change, which tends to create strong opposition among members of the organization [14]. Optimization and improvement are characterized by continuous processes of small changes and adjustments.

Rosemann et al. [15] describe a maturity model to assess and evaluate BPM activities in organizations. Five stages are differentiated from initial state with uncoordinated and unstructured attempts, to optimized BPM being core part of management and incorporating customers, suppliers, distributors and other stakeholders. Following this framework, openness – in terms of systematically involving stakeholders in BPM activities – is a major characteristic of high BPM maturity.

Major characteristics of public administrations, in contrast to private companies, are a high density of legal rules and a larger variety of goals: guarantee of proper legislation and jurisdiction, promotion of economic development, defense of public rights or environmental protection are only some of them [16]. For BPM in local governments, these issues imply more complex processes that contain a multitude of decision and interaction points and that are rarely well structured.

2.2 Open Innovation – Citizen Involvement

The paradigm of 'Open Innovation', coined by Chesbrough [8], tries to address the high demands of innovation processes. Companies find themselves exposed to constantly rising pressure due to higher competition, increase of acceleration and rising customer demands. Research and Development (R&D) divisions are often dysfunctional in coping with such increased pressure. Hence, in contrast to 'Closed Innovation', companies focus on acquisition of external knowledge, e.g. by know-how buy-in or the support of universities. This results in blurring enterprise boundaries, in particular the boundaries of processes in product and service development. In each development phase, external knowledge can be integrated as well as knowledge can be extracted and brought to market as independent products. The outside-in process extends the knowledge base of a company, whereas the inside-out process aims at commercialization of ideas and sale of intellectual property. The coupled process describes work in alliances of complementary partners, where give and take is crucial to success [17].

Chesbrough [8] does not have in mind a certain technique, but wants to achieve a change in culture. Hence, his perspective can potentially be well applied to the public sector. Here, various forms of cooperation can already be found, such as involvement of experts, outsourcing, or public private partnerships. Within the field of e-government there is positive experience in cooperation with companies, in particular in processes with a high degree of routine and little need for discussion and negotiation [18]. Citizens are involved in processes, e.g. by offering them forms on the internet. The cooperation with citizens in reform processes is crucial to increase of acceptance of changes.

2.3 Legitimacy

Legitimacy, being a major concern of governmental institutions, can be achieved by transparency and public participation. Within public policy theory, legitimacy can be defined as 'the capacity of the system to engender and maintain the belief that the existing political institutions are the most appropriate ones for the society' [19]. A state requires the support of its citizens in order to function. An answer to decreasing trust of citizens in their authorities [20, 21] is the increase of transparency, granted by access to information as well as the ability to monitor decision-making processes [22]. However, transparency alone has only little effect [23]. It must be coupled with public participation rights and the ability of citizens to influence decision-making [24].

The rather abstract legitimacy goal of local governments can be concretized in terms of (a) public participation and (b) increase of transparency. Being recognized as a major reform goal, public participation can be used as key instrument in the local government reform processes themselves. In this case, citizens have already the chance to influence the agenda setting and reform process. Furthermore, cooperation with citizens provides them with first-hand information about process contexts and decision-making procedures. Thus, if the increase of transparency is a central reform goal, we may observe high stakes in involving citizens in local government BPM activities in order to offer them these insights. This leads to the first two hypotheses:

> *Hypothesis 1: The reform goal 'increase citizen involvement' leads to co-operation with citizens in BPM activities.*

> *Hypothesis 2: The reform goal 'increase transparency' leads to cooperation with citizens in BPM activities.*

2.4 Employee Orientation

Cooperation with customers can support employees in sense-making of their work and, thus, increase their work motivation. Motivation can be seen as the power that makes people act [25]. More specifically, it is one of several elements of a complex process which can be divided in three parts: definition of a goal which a person strives for, selection of an action that approaches this goal, and execution of the selected action [26]. From a managerial perspective, the central question is how to align the employees' goals with the organization's ones and how to make them act. Intrinsic motivation, may be more sustainable than extrinsic [27]. Such intrinsic motivation can emerge, if the employees perceive their work (environment and results) as useful. In local governments, an understanding of the people they work for – the citizens – can increase intrinsic employee motivation. This approach, known as customer-orientation, is one important element of New Public Management [1]. Based on this argument, the third hypothesis is formulated:

> *Hypothesis 3: The setting of the goal 'increase employee motivation' leads to cooperation with citizens in BPM activities.*

Furthermore, cooperation can qualify employees both by gaining knowledge from customers and by the cooperation process itself. Qualification is gained by education. In addition, in local governments, public participation can increase qualification of employees for the work with citizens as well as provide a better comprehension of the citizens' perspective. Local governments might try to exploit this potential.

Hypothesis 4: The goal 'exploit education potential' derived from cooperation leads to cooperation with citizens in BPM activities.

2.5 Obstacles

In addition to the factors that support citizen involvement tendencies, obstacles can be hypothesized that constrain the cooperation with citizens in BPM activities.

A clear strategy being a long-term oriented plan provides the framework for sensible citizen involvement. Among different definitions and perspectives upon the term, strategy can be seen as development and execution of a plan to achieve a particular goal [28]. Hence, it delivers a framework for tactical or operational actions and decisions which contribute to the super-ordinate goal. 'Privatization' and 'deregulation' are popular catchwords used by politicians to describe reform strategy; however, their meanings may differ from country to country [29]. In local governments within the scope of BPM reform, a clear strategy might be a precondition to a beneficial involvement of citizens. If such a strategy was missing, we might observe less cooperation with citizens in BPM activities as organizations with such trait might not be able to exploit the full cooperation potential.

Hypothesis 5: The lack of a clear reform strategy hinders the cooperation with citizens in BPM activities.

A lack of personnel resources forces organizations to focus on urgent core tasks while additional long-term oriented work might have to be cut or at least limited. Shortage can arise, if the managers of an organization would like to hire additional staff, but they are not found [30]. Besides external factors, internal reasons, e.g. a limited budget – usually found in public sector like in health care or education – can force personnel reduction due to cost pressure. As a consequence of staff shortage, only the essentially needed tasks are fulfilled, others have to be skipped. Local governments can be affected by a lack of personnel resources because of decreasing budgets. Hence, activities that include citizen involvement and that might require a lot of personnel resources (for governance/moderation), might be avoided because everyday work has a higher priority. The following hypothesis takes up this argument:

Hypothesis 6: The lack of personnel resources hinders the cooperation with citizens in BPM activities.

3 Research Methodology

The quantitative study aims at testing the hypothesis discussed in Section 2. The involved data are part of a broader survey which analyzed the reform programs and innovation networks of local governments in Germany. For this survey, a questionnaire has been developed and published on the Internet. People in charge of reforms in German local governments have been invited via email to take part in the survey in spring 2008. A total of 358 complete records were received. This corresponds to a share of about 3% of the total number of local governments in Germany. The survey responds, furthermore, cover all 13 territorial states in Germany and all sizes of local governments. Hence, they deliver a representative picture of German public administration (for a data collection fact sheet see Table 1).

Table 1. Data Collection Fact Sheet

Characteristics	Description
Process of data collection	• Pre-test with three participants (FEB 2008) • Online questionnaire (FEB to MAR 2008) in German language • Invitation via email directly to 8,000 people in charge of local government reforms • Retrospective analysis of non-responses (MAR, APR 2008)
Number of responses	• n = 358 • ~3% of German local governments
Coverage/ Representativeness	• Random sample (8,000 of about 12,250 local governments in Germany, coverage of about 65%) • Municipalities of all 13 territorial states are included • Number of inhabitants range from 1,650 to 996,000 • Retrospective analysis of non-responses: Reasons for non-attendance are mainly lack of time, holiday of respective employee, or basically no willingness to participate in surveys; thus, no bias is identified

The variable corresponding to the 4th hypothesis has already in the questionnaire been dichotomous. All others are originally based on scaled answers with five categories (e.g. for reform goals from "unimportant" to "very important"). To encounter the problem of the heterogeneity of the assessed local governments and to equal the domain of the variables, all values were aggregated to dichotomous variables. (for details on the variable translation see Table 2).

To assess the relationship between the dependent variable and independent variables, a correlation analysis was carried out. The variables entering the correlation analysis contain ordinal values; hence, the selected measure for this analysis is Spearman's rho. Spearman's rho does neither require any assumptions about the underlying frequency distributions of the variables nor do the variables have to be interval measures. After ranking the values of both examined variables the differences between the respective ranks are calculated. The finally calculated measure ranges from -1 to +1 and expresses the strength of the relationship. The higher the absolute value is the stronger is the relation. The sign indicates, whether the correlation is positive or negative. To test for the significance level, the corresponding p-value is calculated, indicating the Type I error. Thus, a low p-value suggests a high probability of the real existence of the assumed relation. Since the directions of the correlations have been assumed in the hypotheses, the one-tailed significance is basis for the calculation of the p-values. All calculations have been performed with SPSS 16.0.

Table 2. Variable Translation

Variable in questionnaire	Domain	Variable in this paper (all dichotomous)
How important are the following potential reasons to conduct administrative reforms?		
Increasing citizen involvement	(1) Unimportant (2) Less important	Reform goal: increase citizen involvement
Increasing transparency	(3) Neutral (4) Important	Reform goal: increase transparency
Increasing employee motivation	(5) Very important	Reform goal: increase employee motivation
Involving external actors in reform activities might have potential advantages. Do you agree or disagree with the following statements?		
"Working together with external actors educates the employees of our local administration."	Citizens (yes / no) (dichotomous)	Goal: exploit education potential
What are major problems of administrative reforms in your local public administrations?		
"There is a lack of a clear reform strategy in our public administration."	(1) Disagree completely (2) Disagree (3) Neutral	Lack of clear reform strategy
"There is a lack of personnel resources to conduct desirable reforms in our public administration."	(4) Agree (5) Agree completely	Lack of personnel resources
How important are the following actors for implementing reforms in the field of business process management in your public administration?		
Individual citizens	(1) Unimportant (2) Less important (3) Neutral (4) Important (5) Very important	Cooperation with citizens (BPM)

4   Results

Concerning legitimacy both hypotheses are confirmed. The reform goal 'increase citizen involvement' is correlated positively with cooperation with citizens in BPM reforms with a value of 0.213. The significance test yields a p-value which is lower than 0.001, hence, the relation between the two variables is highly significant. We can assume the reform goal and the citizen involvement in BPM reforms itself to be correlated in the population (H1). Likewise, a positive correlation between the will to increase transparency and the cooperation with citizens is observed, having a value of 0.144. With a p-value of 0.0036 it is still significant. Thus, the hypothesis stating the reform goal 'increase transparency' leads to closer cooperation with citizens during the process of BPM reform is verified by the results of the research (H2).

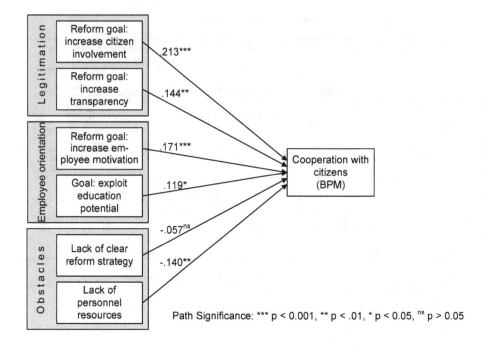

Fig. 1. Statistical Model – Spearman's rho

The same outcome applies to employee-oriented criteria. A positive correlation of 0.177 between the reform goal 'increase employee motivation' and the involvement of citizens is to be found. The p-value of 0.0007 suggests a high significance for the hypothesis to be true (H3). Between the goal to exploit the potential for education of employees derived from cooperation and the citizen involvement a positive correlation is observed as well, having a value of 0.119. With a p-value of 0.0133, this link is still significant, but other factors turn out to be more important (H4).

The obstacles do not seem to be relevant in each case. Although the lack of a clear reform strategy is correlated negatively (-0.057) with cooperation with citizens as assumed, this value is very low. With a p-value of 0.1452 no significance is given. Thus, this hypothesis is not supported (H5). The lack of personal resources is correlated negatively with citizen involvement in BPM activities (-0.140). The p-value of 0.0044 confirms significance. Hence, we can assume that personnel resource shortage is an obstacle to cooperation with citizens (H6).

5   Discussion

5.1   Implications for Theory

The main result of the study is that the core of citizen involvement in local government BPM reforms is the facilitated dialogue which provides mutual comprehension and legitimacy. It follows the theories of BPM maturity [15]. At a high maturity level, prior to cost reduction due to optimized processes is the link to external actors, the communication, and in consequence, the increase of transparency, legitimacy, and employee motivation. Thus, not alone the improved processes and higher efficiency are important as outcome of the involvement of citizens. The key of the cooperation is the communication that happens, the dialogue between administrative employees and the citizens. Public participation aims at the exchange of views, understandings and requirements. Feedback of citizens expressing their needs and revealing current barriers can form the basis for customer-oriented services. Employees can clarify existing practices and provide insights into decision-making to make administrative work more transparent.

Furthermore, the observations go in line with Chesbrough's [8] approach for a cultural change being the underlying condition for open innovation. It is the will and the political commitment which is crucial to the increase of cooperation with citizens. The major trigger for citizen involvement itself is the setting of reform goals which underline this intention: increase of public participation and transparency.

Finally, communication and cooperation with citizens can be used as an instrument to reduce opposition and increase employee motivation. BPM reforms causing radical change tend to generate strong opposition. Hence, the cooperation which is motivated by issues that concern employee motivation or citizen orientation may decrease this criticism and opposition internally. Although the offered education potential is of interest, the emphasis is on other factors, such as employee motivation or legitimacy.

Design theory can be informed by our findings: the importance of the communication itself. Participation techniques and BPM methods must be developed for open process innovation. Such should not primarily focus on optimization of processes on a very detailed level, but provide a more general understanding of the processes, their aims, and their context. Modeling must take place on a higher degree of abstraction, containing modules or building blocks instead of detailed description of each minor step. This approach ensures an increase of transparency and, hence, legitimacy. In addition, such design method must allow for citizens to give appropriate feedback and express their needs. Thus, communication and exchange of views must be in the centre of attention to facilitate mutual comprehension.

5.2 Implications for Practice

In practice, citizen involvement can be a meaningful instrument, but people in charge must be aware that it might not primarily contribute to process optimization in economical terms. The first step of a local government is an analysis of the current situation, that means, to get a rough understanding of the own BPM maturity level and clarify the aim of BPM reforms. If legitimacy or employee motivation is a primary objective, citizen involvement tends to be a very appropriate cooperation partner in BPM activities. However, if required, expectations must be adjusted: the focus is not necessarily on process details themselves, but on communication and the dialogue. The requirements for employees are not mainly business process modeling expertise, but openness and capabilities in collaboration and communication, hence, soft skills. Particularly with regard to the assumption that citizen involvement is time-consuming, local governments must be careful with the assignment of personnel in cooperative BPM and if necessary, rethink their present techniques, not to spend too many resources on inefficient or ineffective cooperation. Nevertheless, cooperation with citizens can be used as a key instrument to increase employee motivation.

5.3 Limitations and Future Research

This paper contains several limitations. Until now, we are only able to draw a picture of the phenomenon for spring 2008, thus, we can only provide a snap-shot. An interesting aspect would be a comparison over the years to be able to identify changes and describe the development of BPM and corresponding reforms in local governments. Therefore, we consider a longitudinal study as a potentially fruitful activity for future research. Furthermore, this paper is limited to a survey of local governments in Germany. To deepen the insights and extend the perspective a comparison with other countries can be made. Concerning the design of citizen involvement methods, we have derived several general proposals. They can set up the framework for effective and efficient cooperation with citizens. The next step would be to concretize these ideas and to develop a cooperative modeling technique in which they are considered.

6 Summary

This paper examines the cooperation of local governments with citizens in BPM activities. Different factors were proven to have an impact on citizen involvement. Legitimacy issues, such as 'increase of public participation' and 'transparency' as reform goals, lead to cooperation. So do the goals 'increase employee motivation' and 'exploit the education potential'. An obstacle to citizen involvement is a lack of personnel resources. The given results show that the objective of citizen involvement in local government BPM reform processes is not cost reduction or high efficiency in business processes, but rather to increase legitimacy and provide mutual bilateral understanding of employees and citizens. Hence, BPM methods in open process innovation should aim at communication and dialogue instead of detailed processes modeling. The study is limited to the German setting at this point of time. Future research could include longitudinal studies and international comparisons. Moreover, the results suggest the development of BPM and modeling methods for citizen involvement pursuing the specific cooperation goals as discussed above. Thus, the presented results can be considered as a design theory [31] for public sector BPM.

References

1. Pollitt, C., Bouckaert, G.: Public Management Reform – A Comparative Analysis, Oxford, UK (2004)
2. Lenk, K.: Der Staat am Draht. Electronic Government und die Zukunft der öffentlichen Verwaltung. Edition sigma, Berlin (2004)
3. Asgarkhani, M.: Digital Government and its Effectiveness in Public Management Reform: A Local Government Perspective. Public Management Review 7, 465–487 (2005)
4. Ridder, H.-G., Bruns, H.-J., Spier, F.: Analysis of Public Management Change Processes: The Case of Local Government Accounting Reforms in Germany. Public Administration 83, 443–471 (2005)

5. Reichard, C.: Local Public Management Reforms in Germany. Public Administration 81, 345–363 (2003)
6. Pratchett, L.: Technological Bias in an Information Age: ICT Policy Making in Local Government. In: Public Administration in an Information Age, pp. 207–221. IOS Press, Amsterdam (1998)
7. Wollmann, H.: Local Government Modernization in Germany: Between Incrementalism and Reform Waves. Public Administration 78, 915–936 (2000)
8. Chesbrough, H.W.: Open Innovation: The New Imperative for Creating and Profiting from Technology, Boston (2003)
9. Niehaves, B.: Verwaltungsreform in Deutschland und Japan - Kooperative Kommunale Reformpolitik im Vergleich. Dissertation der Philosophischen Fakultät, Westfälische Wilhelms-Universität Münster, Münster (2009)
10. van der Aalst, W.M.P., ter Hofstede, A.H.M., Weske, M.: Business Process Management: A Survey. In: van der Aalst, W.M.P., ter Hofstede, A.H.M., Weske, M. (eds.) BPM 2003, vol. 2678, pp. 1–12. Springer, Heidelberg (2003)
11. Zairi, M.: Business Process Management: A Boundaryless Approach to Modern Competitiveness. Business Process Management Journal 3, 64–80 (1997)
12. Scheer, A.-W.: Heilige Kühe schlachten. move Moderne Verwaltung. 2003/11, pp. 26–28 (2003)
13. Breyfogle, F.W.: Leveraging Business Process Management and Six Sigma in Process Improvement Initiatives. Smarter Solutions (2003)
14. Behjat, S.: Prozessmanagement in der Verwaltung. VDM Müller, Saarbrücken (2007)
15. Rosemann, M., de Bruin, T., Power, B.: A Model to Measure Business Process Management Maturity and Improve Performance. In: Business process management: practical guidelines to successful implementations, pp. 299–315. Burlington (2006)
16. Lenk, K., Traunmüller, R., Wimmer, M.: Electronic Business Invading the Public Sector: Considerations on Change and Design. In: 34th Hawaii International Conference on System Sciences (2001)
17. Gassmann, O., Enkel, E.: Towards a Theory of Open Innovation: Three Core Process Archetypes. In: R&D Management Conference (RADMA), R&D Management Conference (RADMA) (2004)
18. Wolf, P., Krcmar, H.: Collaborative E-Government. move Moderne Verwaltung. 2007/5, pp. 12–15 (2007)
19. Lipset, S.M.: Some Social Requisites of Democracy: Economic Development and Political Legitimacy. The American Political Science Review 53, 69–105 (1959)
20. Bock, S.: "City 2030" – 21 Cities in Quest of the Future: New Forms of Urban and Regional Governance. European Planning Studies 14, 321–334 (2006)
21. Jones, M.: Policy Legitimation, Expert Advice, and Objectivity: 'Opening' the UK Governance Framework for Human Genetics. Social Epistemology 18, 247–270 (2004)
22. Héritier, A.: Composite democracy in Europe: the role of transparency and access to information. Journal of European Public Policy 10, 814–833 (2003)
23. King, C.S., Feltey, K.M., O'Neill Susel, B.: The Question of Participation: Toward Authentic Public Participation in Public Administration. Public Administration Review 58, 317–326 (1998)
24. Frost, A.: Restoring Faith in Government: Transparency Reform in the United States and the European Union. European Public Law 9, 87–104 (2003)
25. Maslow, A.H.: A Theory of Human Motivation. Psychological Review 50, 370–396 (1943)

26. Geen, R.G.: Human motivation: A social psychological approach, 1st edn. Wadsworth Publishing, Belmont (1994)
27. Bénabou, R., Tirole, J.: Intrinsic and Extrinsic Motivation. Review of Economic Studies 70, 489–520 (2003)
28. Mintzberg, H.: The Strategy Concept I: Five Ps For Strategy. California Management Review 30, 11–24 (1987)
29. Lane, J.-E.: Public sector reform: only deregulation, privatization and marketization? In: Public Sector Reform: Rationale, Trends and Problems, pp. 1–16. Sage, London (1997)
30. Devine, E.J.: Manpower Shortages in Local Government Employment. American Economic Review 59, 538–545 (1969)
31. Gregor, S.: Design Theory in Information Systems. Australian Journal of Information Systems 10, 14–22 (2002)

Visual Culture and Electronic Government: Exploring a New Generation of E-Government

Victor Bekkers and Rebecca Moody

Erasmus University Rotterdam, Burg. Oudlaan 50, PO Box 1738,
3000 DR Rotterdam, The Netherlands
{bekkers,moody}@fsw.eur.nl

Abstract. E-government is becoming more picture-oriented. What meaning do stakeholders attach to visual events and visualization? Comparative case study research show the functional meaning primarily refers to registration, integration, transparency and communication. The political meaning refers to new ways of framing in order to secure specific interests and claims. To what the institutional meaning relates is ambiguous: either it improves the position of citizens, or it reinforces the existing bias presented by governments. Hence, we expect that the emergence of a visualized public space, through omnipresent penetration of (mobile) multimedia technologies, will influence government-citizen interactions.

Keywords: e-government, visualization, visual culture.

1   Introduction

The outlook of electronic government is changing. The emphasis was primarily on the processing of text and number based data, now however, pictures play an increasing role in the interactions between governments and citizens. The popularity of YouTube which is also being used by governments to inform citizens, illustrates this. From a sociological viewpoint, this trend can be understood in terms of rapid penetration of visual culture in government-citizen-relationships. Although pictures in terms of propaganda or public information services have always been an important policy instrument, the meaning of pictures can go beyond these established practices. Human experiences have become more visual and visualized than ever before, for example, everybody can place their experiences on YouTube. However, the emergence of this visual culture does not depend on the pictures themselves. It is rooted in a tendency to picture and visualize existence, in a more compulsory way: compulsory because pictures create and contest meanings, relate to other meanings in the public domain [21].

In this contribution we theoretically and empirically explore and understand the increasing role which pictures (as visual events) and visualization play in e-government practices and the significance for the involved stakeholders. The question can be asked, whether these pictures give meaning to the relationships between government and citizens and how they (re-)define these relationships [2]. Firstly, we explore the notion of visual culture (section two). In section three we will address the different meanings which pictures have in the shaping of e-government relationships as well how this could be understood. In section four we explore how pictures are used in

M.A. Wimmer et al. (Eds.): EGOV 2009, LNCS 5693, pp. 257–269, 2009.
© Springer-Verlag Berlin Heidelberg 2009

e-government practices, what their meaning actually is and how they are shaped. In section five conclusions will be drawn.

2   Visual Culture: Nature and Backgrounds

Mirzoeff defines "visual culture as being concerned with visual events in which information, meaning or pleasure is sought by the consumer in an interface with visual technologies. [21]

Three developments have contributed to the emergence of a visual culture. Firstly the omnipresent penetration of television in our daily life. In contrast to news papers, television stimulates our association (through amusement and pleasure) much more than the printed word which is more based on reason and order. [6]. Secondly, we can refer to rise of the multi-media networks and systems, in which pictures and videos are integrated with sound and words. The third development is the increased interactivity of these new (multi)media, which comes also forward in the emergence of web 2.0 technologies. Web 2.0 has been called the 'social web', because its content, in terms of the creation and sharing of experiences, can be easily generated by individual users as well as the collective intelligence of users [5] Users are not the passive consumers of content but function as co-producers and co-creators, which presupposes interaction. In expressing these experiences, pictures and videos have become very important (e.g You Tube, MySpace).

Visual technologies are defined as "any form of apparatus designed to be looked at or to enhance natural vision, from the oil painting to the internet" [21] Typical for a visual culture is first, besides textuality, pictures have become increasingly important [21]. An indication is the emergence of a complete industry producing and distributing pictures. [21; 6] Secondly, this visual culture is a post modern culture, implying that it is in essence very fragmentized and disrupted, which adds to the fact that is a dynamic culture. [21] It represents an endless, often real time and thus changing, stream of divergent and convergent (thus) multiple pictures with which people are confronted [6; 8]. This implies that different notions of viewing and interpretation should be taken into account. Visual events are highly contingent; its interpretation depends on the specific (historical) context of the viewer. [21] Thirdly, originally the relationship between a citizen or consumer and these pictures could be understood in terms of 'spectatorship' (with an emphasis on the look, the gaze, the glance and practices of observation). Nowadays, this relationship has become one of reading, of understanding the complex and multiple meaning of pictures that come together in the mind of citizens, thereby creating experiences [21] In the so-called experience economy, consumers are invited to join a open story in which they can participate, adding past of wanted future experiences. [26] Pictures, very often in combination with sound, try to seduce people to be part of this unique story.

3   Visual Culture in e-Government: Different Meanings

From an ecological perspective [2;7] e-government practices are shaped by the unique, and thus local, interaction of different environments (socio, political and cultural and technological) and different stakeholders. In these interactions different meanings are constructed, attached and exchanged [4]. Increasingly, visual events are being created in different e-government practices, while at the same time they give meaning to interactions between government and citizens. Several meanings can be distinguished. Stakeholders may attach a functional meaning to the creation of visual events. The functional meaning consists of the following elements.

First, the classical function of visualization is registration. Through pictures people can register or record people, movements or development in terms of 'freezing' them in time and place. [21] Secondly, visualization can make complicated things rather transparent, in terms of comprehension: one picture can say more than thousands of words. For instance, visualization can make things easier and more understandable, like causes and effects of air pollution. Thirdly, and consequently visualization can also increase the transparency, because it integrates different data in one or a sequence of pictures. In the development of visualized scenarios, relevant information of different data bases can be presented in an integrated way, which can make things (again) easier to understand. Fourthly, visualization facilitates communication. Although a picture says more than a thousand words, people will have different interpretations which are very often an incentive to communicate. Fifthly, visualization facilitates individual and collective learning. Transparency and communication may generate feedback on decisions or arguments.

However, the role visualization may play in e-government practices is not neutral or strictly instrumental. Hence, it is important to address the political meaning of visualization. Visualization supports a process of framing in which social reality is (re-) constructed, thereby including or excluding elements into the constructed picture [28]. In essence this is a political process, in which specific stakeholder try to structure reality in such a way that it may serve their purposes [27; 28] Framing can be seen as an account of ordering that makes sense, because they link facts, values, actions and interpretations in such a way that ambiguity is being reduced and a specific meaning is being created. [9] Hence, visualization is a powerful resource that actors use to manipulate the content and course of their interaction. Consequently, actors attach different meanings to the visualization technologies. [4; 19] In the creation of visual events, used in 21st century e-government, specific biases can be put forward and may be presented as 'reality' [4; 19]. Which 'reality' will be presented as being relevant and who benefits from this kind of representation?

Moreover, in the exploration of the significance of visualization for e-government, another aspect should be taken into consideration, which refers to the combination of visualization with interactivity in relation to the emergence of web 2.0. Web 2.0 does not only stress the importance of citizens as co-producers but also shows us that citizens use their interactive and visual potential in these new technologies to monitor government communications and services by combining individual information, knowledge and experiences, to make processes and outcomes more visible for the general public. In order to do so citizens may also use and exchange pictures. This is the institutional meaning of visualization, because in combination with web 2.0, it may change the established practices and rules in public administration. However, in the literature on the effects of ICT in public administration, there is, repeatedly, empirical support for the so-called 'reinforcement hypothesis' [20] which states that ICT predominantly reinforces the existing interests, positions and frame of references ('bias') of those actors who are already in a powerful positions (but these are not necessarily those providing for the pictures as will become clear later) [1; 23; 24; 25]. Does this also apply to the use of visualization in e-government practices?

4 From Electronic Government to Visual Government: Research Strategy and Empirical Findings

4.1 Research Strategy

In this section we explore several visualized e-government practices in the Netherlands, thereby following the different stages of the policy cycle. In this exploration we assess the following issues:

- the functional meaning which actors attach to the use of visualization in their e-government practice in terms of an instrument or set of tools for registration, transparency, integration, communication and learning;
- the political meaning which actors assess to the shaping of visual event through visualization and the strategic use of visualization in order to achieve specific goals and interests in terms of framing (effects);
- the institutional meaning which actors attach to visualization in relation to the historically established and practices, positions and relationships (effects).

We use a comparative case study approach, in which our empirical findings are based on three data sources: a secondary analysis of research material which has been gathered in other projects, the content analysis of relevant policy documents and the findings that have been based on half open, in-depth interviews with two representatives per case. Through 'triangulation' we have tried to strengthen the validity of our results [29] However, due to the explorative nature of this paper, our research tries to generate findings that contribute to the analytical validity of our research findings, which can be helpful for us to develop new theoretical notions about the use of visual events in e-government practices [29].

4.2 Case Description and Findings

In this section we present several case studies of e-government practices in which visualization is used; practices that can be linked to different policy processes.

Agenda-setting: the Pupils Revolt against the 1040 Norm. Agenda-setting is a process in which specific actors in society try to attract the attention of the general public, policy makers and politicians for their definition of a specific issue in order to put it on the political agenda. [18] Citizens may use ICT to mobilize support and to attract attention. The quality of education has become a widely discussed issue in the Netherlands. In November 2007 pupils revolted against the '1040-hours norm'. This norm refers to the yearly amount of hours pupils have to have education during the first and second years of secondary education. In this revolt, web 2.0 technologies like MSN and YouTube played an important mobilizing role. They partly facilitated local and nation wide protest actions which challenged the educational agenda. The revolt dealt with the idea that schools were not able to fill in these hours, due to a shortage of teachers while the Ministry of Education and its Inspection wanted to hold on to a strict enforcement of the norm. Pupils complained that they had to stay in school, even while no lessons were given.

Visualization played an important role in the mobilization of these youngsters. With their mobile phones, they made pictures and stream videos of local protest actions which were put on You Tube and on Hyves (a Dutch version of MySpace) or were being exchanged by MMS or MSN. For instance, between 29-11-2007 and 06-12-2007, 1720 films were placed on YouTube (Bekkers et al, 2008).

The instrumental meaning of the visualization process was twofold. First, it facilitated the pupil's communication in terms of the (re-)production of the content and course of the protest, in terms of participating in broader movement that generated a collective experience. Second, visualization was also used to record the events that were taking place, almost real time. Through this recording, it was possible to share similar experiences, which gave rise discussion. However, this recording also facilitated these youngsters to freeze the police actions against them. In some cities, small riots occurred and the police reacted very violently. Due to filming, police behavior was made visible and transparent: 'real time' evidence was generated, distributed and made available through all kinds of network sites, which ultimately led to the dismissal of two police officers in Middelburg.

This brings us to the political meaning of visualization. First, youngsters (but also the media) used these films and pictures to frame their claims. They were able to depict themselves as David versus Goliath. This helped them to draw more attention but also to generate the sympathy of the public, several politicians, and the media. Visualization helped them to put forward a specific frame about the goal, the course and the effects of their actions. However, this frame and the presented transparency of the actions were questioned by some politicians and police offers, because the reporting in the pupils was perceived as one-sided: focusing on the 'trill seeking' and picturing the police as 'bad cops'. Secondly, the exchange of pictures in social networks and by instant messaging programs, thereby focusing on the exchange of experiences, facilitated self-organization and co-ordination by these loosely coupled pupils, e.g. leading to a general strike and a large demonstration in Amsterdam. YouTube, Hyves and MSN enabled pupils to mobilize themselves very swiftly and on large scale (it is a generation 'always on'), in which the sharing of visualized experiences played an important role. This created a 'strategic surprise', because the responsible ministry of Education was confused how to react.

The institutional meaning refers to the youngster's combined role of protester and reporter. By acting as reporter they were able to generate an additional view on the content and course of the protest actions, thereby challenging the monopoly of the coverage by the traditional media, which also used the films and pictures that were freely available. Hence, they created their own communication. Furthermore, they showed that is was quite easy for a loosely coupled group to organize themselves as issue group, thereby surpassing established intermediaries like the LAKS (a platform organization of pupils with the ministry which was established in the late 1980's) and political parties.

How did it end? The protest of the pupils was quite successful. The responsible deputy-minister of Education said that she would re-examine the 1040-norm in relation to a broader debate on how to enhance the quality of secondary education.

Policy Development: the Reconstruction of a Public Square in Tilburg. Another case study refers to the development and decision-making regarding the reconstruction of a square in the centre of Tilburg in 2006 [22] According to the municipality, it was, due to discussions on the square's functions as well as the need to increase citizen participation, important to give citizens a vote in the planning of the square. They were asked to voice their preferences (like more terraces, more green, more water). Then the municipality asked city developers to develop plans of which three were chosen. These plans were visualized through the use of geographical information systems and 3-D visualization: named Virtuocity which was made accessible through the internet. By choosing an avatar citizens could walk through the visualizations of the square and to vote for one of the designs. They could discuss the plans in a forum. However, they could not make suggestions to change or combine elements of the plans. The design which gathered most votes was adopted by the municipality. In Tilburg 115.00 visits were registered and 4000 votes were counted.

From a functional perspective, visualization was perceived as an instrument to generate transparency in two ways. One the one hand, Virtuocity made it possible to combine different data, regarding all the different aspects of a square, in an integrated picture. On the other hand, the consequences of complex redesign decisions were made visible in a set of simulations. Not only citizens were able to grasp the redesign of the square at first glance, they were also the experience the square through the eyes of an avatar.

From a political perspective, the way these visualizations were shaped as well as the functions they had to fulfill, were subject to a debate between policymakers, citizens, politicians, architects and the system designers in terms of the (perceived) risks. In Tilburg, we notice that, although the architects were first pleased with the idea of a virtual space for their design, in the end they were rather skeptic. They claim that Virtuocity makes the idea of a design more clear but the way their design was projected was not appreciated, the underlying vision of the design was lacking. Furthermore, the aldermen were afraid of possible one-sidedness in the voter's representation as well as the possibility of fraud. Furthermore, the company that produced Virtuocity (CEBRA) played a powerful role. It had a lot of influence in the way their program was used and how to use it, which also limited the discretion of policy makers. For example, CEBRA preferred a high resolution on screen, but the municipality worried about older computers not being able to handle this high resolution, even though sort of a balance was found, the resolution would still be high.

From an institutional perspective, some interesting changes in practices could be observed. Citizens were primarily seen as voters, who have been given an additional opportunity to participate in a democratic decision-making process. Ultimately, the municipality has accepted the design that gathered most votes. Virtuocity was seen as instrument that could help to introduce elements of direct, participatory democracy and add to the legitimacy of the existing municipal representative democracy. At the same time, the voter turnout was quite low in Tilburg (normally 200.000 inhabitants). One reason was that citizens did not believe the municipality would take their vote seriously. Another reason were some technical problems as well as the fact that only citizen owning a computer and computer skills were able to visit the site and to cast their vote. Citizens complained also about the fact that they have not been addressed as possible co-producers, because they did not have the opportunity to make suggestions within a particular design or to combine elements of the three designs.

Policy Implementation: The Riskmap. After the explosion of a fireworks factory and the knowledge that governments, citizens and first aid agencies were unaware of the locations of risks, a so-called Riskmap was designed [13]. The Riskmap – operational since March 2008 an accessible through the internet- gives an overview of all geographical locations posing a risk to public safety. It will show instances like potentially dangerous, inflammable, explosive and toxic substances as well as core points in transportation which would potentially cause disruption. After selecting a risk the program shows what the risk entails, who is responsible for the risk, the exact location, and the permits. In this way professionals and citizens can get a clear view of the risks in their surroundings. Additionally the Riskmap should be used so that governments can communicate risks to citizens in a clear matter and to help crisis managers and first aid professionals in case of a crisis.

Looking at the functional meaning of visualization, respondents primarily refer to transparency and integration. The risk map not only integrates data stored in different databases into coherent risk and risk management information, it does also make these (often hidden) risks visible in a specific environment. This increased transparency enormously, not only for citizens but also for policy makers and emergency agencies. In case of a fire it becomes transparent for emergency agencies to see whether explosives are located near the fire. Another point is that spatial planners can now very carefully look at where they want to locate buildings, for them it becomes easier to see what a safe place is to build a school. This increased transparency however, also caused a problem. This brings us to the political meaning which stakeholders attach to the increased visibility of risky objects.

There was a large debate on whether the Riskmap itself would not pose a risk, with all the risks accessible for everybody over the world would we not invite terrorist to attack? In the end it was agreed upon that whether or not a Riskmap would exist, terrorists would always be able to get this kind of information. Furthermore, municipalities feared citizens pressuring them in taking all dangerous substances out of their municipalities and that they would feel unsafe. Ultimately, only few complaints by citizens have been made. A reason is that citizens do not make a lot of use of the Riskmap, they claim it makes them nervous or they are not very able to work with the application. The increased transparency also made sure that municipalities became aware of instances in which rules where not applied properly. They feared that when this would be visible, they would be held accountable, so alterations where made. Here we see that because of the existence of the Riskmap rules are executed more accurately.

The institutional meaning of visualization comes forward in the changed government-citizen relationships. Firstly, because now the information on potential risks is easily obtainable for citizens, their information position improved. Secondly, even though citizens do not often complain, since now all the information is transparent, local governments are so afraid that they will that they will make sure that all the rules are applied correctly and that potential risks are taken into account in spatial planning. However, here citizens are not seen as co-producers and the information is only one way, there are no possibilities for interactivity regarding the risks on the website.

Policy Enforcement: Criminals Wanted. During 2008 several police forces have used the internet to publish photos and CCTV-video material, in their prosecution of criminals. An example is www.overvallersgerzocht.nl ('wanted robbers'), on which pictures and videos are published of robberies, sometimes combined with the criminal's voices. The website has led, between the end of 2007 and during 2008, to the arrest of four criminals. Another example is www.politieonderzoeken.nl (police investigations) which is a website of all the police forces together, on which visual and other material are put of cold cases. By making this material accessible for a broader public, the police hope to get new information on cold cases. Since, its start in 2008, two cases have been solved through new information that was given as a reaction to this specific website.

Another channel that has been used is YouTube. For instance, from 16 July until 5 August 2008, the police in Hollands Midden, which started its own You Tube channel placed a video on YouTube, containing 6 minutes of video pictures of an assault on a gas station in Leiden, which have been watched for more than 40.000 times. More then 100 reactions were given, and the case was solved in August. In the slipstream of this success, other videos have been placed on You Tube by the police force. The idea behind this channel is not only to involve citizens in fight against crime, but also to show that the police are able to produce results which may contribute to the safety feelings of citizens.

When looking at the instrumental meaning, the emphasis lies on transparency, by making visual information accessible for the public. This has become easier, due to the increased digital recording of movement in public spaces, in shops, gas stations etc. As a result, citizens may recognize something or may remember something, which is the result of an individual learning process.

Respondents describe the political meaning primarily in terms of the framing power of visualization, thereby showing that the police have been successful in the fight against crime while making use of new instruments. The solved cases are prominent on the website. A banner with 'solved' as well with an explanation how the case is solved (in al the described examples), attracts a lot of visitors. The idea is that positive news will not only seduce people to report more crimes, but that it also contributes to a better image of the police, thereby helping to reduce possible feelings of anxiety. Policymakers but also the public are convinced of the added value of presenting these pictures. Furthermore, also the privacy protection agency does not substantially raise its voice.

The institutional meaning of presenting pictures is that it appeals to citizens as possible co-producers of public safety. The idea is that the fight against crime could be more effective, if the police forces are able to mobilize the knowledge of the public. Furthermore, in doing so, the police want to convince citizens of the idea that the fight against crime is not only the responsibility of the police, but that citizens have their own responsibilities. Moreover, by showing which crimes have been solved, the police also hope to gain public trust.

Policy Evaluation: Monitoring Neighborhood Safety. In April 2006 the police in the city of The Hague introduced the website 'how safe is my neighborhood [17] This website enables citizens to access data about eleven of the most frequent crimes in a specific neighborhood so that they can monitor the results of the actions taken by the police. The idea is that better and more detailed information about the nature of specific crime developments and the outcomes of specific actions would create a better image of the police and its policies as well as to create a larger commitment of the public which may lead to a larger willingness to report crimes. Up till now the number of visits to the site has been a quite a success, although the number of reported crimes did not rise. Citizens appreciate the way in which the information is being presented and made accessible. The police also invite citizens to comment on how to improve the website. Each month, valuable suggestions can win a price. However, a forum for discussion is not provided.

In the creation of this website, visualization was essential. If we look at the functional meaning of visualization we see that visualization is used to increase the transparency of different kinds of crime and their rates. Rather complex and dispersed criminal statistical and geographical data is being represented, integrated and made accessible in one glace, which also helps to reduce complexity. Visualization supports learning, because the website gives additional information on the development of a specific kind of crime during a number of years, also in relation to the measures that have been taken.

Looking at the political meaning, respondents refer to discussion about the 'facts' that are visualized and presented, and thus how 'crime reality' is being shaped by the police. First, the facts that are presented are only based on the reports of citizens on the crimes they have encountered. The 'facts' only represents the registered crime, while the actual state of affairs could be different. Hence, the visual effects that are created are not based on full and reliable information. Secondly, it has been put forward that the visualized information does not take into account the specific context of a neighborhood. For instance, in a neighborhood with a little number of cars parked less cars will be stolen than in an area with a lot of parked cars. Although it is possible to visualize the data per crime type, the combination of all eleven crime types per neighborhood is not possible, which could facilitate a more comprehensive picture. Respondents suggest that the transparency that is being created can be defined as quasi-transparency (decontextualized crime information) as well as fragmentized transparency (only related to specific crime types), which may suit the police's framing of the problem and the policy outcomes. In the fight against crime, also the perception of crime by citizens should be taken into account. How do citizens experience the safety in their neighborhood? The website does not provide a forum in which these experiences can be exchanged or made transparent. Hence, the interactivity of the site is limited.

What is the institutional meaning of the use of visualization in this case? On the one hand, citizens acknowledge that they have the possibility to be better informed, which is demonstrated by the number of website visits. Their information position has been improved. One the other hand respondents perceive that, due to the emphasis on the reported crime rates and the lack of interactivity through which citizens cannot express feelings of unsafety, the policy still dominates the information supply. Citizens are not defined as co-producers in creating a shared picture about the state of affairs in their neighborhood. They are only seen as a possible source of knowledge in relation to the improvement of the website (accessibility, friendliness, representation of information).

5 Conclusions

In this section we first compare the findings of our comparative case studies in order to draw some conclusions. In table 1 these findings are presented. The categories are based on the three types of meanings which stakeholders may attach to the visual events that are used in the described e-government practices. Also attention is paid to the results that these visualized e-government practices have produced.

Firstly, we see that two patterns of functional meanings can be discerned, which depend on the technology used in the visualization process. First, we see pattern in which registration/recording is dominant. The visual events that are presented here,

Table 1. Meanings of visualization in e-government practices

	Pupil's protest 1040 norm	Virtuocity Tilburg	Risk map	Criminals Wanted	Neighbor-hood safety
Policy phase	Agenda-setting	Development	Implemen-tation	Enforcement	Evaluation
Functional Meaning	Recording and communica-tion	Transparency and integration	Transparency, integration and communi-cation	Recording, transparency, communi-cation and learning	Transparency, Integration and learning
Political meaning	Framing of claims and attention; one-sided transparency; common 'story' to facilitate self-organization	Discussion representation of the design and of trust-fulness of voting. Central role program designers	Dominant risk framing by government, no room for citizen input, no debate on useful-ness map	Pictures as a powerful communica-tion instrument and way of framing the police success.	Dominant safety framing by police on registered facts; no room for subjective dimension of safety
Institutio-nal meaning	Support political self-organization and mobili-zation process; counter-balancing framing	Supports political participation as voter, not as co-producer	Improved accountability for safety in spatial planning and correct rule appliance.	Citizens as co-producer of public safety, appealing to public responsibili-ties of citizens. Adding to police legitimacy	Reinforce-ment of the information position of the police; no room for substantial discussion Improved citizen information position
Result	Reconsider-ation of the norm in relation to the quality of education	Acceptance of the design with most votes; low voter turn out, distrust remains	Improved citizen information position, more emphasis on government accountabiliy.	Crime solution by appealing to the citizen's knowledge, decreased feeling of unsafety and better image of police.	Improved citizen information position, no changes in crime reporting

refer to the possibility to show (real-time) experiences, by showing what has happened (protests, police violence, hold ups). The second pattern is primarily focused on the creation of transparency – reducing the complexity of events and developments by making it comprehensible, and the integration of data and databases. In this second pattern geographical information systems (GIS) play an important role. At the same time we notice, due to the dependency on GIS, which are completely controlled by the involved government agencies, the incentive to facilitate communication is rather limited. In all the cases communication seems to appear but the nature of communication differs. Two way communication as a desired effect of visualization seems to appear in those e-government practices in which the internet, especially web 2.0 applications, play an important role (protests against the 1040 norm and internet use in crime fighting), while in the other cases it is one-way communication: from government to citizens.

When we look at the political meaning of visualization in these e-government practices, we may conclude that pictures are used as a powerful resource which governments – but also citizens – use to help to frame specific events or actions in a rather convincing way. However, the transparency that is being created looks, at first glance, overwhelming. Very often the pictures presented, try to enhance, in a compelling way, the legitimacy of specific organizations or their actions. A closer look reveals discussion on the quality of transparency that is being presented. Although a picture may say more than thousand words, the story this picture is telling, is just one story. Therefore, the increased importance, which governments as well as citizens attach to pictures, generates new means of manipulation. At least it is important to take the context into consideration as well as the assumptions that lay behind the making or distribution of these pictures.

When we look at the institutional meaning of visualization, we see a mixed pattern. On the one hand we see that existing and grown practices have been challenged, leading to a changing positions of citizens. Not only are they better informed, they are also asked to take up new and other positions, for instance as co-producer of co-creator, voter or public controller. At the same time, these new positions are taken within a framework in which the initiating governments still impose this framework, with an exception of the pupils protest against the 1040 norm. In all the other cases we may conclude that the creation of the visual events has not led to a weakening of their positions, one could even talk about a strengthening of their position, in the cases in which the police have been involved (criminals wanted and crime monitoring). The latter has also something to do with the strategic use of visualization to improve the legitimacy of those organizations and the trust of the public in them. There seems to be support for the idea that also the visualization adds to the reinforcement of the information and communication positions of those organizations that already have a powerful position. Visualization opens the possibility to create and shape visual events that can be used to present an even more convincing story (in terms of framing) by those stakeholders, which are able to control the use and distribution of pictures but not necessarily the supply of pictures. At the same time, the 1040 norm case shows very convincingly that citizens themselves have also easy access to the creation of these pictures in order to mobilize political and public support as well as to counterbalance the framing of for instance governments, which hardly generates any costs. Hence, we may expect that in the near future, the production and distribution of pictures in the public domain will become an interesting battlefield. This battlefield becomes more interesting, if it citizens are really capable to act as a co-producer or co-creator in e-government process, in which the creation of 'visual facts' may help them to counterbalance the official 'frame' that is put forward by government. Furthermore this the democratizing effect, may be strengthened by the fact that the production and distribution of visual events like photos and videos is rather easy and cheap. For these reasons, it is interesting to investigate how the emergence of a visualized public space, through omnipresent penetration of (mobile) multimedia technologies in our daily life, will influence the nature and course of the interactions between government and citizens in the provision of public services.

References

1. Andersen, K.V., Danziger, J.N.: Impacts of IT on Politics and the Public Sector. International Journal of Public Administration 25(5), 591–627 (2001)
2. Bekkers, V., Homburg, V. (eds.): The information ecology of e-government. IOS Press, Amsterdam (2005)
3. Bekkers, V., Beunders, H., Edwards, A., Moody, R.: De virtuele lont in het kruitvat, Erasmus Universiteit Rotterdam (2008)
4. Bijker, W., et al. (eds.): The social construction of technological systems. MIT Press, Cambridge (1987)
5. Boulos, K.M.N., Wheeler, S.: The emerging Web 2.0 social software: an enabling suite of sociable technologies in health and healthcare education. Health Information and Libraries Journal 24(1) (2007)
6. Castells, M.: The Rise of the Network Society. Blackwell, Cambridge (1996)
7. Davenport, T.H.: Information Ecology. Oxford University Press, New York (1997)
8. Frissen, P.H.A.: Politics, governance and technology. Elgar, Cheltenham (1999)
9. Hajer, Law: Ordering through discourse. In: Goodin, R., et al. (eds.) Handbook of Public Policy, pp. 250–268. OUP Oxford (2005)
10. Alfrink Staking, YouTube,
    http://www.youtube.com/watch?v=xKydYGSQCis&NR=
11. Staking Scholieren Leiden, YouTube,
    http://www.youtube.com/watch?v=1fkjbZ1DNfI&feature=related;
    Leiden Scholieren Staking 2, YouTube,
    http://www.youtube.com/watch?v=1AUq_ZoMClk&feature=related;
    Blesewic staking scholieren part 3, YouTube,
    http://www.youtube.com/watch?v=3SC6T0Ur_wM&feature=related
12. Ik ben tegen de 1040 lesurennorm! Hyves, http://wegmet1040.hyves.net/
13. Risicokaart, Interprovinciaal overleg, http://www.risicokaart.nl/
14. Veroordeelden Gezocht! Politie Amsterdam-Amstelland,
    http://www.veroordeeldengezocht.nl/
15. Overvallers gezocht, Politie, waakzaam en dienstbaar,
    http://www.overvallersgerzocht.nl/
16. Politieonderzoeken.nl, Help politie bij het oplossen van ernstige misdrijven. Politie,
    http://www.politieonderzoeken.nl/
17. Hoe veilig is mijn wijk? Politie Haaglanden,
    http://www.hoeveiligismijnwijk.nl/
18. Kingdon, J.W.: Agendas, Alternatives and Public Policies. Harper, New York (1984)

19. Kling, R.: The Struggle for Democracy in an Information Society. The Information Society 4(1/2), 1–7 (1986)
20. Kraemer, K.L., King, J.L.: Computing and Public Organization. Public Administration Review 46, 488–496 (1986)
21. Mirzoeff, N.: An introduction to visual culture. Routledge, New York (1999)
22. Moody, R.: Assessing the role of GIS in E-government: A tale of E-participation in two cities. In: Wimmer, M.A., Scholl, J., Grönlund, Å., et al. (eds.) EGOV 2007. LNCS, vol. 4656, pp. 354–365. Springer, Heidelberg (2007)
23. Moon, M.J.: The Evolution of E-Government Among Municipalities: Rhetoric or Reality? Public Administration Review 62(4), 424–433 (2002)
24. Norris, P.: A virtuous circle. Cambridge University Press, Cambridge (2000)
25. OECD: The e-Government Imperative. Paris: OECD (2003)
26. Pine, J., Glimore, J.H.: The experience economy. Harvard Business Press, Boston (1999)
27. Snow, D.A., Rochford, E.B., Worden, S.K., Benford, R.D.: Frame Alignment Processes, Micromobilization, and Movement Participation. American Sociological Review 51(4), 464–481 (1986)
28. Stone, D.: Policy Paradox. Norton & Company, New York (1997)
29. Yin, R.K.: Case Study Research. Design and Methods. Sage Publications, London (1994)

On the Origin of Intermediary E-Government Services

Rex Arendsen and Marc J. ter Hedde

Dutch Ministry of Finance, P.O. Box 20201, 2500 EE The Hague; Centre for e-Government Studies, University of Twente, P.O. Box 217, 7500 AE Enschede, the Netherlands
r.arendsen@minfin.nl, m.j.terhedde@gw.utwente.nl

Abstract. The majority of SME's tends to outsource administrative tasks, including their direct relationships with the (electronic) government. Commercial intermediary service providers therefore have to be part of governmental multi channel e-service delivery strategies. This research paper explores the origin, added value and future position of these intermediary organisations with respect to the delivery of e-government services to businesses. Results indicate that (re-)intermediation is more likely to occur within this context than disintermediation is. SME's do not want to be captured within a non-profitable electronic hierarchical relationship with a governmental organisation. The empirical study on the impact of the legal obligation of the use of e-tax services illustrates that SME's instead prefer the 'save haven' of a commercial relationship with an intermediary service provider. Thus creating and fuelling a new market of intermediary e-government services.

Keywords: e-government, SME's, intermediary service providers.

1 Introduction

Large parts of e-government-related policies, planning and research focus on direct service delivery and interaction between governmental organizations and citizens and businesses. In practice however many of these 'customers' rely upon intermediary parties which perform these contacts and transactions with government on behalf of them. Many personal income tax filing e.g. is being supported by social intermediaries [1] like unions or elderly organizations. Citizens also tend to outsource permit procedures to their architect or building contractor. This paper focuses on e-government services for businesses and the role of intermediary service providers within this context.

Especially small and medium sized businesses (SME's) decide to outsource administrative, secondary processes [2]. Important supporting arguments are 'increasing focus on primary products and processes' and 'gaining efficiency benefits'. Commercial intermediaries provide a broad range of administrative and advisory services, which in most cases includes the inherent relationship with governmental organisations. Shipping agencies for example in many cases take care of customs declarations, accountancy firms prepare annual reports, book-keepers fill in and send business tax notices of assessment and salary service organisations calculate and pay social security contributions and report to the statistical department.

M.A. Wimmer et al. (Eds.): EGOV 2009, LNCS 5693, pp. 270–281, 2009.

These types of commercial intermediary organisations play an important role in the day to day (obligated) business data reporting to governmental organisations. They fuel many governmental administrative processes. Allers [3] shows that governmental organisations intentionally bring in these intermediary organisations in order to reduce the amount of contact and data collection points.

From that perspective commercial intermediary service providers are potentially important partners in the development of e-government for businesses. Several European countries have formulated and executed policies with respect to these specific public private partnerships. The Finnish Ministry of Finance began in 1996 an e-service system to improve the electronic data reporting from companies to public authorities, the so called TYVI system [4]. An important element within the Finnish system are the intermediate data brokers which forward business data to the correct authority. In Denmark since 2005 a similar public private data reporting infrastructure exists that focuses on e-invoicing towards governmental organisations. Five private brokers facilitate the transport of all e-invoices to the Danish government [5]. Based on the "Policy Framework for a Mixed Economy in the supply of e-government services" [6] the English government promotes the realization of public, private and voluntary coalitions supporting the delivery of electronic public services. As a result of the legal obligation of electronic business tax filing a new market of intermediary e-tax services has recently developed in the Netherlands [7].

Many governmental organisations at the moment struggle with the question how to design and implement their multi channel e-service delivery strategy [2]. Intermediary service providers ought to be part of such a strategy.

The central research question addressed in this paper is: *what are the origin, added value and future position of intermediary organisations with respect to the delivery of e-government services to businesses?* Answers to the research question help these governments to make better choices and enhance e-service delivery to businesses. Gaining knowledge on this subject is scientifically interesting as well. Little empirical research has been conducted with respect to these intermediary channels in business-to-government domain yet. Answering this research question contributes to the development of the theory of governmental multi channel management.

In the next paragraphs we present successively the theoretical background of our research and the research model and methodology used. We present results of a data mining case study in the Netherlands and discuss their implications for practitioners and researchers.

2 Theoretical Background

The Office of the e-Envoy (UK) defines intermediate organisations as "organisations from the private or voluntary sectors offering services targeted at and tailored to chosen groups of customers, this may be consumers or business" [6]. Van der Meulen et al. [8] use a more general definition: "any organization that mediates the relationship(s) between two or more social actors". Intermediaries provide many functions and roles that cannot be easily replaced, substituted or internalized through direct interactions. Four roles of intermediaries can be defined [9], [10], [11]:

- *matching demand and supply*: bridging the gap between the service requestor's wishes and requirements and the service provider's offers;
- *information processing*: acquiring, aggregating and distributing data;
- *providing trust:* ensuring the accountability of decisions and (added in this paper) the independency within inter-organisational relationships;
- *providing interoperability:* managing an institutional infrastructure used by multiple organisations.

Matching demand and supply: a transaction cost perspective

In case of acquiring a product or service every organisation has the options of internal production or external manufacturing: make or buy, in source or outsource. The transaction costs economics [12] offers a theoretical framework for this business economical assessment. The central element within this theory is the coordination of economical activities: by means of the market of via a specific organisation, a so called hierarchy. A hierarchy is founded within administrative control and management decisions and focuses on internal efficiency [13]. A market is based upon freedom of choice amongst alternatives and focuses on the relationship between business partners. The object of study in this research is the market of intermediary governmental services.

The introduction of ICT within these markets can influence the parameters founding the business economical assessment: the electronic brokerage effect [14]. This effect is being used as one of the important arguments fuelling the hypothesis stating that traditional intermediary organisations will sooner or later disappear; the so called *disintermediation process* [15]. Supported by new technologies buyers and sellers, e.g. can do business in a more efficient manner, within a direct relationship. On the other hand researchers expect new intermediaries to enter these markets, taking advantage of new market characteristics [16]. With respect to e-commerce, this has resulted in the identification of recurring patterns of intermediation, disintermediation, and re-intermediation in terms of a IDR framework [11], [15]. We expect the same patterns are possible related to the e-government context.

Information processing: the administrative burden of businesses

The administrative business-to-government relationship is influenced by numerous information obligations. Businesses are enforced to report data regarding their personnel, turnover, production processes, etcetera. These reporting costs are an administrative burden to many businesses indeed. Allers defines this administrative burden as "compliance cost: private sector costs of complying with regulations" [3]. These information obligation costs hamper economical growth. The reduction of the administrative burden therefore is an important objective within the EU's Lisbon Agenda [17]. Many European countries, amongst which the Netherlands position e-Government as a way to reduce this administrative burden of businesses [18].

Caused by the complexity, scale and diversity of these information obligations many SME's chose however to outsource this data reporting to governmental organisations, thus creating and supporting a market of 'administrative burden related' services. In other words, information obligations are a *burden* to many individual companies but a *business* to others! Contrary to most individual SME's, many of these intermediary service providers are able to gain efficiency benefits out of electronic data reporting relationships with governmental organisations. A professional

(ICT-) organisation enables them to profit from economies of scale and to benefit from the so called electronic integration effect [14].

Arendsen summarizes this into his *intermediary paradox*. Many intermediaries originate and live from the existence of information obligations whereas on the other hand they are the best positioned and equipped to reduce information obligation costs by means of electronic data reporting to governments [2]. In his study he stresses the possible positive effects of competition between intermediary service providers. Lower prices of intermediary services directly lower the administrative costs of individual businesses. Efficiency benefits in that case are passed on in term of lower bills to individual organisations. This is however not an obvious process; studies point to the fact that intermediaries will be reluctant and prefer in those cases enhancement of their service level [2]. Governmental initiatives aiming at the break through of this intermediary paradox will therefore have to influence this market of intermediary providers.

Trust and independency
A third role of intermediary organisations is the provider of trust and independency, for example as a 'trusted third party' with respect to ICT-security services. The notary is an other example of a legally institutionalised trusted third party.

The introduction of inter-organisational systems, like many business-to-government e-services, in most cases leads to chances within the dependency relationships between organisations involved [19]. Especially the more complex edi-based interactions can be characterized as electronic hierarchies [14]. According to Malone, the dominant provider of this electronic hierarchy is best in place to realise significant benefits within this inter-organisational relation. In case of (complex) e-government services benefits will more easily be realised at the side of the dominant governmental provider than on the side of individual SME's [3], [20]. Especially in case of forced adoption of these kind of services, businesses will find it hard to gain benefits [21]. SME's do not want to be trapped in such a non-profitable electronic hierarchical relationship. In case of introduction of e-government services by force/law many of these SME's will probably flee into the 'save haven' of a commercial, market relationship with an intermediary service provider. Thus creating and fuelling a new intermediary services market.

In this paragraph we presented the theoretical foundation of the origin, added value and possible positions of intermediary organisations with respect to the delivery of e-government services to businesses. This analysis has been based on three roles of intermediary organisations. The next paragraph presents a model based on the fourth role depicted earlier: provider of interoperability. This model will be used to present the results of the empirical part of this research.

3 Modelling Intermediary Governmental e-Services

Interoperability is defined as "the ability of ICT systems and supported business processes to exchange data and by that to share information and knowledge" [22]. Figure 1 shows that interoperability asks for coherence on multiple levels. This specific model has been developed by Arendsen based on more general multi-layer frameworks like ISO's Open Systems Interconnection Model [2].

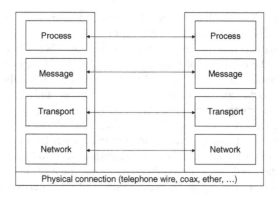

Fig.1. Interoperability services

Coherence at the business level is being captured in terms of *processes*: which organisation start the process, what is the reaction time, and how to deal with exceptions, like e.g. in case of a permit procedure. Electronic *messages* carry the data exchanged. These data have to be defined and recorded in a well structured manner, in a way that they can be exchanged independently from internal data formats. At this level data integration is being organized. Messages have to be *transported* in a reliable way. This asks for systematic tagging with logistical data such as the addresses of sender and recipient and an identification of the message in the 'envelope'. The actual transportation of the messages exchanged takes place via *physical connections*. In the case of electronic message interchange different types of *networks*, like e.g. the Internet, can be used to route the data.

e-Government services for businesses too can be modelled in terms of this multi layer framework. Information obligations state for example timing and content of the messaging required. Data exchange can be facilitated via a governmental website or systems directly connected via the Internet.

In practice two types of commercial intermediaries offer interoperability services in between: communication services providers and business services providers. Both can be positioned within the interoperability model, see figure 2.

The *communication services providers* primarily focus on the logistics part of electronic message interchange, as for instance the routing, archiving and tracking and tracing of data. Till recently these providers often acted as inter-sector (EDI-)hubs servicing e.g. the social security domain (the Belgian Kruispunt bank), the procurement domain (the Danish e-invoice broker WM-data) or the logistics and customs domain (port community systems as Portinfolink in the Port of Rotterdam). These hubs provide network services like availability, security and capacity. Part of their added value consists of the translation between different technical standards. Governmental gateways, like e.g. the UK Gateway or the Dutch Government Transaction Portal can be part of this 'hub infrastructure' and "link information hubs to streamline information and data exchange in the public sector" [18]. This intermediary market is evolving "from traditional dyadic EDI approach towards a web-based integrated data exchange environment within a networked economy" [23].

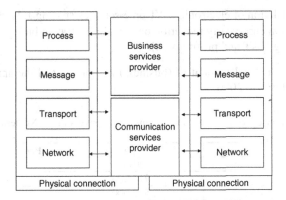

Fig. 2. Intermediary service providers

The *business services providers'* added value lies in the decoupling of business processes and message handling of organisations involved. This group of service providers consists first of all of traditional book-keepers and advisors to which administrative task are being outsourced. Those professionalized offer related communication services as e.g. electronic tax filing via their software system. Additionally, providers like salary service organisations and billing service providers offer high volume B-to-G e-services.

In practice we observe an increase in cooperation between both types of intermediary service providers, as well as with providers of hard- and software systems. New types of intermediary service provides arise, like the *application service providers* (ASP's) which in general provide business functions via the Internet. This 'software as a service' offers e.g. book-keeping functionalities and support the salary administration, including obligated governmental data reporting. These new commercial intermediary service providers are the early adapters of technical innovations like the introduction of open standards and broad band Internet connections.

Fuelled by the three mechanisms described in the former paragraph this results in a vivid market of intermediary e-government services for businesses. The next paragraphs presents some of these depicted market mechanisms in practice, thus illustrating the origin, added value and possible future developments of intermediary service providers.

4   Case Study: Mandatory e-Taxation for Businesses

Starting from 2005 the Dutch Tax Administration obliged individual business by law to file their tax forms in an electronic manner. This legislation concerned the VAT, income and company tax (together called the profit tax) and the wages and social security related taxes (starting from 2006). Arguments behind this strategy were:

- low adoption rates of e-tax filing (<5%) by business and intermediaries;
- efficiency benefits at the Tax Administration (750 fte) [18];

- EU legislation of electronic VAT on e-services starting July 2003;
- 50 million euro yearly reduction on the administrative burden of businesses regarding VAT and profit tax [2].

Table 1 presents the total amount of (business) tax payers and the annual amount of processed tax returns in 2006.

Table 1. Overview of tax types and amount of tax payers in the Netherlands, 2006

Tax type	Tax payers	Processed tax returns
Income tax (incl. citizens)	9.201.000	7.374.000
Company tax	711.000	454.000
Wage related taxation	572.000	6.608.000
VAT	1.231.000	6.190.000

Business Services

The basic process steps within the taxation process are in general: the administration of tax-related data, the calculation of taxes due and the actual filing of the tax form. Next to that, legislation concerning the different business-related tax types often requires specific process implementations. *VAT* i.e. can be filed on a monthly, quarterly or yearly basis, depending on business characteristics. Whereas a paper annual report could accompany the paper *profit tax* form, the electronic version only allows addition of structured data. The newly (2006) introduced *wage related tax* is a combination of data used in taxation, social security and statistics processes. Thus imposing chances on business processes and systems.

As illustrated before in this paper, many different intermediary organisations offer services to individual businesses within these tax-related process chains.

Communication Services

The legal obligation regarding e-taxation affected individual businesses. To support the electronic filing of tax forms, two different electronic communication channels had been opened. The Dutch Tax Administration has been the first in Europe to support tax filing from commercial software systems. Next to that, the tax administration offered e-forms at their website. To many individual companies, outsourcing was a third option. In those cases the intermediary had to chose which of the two communications channels to use.

One year after the introduction, 99% of the business tax forms had been electronically filed.

Research Method

The empirical part of this paper focuses on *the impact of the legal obligation on the market of intermediary (e-tax) services* and hence on the role and added value of these customer commissioned intermediaries [6].

Data collection has been based on more than 20 qualitative and quantitative (in most cases, n>1000) policy reports, and internal and external research reports. In one occasion we had the possibility to add specific research questions.

This data mining case study meets Rasmussen's characterisation of a suitable research method for the study of a contemporary phenomenon within a real-life context: "an exploration … over time through detailed, in-depth data collection involving multiple sources of information rich in context" [24].

5 Results

Business services
Table 2 presents the trend in the outsourcing of tax related administrative tasks by individual businesses. These tasks regard to the tax administration, calculations and the actual tax filing.

The percentage individual businesses handling tax related administrative tasks without external support decreases systematically (a). Till 2005 the percentage individual businesses that outsource all administrative tasks reduces. From 2005, the year of the legal obligation, this percentages rises by 10%-points (c).

Large and small businesses differ significantly. For example, 41% of the smaller businesses and 22% of the larger[1] businesses in 2004 sourced out all administrative (tax-related) tasks. In January 2005 50% of the individual businesses with less than 10 employees outsourced their VAT-declaration, opposite to 5% of the businesses with more than 50 employees.

Table 2. Trends in outsourcing tax processes by individual businesses, n>500

Handling of tax administration tasks by individual businesses	2002	2004	2005	2006	2007
All by themselves (a)	17%	15%	14%	13%	11%
Outsourced some (b)	50%	55%	58%	49%	50%
Outsourced all (c)	33%	30%	28%	38%	39%

Figure 3 illustrates this trend of increasing outsourcing, specified in terms of the individual tax types. The VAT and the wage-related tax show a significant increase in outsourcing.

Communication services
As presented above, to the majority of the individual businesses, an intermediary service provider operates as their communication channel towards the electronic government. Part of the individual businesses directly uses one of the communication channels offered by the Tax Administration, i.e. via a software system or by means of an e-form on the website. Table 3 presents percentages per tax type per channel.

In general more tax declarations are being send by individual businesses via the website than via a software system. (The same holds for the intermediaries which especially during the first introduction phase heavily used e-forms at the website, a channel originally opened to serve only individual businesses).

---

[1] The amount of 50 employees divides the population into large and small businesses.

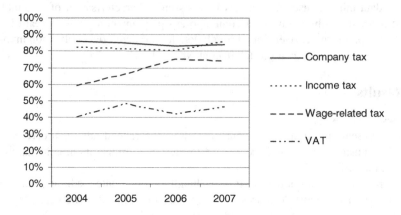

Fig. 3. Outsourcing trends per tax type

Table 3. Direct use of channels by individual businesses, 25<n<270

Channel	VAT		Income		Company		Wage	
	2006	2007	2006	2007	2006	2007	2006	2007
Software	10%	13%	21%	28%	36%	39%	63%	56%
Website	90%	85%	79%	72%	64%	48%	37%	35%
'No idea'	-	2%	-	-	-	13%	-	9%

The increasing *percentages* of use of the software channel (table 3) can be explained by the declining *absolute* population of direct filers (as illustrated above outsourcing has increased). Table 4 in fact shows that related to the total population of individual businesses the use of software tax systems remains rather stable (and low).

Table 4. Trends in use of software tax systems within total population of individual businesses

e-Tax by business software system	2005	2006	2007
VAT	12%[2]	6%	7%
Income tax	6%	4%	4%
Company tax	6%	6%	7%
Wage-related tax	17%	16%	16%

The increase in outsourcing as shown in the beginning of this paragraph, affects mainly the use of the website by individual businesses; whereas the use of software tax systems by individual business is stable within the total population.

New providers entering the market
The legal enforcement of electronic tax filing by businesses has enormously enlarged the market of e-government (tax) services for businesses. From the start we have seen

---

[2] A high percentage of 'does not know' – scores has influenced the accuracy of this figure.

several new commercial intermediaries enter this market[3]. These application service providers offer next to the actual transportation of tax forms, several software supported administrative services; thus illustrating the cooperation trend in paragraph 3. This market is still rather volatile and offers chances for product innovation to many intermediaries. No figures regarding these developments are available yet.

6 Conclusions

The central research question addressed in this paper is: *what are the origin, added value and future position of intermediary organisations with respect to the delivery of e-government services to businesses?* A broad theoretical analysis and an in depth data mining case study provide answers to the research question.

The *origin* of intermediary service providers can be directly addressed in terms of their different roles within inter-organisational relationships.

From a transaction cost perspective we have illustrated that similar to the e-commerce context one may expect dis/re-intermediation (IDR) patterns related to e-government services for businesses. SME's do not want to be trapped in non-profitable electronic hierarchical relationships with governmental organisations. The case study shows for example outsourcing percentages up to nearly 90%.

Legal information obligations are a *burden* to many individual companies but are a *business* to intermediaries. Governmental initiatives aiming at the reduction of the administrative burden have to take this crucial intermediate position into account. They have to deal with the intermediary paradox: lowering bills will positively effect the burden but is not in the intermediary's interest.

To the majority of the individual businesses, intermediary service providers are in fact their communication channel towards the electronic government. The *added value* is either being delivered via communication services like for instance the routing, archiving and tracking and tracing of data or via business services like the decoupling of message handling processes of the organisations involved.

The case study shows that to most individual businesses the use of software systems is hardly an option. Even after legal obligation of electronic tax filing the use of these systems remains stable. This result confirms earlier studies showing most SME's are not able to adopt electronic data interchange with governmental organisations [7], [20].

The case study fuels the hypothesis that especially in case of introduction of e-government services by force/law many SME's will flee into the 'save haven' of a commercial, market relationship with an intermediary service provider. Such an enforcement strategy creates a new market of e-government services and lowers barriers of entry. Thus creating and fuelling a new intermediary services market in which new types of intermediary service provides can arise.

This leads to the overall conclusion that within the e-government context (re-) intermediation is a more likely trend than disintermediation. This points to a *positive future position* of intermediary service providers within the e-government context.

---

[3] See e.g. www.reeleezee.nl or www.creAim.nl

7 Implications

Many governmental organisations at the moment struggle with the question how to design and implement their multi channel e-service delivery strategy.

To policy makers this study presents arguments why intermediary service providers ought to be part of such a strategy. The majority of SME's tends to outsource administrative tasks, including their direct relationships with the (electronic) government. The case study shows that enforcing the use of governmental e-services will probably stimulate this outsourcing process. Thereby strengthening the position of intermediaries in policy discussions regarding the reduction of the administrative burden.

To scientists this study presents an application of the transaction cost theory within the e-government context by illustrating possible effects of the introduction of ICT within the B-to-G relationship. On the one hand results strengthen the hypothesis that (re-)intermediation processes are more likely to occur within this context than disintermediation processes will do. On the other hand this study presents empirical data exploring effects of a legal intervention within the B-to-G context. Opposite to its role as a service provider, governments role as a legislator is hardly ever being used as a research perspective within e-government studies.

References

1. Klievink, B., Janssen, M.: Improving Government service delivery with private sector intermediaries. European Journal of ePractice 5 (October 2008)
2. Arendsen, R.: Geen Bericht, Goed Bericht, dissertation, English summary included, University of Amsterdam (2008)
3. Allers, M.A.: Administrative and Compliance Costs of Taxation and Public Transfers in the Netherlands, dissertation, Rijksuniversiteit Groningen (1994)
4. Hakapaa, S.: E-Taxation in Value Added Taxation in Finland. In: Makolm, J., Orthofer, G. (eds.) E-Taxation: State & Perspectives. Trauner Verlag, Linz (2007)
5. EIPA, eEurope Awards for eGovernment 2005, Winners (2005), http://www.eipa.nl
6. Office of the e-Envoy. Policy Framework for a mixed economy in the supply of e-government services. A consultation document (2003)
7. Arendsen, R., van Engers, T.M.: eTaxation and the Reduction of the Administrative Burden. In: E-Taxation: State & Perspectives. Trauner Verlag, Linz (2007)
8. Meulen, B., van der Meulen, B., Nedeva, M., Braun, D.: Intermediaries Organisation and Processes: theory and research issues. Position Paper for PRIME Workshop, October 6-7 (2005)
9. Bailley, J.P., Bakos, J.Y.: An Exploratory Study of the Emerging Role of Electronic Intermediaries. International Journal of Electronic Commerce 1(3), 7–20 (1997)
10. Janssen, M., Sol, H.G.: Evaluating the role of intermediaries in the electronic value chain. Internet Research. Electronic Networking Applications and Policy 19(5) (2000)
11. Janssen, M., Klievink, B.: Do We Need Intermediaries in E-Government? Intermediaries to create a demand-driven government. In: Proceedings of the fourteenth Americas Conference on Information Systems, ON, Canada, August 14- 17 (2008)
12. Williamson, O.E.: Markets and Hierarchies. Free Press, New York (1975)

13. Brynjolfsson, E., Hitt, L.M.: Beyond Computation. In: Inventing the Organizations of the 21st Century. MIT Press, Cambridge(2004)
14. Malone, T.W., Yates, J., Benjamin, R.I.: Electronic Markets and Electronic Hierarchies. Communications of the ACM 30(6) (June 1987)
15. Chircu, A.M., Kauffman, R.J.: Strategies for Internet Middlemen in the Intermediation/Disintermediation/Reintermediation Cycle, Electronic Markets. The International Journal of Electronic Commerce and Business Media (1999)
16. Clemons, E.K., Reddi, S.P., Row, M.C.: The Impact of Information Technology on the Organization of Economic Activity: the "move to the middle" Hypothesis. Journal of Management Information Systems, 9–35 (1993)
17. European Commission, Better Regulations in the EU: a strategic evaluation, COM(2006) 689 definite, Brussels (November 14, 2006)
18. OECD, Netherlands, OECD e-Government Studies, ISBN 978-92-64-03028-2, Organisation for Economic Co-operation and Development (2007)
19. Boonstra, A., De Vries, J.: Analyzing inter-organizational systems from a power and interest perspective. International Journal of Information Management 25 (2005)
20. Kuan, K.K.Y., Chau, P.Y.K.: A perception-based model for Edi adoption in small businesses using a technology-organisation-environment framework. I&M 38 (2001)
21. Hart, P., Saunders, C.: Power and Trust: Critical Factors in the Adoption and Use of Electronic Data Interchange. Organization Science 8(1), 23–42 (1997)
22. IDABC, European Interoperability Framework for pan-European eGovernment Services, European Commission, 2004/2094, Luxembourg (2004) ISBN 92-894-8389-X
23. Elgarah, W., Falaleeva, J., Saunders, C.S.: Data Exchange in Interorganizational Relationships. The Database for Advances in Information Systems 36 (Winter 2005)
24. Rasmussen, L., Davenport, E., Horton, K.: Initiating e-Participation Through a Knowledge Working Network. In: Kott, L. (ed.) ICALP 1986. LNCS, vol. 226, pp. 96–108. Springer, Heidelberg (1986)

Finding the Right Services for a Citizen Portal
Lessons Learned from the Norwegian Mypage Portal

Karin Furuli[1] and Svein Ølnes[2]

[1] Agency for Public Management and eGovernment (Difi), P.O. Box 8115 Dep,
N-0032 OSLO, Norway
karin.furuli@difi.no
[2] Western Norway Research Institute, P.O. Box 163, N-6851 SOGNDAL, Norway
svein.olnes@vestforsk.no

Abstract. Citizen portals constitute a central part of most countries' eGovernment initiatives and are increasingly important in the move from a traditional way of serving the citizens to online services. But merely duplicating already existing electronic services on a citizen portal is a questionable strategy. An evaluation of the Norwegian self service portal Mypage shows that the vast majority of the users will use the responsible agency's own self service portal. This paper discusses how citizen portals can better serve the citizen needs by adding value to already existing electronic services.

Keywords: eGovernment, Citizen Portals, self service portals.

1 Introduction

Most of the OECD countries, and also a lot of other countries around the world, have established citizen portals with self service for citizens to carry out online services. These portals can be seen as hubs for online public services in providing a single point of access to a number of services. They vary a lot regarding how deep the integration of services is, from a shallow integration of essentially only a central link repository to a deeper integration involving more complex and demanding technological solutions which also pose more challenges to the organizational level.

The term "self service" means that personalization has to be added to the traditional portal. Personalization is of course needed because the mission of a citizen portal is to gather personal data from the users and also present for them stored personal data from the authorities.

Personalization comes in many flavours, from simple methods based on cookies to more advanced methods with passwords and PIN codes and on to strong authentication systems based on PKI technology.

The citizen portals based on the one-stop-shop metaphor is an answer to the need for simplified access to online public services because citizens do not necessarily know which authority is responsible for a specific public service. The most obvious solution to this problem is a simple portal that links to the different authorities and preferably also gives a thematic overview of online services available. Older portals

M.A. Wimmer et al. (Eds.): EGOV 2009, LNCS 5693, pp. 282–292, 2009.

like www.norge.no in Norway, www.denmark.dk in Denmark, and www.help.gv.at in Austria was established with this in mind.

Over time ambitions have grown and many of these citizen portals have tried to solve another question: Why not carry out the online service in the central portal instead of being sent away to the different authorities' own portals? The Norwegian citizen portal Mypage (www.minside.no) was established as an answer to this question and opened its services to the public in mid December 2006, after two years of development. Almost all of the services offered through the Mypage portal could also be carried out on the responsible authority's own portal.

The main question after two years of operation is what type of services is best suited for a citizen portal like Mypage to become a true success in the sense that it adds value to the citizens. The question implies that merely duplicating already existing online services is not the right answer to the citizen needs. Evaluation of two years of Mypage operation shows that this type of citizen portal have problems keeping citizen interest and make them return. What is needed is to identify services that add value to existing online services.

It could be argued that offering the same online services through different portals will only be good because of opening up more channels for the citizens. The case is that developing transaction based online services is costly and the extra cost of providing yet another access point should be justified with a certain amount of users using it. If this number is low one has to question the reasons for establishing the portal.

In this paper we look at the existing services offered by the Mypage portal and discuss what type of services the portal should offer to the citizens in order to add value to the already present online services by various agencies. The insight gained from evaluating Mypage and subsequently laying out a strategy for a renewed self service portal should be of interest for other countries.

2 About Citizen Portals

Establishment of a citizen portal can be a part of reaching the government's goals in eGovernment and use of information and communications technology.

E-government can be thought of in terms of three distinct spheres; the administrative sphere, the civil society sphere, and the formal politics sphere [5]. Since the three spheres are interrelated, a change can influence all spheres. E-government strategies have impact on the way governments interact with citizens [1]. The development and implementation of e-government also causes impact and change in the structure and functioning of public administration [12].

A portal can be described as a web site that acts as a starting point for different services, such as mailbox, search engines, news and information [2]. Horizontal portals aim to serve as many internet users as possible. Verticale portals are specialised on specific market and subject areas, also called vortal [8]. A citizen portal can be viewed as both vertical and horizontal. It is horizontal in the sense that it aims to reach all inhabitants and vertical due to the fact that it shall provide public information and services from both municipalities and governmental agencies. Citizen portals have inhabitants as audience, and the relationship between the the citizen and the public is the main focus.

E-government can involve relationships between government and different levels of constituents. The relations can be between:

- government and businesses (G2B)
- government and other government institutions (G2G)
- government and employees (G2E)
- government and citizens (G2C).   [10;6].

The focus in this paper is on G2C, the citizens' relationship to government. Citizens can have various relations to the government and to the different parts of it. In one role the citizen can act as a tax payer and in another role as a parent [4]. Some citizen portals have included business oriented information and services as well (G2B). Information and services can be thematically organized (for example "School and Education" or "Health"). Information and services that are related to each other can be organized in the same theme, for example "My economy" or "My Health". In addition to this, information and services can also be sorted alphabetically or presented as "Most visited" or "Last visited" etc.

Each year comparative studies of the national offerings of electronic information and services are carried out. Among others the UN and EC publish annual studies, and according to the survey carried out by the UN in 2007 [14] the top five advanced nations in eGoverment (Web measure index) were:

1. Denmark
2. Sweden
3. USA
4. Norway
5. France

It is of interest to look at the nations that are considered to be the best in order to see what kind of solutions they have chosen. The Danish citizen portal - Borger.dk have collected information and services in one single portal. Business services has its own portal, like in Norway. Late 2008 Borger.dk was extended with a "My Page" part that includes electronic services that requires authentication with digital signature.

Sweden closed down their citizen portal Sverige.se, in march 2008. The portal consisted of some digital self-services, in addition to information structured after life situations. Sweden.no has been rebuilt and the mission of the portal is to make it easy to find information about Sweden in English as well as other languages. There are five organizations behind Sweden.se with an overall responsibility for promoting Sweden abroad: the Swedish Institute (which produces, develops, maintains and operates the portal), the Swedish Government Offices including the Ministry of Foreign Affairs and the Ministry of Enterprise, Energy and Communications, the Invest in Sweden Agency, the Swedish Trade Council and VisitSweden.

Verva, The Swedish Agency for Administrative Development, was established in 2006 in an attempt to strengthen the work on e-Government. It was closed down by the end of 2008 and the different tasks transferred to other agencies, most notably Statskontoret. This move coincides with the closure of sweden.se as a portal and can be interpreted as an admittance of a wrong approach to the governance of the eGovernment policy. In all fairness it also has to be added that this was to be expected

since the Government had given Verva neither the tools needed nor a concrete definition of the e-government mission [13].

3 About Mypage

Mypage was launched in December 2006, after two years of deveopment. The initiative came from the Ministry of modernization (now: Ministry of Government Administration and Reform). The Agency for Public Management and eGovernment
managed the portal.

The vision of Mypage is to contribute to a simpler and more effective dialogue between citizens and the public sector. Another aim is to give an overview of what information the individual agencies hold about the individual citizen [11]. Mypage is
part of Norway.no, which acts as a gateway to public sector information in Norway,
both from the Government and its agencies and the municipalities.

Mypage is a common entrance to public e-services on the Internet, and the portal is
the citizens' public service office on the Internet. Mypage is a collection of e-services,
personalized for the citizens and as such it offers interaction with the Government.
For the governmental agencies and municipalities Mypage is a supplement to their
own portals.

Mypage consists of services offered by municipalities and public agencies. The
services are owned by the municipalities and public agencies, Mypage presents the
services and contains information required to personalize the citizen's own page.

The citizen has to authorize himself to get access to Mypage. The current public
authentication method MyID (My identification) is based on PIN-codes issued by the
tax authorities. There are work in progress to establish a new public solution, where
private suppliers also can deliver electronic identification. The current solution for
authentication can also be used by agencies and municipalities which currently have
no services in the citizen portal. MyID is now used by 1 200 000 citizens (by 1st of
May 2009).

There are four different types of services on Mypage today:

- Transaction services (for instance applying for kindergarten or credit on loan
  given to students). The services are executed on the service owners' own web
  site.
- Messaging services. This kind of service supports secure communication between the citizen and the service owner.
- Register services give the citizens a view of information about themselves held
  in public registers, for example an overview of applications sent to the municipality or how much pension one has earned.
- Calendar services in Mypage offers the citizen an overview over important dates
  and deadlines. The calendar shows important dates (for example delivering tax
  return).

By 1st of May 2009 about 620 000 unique users have logged in to Mypage. 65 municipalities and 12 public agencies offer services to the citizen portal.

The fact that the electronic services offered through Mypage also can be found on the different agencies' own portals makes it interesting to see what portion of the citizens access the services through the different channels.

A study in 2008 [16] as part of a working out a new strategy for Mypage, found that most users went to the responsible agency's own portal to carry out the specific electronic service:

Table 1. Use of different channels for carrying out specific electronic services

Service	Agency users	Mypage users	Percentage Mypage
Change of tax information	247 688	27 250	11
Request for health insurance card	437 071	21 425	5
Information about personal doctor	1 072 069	153 103	12
Change of address	86 000	44 271	34

Even if quite a lot of the citizens use the services on Mypage today, and thus are increasing the use of electronic services, the main question is if Mypage gives added value to the citizens. Are there other ways to present services or are there other types of services that can add more value to the citizens when presented in a citizen portal?

4   Proposed Services for a Citizen Portal

Our study of the Norwegian Mypage portal show that ordinary electronic services that already exist on the responsible agencies' own portals will not give any added value to the citizens if offered also on a citizen portal. Our evaluation also shows that building a citizen portal with this kind of services is questionable in terms of costs and benefits. People tend to use the agencies' own service portals, especially if the service provider is one of the major agencies.

There is of course a reason to help those who do not know which agency provides a specific service. But there are other and cheaper ways to help these citizens. An ordinary link portal would do the same job, providing the necessary information and links to the right agencies and their services. This is the kind of help the traditional public portals like for instance www.norge.no and www.denmark.dk provides.

A citizen portal should offer more than just duplicates of already existing electronic services. It should offer an added value that a public agency itself cannot do and that has to be carried out from a central point.

4.1   Compound and Process Oriented Services

Quite a few public services involve more than one organization. Compound services have so far been offered separately from each organization with (almost) no transfer of information or help in progress for the user. Each involved organization has solved the problem isolated inside their own silos. Clearly this is not the way to handle compound services. Some rudimentary attempts have been tried out, but a sustainable solution to this challenge has not yet been developed.

The ability to present a compound service for the users so that it looks and behaves like one service and not several more or less interlinked ones is what characterises the fourth step in Layne & Lee's Four Stage Model [9] of eGovernment services.

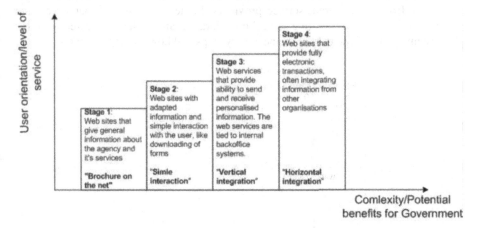

Fig. 1. The Four Stage Model by Layne & Lee

The fourth stage of the Four Stage Model involves services often integrating information or parts from other organizations. These services must be orchestrated in such a way that the service presents itself as a whole to the user. In order to achieve this it must be a central coordination from either one of the service providers or from a level above each service provider. In practice reaching stage four has proven difficult because of the interoperability challenges. Less than 5% of the municipalities have services at the fourth stage. Among governmental agencies less than 10% provide services at stage four [3].

Here is where a citizen portal has a mission. Compound services are difficult to solve at an organizational level alone, it needs to be looked at the challenges at a higher level. The citizen portal could orchestrate the process of building together compound services involving more than one organization by offering a framework, an architecture, for compound services. In offering compound services it is also very important to show the progress of the service delivery because the sequence in which the different parts of the service are carried out is not arbitrary. The accompanying guidance to the process is about as important as the service itself and is also a pedagogical challenge.

We will use the service *obtaining a driving license* as an example of a compound service. In Norway this service involves at least four organizations, of which there are also private agencies involved: The National Road Authority as the main organization, the local municipality, a (private) driving school, the Police Authorities, and the primary health service which is partly public and partly private. The process of obtaining a driving license is also important because the different steps have to be carried out in a certain sequence.

In a joint project between the National Road Authority, a local municipality and the Norwegian public portal www.norge.no modelling this compound service was one of the main tasks [15]. The process of obtaining a driving license was modelled with the use of the semantic technology Topic Maps, an ISO standard for knowledge representation (ISO 13250:2003). The semantic supported model enabled to guide the user through the process in a correct sequence and at the same time coupled the service parts from the different service providers. Some of the service parts were not possible to carry out online (e.g. a health declaration and a character reference), but the system informed the user of the necessary steps and how to carry them out.

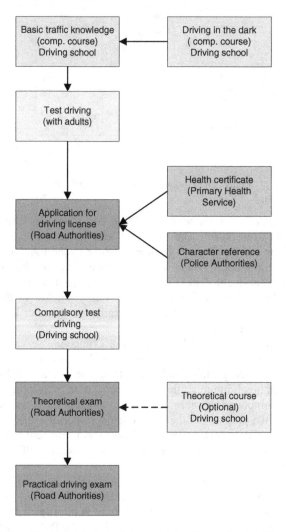

Fig. 2. A simplified model of obtaining a driving license (car) in Norway [15]

The figure above shows a simplified model of obtaining a driving license for a car in Norway. The different colours represent different authorities/responsibilities.

The above example put the main focus on modelling the compound service and did not spend many resources on implementation other than developing mock-ups showing the possibilities. The compound service was modelled using the semantical technology standard Topic Maps. Using this standard it was relatively easy to model a compound service in a way that also took care of the progress challenge.

A compound service like this typically involves several organizations and is challenging in terms of interoperability. It involved interoperability at all levels described by EU's IDABC [7] like technical (agreement on formats etc.), semantic (agreement and harmonization of vocabulary and ontologies), and organizational in terms of the different parties agreeing on the provision and the maintenance of the service. We think this best can be done when introducing a level above the organizations orchestrating the whole process.

The responsibility for the different parts of the service should be clearly stated. But tying the different parts together to a new compound electronic service also introduces new challenges in terms of support for the process as a whole. This is very important and must not be underestimated or else one can easily end up in a situation where the user is thrown back and forth between the organizations involved. The citizen portal must take a responsibility here and also provide a first stop support service. This is an essential part of the organizational interoperability.

Compound services seem to be obviously suited for citizen portals, but there are also other types of services that such portals should investigate. Examples of other suitable services for these portals are secure messaging services and secure access to personal information held by different public bodies.

Starting with the last example Mypage already from the start provided citizens with access to personal information held by different public bodies. On Mypage a citizen can view the address registered in the National Registry, the properties registered in the National Land Register, and registered vehicles at the National Road Authority. Whether this should be called a service is questionable but the question of "what is a service" is too comprehensive to be discussed here, it is a topic in its own for discussing in another paper [16].

4.2 Easy Access to Personal Information

The provision of relatively easy access to this information led to both obviuous and surprising results. The obvious result was that a lot of the registered information was corrected by the citizens, not directly but via emails and telephone calls to the Mypage. The surprising result was that a lot of citizens discovered detailed personal information that they did not know existed. For instance, a lot of property information came as a surprise to many users. They were not aware of all their properties, in other words properties were disclosed for them that they did not know existed.

Easy access to personal information helps citizens find out what the public sector holds of information about them as a whole. This is a right each person is granted according to the privacy law but it is important that this is solved in a user friendly way with as low barriers to the users as possible. This is probably best done through a central citizen portal and not on each agency's own portal. At least the people behind the European eGovernment Award thought so when they awarded Mypage the prize for best service in the category "Participation and transparency" in 2007[1]. Although the information gathered on Mypage is obtainable also through each agency's own web portal it gives meaning to be able to access this information from a single point.

The experiences with this part of Mypage have shown the importance of disclosing personal information held by the public authorities. It is important that citizens can get easy access to the information held by public authorities in order to secure correct information and thus improve the data quality. In most cases the citizen himself knows better what the right information is and what is not. But in some cases the citizen in fact does not know of information that should be known to him. In this case a self service portal serves an important duty in informing the citizens. The next step in improving this kind of services would be to provide for easy maintenance of the information for the users themselves.

The third kind of services a citizen portal should focus on is services that depend on a central coordination and cannot and should not be offered by the different public agencies themselves. Security services are obvious here, but they are a prerequisite for a self service portal in the first place so we will not discuss them here. We will instead describe the public inbox as an example of a service that needs to be coordinated from a single, central point.

4.3 E-mail Inbox

The public inbox is a secure email inbox where citizens can receive mail from different public bodies. There is a huge potential for reducing costs if public sector can communicate with most citizens electronic instead of by sending physical mail. The provision for a central public inbox would also lessen the confusion caused by different agencies operating their own inboxes. The public email inbox could also be extended to include communication from private sector as well, but in this example we concentrate on public sector communication.

The argument for having one central email inbox instead of each public agency communicating directly with the citizens can be found in the related physical service. You only have one mailbox for all your mail and it is quite clear that the Tax Authorities or the Social Welfare Authorities cannot put up their own mailboxes on your mailbox stand. Strangely this is the case for electronic communication. Several authorities are establishing their own channels for delivering electronic mail to citizens. Seen from their own isolated perspective these initiatives are successful because it both reduces mail handlings and costs and the quality of communication can be improved.

What is seen as a success in a public agency is not necessarily best for society as a whole. We think the case of public inboxes is in this category. For the individual user a good functioning electronic channel to a public agency is at first a benefit, but when agency number three and four, not to mention number fifteen and twenty, has established their own channels, the picture looks different. The challenge calls for a solution where the user is in the centre and the different agencies cooperate to deliver a communications solution as a whole.

---

[1] http://www.epractice.eu/egovernment2007

Although Mypage was established with a message component built into it, this function has not been much used. There are several reasons for this. The message function is not a complete public email inbox solution and there has not been enough pressure to ensure different agencies to route their communication through the Mypage portal instead of their own self service portals.

When discussing a central email inbox it is also very important to distinguish between the archiving process and the communication process. Archiving should of course still be the individual agency's responsibility and the central public email inbox should only be a window into the archives of all the public agencies.

Denmark is probably the leading country for this type of service. Their e-Boks service now has 1,5 million users out of a total population of 5,5 million people.

5 Conclusion and Further Research

Our work with the citizen portal Mypage in the two years of operation has shown that although it has attracted many users, the vast majority of them prefer to use the responsible agency's own self service portal to carry out electronic services. Working on a new strategy for Mypage we suggest that a citizen portal should not duplicate already existing electronic services but instead offer services that give the users an added value compared to the different agencies' own services. This can be compound services where more than one organization is involved. We also point to easy access to personal information held by public bodies as a natural responsibility for a citizen portal and finally we think services like a common electronic mailbox is best solved when offered through such a portal.

Our work with a new strategy for Mypage has shown that there are many issues that need to be further examined in order to better understand the premises for building a successful citizen portal. We think it is important to have better knowledge about citizen portals as a part of national eGovernment initiatives. Such initiatives tend to be costly and more knowledge about the issues can better ensure that the goals will be met and that the effects of the initiatives will be greater. All in all we think a better understanding of the way citizen portals function will help to get more benefits from the resources put in. As such a broader and deeper survey of some national citizen portals would be interesting.

We should also listen more carefully to the users of citizen portals. A broader survey could help us find answers to what services would benefit them the most. How should citizen portals be build to meet the expectations from the users? Where should one start when building such portals? Should shared components be developed first or should the portal be established first as a driver for developing these shared components?

Another approach worth looking at is what stakeholders a citizen portal have and if they have common interests in the portal. If they do not have the same interests, how should conflicts be managed and solved? These and other questions should be turned into research questions for further evaluations and better knowledge and understanding of what gives a successful citizen portal.

References

1. Chen, Y.N., Chen, H.M., Huang, W., Ching, R.K.H.: E-Government Strategies in Developed and Developing Countries: An Implementation Framework and Case Study. Journal of Global Information Management 14(1), 23–46 (2006)
2. Davis, W., Benamati, J.: E-commerce basics Technology Foundations and E-Business Applications. Addison Wesley, USA (2003)
3. Fornyings- og administrasjonsdepartementet: Stortingsmelding nr 17 (2006-2007) Et informasjonssamfunn for alle. Fornyings- og administrasjonsdepartementet, Oslo, Norge (2006)
4. Furuli, K., Kongsrud, s.: My page and Borger.dk - A Case Study of two Government Service Web Portals. In: European Conference on eGovernment, Haag (2007)
5. Grönlund, Å.: What's In a Field – Exploring the eGoverment Domain. In: Proceedings from the 38th Hawaii International Conference on System Sciences, Hawaii, USA (2005)
6. Hiller, J., Bélanger, F.: Privacy strategies for Electronic Government. In: Abrahamson, M.A., Means, G.E. (eds.). Rowman and Littlefield Publishers, Oxford (2001)
7. IDABC (2004): European Interoperability Framework for Pan-European eGovernment Services, Luxembourg (2004),
   http://ec.europa.eu/idabc/servlets/Doc?id=19529
8. Laudon, K.C., Traver, C.G.: E-commerce business technology society. Addison-Wesley, USA (2001)
9. Layne, K., Lee, J.: Developing fully functional E-government: A four stage model. Government Information Quarterly 18, 122–136 (2001)
10. Long, Y.A., Siau, K.: Using social development lenses to understand e-government development. Journal of global management 14(1), 47–62 (2006)
11. Moderniseringsdepartementet: eNorge 2009 – det digitale spranget. Moderniseringsdepartementet, Oslo, Norge (2005)
12. Snellen, I.: Electronic commerce and bureaucraties. In: Proceedings of the 11thInternational Workshops on Database and Expert System Application, pp. 285–288 (2000)
13. Stabsutredningen (2008): Ett stabsstöd i tiden. SOU 2008:22. (Up to date support agencies) (2008)
14. United Nations (2008): UN e-Government Survey 2008. From e-Government to Connected Governance. Tilgjengelig,
   http://unpan1.un.org/intradoc/groups/public/documents/UN/
   UNPAN028607.pdf (Siste sett: 2. February 2009)
15. Ølnes (2006): Emnekart og tenesteprosessar. Vestlandsforsking, Sogndal (2006),
   http://www.vestforsk.no/www/show.do?page=12&articleid=1284
16. Ølnes and Gulbrandsen: (2008) Strategy for Mypage and Norge.no. Vestlandsforsking, Sogndal (2008),
   http://www.vestforsk.no/www/show.do?page=12&articleid=2188

The State of Client-Centered Public Service Delivery in the Netherlands

Jurjen Jansen[1], Sjoerd de Vries[1], Thea van der Geest[1], Rex Arendsen[2], and Jan van Dijk[1]

[1] University of Twente, Center for e-Government Studies
P.O. Box 217, 7500 AE Enschede, The Netherlands
{j.jansen,s.a.devries,t.m.vandergeest
j.a.g.m.vandijk}@utwente.nl
[2] Dutch Ministry of Finance
P.O. Box 20201, 2500 EE The Hague, The Netherlands
r.arendsen@minfin.nl

Abstract. Businesses and citizens demand a better and more client-centered way of service delivery from public organizations. As society becomes more complex, dynamic and diverse, public organizations need to adapt to this demand. Conversely, our perception is that public organizations might still treat their target groups as one. However, the need for client-centered public service delivery is growing. This is widely debated in literature. Nonetheless, little empirical evidence is available about the state of client-centeredness of public organizations. The objective of the present study is to identify the state of client-centered public service delivery in the Netherlands. In order to research this topic 400 people from 194 Dutch public organizations were invited to complete an electronic questionnaire. 105 people responded. According to the respondents the state of client-centeredness is acceptable. However, only 25% of the public organizations seem to take differentiation as the point of departure for their service delivery.

Keywords: Client-centeredness, public service delivery, public organizations, government, differentiation, segmentation.

1 Introduction

"The citizen does not exist, therefore differentiation is needed" [1, p.23]. This quotation about citizenship in the Netherlands shows that there is a need for a client-centered approach. Because people are different, public organizations can only succeed in getting things done by adapting to the behavior and preferences of their target groups.

Although differentiation is needed it is assumed that public organizations treat their target groups equally. At the point of departure for policy making the question rises what 'the' citizen wants and wants not, what he thinks is user-friendly and which needs he has. Clearly, citizens have the need for a non-equal approach.

We studied client-centeredness in two projects. Recently, for example, the Dutch Tax Administration has developed a new segmentation model of citizens which is

M.A. Wimmer et al. (Eds.): EGOV 2009, LNCS 5693, pp. 293–304, 2009.
© Springer-Verlag Berlin Heidelberg 2009

being implemented in their communications and service delivery processes at the moment. In 2007 the city of Enschede started with a so-called forms squad. This squad visits people who are living under the poverty line and who do not make use of social benefits. The forms squad assists people filling in difficult forms or addresses them the possibilities to apply for social benefits. The squad is furthermore multicultural in order to give better interpretations to language or cultural differences.

The objective of the present study is twofold: to identify the state of client-centeredness and to determine if differentiation is the starting point for public organizations in approaching their target groups. This study concentrates on the service deliverer. In the next study we expect to focus on the receiver of public services, i.e. citizens and businesses. The following research question is addressed in this paper: *What is the state of client-centered public service delivery in the Netherlands?*

Public organizations can learn from private organizations that have gone through the development of undifferentiated mass marketing, via segmented marketing, to one-on-one marketing in the last 50 years. A relevant question is if public organizations have taken notice of this trend.

The need for adopting a client-centered approach by public organizations is growing. Van Duivenboden and Lips [2] appeal that there are three explanations why client-centeredness gets more attention in public service delivery. These are: changing expectations from citizens, a complex societal environment that calls for different ways of direction and a differentiating offer of public services by using ICTs. This need is furthermore prompted by the ongoing bureaucratic procedures and the increase of electronic service delivery which is recognized to be abstract and impersonal. And by society which becomes more complex, dynamic and diverse.

Client-centeredness is a multi-faceted concept. In order to put client-centeredness into operation we utilize the segmentation concept. Segmentation is chosen, because it is a common technique for differentiation. However, little is known about segmentation in a public organizational context. Although there is experimented with several segmentation techniques it is rather difficult to apply segmentation models successfully. Two important reasons are: the generic character of segmentation models and the small scientific basis on which the segmentation models are based.

2 Client-Centered Public Service Delivery

For private organizations it is well-known that in order to provide consumers products and services research needs to be conducted on the wishes, expectations and needs of the (wished-for) target group. Public organizations are increasingly recognizing that they need to take the characteristics of their target groups into account. This means that one needs to understand who the target group is and what kind of relationship they have with the organization [3].

When meeting this kind of understanding and acting to it we speak of client-centeredness. The definition that we give to client-centeredness is: to put a target group at the central stage and to take into account their characteristics, situation and perceptions in order to pinpoint service delivery, enforcement and communication activities.

In order to describe the state of client-centered public service delivery the definition of state needs to be clear-cut. We propose that the state of client-centered service delivery mainly consists of the vision of the organization and of four concrete implementation steps which we identify as: goals, motives, conditions and design. These concepts are further explained within this section.

Visions. With regard to visions we define two broad concepts, namely: a client-centered vision and an organization-centered vision. A client-centered vision in our study consists of one basic stage, i.e. focusing on the average client, and three (more) advanced stages, namely: taking different segments, individuals or the question of the client as the point of departure for service delivery. The starting point for service delivery from an organization-centered vision consists of the following three stages: the organizational structure, the internal processes or the products and/or services. The formulation of the identified visions is inspired by research of Thomassen [4].

Goals. Based on Besamusca-Jansen [5] we refer to four goals of client-centeredness for public organizations: improving the effectiveness of service delivery, improving the internal efficiency of the organization, improving the image of the organization and offering new challenges for managers and employees of the organization. It can be noticed that these goals are primarily internal goals. This is justified, because this study comprehends with the service deliverer. When researching the receivers of public service delivery, e.g. citizens and businesses, other goals would be more appropriate. In that case one could think of goals about: user-friendliness, accessibility, transparency, and the like.

Motives. Besides formulating goals around client-centeredness, organizations can also be triggered by motives to adopt a client-centered approach. Thomassen [4] addresses three motives. The first motive is internal pressure, i.e. (new) policy makers can put client-centeredness (back) on the agenda. The second motive is the introduction of free market processes. However, in a government context this is only possible for semi-government organizations, like hospitals and power companies. A third motive is pressure from national politics, e.g. regulations, or pressure from internal management, e.g. targets and goals.

Conditions. For an organization to be or to become a client-centered organization some conditions need to be met. Thomassen [4] has identified six conditions. Five of these come back in the results section and are formulated as follows: knowing the target group, knowing what the target group wants, delivering what the target group wants, improving the service delivery to the target group continuously and coaching employees of the organization to work in a client-centered way.

Design. Public organizations are more aware that their target groups are heterogeneous [4]. Public organizations could increase researching the differences and similarities of their target groups and use these results to segment their target groups. According to Akerboom et al. [6] segmentation is needed in the public sector. They give the example that the population can not longer be addressed with only one message. They state that in this way the groups that need the message the least will be reached while it is important to reach that group that needs it the most. The design of client-centeredness is narrowly related with segmentation. Because of this, segmentation deserves additional attention.

In this study client-centeredness is cultivated around segmentation. This concept is introduced by Wendell Smith in 1956. It was introduced to change the scope from a mass marketing to a more client-centered marketing approach [7], [8]. The definition of segmentation that Smith gave at that time was: *"Market segmentation involves viewing a heterogeneous market as a number of smaller homogenous markets, in response to differing preferences, attributable to the desires of consumers for more precise satisfaction of their varying wants"* [9; cited in 10, p.3].

After more than two generations of research about this topic, segmentation both in practice as in science has made a lot of progress. Nowadays, topics like customer relationship marketing and one-on-one marketing are predominant. However, according to Professor Bijmolt [in 11, p.8] segmentation is not an outdated concept. He states that *"the underlying idea that not all consumers are equal, but also are not all different, is still relevant today"*.

In a literature review on user-profiling [12, p.14] the following definition of segmentation is given. *"Segmentation is the process of dividing a population into groups on the basis of similarities in user-related information of individuals"*. This definition pulls segmentation out of the marketing scope and defines it as a broad concept that can be applied in all kinds of situations. It also concentrates more on the similarities within groups than on differences between groups. In segmentation exercises it is the similarities that count [13]. It is thus this definition that will be used in this paper.

In this paper a distinction is made between four general forms of segmentation, which will be referred to as: geographic, demographic, psychographic and behavior segmentation. This division is based on Kotler's [14].

The first form of segmentation, geographic segmentation, is the oldest and the easiest form of segmentation. The assumption is that people have different needs on the basis of where they live [13]. This means that people who live near each other appear to have the same characteristics [10].

The second oldest and most occurring form of segmentation is demographic segmentation [15], [16]. Demographic segmentation assumes that people who have the same demographic characteristics, e.g. age, gender and income, act the same [15]. It is an often used exercise, because it is relatively easy to use, cheap and gives a quick overview of the market [17], [12]. However, some studies have shown that demographic segmentation became unpractical to use, because there is too much variation within the segments [18], [19], [20].

The third, and newer, form of segmentation is psychographic segmentation. According to Cahill [13] psychographic segmentation starts with a distinction between activities (e.g. job and hobbies), interests (e.g. family and media-use) and opinions (e.g. about socials issues, politics and products). He furthermore states that values should be added to this list, because of its relevance. All four variables combined together can be interpreted as lifestyle and sometimes reflect ones personality. As Beane and Ennis [21] note, psychographic segmentation directs more to someone's inner side than somebody's external appearance.

The fourth and last form of segmentation is behavior segmentation. The goal of this kind of segmentation is to identify different types of behavior that could have implications for different (marketing) purposes [21].

Segmentation is a common practice used by private organizations. It is, however, unclear how much it is used by public organizations. There is also no empirical basis to decide which of these segmentation forms work for public organizations and which do not. Despite this, we try to investigate to what extent public organizations have adopted segmentation forms.

3 Methods

In this section we describe the research approach. We take a look at the research population first and then take a look at the method for data collection.

The research population concerns national and local public organizations in the Netherlands. All public organizations are identified as government organizations. The kind of public organizations that were approached during this study were: ministries (N=13), administrative bodies (N=9), provinces (N=12) and a stratified sample of municipalities (N=160). The municipalities were split up in three categories, namely: small, i.e. less than 20.000 inhabitants (n=60), medium, i.e. between 20.000 and 100.000 inhabitants (n=75), and large, i.e. over 100.000 inhabitants (n=25).

The respondents for this study needed to be involved in communication or service delivery processes, with a preference for respondents that were responsible for client-centeredness in their organization. This means that more than one e-mail address could be obtained for each public organization. The names and e-mail addresses of the respondents were gathered by means of looking for them on related websites or by calling directly to the specific organizations. It was rather difficult to find the right people, especially for the municipalities. This was mainly due to the difference in website and organizational structure and because of large differences in the naming of departments and job titles. Eventually, 400 e-mail addresses were gathered.

In order to answer the research question an electronic questionnaire was set up. The questionnaire was constructed around the five identified aspects (visions, goals, motives, conditions and design) of client-centeredness, i.e. our conceptual model. Before the questionnaire was sent out to the respondents it was qualitatively pre-tested by three people who belong to the population of interest. The questionnaire was furthermore personalized in order to receive a higher response rate.

4 Results

In this section the results of the electronic questionnaire are described. The questionnaire could be filled in from the beginning of December 2008 till the end of January in 2009. This period is relatively long, but was needed considering the holidays in that timeframe. On December 15th and January 15th a reminder was sent out to the respondents who had not filled in the questionnaire. At the end of January an effective response of 26.3% (N=105) was gathered. However, when taking the number of approached organizations into account (194) the response is 54.1%.

The administrative bodies, the medium and the large municipalities are represented the strongest by respectively 66.7, 68 and 60 percent. Besides that, representatives of one of thirteen ministries, one third of the provinces and 46.7% of the small-sized municipalities filled in the questionnaire. Of the total response, 1% belongs to the ministries, 5.7% to administrative bodies, and 3.8% to the provinces. 26.7%, 48.6% and 14.3% belongs respectively to small, medium and large municipalities. From our perspective this response is adequate to give a global insight in the state of client-centeredness in the Netherlands.

4.1 Client-Centered Public Service Delivery: Visions

Respondents were asked what the vision of their organization is about service delivery. The respondents could only choose one of the presented levels. In our opinion level 1 to 3 indicate an organization-centered vision, whereas level 4 to 7 point toward a client-centered vision.

Table 1. Visions of client-centeredness (N=105)

Levels of centrality	Percentage
1 Organizational structure	1.0
2 Processes	6.7
3 Products/services	19.0
4 Average client	37.1
5 Segments	12.4
6 Individuals	11.4
7 Client-steering	4.8
8 Do not know	1.0
9 Other	6.7

As can be seen from table 1, more than a quarter of the respondents has adopted an organizational-centered vision. Over a third of the respondents take on a basic level of client-centeredness, i.e. the average client. Approximately 25% make use of differentiation, i.e. segments and individuals, as the point of departure for their service delivery. 5% of the approached organizations point out that the client steers the process of service delivery.

4.2 Client-Centered Public Service Delivery: Goals

Respondents that made clear that their organization has adopted a client-centered approach were asked for what goals they had in mind when adopting such an approach. They had the opportunity to select more than one goal. Therefore, the percentages do not add up to 100.

Almost 80% of the respondents mention improving service delivery to their target groups as the most important goal for client-centeredness. Between 40 and 50 percent of the respondents articulate that improving effectiveness of service delivery, improving efficiency of service delivery and improving the image of the organization are also important goals to adopt a client-centered approach.

Table 2. Goals for adopting a client-centered approach (n=70)

Goals	Percentage
Improving service delivery	77.1
Improving effectiveness	48.6
Improving image	44.3
Improving efficiency	42.9
Improving relationships	22.9
Reducing costs	10.0
Other	1.4
Do not know	0

The respondents who mentioned that their organization had not adopted a client-centered approach were asked for reasoning. They also had the opportunity to select more than one option.

Table 3. Reasons for not adopting a client-centered approach (n=30)

Reasons	Percentage
Other	40.0
Not ready	36.7
Too little knowledge	23.3
Current way is more effective	10.0
Privacy matters	10.0
Costs too much time	6.7
Obstructed by the organization	6.7
Do not know	3.3
Current way is more efficient	0
Costs too much money	0

The reasons that were mentioned the most in relation to not having adopted a client-centered approach are that they are just not ready for it and that there is too little knowledge in order to put a client-centered approach into action. Over a third of the respondents gave another reason for not having adopted a client-centered approach. About 50% of these respondents made clear that activities in their organization are organized in order to employ a client-centered approach, but that they are not realized yet. A third of these respondents made clear that it is rather difficult to adopt a client-centered approach, because of the way certain products, processes and regulations are designed.

The respondents (n=30) were also asked what the likelihood is that their organization will adopt a client-centered approach in the next five years. Almost 90% is positive that they will.

4.3 Client-Centered Public Service Delivery: Motives

Besides formulating goals it is also possible that public organizations are triggered by motives in order to adopt a client-centered approach. The motives defined within this paper are: 1) influence from targets/goals, 2) influence of ICT developments, 3) influence from the own organization, 4) influence of regulation policies, 5) influence from the target group, and 6) influence from national politics. The respondents rated these propositions on a seven point Likert scale ranging from (1) not applicable at all to (7) fully applicable.

Table 4. Motives for adopting a client-centered approach (seven point Likert scale)

Proposition	Much (5-7)	Moderate (4)	Little (1-3)	n
1 Targets/goals	95.7%	1.4%	2.9%	70
2 ICT developments	62.9%	17.1%	20.0%	70
3 Own organization	52.8%	12.9%	34.3%	70
4 Regulation policies	38.5%	21.4%	37.1%	70
5 Target group	32.8%	28.6%	37.1%	70
6 National politics	18.8%	15.7%	65.7%	70

Table 4 shows that the biggest influence for adopting a client-centered approach is the internal targets or goals. National politics and the influence of the target group have little to do with the motives of public organizations to adopt a client-centered approach. The other three reasons are of small influence.

4.4 Client-Centered Public Service Delivery: Conditions

Not only the goals and motives are important for a client-centered organization. According to Thomassen [4] public organizations need to meet different conditions in order to become a client-centered organization. The conditions are translated into the following propositions: 1) my organization improves its service delivery to the target group continuously, 2) my organization knows who its target group is, 3) my organization coaches me and my colleagues to work in a client-centered way, 4) my organization knows what the target group wants, and 5) my organization delivers what the target group wants. In some cases the population is less than 105. This means that the respondents have filled in that they do not know the answer.

Table 5. Conditions for client-centeredness (seven point Likert scale)

Proposition	Much (5-7)	Moderate (4)	Little (1-3)	N
1 Continuous improvement	92.3%	2.9%	4.8%	105
2 Knowing the target group	91.4%	3.8%	4.8%	105
3 Coaching employees	82.6%	8.7%	8.7%	103
4 Knowing needs of target group	78.1%	13.3%	8.6%	105
5 Delivering needs of target group	63.8%	27.6%	8.6%	105

Table 5 illustrates that the propositions are all above the neutral level. This means that the public organizations continuously improve their services to their target groups and know who its target groups are. They also, but to a smaller extent, know and deliver what their target groups want. According to Thomassen [4] a client-centered organization starts with client-centered employees. Public organizations are coaching their employees in this. These results show that, on average, public organizations do a reasonable to good job qualifying the conditions to be or to become a client-centered organization.

4.5 Client-Centered Public Service Delivery: Design

An important part of this research is to identify the design or adopted forms of client-centeredness. The following six forms are identified: 1) segmentation of one, i.e. individuals get tailored products or services, 2) no segmentation, i.e. everyone gets the same products or services, 3) geographic segmentation, 4) demographic segmentation, 5) behavior segmentation, and 6) psychographic segmentation.

Table 6. Design of client-centered service delivery (seven point Likert scale)

Proposition	Much (5-7)	Moderate (4)	Little (1-3)	n
1 Segmentation of one	68.3%	19.2%	12.5%	104
2 No segmentation	50%	19.2%	30.8%	104
3 Geographic	20%	19%	61%	105
4 Demographic	18.1%	25.7%	56.2%	105
5 Behavior	10.7%	15.5%	73.9%	103
6 Psychographic	9.6%	13.5%	77%	104

As shown in table 6, public organizations in general make little use of geographic, demographic, behavior and psychographic segmentation forms. Public organizations are more occupied applying the same services to all, but are, conversely, also trying to deliver tailored services to their target groups.

5 Conclusion and Discussion

This study began with the premise that little is known about the state of client-centered public service delivery in the Netherlands. Within this section the research question is briefly answered, a discussion about the study is outlined and directions for future research are given. Before answering the research question we first take a look to the five points for the state of client-centeredness.

5.1 Conclusion

Visions. The results lead us to the conclusion that more than a quarter of the public organizations do not organize their communication and service delivery in a client-centered way. This means that nearly two-thirds has adopted some level of client-centeredness. However, over a third of the public organizations base their service delivery on the average client, i.e. a basic form of client-centeredness. Just 25% make use of differentiation. In about 5% of the cases the client steers the process of service delivery. This previous point is an important aspect for the central government in the Netherlands. According to their policy plan public organizations need to make a transfer to this way of service delivery.

Goals. The results suggest that the most important goal for adopting a client-centered approach is improving the service delivery to the target group. Other goals were: improving the effectiveness of service delivery, improving the efficiency of service delivery and improving the image of the organization. Organizations that have not adopted a client-centered approach explained that they are not ready for it (yet) and that they have too little knowledge in order to adopt a client-centered approach.

Motives. The most mentioned motive for becoming a client-centered organization is the influence of internal targets or goals, i.e. an inside-out perspective. The motives do not or barely come from an outside-in perspective. This is surprising considering the positive vision of public organizations about client-centeredness.

Conditions. Public organizations in the Netherlands know their target groups and continuously improve their services to them. The results furthermore show that, on average, public organizations do a reasonable to good job qualifying the conditions to be or to become a client-centered organization.

Design. Public organizations make little use of the general forms of segmentation. Instead, they try to deliver their services in a tailored way. The majority also delivers equal services for everyone, which seems to be a contradiction.

To draw conclusions and to answer the research question it can be summarized that according to the respondents the state of client-centeredness is acceptable.

5.2 Discussion

In this study some points of discussion can be addressed. Although we try to sketch the state of client-centered public service delivery in the Netherlands it needs to be taken into account that the results are mainly based on municipalities. The sample of the other public organizations is small. It could thus be that some results are skewed. Furthermore, the medium-sized municipalities were slightly over-represented while the small-sized municipalities were slightly underrepresented.

Also the method of data collection can be judged. An electronic questionnaire is an adequate tool, but it cannot be guaranteed that all respondents were the right ones to speak on behalf of their organization.

Furthermore, the visions of service delivery in section 4.1 could be difficult to fill in. Respondents may have answered this question for the whole organization or for a certain department or service. Some departments or services could be more client-centered than others.

Some might argue that the propositions in section 4.4 are too vague and that more specific propositions would improve the quality of the questionnaire. However, in order to limit the length of the questionnaire we needed to omit some in-depth questions.

In conclusion, according to our opinion the state of client-centeredness is not as far as we have hoped. Around two-thirds of the public organizations do not come further than taking the average client as the point for departure for the communication and service delivery. Moreover, only 25% makes use of differentiation.

5.3 Future Research

Because client-centeredness within public organizations is just in the early stage, more insights are desirable. Therefore, future research is needed. It is first of all essential to define the concepts used in this study more thoroughly in order to create a theoretical framework around client-centeredness. This is currently missing in scientific literature.

It is necessary to identify how public organizations implement a client-centered approach in their daily practices. It is furthermore important what a client-centered approach produces, i.e. what are the effects of adopting a client-centered approach, both for the organization and for the target groups?

Additionally, it is necessary to do more research on the differences and similarities between public and private organizations in the field of client-centeredness. Private organizations have, for example, more freedom in the way they deliver services and approach target groups. It is also valuable to identify if the target groups of public organizations really want to be treated in a client-centered way or in similar ways like private organizations treat them. Perhaps they do not have a need for this?

In order to interpret these results international studies should be executed. When benchmarking the results it will be possible to draw conclusions about how well public organizations in the Netherlands are really performing on client-centeredness.

To conclude, it is worthwhile to identify more specific forms of client-centered approaches. Examples of specific forms are disadvantaged groups (e.g. people with low income, people with low education and disabled people), risk groups, channel preferences and digital skills. Organizations that address themselves not to be a client-centered organization could meet these more specific forms. Does this make them a client-centered organization then?

References

1. Commission of Future Public Communication: In Dienst van de Democratie [Serving Democracy] (2001),
   http://www.minaz.nl/dsc?c=getobject&s=obj&objectid=92001
   (retrieved December 4, 2007)
2. van Duivenboden, H., Lips, M.: CRM in de Publieke Sector: Naar een Klantgerichte Elektronische Overheid [CRM in the Public Sector: Towards a Client-Centered Electronic Government]. Holland Management Review 85, 45–57 (2002)
3. van Duivenboden, H., Lips, M.: De Vraaggerichte Elektronische Overheid [Question-Oriented Electronic Government]. Bestuurskunde 11(8), 355–363 (2002)
4. Thomassen, J.-P.: De Klantgerichte Overheid [Client-Centered Government]. Kluwer, Deventer (2007)
5. Besamusca-Jansen, M.: Klantgerichte Dienstverlening in Non-Profit Organisaties [Client-Centered Service Delivery in Non Profit Organizations]. Uitgeverij Nelissen, Baarn (1997)

6. Akerboom, M., Butzelaar, E., van der Noort, W.: Gerichte Communicatie op Basis van Segmentatieonderzoek: Een Verkenning [Tailored Communication Based on Segmentation Research: An Exploration] (2002), http://www.communicatieplein.nl/dsc?c=getobject&s=obj&object id=126985 (retrieved April 8, 2008)
7. Brodie, R.J., Coviello, N.E., Brookes, R.W., Little, V.: Towards a Paradigm Shift in Marketing? An Examination of Current Marketing Practices. Journal of Marketing Management 13(5), 383–406 (1997)
8. Lemon, K.N., Mark, T.: Customer Lifetime Value as the Basis of Customer Segmentation: Issues and Challenges. Journal of Relationship Marketing 5(2/2), 55–69 (2006)
9. Smith, W.: Product Differentiation and Market Segmentation as Alternative Marketing Strategies. Journal of Marketing 21, 3–8 (1956)
10. Wedel, M., Kamakura, W.: Market Segmentation: Conceptual and Methodological Foundations. Kluwer Academic Publishers, United States of America (2000)
11. Mulder, H.: Marktsegmentatie in Nederland [Market Segmentation in the Netherlands]. The Circle of Customer Knowledge, Groningen (2006)
12. van Dijk, J.A.G.M., Ebbers, W.E., Fennis, B.M., van der Geest, T.M., Loorbach, N.R., Pieterson, W.J., Steehouder, M.F., Taal, E., de Vries, P.W.: Alter Ego: State of the Art on User Profiling (2005), http://www.ibr.utwente.nl/egov/docs/2005-Alter_Ego_SOTA.pdf (retrieved December 4, 2007)
13. Cahill, D.J.: Lifestyle market segmentation. Haworth Press, New York (2006)
14. Kotler, P.: Principles of Marketing. Prentice Hall, Englewood Cliffs (1980)
15. Fu, J.-R., Chao, W.-P., Farn, C.-K.: Determinants of Taxpayers' Adoption of Electronic Filing Methods in Taiwan: An Exploratory Study. Journal of Public Information 30, 658–683 (2004)
16. Badgett, M., Stone, M.: Multidimensional Segmentation at Work: Driving an Operational Model that Integrates Customer Segmentation with Customer Management. Journal of Targeting, Measurement & Analysis for Marketing 13(2), 103–121 (2005)
17. Rao, V.R., Steckel, J.H.: Analysis for Strategic Marketing. Addison Wesley Longman, Inc., Amsterdam (1998)
18. van Raaij, W.F., Verhallen, T.M.M.: Domain-Specific Market Segmentation. European Journal of Marketing 28(10), 49–66 (1994)
19. Hessing, E., Reuling, A.M.H.: Waarden in Nederland: Segmentatie van Doelgroepen [Values in the Netherlands: Segmentation of Target Groups] (2003), http://www.moaweb.nl/bibliotheek/jaarboeken/2003/jaarboek-2003-10.pdf (retrieved December 4, 2007)
20. Buttle, F.: Customer Relationship Management: Concepts and Tools. Elsevier, Amsterdam (2007)
21. Beane, T.P., Ennis, D.M.: Market Segmentation: A review. European Journal of Marketing 21(5), 20–42 (1987)

Impact of Information and Communication Technologies on School Administration: Research on the Greek Schools of Secondary Education

Anna Saiti[1] and Georgia Prokopiadou[2]

[1] Harokopio University, Athens, Greece
[2] University of Athens, Athens, Greece
asaiti@hua.gr, gproko@ionio.gr

Abstract. Information and Communication Technologies (ICT) may be considered as a synonym for the modernization of all organizations, including school units, as they provide for advanced and updated technological tools and applications. Nowadays, the implementation of new technologies in the schools of secondary education in Greece has been rapidly increasing. This adoption of ICT reinforces the teaching process, but also facilitates administrative transactions. The current research aims to determine the level of technological infrastructure present in the secondary schools of Greece, to what extent this equipment meets their administrative needs, to study the role of the school libraries in their contribution to the modernization of school administration, and to examine the conditions that influence the implementation of ICT in school management.

Keywords: Information and Communication Technologies (ICT), School Administration, School Libraries, Information Literacy, Computer Literacy.

1 Introduction

The usage of Information and Communication Technologies (ICT) in the school environment is considered to be part of the extensive technological modernization of administration and education, as well as of the Information Society's action for electronic government (eGovernment) and electronic learning (eLearning). Within this framework, the introduction of innovative technological applications in schools is connected with changes, not only at the level of teaching and learning, but also in the fulfillment of schools' administrative tasks. As Mooij et al. [1] indicate, ICT enters the school environment progressively, with the objective of adopting technological applications not only in the teaching and learning process or in the monitoring of students' progress but also in school administration, in the school library, and generally in the management of the whole school, as an organization. Moreover, according to Michaelidis [2], ICT in schools are examined in three respects: as an administrative and management tool, as a teaching medium, and as a learning object. As such, the implementation of ICT in the school environment may be characterised as having three primary functions, with new technologies as the focal point: Administration – Library – Teaching.

M.A. Wimmer et al. (Eds.): EGOV 2009, LNCS 5693, pp. 305–316, 2009.

Taking note of the fact that a wide range of studies and research have taken place on the introduction and implementation of ICT in teaching and learning indicatively [3], [4], this study focuses on the impact of ICT on school administration and the school library. Starting with school management, we may notice that the new technological applications and the rapidity of their renewal require new organizational models and functions that form a significant part of administrative service [5]. More specifically, the adoption of contemporary technological tools in school management considerably affects the methods and the mediums used for administrative transactions. The system of manual procedures - where official records are composed and handled with traditional/conventional means - are being replaced by electronic and digital processes, according to which ICT provides for the ability to adopt advanced technologies for the creation, organization, maintenance and circulation of official information. The focal point of an electronic/digital administration is the way in which data, produced within administrative actions, are handled and managed.

Thus, within school administration, ICT is implemented for the development of electronic applications for the management of administrative transactions and records, as well as for the rendering of well-organized and prompt information services (i.e. electronic register, electronic curriculum, digital lesson material, electronic monitoring of school progress). As Haddad et al. [6] point out, ICT:

- assists school administration in the efficient management of official functions, in the enhanced supervision of student progress, as well as in the improvement of school resources management,
- contributes to an easier and friendlier management of complicated and multilevel administrative transactions, and
- promotes communication between school units, parents, and principal administration, and therefore cultivates responsibility on the part of school management, transparency in administrative actions, as well as the interlinking of school networks.

Hence, the modernization of school administration may be considered as the key for the extensive transformation and the overall reorganization of services in education [7]. Present-day technology provides for upgraded tools for e-Services that facilitate administrative transactions and ensure efficient sharing of information between members of the school community. To be more specific, ICT provides the means for administrative transactions to be accomplished with electronic management tools, in a digital environment, which is composed of decentralized, yet interlinked, web-based services. Within this digital information pool, the carrying out of administrative transactions is realized in real time, and therefore:

- ensures efficient data flow, instant information services for educators, students, parents, plus time saving in the execution of the necessary procedures,
- eliminates space and time restrictions [7], and reinforces the information access rights of the school community, and its participation in the administrative actions.

Moreover, the introduction of ICT in education also has a significant influence on the school library, which may contribute to the management and exchange of administrative information (based on its proficiency in information handling) and also to the training of students on information literacy skills. As Smalley [8] highlights, nowadays electronic information management requires a set of skills which, however complicated, are necessary for the school's academic and professional achievement. To meet this challenge, schools are required to teach young people not only computer and web-based applications but also information literacy, in order to be able to interact with the demanding information environment of modern professional and social life.

However, several parameters considerably affect the implementation of new technologies in the school environment [9]. For example, the opinions and attitudes of school educators and principals with regard to ICT adoption influence the extent and quality of technological applications' usage. Moreover, the level of the school community's familiarization with ICT, namely their possession of the necessary information skills and abilities, is a key factor for the efficient and effective introduction of new technological tools and applications within school administration. Finally, apart from the human factor, ICT initiation requires certain technical and financial competences in terms of suitable infrastructures and building requirements, ongoing and in-house technical assistance and the ability to upgrade and update the existing equipment, software and electronic applications, according to new technological developments.

The current study focuses on the contribution of ICT to the administration of Greek secondary schools, as well as on the role of the school library in electronic information management. The depiction of the schools' ICT current condition may highlight the deficient fields and indicate the measures that need to be taken on national level, in order to ensure effective and efficient school administrations. Besides, the findings of researches like this may help the principal authorities to base their decision making and the drawing of their strategic plan on real facts and outcomes. Within this framework, this article aims to:

- determine the extent to which new technologies are used in school administration,
- find out if the school libraries have the ability to provide students with information skills and to contribute to the modernization of school management,
- examine the parameters influencing the adoption and implementation of new technologies in Greek secondary schools and finally propose indicative solutions.

2 Data and Methodology

A survey was conducted to collect primary source data for the paper. Questionnaires were administered to 240 secondary educators. From those, 188 questionnaires were fully completed (response rate: 78.3%). The sample was randomly selected from 8 Greek regions (including the metropolitan region of Attiki, Athens). Since the data are not sufficiently rich to allow for a deeper analysis, further analysis is needed in order to confirm the results. The statistical analyses used included:

- Descriptive statistics (percentages);
- Ordinary Least Squares (OLS) as the estimation method, since the essential task was to apply a model to a particular available set of data in order to establish the required initial values of the coefficients.

3 Results: Presentation of Educators Perceptions

From the sample of 188 secondary educators in question, a considerable number of the respondents (76.1%) reported that the introduction of ICT in education was of vital importance for school administration. When questioned about the types of technological equipment that their school used solely for administrative purposes, the responses were ranked as follows: 99.5% had a PC, 93.6% had the internet, 91.0% had peripheral gadgets, such as printers, scanners, etc., 26.6% had an intranet and just 2.7% had video-projectors. Moreover, regarding technical support for this equipment, over half of the respondents (61.7%) reported that this was carried out by an expert educator in ICT, 36.2% stated the ICT office of the prefecture, 25% noted a technician from a private company and only 4.3% indicated a person appointed by the prefecture authorities exclusively for technical support. Concerning the extent to which the available technological equipment and applications in their school covered their administrative needs, over half the responses (66.0%) indicated that they were adequately covered by the available resources, while 16.5% claimed that it only partially, or not at all, the available equipment of their school cover their administrative needs.

Those who responded either "not at all" or "partially" in the last question were asked to specify the reasons for the lack of technological equipment in their schools. Their answers focused mainly on two reasons: limited financial support from the State (31.9%) and poor management on the behalf of the Ministry of Education in the distribution of the available equipment to secondary schools (28.7%).

When asked to what degree the educators were familiar with the use of computers, the distribution of responses was as follows: 47.9% claimed they were "adequately familiar", 27.7% reported their experience with computers was "more than adequate", 20.7% reported "little familiarity" and only 3.7% were not familiar at all with the use of a computer. More particularly, for those who answered either "more than adequate" or "adequate", they were asked to give the main reason for their proficiency in using computers. The responses focused on two major points: attending training programs of the Ministry of Education in computer science (42.0%) and personal interest (62.2%). On the contrary, for those who quantified their knowledge and familiarity with computers as either "little" or "none at all", a question was included regarding the reasons for this. There were three main responses: the training program they had attended was inadequate (8.0%), they were approaching retirement (6.4%) or they had not attended any relevant training program because there was no such program in their area (5.9%).

When asked whether or not their school had an organised electronic library, the vast majority (78.2%) answered negatively and the rest (21.8%) responded positively. For those who answered positively, the majority (21.8%) stated the educators' staff room as the place for the school library, 20.2% identified a specially designated room and 2.1% stated a room such as a laboratory or a multiple purpose room.

As for the most significant factor impacting on the effectiveness of the school library, the majority of the respondents (47.9%) identified the appropriateness of the school library's location. Another factor that appears to play a significant role, according to 22.9% of the educators, is the appointing of experienced personnel/ librarians.

When asked to identify, in order of significance, the factors that contribute to the effective introduction of ICT in the school administration, the responses focused mainly on three aspects: a suitable place for the location of technological equipment (27.1%), appropriate planning by the Ministry of Education for the distribution and the maintenance of technological equipment (26.6%), and the training and instruction of the educators on the use of ICT (22.9%).

Table 1[1] presents the results on the extent to which ICT meets the school's administrative needs.

Table 1. OLS dependent variable for the degree to which the school administrative needs are covered via existing ICT

Variables	Estimated Coefficient	S.E.
C	2.425***	0.270
Technological equipment is located in the school principal's office	0.271*	0.161
Technological equipment is located in the computer room	0.060	0.093
Technical support is provided by an educator expert in ICT	-0.003	0.114
Technical support is provided by an expert from a private company	-0.203*	0.115
Technical support is provided by the ICT office of the prefecture	-0.126	0.110
Mean value of school technological equipment exclusively for administrative use	0.125*	0.070

Model 1 McFadden R^2 = 0.061, Log Likelihood= -171.8785
*** denotes significance at 1%, * denotes significance at 10%, * S.E. denotes Standard Error.

It is clear from table 1 that three independent variables are significant for the degree to which the school administrative needs are covered via the existing ICT. These were: technological equipment located in the school principals' office, when technological support is provided by an expert from a private company, and the mean value of school technological equipment used exclusively for administrative purposes. In particular, when technological equipment is located in the school principal's office, the school administrative needs are more likely to be covered via the existing ICT. Moreover, when the school unit has more technological equipment, the possibility of covering the school administrative needs is increased. In contrast, the significant variable regarding the technological support provided by an expert from a private company had a negative sign, indicating that in such a case, the possibility of covering the school administrative needs is reduced. The latter result is rational, since the representative of a private company would not always be available for technical support. On

---

[1] Both models had been tested for heteroscedasticity and they were free. Further information about the variables included in the models is available from the authors upon request.

such occasions, the educators may be reluctant to use the ICT for the purpose of covering the school's administrative needs.

Table 2 presents the determinants of the level of familiarization with computer use. Empirical results from table 2 indicate that five independent variables were significant determinants for the degree of secondary educators' familiarization with computer use. In particular, the age of the respondents had a negative sign, indicating that younger people tend to be more familiar with computer use. Moreover, since the variable of gender is significant with a positive sign, the results suggest that male educators are more likely to be more familiar with computer use than female educators. Given that the perception of educators regarding the degree of importance for the introduction of ICT in school administration is significant with a positive sign, then those educators who believe strongly that the introduction of ICT is of vital importance for the school administration are more likely to be more familiar with computer use. Finally, the dummy variables for the school area are significant with a positive sign, indicating that those educators whose school is located in an urban and semi-urban area are more familiar with the use of computers than those colleagues whose school is located in a rural area.

Table 2. OLS regression model regarding the determinants for educators' level of familiarization with computer use

Variables	Estimated Coefficient	S.E.
C	2.283***	0.621
Age of respondents	-0.025***	0.009
Gender of the respondents	0.234**	0.107
D1area	0.626***	0.148
D2area	0.488***	0.179
The family status of the respondents	0.035	0.123
Years of teaching experience in the public secondary education	-0.007	0.011
Years of teaching experience in the same school	-0.008	0.010
The degree of importance for the introduction of ICT in school administration	0.344***	0.117

Model 1 McFadden $R^2 = 0.251$, Log Likelihood= -196.5451
*** denotes significance at 1%, ** denotes significance at 5%, * S.E. denotes Standard Error.

4 Discussion

Regarding ICT utility in school management, the research data show that the vast majority of educators consider new technologies to be extremely important for the efficient running of school administration. This result is confirmed by a relevant study [10], according to which the majority of the sample educators believe in the usage of technological applications for the improvement of school administration, as ICT rids school management of bureaucratic problems that hinder a school's smooth functioning, thereby reducing its effectiveness. Additionally, the results of more theme-related surveys [11], [12] partially strengthen the aforementioned opinion, due to the fact that they reveal the positive attitude of educators towards the usefulness of ICT in contemporary education.

Of particular interest is the discovery concerning the types of technological equipment that schools maintain exclusively for administrative use. According to our findings, the vast majority of the schools sampled have adequate infrastructure on computers and peripheral gadgets (printers, scanners, etc.). Furthermore, almost all schools sampled have internet connectivity. These findings do not come as a surprise, as several programs such as 'Information Society action' provide schools with sufficient technological equipment and applications. Other research that was conducted in the European Union in 2006 [13] confirms this result, with the vast majority of schools having computers and internet connectivity.

Regarding the location of the equipment for administrative use, our research reveals that in the vast majority of the schools sampled, this equipment is housed within the principal's office. This finding may be attributed to the fact that the principal is the qualified and responsible person for the school's administrative processes. Indeed the location of the equipment is a vital parameter for the implementation of new technologies in everyday administrative work whereby prompt access to the available infrastructure facilitates, reinforces and increases the usage of technological equipment and applications. International studies raise the availability and accessibility issue as one of the practical factors that influence the extent of technological equipment usage [14], [15], demanding strategic decisions on the behalf of school leadership regarding the equipment location and function [16], [17]. According to Ritchie et al. [18], physical obstacles, such as the location of computers and gadgets in places not easily and promptly accessible, negatively affect the usage of the available equipment. This opinion is reinforced by the findings of other relevant research [19], according to which there is a close relationship between the exploitation of ICT abilities and computer availability, stating that the location of the school equipment is directly connected with the extent of its usage.

With reference to an in-house expert exclusively for technical assistance, in our research there was not a single one among the vast majority of the schools of our sample. This finding may be considered as negative since, in several studies [20], [21], ensuring the quality and permanency of technical assistance constitutes one of the important factors for the efficient introduction and exploitation of new technologies' capabilities. Within this framework, the existence of an in-house expert for the rendering of technical assistance may be considered as a contemporary demand for the school units [13]. Other research conducted in England [22] remarked on the need for satisfactory technical assistance, in order to maintain the equipment at reliable levels. As Mahony [23] and Carter [24] underline, the lack of sufficient technical support considerably affects the usage of new technologies on the part of educators.

Regarding the extent of educators' satisfaction on the availability of technological equipment for administrative tasks, our research shows that the majority of the sample is satisfied or more than satisfied. This finding comes as no surprise, due to the fact that the school units have adequate means in technological infrastructure, as we have already identified. Furthermore, this result is in agreement with the findings of a relevant study from the United Kingdom, in which the level of educators' contentment from the available equipment was sufficiently high [25].

Concerning the level of familiarization with the usage of computers, our research reveals that the majority of the educators have adequate or more than adequate knowledge. This finding may be characterized as positive, since the ability to use the available technological equipment is considered one of the parameters that influence the efficient and effective introduction of ICT within the school environment [26], [27]. The aforementioned result is in agreement with the findings of other relevant research [28], according to which Greek educators appear to have increased levels of self-confidence, regarding their abilities in computer usage.

With reference to computer literacy level and educator's age, the OLS model shows that younger people tend to be more proficient in the usage of computers. This result is confirmed by the findings of relevant research, according to which people at a younger age feel more familiar with the implementation of ICT, have greater self-confidence in their technological skills, as well as more positive attitude towards new technologies [13], [29]. A possible explanation for this result may be the fact that the younger educators are more likely to have used computers, and generally new technologies, from the time of their student life, and they have received the necessary training via universities' curriculum [23]. Moreover, educators that are about to be retired may not have the same interest as their younger colleagues in acquiring new knowledge and skills.

Additionally, the OLS model on the level of computer familiarization and the gender of educators reveals that male educators are more likely to be proficient in the usage of new technologies. This finding is in agreement with the results of relevant research in which: (a) male educators feel more confident in their computer abilities [30], (b) retain a more positive attitude towards ICT [29], and (c) use new technologies more often as an information tool in their everyday work [19].

The findings of the second OLS model are of particular interest, according to which the educators that believe strongly in the importance of ICT in school administration are more likely to be more than adequately familiar with the use of computers. This result comes as no surprise, as the educators' opinions and attitudes influence the extent and quality of ICT usage. Therefore, the educators who are positively disposed towards ICT tend to be involved, or interested to be systematically involved, with the new technological tools and applications. Through this greater interaction they acquire more technological skills, thus enhancing their familiarization.

Furthermore, our research shows that educators' computer literacy is associated with their participation in a relevant training program. This finding is confirmed by a relevant study [31], in which the majority of the sample stated that they had acquired the necessary technological skills via training programs. Within this framework, international research [16], [26] considers the ICT training issue to be a vital one, not only for providing the educators with the required skills and knowledge, but also for introducing ICT effectively within the school environment.

Besides training programs, our research reveals another key factor influencing educators' computer knowledge: their personal interest in computers. This finding is confirmed by Simpson's et al. [32] study, which highlighted that the technological skills and the extent to which new technologies are used depends significantly on personal interest, on the level of enthusiasm, and the feeling of commitment possessed by educators. In particular, several studies [32], [33] remark that using computers at home contributes to the proficiency in technological applications and to the acquisition of self-confidence in technological skills and knowledge.

Regarding the existence of an organized electronic school library at their school, the majority of the sample answered negatively. This result may be characterized as negative, since the contribution of the school libraries in education is formative. They provide mental and physical access to various information sources, offer guidance and encourage students in the usage of a range of information, and collaborate with the school's educators, in order to support their teaching and to satisfy the information needs of all students individually (student-centered learning) [34]. Furthermore, school libraries play a significant role in acquiring information literacy [35] by expanding teaching and learning boundaries, and by providing information skills. However, ICT is a key factor for the promotion of the school libraries' contemporary aim, as it facilitates user access to information sources and provides for simultaneous query and retrieval from several information databases [36].

Concerning the location of the school library, our research reveals that in a significant number of schools, the library is housed in the educators' room, and not in a separate room used exclusively for the needs of the school library. This finding may be considered as negative, given that the provision of a specially designated room is thought to be one of the significant parameters for the effective and efficient function of the school library [37]. Indeed, according to international studies [38] the library room must satisfy concrete specifications, regarding the size (square meters) and the design (study seats available), in order to serve the school community's needs, and to offer its members an attractive environment for study, creative work, etc. Within this framework, the Greek Ministry of Education [39] has defined explicit criteria and detailed specifications for the location of school libraries. In the case of the present study, having the library located in the educator's room may be due to the lack of free space for its transformation to a school library, and/or to the shortage of State financing for establishing a suitable place, according to the Ministry of Education's specifications.

Of particular interest is the finding on the parameters that contribute to the efficient running of the school library, according to which the three main factors are: a suitable location for the school library, the presence of a librarian, and State financing. These findings are in agreement with the results of other relevant research [37] in which the sample of educators gave recommendations for the effective functioning of a school library. These included the establishment of a specially designated room, adequate State financing, and appropriate staffing with a librarian. Furthermore, a related study [40], as well as the international specifications of the International Federation of Library Association (IFLA)/ UNESCO [41] highlighted the aforementioned parameters as some of the most important factors for the efficient and effective running of a school library.

Regarding the essential conditions for the well-organized and proficient usage of ICT in school administration, our research data show the establishment of a suitable place for the housing of ICT to be a primary concern, followed by the Ministry of Education's appropriate planning for the distribution and maintenance of the technological equipment among secondary schools, as well as the training and instruction of educators on ICT usage. Based on these findings, we may state that several parameters contribute, to varying extents, to ensuring the effective introduction of new technologies in the school environment. In practical terms, this means that fulfilling one factor alone does not necessarily bring about the successful adoption of technological initiatives in everyday work. However, it would result in the definition of a more appropriate framework for the "modification" of school administration from its more traditional form to a more advanced and upgraded technological environment.

5 Conclusions

In conclusion, we may observe that the usage of new technologies in school administration is vital in order to upgrade its administrative processes. However, educators, due to an unfavorable environment, are not in a position to fully exploit all the available technological resources for the improvement of administrative tasks. It would seem that the successful introduction of ICT into the school environment is dependent on the above-mentioned factors. This exposes the need for changes in school strategy and culture, not only on the behalf of the State, but also on the behalf of the school community members.

Within this framework, we propose, among else, the creation and adoption of a nationally accepted ICT policy for school administrations, the ensuring of sufficient financial support, as well as the implementation of continuous training programs.

References

1. Mooij, T., Smeets, E.: Modelling and supporting ICT implementation in secondary schools. Computers and Education 36, 265–281 (2001)
2. Michaelidis, P.G.: Improvisation: an alternative and heretic approach for computer science in schools. In: Dimitrakopoulou, A. (ed.) Information and Communication Technologies in Education: 3rd Pan-Hellenic Conference Proceedings. Kastaniotis Publications, Rhodes (2002) (in Greek)
3. Simatos, A.: Technology and education: supervisory teaching mediums' selection and usage. Pataki Publications, Athens (2003) (in Greek)
4. Solomonidou, C.: New trends in education technology: constructive and contemporary teaching environments. Metechmio, Athens (2006) (in Greek)
5. Anastasiades, P.S.: Towards the global information society: The enactment of a regulatory framework as a factor of transparency and social cohesion. In: Shafazand, H., Tjoa, A.M. (eds.) EurAsia-ICT 2002. LNCS, vol. 2510, pp. 527–535. Springer, Heidelberg (2002)
6. Haddad, W., Jurich, S.: ICT for education: potential and potency. In: Haddad, W., Drexler, A. (eds.) Technologies for education: potentials, parameters, and prospects. Academy for Educational Development and Paris, Washington (2002)
7. Schelin, S.H.: E-Government: an overview. In: Garson, G.D. (ed.) Public Information technology: policy and management issues, pp. 120–137. Idea Group Publishing, Hershey (2003)
8. Smalley, T.N.: College success: high school librarians make the difference. The Journal of Academic Librarianship 30(3), 193–198 (2004)
9. Pelgrum, W.J.: Obstacles to the integration of ICT in education: results from a worldwide educational assessment. Computers and Education 37, 163–178 (2001)

10. Kinigos, P., Karageorgis, D., Vavouraki, A., Gavrilis, K.: Educators' opinions on "Odyssea" for ICT usage in education. In: Komis, V. (ed.) Information and Education Technologies in Education: 2nd Pan-Hellenic Conference Proceedings. New Technologies Publications, Patra (2000) (in Greek)
11. Karagiorgi, Y.: Throwing light into the black box of implementation: ICT in Cyprus elementary schools. Educational Media International 42(1), 19–32 (2005)
12. Hadjithoma, C., Karagiorgi, Y.: The use of ICT in primary schools within emerging communities of implementation. Computers & Education, Article in Press (2008), doi:10.1016/j.compedu.2008.06.010
13. Empirica. Benchmarking access and use of ICT in European schools 2006: final report from head teacher and classroom teacher surveys in 27 European Countries. European Commission, Information Society and Media Directorate General (2006), http://ec.europa.eu/information_society/eeurope/i2010/docs/studies/final_report_3.pdf
14. Tearle, P.: A theoretical and instrumental framework for implementing change in ICT in education. Cambridge Journal of Education 34(3), 331–351 (2004)
15. Franklin, C.: Factors That Influence Elementary Teachers Use of Computers. Journal of Technology and Teacher Education 15(2), 267–293 (2007)
16. Flanagan, L., Jacobsen, M.: Technology leadership for the twenty-first century principal. Journal of Educational Administration 41(2), 124–142 (2003)
17. Vandenbroucke, F.: Competences for the knowledge society: ICT in education initiative, 2007-2009. Vlaamse Overheid (2007)
18. Ritchie, D., Rodriguez, S.: School administrators and educational technologies: narrowing the divide. Technology, Pedagogy and Education 5(1), 107–114 (1996)
19. Tondeur, J., Valcke, M., van Braak, J.: A multidimensional approach to determinants of computer use in primary education: teacher and school characteristics. Journal of Computer Assisted Learning 23(3), 197–206 (2008)
20. Eteokleous, N.: Evaluating computer technology integration in a centralized school system. Computers & Education 51, 669–686 (2008)
21. McGarr, O., O'Brien, J.: Teacher professional development and ICT: an investigation of teachers studying a postgraduate award in ICT in education. Irish Educational Studies 26(2), 145–162 (2007)
22. Waite, S.: Tools for the job: a report of two surveys of information and communications technology training and use for literacy in primary schools in the West of England. Journal of Computer Assisted Learning 20, 11–20 (2004)
23. Mahony, C.O.: Reaping ITEM benefits. Information Technology and Educational Management in the Knowledge Society 170, 23–36 (2005)
24. Carter, D.: Distributed practicum supervision in a managed learning environment (MLE). Teachers and Teaching 11(5), 481–497 (2005)
25. Kitchen, S., Finch, S., Sinclair, R.: Harnessing technology schools survey 2007. National Centre for Social Research (2007), Διαθέσιμο στο: http://www.becta.org.uk
26. Wood, E., Mueller, J., Willoughby, T., Specht, J., Deyoung, T.: Teachers' perceptions: barriers and supports to using technology in the classroom. Education, Communication & Information 5(2), 183–206 (2005)
27. Dawson, V.: Use of information communication technology by early career science teachers in Western Australia. International Journal of Science Education 30(2), 203–219 (2008)

28. Paraskeva, F., Bouta, H., Papagianni, A.: Individual characteristics and computer self-efficacy in secondary education teachers to integrate technology in educational practice. Computers & Education 50(3), 1084–1091 (2008)
29. Jimoyiannis, A., Komis, V.: Examining teachers' beliefs about ICT in education: implications of a teacher preparation programme. Teacher Development 11(2), 149–173 (2007)
30. Galanouli, D., Murphy, C., Gardner, J.: Teachers perceptions of the effectiveness of ICT-competence training. Computers & Education 43, 63–79 (2004)
31. Soulis, S.: Special pedagogic and computer science: attitudes of special educators towards computer usage: conclusions from a pilot research from Epirus region. 1st ETPE Conference, Ioannina (1999) (in Greek), http://www.etpe.gr
32. Simpson, M., Payne, F., Condie, R.: Introducing ICT in secondary schools: a context for reflection on management and professional norms. Educational Management Administration & Leadership 33(3), 331–354 (2005)
33. Tearle, P.: A theoretical and instrumental framework for implementing change in ICT in education. Cambridge Journal of Education 34(3), 331–351 (2004)
34. Stoll, A.: Framing the library power automation: current and future implications. In: Zweizig, D.L., et al. (eds.) Lessons from library power: enriching teaching and learning: final report of the evaluation of the National Power Initiative. Libraries Unlimited, Englewood (1999)
35. Turner, P.M.: Helping teachers teach: a school library media specialist's role. Libraries Unlimited, Englewood (1993)
36. Murphy, C.: The time is right to automate. In: Murphy, C. (ed.) Automating school library catalogs: a reader. Libraries Unlimited, Englewood (1992)
37. Saitis, C., Saiti, A.: School libraries in Greece: A comparative study of public primary schools in rural and urban areas. Library & Information Science Research 26, 201–220 (2004)
38. Zweizig, D.L., et al.: Lessons from library power: enriching teaching and learning: final report of the evaluation of the National Power Initiative. Libraries Unlimited, Englewood (1999)
39. Ministry of Education, School library: principals (part A'). Athens (2003) (in Greek)
40. Bernhard, P., Willars, G., Pemmer Sætre, T.: School libraries: today and tomorrow. IFLA School Library Section. The school library: today and tomorrow (2002), http://www.ifla.org/VII/s11/pubs/SchoolLibrary_today_tomorrow.pdf
41. IFLA/ UNESCO, School library guidelines (2002), http://www.ifla.org/VII/s11/pubs/sguide02.pdf

From National to Supranational Government Inter-Organizational Systems: An Extended Typology

Boriana Rukanova[1], Rolf T. Wigand[2], and Yao-Hua Tan[1]

[1] Faculty of Economics and Business Administration, Vrije Universiteit Amsterdam,
De Boelelaan 1105, 1081 HV, Amsterdam, The Netherlands
{brukanova,ytan}@feweb.vu.nl
[2] Departments of Information Science and Management,
University of Arkansas at Little Rock,
2801 South University Avenue, Little Rock, Arkansas 72204-1099, USA
rtwigand@ualr.edu

Abstract. While inter-organizational systems (IOS) driven by supranational government (here referred to as supranational IOS or SN IOS) are increasingly being developed in practice, this phenomenon remains largely unexplored in the existing literature. What makes SN IOS specifically interesting is that their development and implementation is driven by supranational bodies (rather than businesses or national governments), implying that Member States have given up some of their decision-making power to higher level bodies and are bound to implement the decisions of these bodies. A key question then becomes: Are the processes for standards and system development and adoption of SN IOS distinct from IOS processes driven by businesses or national governments and, if so, what makes them different? Building on a novel typology and a case study of one SN IOS, our findings suggest that both industry and SN IOS exhibit similarities in terms of the role that intermediary organizations play as well as the processes through which standards are negotiated. These similarities can be used for transferability of knowledge between the two domains. We also demonstrate that there are inherent differences in terms of drivers, focus, approach, adoption incentives and the role of national governments. These differences require further attention and different considerations.

Keywords: supranational IOS, typology, standards, eGovernment.

1 Introduction

During our investigation of the inter-organizational systems (IOS) used to control cross-border trade activities we became acquainted with the introduction of a supranational government IOS (SN IOS) in Europe, called the New Computerized Transit System (NCTS), which is an example of one of the numerous supranational systems that are currently being introduced in practice [6]. The authors were surprised by the nature and scale of this IOS development. We found that there is a legal obligation at the EU level that a transit system needs to be developed and implemented in all Member States and businesses involved in transit. The new transit procedures as well

M.A. Wimmer et al. (Eds.): EGOV 2009, LNCS 5693, pp. 317–327, 2009.

as the system requirements were then defined at the EU level, where representatives of all the 27 Member States took place in the committees for defining the legal and system requirements. Subsequently, the governments of all Member States were obliged by law to develop national systems based on the EU specifications, resulting in 27 interconnected national systems. Finally, all the businesses involved in handling transit goods were also obliged by law to develop an interface towards the system of their national transit authorities. This illustrates the scale, but also the supra-national character of this IOS development.

What makes such SN IOS especially interesting to study is that their development and implementation is driven by supranational bodies (rather than businesses or national governments), implying that Member States have given up some of their sovereignty and decision-making power to a higher level body and are bound to implement the decisions of this higher-level body at their respective national level. In this process Member States are driven by their own agendas, which are often diverging and even conflicting with that of the supranational government and this results in different political dynamics when it comes to system development and adoption. A key question then becomes: Are the processes for standards and system development and adoption of SN IOS distinct from IOS processes driven by businesses or national governments and, if so, what makes them different? In order to address this question we develop below a novel uniform and integrative typology of IOS and provide an in-depth case study of the development and adoption of such an SN IOS. We pay specific attention to the political processes taking place during the development and subsequent adoption of the system as well as the interactions among supranational and national bodies, and businesses.

The remainder of this paper is structured as follows. In Section 2 we present our theoretical framework, while in Section three we discuss the research methodology. The case findings are presented in Section 4 and we end the paper with discussion and conclusions.

2   Theoretical Framework

In this section we provide a review of IOS studies, where the development and adoption processes are driven by industry or national governments. In the context of IOS, interoperability at both technical and organizational level is of key importance [11] and standards play a major role in achieving that. We therefore also pay specific attention to the processes of standards development and adoption. The typology we derive in section 2.2 aims to clarify where SN IOS stand with respect to other IOS studied today and to provide conceptual clarity for the follow-up analysis.

2.1   Literature Review

Early on IOS was defined as "an automated information system shared by two or more companies" [4, p. 134]. This definition of IOS clearly indicates a focus on the use of information systems (IS) to support business-to-business interactions between and among companies and the role of government is seldom the focus of the analysis. Fifteen years later, by looking at the IOS literature retrospectively, [10] observe that inter-organizational systems research has dealt mainly with micro-level business-to-business interactions. In their criticism of the then-available IOS literature, [10] point out that the work has tended to a large extent to ignore the relationships between analysis at a level of individual firm and analysis at a broader industry level. To overcome the above-mentioned limitations, a number of researchers have tried to shift the analysis of IOS implementation and adoption and to move beyond the micro-level business-to-business interactions towards an industry focus [10, 15, 18, 12]. The *Journal of Information Technology* devoted an entire issue to this topic [9]. [10] propose a multi-level analysis consisting of three levels: individual industry units; the industry group itself, and the remote environment. Moreover, [14] argue that one needs to explore industry level consequences. They show how IOS can have influences extending beyond the organization or the immediate pair of organizations implementing them. [15] identify three types of industry level phenomena when examining the use of inter-organizational IT-driven coordination systems: performance effects, structural effects and collective actions. Standards are key to any IOS but they become even more important when multiple players are involved, which is the case with of industry. [12] provide further investigation of industry-wide information systems standardization as collective action and they point out the importance to study both cycles of standards development and standards diffusion, as they are interrelated. Regarding [10], standardization bodies are seen as industry units, part of an industry group. Most research in this setting demonstrates that overall businesses are the drivers for the development of IOS. When reflecting on the role of government in the above-mentioned studies (both focusing on limited B2B interactions as well as those with industry focus), government is either not discussed at all or is seen as part of the remote environment [10]. For the purpose of the present study, however, government is at the focal core of our investigation.

It has already been acknowledged that the issue of IOS in the public sector and its interaction with private businesses has received limited attention [13]. Nevertheless the literature reveals studies where in the context of cross-border trade IOS developments are initiated and driven by national governments (e.g., Singapore's TradeNet [16] and the 'e-export" system in Denmark [2]). When government introduces a system to communicate with trade entities, the goal of the systems is to support government-to-business (G2B) interactions such as launching an import or an export declaration. This differs when compared to traditional IOS, where the purpose for developing a system is to be used by companies (see the definition by [4] above) in support of their business-to-business interactions. In IOS developments driven by national governments, regulation and political agenda drive these developments [1]. And while in B2B contexts the adoption of IOS is driven by business drivers, in B2G settings, governments have the power to impose an IOS by making the system obligatory by law [2, 9]. While such studies explicitly acknowledge the role of government, they remain limited to the national context.

With the increasing complexity in areas where IOS are applied, we recognize studies focusing on transnational information systems [5]. Transnational information systems (TIS) are defined as "information systems that transcend both national and organizational boundaries" [5, p.17]. These studies emphasize specifically the crossing of national boundaries, where confrontation between different national cultures, judicial systems and political priorities become visible. While these studies explicitly acknowledge the need to consider the cross-national boundaries nature of these IOS, they do not explicitly reflect on the role of supranational government bodies and how they influence the collective action processes related to standards, system development and adoption.

Supranational means above states or nations, implying that decisions are made by a process or institution that is largely (but not entirely) independent of national governments. The subjects (in the case of the EU these are the Member State governments) are then obliged to accept these decisions [3]. While in political science the debate about supranational governance and the EU has been going on for years, it has not yet been addressed in the IOS field. Here we use the term supranational government IOS to refer to IOS, where decisions about the development and adoption of IOS in Member States and businesses are to a large extent influenced and driven by supranational bodies. In such situations, Member States are bound to implement the system, whether or not they fully agree with it, and their role as powerful players which can impose national systems diminishes in the role of an intermediary, maneuvering between the interests of its national businesses and those of the supranational bodies.

2.2 Typology of IOS

Figure 1 is an attempt to provide a consistent typology of IOS, while building on earlier research reviewed in the above. The studies discussed in Section 2.1 are often in isolation of one another. Therefore, this typology aims to propose a systematic way of viewing these efforts to date. In doing so, we aim to be better able to distinguish SN IOS from other types of IOS. In building this typology we use two dimensions: levels and scope. With respect to levels, we distinguish between businesses, government level 1 (national government) and government level 2 (supranational government). With respect to scope we distinguish between national and transnational, where for transnational we rely on the definition of [5] where IOS cross national boundaries. The resulting typology consists of five blocks and interactions between these blocks. To understand the typology it is important to realize the interactions between higher levels in the typology with the lower levels, as they capture the government's influence on IOS decisions.

Table 1. Key interactions from the typology

Interactions block 2 and 1	Interaction between government and businesses at the national level.
Interactions block 5 and 4	Interactions between supranational government and national governments in transnational context.
Interactions block 5, 4, and 3	Interactions between supranational government, national government and businesses in transnational context.

In cases when we have interactions between blocks 5 and 4 as well as between 5, 4 and 3 we will have cases of supranational IOS or supranational bodies are able to impose decisions about IOS on the lower levels. It is these types of systems and interactions that are of focal interest to our present study.

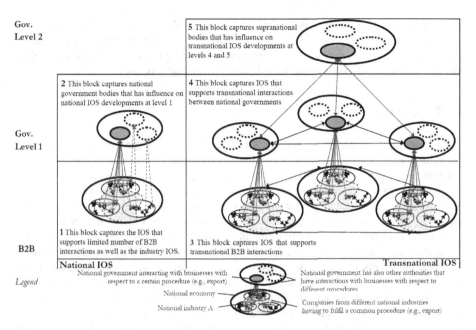

Fig. 1. Typology of IOS and the role of government

3 Methodology

In our study we build on the interpretative tradition that is well established in IS research [17]. The study presented here is part of the EU-funded ITAIDE research project (www.itaide.org), which aims to propose innovative solutions for cross-border trade. Four European Living Labs provide the real-life settings in which eCustoms solutions are developed. The Dutch "Beer Living Lab" (BeerLL) focused on the analysis of the procedures for export of excise goods and we analyzed current EU initiatives aiming to introduce an EU-wide system (called EMCS) for information exchange concerning excise-free goods. This system is still in the early stages of its development. During interviews with experts involved in the BeerLL we learned about another system, the New Computerized Transit System (NCTS), which was introduced in 2005 for transit goods and was considered similar to EMCS. Thus we conducted the NCTS study as a contextual study for the BeerLL. The data collection included multiple sources of evidence such as exploratory interviews, participation in meetings and brainstorming sessions (most of them were recorded) and document analysis. Data was collected during the period of January 2006 to December 2007. We gained contextual knowledge about the Customs domain via the Beer LL. The authors attended 19 work meetings, 5 brainstorming sessions, and conducted 23 interviews with BeerLL participants. Subsequently, our contacts from Dutch Tax arranged access to experts from Dutch Tax, who were involved in the development and implementation of the NCTS system (both at national and EU levels). We conducted 11 additional interviews with key people involved in the project. We also reviewed multiple documents related to the NCTS case and earlier studies on that matter. To analyze and discuss the supranational IOS development that we observe in the NCTS case, we build on the earlier IOS research as well as the typology discussed in section two. We pay specific attention to the collective action processes related to standards and systems development and adoption as well as the role that national and supranational bodies play in that process.

4   Case Analysis

This case study focuses on the transit procedure in Europe and the subsequent introduction of a supra-national EU-wide system called New Computerized Transit System (NCTS) to support this very procedure. Transit meant suspension of the obligation of payment of duties at the border. The import duties are used to finance the budgets of government, thus part of the transit procedure includes control mechanisms to ensure that such suspension of payments of duties at the border is granted correctly. This procedure was traditionally paper-based. Fraud reached such a high level that the European Parliament decided to launch an official inquiry to find out sources and levels of fraud. As a result of that inquiry, one major recommendation towards the customs authorities and the European Commission was to replace the paper-based procedure with electronic message exchanges. There were already several attempts to use computers for the exchange of transit information but they were not successful, as the issue was not high on the political agenda. When the recommendations of the European Parliament were published, there was already a third project in progress, which aimed to develop a computerized system for transit called the New Computerized Transit System (NCTS). The idea behind the NCTS was that legal and systems specifications would be developed at the EU level and the systems based on these specifications would subsequently be implemented by all Member State governments and businesses, dealing with transit goods. The resulting system is a supranational IOS system for exchange of information about transit, the development and adoption of which was largely driven and influenced by EU bodies.

4.1   Collective Actions for Development of NCTS (Standards and Systems)

We identified three developments at the EU level with different goals and different sub-sets of participants and these can be seen as separate collective action initiatives.

Collective action for defining the new legal procedures. The goal of the first initiative was to define new legal procedures for transit. In this development, two separate groups joined forces. The Member States of the EU formed part of the Community Transit Working Group and the work done within this Working Group was limited to the EU Member States. In addition, EFTA countries (who were not part of the EU but were part of the European Free Trade Association) were also interested in participating in the definition of the new transit procedures and this was accomplished in the Common Transit Working Group. This Working Group had a broader scope of membership, as it included the EU Member States as well as the EFTA countries. The Community Transit and the Common Transit had a different voting structure as well as a different legal basis which made the negotiations difficult. The processes in these committees were driven by different political interests and it was not in the power of one single government to make a decision, the decisions are made collectively. For example, in the Common Transit meeting the European Commission had to come up with one vote on behalf of all the EU Member States. There were examples of situations, however, where one member state did not fully support the position of the European Commission and was using informal channels to join forces with EFTA countries. This process required compromise and political maneuvering, where Member States were stuck in the middle between the need to cooperate in order to define the new procedures and the need to compete in order to preserve their national interests.

Collective action for the development of system specifications. While the Transit committees were busy with specifying the new transit procedures, a separate Working Group was established to develop the standard for the development of the computer system to be used for the exchange of transit data. One of the complications for the development of the NCTS was that all EU Member States had to have different experts represented in the discussions, resulting sometimes in three or four representatives per country. Furthermore, EFTA countries were also represented. This meant that a large number of people took part in the meetings. The detailed matters to be discussed with larger groups of people made the progress of the discussion very difficult. It was expected that as the documents that needed to be exchanged were already defined (i.e. Single Administrative Document) and used for the paper processes it would be very easy to build a computerized system. It turned out, however, that the different countries had different interpretations of the law. Accordingly, between 1995 and 1997 much time was spent to agree on common definitions and it was not expected that it would take so long to reach agreements. While ultimately the Working Group developed the specifications, the process of reaching agreements was challenging due to the large number of people involved, different national interpretations as well as different views on the project's scope. The next task was to develop applications conforming to these requirements. Some countries preferred to develop their own applications, while other countries preferred to participate in the development of a joint system. While a joint solution was not found, a compromise was agreed upon, i.e. it was decided that both options will be allowed.

Collective action for the development of a common system. The European Commission took the responsibility for the development of the common system. The Commission wanted to make sure that there is a system available and any country wanting to use it can do so. The Commission was providing the financial resources. During that process the Commission needed to select a software company. The software company was selected by the Commission via a tender process, where the Commission was the main contractor. For the development of the common application a special temporary organization called Minimal Common Core User Group (MUG) was created. The goal of that group was to discuss the development of the common system as well as implementation problems and experiences. From the countries, which were working with the Commission for the development of the common system, some were fore-runners and actively participating in the processes and the decision-making, while others were followers. One such country is the Netherlands handling large volumes of transit goods. The Netherlands made a political decision to participate actively, in order to ensure that its interests are discussed and taken into account in the development.

4.2 The implementation of the NCTS in One Member State (The Netherlands)

Although the common system was developed centrally, each participating country was responsible for the national implementation of the system. Here we will present the experience with the adoption of the common system in only one member state, i.e. the Netherlands. We will touch upon both technical and socio-political aspects with respect to adoption.

Although the Netherlands made a political decision to participate in the development of the common system and to put much effort in working with the Commission during the development, it turned out that it is rather difficult to embed the common application in the existing technical infrastructure of Dutch Tax. This initiated a struggle where the politicians advocated the pro-European view and wanted to be a fore-runner in the developments were confronted with the IT people who saw the technical dangers and limitations of this approach. Nevertheless, the implementation had to continue, as commitments had been made on the political level. It is important to mention that Dutch Tax installed a special function- national transit coordinator, performing a mediating role between the businesses and the EU. His role was to communicate to trade the changes that the EU is requiring, but at the same time he was attentive to the concerns of trade and was bringing these concerns into the discussions at the EU level. This mediating role of the Dutch government became also very important during the adoption stage and this illustrates how national government played a mediating role among the IT people, the businesses, the technology providers of the common application and the committees in Brussels.

In the period after the national pilot, the system was available but the companies were reluctant to use it: they were used to work with the old process, the system was not made obligatory yet, and there was a need to obtain a license to be able to use the system. In addition the introduction of the electronic system was considered as restricting to some extent the freedom of the companies and there was a possibility that failure in the system will interfere negatively with the logistics processes. In 2003 representatives of the Commission visited the Netherlands. It was expected that the Netherlands with large volumes of trade would require many electronic messages but that was not the case, as only few companies had adopted the system. It was recommended by the Commission that the Dutch government had to take actions and ensure adoption. This illustrates a situation where the Member States were willing to take more liberal approaches towards the adoption of the NCTS system from businesses; they were forced, however, by the higher-level authorities to make the system obligatory as there were binding legal obligations established at the EU level to have the system adopted by 2005. After the recommendations from Brussels, the Netherlands had to take actions to ensure adoption by 2005. The Dutch government played a mediating role between businesses and the EU in order to solve the problems that were encountered. At the same time it tried to protect its national interests and negotiate terms that were more acceptable to businesses.

5 Discussion and Conclusions

The NCTS case discussed above presents a detailed account of the development and implementation of one SN IOS and demonstrates the distinct role that supranational government can play in influencing decisions about IS on the levels of national governments and businesses. Below we reflect on the processes related to the standard and systems development and adoption, as well as the role of supranational bodies and national governments in that process. When discussing our findings, we draw a comparison with studies that focus on IOS adoption processes driven by industry or national governments.

Similarly to what is observed in industry-focused IOS studies [12] in the NCTS case we see that collective action is essential for the *development* of IOS standards and systems. In the industry-focused IOS research, the role of the supporting organizations such as standardization bodies has been identified as very important [10] and they have been identified as key players in the process of mobilizing collective action [18, 12]. Similarly, in the NCTS case we also observe collective activities by representatives of the EU Member States for the development of the legal procedures, the system specifications as well as for the subsequent development of the common application. If we look at the drivers for setting up such supporting organizations in industry IOS and in the case of supranational IOS, we see, however, some differences. While on an industry level, businesses are the driving force for setting standardization bodies and are actively involved in the process of standards setting, in the NCTS case, the committees were set-up by the government and government representatives of all the EU Member States. Businesses have no decision-making power in this process but are those who have to bear the consequences. In addition, the industry standardization efforts focus on a specific industry, whereas in the supranational case discussed here the focus is on a specific procedure (in our case 'transit') rather than on a specific industry. Furthermore, the approaches of these initiatives differ also. While in the industry case, the initiatives for standard development often emerge bottom-up, driven by the needs of the businesses, in the NCTS case we see that the initiative for setting up the legal and system specifications were started top-down and it was obligatory for all Member States to participate.

Looking at the way standards and systems are *adopted*, we can see differences in the case of industry, compared to supranational IOS. With respect to industry, the adoption of a standard for IOS is defined by business drivers. In an industry setting, the adoption approach is very much bottom-up and companies often wait for other companies to adopt the standard first [12]. Thus, although a standard may offer considerable advantages to businesses, whether it will ultimately be adopted is unclear. In the literature on IOS driven by national government we see examples of a completely different approach, top-down instead of bottom up, where national government can make systems obligatory by law [2,8]. Similarly, in the NCTS case we also see that the top-down approach is applied, ensuring the adoption of the standards and the systems in all the governments of the EU Member States as well as all the respective businesses involved in trade with transit goods. It is interesting to note, however, that the role of the national government has changed. In case of supranational systems, the national government is not the powerful actor who can impose systems, as these decisions come from a higher level (in our case the EU).

326	B. Rukanova, R.T. Wigand, and Y.-H. Tan

In the context of national IS implementation, [14] bring the attention to the difficult political processes taking place when the control of IS is spread over several levels. They examined the paradoxical nature of inter-municipality collaboration, which combines competition and cooperation, autonomy and interdependence. The authors suggest that in that process, local municipalities may loose some of their independence and power. On a different scale (i.e. supranational) our study brings us to similar observations. While national governments are quite powerful on a national level, on a supra national level they are but only one player in the process and the power gets more dispersed [8]. In the NCTS case, both with respect to standard and systems development as well as with respect to adoption, national governments were stuck between the demands of the supranational bodies and the national interests of trade. These processes were characterized with constant struggle between cooperation and competition between member states, as Member States also try to protect their national interests in negotiations.

We started this contribution with the motivation that while SN IOS are increasingly being introduced in practice, there is a lack of theoretical understanding of the processes driving the development and adoption of such systems. Thus a key question explored here is: Are the processes for standards and system development as well as adoption of SN IOS distinct from IOS processes driven by businesses or national governments and, if so, what makes them different?

This article's contribution is threefold. First of all, by providing an integrated typology, we conceptually clarify the positioning of SN IOS, compared to other types of IOS studied today. Second, we present an in-depth case study, providing insights into how such SN IOS are actually developed and adopted. Third, we identify that while there are areas where the development and adoption processes exhibit similarities to IOS developments driven by industry or national governments, there are also aspects where SN IOS seem to be different. Areas where differences can be identified include the drivers for setting up the supporting organizations (business vs. government), focus (industry vs. procedure), approach (bottom-up vs. top-down), and adoption incentives (business vs. legally driven). In addition, an important finding of our study is that the role of national government diminishes from a very powerful player in the adoption arena to an intermediary actor, which needs to maneuver between the national interests of the businesses and those of the supranational bodies. Future research could further examine the specifics of SN IOS and the role of national governments in that process. Understanding the underlying complex political processes that take place in the arena of SN IOS can provide businesses and national governments with a better comprehension of how to intervene in these processes to achieve outcomes more favorable to them.

Acknowledgements

This research is part of the integrated project ITAIDE (Nr. 027829), funded by the 6th Framework IST Programme of the European Commission (see www.itaide.org). The ideas and opinions expressed by the authors do not necessarily reflect the views/insights/interests of all ITAIDE partners.

References

1. Andersen, K.V., Henriksen, H.Z., Rasmussen, E.B.: Re-organizing government using IT: The Danish model. In: Nixon, P.G., Koutrakou, V.N. (eds.) E-government in Europe: Re-booting the state, pp. 103–118. Routledge, London (2007)
2. Bjørn-Andersen, N., Razmerita, L., Henriksen, H.Z.: The Streamlining of Cross-Border Taxation Using IT -The Danish eExport Solution. In: Makolm, J., Orthofer, G. (eds.) E-Taxation: State & Perspectives, pp. 195–206. Trauner Verlag, Linz (2007)
3. Bomberg, E.E., Peterson, J., Stubb, A.: The European Union: How does it work? Oxford University Press, USA (2008)
4. Cash, J.I., Konsynski, B.R.: IS redraws competitive boundaries. Harvard Business Review 63(2), 134–142 (1985)
5. Cavaye, A.L.M.: An exploratory study in investigating transnational information systems. Journal of Strategic Information Systems 7(1), 17–35 (1998)
6. European Commission: Electronic Customs Multi-Annual Strategic Plan (MASP), Rev. 8 (2007)
7. Gregor, S.: The nature of theory in information systems. MIS Quarterly 30(3), 611–642 (2006)
8. Henriksen, H.Z., Rukanova, B., Tan, Y.-H.: Pacta Sunt Servanda But Where is the Agreement? The Complicated Case of eCustoms. In: Wimmer, M.A., Scholl, H.J., Ferro, E. (eds.) EGOV 2008. LNCS, vol. 5184, pp. 13–24. Springer, Heidelberg (2008)
9. Iacono, S., Wigand, R.T.: Information technology and industry change: View from an industry level of analysis. Journal of Information Technology 20(4), 211 (2005)
10. Johnston, R.B., Gregor, S.: A theory of industry-level activity for understanding the adoption of interorganizational systems. European Journal of Information Systems 9(4), 243–251 (2000)
11. Kubicek, H.P., Cimander, R.: Three dimensions of organizational interoperability: Insights from recent studies for improving interoperability frame-works. European Journal of ePractice 6, 1–12 (2009)
12. Markus, M.L., Steinfield, C.W., Wigand, R.T., Minton, G.: Standards, Collective Action and IS Development-Vertical Information Systems Standards in the US Home Mortgage Industry. MIS Quarterly, Special Issue on Standards and Standardization 30, 439–465 (2006)
13. Schooley, B.L., Horan, T.A.: Towards end-to-end government performance management: Case study of interorganizational information integration in emergency medical services (EMS). Government Information Quarterly 24(4), 755–784 (2007)
14. Sorrentino, M., Ferro, E.: Does the answer to eGovernment lie in intermunicipal collaboration? An exploratory Italian case study. In: Wimmer, M.A., Scholl, H.J., Ferro, E. (eds.) EGOV 2008. LNCS, vol. 5184, pp. 1–12. Springer, Heidelberg (2008)
15. Steinfield, C.W., Markus, M.L., Wigand, R.T.: Exploring interorganizational systems at the industry level of analysis: Evidence from the us home mortgage industry. Journal of Information Technology 20(4), 224 (2005)
16. Teo, H.H., Tan, B.C.Y., Wei, K.K.: Organizational transformation using electronic data interchange: The case of TradeNet in Singapore. Journal of MIS 13(4), 139–165 (1997)
17. Walsham, G.: Interpreting information systems in organizations. John Wiley and Sons, Chichester (1993)
18. Wigand, R.T., Steinfield, C.W., Markus, M.L.: IT Standards Choices and Industry Structure Outcomes: The Case of the United States Home Mortgage Industry. Journal of MIS 22(2), 165–191 (2005)

eGIF4M: eGovernment Interoperability Framework for Mozambique

Pavel Shvaiko[1], Adolfo Villafiorita[2], Alessandro Zorer[3],
Lourino Chemane[4,6], Teotónio Fumo[4], and Jussi Hinkkanen[5]

[1] TasLab, Informatica Trentina S.p.A., Trento, Italy
pavel.shvaiko@infotn.it
[2] Fondazione Bruno Kessler IRST, Trento, Italy
adolfo@fbk.eu
[3] Create-Net, Trento, Italy
alessandro.zorer@create-net.org
[4] UTICT - ICT Policy Implementation Technical Unit, Maputo, Mozambique
{chemane,tfumo}@infopol.gov.mz
[5] Ministry of Science and Technology, Maputo, Mozambique
jussi.hinkkanen@mct.gov.mz
[6] DSV, University of Stockholm, Stockholm, Sweden

Abstract. Harmonizing decentralized development of ICT solutions
with centralized strategies, e.g., meant to favor reuse and optimization
of resources, is a complex technical and organizational challenge. The
problem, shared by virtually all the governments, is becoming a priority also for countries, such as Mozambique, that have started their ICT
policy relatively recently and for which it is now evident that — if no
particular attention is devoted to the interoperability of the solutions being developed — the result will rapidly become a patchwork of solutions
incompatible with each other. The focus of the paper is on formulation
of eGIF4M: eGovernment Interoperability Framework for Mozambique.
The framework is based on a holistic approach. It builds on top of the
existing experiences in eGIFs all over the world and it addresses some
specific needs and peculiarities of developing countries, like Mozambique.
The result is a comprehensive framework based on: (*i*) a reference architecture along with technical standards, (*ii*) a standardization life cycle,
(*iii*) a maturity model, and (*iv*) some key actions meant to make the
initiative sustainable in the longer term.

1 Introduction

The government of Mozambique initiated the development of a national ICT
policy in 1998, by establishing the ICT Policy Commission, whose work resulted
in the release of the national ICT Policy in 2000 and, subsequently, its implementation plan. The plan, approved in 2002 identifies eGovernance as a strategic
area for the development of the country. One of the final goals here is to switch
to a *citizen-centric* government, that is, to a state of affairs in which the government delivers integrated services focused on the needs of citizens and private
sector and where these are able to interact with government in a manner, time
and place of their choice [5,11,21,30].

M.A. Wimmer et al. (Eds.): EGOV 2009, LNCS 5693, pp. 328–340, 2009.

Having adopted a comprehensive approach in the implementation of this vision, many government departments started, since 2000, implementing various ICT initiatives (e.g., Public Servants Information System, State Financial Information System, Enterprise Licensing and Cadastre Information System, Information System of the Administrative Tribunal, eLand Registry and Management Information System) and several projects related to a functional analysis and process re-engineering of government departments. It became clear quite soon that without proper governance and guidance, and without the definition of a proper interoperability framework, eGovernment services in Mozambique would soon be based on a patchwork of incompatible and closed systems, not differently to what happened to other countries.

Several interoperability frameworks have been defined in the world. We mention Australia, Germany, UK, New Zealand, Greece, EU, Ghana, and South Africa [2,3,7,8,22,23], to name a few. The works in [25,26,27] provided a concise comparative survey of some selected eGIFs and a general guidance on implementing an interoperability framework. Notice that common to nearly all eGIFs is the definition of standards to adopt (see, e.g., [3]). Slightly less common is the definition of a reference architecture to achieve interoperability, typically based on service oriented architectures (see, e.g., [28]), and addressed only by a part of the eGIFs are organizational, managerial, and technical aspects related to maintenance in the longer term of the frameworks (see, e.g., [8]). Finally, it is worth noting that the work in [18] has been selected by EU as a good practice case for eGovernment interoperability at local and regional levels.

By building on top of the achievements from the various eGIFs in the world and as a part of implementation of the eGovernment strategy of Mozambique, we propose a systematic and comprehensive approach to interoperability in Mozambique, called eGIF4M. The approach is devised to facilitate its early adoption and to be sustainable in the longer term. We achieve this by addressing specific risks and opportunities of Mozambique, which are also shared by other developing countries. The contributions of the paper include: (*i*) the service delivery architecture along with technical standards, (*ii*) a standardization lifecycle, (*iii*) an interoperability maturity model, and (*iv*) a set of support actions needed to ensure sustainability of eGIF4M. Notice that the uniqueness of the eGIF4M approach (compared to the other eGIFs mentioned above) is due to both: the consideration of all technical, organizational and process aspects, which in our opinion are needed to effectively and successfully deal with interoperability in the public sector along with supporting the development of the country, and the novelty of some of the support actions, such as the Maputo Living Lab.

The remainder of the paper is organized as follows. Section 2 provides the objectives of the work. Sections 3-8 elaborate in detail the various aspects of eGIF4M, including: the approach (Section 3), the service delivery architecture (Section 4) and its feasibility (Section 5), a standardization lifecycle (Section 6), an interoperability maturity model (Section 7), and the support actions (Section 8). Finally, Section 9 reports the major findings of the paper and outlines future work.

2   Fostering Interoperability in Mozambique

The objective of eGIF4M is the definition of the concrete steps to enable inter-operability across the Mozambique's public administration. By *interoperability* we mean here the capability of (two or more) systems to exchange seamlessly data, information, and knowledge. eGIF4M, therefore, is a central milestone for improving efficiency and effectiveness of government services and it is a key-enabler for switching the government to a citizen centric approach, a strategic goal of the country.

Besides the criticalities experienced by many countries all over the world in implementing their eGIFs (see, e.g., [28], for an overview), eGIF4M also needs to take into account some specific issues and opportunities, typical of countries experiencing a fast development, among which:

Governance: ICT projects are often supported by international donors and the resulting governance process is more complicated than that of other projects. The possibility to enforce common architectural solutions and standards on these projects, for instance, is limited, requires strong political commitment and clearly defined organizational roles.

Skills: the limited availability of specialized technical ICT and managerial skills in the country implies a strong dependence on external support to implement and manage the ICT projects. Without establishing a transition path to provide the necessary competencies to the local context and to gradually increase and enlarge the base of ICT skills, there is a risk of not becoming able to control the convergence of eGovernment projects on the interoperability framework.

Sustainability: The traditional approach of setting up specific projects to re-spond to the needs of government agencies is not suited for a long term initiative like eGIF, while most of the results are envisioned from three to five years. Hence, management of eGIF4M requires the setup of conditions that allow for operation in a multi-year perspective.

At the same time the implementation of an interoperability framework can re-duce some of the typical barriers faced by small and medium enterprisers (SMEs) in ICT projects. For instance, by having governments' solutions based on open standards, SMEs have more possibilities to compete or cooperate with bigger players. Thus, eGIF4M can be an opportunity for local companies to join the development of the eGovernment framework and in strengthening international connections and networking.

3   eGIF4M: The Approach

The risks and opportunities mentioned above require setting up a framework that refines existing approaches to be tailored to the specific needs and constraints of Mozambique. eGIF4M is therefore based on the following key actions:

Technical implementation, organized in two key areas:

- Implementation of an architectural framework (the eGIF4M *service delivery architecture*) based on a government service bus, where all the systems will converge to interoperate. We envisage the development of the architecture to be guided by a specific government unit. This helps drastically simplify the interoperability implementation process and reduce the dependencies, the expectations, and the needs for strong coordination with donor funded projects.
- Specification of the *standards* to be adopted at each level of the architecture, if applicable, and definition of a *life cycle for the standards*, to accommodate evolving eGovernment projects and innovation in technologies. Notice that the life cycle is an essential aspect to favor maintenance of the framework in the long run.

Organizational implementation, structured in:

- Definition of an *interoperability maturity model*, which measures the level of compliance and of adoption of eGIF. This information is essential to quantify and make visible the benefits (or disadvantages) of eGIF and can be used as an important tool for the setup of incentivation mechanisms for the more virtuous projects.
- Setup of an *organizational structure* and of the decision processes to manage eGIF4M, to monitor its execution, and to maintain and enforce it in the longer term.

Systemic support actions, meant as the set of activities to favour the growth of local skills and capabilities, to help create and disseminate a culture of interoperability, to help increase international networking of local companies and universities, and to create a virtuous cycle among public institutions, higher education, and private companies.

4   The eGIF4M Service Delivery Architecture

Figure 1 describes the eGIF4M service delivery architecture. It will serve as the basis for interoperation of data, systems, and processes. The architecture is based on a Government Service Bus and follows the standard SOA (service-oriented architecture) and EDA (event-driven architecture) approaches. We distinguish:

- *Users*, who are the actual service recipients that can be individuals, representatives of a private sector, such as SMEs, state agents, and so on.
- *Channels* that deliver the services, e.g., one-stop-shop, telephone, Internet.
- *Services* that are offered by eGovernment, such as legal entity services and civil identification services. Notice that access to the services offered either via a government portal or application interfaces might require authentication and authorization procedures.
- *Government service bus* is the core of the interoperability. It is constituted by two main components, the common information platform (providing interoperability of data and processes), and the common communication platform (that provides network and infrastructure). Of these two components,

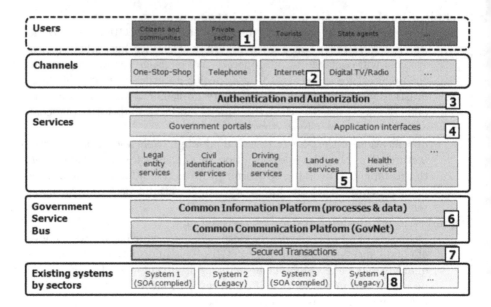

Fig. 1. The eGIF4M service delivery architecture

the latter has already been implemented. As a matter of fact, within the GovNet project, in its fifth year of operation, more than 140 government institutions from central (ministries), provincial, and district levels are now interconnected [6,17].

- *Existing systems by sectors* represent existing information systems. Some examples include: Enterprise Licensing and Cadastre Information System, State Financial Information System, eLand Registry and Land Management Information System.

The implementation of the architecture described in Figure 1 relies upon the identification and allocation of standards to the various architectural components. eGIF4M, therefore, starts from a taxonomy illustrated in Figure 2, which organizes standards in: (*i*) networks and infrastructures, (*ii*) process interoperability, and (*iii*) semantic data interoperability and allocates them to the architectural components. These areas are then further developed according to the seven layers covered by UNDP [27]. In parenthesis we indicate the number of standards considered in each area (only a subset of which is shown in Figure 2).

We now consider a scenario from the land management application following the path of eight items marked by numbers in rectangles in Figure 1. Notice that items 1-5 can be grouped under the front-office heading, while items 6-8 represent back-office. Suppose there is a private company that provides mediator services for renting land parcels, and there is a farmer that wants to rent one for agricultural use with the help of this company (item 1). The farmer has several choices among various land parcels, and, hence, asks the company first

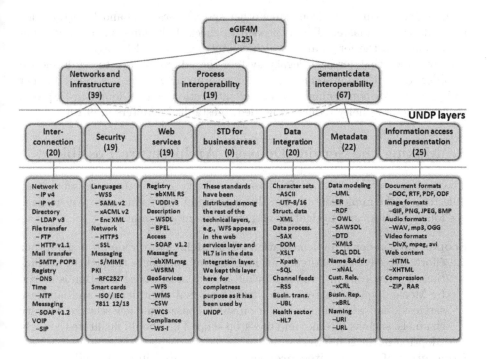

Fig. 2. Overview of the eGIF4M standards

to provide the maps of the identified areas to study them in order to make an informed decision with respect to which land parcel to rent. To process the request of the farmer, the company uses internet (item 2: IP v4[1]), passes through the necessary authentication and authorization procedures (item 3: LDAP[2]) and interacts in a secured way (item 7: SAML[3]) via the exposed application interfaces (item 4: SOAP[4], WMS[5]) of the land use services of the government (item 5) with the eLand Registry system (item 8). In turn, item 6 provides the interoperability glue at the process, data, and infrastructure levels that is necessary to process the request. For example, to describe metadata about geo-data it is used ISO 19115[6], while for describing metadata about geo-services it is used ISO 19119[7] (as required by CSW[8]), a map request is handled with WMS, etc. This request

---

[1] http://www.ietf.org/rfc/rfc0791.txt

[2] http://www.ietf.org/rfc/rfc1777.txt

[3] http://www.oasis-open.org/committees/tc_home.php?wg_abbrev=security

[4] http://www.w3.org/TR/2007/REC-soap12-part1-20070427/

[5] http://www.opengeospatial.org/standards/wms

[6] http://www.iso.org/iso/iso_catalogue/catalogue_tc/
catalogue_detail.htm?csnumber=26020

[7] http://www.iso.org/iso/iso_catalogue/catalogue_tc/
catalogue_detail.htm?csnumber=39890

[8] http://www.opengeospatial.org/standards/cat

requires integrating data from some other systems beside eLand Registry, such as the forestry cadaster. This is needed to check if the land parcel under consideration is in the forest area, which cannot be exploited for agricultural use. Finally notice that for each legacy system the adaptors have to be developed in order to use these systems under the government service bus. Some further technical details concerning: geo-service integration can be found in [31], and semantic heterogeneity reduction needed to establish adapters in [9,10].

5   Making the Service Delivery Architecture Possible

The implementation of the eGIF4M service delivery architecture represents a key milestone in the implementation of the interoperability framework. We envisage the following risks and mitigation actions in its implementation:

Scope: full top-down implementation of the architecture requires a significant effort. We envisage, instead, an incremental approach, through the definition of a few (one or two) significant case studies, whose selection is driven by Mozambique's strategic priorities (e.g., civil identification and land use services), and whose implementation will be based on a few selected delivery channels, such as Internet and one-stop shop. This should facilitate the early adoption of the framework.

Coherence of the architecture: keeping coherence, simplicity and efficiency of the architecture requires clear ownership in the setting up of the vision and in the definition of the strategic lines of development. For this reason a specific task force within a suitable government unit has to be responsible and accountable for its development.

Migration: in order to be of any use, legacy systems will have to converge (technically, e.g., via adaptors) on the government service bus. The framework uses the maturity model as a tool to measure compliance of the projects with the vision; defines technical standards to which projects migrate and proposes managerial standards (e.g., minimal technical documentation) that will also allow to have third parties migrate solutions, if necessary.

6   Keeping the eGIF4M Healthy

In the longer term the standards that we have allocated to the various components of the architecture will have to evolve, e.g., to better accommodate changing requirements of the government and changing technologies, while, at the same time, to maintain some control.

This is achieved in eGIF4M by defining a life cycle for standards, coherently to what also has been proposed by several other eGIFs. The life cycle builds on top of the work in [28] and includes the following states:

Emerging: it includes all the standards that the government is considering for introduction.

- *Future*. It encompasses all the standards that are not in use in the government (and not included in any of the states below) - no matter what the reason is (not needed, future consideration, and so on).
- *Assessed*. The standard has been evaluated and approved by the eGIF4M task force (§5) for experimental introduction, though is not yet in use.
- *Experimented*. An assessed standard has been deployed and it is in use in a controlled environment (e.g., in the scope of a new project; by some government agencies). The experimentation has the goal of assessing usefulness of the standard. The standard runs in parallel with other *Current* standards. A deadline is defined for a final assessment and evaluation, which will lead to a change of state (e.g., from *Experimented* to *Future*; from *Experimented* to *Current*).

Current: it includes all the standards that the government is currently using. We distinguish two levels that encode the prescription for the standard.
- *Possible*. It refers to a standard that can be used for data and services. Adoption is not compulsory. A standard can be kept in this state to, e.g., improve flexibility (not all the agencies have the possibility of switching to a corresponding mandatory standard, or it might not make sense for them to switch to the standard), while, at the same time, moving towards a common reference framework.
- *Mandatory*. The standard is officially adopted. Government bodies are required to deliver services and documents using the mandatory format.

Fading: it includes all the standards that are not in use anymore. When a format is in the *fading* state, no new document or service can be produced in the *faded* format. Furthermore, we distinguish two sub-cases, according to the policy chosen for historical data:
- *Disappearing*. Government bodies are required to migrate all data to the new format. A deadline is set for the migration.
- *Remaining*. Old data does not need to be migrated. The government ensures the readability of the format by maintaining support for the applications that handle the data.

7   eGIF4M Interoperability Maturity Model

One important aspect of eGIF4M is providing the ability to measure the level of adoption and diffusion of the interoperability framework. Such capability, in fact, allows decision makers and program managers to understand more precisely the level of adoption, the impact, and the success of eGIF4M. Moreover, it allows to plan actions meant to improve the delivery of services through the adoption of the interoperability framework.

Various models exist to measure the maturity of organizations in developing systems (e.g., CMMI [13], ISO/IEC 15504 [1], Bootstrap [16], Trillium [4]) and, more specifically, to measure the level of interoperability, see, e.g., [20,29]; see also the family of standards identified by SEI [12,19,24] as well as the works in [14,15] for surveys. All models share a common approach which is based on:

- identification of the *targets of evaluations*, for which the maturity level has to be determined (for instance, an organization or a system);
- a set of *maturity levels* (for instance, initial, managed, defined, measured, and optimized);
- a *set of goals*, that defines what has to be measured (for instance, procedures, applications, infrastructures, and data).
- a *method* to determine the maturity level. This can be accomplished, for instance, by assigning the maturity level demonstrated by the target of evaluation in achieving each goal. A transformation function, e.g., as a (weighted) average of the scores, can be used to determine the total level of maturity.

The approach we propose in eGIF4M, see Table 1, is based on an adaptation of some of the models described above to provide a measurement system which is closer to the needs of Mozambique. Specifically, the model has two targets of evaluation: (*i*) organizations, and (*ii*) software development (system) projects. Notice that targeting projects is a peculiarity of eGIF4M, which allows to more easily manage inter-departmental projects and to raise awareness of interoperability as early as possible in the development cycle.

The assessment of (software development) projects is performed on the most recent artifacts (e.g., requirements, design, prototype, implementation) and is meant to measure two dimensions: level of data interoperability (for which we revised the Conceptual Interoperability levels of the LISI approach [24]) and technical maturity, meant as the level of adoption of standard technologies for the development (for which we devised specific goals, being loosely inspired by the work in [20]).

Table 1. eGIF4M Interoperability Maturity Model

The assessment of organizations is based on the PAID attributes (Process, Applications, Infrastructure, and Data) of the LISI model. For the process and the infrastructure we adapted the LISI model, whereas for the applications and the data attributes we reused the model adopted for projects.

We expect various benefits from the adoption of the model, among which the possibility of measuring the penetration of interoperability at different levels of granularity (government, agency, and systems), the identification of criticalities in the implementation of the framework, and raising awareness on interoperability opportunities and advantages.

8 Support Actions

Organizational structure for the whole initiative. eGIF4M includes a complex set of initiatives, which needs a well defined cross-departmental organization and clear horizontal processes to be managed and coordinated. To achieve that, two kinds of organizations need to be established. The first is an inter-agency and inter-ministry committee, responsible for defining the enforcement policies and incentives for the diffusion of standards, and to monitor the eGIF4M implementation and impact. The second is an operational group in charge of the execution of the framework and in charge of the implementation of eGIF4M (§5).

Dissemination, networking and higher education. One of the key issues in implementing a sustainable eGIF initiative in a developing country like Mozambique is to grow the skills of the local players, both in the public and private sector, and to better connect them with international initiatives. The plan for dissemination, higher education, and mobility initiatives in eGIF4M therefore includes aspects related to increasing national and international visibility of eGIF4M and the definition of exchange programs between Mozambique's and international universities.

Living lab **to connect user institutions, research centers and local companies.** To combine some of the actions previously described and to create a stable infrastructure in which public initiatives, education, and private companies can exchange experiences, eGIF4M is strongly tied to the Maputo Living Lab (LLM) initiative, that has recently become part of the European network of Living Labs[9]. This is a system for building future economy in which real-life user-centric research and innovation will be a normal co-creation technique for new products, services and societal infrastructure. We expect LLM to become the reference point for the strengthening of national and international networking of local companies and the place for the exchange of best practices.

9 Conclusions

Several frameworks have been proposed and adopted by different countries to address issues and costs due to the lack of interoperability in public agencies

---

[9] http://www.openlivinglabs.eu/

and in government's ICT systems. Approaches and scope vary quite a bit, to reflect the different allocation of responsibilities between central and peripheral agencies, the level of automation, and the maturity of eGovernment services. In this paper we have discussed the main actions we envisage for the implementation of eGIF4M, part of a wider eGovernment initiative whose implementation started in 1998. The framework is based on several key actions (implementation of the government service bus, monitoring and control through the interoperability maturity levels) and on a set of wider-scope actions, such as living labs. All actions are based on the definition of the standards to adopt and of their life cycle, coherently with what happens in various other eGIFs.

We expect various benefits from the adoption of the framework, among which the main is governing a transition to more interoperable solutions, while, at the same time, allowing for a certain independence in the choice and development of ICT solutions, which is one of the priorities of the country. The possibility of measuring the penetration of interoperability at different levels of granularity (government, agency, etc.) and using the information to guide decision making, the increased efficiency coming from the implementation of a citizen-centric government (for whose implementation interoperability is essential), together with the broader actions suggested in the framework, constitute a further opportunity to sustain and accelerate the growth of the country which, in the last ten years, has experienced a steady economical growth in the two digits range.

Future work includes at least: (i) actual implementation of the framework proposed in order to obtain practical evidence of the eGIF4M strong and weak aspects, and (ii) drawing general implications from the empirical eGIF4M experiences which can be useful also for the other similar initiatives in the world.

Acknowledgements. This work was funded by the Italian Cooperation[10]. We appreciate support and useful suggestions from Fausto Giunchiglia, and the Common Communication Platform and Interoperability Framework Working Group of Mozambique on the themes of the paper.

References

1. ISO/IEC 15504: Information technology - software process assessment part 7: Guide for use in process improvement (1998)
2. Australian government technical interoperability framework,
   http://www.agimo.gov.au/publications/2005/04/agtifv2/#
   Australian20Technical20Framework (2005)
3. New Zealand e-government interoperability framework (2008),
   http://www.e.govt.nz/standards/e-gif/e-gif-v-3/e-gif-v-3-total.pdf
4. Bell Canada. The trillium model (1994),
   http://www2.umassd.edu/swpi/BellCanada/trillium-html/trillium.html
5. cc:eGov. A Handbook for Citizen-centric eGovernment (2007),
   http://www.epractice.eu/document/4227
6. Chemane, L., Taula, R., Carrilho, S.: MCDM framework and the selection of network topology – GovNet case study. In: Proc. of IST-Africa (2006)

---

[10] http://www.italcoopmoz.com/

7. Bundesministerium des Innern. Standards and architectures for e-government applications, vol. 59. KBSt Publication Series (2003). ISSN 0179-7263,
   `http://www.apdip.net/projects/gif/country/GE-GIF.pdf`
8. eGovernment Unit. e-government interoperability framework version 6.1 (2005),
   `http://www.govtalk.gov.uk/documents/eGIF%20v6_1%281%29.pdf`
9. Euzenat, J., Shvaiko, P.: Ontology matching. Springer, Heidelberg (2007)
10. Giunchiglia, F., Yatskevich, M., McNeill, F., Pane, J., Besana, P., Shvaiko, P.: Approximate structure preserving semantic matching. In: Proc. of ODBASE (2008)
11. Gov3. Citizen Centric Government – Global Best Practices in Delivering Agile Public services to Citizen and Business (2006),
    `http://www.intel.com/business/bss/industry/government/citizen_wp.pdf`
12. C4ISR Interoperability Working Group. Levels of Information Systems Interoperability (LISI). Department of Defense (1998)
13. Software Engineering Institute. Capability maturity model integration (2009),
    `http://www.sei.cmu.edu/cmmi/`
14. Software Engineering Institute. Guide to Interoperability (2009),
    `http://www.sei.cmu.edu/isis/guide/index.htm`
15. Kasunic, M., Anderson, W.: Measuring systems interoperability: Challenges and opportunities. Technical Report CMU/SEI-2004-TN-003, Software Engineering Institute (2004)
16. Kuvaja, P., Simila, J., Krzanik, L., Bicego, A., Koch, G., Saukonen, S.: Software Process Assessment and Improvement: the BOOTSTRAP approach. Blackwell Publishers, Oxford (1994)
17. Mapsanganhe, S., Chemane, L.: GovNet e-mail system capacity planning. In: Proc. of IST-Africa (2007)
18. Marcucci, L., Kluzer, S., Nicolini, A., Cimander, R.: ICAR - a system for e- enabled cooperation among regional, local and national administrations in Italy. European Commission (2006),
    `http://www.egov-iop.ifib.de/downloads/GPC_ICAR_Italy.pdf`
19. Morris, E., Levine, L., Meyers, C., Plakosh, D., Place, P.: Systems of systems interoperability. Technical Report CMU/SEI-2004-TR-004, ESC-TR-2004-004, Software Engineering Institute, Carnegie Mellon University (2004)
20. NETHA. Interoperability Maturity Model. National E-Health Transition Authority Ltd. (2007)
21. Council of Ministers. Public sector reform strategy. Council of Ministers Publication, Maputo, Mozambique (2006)
22. Government of South Africa. Minimum interoperability standards (MIOS) for information systems in government (2007),
    `http://www.i-gov.org/images/articles/4760/MIOS_V4.1_final.pdf`
23. Papadakis, A., Rantos, K., Stasis, A.: The realization of the greek e-gif. Presented at Secondo Vertice Europeo sull'Interoperabilit a nell'iGovernment (2008)
24. Tolk, A., Muguira, J.A.: The levels of conceptual interoperability model. In: Fall Simulation Interoperability Workshop, Orlando, Florida (2003)
25. United Nations Development Programme (UNDP). e-Government Interoperability: A Review of Government Interoperability Frameworks in Selected Countries. UNDP Regional Centre in Bangkok (2007)
26. United Nations Development Programme (UNDP). e-Government Interoperability: Guide. UNDP Regional Centre in Bangkok (2007)
27. United Nations Development Programme (UNDP). e-Government Interoperability: Overview. UNDP Regional Centre in Bangkok (2007)

28. United Nations Development Programme (UNDP). e-Government Interoperability: e-Primers for the Information Economy, Society and Policy. UNDP Regional Centre in Bangkok (2008)
29. University of Albany. Sharing Justice Information: A Capability Assessment Toolkit (2005)
30. UTICT. Estratégia da política de informática em Moçambique. UTICT Publication, Government of Mozambique, Maputo, Mozambique (2000)
31. Vaccari, L., Shvaiko, P., Marchese, M.: A geo-service semantic integration in spatial data infrastructures. International Journal of Spatial Data Infrastructures Research (2009)

Metadata Sets for e-Government Resources: The Extended e-Government Metadata Schema (eGMS+)

Yannis Charalabidis, Fenareti Lampathaki, and Dimitris Askounis

National Technical University of Athens, 9 Iroon Polytechniou, Athens, Greece
{yannisx,flamp,askous}@epu.ntua.gr

Abstract. In the dawn of the Semantic Web era, metadata appear as a key enabler that assists management of the e-Government resources related to the provision of personalized, efficient and proactive services oriented towards the real
citizens' needs. As different authorities typically use different terms to describe
their resources and publish them in various e-Government Registries that may
enhance the access to and delivery of governmental knowledge, but also need to
communicate seamlessly at a national and pan-European level, the need for a
unified e-Government metadata standard emerges. This paper presents the creation of an ontology-based extended metadata set for e-Government Resources
that embraces services, documents, XML Schemas, code lists, public bodies
and information systems. Such a metadata set formalizes the exchange of information between portals and registries and assists the service transformation
and simplification efforts, while it can be further taken into consideration when
applying Web 2.0 techniques in e-Government.

Keywords: metadata element set, e-Government resources, service definition,
e-GMS, semantic interoperability.

1 Introduction

Today, modernizing government strategies, such as the i2010 e-Government Action
Plan, require better use of official information, joined-up systems and policies, and
services designed around the needs of citizens. The evolution of Internet at the same
time gives way towards building a Semantic Web that enables seamless communication between machines [4]. In this context, creating and populating rich semantic
metadata on the Web has been commonly accepted as the route leading to the e-
Government Semantic Web vision [11]. Metadata is a fundamental concept in building governmental digital collections or public information centres that describe and
categorize e-government resources online [29]. According to [6], metadata can be
defined as "data about data" and can exist in multiple levels:

- Syntactic metadata describe non-contextual information about content and
  provide very general information, such as the document's size, location or
  date of creation.
- Structural metadata provides information regarding the structure of the content, how items are put together or arranged.

M.A. Wimmer et al. (Eds.): EGOV 2009, LNCS 5693, pp. 341–352, 2009.

- Semantic metadata add relationships, rules and constraints to syntactic and structural metadata. Such metadata describe contextually relevant or domain-specific information about content based on a domain specific metadata model or ontology, providing a context for interpretation.

Over the years, e-Government initiatives across Europe have tried to describe services and other resources (e.g. document collections) for use by systems and applications to serve citizens, business and administration agencies [8]. However, proposing a set of structural and syntactic metadata for e-Government resources is not adequate and effective to help services discovery and knowledge sharing [11], [16] leading to the conclusion that web-based resources and their mutual relationships can still be considered rather ungoverned [24].

In this direction, the present paper proposes a metadata set for describing e-Government resources gaining experience from relevant e-Government Metadata standardization efforts. Effectively applied in the context of the Greek e-Government Interoperability Framework [14] and the Interoperability Registry Prototype implementation [27], the proposed metadata set is customized on the particular needs of the e-Government services, documents, XML Schemas, code lists, public bodies and information systems and formalizes their meaning. It further contributes to accelerate the exchange and retrieval of service-related information by governmental sites on the fly and to enhance the perspective over service provision guiding any transformation effort [11].

The structure of the present paper is as following: Section 2 describes the current state of the art in e-Government metadata schemas and standards, analyzing the main elements contained in most implementations worldwide. Section 3 presents an overview of the ontology that synthesizes the proposed metadata set creation, while the actual metadata sets for services, documents, XML schemas, code lists, public bodies and information systems are outlined in Section 4. Conclusions upon the merits and limitations of the approach, as well as next challenges to be tackled are provided in Section 5.

2 Relevant Work

Standardizing metadata sets for describing web resources has attracted great interest both from research and practical reality, as indicated in the following initiatives:

- *Dublin Core Metadata Initiative (DCMI)* [13] provides simple standards to facilitate the finding, sharing and management of information that extends over a broad range of purposes and business models.
- *United Kingdom's e-Government Metadata Standard (UK eGMS)* [21] lays down the elements, refinements and encoding schemes to be used by government officers when creating metadata for their information resources or designing search interfaces for information systems.
- *Australian Government Locator Service (AGLS)* Metadata Element Set [2] provides a set of metadata elements designed to improve the visibility, accessibility and interoperability of online information, organizations and services.

- *New Zealand Government Locator Service (NZGLS)* Metadata Element Set [28] originally designed for use by any governmental agency wishing to make information sources or services more readily discoverable is suitable for more general use.
- *IDABC Management Information Resources for e-Government (MIREG)* [15] came to supplement MOREQ (Model Requirements for the Management of Electronic Records) results and aimed to develop extensions to the Dublin Core for government information based primarily on the national metadata recommendations of the Member States' public administrations.
- *CEN/ISSS Workshop on Discovery of and Access to e-Government Resources (CEN/ISSS WS/eGov-Share)* [8] presents the ontology for the description of e-Government resources (Services, Process descriptions, Standards and interoperability frameworks, (Requirements) documents) and the metadata schema that is used in its work.

However, such metadata standards and schemes for network resources apply mainly to documents, electronic archives and public sites or do not cover all the requirements for service-related modeling, as indicated in the following figure.

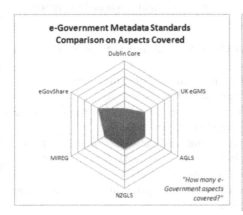 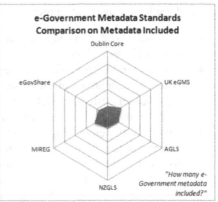

Fig. 1. e-Government Metadata Standards Coverage

Research papers that have provided sets of metadata and ontologies for modeling services, such as [4], [9], [16], [23], [24], [30], as well as relevant initiatives for describing spatial information [16] and standards [17] have also been taken into account. However, despite the fact that a set of international standards and protocols, such as RDF (Resource Description Framework), OWL (Web Ontology Language), Atom Syndication Format, RSS (Really Simple Syndication), SKOS (Simple Knowledge Organization System) and XTM (XML Topic Maps), accompanies such metadata initiatives in order to formally depict e-Government metadata, a complete solution requires such a wide range of different technologies that to date have not rallied around a standard metadata representation [26].

The main emerging conclusions from studying the underlying state of the art thus include:

- Lack of a comprehensive, yet easy to use standardized metadata schema for e-Government resources that adopts a "follow-the-service" approach and captures the semantics of all the service-surrounding information, such as XML Schemas and code lists.
- Lack of orientation towards transforming services and real time service provision at web front-ends.
- Lack of easily accessible glossaries and predefined code lists for use in such metadata definitions, that resolve language issues as all the relevant metadata descriptions need to be in local language (for the government officials to understand, modify and approve) and at least in English (for easiness of communication with other governments and practitioners).

3   The e-Government Ontology

The definition of the proposed extended e-Government Metadata Standard is driven by the e-Government ontology and emphasizes on the formalization and the representation of the following basic entities – classes:

- *Services* provided in conventional or electronic means by the public authorities to the citizens and businesses.
- *Documents*, in electronic or printed format, that constitute the inputs or outputs of a service or are involved during their execution.
- *Information Systems*, which support the service provision and encompass the web portals as well as the back-office and the legacy systems.
- *Public Bodies* embracing all the service points and the authorities of the public sector that provide services, issue documents, create XML Schemas and code lists and own supporting information systems.
- *Web Services* for the interconnection and the interoperability among information systems during a service execution.
- *Legal Framework* that regulates the service provision, the documents issuance and the overall operation of the public bodies.
- *XML Schemas* and *Code Lists* with which the electronically exchanged documents comply and which are exploited in web services.

The following figure presents an abstract overview of the e-Government Ontology which is described in detail in [9] and [27]. The basic clusters of attributes are provided within each class, as well as the main relationships between them giving way to further analysis in Section 4. It needs to be noted that as far as the class Web Service is concerned, the proposed approach adopts the metadata definition prescribed in the OWL-S standard.

Additional classes of the ontology, completing the representation but not presented in further details in the present paper, are the following:

- Classes representing service types, document types, information system types, the (functionally oriented) service category list, and relevant categorization elements.
- Classes representing activity steps (start, finish, decisions, etc), giving the ability for in-depth description of the service flows.
- Classes for representing user-oriented elements, such as life events and business episodes.
- Classes holding information on various characteristics of services and documents, such as authentication methods, ways of service provision, levels of service sophistication, etc.

The majority of the above additional classes constitute an important addition to existing ontologies, such as the eGMS or the CEN/ISSS, providing for automated reconciliation and semantic matching of relevant annotations among systems of different organizations, directly contributing to semantic interoperability achievement. They have been modeled as Controlled Lists in the metadata sets that follow in the next chapter.

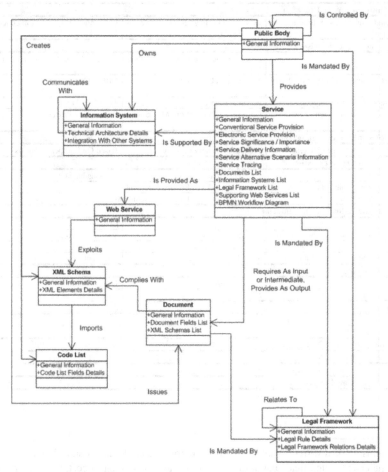

Fig. 2. e-Government Ontology Partial Class Diagram

4   The Extended e-Government Metadata Schema (eGMS+)

4.1 Services

The metadata set customized to the conventional and / or electronic services' requirements consists of 9 groups and is provided in the following table. It needs to be noted that the metadata definition of a service needs to be accompanied by the BPMN (Business Process Modelling Notation) diagram of its workflow.

Table 1. Metadata Set for Services[1]

General Information		
Identifier	Title	Responsible Public Body
Final Service (*)	Addressee (*)	Type (*)
Aggregation (3 level-GCL) (*)	Life Event (*)	Business Episode (*)
Service In Abstract Level (*)	Parent Service	Service Delivery Channels (*)
Conventional Service Provision		
Demand On Physical Presence In Submission (*)	Demand On Physical Presence In Receipt (*)	Conventional Authentication Method (*)
Electronic Service Provision		
Website	Electronic Service Delivery Method (*)	Current Online Sophistication Level (*)
Target Online Sophistication Level (*)	Multilingual Content (*)	Offline Operation (*)
Progress Monitoring Support (*)	Personal Data Level (*)	Trust Level (*)
Required Authentication Level (*)	Current Authentication Mechanism (*)	Registration Process (*)
Service Significance / Importance		
Transactions Volume (per year)	Frequency of Service Requests	Based On European Policies (*)
Service Delivery Information		
Delivery Cost	Delivery Time	Responsible Department
Responsible Public Servant		Service Preconditions
Related Announcements		Related Attachments
Service Alternative Scenaria Information[2]		
Identifier	Title	Conditions
Resources for Public Administration	Resources for Addressee	Total Resources
Cost for Public Administration	Cost for Addressee	Total Cost
Time for Public Administration	Time for Addressee	Total Time
Service Tracing		
Source	Date. Published	Date. Modified
Date. Valid (From-To)	State (*)	Language (*)
Documents List		
Identifier	Title	Position In Service (*)	Mandatory (*)
Replaces Document		Self-appointed Call (*)	
Information Systems List		
Legal Framework List		
Supporting Web Services List		
BPMN Workflow Diagram		

---

[1] The fields marked with (*) take values from appropriate predefined, controlled lists.

[2] It includes computed fields based on the step-by-step calculation of cost, time and resources, taking into account the possibility of faults.

4.2 Documents

The metadata set that accompanies the documents claims novelty in incorporating the documents fields' definition that guides the XML Schema design and the code lists creation at later stages.

Table 2. Metadata Set for Documents

General Information		
Identifier	Title	Creator
Publisher	Type (*)	Subject
Coverage	Format (*)	Language (*)
Addressee	Audience	Mandate. Authorizing Statute
Source	Date. Published	Date. Modified
Date. Valid (From-To)	State (*)	
Document Fields List		
Name	Description	Aggregation
Filled In By	Mandatory (*)	Complex Type (*)
Multiple Values (*)	Predefined Values from Code List	
Type (*)	Length	
XML Schemas List		

The metadata set built around XML Schemas is further customized according to the type of the XML Schema [10] and has been based on the UN/CEFACT Core Components Technical Specification.

Table 3. Metadata Set for XML Schemas

General Information		
Identifier	Title	Creator
Version	Type (*)	Format (*)
Date. Published	Date. Valid (From-To)	State (*)
XML Elements Details		
Unique Identifier	Name	Dictionary Entry Name
Type (*)	Version	Definition
Object Class Term Qualifier	Object Class Term	Property Term Qualifier
Property Term	Associated Object Class Term Qualifier	Representation Term (*)
Date Type Qualifier	Primitive Type (*)	Qualified Data Type
Cardinality Min	Cardinality Max	Facets (i.e. Pattern, Length, Min/Max Length, Enumeration, Total Digits, Fraction Digits, Min/Max Inclusive/Exclusive)
Context: Business Process	Context: Organization	Context: Region (*)
Business Term	Example	Remarks

As far as the approved code lists are concerned, the requirement for bilingual content has been fulfilled in the metadata set depicted in Table 4.

Table 4. Metadata Set for Code Lists

General Information		
Identifier	Title	Creator
Version	Description	Application Field (*)
Type (*)	Format (*)	Date. Published
Date. Valid (From-To)	State (*)	
Code List Fields Details		
Unique Identifier	Name	Dictionary Entry Name
Component Type (*)	Version	Enumeration Value
Name in English	Definition in English	Name in Greek
Definition in Greek	Related Field	Representation Term (*)
List Qualifier(s)	Primitive Type (*)	
Active Flag (*)	Date. Valid (From-To)	

4.3 Public Body

The public bodies' metadata information creates a basic profile around service providers and recognizes their structure and dependencies through the properties as depicted in the following table.

Table 5. Metadata Set for Public Bodies

General Information		
Identifier	Title	Acronym
Type (*)	Supervisor Public Organization	Description
Location	Website	State (*)
Contact Details	Remarks	Date. Valid (From-To)

4.4 Information Systems

Apart from the general information, the metadata set for Information Systems dives into details around the technical architecture of a system, its sub-systems and the communication / integration capabilities with other systems either within or outside the boundaries of the public organization.

Table 6. Metadata Set for Information Systems

General Information		
Identifier	Title	Owner Organization
Contractor	Project	Description
Type	Users (Total Number)	Date. Acquired
Date. Modified	Date. Valid (From-To)	State (*)
Preservation Mechanism (SLA)	Contact Details	Website
Technical Architecture Details		
Database Management System	Application Level	Network Infrastructure
Authentication Mechanism (*)	Security Mechanism (*)	Technical Standards (*)
Integration With Other Systems		
Identifier	Title	
Integration Mechanism (*)	Communication Frequency	

4.5 Legal Framework

The Legal Framework metadata span into general information around the framework, details about the legal rules it contains and its relations with other legal frameworks, such as legal frameworks it amends, replaces or suspends.

Table 7. Metadata Set for Legal Framework

General Information		
Identifier	Title	Official Journal Identifier
Official Journal Page Numbers	Application Field (*)	Application Status (*)
Type (*)	Language (*)	Date. Issued
Date. Signed	Date. Valid (From-To)	Relevant Attachments
Legal Rule Details		
Identifier	Title	Description
Legal Framework Relations Details		
Legal Framework Identifier	Relation Type (*)	

4.6   Controlled Lists

In order to avoid populating the metadata set with unstructured information, a set of controlled lists has been created and an indicative extract is provided in the following table.

Table 8. Indicative Enumeration Controlled Lists

Government Category List (1st Level out of 3)		
City Planning and Land Registry	Civilization and Free Time	Education and Research
Environment and Natural Resources	Finance and Economy	Health and Social Care
Information and Communication	International Affairs and European Union	Justice, State and Public Administration
People, Communities and Way of Living	Public Order and Defence	Services for Companies
Transportation Means, Trips and Tourism	Work, Insurance and Pension	
Service Type		
Request	Information Discovery	Declaration
Return	Registration	Participative Actions
Permit / Licence	Certificate Issuance	Payment
Life Event		
Birth	Marriage	Divorce
Death in Family	Sickness	Employment
Dismissal	Retirement	Property Acquisition
Property Loss	Residence Change	Education
Travel Abroad	Military Service	Other …
Not Applicable	Unknown	
Conventional Authentication Method		
Identity Card	Passport	Driving Licence
Identity Certificate	Social Insurance Card	Other
Not Required	Unknown	
Electronic Authentication Method		
Username / Password	Soft Digital Certificate	Hard Digital Certificate
Other	Not Required	Unknown
Service Delivery Method		
Service Provider Premises	Single Points of Contact (Citizen Service Centers in Greece)	Call Centers
Mail	Internet	Mobile Phone
Digital TV	Other	Unknown
Electronic Service Delivery Method		
Internet Browser	Web Service	Desktop Application
Other	Unknown	
Document Type		
Application	Licence	Certificate
Request	Receipt	Declaration
Notification	Decision	
Other	Unknown	

5 Conclusions

Utilizing practices and standardization from the e-Government domain internationally, the presented approach is claiming novelty in conceptualization of an ontology-based extended metadata set embracing the e-Government knowledge, from services and documents to code lists and information systems. It brings the power of annotating services with commonly agreed metadata into the exchange and the retrieval of service-related information stored in Interoperability Registries by governmental sites on the fly. As the need for transforming services to obtain a more citizen-centric orientation based on their real needs and life events is more and more stressed, the proposed approach has already included metadata around service delivery scenaria that can guide any business process re-engineering effort in the public sector.

Problems faced during the adoption and application of the proposed metadata set were not trivial and have to be to be taken in mind during relevant attempts by government officials and practitioners. Such a large metadata schema for each service a public body provides, every document that is exchanged during service provision and every information system involved, not to mention the XML Schemas and code lists required documentation, inevitably requires additional effort on behalf of the public servants both in the creation and the maintenance phase. The adoption of a common "governance policy" over metadata appears as a worthwhile track towards this direction. Language issues also need to be taken care of early in the process, as the provision of pan-European e-Government Services is already on the way. Finally, adequate time and effort should be spent for educating and working together with government officials at various levels, for obtaining a common perspective over the metadata set.

As the proposed metadata set is incorporated into the Greek e-Government Interoperability Framework [14] and the Interoperability Registry Prototype implementation [27], future steps along our work mainly include exploration of how such a metadata set as the proposed one can: (a) be exploited in intelligent governmental service front-ends that enhance end users experience and have recently started to gain momentum at the international research scene [6], mainly when it comes to provided public services cataloguing and user groups profiling information, and (b) be further elicited in order to take into account service addressees' feedback when creating the service alternative scenaria.

References

1. Aktas, M.S., Fox, G.C., Pierce, M., Oh, S.: XML Metadata Services. Concurrency Computat. Pract. Exper. 20, 801–823 (2008)
2. Australian Government, National Archives of Australia, AGLS Metadata Standard, Version 1.3,
   http://www.naa.gov.au/records-management/publications/
   AGLS-Element.aspx
3. Balani, N.: The future of the Web is Semantic - Ontologies form the backbone of a whole new way to understand online data, IBM White Paper,
   http://www.ibm.com/developerworks/web/library/wa-semweb/

4. Barone, A., Di Pietro, P.: Semantic of e-Government Processes: a Formal Approach to Service Definition (Arianna). In: Proceedings of eGovINTEROP 2006, Bordeaux, France (2006)
5. Berners-Lee, T., Hendler, J., Lassila, O.: The semantic web. Scientific American 284(5), 34–43 (2001)
6. Cantera, J.M., Reyes, M., Hierro, J., Tsouroulas, N.: White Paper on Service Front-Ends in the Future Internet of Services and Next Generation SOA,
   http://www.nexof-ra.eu/sites/default/files/nxt_gen_soa_
   workingdraft_21july2008.pdf
7. Cardoso, J., Sheth, A.: The Semantic Web and its Applications. In: Cardoso, J., Sheth, A. (eds.) Semantic Web and Beyond: Computing for Human Experience, Semantic Web Services, Processes and Applications. Springer, Heidelberg (2006)
8. CEN/ISSS Workshop on Discovery of and Access to e-Government Resources (CEN/ISSS WS/eGov-Share): Sharing e-Government resources: a practical approach for designers and developers,
   http://www.cen.eu/cenorm/businessdomains/businessdomains/iss
   s/workshops/wsegovshare.asp
9. Charalabidis, Y., Askounis, D.: Interoperability Registries in e-Government: Developing a Semantically Rich Repository for Electronic Services and Documents of the new Public Administration. In: Proceedings of the 41st Hawaiian International Conference of System Sciences, HICCS 2008, Hawaii (2008)
10. Charalabidis, Y., Lampathaki, F., Askounis, D.: Unified Data Modeling and Document Standardization Using Core Components Technical Specification for Electronic Government Applications. Journal of Theoretical and Applied Electronic Commerce Research 3(3), 38–51 (2008)
11. Charalabidis, Y., Lampathaki, F., Psarras, J.: Combination of Interoperability Registries with Process and Data Management Tools for Governmental Services Transformation. In: Proceedings of the 42nd Hawaiian International Conference of System Sciences, HICCS 2009, Hawaii (2009)
12. Chen, L., Shadbolt, N.R., Goble, C., Tao, F.: Managing Semantic Metadata for Web Grid Services. International Journal of Web Services Research 3(4), 73–94 (2006)
13. Dublin Core Metadata Element Set, Version 1.1,
   http://dublincore.org/documents/dces/
14. Greek Ministry of Interior, Greek e-Government Interoperability Framework,
   http://www.e-gif.gov.gr/
15. IDABC Management Information Resources for e-Government,
   http://ec.europa.eu/idabc/en/document/3615/5585
16. INSPIRE (Infrastructure for Spatial Information in Europe) Draft Implementing Rules for Metadata (Version 2),
   http://inspire.jrc.ec.europa.eu/reports/
   ImplementingRules/draftINSPIREMetadataIRv2_20070202.pdf
17. ISO/IEC WD 24706 Information technology – Metadata for technical standards and specifications documents,
   http://jtc1sc32.org/doc/N1251-1300/32N1257-WD24706.pdf
18. Lampathaki, F., Charalabidis, Y., Sarantis, D., Koussouris, S., Askounis, D.: E-Government Services Composition Using Multi-faceted Metadata Classification Structures. In: Wimmer, M.A., Scholl, J., Grönlund, Å. (eds.) EGOV 2007. LNCS, vol. 4656, pp. 116–126. Springer, Heidelberg (2007)

19. Missier, P., Alper, P., Corcho, O., Dunlop, I., Goble, C.: Requirements and Services for Metadata Management. IEEE Internet Computing 11(5), 17–25 (2007)
20. NISO: Understanding Metadata,
    http://www.niso.org/publications/press/
    UnderstandingMetadata.pdf
21. Office of the e-Envoy, e-Government Metadata Standard, Version 3.1,
    http://www.govtalk.gov.uk/documents/eGMS%20version%203_1.pdf
22. Osimo, D.: Web 2.0 in Government: Why and How? European Commission Joint Research Centre Scientific and Technical Reports (2008)
23. Palmonari, M., Viscusi, G., Batini, C.: A semantic repository approach to improve the government to business relationship. Data & Knowledge Engineering 65, 485–511 (2008)
24. Peristeras, V., Tarabanis, K.: Governance Enterprise Architecture (GEA): Domain Models for E-Governance. In: Proceedings of the ICEC 2004, Sixth International Conference on Electronic Commerce (2004)
25. Schroth, C.: The Internet of Services: Global Industrialization of Information Intensive Services. In: Proceedings of IEEE International Conference on Digital Information Management (ICDIM 2007), Web X.0 and Web Mining Workshop, Lyon, France (2007)
26. Smith, J.R.: The Search for Interoperability. IEEE Multimedia 15(3), 84–87 (2008)
27. Sourouni, A.-M., Lampathaki, F., Mouzakitis, S., Charalabidis, Y., Askounis, D.: Paving the way to eGovernment transformation: Interoperability registry infrastructure development. In: Wimmer, M.A., Scholl, H.J., Ferro, E. (eds.) EGOV 2008. LNCS, vol. 5184, pp. 340–351. Springer, Heidelberg (2008)
28. State Services Commission, NZGLS Metadata Element Set, Version 2.1,
    http://www.e.govt.nz/standards/nzgls/standard/
    element-set-21/nzgls-element-set-2-1.pdf
29. Tambouris, E., Manouselis, N., Costopoulou, C.: Metadata for digital collections of e-government resources. The Electronic Library 25(2), 176–192 (2007)
30. Vassilakis, C., Lepouras, G.: An Ontology for e-Government Public Services. In: Encyclopedia of E-Commerce, E-Government and Mobile Commerce, pp. 865–870 (2006)

Bidding for Complex Projects: Evidence from Italian Government's Acquisitions of IT Services

Gian Luigi Albano, Federico Dini, and Roberto Zampino

Consip S.p.A., Italian Public Procurement Agency, Via Isonzo 19/e,
00198 Roma, Italy
gianluigi.albano@tesoro.it, federico.dini@tesoro.it,
roberto.zampino@tesoro.it

Abstract. Public buyers are often mandated by law to adopt competitive procedures to ensure transparency and promote full competition. Recent economic
literature, however, suggests that open competition can perform poorly in allocating complex projects. In exploring the determinants of bidding behavior in
tenders for complex IT services, we find results that appear consistent with theory. Our analysis shows that price and quality are linked in a puzzling way:
high quality is associated with low prices. We also find that quality proposals
are mainly explained by suppliers' experience. Results suggest that scoring
rules at the basis of the tendering process might fail to appropriately incorporate
buyers' complex price/quality preferences.

Keywords: procurement, tenders, scoring rules, IT contracts, complex projects.

1 Introduction

Public buyers often use competitive bidding to select contractors. Competitive bidding
was already popular among private procurers, and today is a central principle in public
procurement regulations worldwide, in particular in Europe and in the U.S.. Competition in fact allows buyers to pursue cost minimization and to ensure transparency.

However, when procurement involves a complex project, economic theory suggests
that competition may not be the best allocation mechanism ([9] Goldberg 1977, [12]
Manelli and Vincent 1995). Empirical evidence on construction procurement, for instance, highlights the potential limits of sealed-bidding: these stem from unexploited
communication between buyer and suppliers ([3] Bajari, McMillan and Tadelis, 2008)
and to the difficulties in capturing post-contract adaptation costs ([5] Bajari and Tadelis,
2001). One critical point for the buyer is to precisely describe (many) quality dimensions
that are often unverifiable and that can sometimes be only partially known in the bidding
stage (e.g., functionalities of a new software to be developed). More precisely, the issue
is how to design a scoring auction, i.e., how to appropriately incorporate the buyer's
price/quality preference in the tender design. Scoring auctions[1] i.e., tenders in which both

---

[1] Henceforth we will use competitive bidding, competition, tenders and auctions as synony-
mous. Scoring auctions, which refer to the most economically advantageous criterion of the
European public procurement legislation, are used to define competitive process in which
both price and quality matter.

M.A. Wimmer et al. (Eds.): EGOV 2009, LNCS 5693, pp. 353–363, 2009.

price and quality matter, are quite common in the practice of public procurement. They are particularly appropriate for commercial/standardized items ([6] Che, 1993), such as laptop and printers, that is when quality can be easily measured and well captured by a suitable scoring rule. Scoring auctions instead may not perform well in complex projects as they "force" the buyer to give a precise shape to the scoring rule to account for complicated, often unknown, price/quality preferences.

In Italy, the Ministry of Economy and Finance (MEF) selects the contractors of IT services through scoring auctions. Since 1997 Consip operates in the behalf of the MEF, being in charge to organize tenders and award contracts. IT services contracts are often "general purpose", i.e., they include a large variety of activities, such as maintenance of systems and applications, developments of new applications, IT consultancy. Quality proposals consist in providing effective and flexible teams of professionals and technological solutions to best fit the various needs of the MEF. The selected contractor is called to "shape" the several elements of the proposed projects to best meet the buyer's needs.

In this paper we explore the suppliers' behavior in bidding for complex IT projects. After presenting some descriptive statistics, we address the issue of potential consequences of using competitive procedures when theory advises against doing that. More precisely, our research questions are: i) can observed bids tell us something about how well the awarding mechanism captures the buyer's price/quality trade-offs ii) what is (if any) the relationship between price and quality?

To answer these questions we exploit a unique dataset of contracts for professional IT services that Consip awarded on behalf of the MEF. In particular, we use the complete set of 20 contracts awarded by Consip in the period 1998–2007 in the sector of IT development and consultancy. We find no evidence of a tension between price and quality in submitted price/technical bids: data exhibit a puzzling negative correlation between quality and price, such that higher quality is associated to lower prices. Although not conclusive, the results put at least some doubts on the suitability of scoring auctions for capturing complex price/quality trade-offs. Regression analysis also shows that *incumbency* is an important determinant of ex-ante submitted quality, suggesting that past experience plays a key role in explaining bidding behavior.

The rest of the paper is organized as follows. Section 2 surveys some recent empirical literature. Section 3 describes the institutional context and the contract awarding process. Section 4 overviews the dataset and presents some basic statistics. Section 5 illustrates the results of the empirical analysis. Section 6 draws the concluding remarks.

2   Related Literature

This paper is related to the empirical literature on bidding in procurement auctions. There are several papers exploring important issues in (public) procurement. For instance, [4] Bajari, Houghton and Tadelis (2007) and [5] Bajari and Tadelis (2001) estimate the importance of renegotiation and adaptation costs in the procurement of highways paving works in the U.S.. When projects are complex and the contractual design is incomplete, "softening competition" e.g., negotiating with a restricted pool of suppliers, may be appropriate for selecting the most efficient supplier. This view finds support also in [3] Bajari, McMillan and Tadelis (2008), who compare auctions with negotiations by examining a comprehensive data set of private sector building contracts in the U.S.

There is, however, lack of empirical investigations on how scoring auctions (scoring rules) and other key factors such as incumbency affect bidding behavior.

First attempts to explore such issues are in [11] Lundberg (2005), although in a completely different setting of legal regulation of tender procedures, and in [13] Zhong (2007) who explores some key issues in online procurement auctions for manufacturing goods from a large buyer in the high-tech industry. He characterizes the suppliers' bidding behavior to examine the effect of incumbency on bidding. His most interesting finding is the biased towards the incumbent suppliers, but in a setting where (in contrast to our case) the buyer is not committed to a specific scoring rule.

3 The Institutional Context

Consip was created in 1997 with the mission to provide the MEF with ICT solutions, technologies and services. One important task of Consip is to manage ICT acquisitions to evolve and maintain the whole IT infrastructures supporting the MEF activities. Consip is today mandated to: define needs/solutions, organize tenders, appoint evaluating committees, evaluate suppliers' proposals, award and manage contracts, and finally, monitor suppliers' performances. In compliance with the EU Directive 2004/18 all these contracts are awarded through open competitive procedures, usually with the *most economically advantageous tender* (MEAT).

Quality is crucial for IT services contracts. It often accounts for more than 50% of the total weight. Evaluation of proposals is largely based on "discretional" components e.g., adequacy of IT solutions and organizational structures to fit the MEF's needs. The "typical" contract requires that contractor sets up a team of professionals (the chief of the project, senior consultants, junior consultants, function analysts, programmers, etc.), IT equipments and technological solutions to achieve both high quality standards and sufficient flexibility to manage heterogeneous activities. Tenders are evaluated on the basis of following main aspects: i) organization (e.g., how professionals are organized and deployed to best perform tasks); ii) solutions (e.g., software, methodologies and tests for development activities); iii) quality (e.g., quality plans, type-documents released such as users' guides).

3.1 Tenders Evaluation: The Role of Committees

Tenders are evaluated by ad-hoc committees. The committee judges whether and how the organizational setting and proposed solutions are suitable to perform the various activities provided for the contract. At the end of the evaluation process, the committee assigns the technical scores for each supplier. These scores are disclosed in a public session with suppliers. In the same session the committee opens the sealed envelopes containing price bids and publicly announces the submitted prices. One important point is the composition of the committees: this is regulated by the law. Until 2006 the legislation provided for committees to be mixed, i.e., composed of both purchasing administration's employees (insiders) and external professionals, such as full professor or recognized experts (outsiders). Since 2007 committees consist of all insiders. In our analysis we will account for such change to capture the potential differences in quality evaluation under the two regimes.

4 Data

4.1 Bids and Scores

Our analysis is based on a unique set of 20 contracts that Consip awarded in the period 1998–2007. Analyzed contracts total value amounts to € 428,7 millions, 4,6% of total Italian expenditure on IT services in 2006 (private and public sectors amount to € 9,3 billions).

The simple ranking of contracts by raffled off technical scores[2] shows that quality is very important. Note that more than 60% of contracts are skewed on the technical side. In the majority of contracts quality weighs at least 60%. Contracts in which quality is at least 50% are 85% of total contracts. Symmetrically, the frequency distribution of financial scores shows that 60% of lots has been faced with scores until 40 points, or 85% under 50 financial scores.

Table 1. Frequency distribution of available Technical Score

α	<50	50-59	60-69	≥70
N.	3	5	8	4
%	0.15	0.25	0.40	0.20

Table 2. Frequency distribution of available Financial Score

β	≤30	31-40	41-50	>50
N.	4	8	5	3
%	0.20	0.40	0.25	0.15

Table 3 and 4 present the frequency distribution of observed relative scores effectively achieved by competitors. The relative score is equal to $\frac{Actual\_Score}{Max\_Score}$. The central technical score ranges (51-60 and 61-70) represent the 50% of technical proposals, whereas 62% of technical proposals obtained scores over 60. Overall average technical score is 66.17, median is 65 and standard deviation is 14.67. Statistics also show that there is a limited number of bids (9 out of 132) that are in the highest score range (91-100).

Things are quite different if we analyze the frequency distribution of relative financial scores. The first two higher ranks (81-90 and 91-100) together account for the 51% of proposals, while the 75% are over 50. Furthermore, both the mean and the standard deviation (72.60 and 25.43 respectively) are greater with respect to the technical scores. Price bids exhibit much more dispersion than quality bids, even if bidders seem to achieve higher ranks of financial scores more easily rather than analogous levels of technical scores.

---

[2] Henceforth, we will use score(s) and point(s) interchangeably. This holds also for lot(s) and contract(s).

Table 3. Frequency distribution of relative Technical Score

rank	<=40	41-50	51-60	61-70	71-80	81-90	91-100
N.	5	13	31	36	19	19	9
%	0.04	0.10	0.23	0.27	0.14	0.14	0.07

	Summary Statistics	
Mean	Median	St. Deviation
66.17	65.00	14.67

Table 4. Frequency distribution of relative Financial Score

rank	<=40	41-50	51-60	61-70	71-80	81-90	91-100
N.	18	15	8	9	15	24	43
%	0.14	0.11	0.06	0.07	0.11	0.18	0.33

	Summary Statistics	
Mean	Median	St. Deviation
72.60	80.81	25.43

Table 5. Score matrix

		Winners' Technical Score	
		Best score	Not best
Winners' Financial	Best score	5	2
Score	Not best	11	2

Interestingly, suppliers do not win submitting outstanding financial proposals. The score matrix shows that the winner obtains the highest technical score in 16 cases out of 20, whereas only in 7 cases she gets the highest financial score. This suggests that suppliers mainly win contracts by promising relatively more (ex-ante) quality rather than submitting low price, so much so they win 11 times thanks to the best technical score, without achieving the best financial ones.

4.2 Scoring Rules

Contracts for IT services often contain many aspects of quality. Buyers usually deal with such a multidimensional problem by awarding contracts with MEAT criterion. MEATs are concretely performed through scoring rules which transform the price (and/or qualitative aspects) into a score. Thus the contract is awarded to the supplier with the total highest score. As a preliminary analysis, fig. 1 shows how rebates of winners increase on average when the scoring rule is *linear* with respect to other rules.

A scoring rule is linear if the score increases proportionally as the price declines. This type of scoring rule belongs to the family that we may call *independent* scoring rules: in this case the bidder's score depends on her bid only. *Interdependent* scoring

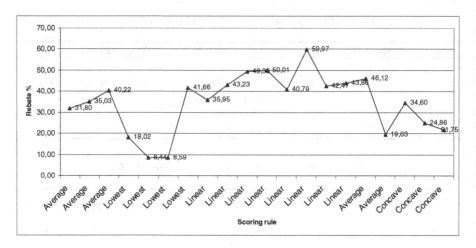

Fig. 1. Rebates of winning bidders and scoring rules

rules, instead, are such that the score of any bidder also depends on some (or all) other bids (e.g., the lowest bid, the highest bid, the average bid, etc.).[3]

In our dataset the latter type of rule leads to higher submitted prices on average. Such a difference may stem from the unpredictability of the score for interdependent scoring rules. Linear (and thus predictable) scoring rules, on the contrary, allow suppliers to compute easily the score for any possible price bid. This, in turn, enables them to choose the optimal price/quality bidding strategy.[4] Interdependent scoring rules tend to yield significant lower rebates on average – about 27% with respect to 46% – than independent scoring rules.

In particular, lowest and/or average price-based scoring rules induce suppliers to submit bids as close as possible to what they expect the best or the average price will be. The more precise this estimate the more chances the supplier has in achieving an

---

[3] See [6] Che (1993) and [2] Asker and Cantillon (2008) for theoretical implications and properties of scoring auctions. See also [7] Dimitri, Dini, Pacini and Valletti (2006) for an in-depth analysis on the design of scoring rules. The linear scoring rule is a very simple way to transform price bids into a score. This rule is described by [...]": $PriceScore = nn * \frac{(\text{Re} \, serve \, Price - PriceBid)}{(\text{Re} \, serve \, Price - PriceThreshold)}$, where the price threshold is a percentage of the reserve price that the procurer may want to introduce in order to stimulate competition on price" and nn is the available max financial score.

[4] Two things is worth stressing. First, the procurement environment we are considering refers to the IPV (*Independent Private Value*) model. In this type of (auction) model, project's costs depend on the supplier's intrinsic *efficiency* (e.g., organizational efficiency). In CV (*Common Value*) models, instead, costs are influenced by others' costs estimates. Our assumption of IPV relies on the idea that the potential heterogeneity in information on the procurement environment affects more the *ability* of suppliers to write a comprehensive technical proposal than the *costs* of the projects itself. Second, CV model *de facto* makes costs/evaluation of the contract interdependent. Such an interdependency should not be confused with that of the scoring rule, which refers to the interaction of suppliers' bids when applying a certain type of scoring rule.

high score. The uncertainty, however, may trigger a precautionary behavior on the price side. Both effects may induce suppliers to bid higher prices and thus to increase purchasing costs for the buyer.

The effects of interdependent scoring rules has not been studied systematically by the theoretical literature. First indications from [1] Albano et al. (2007) suggest that interdependent scoring rules might facilitate some form of coordination among bidders. Lower dispersion found in submitted bids when scoring rules are interdependent might not conflict with the authors' findings.

5 Empirical Analysis

In this section we use the dataset to explore the main factors explaining suppliers' bidding behavior. Our estimates are based on a reduced form OLS regression approach, which allows us to focus more on the directions rather than magnitude of the effects. Our reduced form model is the following linear model:

$$y_i = \alpha + x'_{i,k}\beta_k + \varepsilon_i . \tag{1}$$

and $k = 1, \dots K$ indexes all our explanatory variables x, while $i = 1, \dots N$ indexes the observation units. A cross-section estimate is carried out on 132 observations submitted for winning 20 contracts (summary of statistics are in table 6).

The list of variables includes the following:

Number of bids. The number of actual bids proxies the level of the ex-ante expected competition in the tender. In mature markets, as that of IT services, suppliers are likely to know each other, and thus to infer potential participants to a tender. Therefore, bids inform about what suppliers know on the level of competition in the tender. In general, this variable can be an important determinant explaining bidding behavior. Standard auction theory (independent private value) suggests that, all else being equal, price (competition) tends to increase with the number of actual bids (in procurement, the price decreases with participation).

Scoring rules. This is a binary variable, 1 for independent and 0 for interdependent scoring rules, respectively. Our conjecture is that independent scoring rules should stimulate competition on the economic side more than interdependent, since suppliers can calculate ex-ante the change of the score associated to a variation of the price bid.

Interdependent scoring, instead, complicates bidding and the conjectures suppliers make about other competitors' bidding behavior. In average scoring rules, for instance, suppliers are induced to guess the average price in order to bid as close as possible to it. This tends to concentrate prices around the average guessed level rather than the lowest possible level.

Experience. This is measured by the number of previously won contracts for any bid i at any given time t, by each bidder. We expect more experienced suppliers to better know the procurement environment and thus, ceteris paribus, to offer proposals that better fit the various needs of the buyer. Expert suppliers are expected to be better informed about the real MEF's needs and how to put this knowledge into more comprehensive technical offers. These should yield higher technical scores with respect to less (or non-)experienced suppliers.[5]

Committees. This is a binary variable, equal to 1 for all-insiders committees and 0 for mixed committees (insiders + outsiders). This is a control variable capturing possible technical score variability due to different evaluation approaches under the two types of committee described above.

Bids and scores. We use technical scores to proxy the ex-ante quality offered by suppliers. Rebates, financial scores and the price/reserve price ratios are alternative measures of economic effort.

Table 6. Summary statistics of variables

Variable	Mean	St. Dev.	Min	Max	Obs
Bids per contract	7.56	2.63	3	12	132
Experience	1.73	2.29	0	10	136
Tech. Score (relative)	66.17	14.72	29.17	96.82	132
Financ. Score (relative)	72.60	25.53	0	100	132
Rebates	33.15	13.78	0.37	59.97	132
Reserve Price	21,5 € Mln	1.88e+07	0,491 € Mln	70,3 € Mln	20

5.1 Testing for Price/Quality Trade-Off

In this section we investigate whether and how quality is explained by price, controlling for the key elements of the tender design (namely the type of scoring rule and the number of bidders). We measure quality with the suppliers' actual technical score. Another research question is to identify possible incumbent effects measured by the suppliers' past experience. The equation we estimate is the following:

$$Tech\_Score_i = const + \beta_1 Financial\_Score_i \, [Rebate_i; \, Bid\_Price/Res\_Price_i] + \qquad (2)$$
$$\beta_2 \Sigma_t Winning_{it} + \beta_3 N\_Bids_i + \beta_4 Scoring\_Rule_i + \beta_5 Committee\_dummy_i + \varepsilon_i \, .$$

We performed 5 regressions[6] with alternative measures of the price bid: financial score, rebate and relative price (price bid/reserve price). All regressions suggest that price does explain quality. Coefficients are all statistically significant. However, a

---

[5] Contractor's superior information about the procurement environment does not necessarily imply that the correct theoretical model to analyze data is common value. Talks with practitioners and contract managers, suggests that superior information does not affect significantly the suppliers' evaluation of the contract, rather their *ability* to write suitable and "well-crafted" projects/proposals. Therefore, superior information affects the technical score achievable by suppliers via best fitting proposals.

[6] Tests indicate that the estimated model is not affected by multi-collinearity for independent variables. F-test indicate that all variables should be included in the regression. Goodness of estimation: despite parsimony, the model is able to explain up 30%-35% of total variance. Further testing rejects the hypothesis of non-normality in estimated residuals, therefore supporting the choice of a linear model for our data. These considerations hold also for the price regressions.

puzzling positive link is predicted between quality and price: *higher quality is associated to lower prices and vice versa.* The sign in this relation seems to reject the classical paradigm of a "price-quality trade-off" in submitted bids. Nevertheless, this could be not so surprising because of some arguments already mentioned above.

One first explanation is the difficulty for the buyer to incorporate complex price/quality trades-off in the tender design. Since quality is the ability of professionals and how they are deployed to best perform tasks, it turns out quite hard for the buyer to give precise economic evaluation to quality of such dimensions, and thus shape correctly the scoring rule. Price and quality may thus end up exhibiting a perverse relationship.

The results might also be driven by the presence of non-contractible quality considerations. Since many quality dimensions are hard/costly to monitor ex-post, suppliers may anticipate this in the bidding stage and offer low prices for the "promise" of outstanding quality (yielding high technical scores), which will be a lower ex-post effective quality. A similar effect is studied in theory by [10] Kim (1998). Non-contractible quality implies transaction costs for contract enforcement and difficulties to ensure that the project is of the desired high quality. In this framework the author points out that if the buyer commits himself to a firm fixed price contract, the contractor may provide low quality in order to cut down on production costs.

A third explanation is related to discretional evaluation of bids on committees side. This acts as *shock*. For a given quality a supplier may receive either a lower or higher technical score depending on the subjective evaluation of the committees, therefore altering the true relationship between price and quality. Despite we have introduced a committees dummy for different types of committees, we have not been able to isolate the potential shock effect.

5.2 The Role of Other Variables

Estimates suggest that independent scoring (linear and concave)[7] reduces technical score (the sign of coefficients is always negative as reported in table 7). Independent rules allow each supplier to determine his financial score unloosed from his competitors' behavior. This provide him with a clear incentive to improve the price offer. It is worth noting, on the contrary, that interdependent rules (lowest bid and average scoring) introduce uncertainty also on the price side. Scores become unpredictable because of the simultaneous presence of both discretional evaluation of technical side and interdependent price scoring on the economic side. In this context, incentives for the suppliers to shift effort from quality towards price improvements are expected to be weaker since they cannot know the "rate of return" in terms of financial score.[8]

---

[7] Concave scoring is such that the score increases less than proportionally as price declines. A standard concave scoring can be as follows: $S_i = [1 - (P_i/Pb)^\alpha] \cdot PE$. Where S_i is the score obtained by bidder "i", P_i is the price submitted by bidder "i", Pb is the reserve price, α measures the slope of the curve and PE is the weight of price in the tender. Concave scoring clearly discourages bidders to bid aggressively, as soon as the incremental score is made negligible (depending on α) for marginal reductions of P_i.

[8] With independent scoring rules such a shift can indeed pay: rather than offering X additional consultants at a cost of say € 250.000, to get an uncertain incremental technical score, the supplier can easily compute the (certain!) incremental score associated to a price reduction of the same amount.

Table 7. Technical score regressions

Tech_Score$_i$	OLS				
	I.	II.	III.	IV.	V.
Financial_Score$_i$	0.156*** (3.24)	-	-	-	-
Rebate$_i$	-	0.389*** (3.72)	0.364*** (3.47)	0.244** (2.44)	-
Bid_Price/Res_Price$_i$	-	-	-	-	-38.91*** (-3.72)
$\sum_t$ Winning$_{it}$	3.07*** (6.55)	3.414*** (7.15)	3.55*** (7.44)	3.01*** (6.23)	3.414*** (7.15)
N_Bids$_i$	-1.41*** (-2.86)	-0.854** (-1.97)		-1.266*** (-2.91)	-0.854** (-1.97)
Scoring_Rule$_i$	-5.12** (-2.00)	-9.625*** (-3.49)	-11.11*** (-4.14)		-9.625*** (-3.49)
Committee_dummy	-8.964*** (-3.76)	-2.676 (-1.03)	-2.857 (-1.09)	-1.739 (-0.65)	-2.676 (-1.03)
Constant term	67.202*** (16.27)	61.092*** (12.62)	56.252*** (13.34)	63.158*** (12.60)	100.00*** (12.08)
Adj. R^2	0.33	0.35	0.33	0.29	0.35
F-test	14.09	15.06	17.46	14.51	15.06
N. Obs.	132	132	132	132	132

t-Statistic shown in parentheses; significant levels at *0.10, **0.05, ***0.01.

The variable $\sum_t$ Winning$_{it}$ summarizes the number of past contracts awarded to each bidding supplier. Experience/learning is what the supplier have learnt in executing the contract. Learning can be important in complex procurement like the ones we are considering. The incumbent learns how to make a "custom tailored" proposals and thus to exploit this superior information in subsequent tenders. Winning one additional contract is associated to supplier's improvement of the relative technical score by roughly 3.1-3.6 points, about 6% of relative technical score on average.

The number of submitted bids has a negative impact on the technical score. A first possible explanation is that more participation shifts the players' efforts towards price-competition rather than technical-competition. Again, the expectation that quality improvements may not be appropriately rewarded (or will do less than price improvements) may induce suppliers to shift effort from quality to price when expecting higher participation. Scoring rule and expected participation appear to interact, and to operate in the same direction.

Despite statistical significance is achieved only when using the financial score as covariate, the composition of *committees* seems to affect technical scores in the conjectured direction. Internal committees are associated to a lower average technical score. Insiders tend to reward quality proposals less than outsiders. One explanation is that risk-averse external members, who typically "know less" about the procurement context, may over-reward technical proposals to avoid appeals from suppliers.

6 Conclusions

In this paper we explored the determinants of suppliers' bidding behavior, using a unique dataset of contracts for IT services that Consip awarded on behalf of the Italian Ministry of Economy and Finance. Although evidence is based on a small number of observations, the analysis may provide some indications. In a framework of competitive tendering to allocate complex IT projects, we find no tension between price and quality in observed bids. Price and quality appear related in a puzzling way: higher quality is associated to lower prices. These results may be stemmed from the difficulty for the buyer to adequately describe and incorporate her price/quality preferences into the tender design (and more precisely in the scoring rule).

Another finding is that past experience appears to be among the most important determinants of quality proposals. Superior information on the procurement environment can significantly increase the suppliers' chances to achieve high technical scores and thus to win the contract.

References

1. Albano, G.L., Bianchi, M., Spagnolo, G.: Bid Average Methods in Procurement. In: Piga, G., Thai, K. (eds.) The Economics of Public Procurement. Palgrave (2007)
2. Asker, J., Cantillon, E.: Properties of Scoring Auctions. Forthcoming, Rand Journal of Economics (2008)
3. Bajari, P., McMillan, R., Tadelis, S.: Auctions vs. Negotiation in Procurement: An Empirical Analysis. Forthcoming, Journal of Law, Economics and Organization (2008)
4. Bajari, P., Houghton, S., Tadelis, S.: Bidding for Incomplete Contracts: An Empirical Analysis of Adaptation Costs. NBER Working Paper No. 12051 (2007)
5. Bajari, P., Tadelis, S.: Incentives Versus Transaction Costs: A Theory of Procurement Contracts. Rand Journal of Economics 32(3), 287–307 (2001)
6. Che, Y.-K.: Design Competition through Multidimensional Auctions. Rand Journal of Economics 28, 668–680 (1993)
7. Dimitri, N., Dini, F., Pacini, R., Valletti, T.: Scoring Rules. In: Dimitri, N., Piga, G., Spagnolo, G. (eds.) Handbook of Procurement. Cambridge University Press, Cambridge (2006)
8. Georgia Institute of Technology,
   http://smartech.gatech.edu/bitstream/1853/19765/1/
   zhong_fang_200712_phd.pdf
9. Goldberg, V.P.: Competitive Bidding and the Production of Precontract Information. Bell Journal of Economics 8, 250–261 (1977)
10. Kim, H.I.: A Model of Selective Tendering: Does Bidding Competition Deter Opportunism by Contractors? Quarterly Review of Economics and Finance 3(4), 907–925 (1998)
11. Lundberg, S.: Auction Formats and Award Rules in Swedish Procurement Auctions. CERUM Working Paper No. 79 (2005)
12. Manelli, A.M., Vincent, D.R.: Optimal Procurement Mechanisms. Econometrica 63(3), 591–620 (1995)
13. Zhong, F.V.: Empirical Analyses of Online Procurement auctions: Business Value, Bidding Behavior, Learning and Incumbent Effect. Ph. D. Dissertation, College of Management. Georgia Institute of Technology (2007)

Role-Based and Service-Oriented Security Management in the E-Government Environment

Chien-Chih Yu

Dept. of MIS, National ChengChi University, Taipei, Taiwan
ccyu@mis.nccu.edu.tw

Abstract. This paper proposes a role-based and service-oriented security management framework suitable for the e-government operating environment. Based on user roles and functional classes of e-government services, security threats and vulnerabilities related to e-government systems and applications are identified. In the mean time, security requirements as well as appropriate mechanisms for preventing, detecting and recovering from security attacks are specified. Also provided are suggestions and guidelines for planning and controlling e-government security policies.

Keywords: E-government, role-based, service-oriented, security management.

1 Introduction

E-government (EG) emphasizes on adopting the information and communication technology (ICT) to facilitate the access and utilization of government information and services for citizens, businesses, and government agencies [12]. The aims of e-government initiatives have been set to provide one-stop quality public services and value-added information to citizens and businesses, to enable government agencies working together more efficiently, and to achieve internal efficiency and effectiveness of operations [13]. Creating public value and trust has been identified as a strategic goal for designing e-government systems [4]. People in leading countries of e-government readiness have increasingly used EG services to file tax returns, pay parking tickets, register vehicle, and exchange document online. On the other hand, the UN's 2008 e-government survey points out that although the progress is slow, governments around the world are moving forward in e-government development, and in terms of e-participation, there is a modest upward movement with 189 countries online in 2008 as compared with 179 in 2005 [22]. Connected governance which is aimed at improving coordination between government agencies, deepening consultation and engagement with citizens, and allowing for a greater involvement with multi-stakeholders regionally and internationally has been indicated as the second generation e-government paradigm. Involving with various user types and interactions, e-government system environments encompass internet for public users, intranet for internal users of specific government functions, extranet for inter-organizational government users across functional boundaries, and network integrations for complex two-way transactions between public users and government

M.A. Wimmer et al. (Eds.): EGOV 2009, LNCS 5693, pp. 364–375, 2009.

agencies [13,16]. In the process of developing, managing, and delivering e-government information and services to internal, inter-organizational, as well as public users, information system security and user privacy have often been considered as critical success factors for ensuring the creation of organizational efficiency and effectiveness, as well as public values and trust [11,12]. Maintaining collective security that requires security concerns be addressed at each level of the government's information infrastructure has been indicated as the most crucial element among all government functions [7]. Information security, in its basic meaning, reflects the requirements that information is maintained in the right form, and can only be accessed in the right way by the right (identified/authenticated) people doing the right (authorized) things. Information system security, in general, focuses on the protection of information systems against unauthorized information access and modification, on the prevention of denial of services to authorized users, as well as on the detection of and recovery from security attacks. Generally speaking, security threats to information systems include sniffing, monitoring, interference, taking over/hijacking, overloading, and damaging in the system and network levels, eavesdropping, modification, replacement, destruction, misuse, spoofing, repudiation, and denial of service in the data and application levels [8,9,20,23]. Basic security requirements often mentioned for systems and networks include availability, confidentiality, integrity, reliability, accuracy, authentication, non-repudiation, and privacy. Major security techniques used include password, digital signature, data encryption, virus scan, firewall, intrusion detection system, database backup and recovery, etc. From the risk management perspective, steps for planning security policies include identifying security threats, vulnerabilities, and risks associated with systems and services; assessing impacts of potential security incidents; and selecting and implementing appropriate security measures to prevent and control risks. Existing e-government related security reports show that government websites of both local and national levels are vulnerable to a wide range of attacks including SQL injection, viruses, spyware, and the others [19,21]. The partial progress towards making sure whether the EG services are secure masks a deeper uncertainty about authentication, privacy, and the changing relationship between governments and citizens. Therefore, providing e-government services securely is widely recognized as the key to start an e-government initiative. Since e-government operational processes may considerably involve interconnection, integration, and interoperability of systems and services across multi-level and multi-function organizational boundaries in the government environment. It is necessary to develop a e-government security framework for guiding the identification and organization of security requirements for different government systems and services, as well as the formulation of a unify security policy [12]. Although a great deal of previous research works have addressed web security issues and methods in the technology aspect, nevertheless, it has been noted that security-related research efforts in the e-government domain are still in the initial stage [3,6,9,10,14,20]. More comprehensive studies are needed to explore the security focused framework, requirements, mechanisms, and policy making issues that strongly affect the success of e-government initiatives [2,8,12,19].

The objectives of this paper are to identify security requirements of e-government systems based on user roles and service types, to propose an integrated e-government security management framework, and to provide suitable mechanisms for preventing and detecting security attacks. Also provided are suggestions for planning and evaluating e-government security policies. The remainder of this paper is organized as follows. In section 2, a brief literature review on e-government related security issues is provided. In section 3, an adoptable EG security management framework is presented, and security threats and requirements with respect to users, services and systems are specified. Section 4 presents suitable security control mechanisms for handling the identified security requirements. Section 5 provides a guideline for planning and controlling e-government security policies. A conclusion and future research directions are provided in the final section.

2 Literature Review

In the e-government security related research literature, Joshi et al (2001) report that, in the digital government's multidomain environment, the goals of information system security include confidentiality, integrity, availability, accountability, and information assurance, besides, key mechanisms of the information security infrastructure consist of authentication, access control, and audit [19]. They also indicate that the role-based access control (RBAC) models with features such as policy neutrality, principle of least privilege, and ease of management can provide a generic framework for expressing diverse security requirements. For dealing with security problems, Lambrinoudakis et al (2003) first classify e-government services into four types, namely, e-university, e-voting, e-collaboration, and e-transaction, according to the similarity of their security requirements [12]. They then identify a set of common security requirements including system availability, performance, management of privileges, authentication, integrity, logging, confidentiality, non-repudiation, and secure storage, as well as additional security requirements including public trust, anonymity, and untracability specifically for eligible voters of the e-voting system. A public key infrastructure (PKI) based security approach is proposed for fulfilling the security requirements of e-government services. Kaliontzoglou et al (2005) propose an architecture of a secure e-government platform for small-to-medium sized public organizations based on web services [8]. The architecture comprises five major groups of services including Core web services, User interfaces, Security services, Legacy applications support, and Web services management. Basic security services of authentication, integrity, confidentiality, and non-repudiation are implemented by utilizing cryptographic operations including digital signatures, encryption, and time-stamping that are based upon related W3C and OASIS protocols. Smith and Jamieson (2006), when investigating the key drivers and inhibitors for information system security and business continuity management in e-government, identify four key issues for implementing e-government IS security that include active management support, appropriate funding, awareness and training [18]. For discussions about specific security issues, Kesh and Ratnasingam (2007) propose an IT security knowledge architecture which consists of stakeholders, knowledge dimensions, knowledge characteristics, and knowledge resources as components [9]. Stakeholders are classified into external organizational entities and internal organizational members. Specifically for an internal security technician, identified knowledge dimensions related to the stakeholder include to configure firewalls, to implement security software, and to diagnose/troubleshoot problems. Grimsley and Meehan (2007), in proposing an evaluation-led design framework for EG information systems, argue that public value should focus on clients' experiences of service provision and outcomes that build up the base of public trust [4]. Three suggested experiential dimensions for measuring trust in the EG context include informedness, personal control, and influence. Belanger and Carter (2008) point out that EG services will only be adopted if citizens consider them as trustworthy [1]. They propose a EG trust model that consists of disposition of trust, trust of the government, trust of the Internet, and perceived risk as constructs for conducting citizen survey. Yu (2008) propose a value-centric EG service framework that encompasses 7 generic service functions, namely, profile management, security and trust management, information navigation and search, transaction and payment, participation and collaboration, personalization and customization, as well as learning and knowledge management [24]. The security management services include public key management, certificate authorization, digital signature and authentication, as well as other security control services. Trust management services, on the other hand, allow citizens, businesses, government agencies to register and attain authorized trust seals and certificates, as well as to access privacy statements.

Although methods and processes for maintaining information system security and improving information security management across all functions and levels of government agencies, as well as for protecting privacy and preventing fraud in e-government applications have been considered as essential issues, previous research works in this field are still too rough and diversified. Critical issues regarding to the requirement assessment, architecture design, policy planning and operational control of e-government security have not yet been fully developed, and therefore, need to be further explored.

3 Security Management Framework and Requirements

In order to efficiently and effectively identify EG security requirements, we first identify user roles, services categories, and system assets in the EG environment, and then propose a role-based and service-oriented framework for directing security management. Based on the framework, security threats and vulnerabilities with impact assessment, and mainly the security requirements can be identified and organized in a structural way. Furthermore, suitable countermeasures to protect critical assets can be selected, and appropriate as well as flexible security policies can be formulated. This research is carried out through conducting an extensive literature review and a series of case studies on multiple level governments.

3.1 EG Environment and the Security Management Framework

User and service classification in the EG environment have been viewed from various perspectives in the literature. For instances, EG user groups have been characterized in terms of actor types that include service customers, service operators, and system administrators [12], or in terms of user roles such as citizens, businesses, community members, employees, government agents, and government service chain participants

[24]. As for EG service classification, a variety of views have been used including the 5 service categories approach that consists of Government-to-Citizens (G2C), Government-to-Businesses (G2B), Government-to-Government (G2G), Government Internal Efficiency and Effectiveness (IEE), and Overarching Infrastructure [13], the 4 service suites approach that comprises e-university, e-voting, e-collaboration of governmental departments, and web-based public services (transaction and payment) [12], as well as the 7 service functions approach that contains profile management, security and trust management, information navigation and search, transaction and payment, participation and collaboration, personalization and customization, and learning and knowledge management [24]. Vulnerability dependent information system assets identified in previous works to be securely controlled include information assets, service assets, software assets, physical system assets, and network assets [12,21]. By integrating multiple perspectives from the literature and practices, we identify citizens, businesses, government employees, and government agents as EG service receivers for G2C, G2B, G2E, and G2G systems respectively. Government agents in multiple-function and multiple-level governments also have their roles as service operators and system administrators that are responsible for providing services as well as managing, monitoring and controlling service delivery procedures. Figure 1 shows such an EG operating environment comprising of multiple user types, multiple service systems, and a government portal as the commonly access point.

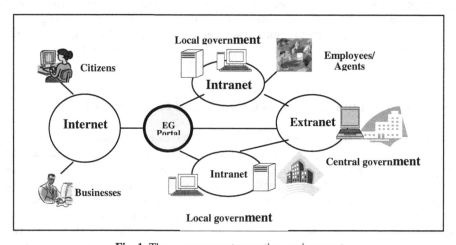

Fig. 1. The e-government operating environment

Based on the literature review and case studies conducted in multiple government levels including a local-level city government, 2 ministry-level functional governments, and a government sponsored security control center, we develop a role-based and service-oriented framework for EG security management as shown in Figure 2. Asset levels for security control include information level, application level, system level, and network level. In the application level, types of service functions identified for various user roles include e-Profile, e-Information, e-Transaction, e-Participation, e-Personalization, e-Learning, and e-Trust. Security requirements for protecting information asset, user-based application services assets and web services assets, software and hardware systems assets, as well as communication and network asserts can be identified accordingly. Service classes associated with the user-role and service-oriented applications within the application level of the security management framework are described in more detail as follows.

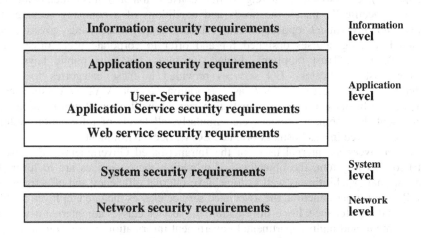

Fig. 2. The EG security management framework

For citizens as public users, i.e. service receivers, of the G2C application systems in national, municipal, or local levels, the service functions include e-Profile, e-Information, e-Transaction, e-Participation, e-Personalization, e-Learning, and e-Trust. Service classes in e-Profile include personal file creation and maintenance. Service classes in e-Information include information navigation and search services for accessing news and announcement, multi-level government information, job offers and tourism information, etc. Service classes in e-Transaction contain transaction and payment services for conducting tax processing, registration and certification (e.g. birth, marriage, car, land), permit application (e.g. driver license, passport), booking and reservation (e.g. tours, healthcare), social security contribution and welfare compensation, etc. E-Participation represents service classes in community forum and meeting participation, as well as online voting, etc. E-Personalization contains service classes for creating personalized pages, requesting personalized consultation and recommendation, etc. Service classes in e-Learning allow citizens to access course materials and perform learning activities online. E-Trust is responsible for offering service classes for applying digital signatures, obtaining public keys, and accessing privacy statements, etc. All levels of EG related information system assets including information, applications and services, computer systems and communication networks are involved. Service functions and classes in this sector can also be extended to serve user groups such as schools, communities, non-profit organizations, and special interest groups (SIGs), etc.

For businesses as public users, EG services are delivered from multi-level G2B systems. Business-oriented service functions and categories include e-Profile (business profile creation and maintenance), e-Information (news and announcement, multi-level government information and regulation), e-Transaction (tax processing, registration and certification, permit application, social contribution for employees, business data submission, customs declarations, financial transfer and payment processing), e-Participation (government project bidding, public procurement participation), e-Personalization (e.g. online consultation and recommendation for processes specifically match the needs and conditions of a company seeking for trading and investment opportunities), e-Learning (e.g. accessing government-sponsored training courses designed for and offer to corporate users of specific industries), and e-Trust (applying digital signatures, obtaining public keys, and applying trust certificates). EG services provided in these categories focus on facilitating business activities such as corporation tax and VAT processing, new company and business properties registration, permit application of construction and environment development projects, etc. Similarly, all levels of information system assets are involved in this business-oriented EG service environment.

For employees as internal users of the Intranet-based Government-to-Employee (G2E) (or IEE) system, the objectives of providing these services are to leverage organizational capabilities as well as to achieve internal efficiency and effectiveness. For e-Profile service function, the associated service classes include employee profile creation and maintenance. For e-Information, the service classes are internal news and announcement, and multi-departmental government information. For e-Transaction, a variety of service categories include payroll and benefits, document interchange and approval, knowledge sharing and management, online recruitment and human resource integration, as well as integrated access to organizational databases and applications. For e-Participation, service classes consist of internal community participation as well as internal communication and collaboration that provide services such as email, bulletin board, video conferencing, and project management etc. For e-Personalization, personalized page, personalized consultation, and personalized knowledge base for individual employee and staff are major service categories. For e-Learning, service classes focus on conducting internal education and training. As for e-Trust, key service classes include internal audit, evaluation and performance control. Within the Intranet environment, EG related information system assets also include information, services, systems and networks.

For government agents as the inter-organizational users within and across government functions, the associated Extranet-based G2G system handles vertical and horizontal service integration of the government service chain with the aim set to achieve efficiency and effectiveness of the entire chain. These users are mainly service operators and system administrators that are responsible for managing and delivering government services to the public users. Service categories and related service functions provided by the vertical and horizontal G2G system include agency profile creation and maintenance for e-Profile, inter-organizational news and announcement, and multi-institutional government information for e-Information, inter-organizational database access and integration, document interchange and approval, integrated information and knowledge management, integrated budget and financial management, integrated personnel administration, etc for e-Transaction, inter-organizational communication and collaboration such as participating in join conference, join purchases, and multi-project management and control for e-Participation, personalized page, reporting, consultation, knowledge management, and decision support for chief government officers for e-Personalization, inter-organizational education and training for e-Learning, as well as inter-organizational key management and certificate authorization for e-Trust. All level of information system assets are also involved.

3.2 Security Threats, Requirements, and Mechanisms in the EG Environment

Vulnerabilities in the EG environment have multiple aspects. Eventually, vulnerabilities may exist related to users, trust models, application system design and implementation, service and system operation, software and hardware, recovery methods, and cryptography technologies, etc. Security threats in the EG information systems environment include eavesdropping, modification, replacement, destruction, and misuse in the information asset level, spoofing, repudiation, manipulation, and denial of service in the application and service assets level, as well as sniffing, monitoring, interference, taking over/hijacking, overloading, damaging, and corruption in the system and communication assets levels. Basic security requirements often mentioned for information systems and networks include availability, confidentiality, integrity, reliability, accuracy, authentication, non-repudiation, and privacy. Major identified security requirements are described below.

Availability: To ensure that information, information accessing channels, service functions and systems are available when requested.

Confidentiality: To ensure that information and documents are only available to authorized people and systems.

Integrity: To ensure that information is accurate and timely, and can only be modified by authorized people and systems.

Reliability: To ensure that service and system functions as well as outcomes are consistent and continuously operated.

Accuracy: To ensure that data and information are accurate.

Authentication: To ensure correct identities of users, documents, services, and systems.

Non-repudiation: To ensure that evidence are collected and managed to prevent repudiation acts.

Privacy (anonymity and untracability): To ensure that access to user accounts is restricted to authorized individuals and that the private user information is protected from unauthorized use.

Trust: To ensure that users are well-informed, information is accurate, transactions are secure, and systems are reliable.

Access control (authentication, authorization, and accounting): To ensure that only authenticated people with authorized actions can be executed, and that the accounts are simultaneously updated and maintained.

System Continuity (logging, backup and recovery): To ensure that systems can be continuously operated without stop.

As an example, the security requirements of a G2C system for accessing, delivering, and controlling the 7 service functions by citizens, service operators, and system administrators respectively are identified and organized in Table 1. Similarly, security requirements for the G2B, G2E, and G2G systems can be structurally identified using the same user-service security management framework.

Table 1. Security requirements for the G2C system

Service Functions	Citizen Users' Requirements
e-Profile	Authentication, Availability, Integrity, Confidentiality, Privacy
e-Information	Availability, Integrity, Accuracy, Trust
e-Transaction	Authentication, Availability, Integrity, Confidentiality, Trust, Privacy, Non-repudiation
e-Participation	Authentication, Availability, Integrity, Confidentiality, Trust, Privacy
e-Personalization	Authentication, Availability, Confidentiality, Trust, Privacy
e-Learning	Authentication, Availability, Confidentiality, Trust, Privacy
e-Trust	Authentication, Availability, Trust, Privacy
Service Providers' Requirements	Authentication, Availability, Integrity, Access control, Reliability, Continuity
System Admin. Requirements	Authentication, Availability, Integrity, Access control, Reliability, Continuity

4   Security Control Mechanisms

Major security techniques and management services commonly used in the information system environment include ID and password management, data encryption, public key management, digital signature and digital envelop, certificate authorization, authentication and access control, virus and intrusion detection, as well as backup and recovery, etc. Trust management services, on the other hand, include trust seals and certificates, as well as privacy control and statements.

Table 2. Security requirements and control methods

Security Requirements	Security Threats	Security Measures
Integrity	Illegal modification, replacement, deletion of data, Destruction of applications, Denial of service	Serial Number Control, Time Stamping, MAC Code, Digital Signature,
Confidentiality	Eavesdropping, Sniffing Illegal monitoring	Data Encryption Methods, Digital Envelope
Authentication	Transaction spoofing	User ID, Password, Digital Signature
Non-repudiation	Denial of Message Sending or Transaction Making	Digital Signature, Digital Envelope, Time Stamping,
Privacy	Disclose and unauthorized use of personal data, Illegal monitoring and tracking of personal behavior, Eavesdropping and Sniffing	Proxy, Data Encryption Methods, Anonymity mechanism
Access Control	Illegal user access, Misuse of data	Qualified Systems and Software, User ID, Password, Firewall, Intrusion Detection System, Trans. Logs
System Continuity	Denial of service, Database and system corruption	Logging, Time Stamping, Backup and Recovery

For handling security requirements of authentication, access control, integrity, confidentiality, and non-repudiation, cryptographic methods used include data encryption, digital signatures, and time-stamping that are based upon W3C XML Signature Recommendation (XML-DSIG), W3C XML Encryption draft standard, and OASIS WS Security (WSS) protocols. EG specific security and trust functions such as assurance of long term validity of electronic signature, establishment of trust chains, key integration and management, as well as access control are based on public key technologies including XML Advanced Electronic Signatures (XAdES), XML key Management (XKMS), OASIS eXtensible Access Control Markup Language (XACML), and OASIS Security Assertion Markup Language (SAML) etc. Table 2 lists major security requirements as well as related threats and control mechanisms.

5 Security Policy Planning and Control

The international standard of information security management ISO/IEC 17799 has provided a guideline for describing security policies, and has been adopted in many countries for managing information system securities [17,18]. Adapting the international standard to the proposed security management framework, we suggest the following steps for planning unified security policies. The first step is to identify the objectives and principles of the EG security management. The second step is to identify information system assets for protection. The third step is to specify user-service based application services for EG systems of different government levels and functions, as well as their associated security requirements. The fourth step is to analyze the risk levels and impacts. The fifth step is to select suitable security protocols and mechanisms for preventing, detecting and recovering from the occurrence of risk events. The sixth step is to decide on setting priorities and allocating budgets for implementing the selected security measures. The seventh step is to set up control points, control procedures, audit trails, and performance measures for conducting security control.

Three stages of EG information system security control are prevention, detection, and recovery. The first stage is to prevent the information systems and related assets from being attacked by setting up firewalls, implementing access control, scanning virus, performing vulnerability check, and controlling mobile codes distributed in the Internet and communication networks, etc. Once the systems have been attacked, the second stage is to detect the intrusions and take immediate actions such as making alarm, disconnecting intruders or removing viruses, diagnosing problems, assessing impacts, and suggesting solutions. Provided that the systems have been damaged, then the third step is to activate a disaster recovery procedure for repairing or restoring corrupted data, documents, services, and/or systems. In general, for effectively controlling and maintaining transaction trails for auditing, system and transaction logs need to be designed and created with appropriate formats. These log files record processed transactions and time sequences, as well as user-provider acknowledgments of service operations. Consequently, these logs provide evidence that transactions are recorded in the correct accounting period with electronic time stamps. Furthermore, acknowledgments between service receivers and providers ensure that transactions are recorded at a timely basis and accompany messages are genuine, understood by both parties, and have not been altered. In addition, using with database and application system backups, a damaged application system can be recovered to its most current status.

6 Conclusion

In this paper, we present a user-service based security management framework for e-government systems. Security threats and requirements are identified based on information system asset levels including information, application, system and network layers. The application level requirements are further classified by user roles and service functions of the G2C, G2B, G2E, and G2G systems. User roles identified include citizens and businesses as external users, employees as internal users, as well as multi-level and multi-function government agents as vertical and horizontal integrators, service operators, and system administrators. Unified service functions specified for various systems include e-Profile, e-Information, e-Transaction, e-Participation, e-Personalization, e-Learning, and e-Trust. In different types of EG service systems, service categories within each generic service functions are varied to meet the needs of the system users and environment. The contribution of this research is that the proposed security management framework and process serve as guidelines for efficiently and effectively specifying EG specific security threats, requirements, and control mechanisms, as well as for systematically planning and controlling EG security policies. Future research works include conducting case studies regarding different EG system types in various government levels to validate the completeness and usefulness of the proposed security management approach.

References

1. Belanger, F., Carter, L.: Trust and Risk in e-Government Adoption. Journal of Strategic Information Systems 17(2), 165–176 (2008)
2. Cansell, D., Gibson, J.P., Mery, D.: Refinement: A Constructive Approach to Formal Software Design for a Secure e-Voting Interface. Electronic Notes in Theoretical Computer Science 183, 39–55 (2007)
3. Chang, E., Dillon, T.S., Hussain, F.: Trust Ontologies for e-Service Environments. International Journal of Intelligent Systems 22(5), 519–545 (2007)
4. Grimsley, M., Meehan, A.: E-government Information Systems: Evaluation-led Design for Public Value and Client Trust. European Journal of Information Systems 16(2), 134–148 (2007)
5. Guo, X., Lu, J.: Intelligent E-Government Services with Personalized Recommendation Techniques. International Journal of Intelligent Systems 22, 401–417 (2007)
6. Jaamour, R.: Securing Web Services. Information System Security 14(4), 36–44 (2005)
7. Joshi, J.B.D., Ghafoor, A., Aref, W., Spafford, E.H.: Digital Government Security Infrastructure Design Challenges. IEEE Computer 34(2), 66–72 (2001)
8. Kaliontzoglou, A., Sklavos, P., Karantjias, T., Polemi, D.: A Secure e-Government Platform Architecture for Small to Medium Sized Public Organizations. Electronic Commerce Research and Applications 4(2), 174–186 (2005)
9. Kesh, S., Ratnasingam, P.: A Knowledge Architecture for IT Security. Communications of the ACM 50(7), 103–108 (2007)

10. Kobsa, A.: Privacy-enhanced Personalization. Communications of the ACM 30(8), 24–33 (2007)
11. Ksiezopolski, B., Kotulski, Z.: Adaptable Security Mechanism for Dynamic Environments. Computers & Security 26(3), 246–255 (2007)
12. Lambrinoudakis, C., Gritzalis, S., Dridi, F., Pernul, G.: Security Requirements for e-Government Services: A Methodological Approach for Developing a Common PKI-based Security Policy. Computer Communications 26(16), 1873–1883 (2003)
13. Lee, S.M., Tan, X., Trimi, S.: Current Practices of Leading e-Government Countries. Communications of the ACM 48(10), 99–104 (2005)
14. Lim, B.B.L., Sun, Y., Vila, J.: Incorporating WS-Security into a Web Service-based Portal. Information Management and Computer Security 12(2/3), 206–216 (2004)
15. Lioudakis, G.V., et al.: A Middleware Architecture for Privacy Protection. Computer Networks 51(16), 4679–4696 (2007)
16. Pardo, T.A., Tayi, G.K.: Interorganizational Information Integration: A Key Enabler for Digital Government. Government Information Quarterly 24(4), 691–715 (2007)
17. Saint-Germain, R.: Information Security Management Best Practice Based on ISO/IEC 17799. The Information Management Journal 39(4), 60–66 (2005)
18. Smith, S., Jamieson, R.: Determining Key Factors in E-Government Information System Security. Information Systems Management 23(2), 23–32 (2006)
19. Stibbe, M.: E-Government Security. Infosecurity Today 2(3), 8–10 (2005)
20. Swart, R.S., et al.: Dimensions of Network Security Planning for Web Services. Journal of Information Privacy and Security 1(1), 49–66 (2005)
21. Tanaka, H., Matsuura, K., Sudoh, O.: Vulnerability and Information Security Investment: An Empirical Analysis of e-Local Government in Japan. Journal of Accounting and Public Policy 24(1), 37–59 (2005)
22. United Nations: United Nations e-Government Survey 2008: From e-Government to Connected Governance. United Nations Publication (2008),
    http://unpan1.un.org/intradoc/groups/public/documents/UN/UNPAN028607.pdf
23. von Solms, B.: Information Security - A Multidimensional Discipline. Computers & Security 20, 504–508 (2001)
24. Yu, C.C.: Building a Value-Centric e-Government Service Framework Based on a Business Model Perspective. In: Wimmer, M.A., Scholl, H.J., Ferro, E. (eds.) EGOV 2008. LNCS, vol. 5184, pp. 160–171. Springer, Heidelberg (2008)

IT Enabled Risk Management for Taxation and Customs: The Case of AEO Assessment in the Netherlands

Jianwei Liu[1], Yao-Hua Tan[1,2], and Joris Hulstijn[1]

[1] Vrije Universiteit Amsterdam, Faculty of Economics and Business Administration,
Information Systems Group, 1081 HV Amsterdam, the Netherlands
[2] Technical University Delft, Dept. of Technology, Policy and Management
jliu@feweb.vu.nl, ytan@feweb.vu.nl, jhulstijn@feweb.vu.nl

Abstract. Building collaborative relationships with trusted businesses is a long-term strategy for EU governments. Recently, for the EU Tax and Customs Administration (TCA), the realization of this goal has become more visible with the emerging concept of the Authorized Economic Operator (AEO). Businesses in the member states can apply for the AEO certificate. When it is being granted, simplified control procedures and trade facilitation will be provided by the TCA. A possible "win-win situation" can be achieved, with increased trade efficiency and lowered administrative burden. However, without proper selection of trusted business partners, governments may be worse off due to the adverse selection problem caused by information asymmetry. In this paper, we analyze the cause and effect of the adverse selection in the Government-to-Business relationship building. Further, we show that an IT enabled risk assessment approach can effectively eliminate the G2B information asymmetry and solve the adverse selection problem. The AEO assessment approach of DutchTCA is analysed to give a real life application on how IT is enabling the general risk management approach of the DutchTCA.

Keywords: G2B relationship building, adverse selection, risk management, AEO.

1 Introduction

One of the key visions for e-government is to enhance government relationship with businesses and citizens: turning a government service into a self-service, for better participation, enhanced efficiency and lowered administrative burden. Tax and Customs administrations facing the challenge of growing trade volumes and increased security requirements are now adopting this vision, by applying advanced information technology (IT) to achieve the objective of building new collaborative relationships with businesses. The collaborative relationship means to change the G2B relationship from the traditional "control and command" to a more "trust-based" relationship, which includes replacing the traditional labour intensive customs controls with businesses' "self-control" regarding to customs issues. To realize this transformation, the EU Directorate-General of Tax and Customs has made a major effort to develop and promote the concept of the Authorized Economic Operator (AEO) for European

M.A. Wimmer et al. (Eds.): EGOV 2009, LNCS 5693, pp. 376–387, 2009.

businesses [1]. The underlying idea is that if businesses can prove to the TCA that they are in control of the tax and security aspects of their own business processes, then they will be AEO certified by the TCA, which brings them the benefits of less physical inspections, fast customs clearance procedures and trade facilitation by the TCA. The aim is to achieve a win-win situation for both government and businesses, with trade simplification and lowered administrative burden.

However, because businesses typically have better information about themselves than the government (information asymmetry), problems of *moral hazard* and *adverse selection* may occur. Moral hazard means that businesses tend to act opportunistically and inappropriately; adverse selection means that good companies are driven out of the market by bad ones (For details see, [2], [3] and [4]). In Section 2, we investigate how adverse selection may have a negative effect on the AEO certification process in the sense that, due to information asymmetry between the government and businesses, the government can be misled, and will certify companies that are actually not in control. If this happens, the good companies who are in control will perceive this as unfair competition, leave the market, and will no longer apply for the AEO certificate. Hence, a so-called "lemons market" for AEO certificates may be created, which would make the certificate virtually useless. In Section 3, we argue that, by applying an IT enabled risk assessment approach, the adverse selection problem in the AEO certification process can be effectively reduced, enhancing the trust relationship between government and businesses. Businesses can show to the government that they are "in-control" by sending a positive *signal* to the government based on their business information systems and internal control quality. There is also a second role of IT: when businesses use IT enabled decision support systems to perform the AEO self-assessment, the quality of the self-assessment increases, and hence the strength of the positive signal can be further enhanced. Based on this, governments are better able to perform a risk assessment, to *screen* and differentiate trustworthy businesses from opportunistic ones and entitle the AEO certificate only to the good ones. In Section 4, we analyse a case study with DutchTCA of the AEO certification procedure. We analyzed what role IT is playing in the risk management for the AEO assessment. Based on this case study, we provide recommendations for EU policy making on AEO certification.

2 Asymmetric Information in G2B Relationships Forming

To form any kind of relationship, information sharing is essential. In an ideal world we assume information is shared equally and transparently among the parties. However in the real world, due to lack of communication channels and hidden incentives for sharing or hiding information between parties, information is normally spread in an asymmetric way. Information asymmetry occurs when one party has more or better information than the other party. Typically, two problems are triggered by asymmetric information, namely, moral hazard and adverse selection ([2], [3] and [4]).

Moral hazard refers to "situations where one side of the market can't observe the actions of the other. For this reason it is sometimes called a hidden action problem" [5]. It arises because an individual or institution in a transaction does not bear the full consequences or can hide the consequences of its actions without the counter party knowing it, and therefore has an incentive to act inappropriately. Tax fraud can be seen as a typical moral hazard problem in G2B relationships. For example, in VAT (Value Added Tax) collection, two parties are involved: a company who is obliged to declare VAT and pay the tax; and a tax office which audits the tax declaration and collects the VAT. Under the assumption of perfect information, the tax office obtains complete information and knows about the company's exact operation; the company reports and pays the correct amount of VAT (Figure 1a). However, in the real world the company has better information about its own operating details than the tax office, and thus may have incentives to hide and even falsify certain information from the tax office to get tax advantages. If such an incentive is present, or the penalty of defaulting is not severe enough, the company might choose tax evasion--- a moral hazard problem is caused (Figure 1b). In a previous paper [6] we have discussed the issues of moral hazard in detail. In this paper we focus on the second problem: adverse selection.

Fig. 1a. Ideal situation (Perfect information)   **Fig. 1b.** Moral hazard (Asymmetric information)

Adverse selection refers to a failing market due to information asymmetries between buyers and sellers, where "bad" products or customers are more likely to be selected rather than the "good" ones. A famous example of adverse selection is illustrated by [2] for the second-hand car market, which is referred to as a "lemon market". Buyers of second-hand cars typically do not have the expertise to know whether a car is a "lemon" (bad car) or a "cherry" (good car), so they are willing to pay an average price that lies in between the lemons and cherries. However, with such a price, the good car dealers are not willing to sell the cars with premium quality. As a result, cars with lower than average quality will be sold: the "cherries" are driven out and "lemons" will dominate the market.

In the G2B relationship, adverse selection can occur when government bodies select private partners and grant certificates. The Authorized Economic Operator (AEO) certificate may serve here as a good example. The idea of AEO is that each EU Member State Customs Administration can establish partnerships with private companies and certify them with the AEO status. The involvement of the companies in AEO will enhance a win-win situation for the safety and security of international trade: on the one hand government can do less physical checks and use limited personnel for other tasks, and on the other hand the certified AEO companies will enjoy tangible benefits such as fast customs clearance and simplified procedures (e.g. containers of AEO companies will not be inspected by the customs when they pass the EU border) [7]. AEO can be seen as an extra Customs control instrument that enhances the Customs control while it does not introduce extra control burden for the government. More specifically, it is a form of government delegating certain control tasks to collaborative businesses and in return giving these businesses trade simplification.

A critical issue here is that the AEO certificate is quite unlike other governmental requirements; it is voluntary rather than mandatory: "It requires … no obligation for economic operators to become AEOs, it is a matter of the operators' own choice..." [1]. Companies can make their own decisions on whether or not to qualify for the AEO certificate, based on company strategy. In addition, in spite of the facilitations AEO companies may have, the AEO certificate is not cost free. Companies have to make considerable investments (around 50K euros for small, up to a couple of million euros for large companies) to achieve and maintain the certificate. Hence, we can see AEO as a free will certificate "market", with entry cost and associated benefit.

The problem raised here is that if the government can not effectively differentiate companies from the two streams, a similar adverse selection problem like in the second-hand car market may occur. The "good" (trustworthy and compliant) companies are not willing to join when they see no fair value for them to participate: as one of the inter-viewed companies (a Netherlands-based international brewery) said "We are already a compliant company with a good reputation, and our current procedure is simpler than that of others anyway, why should we invest more to get the AEO certificate?". On the other hand, the "bad" (opportunistic and fraudulent) companies may see more benefits (less checking and simplified procedure may create an easier way of committing fraud), less cost (they can make a false report to show the fulfilment of the requirements), and thus are more willing the get the certificate (See Figure 2).

The original aim of the government is to focus control effort on potentially fraudu-lent companies, and limit the number of physical inspections and simplify the proce-dures for trusted companies with an AEO certificate. As indicated in the interview with the Dutch Tax and Customs Administration (DutchTCA):"If companies are al-ready in good control themselves, why should we waste our resources to exert extra control on them?" However, the consequences of the adverse selection problem may diverse from government's expectation. The situation may even deteriorate, when more "bad" companies obtaining the AEO certificate but committing fraud neverthe-less --- a market of "lemons" will be created and the public will lose their trust in the government. Nevertheless, there are remedies for the adverse selection problem. One possible solution is to apply an IT-based risk management approach for effective *sig-nalling* and *screening*, which will be discussed in the next section.

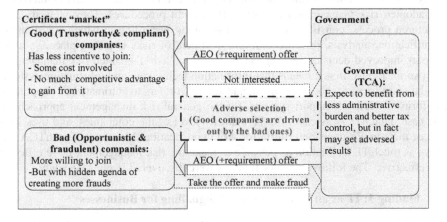

Fig. 2. Adverse selection caused during AEO certification procedure

3   IT-Based Risk Management for Effective Signalling and Screening: The Case of AEO Assessment in the Netherlands

O'Reilly [8] indicates that the quality of decision making increases with the decision maker's information level. However, if the quality of information itself can hardly be evaluated, information behaviour (information seeking and information encountering activities) can have important signalling effects on observers [9]. *"Signalling"* has been considered as one of the most important strategies of solving asymmetric information problems in the job market and capital market, e.g., [3, 10]. The general idea behind signalling is that one party (informed party) conveys some meaningful information (signal) about himself to another party (under-informed party). Due to this extra information, the under-informed party is able to classify the counter parties as good or bad and make sensible selection decisions. *"Screening"* is another way of dealing with adverse selection, but in contrast to signalling, now the under-informed party moves first. It means that the under-informed party can induce the other party to reveal their information, for instance by providing a menu of choices in such a way that the choice depends on the private information of the other party [4]. An example in the job market, a job candidate will send his CV with education level and working experience to the employer to signal that he is the most suitable candidate; at the same time, employers will arrange their own interviews and assessment procedure to screen the candidates and test their abilities.

With our case study, we investigate a possible solution for the AEO adverse selection problem. We undertook in-depth interviews with DTCA on their general AEO assessment approach. Semi-structured interviews were used as the primary method for the data collection [11, 12]. We conducted seven interviews with DutchTCA and attended one auditing visit with DutchTCA to an AEO applicant company. In total we interviewed ten persons from DTCA and three from the company. The interviewees typically have an auditing or EDP auditing background. Interviews were tape recorded with the informants' prior agreement, then transcribed for participant's feedback and our analysis. We discovered that IT-enabled risk management may effectively eliminate the information asymmetry for G2B relationship building. DutchTCA has adopted risk management as part of their audit procedures. They view it "as a structured process, consisting of well-defined steps, according to which a systematic identification, analysis, prioritization and treatment of risks is taking place, so as to support improved decision-making" [13]. The so-called IT-enabled risk management has two meanings: first it means that information technology and information systems are the main focus for the assessment, and second it refers to automated IT support, in the form of decision support systems, for the general risk management approach. In this case, DutchTCA assesses the IT maturity level of the companies, and uses it as one of their major decision criteria for AEO certification. Moreover, DutchTCA deploys as much IT facilitation as possible to make the risk management more efficient and effective. The following major findings were discovered in our case study.

3.1   Finding 1: IT as an Effective Way of Signalling for Businesses

Application of advanced IT may serve as a effective way of signalling for businesses to indicate their types, which will enable the government to effectively differentiate "good" from "bad" companies for certification. One of the major concerns for the government in the AEO certification is the supply chain safety and security. Gutierrez and Hintza [14] argue that supply chain security can be implemented via facility management, cargo management, human resource management, information management and business network and company management systems. IT facilitation can enhance all five perspectives: 1) for facility management, the use of IT has greatly improved inventory management and control. IT-based access control procedures and technologies (e.g., PKI security, smart cards) enhance facility protection and monitoring functionality; 2) for cargo management, the use of cargo tracking and tracing and anti-tampering technologies (e.g., bar code, RFID, GPS tracking, smart container seals) and cargo inspection technical solutions have enhanced cargo management; 3) for human resource management, most modern organizations apply Enterprise Resource Planning (ERP) system for better HR management, information dissemination and responsibility assignment; 4) for information management system, real time information recording and secure data exchange have been adopted by many organizations; 5) for business network and company management system, most companies have already built up a company security management system and business partner evaluation system for better risk management. IT-based control for supply chain security can significantly lower labour costs and data error rates associated with scanning items and extended identification to individual items. The systems can provide quality information that enables companies to track literally billions of objects across the value chain, increasing the efficiency of individual processes, improving asset utilization, increasing the accuracy of forecasts, and improving the ability of companies to respond to changing conditions of supply and demand [15].

With our case study we find that there are two main signals that a company can send to the government to prove their security status: 1) the use of integrated IT applications for supply chain management (e.g., well implemented ERP system, just-in-time (JIT) programs, electronic data interchange (EDI), and point-of-sale data sharing programs) and, 2) the use of IT applications for security control (e.g., application of GPS, Radio Frequency Identification (RFID) and smart seal technology). To apply for AEO status, companies must first fill in a self-assessment. Part of the self assessment is a risk analysis, detailing the security threats and their impact for a specific company. In addition to the above mentioned general IT systems, companies can also run the self-assessment via an automated toolset, which is yet another enhanced signal to the government. In our case, an automated self-assessment tool "Digiscan", developed by Deloitte, was used. The Digiscan tool is an expert system that is based on the AEO guidelines and criteria issued by the EU. It is a rule based system, to supports companies to identify in their own organization cases of potential Customs related risks. The system consists of facts, decision rules, and a rule interpreter. All facts are stored in a database and the evaluated risks are described in abstract mathematical rules. A rule consists of one or more facts (preconditions) connected with each other and actions. Rules in the form of IF "x" THEN "y" are particularly suitable. These rules are the basis for the computer-assisted analysis of risk cases. Digiscan supports the company's AEO self-assessment in an interactive question-answering style. The system generates, based on the AEO Guidelines, a sequence of questions that help the company to improve the quality of their self-assessment. As Digiscan supports a risk based, systematic and objective description of the business, the quality of the business self-assessment can be perceived better than without it. The end result of the Digiscan supported self-assessment is a so-called summary result which ranks the company on a 1-5 scale for various risk indicators. This summary can be used by DutchTCA for further evaluation. Currently, the value of automated tools to assist in self assessment is under still debate. Potentially, such tools could enhance the reliability of the self assessment. Using the tool would then count as a signal that the company takes compliance seriously. However, the current version of the tool, an automated questionnaire, may not be suited for the purpose of conducting a thorough risk analysis and self assessment. Therefore, DuchtTCA and Deloitte are currently discussing adjustments, both to the tool and to the way its evidence is being used in auditing.

3.2 Finding 2: IT Support for Effective Screening by the Government

Instead of passively receiving "signals" from applicants, DutchTCA also actively *screen* companies by including the specific IT requirements in the AEO selection criteria that all applicants have to fulfil in order to get the certificate. In our research project we discovered in various cases that two principles are essential for explaining the supporting role of IT for AEO self-assessment; namely (1) *Real-Time Monitoring* and (2) *Information Sharing*. **Real-time monitoring** means that IT is used to monitor continuously the location and state of the cargo. For example, in one of the pilot projects that are part of our research project, a smart container seal, TREC (Tamper-Resistant Embedded Controllers), was introduced. The TREC sends information via encrypted GSM or satellite communication about the precise location and unauthorized opening of the container (opening without proper digital certificate). This information is typically received by the owner of the container, or the carrier who is transporting this container. However, when this TREC information can also be shared with the TCAs, the government will have most of the relevant information needed to execute its fiscal and security control tasks. **Information sharing** is done via a service-oriented architecture that gives the DutchTCA direct access to the data bases of the owner and the carrier, to read the stored TREC data about the container.

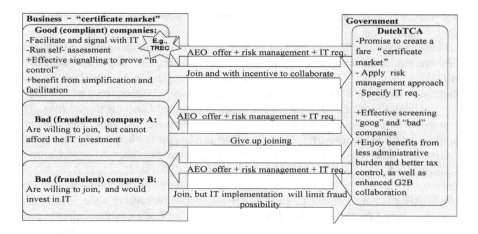

Fig. 3. IT based risk management for AEO certification

Hence, if this type of IT is referred to in the AEO self-assessment of a company, then the government knows that containers from such a company are unlikely to be used to smuggle goods, and hence they do not have to physically inspect these containers at the border. In this way, the right type of IT can support the AEO certification process. DutchDTA will not require specific IT solutions, to avoid being biased towards specific IT vendors, but they could recommend generic types of IT solutions, like smart container seals or service-oriented architectures. With the risk based and IT enabled screening from the government side internal control signalling from the business side, the adverse selection is tackled. Figure 3 presents the changes: for the "bad" company (A), as the signalling costs of implementing the required IT solution will outweigh the potential fraud benefit, he will decide not to apply for the AEO certificate. Anyhow, if the "bad" company (B) would like to have simplified tax and customs procedure and decides to apply for the AEO certificate, he must be compliant with the IT requirements of the government. Moreover, the implementation of the advanced IT solution itself will minimize the fraud possibilities of the "bad" companies and may finally transfer the "bad" companies to "good" ones. The market can correct itself such that "good" companies join and the "bad" ones may leave the market.

3.3   The Role of IT in the DutchTCA AEO Risk Management

It is agreed that a systematic and clear step plan is required for the auditors in the AEO certification process to make an un-biased professional judgment. Our findings from the interviews indicate that DutchTCA mainly relies on a risk management approach for the AEO certification. The purpose of using a risk management approach is to focus customs' control activities and their limited resources, in particular, on specific risks that are not sufficiently covered by measures taken by the businesses. Therefore, they have to assess the economic operator's organization, processes, procedures, administration, and so on. The main model used by DutchTCA is the AEO COMPACT Model [16], which requires that the AEO applicants implement, in accordance with their business model and risk analysis, the systems, procedures, conditions and requirements established in the Community Customs Code and the AEO Guidelines [16]. Figure 4 represents the risk management approach, underlying the AEO certification process, which we elicited based on our interviews. We focus on the IT enabled steps (steps with a * sign at the beginning) and skipped the details in rest of the analysis below.

a) **Determine fulfilment of formal (legal) conditions (details skipped)**
As the first step of AEO assessment, DTCA have to determine whether the formal conditions related with the procedure or facilitation for the company is fulfilled. If the applicant cannot fulfill the formal legal conditions, the application will be refused.

b) ***Understand the business (of an operator) through examination of:**

- From Customs internal sources
- ❖ *IT enabler: Primarily based on DutchTCA's own internal database (National Risk Database) and filing system (RBpro) for effective internal screening.*

The National Risk Database (RDB) is a computerized method for recording and considering risks in the fiscal process. The RDB application is accessible to all staff members of the DutchTCA. In the RDB the whole 'lifecycle' of a risk is recorded. After the introduction of the risk, the results of coverage are recorded in RDB in almost the same terms as used during the phase of the preliminary investigations. Every tax official can consult the risk database at any moment to see if a certain risk is already recorded, as well as which risks are recorded in the base.

RBpro is an automated filing system which contains the entire AEO applicant's existing Customs certificates, basic information of the company and its historical compliance record (e.g., whether the company has violated the law and to which extent); and information can also be retrieved from company historical data profiles gathered in the past through customs import and/or export systems, VAT or other information from the tax services.

- From external sources: via the Internet, companies' annual financial reports, and auditors report on internal control, etc. and via communication with Chambers of Commerce and Central Statistics (under Dutch law, DTCA has no right accessing it)

❖ *IT enabler: Use of XENON web robot for effective external screening*
  XENON is a business intelligence software tool, which is used by DutchTCA since 2004. It is an Internet (web) robot, which not only detects unknown tax evaders, but also other probable non-compliant events such as the unauthorized use of brand names or illegal diversion of trade.

c) **Clarify the customs' objectives (details skipped)**

- General objectives: are the fiscal as well as the security requirements of the Community Customs Code implemented?
- Specify additional objectives based on the type of AEO certificate

d) ***Identify risks (which risks might influence the customs' objectives)**

  Determine which of the potential risks are relevant for the particular operator, its business processes and supply chain.

❖ *IT enabler: Deploy business signal based on automated self-assessment (Digiscan)*

In this step, DutchTCA mainly uses the applicant's AEO self-assessment summary compared with the actual information achieved from the "understanding business" step to address the risk indicators and corresponding points of attention. The self-assessment summary is based on the AEO guidelines, which can be automated assessed by the Digiscan tool. Digiscan deploys a rule based system, with which it is possible to identify cases with potential Tax & Customs risks using a rule based decision system. Risk indicators, risk description and points of attentions which should guide the customs officials as well as the operators themselves are indicated in the Digiscan. Under further development, the Digican may effectively reflect the company's information systems and internal control maturity level, and thus it can used by DutchTCA for further decision making and evaluation.

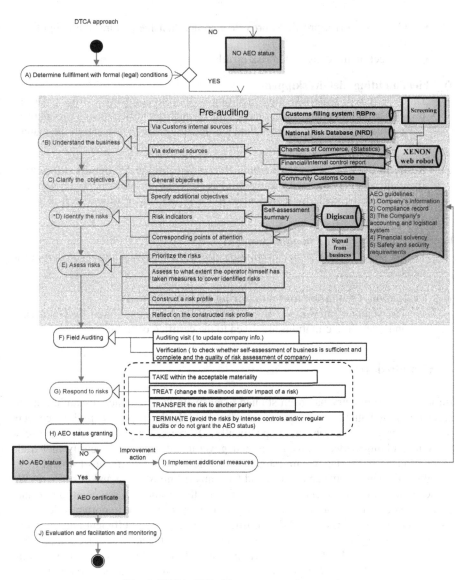

Fig. 4. DTCA AEO risk management approach

e) Assess risks (which risks are the most significant) (not fully implemented by DutchTCA at the current stage yet)

This step of the risk mapping approach is described by the AEO compact model [16] as:

- Prioritize the risks identified in step 3 through evaluation of the impact on customs objectives and the likelihood of the risk materializing.
- Assess to what extent the operator himself has taken measures to cover identified risks and in which way the operator prioritized the different types of risks.

- Construct a risk profile to provide a comprehensive picture of all significant risks.
- Reflect on the constructed risk profile

f)   Field auditing (details skipped)
DutchTCA will undertake field auditing at the the company's offices. During this phase auditors determine whether the controls identified during pre-auditing have actually been implemented, and are operating effectively and in the manner described by the client.

g)   Respond to risks: what to do about the (remaining) risks (details skipped)
Evaluate whether the AEO status is to be rejected or adjustments or improvements are to be made by the operator to cover the risk or to reduce it to an acceptable level.

h)   AEO status granting (details skipped)
In this step DutchTCA make granting decisions based on the results from the auditing.

j)   Evaluation, facilitation and monitoring (details skipped)
The status of an AEO is regularly evaluated and monitored by DutchTCA and relevant facilitations are given to the certified operator.

4   Conclusions

Information asymmetry has been studied extensively in economics research, but has received limited attention in the e-government field. In this paper we used the concept of asymmetric information, more specifically adverse selection, to analyze the relationship building between businesses and government regarding security and trade facilitation. In particular, we investigated the role of AEO certificates to build trust-based relationships between the Tax and Customs Administration and businesses. We argued that risk management can help to mitigate the problem of asymmetric information. In particular, we argued that IT plays in various ways an important role in this risk management to make the AEO certification process more efficient and effective. With effective signalling and screening, IT can mitigate the adverse selection problem for the G2B relationship building. A real life case of the AEO assessment in the Netherlands is presented in the paper, in which we showed how IT is included in the general risk management of the DutchTCA. The findings from this paper may provide valuable knowledge for the EU governments to further validate the AEO certification procedure, and provide a better understanding of the G2B relationship building.

Acknowledgements

The research of the first author was partially funded by the integrated project ITAIDE of the 6th Framework of the IST Programme.

References

1. EU Commission: Authorised economic operators—guidelines. Risk Management, Security and specific controls.DG Taxtion and Customs Union, Brussels (June 29, 2007),
   http://ec.europa.eu/taxation_customs/resources/
   documents/customs/policy_issues/customs_security/
   AEO_guidelines_en.pdf
2. Akerlof, G.A.: The Market for "Lemons": Quality Uncertainty and the Market Mechanism. The Quarterly Journal of Economics 84, 488–500 (1970)
3. Spence, M.: Job Market Signaling. The Quarterly Journal of Economics 87, 355–374 (1973)
4. Rothschild, M., Stiglitz, J.: Equilibrium in Competitive Insurance Markets: An Essay on the Economics of Imperfect Information. The Quarterly Journal of Economics 90, 629–649 (1976)
5. Varian, H.R.: Intermediate microeconomics: a modern approach. WW Norton & Co., New York (2002)
6. Liu, J., Tan, Y.-H.: Moral hazard and G2B control procedures redesign. In: Proceedings of the 9th Annual International Conference on Digital Government Research (DG.O 2008), Montreal, Canada. ACM International Conference Proceeding Series, vol. 289, pp. 421–422 (2008)
7. EU Parliament: Amending Council Regulation (EEC) No 2913/92 establishing the Community Customs Code. Official Journal of the European Union L 117/13 648/2005 (2005)
8. O'Reilly, C.A.: The use of information in organizational decision making: A model and some propositions. Research in Organizational Behavior 5, 103–139 (1983)
9. Feldman, M.S., March, J.G.: Information in Organizations as Signal and Symbol. Administrative Science Quarterly 26, 171–186 (1981)
10. Gertner, R., Gibbons, R., Scharfstein, D.: Simultaneous Signalling to the Capital and Product Markets. The RAND Journal of Economics 19, 173–190 (1988)
11. Eisenhardt, K.M.: Building theories from case study research. The Academy of Management Review 14, 532–550 (1989)
12. Yin, R.K.: Case Study Research: Design and Methods. Sage Publications Inc., Thousand Oaks (2003)
13. EU commission (Fiscalis Risk Analysis Project Group): Risk Management Guide for tax administrations (2006),
    http://ec.europa.eu/taxation_customs/resources/
    documents/taxation/tax_cooperation/gen_overview/
    Risk_Management_Guide_for_tax_administrations_en.pdf
14. Gutierrez, X., Hintsa, J.: Voluntary Supply Chain Security Programs: A Systematic Comparison. In: The International Conference on Information Systems, Logistics and Supply Chain, Lyon, France, May 15-17 (2006)
15. Davenport, T.H., Brooks, J.D.: Enterprise systems and the supply chain. The Journal of Enterprise Information Management 17, 8–19 (2004)
16. EU Commission: Authorised economic operators: The AEO COMPACT model. DG Taxtion and Customs Union. In: Directorate-General, T.A.C.U. (ed.), vol. TAXUD/2006/1452. Brussels (June 13, 2006),
    http://ec.europa.eu/taxation_customs/resources/
    documents/customs/policy_issues/customs_security/
    AEO_compact_model_en.pdf

Professional Presentation in Austrian E-Government

Arne Tauber and Thomas Rössler

Institute for Applied Information Processing and Communications,
8010 Graz, Inffeldgasse 16/a
{arne.tauber,thomas.roessler}@iaik.tugraz.at

Abstract. Mandates are a fundamental vehicle for carrying out public administration and are an indispensable requirement for conducting transactions on someone else's behalf in legal or business matter. Austrian eGovernment initiatives have introduced electronic mandates early. However, a special case is the submission of professional representatives when conducting transactions on someone else's behalf. In this paper we introduce a solution allowing professional representatives the representation of both natural persons and corporate bodies by means of complementing existing tools and technologies for adequate online identification and authentication.

Keywords: e-Government, Identification, Mandates, Professional Representation.

1 Introduction

During the last years, electronic Government (eGovernment) achieved a fairly high acceptance in being an alternative to traditional means of accessing public services. 7 x 24 availability, accessibility, reduced costs, resources and retention periods paved the way for a deployment of eGovernment applications on the large scale. Thus significant progress could be achieved in many EU member states so that eGovernment and its underlying technologies — e.g. smartcards, certificates for electronic signatures, etc. — are widely deployed. This finally led to a broad range of e-Government applications serving all kind of transactions: from citizens to administrations (C2A), businesses to administrations (B2A) as well as administrations to administrations (A2A).

Austria was one of the first EU member states adopting the EU Signature Directive [1] into domestic law by enacting the Austrian signature law in 2000 [2]. Efforts made so far have been confirmed by a benchmark of the European Commission Directorate [3]. A 100% fully online availability for every measured service was achieved. This means that citizens or businesses can access all measured services by electronic means.

Representation is a fundamental vehicle in everyday's life. In order to attest that a person is empowered to represent another one, mandates are used. Mandates are required in several scenarios, for example with respect to court proceedings, bank transactions or trading operations. Frequently used mandates are e.g. the commercial procuration when conducting commercial transactions on behalf of a company or a postal mandate when receiving consignments or deliveries on someone else's behalf. Mandates are of great importance in traditional means of carrying out public administration.

M.A. Wimmer et al. (Eds.): EGOV 2009, LNCS 5693, pp. 388–398, 2009.

Austria has identified the need for equivalence in electronic processes early. Thus, electronic mandates are among the main concerns in Austrian eGovernment initiatives since its early stages and are a core part of the Austrian eGovernment Act [4].

In contrast to representations established by mandates so called professional representations are a special case in Austrian legislation. For example, a written mandate for empowering a lawyer to act on a client's behalf is not necessarily required as they are legally accredited for representation. Lawyers have the most comprehending power of representation and can act on behalf of natural persons as well as corporate bodies in front of all Austrian courts and public administrations without having an explicit mandate. With limitation to dedicated functional areas several other occupational groups can act as so called professional representatives, e.g. notaries and architects.

Although electronic mandates and the recognition of professional representatives by electronic means have been specified quite early, most of today's employed eID based public services do not provide support for representations at all. More often than not, the declaration of acting as professional representative has to be communicated to the relying party out-of-band. However, open source tools are employed backing the implementation of eGovernment applications to allow entity identification and authentication based on electronic mandates. In this paper we discuss a solution for a seamless integration of professional representation without the need of tailoring already employed eGovernment applications in order to foster take up and reduce hurdles for providers of eGovernment services.

The rest of this paper is organized as follows. In section 2 we briefly introduce the Austrian eID concept and technologies and tools for online identification and authentication are discussed as well. In section 3 we discuss the Austrian approach of introducing electronic mandates and how mandates can be used for online identification and conducting transactions on someone else's behalf. We discuss requirements, challenges and security considerations of the presented solution in section 4. Finally, conclusions are drawn.

2 Identification and Authentification

Austrian eGovernment services require entity identification and authentication of high quality as well as qualified electronic signatures for signing applications. The Austrian Cabinet Council adapted the European Electronic Signature Directive in 2000 with the enactment of the Austrian Signature Law by introducing qualified electronic signatures based on qualified certificates. Qualified electronic signatures have the same legal impact as handwritten signatures. The eGovernment Act - enacted on 1th March 2004 – provides the basis for employed eGovernment applications and underlying tools and technologies as well. First, we give a short overview of the citizen card - the Austrian security architecture for online identification and authentication. Then we introduce how citizens can uniquely be identified by so called source personal identification numbers (sourcePIN) and sector specific personal identification numbers (ssPIN). Finally, authentication for public authorities and available tools for online identification are discussed.

2.1 Citizen Card

Web browsers are a frequent tool of choice when accessing eGovernment applications, but do not provide a standardized interface for accessing X.509 certificates by means of cryptographic service providers (CSP). Strong cryptographic support within web browsers is mostly limited to SSL/TLS client authentication and hence does not fulfill the requirements for qualified electronic signatures. Thus, Austria has chosen to develop an open interface called "Security Layer" [5] for a seamless integration of cryptographic functions within web browsers. The "Security Layer" concept provides a standardized interface on a high abstraction level based on the hypertext transport protocol (HTTP). In this way it can easily be accessed by conventional web-forms. A middleware implementing the "Security Layer" interface is called "citizen card environment" and must provide several functions for the underlying security token called "citizen card". Such functions include the read-out of data storage containers (so called "Infobox" container) as well as the creation of qualified electronic signatures according to the XMLDSIG standard [6] and the Austrian signature law. A citizen card could be a smartcard or any other device that fulfills the requirements for secure signature creation devices (SSCD) [7].

2.2 Source Personal Identification Number (sourcePIN) and Identity Link

In Austria every citizen is assigned a unique identification number held in the base registers – the Central Residents Register (CRR) and the Supplementary Register for persons who do not have a registered address in Austria. For data protection reasons public authorities are not allowed to use this unique number within the scope of eGovernment applications. A derivation of this unique identification number (e.g. CRR number) - based on a Triple-DES encryption - must be used instead. The derived number is called "source personal identification number" (sourcePIN). The calculation of sourcePINs is carried out by the sourcePIN register authority which is under the control of the Austrian Data Protection Commission. Although its name implies it, the sourcePIN register authority does not run a register of sourcePINs as sourcePINs must be discarded immediately after their creation. SourcePINs are allowed to be stored on citizen cards only. In contrast to natural persons, the sourcePIN of corporate bodies is equivalent to their unique identification number (e.g. number of their entry in the Register of Company Names) as they are not of concern of specific data protection policies.

Identification is based on an XML record called "identity link". This record holds a security assertion markup language (SAML) [8] token including the citizen's personal data like given name, surname and date of birth and sourcePIN as well as the citizen's public key of her qualified signature certificate. By signing this XML record the sourcePIN register authority establishes a direct link between the citizen card holder and her sourcePIN. The identity link is finally stored in a particular infobox-container called "IdentityLink" on the citizen card.

2.3 Sector Specific Personal Identification Number (ssPIN)

In order to prevent data abuse public authorities are not allowed to persistently store the sourcePIN of natural persons. A one-way derivation – the sector specific personal identification number (ssPIN) - of the sourcePIN is required for each administrative sector. The ssPIN is calculated by applying a SHA-1 hash function to the concatenation of the sourcePIN and the administrative proceeding code. Thanks to this approach a citizen is still uniquely identified within each administrative sector, however, her very unique sourcePIN is not revealed (due to the hash function applied, the sourcePIN underlying a ssPIN cannot be determined).

2.4 Authentication for Public Authorities

The Austrian eGovernment act states that "An official signature, being the electronic signature of a public authority, is an electronic signature within the meaning of the Signature Act, the peculiarity of which is indicated by an appropriate attribute in the signature certificate"[9]. This legal definition has been taken from the eGovernment Act. Using object identifiers (OID) to define appropriate attributes is a common practice in public key infrastructure (PKI). The object identifier "1.2.40.0.10" has been registered as "Austrian eGovernment OID" and public administration has been assigned the sub-tree "1.2.40.0.10.1" meaning that certificates having an OID with such a starting value are authenticated as public authorities.

2.5 Module for Online Applications–Identification (MOA-ID)

Public authorities can easily enable secure online identification and authentication for their eGovernment applications by integrating an open source module called MOA-ID [10] (Module for Online Applications – Identification) provided by the platform Digital Austria. A MOA-ID login is a dual-step identification and authentication process. In a first step the identity link is read out and checked for authenticity by verifying the XMLDSIG signature of the sourcePIN register authority. In a second step the citizen has to create a qualified electronic signature for authentication purposes. All cryptographic processes and the communication between the citizen's web browser and the relying party (MOA-ID) are handled by the citizen card environment middleware using a HTTPs based secure channel.

3 Mandates in eGovernment–The Austrian Approach

Mandates are a fundamental vehicle of public administration and the private sector as well. As in traditional means of carrying out public administration mandates are of great importance. Thus, the Austrian eGovernment movement developed an XML-scheme for creating electronic mandated [11] in order to have an equivalent vehicle by electronic means. According to Austrian law the power of representation is legally established as soon as the mandator grants such a power. A mandate – regardless of in oral or written form - is the according legal instrument. Mandates are granted unilateral, i.e. the representative's consent is not necessarily required. In this section we discuss the Austrian approach of introducing electronic mandates. First, a technical insight into electronic mandates is given. We further show how electronic mandates can be used in online transactions. Finally we give a brief overview on how the Austrian eGovernment law handles professional representation.

3.1 Technical Bases

Electronic mandates are represented as an XML structure containing the identification data of both the mandator and the representative. Analogous to the identity link it holds the sourcePIN as well as other identification data like given name, surname and date of birth. In Austrian law mandates are not bound to a particular legal form, therefore an additional field for the purpose is preserved. Even if an arbitrary content basically hampers automated processing of electronic mandates, most standard cases can be covered, e.g. the commercial procuration.

Figure 1 illustrates a simplified XML structure of an electronic mandate.

```
<Mandate MandateID="441 (1) " xmlns="">
   <StatusInformationService>http://rev.szr.gv.at/RevocationServ(2)</StatusInformationService>
   <Representative>
     <pr:PhysicalPerson>
       <pr:Identification>
         <pr:Value>CDP7GEMabMMR8jlwyAxh3(3)</pr:Value>
         <pr:Type>urn:publicid:gv.at:baseid</pr:Type>
       </pr:Identification>
       <pr:Name>
         <pr:GivenName>John</pr:GivenName>
         <pr:FamilyName>Doe</pr:FamilyName>
       </pr:Name>          (4)
       <pr:DateOfBirth>1980-01-01</pr:DateOfBirth>
     </pr:PhysicalPerson>
   </Representative>
   <Mandator>(5)</Mandator>
   <SimpleMandateContent>
     <TextualDescription>mandat(6)ontent</TextualDescription>
   </SimpleMandateContent>
   <dsig:Signature(7)</dsig:Signature>
</Mandate>
```

Fig. 1. Simplified XML structure of an electronic mandate

As shown in figure 1 an electronic mandate contains the following elements:

1. A m*andate ID* to uniquely identify the mandate.
2. A *Uniform Resource Locator (URL)* referring to the mandate status information service of the sourcePIN register. Mandates can be revoked by the mandator in a similar way to X.509 certificates in PKI. Analogous to online certificate status protocol (OCSP) services, the sourcePIN register authority provides a service for checking the revocation status of an electronic mandate.
3. The representative's *sourcePIN*.
4. The representative's *given name, family name and date of birth*.
5. The mandator's *sourcePIN, given name, family name and date of birth*.
6. A textual description of the *purpose*.
7. *(Enveloped XMLDSIG) digital signature*: an electronic mandate is only authentic if it is signed by the sourcePIN register authority.

3.2 Storing a Mandate within the Citizen Card

For concerns of authenticity electronic mandates can only be issued at the web site of the Austrian source-PIN register authority and requires a citizen card based login. The XML structure of the mandate is signed according to the XMLDSIG standard with a particular X.509 certificate bound to the source-PIN register authority. Each citizen card environment middleware must support an infobox data container called "Mandates" for a persistently storage of electronic mandates.

3.3 Mandates in Online Authentication

MOA-ID is capable of handling electronic mandates by reading out the infobox container "Mandates" along with the identity link and verifying the mandate using the open source module MOA-VV [12]. This process comprises signature and revocation information verification as well as a congruence check between the identity link sourcePIN and the representative's sourcePIN.

3.4 Professional Representation

In Austria professional representatives do not need a particular mandate to act on someone else's behalf. In order to introduce this principle in eGovernment as well, the Austrian eGovernment act states that the power of representation of a professional representative must be evident by an appropriate attribute in the representative's signature certificate. Analogous to the OID for public authorities, a dedicated sub-tree of the Austrian eGovernment OID has been assigned to professional representatives and starts with the value "1.2.40.0.10.3". Each group of professional representatives, i.e. lawyer, notary, etc., is assigned a further sub-tree, e.g. the law society is responsible for administrating OIDs starting with "1.2.40.0.10.3.2".

In order to conduct online transactions for someone else's behalf the professional representative must be identified according to the Austrian eGovernment act following the citizen card concept. In addition to this, the certificate provided during the authentication step has to be proven whether it contains an adequate OID or not. However, the OID provided by the representative's certificate just attests she is a lawful acting professional representative. There is a need for further essential attributes of the mandator, such as the mandator's sector specific personal identification number (ssPIN) or her first-name and surname.

The next section introduces an extension for MOA-ID giving professional representatives a way to conduct online transactions on someone else's behalf following the technical process described before.

4   Integration of Legal Professionals in Online Identification

In this section we introduce a solution called "MOA-ID Compatibility Mode" to allow professional representatives to act on someone else's behalf in online transactions. The term "Compatibility Mode" arises from the fact that if eGovernment applications are already aware of handling electronic mandates, submissions by professional representatives could seamlessly handled without any further effort for the application or service provider. We discuss challenges and requirements, the solution developed and data protection considerations in the remainder of this section.

4.1 Challenges

Deployed eGovernment applications based on MOA-ID are already aware of handling mandate-based entity identification and authentication. A redesign of the existing interface is therefore not desirable. We rather aim at a compatible solution allowing already employed applications to handle professional representatives in the same way as a conventional mandate based identification. To support the representation of both natural persons and corporate bodies is a major concern.

Professional representatives usually act in place of many clients. For them it is therefore not desirable to hold mandates for each mandator within the citizen card environment. This was also the reason why OIDs are used to recognize professional representatives electronically instead of using explicit mandates. Although a professional representative does not need to show explicit mandates to act for her mandator, the proposed approach makes use of temporary electronic mandates to the eGovernment application.

For each new representation act a temporary mandate is generated, passed to the application and discarded afterwards by MOA-ID. In other words, the structure of mandates is just used as a technical vehicle to inform the eGovernment application that the professional representative is acting in the name of her mandator. In contrast to explicit mandates temporary mandates are not digitally signed by the source-PIN register authority and cannot be used in any other case than in connection with the affected eGovernment application. In other words, the legal basis for a professional representation is already and sufficiently established by the professional representative's OID in her qualified signature certificate. The temporary electronic mandate is used as an interface only.

4.2 Compatibility Mode Solution

Figure 2 illustrates the MOA-ID login process in case of professional representation.

A MOA-ID login process is carried out in seven steps as shown in figure 2. These steps are as follows:

1. The professional representative is accessing the MOA-ID login page of the eGovernment application she aims to use in the name of her mandator (also referred to as relying party). A dummy mandate identifying him as professional representative is sent along with the identity link to MOA-ID using his citizen card environment. A citizen card environment could also provide a "professional representation modus" sending the dummy mandate automatically on each MOA-ID login. The dummy mandate does not contain any identification data. It only serves as a flag for MOA-ID indicating to switch into compatibility modus. The dummy mandate as technical vehicle is required as the qualified signature certificate is not yet available at this point and therefore the intention of representation is not evident.

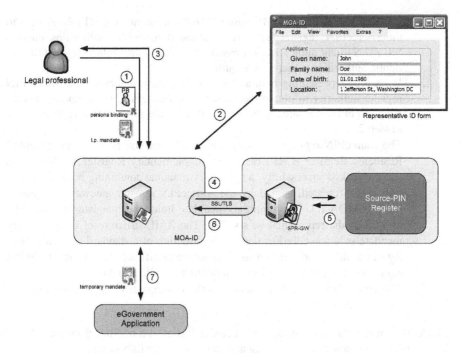

Fig. 2. MOA-ID login process in case of professional representation

2. MOA-ID recognizes the fact that a professional representative is carrying out a login process and opens a new browser window showing a form for entering the mandator's identification data. first name, surname and date of birth must be provided in case of representation of natural persons. Address or CRR number can be supplied optionally. Corporate bodies require the submission of the sourcePIN, e.g. the number of their entry in the Register of Company Names or of their entry in the Central Register of Associations.

3. If the mandator's identification data is correctly submitted, MOA-ID prepares an XML signature request containing a SAML structure with the submitted data. In contrast to the traditional login process the representative's SAML data are replaced by the mandator's ones. The representative's SAML data are additionally provided to have the choice of signing both identification data sets. In this way existing MOA-ID applications remain fully compatible. The request signed by the professional representative with his citizen card is then sent back to MOA-ID for signature verification.

4. An additional check for the presence of the professional representation OID in the qualified signature certificate is made besides signature verification. In order to obtain the mandator's sourcePIN a request for a temporary mandate is sent to the sourcePIN register authority. Direct access to the source-PIN register authorities requires a amount of configuration work for public authorities. The request is therefore sent along with the professional representative's qualified electronic signature to a so called source-PIN register

gateway [13] using an XML-based SOAP document over HTTPs. Access to the sourcePIN register gateway is allowed to public authorities only; a SSL/TLS client authentication based on a certificate containing the OID for public authorities is therefore required.

5. In case of representing natural persons the gateway contacts the sourcePIN register authority to obtain the mandator's sourcePIN. For corporate bodies the sourcePIN has already been provided by the professional representative in step 2.

6. The sourcePIN register authority searches for natural persons in the Central Residents Register (CRR) or in the Supplementary Register. If the person can be tracked successfully, a temporary mandate containing both identification sets is created, signed by the sourcePIN register gateway and passed back to MOA-ID. The temporary mandate holds the mandator's sourcePIN as well as the representative's ssPIN. The XML structure of the temporary mandate is technically identical to the structure of a standard authentic mandate and differs only in the used signature certificate. Due to the technical equivalence it can be used like a standard authentic mandate.

7. The temporary mandate is passed to the eGovernment application and discarded afterwards.

MOA-ID provides the same identification credentials as in a traditional mandate-based login process. In this way eGovernment applications remain fully compatible.

4.3 Data Protection Considerations

Data protection is one of the most important principles of eGovernment law. In cases of professional representation the sourcePIN register authority is allowed to temporarily provide the mandator's sourcePIN to eGovernment applications. Hence, public authorities are not allowed to store sourcePINs persistently, they can only be used for further processing, e.g. the calculation of sector specific sourcePINs. MOA-ID meets this requirement and discards every temporary mandate after passing it to the application.

SourcePINs are very sensitive data and citizens need to have certainty that their data is well protected. The eGovernment Act states that public authorities can only query sourcePINs in case of professional representation. It is obvious that neither public authorities nor professional representatives should get to arbitrarily query sourcePINs. The sourcePIN register gateway thus provides a dual security channel for authenticating incoming requests. First, the communication between the relying party and the gateway is based on a SSL/TLS client authentication requiring a client certificate having the public authority OID. This guarantees that only public authorities can query sourcePINs. The request must also include a single-serving qualified electronic signature of a professional representative and cannot be used twice for authentication. In this way replay attacks are prevented and public authorities are not able to arbitrarily query sourcePINs without a professional representative's qualified electronic signature.

5 Conclusions

The paper introduced an approach integrating professional representation seamlessly into employed eGovernment applications. General requirements and challenges have been discussed and the implementation made so far for carrying out public administrations by professional representatives.

In most cases deployed applications already provide a MOA-ID based online identification and authentication capable of handling electronic mandates. For concerns of backward-compatibility an approach extending the established infrastructure for querying temporary sourcePINs has been made by means of using conventional electronic mandates as technical vehicle for identifying professional representatives. With this approach deployed eGovernment applications remain untouched. A one-time upgrade of MOA-ID allows relying parties the easy integration of professional representation without the need of tailoring existing eGovernment applications.

The paper discussed access concerns regarding the sourcePIN register gateway allowing the query for temporary sourcePINs. This has been complemented by data protection considerations for this core part covering crucial exposure of sourcePINs in terms of temporary use. Finally, access restrictions to the gateway by means of a dual security channel requiring a certificate with public authority identifier as well as a certificate with professional representation identifier have been discussed.

References

[1] European Parliament and Council, Directive 1999/93/EC on a Community framework for electronic signatures

[2] Austrian signature law: Bundesgesetz über elektronische Signaturen (Signaturgesetz – SigG), BGBL. I Nr. 190/1999, BGBL I Nr. 137/2000, BGBL. I Nr. 32/2001, BGBL. I Nr. 8/2008(in German)

[3] European Commission, Directorate General for Information Society and Media, The User Challenge Benchmarking The Supply of Online Public Services, 7th Measurement (September 2007)

[4] The Austrian E-Government Act: Federal Act on Provisions Facilitating Electronic Communications with Public Bodies. Art. 1 of the Act published in the Austrian Federal Law Gazette, part I, Nr. 10/2004

[5] Leitold, H., Hollosi, A., Posch, R.: Security Architecture of the Austrian Citizen Card Concept. In: Proceedings of 18th Annual Computer Security Applications Conference (2002)

[6] Eastlake, D., Reagle, J., Solo, D.: XML Signature Syntax and Processing, W3C Recommendation (2002)

[7] European Committee for Standardization: Security Requirements for Secure Signature Creation Devices (SSCD-PP), CWA 14169 (2002)

[8] Cantor, S., Kemp, J., Philpott, R., Maler, E.: Assertions and Protocols for the OASIS Security Assertion Markup Language (SAML) V2.0, OASIS Standard (March 15, 2005)

[9] Hollosi, A., Leitold, H., Rössler, T.: Object Identifier der öffentlichen Verwaltung (2007) (in German)

398   A. Tauber and T. Rössler

[10] Schamberger, R., Karlinger, G., Moser, L.: Spezifikationen Module für Online Applikationen – ID (2007) (in German)
[11] Rössler, T., Hollosi, A.: Elektronische Vollmachten Spezifikation 1.0.0 (2006) (in German)
[12] Scheuchl, A.: MOA-VV Spezifikation Version 0.9.9 (2005) (in German)
[13] Tauber, A.: Stammzahlenregister Gateway (sourcePIN register gateway) – Spezifikation, Version 1.0.0 (2008) (in German)

Explaining the Behavioral Intention towards BI Implementation in Public Administrations – A Principal-Agent Theory Approach

Jörg Becker, Philipp Bergener, Łukasz Lis, and Björn Niehaves

European Research Center for Information Systems, University of Münster,
Leonardo-Campus 3, 48149 Münster, Germany
{joerg.becker,philipp.bergener,lukasz.lis,
bjoern.niehaves}@ercis.uni-muenster.de

Abstract. Business Intelligence (BI) is an established instrument to support public administrations in their management tasks by increasing their information level. BI is of special interest in the context of introducing accrual accounting in public administrations as this affects the information level of different stakeholders, leading to a possible decrease for municipal councils. The principal-agent theory can help to explain different behavioral intentions of the stakeholders concerning the introduction of BI. We employ a single qualitative case study to analyze these behavioral intentions. It shows that the introduction of accrual accounting did decrease the information level of the municipal council making the principal-agent problems possible. Furthermore, it shows that BI might be a solution for this problem. Therefore, council members show the behavioral intention to support the BI implementation while administration staff members rather resist it. Based on these finding, we discuss implications for practice and future research.

Keywords: eGovernment, Business Intelligence, Empirical Study, Organizational Change, Principal-Agent Theory.

1 Introduction

Business Intelligence (BI) is an established instrument which can support public administrations in their strategic management tasks. Business Intelligence has been proven a successful instrument to provide the strategic management with information in a useful form. Hence, it can also be an appropriate instrument for municipalities to transform the information provided by accrual accounting in a form which is easily accessible for the political leadership of public administrations [1]. Thereby, it can help to increase the information level in these positions [2].

In the context of introducing accrual accounting BI is an important instrument. In a move towards New Public Management, most German federal states are committing their municipalities to implement accrual accounting until 2012. In the long term, the introduction of instruments like contract management, budgeting and controlling which have be proven successful in the private sector promise higher information

M.A. Wimmer et al. (Eds.): EGOV 2009, LNCS 5693, pp. 399–411, 2009.
© Springer-Verlag Berlin Heidelberg 2009

levels for the municipal council [3, 4]. In the short term, the honorary council members are confronted with a new, diminished budget layout they are not used to, leading to a decreased information level. BI presents an instrument, which can provide the council with targeted, indivdual information and help to overcome this problem.

Principal-agent theory can help to understand different behavioral intentions towards BI implementation in public administrations. Though Business Intelligence could help municipal councils to increase their information level and will therefore be supported by council members, public administration staff might resist the introduction, as they could lose a possible information advantage compared to the council. Understanding behavioral intentions, especially possible resistance, towards BI implementation is crucial for a successful BI implementation process. In this paper we aim to analyze the behavioral intention towards the introduction of Business Intelligence from the perspective of the principal-agent theory, as this theory is very well suited to explain problems arising from information asymmetries and has already been successfully applied in the domain of public administration [5]. We strive to answer the research question of:

In how far can the principal-agent theory aid to analyze and explain the behavioral intention towards a Business Intelligence implementation in public administrations?

In order to answer this research question we employ a single, qualitative and interpretive case study. The remainder of the paper proceeds as follows: In the second section, we discuss the related work, especially the principal-agent theory and its application in the public sector as well as the concept of behavioral intentions. Subsequently, we develop a research model with the underlying hypotheses of this study. After describing the research methodology in the third section, the case data gathered in a municipality in Germany, is presented in Section four. In the fifth section, the findings and implications are discussed and interpreted against the underlying hypotheses. The paper concludes with a summary of the major results.

2   Theoretical Foundation

2.1   Behavioral Intention

Behavioral intention is a key variable to research on technology adoption and diffusion. Information Systems literature has developed a rich body of knowledge explaining the user adaption of information technology (For an overview see[6]). Theory development in adoption and diffusion research, so far, mainly examines individual-psychological variables for explain behavioral intention, revolving around individual-psychological concepts such as ease of use, usefulness, or attitude. However, while the merits of this theory approach lie in its wide-range applicability, explanatory potential in terms of the institutional setting of a behavioral intention situation is neglected. Here, we argue that an analysis of such circumstantial institution have the potential to shed new light on technology adoption and diffusion.

Public sector organizations are characterized by specific and effective institutions. E-government can be regarded broadly as the design, adoption, and assessment of IS in government organizations. This view opens up for an external, customer-oriented perspective as well as for an organization-internal perspective on technology adoption and diffusion. In the former, behavioral intention has as well been successfully applied as a predictor of technology acceptance, for instance, by [7]. However, we identified that studies focusing on IS adoption within a public organization are rarely to be found [8, 9]. Here, we argue that within the realms of public organizations, institutions are most effective and, too, most specific to the sector of analysis. In that respect, the question arises of which institutional theories bear potential for utilization in e-government adoption and diffusion.

2.2 Principal-Agent Theory

Principal-agent theory – also known as agency theory – is concerned with a general agency relationship between two parties. One party (the principal) concludes an agreement with another party (the agent), in the expectation that the agent will subsequently choose actions that lead to outcomes desired by the principal [5]. The relationship between both parties is governed by an imaginary contract specifying what the agent should do and what the principal must do in return [10, 11]. In such relationships, a series of problems arise. The principal-agent problem occurs when (a) the principal and the agent have partly differing goals and (b) it is costly for the principal to receive accurate information about the actual behavior of the agent. Situation (a) is usually referred to as a goal conflict. Situation (b) results in the parties' different information levels and thus leads to an information asymmetry [12]. Two issues have been identified in the literature as typical for an agency relationship. The *moral hazard* phenomenon arises when some outcome-influencing actions of the agent are too costly to be observed. The agents might then be personally motivated to take different actions than they would take if they were observed by the principal [13]. Usually, there exist some unobservable, uncontrollable outcome-influencing factors, which vary in time. As the agents prefer less effort to more, they are able to mask their own *shirking* with random variations of those factors [14]. The *adverse selection* issue refers to a situation when the agent's skills (characteristics) are not observable. The principal is then likely to hire lower skilled agents who falsely claim the requisite skill level [15].

In the literature, two main measures have been identified which increase the probability that the agent will behave in the interests of the principal. First, outcome-based contracts, i.e. co-aligning the preferences of the agent with those of the principal through allowing the former to participate in the outcome, can effectively curb agent opportunism [16]. Second, when information systems informing the principal about the agent's behavior are implemented, the agent is more likely to behave in the interests of the principal [17].

2.3 Principal-Agent Theory in Public Administration

In the domain of public administration – or synonymously public bureaucracy –exist an extensive chain of pairwise principal-agent relationships. They can be identified between citizens and politicians, politicians and public administration heads, and public administration heads and their staff [5]. Between politicians and public administration staff exist information asymmetries. Niskanen [18] argues that the combination of informational monopoly and knowledge about legislative needs allows bureaucrats to prepare budget-output packages that are presented to politicians as take-it-or-leave-it proposals. As public administration staff is usually paid salary, which is due to governmental regulations, there is no opportunity to bind them directly to the (monetary) results of their efforts. Moreover, the outcome is hard to measure [5]. Hence, there exists a principal-agent problem with its dangers of moral hazard and adverse selection [19].

In the move of New Public Management (NPM), a trend arose in the domain of public administration to implement some mechanisms originating from the private sector [3]. Costs, which had been previously aggregated, pooled, or not measured at all, are increasingly categorized and analyzed. This process is referred to as *accountingization* [4]. In particular, most German federal states committed their municipalities to move from cash-basis accounting to accrual accounting. Although the principal (politicians in the city council) does not pay the agent (public administration staff) direct commission on the realized outcome, the agents have to commit themselves on a specific outcome level they aim at.

Business Intelligence (BI) systems are information systems that support decision-making through aggregating data, and enabling to analyze and disseminate the relevant information among decision-makers [20-22]. In the domain of public administrations, such systems can be implemented in order to inform the principal about the outcome realized by the agent [1]. Waterman and Meier [2] state that eliminating the information asymmetry through implementation of information systems can increase administration efficiency if the principal and the agent establish a cooperative relationship and support each other.

2.4 Research Model

The principal-agent theory provides a theoretical framework for our analysis of the behavioral intention towards BI implementation in public administrations. We study the information balance between the city council (principal) and the public administration staff (agent) before and after the move from cash-basis accounting to accrual accounting. This change was required by federal state law and took place for the studied case in 2003. Furthermore, we study the expectations and intentions of both sites towards a possible introduction of BI. The main elements of our research and their relationships are presented in Figure 1. The time dimension is visualized vertically while the horizontal axis is used to present causalities between certain events, the information level of both involved parties and their behavioral intention.

In particular, we analyze the information level of both principal and agent before 2003 (cash-basis accounting) and at present (accrual accounting without BI) and compare them. We formulate the following hypothesis:

H_1: *The implementation of accrual accounting leads to less information for the city council (principal).*

As we assume that the implementation of the accrual system does not decrease the information level of the public administration staff, we expect to find an information asymmetry for the benefit of the agent. Further, we analyze the information level of both involved parties in the case of a BI implementation (accrual accounting with BI) and pose the following hypothesis:

H₂: The implementation of BI would lead to more information for the city council (principal).

Again, as the public administration staff members deal with the original information on a daily basis, we assume that an information system implementation cannot change their information level. Hence, we expect a decrease of the information asymmetry after a BI implementation. As this fact has substantial consequences for both principal and agent, we formulate the following propositions:

H₃: Due to the expected improvement of the information supply, the city council (principal) shows the behavioral intention to support BI implementation.

H₄: Due to the expected loss of information privileges, the public administration staff (agent) shows the behavioral intention to resist BI implementation.

H₃ and H₄ concern the behavioral intentions of both principal and agent towards the implementation of a BI system. In particular, we assume that the principals support such a move in the hope to improve their own information level and be able to influence the agent's actions. On the contrary, the agents resist an implementation as they fear to lose their information privileges.

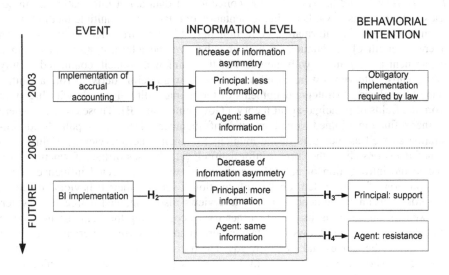

Fig. 1. Research Model

3 Research Methodology

Methodology selection. Case studies are a well established method in qualitative IS research methodology. They study contemporary events in their natural surroundings using multiple methods of data collection. The researcher exercises no experimental control over the studied phenomenon and therefore does not influence analyzed developments or behaviors [23-25]. Hence, case study research is well suited to analyze temporal, organizational developments like the implementation of accrual accounting in German municipalities as this is a currently ongoing process. Literature distinguishes different types of case studies including single case studies. Single case studies are, amongst others, applicable in situations where a revelatory case or a leading case example is studied, which provides valuable insights for future similar cases [23, 25]. This condition holds for an ongoing process like the introduction of BI in public administration in combination with accrual accounting. Single case studies have been applied successfully in eGovernment research [26].

Case selection. To answer our research question we employed the case of a municipality in Lower Saxony, Germany. This municipality has about 12,000 inhabitants, about 27 full time staff members in the core administration and a municipal council consisting of 26 honorary members. This case is especially suited for our research since (1) due to its size, the studied municipality is representative for a large number of public administrations in Germany, and (2) this municipality has already implemented accrual accounting and has introduced an ERP system in this process, thereby providing the technological basis BI systems can build upon. Hence, the presented case constitutes a leading case example for other municipalities facing the same challenges in the future.

Data collection and analysis. For the collection of data about information asymmetries and intentions towards the implementation of a BI system multiple methods were applied. Core of the information collection were 12 semi-structured interviews of an average length of 42 minutes, 6 with members of the administration (including 5 department heads) and 6 with members of the municipal council, conducted in July 2008. Those interviews were based on an interview guideline derived from an initial stage of analysis of strategic documents of the municipality alongside with literature from the fields of principal-agent theory, eGovernment and BI. Those concepts where further refined in a joined workshop with staff members of the municipality's administration as well as members of the municipal council. The interview guideline contained questions about the current information level, changes of the information level due to the introduction of accrual accounting as well as expected influence of the introduction of a BI system on the information level and their behavioral intention towards such an implementation. The interviews also contained a free part, which allowed for an open discussion of further issues concerning the items brought up in the interviews. All interviews were tape-recorded and transcribed afterwards resulting in 84 transcribed pages and 54,883 words. The transcripts were then analyzed by two researches who were not involved in the interviewing process, each searching independently for text passages supporting or dissenting with hypotheses (Qualitative Content Analysis). The findings were then discussed and consolidated with the support of a third researcher.

4   Results

4.1   Accrual-Basis Accounting and Information Level

"The studied municipality moved from cash-basis accounting to the accrual system as required by state law. We experience a changed information level. Many

colleagues, who have already been in the council for many election periods, miss the old transparency, those detailed budget items. One could look for an item and ask how the money was spent." (Councilor III)

As the honorary councilors do not work with the operational systems, the main problem seems to be the new budget layout, which provides less information. The councilors got used to the old cash-basis budget over the years and stress they were able to find detailed information about single budget items and make further inquiries about expenditures. As the accrual-basis budget gives an aggregated overview, they are not able to see detailed information about singular cash flows.

„One often has the feeling that it is the administration staff that has an overview rather than the council members, who only occasionally deal with the budget." *(Councilor I)*

The city council members feel they are presently less informed and think that the administration staff has gained information advantages from the move to accrual accounting, because of their daily experience with the operational systems.

„I think the council members' reception is that they used to be better informed, because they were able to deal with the matter better." (Administration staff A)

The administration staff shares this view. The staff members think the city councilors used to have more information and were able to handle it better.

4.2 BI and Information Level

The intended implementation of a Business Intelligence (BI) solution would lead to a better information supply for the city council members.

„I hope that we receive more information. This is what a BI system is ultimately for. [...] I think that the council will be strengthened." (Councilor IV)

The councilors expect to receive more information from the BI system and hope for a change in their information supply. They see an opportunity to strengthen their position.

"Certainly, the position of the council will be strengthened insofar as we will be able to contribute to the decision-making process ourselves. At the moment, we get something we can vote on, we can ask for additions, but we don't have the information to actively play a part in the decision-making process from the very beginning." (Councilor II)

At present, the city council members miss the opportunity to actively pull information in an autonomous way. As the new budget layout provides less detailed information, such inquiries seem necessary. The decision-making process is currently usually triggered by the information pushed from the administration staff and the councilors would welcome more autonomy. The alternative to independently pull information from the BI system would let them initiate decision-making processes themselves.

"When we implement a BI system there will be targeted reports that the council is actually interested in. [...] It will be a benefit for the council members." (Administration staff B)

The administration staff members see an advantage of the BI system for the council members. Such a structured solution would increase the precision of the information supply so that more information reaching the councilors would actually satisfy their information needs.

4.3 Behavioral Intention towards BI Implementation – Principal (City Council)

As some of the city council members have already gained professional experience with BI solutions, the council seems to support the implementation in the municipality.

> „I am shaped by my professional experience and in the beginning you are skeptical, because you are the one to do the work, but today you clearly appreciate the transparency and the alignment of goals and measures." (Councilor III)

The councilors praise BI as providing more transparency and leading to better and easier decision-making. Apparently, there are differences between the council and the administration staff on two main issues concerning the intended BI implementation.

> „The council sees precisely a decrease of workload. Doesn't the administration staff perceive it so as well?" (Councilor V)

First, the councilors expect an alleviation of workload for all participants and seem to be surprised that this view is not shared by the administration staff.

> „But when they work reasonably, they don't have to be afraid of control. Certainly, a BI system is controlling. But this is what it is for." (Councilor IV)

Second, the council members admit a BI solution could potentially give them the opportunity to supervise the administration staff's work. However, they don't seem to see a problem there but rather a normal situation.

4.4 Behavioral Intention towards BI Implementation – Agent (Administration Staff)

The administration staff perceives the two already mentioned problems concerning the intended BI implementation.

> "It will be more work for us because of further inquiries that will come. Perhaps, this information is already in the report, but they don't read it. When we have to answer all those inquiries, it will be more work for us." (Administration staff C)

The administration staff members fear more workload that would not always be founded and think the councilors would not appreciate this additional work.

> "You just know that you will be a bit more controlled through this system." (Administration staff D)

The second issue is the arising possibility of work supervision and benchmarking with other positions and municipalities.

> "I think no one of us can claim that they never thought: 'It can also lead to the situation that you are benchmarked with other municipalities and other positions.'

The opportunity is clearly there. One definitely can't deny it. I am not so anxious myself but my colleagues are, I think." (Administration staff C)

Many administration staff members seem to fear benchmarking opportunities. However, they do not explicate their own fears directly, but refer to other concerned colleagues.

5 Discussion

5.1 Findings

The implementation of accrual accounting without a complementary BI system decreased the information level of the city council. The obligatory implementation of accrual accounting is supposed to provide better information about costs aggregated on their respective so-called products and thus give the city council a more outcome-oriented view of the actual state of their municipality. However, our interviewees confirmed the opposite result of this particular change. The councilors miss the much more detailed old budget layout, which they were used to. In terms of the agency theory, the principal used to be provided with information on the behavior of its agent. Accrual-basis budget layout, as required by German federal state law, does not provide this detailed information any more. The councilors are not able to observe the behavior of the administration staff members. The sole implementation of accrual-basis accounting decreased the information level of the city council. This confirms our hypothesis H_1.

The city council's decreased information level led to an information asymmetry. The administration staff deals with the new accounting system on a daily basis and is forced to understand it. Due to this on-the-job experience, the information level of public administration staff did not change. Hence, an information asymmetry arose between the city council and the administration staff, which gives the latter clear information privileges. The personal interests of the administration staff members are not co-aligned with the outcomes desired by the council. Moreover, the staff has no incentives to handle in the interests of their principal. Staff members are able to initiate decision-making processes by preparing own dedicated voting proposals. Both solutions of the principal-agent problem proposed by the theory, outcome-based contracting and exploring agent behavior using information systems, are not applied. As the administration staff, like every worker, prefers less effort to more, the issue of moral hazard arises. Moreover, the councilors have only limited opportunities to assess the staff members' skills and the quality of their work. This makes the adverse selection issue feasible.

A BI system build on top of the accrual accounting base provides an opportunity to reduce the information asymmetry. The city council expects the implementation of a complementary BI system to increase their information level. A BI system would provide information about current financial expenditures and place them in relation to performance figures and respective goals. This would lead to a coherent view of municipal goals and the related current and scheduled administrative measures. Such system would reduce the information asymmetry and provide the councilors with an instrument increasing the probability that the public administration staff behaves in the interests of the city council. Both the behavior and the respective outcome of the administration staff would be observable by the city council members. Moreover, as the councilors would have the opportunity to actively pull needed information, they would be able to initiate decision-making processes themselves and don't have to rely on the administration staff's proposals. Our second hypothesis H_2 can be confirmed.

As a BI system would improve the councilors' information level, they show the behavioral intention to support this step. The sole implementation of accrual-basis accounting decreased the information level of the city council members and induced an information asymmetry for the benefit of the public administration staff. The councilors expect that an implementation of a BI system would reduce the information asymmetry and the principal-agent problem of moral hazard on the side of the administration staff. As the councilors expect more transparency and easier decision-making with less effort, they support an implementation of a BI system. Our third proposition H_3 regarding the behavioral intention of the city council towards a BI implementation can be confirmed.

As public administration staff members are unwilling to lose their information privileges, they show the behavioral intention to resist BI implementation. The implementation of BI would reveal the actions and the respective outcome to the city council members. This would make their behavior observable reducing the opportunity to shirk. Moreover, as the outcome of their work would be measured and registered, benchmarking would be feasible. This way, not only the actions but also the skills of public administration staff members would be revealed. Both principal-agent issues of moral hazard and adverse selection would be reduced or even eliminated. Public administration staff would be increasingly forced to behave in the interests of the city council. Moreover, the staff members expect an increased workload due to the BI implementation. Consequently, the public administration staff shows the behavioral intention to resist a BI implementation. Our fourth proposition H_4 can be confirmed.

5.2 Implications for Practice

Our findings suggest that the sole implementation of accrual accounting without a complementary BI solution can actually decrease the information level of the city council members. As a result, an information asymmetry between the council and the public administration staff can be induced leading to a principal-agent problem with its issues of moral hazard and adverse selection. The probability that the staff members behave in the interests of the city council, decreases. The additional implementation of a BI system is perceived as reducing the information asymmetry and the probability that the administration staff behaves in the interests of the council increases. We derive the following implications for the practice.

Federal public policy. The implementation of accrual accounting is required by law in most German federal states. However, our study suggests that this step alone is not reasonable and thus not advisable. It should be taken into consideration whether the hitherto optional implementation of a BI system is to be made obligatory and required by law as well.

Local implementation strategy. Local politicians who plan to implement accrual accounting as required by law are advised to consider the synchronous implementation of a complementary BI system. Otherwise, the information level of the city council is likely to decrease and the administration staff members might not behave in the interests of the principal.

Outcome-based contracting. When accrual accounting with a complementary BI system are implemented, the outcome of the administration staff actions is measurable and observable by the city council. This provides the technical opportunity to implement outcome-based contracting. This way the probability that the administration staff behaves in the interests of the city council is increased.

6 Summary

BI is an instrument, which can help to support strategic management tasks by supplying an easy access to relevant information. This is especially important given the current situation in which many public administrations across Europe implement accrual accounting.

In this paper we employed a single, qualitative case study in a pilot municipality which has already implemented accrual accounting to analyze the behavioral intention towards the introduction of BI of both councilors and administration staff from a principal-agent-perspective. Our findings show that, (1) the introduction of accrual accounting in the municipal administration has led to a decrease of the information level of the studied council due to diminished budget layout. The administration staff, in contrary, shows no such decrease. This leads to a principal-agent situation of information asymmetry. The council can neither observe the administrational staff behavior nor control the outcome of their work. (2) it became clear that BI is perceived as an instrument to address the information asymmetry problem as it can supply additional, interactive information to the councilors in form of easy-to-read reports. Therefore, (3) council members support the introduction of a BI system as it would increase their information level. On the other hand, (4) the administrational staff is not supportive of a BI implementation as it would eliminate their information privilege forcing them to act according to interest of the council.

The main limitation of the presented approach is the application of only a single case. A single case cannot provide generalizable results but allows studying current, leading cases as an outset for theory creation. Nevertheless, the basic conditions of the presented case are similar for a large number of municipalities, in terms of size (less than 20.000 inhabitants) as well as for the existence of a principal-agent relationship between administration and council. To generalize the findings of further case studies have to be conducted, varying the size of the municipality as well as considering other German and also European setting. For practice our findings suggest that the implementation of accrual accounting alone might not sufficient but should be accompanied by BI to ensure no information asymmetries arise. This implies for the federal government level that the implementation of BI could be made obligatory along with introduction of accrual accounting. Politicians on the local level are advised to consider a simultaneous implementation of accrual accounting and BI. Moreover, this should be accompanied by the utilization of instruments like outcome-base contracting to further ensure that the administration staff behaves according to the council's interest.

References

1. Bozeman, B., Bretschneider, S.: Public management information systems: theory and prescription. Public Administration Review 46, 475–487 (1986)
2. Waterman, R.W., Meier, K.J.: Principal-Agent Models: An Expansion? Journal of Public Administration Research and Theory 8, 173–202 (1998)
3. Hood, C.: The 'New Public Management' in the 1980s: Variations on a Theme. Accounting, Organizations and Society 20, 93–109 (1995)
4. Power, M., Laughlin, R.: Critical theory and accounting. In: Alvesson, M., Wilmott, H. (eds.) Critical Management Studies, pp. 113–135. Sage, Thousand Oaks (1992)
5. Moe, T.M.: The New Economics of Organization. American Journal of Political Science 28, 739–777 (1984)
6. Dinev, T., Hu, Q.: The Centrality of Awareness in the Formation of User Behavioral Intention toward Protective Information Technology. Journal of the Association for Information Systems 8, 386–408 (2007)
7. Carter, L., Bélanger, F.: The utilization of e-government services: citizen trust, innovation and acceptance factors. Information Systems Journal 15, 5–25 (2005)
8. Chappelet, J.L.: The appropriation of e-mail and the Internet by members of the Swiss Parliament. Information Polity: The International Journal of Government & Democracy in the Information Age 9, 89–102 (2004)
9. Narro, A.J., Mayo, C., Miller, A.F.: Legislators and constituents: Examining demographics and online communication tools. Information Polity: The International Journal of Government & Democracy in the Information Age 13, 153–165 (2008)
10. Jensen, M., Meckling, W.: Theory of the firm: Managerial behavior, agency costs, and ownership structure. Journal of Financial Economics 3, 305–360 (1976)
11. Perrow, C.: Complex organizations. Random House, New York (1986)
12. Eisenhardt, K.M.: Agency Theory: An Assessment and Review. The Academy of Management Review 14, 57–74 (1989)
13. Demski, J., Feltham, G.: Economic Incentives in Budgetary Control Systems. Accounting Review 53, 336–359 (1978)
14. Alchian, A., Demsetz, H.: Production, Information Costs, and Economic Organization. American Economic Review 62, 777–795 (1972)
15. Akerlof, G.A.: The Market for 'Lemons': Quality Uncertainty and the Market Mechanism. Quarterly Journal of Economics 84, 488–500 (1970)
16. Jensen, M.: Organization Theory and methodology. Accounting Review 56, 319–338 (1983)
17. Fama, E.: Agency problems and the theory of the firm. Journal of Political Economy 88, 288–307 (1980)
18. Niskanen, W.A.: Bureaucrats and politicians. Journal of Law and Economics 18, 617–643 (1975)
19. Mitnick, B.M.: The Theory of Agency: The Policing "Paradox" and Regulatory Behavior. Public Choice 24, 27–42 (1975)
20. Luhn, H.P.: A Business Intelligence System. IBM Journal of Research and Development 2, 314–319 (1958)
21. Power, D.J.: A Brief History of Decision Support Systems, http://DSSResources.COM/history/dsshistory.html
22. Shim, J.P., Warkentin, M., Courtney, J.F., Power, D.J., Sharda, R., Carlsson, C.: Past, present, and future of decision support technology. Decision Support Systems 33, 111–126 (2002)

23. Benbasat, I., Goldstein, D.K., Mead, M.: The Case Research Strategy in Studies of Information Systems. MIS Quarterly 11, 369–386 (1987)
24. Lee, A.S.: A Scientific Methodology for MIS Case Studies. MIS Quarterly 13, 33–52 (1989)
25. Yin, R.K.: Case study research. Sage, Thousands Oaks (2003)
26. Silva, L., Hirschheim, R.: Fighting against Windmills: Strategic Information Systems and Organizational Deep Structures. MIS Quarterly 31, 327–354 (2007)

Author Index